International Handbook of Education
for the Changing World of Work

Rupert Maclean · David Wilson
Editors

Chris Chinien
Associate Editor

International Handbook of Education for the Changing World of Work

Bridging Academic and Vocational Learning

 Springer

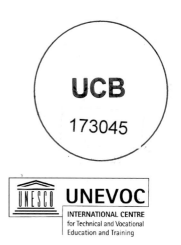
UNEVOC
INTERNATIONAL CENTRE
for Technical and Vocational
Education and Training

Editors

Dr Rupert Maclean
UNESCO-UNEVOC
International Centre for Education
Hermann-Ehlers-Str. 10
53113 Bonn
Germany
r.maclean@unevoc.unesco.org

Professor David Wilson
University of Toronto
Canada

Associate Editor

Dr Chris Chinien
Workforce Development Consulting
Montreal
Canada

ISBN: 978-1-4020-5280-4   e-ISBN: 978-1-4020-5281-1

Library of Congress Control Number: 2008930131

Printed on acid-free paper

9 8 7 6 5 4 3 2 1

springer.com

Contents

v

Part II   The Changing Context of Work and Education

Section 1   Changing Workplace Requirements: Implication for Education
Margarita Pavlova and L. Efison Munjanganja

Section 2   Education and Training in Informal Economies
Madhu Singh

VOLUME 2

**Part III   Education for the World of Work: National and Regional
Perspectives**

Section 3   Reforming National Systems of Vocational Education and Training
David Atchoarena and Peter Grootings

VOLUME 3

Part IV   **The Management of TVET Systems**

Section 6   **Policy and Management of TVET Systems**
               Rupert Maclean and Chris Chinien

Part V   Teacher Education for Vocational Education and Training

Section 8   The TVET Profession
Stephen Billett

VOLUME 4

Part VI   **Education for Work: Research, Curriculum Development**
and Delivery

VOLUME 5

**Part VII   Learning for Life and Work: Bridging Academic and Vocational
           Education**

**Section 12   Participation in Formal Programmes of Learning and Skills
             Development**
           Rupert Maclean and Hendrik van der Pol

Section 14 The Skills Debate in an Ageing Society
          Tom Karmel and Rupert Maclean

VOLUME 6

Part VIII   **Lifelong Learning for Livelihoods and Citizenship**

Section 15   **Adult, Continuing and Lifelong Learning**
Chris Chinien and Madhu Singh

VOLUME 2

Part III
Education for the World of Work:
National and Regional Perspectives

Section 3
Reforming National Systems
of Vocational Education and Training

David Atchoarena

UNESCO International Institute for Educational Planning, Paris, France

Peter Grootings

European Training Foundation, Turin, Italy

Chapter III.1
Overview: Changing National VET Systems through Reforms

David Atchoarena and Peter Grootings

1 Introduction

The future of technical and vocational education is generating heated debate nearly everywhere in the world. Of course, this concern is not new, but globalization, the collapse of planned economies and the failure of development policies in the fight against poverty have put it back at the centre of national and international policy debates. As a result, vocational education reform constitutes a vibrant area of public policy and research.

In many countries the issue is no longer about partial and isolated change measures but rather about changing overall systems. This means not just addressing all the different building blocks of national systems (system-wide), but increasingly even how vocational education and training systems are functioning (system-deep). The role and place of vocational education and training as part of overall lifelong learning systems is on the agenda, even though individual countries are at different stages of readiness to face the challenge.

This section gives an overview of some of the key issues and developments in vocational education and training around the world at the start of the twenty-first century. It looks in particular at what exactly drives current attempts to change national systems and makes an attempt to identify some commonalities. The section will pay special attention to more recent approaches and initiatives that countries are using to trigger off system-wide and system-deep reforms, such as the development of national qualifications frameworks, regional co-operation and knowledge-sharing, improving accountability and making better use of research. The section includes also a number of country case studies to illustrate the extent to which the various general and specific drivers operate in particular country contexts.

Together, the chapters of this section provide evidence for the fact that everywhere there is not just one specific but a complex constellation of drivers at work that include economic, technological, political but also—and perhaps increasingly—educational ones. The emphasis given to each of these differs from country to country depending on existing institutional and political environments and, of course, also on outcomes of past policies. However, even though there is no easy way to identify what works best, there is still a lot to be learned from other countries. The chapters that follow have been selected within such a policy-learning perspective.

R. Maclean, D. Wilson (eds.), *International Handbook of Education for the Changing World of Work*, DOI 10.1007/978-1-4020-5281-1_III.1,
© Springer Science+Business Media B.V. 2009

2 Old, New and Continuing Issues and Their Changing Contexts

At the turn of the twenty-first century, some of the old contextual issues that launched vocational education and training policy debates have re-emerged, such as: youth unemployment in developed countries and poverty in developing ones; the low status of vocational education as compared to general and higher education; and the need to adapt curricular programmes to new learning requirements.

Some new issues have emerged as well, such as: (a) the need for reform of vocational education in transition countries; (b) the impact of globalization; (c) demographic developments leading in most industrialized countries to a rapidly ageing workforce, (d) in many developing countries, an increasing number of young people seeking access to education and work; and (e) the discourse on developing lifelong learning systems in response to these overall challenges.

Indeed, some issues seem to be everlasting, such as: (a) the need for occupational flexibility given changing product markets, technologies and work organizations; (b) the role of the State versus that of the private sector; and (c) the need to secure relevance, efficiency and effectiveness of vocational education and training generally. But old and new policy issues are now arising in completely different policy environments and will therefore also be discussed and treated differently.

3 Short-Term Versus Long-Term Objectives

Governments' interventions in the field of vocational education and training have always been motivated by a mix of short- and long-term motives, with the short-term issues often becoming dominant simply because they are political priorities. This has happened in many European countries where the fight to combat youth unemployment during the 1970s and 1980s frequently led to series of ad-hoc measures to get young people away from the labour market. Improvements of overall quality, relevance and status of vocational education became difficult because of the dominant concern for reducing school drop-out and providing basic qualifications to low school achievers. These measures have taken place in many countries at the cost of developing a high-quality overall vocational education and training system that would provide in a balanced way qualified people at all levels of ability. Sometimes, the—certainly unintended—effect of many short-term measures has been to further decrease the status of vocational education by signalling that training is really for those who do not succeed in education.

Nowadays, in many—impoverished—transition countries, there is a similar tension between short-term attempts to preserve the social welfare function of vocational schools and the long-term one of addressing the reform of their qualification function. A dramatic lack of resources forces countries to make choices—and choices are by necessity focused on issues of immediate concern. As a result, in many cases, public vocational schools find themselves increasingly trapped in a vicious cycle of becoming schools for children of the poor without being able to provide them with the knowledge, skills and competences to prevent or escape from poverty. Also here, overall improvement of qualification levels and a balanced provision of qualifications that emerging labour markets are demanding is not properly addressed. Also here, vocational education—already of low status—finds it increasingly difficult to be seen as an attractive alternative for general and academic higher education.

Most developing countries are still caught in the middle between a plethora of local, NGO-driven and often unsustainable development initiatives, regularly including training and national education policy reforms advised by international donors. Both regularly lack local ownership and are dependent on resources and capacities offered by donors. The importance given to vocational education and training has changed over time in international donor policies with periods of heavy investments in large public training systems (basically buildings and equipment) followed by market-driven short-term training measures aimed at satisfying the needs of the private sector. None of these approaches has as yet been able to properly address the varied learning needs of people working in different positions in either the formal or informal economies of the countries.

4 Reform Histories

Some countries have gone through various waves of vocational education reform since the 1970s when the first period of extensive industrialization came to an end and traditional vocational education and training systems that prepared for highly standardized and—often very simple—occupations sought to adapt to changing economic and employment conditions. Some have been more successful than others. A number of countries, in particular those in which vocational education was well established and respected, both among employers and students, have kept their systems fairly stable and have merely sought to gradually optimize what existed.

Yet others have missed out on the need to adapt to modernization needs during the 1970s, such as many developing countries and all of the centrally planned countries of Eastern Europe and the former USSR. Whereas the latter are currently undergoing a difficult process of systemic reforms of their systems, many developing countries have remained highly dependent on educational policies and priorities provided by international donor institutions that had become increasingly anti (public) vocational education and training.

In the same period, on the other hand, several countries in South-East Asia have managed to establish effective ways of developing the knowledge, skills and competences of their populations.

5 Common Trends and Developments but No Convergence

This great diversity of contexts, objectives and histories makes it complex to assess vocational education policies, but it seems that there are nevertheless some commonalities in current reform thinking. There is an increasing attention to embedding vocational education and training in local or regional development, for mobilizing and continuously improving competences and, hence, for improving the quality of learning processes and outcomes.

There is also an increased appreciation for the fact that a new balance needs to be found between local development and innovation, on the one hand, and overall national quality assurance frameworks, on the other. In addition, there is a growing concern, motivated by globalization and migration trends, that the reforms of national vocational education and training systems need to be placed in an international perspective. The international dimensions of vocational education and training are becoming more and more important—in a way similar to what has already happened with higher education and, indeed, employment systems and labour markets.

Finally, and perhaps only in embryonic forms, there is increasing attention and concern for those for whom education and training is in the end all about: learners, and the teachers and trainers that assist them in developing the knowledge, skills and competences that they need. This new concern is very much based on a better understanding of why so many of the previous attempts to reform vocational education and training systems have not brought the anticipated results. They usually were designed *for* people and not *with* them; they also tended to focus on structures and institutions rather than on the people involved.

These common strands are present in most of the policy debates and developments in vocational education and training around the globe, though not in the same ways and not to the same extent. They also do not point in any way to convergence of systems and policies. While the challenges become increasingly similar, policy responses remain specific.

6 Back to Core Business?

The increased attention to learners and learning approaches mentioned earlier is only one element in the current discourse on vocational education and training reform. However, it is important to note that this return to what can easily be called the 'core business' of education and training systems follows earlier reform initiatives that focused on other aspects: (a) their governance (through increased involvement of social partners); (b) administration (through decentralization and increased accountability of education and training institutions); (c) funding (involving the private sector and students and their parents in financing arrangements); (d) assessment (giving more attention to learning outcomes and separating assessment from teaching and learning); (e) quality assurance and transparency (such as through developing national qualification standards and frameworks); (f) mobility, openness and pathways (such as through recognition of prior learning and restructuring of educational sub-systems); and (g) curriculum reform (making curricula more flexible and competence based).

A return to the core business of education and training also signifies increased attention for those who are actually learning and helping them to learn. This is remarkable, since the earlier reforms have concentrated on the roles and responsibilities of other actors and stakeholders: social partners, administrators, assessors, people working in educational support institutions and professionals outside the schools. In fact, in several countries, earlier reforms were directed at making the outcome of vocational education and training less dependent on teachers and trainers, such as by moving from so-called input-based to outcomes-based standards, by stressing involvement of the private sector, giving greater importance to work-based learning and separating learning from assessment.

Currently, there seems to be a reversal of this trend—or at least a remarkable shift in emphasis. Teachers and trainers are increasingly becoming recognized in their dual role of educational professionals and of stakeholders in reforms. They are again seen to be important for organizing learning processes, but the nature of learning processes has changed from being teacher-centred to student-centred. They also become appreciated as stakeholders in reform and without whose contribution nothing would really change in the classroom. One of the major challenges that countries are facing, therefore, is to bring these different stakeholders and focuses of attention together in an overall and coherent reform policy that will enable education and training systems to help people develop the knowledge, skills and competences that are needed to survive and prosper in a globalizing world.

7 From Partial to Overall System Reforms?

The issue of developing overall and coherent reform policies has yet another dimension that needs to be examined. The increasing need to pay attention to the quality of learning contents and processes does not mean that this can be simply added on to the list of policy measures undertaken so far. On the contrary, focusing on learners, learning processes and those who should enable and facilitate learning may well require a fundamental rethinking of those aspects of education and training systems that have until now in most countries been given priority.

For example, decentralization becomes more than merely giving more administrative autonomy to lower levels in the system. It will also imply improving the capacity for schools to dialogue and co-operate with other organizations involved in education and training at the local level and to be able to identify and cater for the learning needs of divergent groups of people. Moreover, it will require developing capacities at school level for initiating and implementing innovations in response to the education and training needs of the local communities that they are part of. This, in turn, will have implications for the functioning of national and often centralized support institutions, as it will have consequences for the ways in which national authorities fund and promote such school-based innovation and development work. But decentralization of this kind can only be successful and productive when it is framed by overall national qualification standards and frameworks that can secure adherence to agreed quality standards across the country, or groups of countries. Otherwise, decentralized initiatives may put the very existence of transparent national systems with open pathways at risk. Obviously, for these very reasons in many countries the move towards new learning contents and approaches is a heavily debated one.

Generally, awareness of 'whole-system' reforms has undoubtedly increased, however, and the search is for those interventions that can 'drive' overall reform by triggering off related changes in how the vocational education and training systems operate in a particular context.

Changing individual aspects of vocational education and training systems will have little impact if other aspects remain untouched. This understanding has been a strong factor in the current drive for system-wide or whole system reforms. It has also led to a rethinking of the logic or rationale along which systems were structured and functioning. This, as a matter of fact, appears to be the most difficult dimension of education and training reform as it implies fundamental redefinitions of the roles that key actors and stakeholders are playing. Successful reforms therefore require that sufficient space, time and resources are devoted to enabling reform learning to take place. Neither institutions, organizations nor individuals change from one day to the next.

8 Balancing Major Reform Drivers

Carnoy determines the global challenges for educational planners in this way:

> Globalization together with new information technology and the innovative processes they foment are driving a revolution in the organisation of work, the production of goods and services, relations among nations, and even local culture. These changes put a lot of pressure in education to change (1999, p. 14).

He also identifies three types of reform as responses to the pressures of globalization by the education sector: competitive-driven reforms; finance-driven reforms; and equity-driven reforms (1999, p. 37).

- The basic characteristics of the *competitive-driven reforms* are an emphasis on the macro issues of the education system. Changes are introduced in the area of administration and management (decentralization, privatization, management of resources). Emphasis is put also on the issues of meeting the standards of achievement, and on teacher recruitment and training. The main purpose of this type of reform is to increase the quality of education in order to produce a better educated labour force.
- *Finance-driven educational reforms* have as a main target the reduction of public expenditure on education and making the use of public funds more efficient and effective. These reforms are advocated by the International Monetary Fund and the World Bank, in particular with regard to developing and transition countries, and try to shift funding from secondary to basic education, expand the secondary sector through privatization, especially its technical and vocational part, and to reduce the cost of public education by increasing the teacher/pupil ratio.
- Finally, *equity-driven reforms* place more emphasis on equality of educational opportunities and on basic education, with the latter taking on a wider meaning than basic literacy only. These reforms aim at integrating marginalized groups in society and at reducing social exclusion and poverty.

It is probably true to say that since the 1970s equity-driven reforms (including the ones that focused on reducing youth unemployment) have increasingly made way for reforms driven by finance and competition considerations, or combinations of the latter. This is equally true for developed countries as for developing countries, where reforms have been driven largely by the international donor community. It has also been the case for the reform of VET systems in transition countries that have found themselves in the same 'receiving' situation, at least until very recently. The challenge that most countries are facing now, however, is to find a proper balance between all three types of reform: (a) they need to develop a well-educated labour force in order to secure sustainable growth and welfare; (b) they also need to make their education and training systems affordable in the mid and long terms; and (c) they need to secure social cohesion through education and training in order to develop a certain degree of political stability.

9 Specific Drivers Remain Country Specific

Whereas globalization forces increasingly create an overall environment of policy challenges to which all countries have to respond, priorities and emphasis on particular aspects continue to differ. However, there is also an increased interest in international or regional co-operation and exchange. Indeed, one of the most exciting developments is exactly the growing interest of countries to learn from others. But changes are occurring here as well.

Even though short-term action may often still be dominant, there is a growing tendency to consider whole-system reforms instead of addressing isolated aspects by single and unco-ordinated measures. This has necessitated, as mentioned earlier, a broader involvement of stakeholders at all levels of the system, including those working inside schools and training centres. Moreover, the very need for ownership, fit-in-context and sustainability has also led to a review of traditional international assistance and co-operation that was largely based on policy copying and best-practice emulation. Instead, active policy-learning, local capacity-building and approaches that aim at helping-countries-to-help-themselves have emerged as part of the international co-operation rhetoric.

Having said this, it is clear that countries differ in the extent to which they have created favourable conditions—such as through earlier reform initiatives—to address the new challenges. For example, there are countries that have traditionally or as a result of recent reforms given schools high levels of autonomy, improved the dialogue with social partners, strengthened innovative and development capacities of schools and teachers, created open pathways for everybody all through their education and training systems and have sufficient budgets to continue further development and innovation. These countries are clearly better equipped to face the challenge of improving the quality of learning and learning processes than those countries where reforms have aimed at different objectives having no immediate relation with organized learning. The latter will have to combine the development of an enabling environment with seeking to improve the quality of learning processes and outcomes.

This also reminds us that giving emphasis to particular aspects in one country may not have the same 'driver' impact as in another country. An example of this is the current discourse on learning outcomes.

In countries where there has been a strong tradition of paying attention to the quality of learning processes, such as in countries that favour vocational didactics, giving more emphasis to learning outcomes may in fact contribute to improving their quality even further. In countries that have given more weight to assessment processes and where there is little or no tradition in the professionalization of vocational teachers and trainers, this may result in a further refinement of assessment criteria and procedures and a continued neglect of learning processes.

Thus, drivers do not have automatic trigger effects, nor are the effects that they may generate always the same. Also here, the existing context plays its role. Of course, these are not natural laws and an understanding of possible impact and unintended effects may very well help to achieve success even though the existing environment is not optimal. Placing past and on-going reform experiences in their proper context of time and space may therefore lead to better national reform policies in the future. This is what policy-learning is about.

10 Overview of the Contributions

This section presents contributions that cover some of the more recent debates and developments on vocational education and training reform from different parts of the world. The chapters that follow provide illustrations of how different drivers for change operate in different contexts and may—or may not—prompt related changes in the overall system of vocational education and training of a country. They include analyses of a variety of country-specific developments, of thematic issues and of reform strategies and approaches. They neither cover the whole world nor all the key thematic issues. We have had to be pragmatic and selective. Together, the chapters do give a reasonably good overview of the key aspects that will need to be taken into account for long-term VET reform policies in any country in the world.

The analyses provided should not be seen as presenting best practices that can easily be copied or emulated elsewhere. On the contrary, and we have stressed this already several times before, these are all context-bound reviews and case studies from particular environments and specific periods in time. Nevertheless, they contain valuable experiences that may function as eye-openers and provoke policy-learning. Above all, they show that different aspects of vocational education and training are intimately interconnected and that isolated and partial measures may have undesirable—even if unintended—consequences if the overall challenge of any reform of vocational education systems is not firmly kept in mind. The objective is to have a system in place that enables people to learn the knowledge, skills and competences that are useful and relevant for them to live a decent life through decent work.

III.2 *Latin America's Efforts in the Vocational Training of Young People from Poor Backgrounds,* by **Claudia Jacinto**

Across the world, youth unemployment remains a sensitive issue. In a context of global educational expansion, early school-leavers face an increased risk of exclusion. School-to-work transition constitutes a fertile research field for investigating social and educational change. It also constitutes an active domain of public policies. But education is only one of the variables that determine school-to-work transition. Social characteristics, such as ethnicity, gender, socio-economic status or rurality, have a significant impact upon the work prospects and the life experiences of young people.

As illustrated by the experience of Latin America, targeted programmes are sometimes implemented as part of broader social policies for youth. In this region, many youngsters leave school with few or no qualifications. In the context of an overall increase of educational levels, the costs of dropping out are higher than ever because—as in other parts of the world—employment opportunities for the unskilled have diminished. While increasing participation in vocational courses cannot be an end in itself, VET is sometimes used as a strategy that helps to keep children and youth off the streets. The large numbers who are neither in education, work nor training are increasingly seen as contributing to the incidence of juvenile crime, teenage pregnancy and drug abuse.

There is currently an extensive debate regarding the focus of these programmes and their contribution to the social integration of young people. Many people are asking themselves whether: (a) it would be better to reintegrate these young people into a formal education system so that they can be guaranteed access to twelve years of education; (b) vocational training alone may create an opportunity for these young people to find a decent job, or produce livelihoods with enough income to pull them out of poverty; (c) the initiatives have been adequately linked to a range of public policies; (d) it has been possible to overcome the tendency to create 'supply side' courses that do not take sufficient account of the actual demands of the labour market; and so on. The central question for the author is to what extent and by which means these initiatives can contribute to generate a valuable 'second opportunity' for young people from low-income households with low educational backgrounds. The answer is a cautious 'yes', but only if these measures lead people into qualifying paths that provide access not only to work, but also to further education and training.

III.3 *Accountability and Career Technical Education (CTE) Policy: A Brief Review of Six States of the United States,* by **Joshua D. Hawley and Alexandra de Montrichard**

These authors address accountability, an issue that has come to the fore as part of the 'new public management' discourse and the reform of the state and the public sectors for which it used to be responsible, including in many countries vocational education and training.

Accountability is a critical issue for state and federal government in the United States. The approach under the current policy regime is to consolidate the requirements for accountability under the Consolidated Annual Report (CAR) framework. However, there are continuing problems creating an appropriate accountability framework for career and technical education (CTE), as vocational education is referred to in the United States. The development of academically oriented CTE under the most recent legislation has forced states and the federal government to confront the contradictory goals of preparation for the labour market (career development) and further studies (college preparation). As an academic programme, CTE needs to be responsible for ensuring that all young people have basic skills, while also being adequately prepared for success in the labour market.

Accountability is the practice of holding schools, districts and teachers responsible for providing quality education and holding students responsible for their performance. As part of the push to hold school systems accountable, standards and (to varying degrees) accountability systems were developed both at the state and federal levels. This is a development that has also taken place in many other countries, for example through the change from so-called input to outcome standards as the basis for funding. The big question everywhere remains how a system can be developed that measures outcomes in such a way that this also leads to improvement of the educational process: what educators would call a formative assessment approach.

III.4 The Regional Perspective of Vocational Education and Training, by Mike Coles and Tom Leney

Coles and Leney argue that actions taken to strengthen regional co-operation are among those that shape national VET systems. An important reason for this is the fact that, increasingly, countries in a region (such as Europe) are confronted with similar pressures for change. As the authors also stress, it is probably not the case that common pressures would lead to common responses through reform. The country or regional context will require bespoke solutions. However, the elements of changing VET infrastructure might be expected to show some commonality and the process of change itself could have features that are created through policy-learning from reforms and trials in other countries and regions.

First experiences with a co-ordinated approach to policy-learning, the European Union's Open Method of Co-ordination (OMC) and a review of a number of more specific cases, including the European Qualifications Framework, illustrate some of the obstacles that are to be found on the way towards making regional co-operation transform itself into knowledge-sharing and policy-learning.

III.5 *Vocational Education, Training Reform and Regional Integration in the Middle East,* by **Munther Wassef Masri**

Chapter 5 takes the issue of regional co-operation to a more operational level based on recent experiences from the Middle East, a region that has traditionally profited from the presence of regional agencies and projects. There are a number of 'do's' and 'don'ts' that emerge from that experience, especially in terms of ensuring that regional co-operation leads to local ownership and context-fit of reform initiatives.

National stakeholders rarely have the means or capacities to initiate or co-ordinate knowledge-sharing and joint involvement in projects and are therefore depending, as is the case with the European Union countries, on supra- or international agencies. The Arab world has developed its own regional institutions and there are yet other multilateral and bilateral ones as well. Even so, as is clear from history, the mere presence of such agencies does not guarantee effective reforms. But the growing need for VET reform within countries may also lead to a better use of the opportunities that such regional institutions offer for better policy development and implementation.

III.6 *The Influence of Qualifications Frameworks on the Infrastructure of VET,* by **Mike Coles and Patrick Werquin**

Chapter 6 examines the ways in which the existence of a qualifications framework influences several structural aspects of VET, such as management of the supply and demand for skills, the institutional arrangements, the financing of VET and the way the VET system interfaces with other learning systems and VET in other countries. Given this potential impact, developing national qualifications frameworks can provide strong tools for reforming national VET systems.

The authors illustrate how this may work: qualification frameworks make explicit the relationship between qualifications. They aim to increase transparency and to show potential progression routes; they can become the basis of credit-transfer systems. They are overarching tools that can be used to engage all stakeholders in developing and co-ordinating the qualifications system. Often they are used as tools for regulation and quality assurance. At the same time, a qualifications framework can open opportunities to potential learners, because it makes progression routes clear and can offer the opportunity to rationalize qualifications by reducing the overlap between them. In all of these ways, frameworks create an environment where the whole qualifications system can be reviewed. This means that the management of the qualification framework can be used as a tool to enhance many policy responses that countries are adopting in response to the lifelong learning agenda—of which VET is a very important component. It is rather a decisive component when it comes to global economic performance and coping with emerging issues.

III.7 Reforming Skills Development, Transforming the Nation: South African Vocational Education and Training Reforms, 1994–2005, by Simon McGrath

However, national qualifications frameworks (NQF) do not always easily fulfil these promises, as is shown by the case of South Africa.

In an era where vocational education and training reform is common, South Africa provides one of the most striking national case studies of the complex interplay between international discourses of both economic change and VET reform and historical and contemporary forces at the national level. Moreover, the twin imperative of economic and social focus for VET is made particularly complex and challenging by the legacy of *apartheid.*

The author concludes from his review that the transformation of the VET system in South Africa has proved far more complex than was realized at the point of departure. Developing new institutions, creating a workable NQF, transforming funding and delivering new programmes have all been attempted at the same time as expanding the system and radically reforming access. Inevitably, too, South Africa has found itself faced with many of the tensions that affect VET systems globally, most particularly the difficulty of balancing social and economic imperatives and of ensuring that national departments of education and labour work together effectively.

The country now faces the challenge of reviewing the whole process in such a way that the key successes are allowed to continue. The elements of the system that need radical overhaul can be identified or abandoned. Honest self-reflection needs to be carried out with maintenance of public support for the system. If such a process can be successfully negotiated, McGrath argues, then the South African skill revolution may come to a truly successful conclusion.

III.8 Reform of Vocational Education in the Russian Federation, by Olga Oleynikova and Anna Muravyeva

The Russian Federation has not yet reached this point, as the authors of Chapter 8 make clear. Tensions between the qualifying and social protection role of vocational education and training institutions remain one of the big challenges yet to be solved. Moreover, only fairly recently, wider reform requirements have become understood after an initial phase in which the inherited VET system was merely allowed to survive while administrative responsibilities were transferred to regional levels, without the necessary financial, institutional and human resources to enable the system to adapt to radical changes during the transition period.

The authors end on an optimistic note. There may not have been much of a national VET reform policy until now, but at the same time a wealth of experience has been acquired at local levels, where schools have been forced to act, often profiting from international assistance. Given the wide range of good practices that exist in individual VET schools that could serve as a resource for developing modern and effective models of VET in the country, the authors argue that networking of VET schools should be encouraged to enhance information exchange and sharing of good practices. This seems to be the only feasible way to envisage a continuation of on-going reforms and modernization efforts.

III.9 Vocational Education in the Netherlands: In Search of a New Identity, by Jan Geurts and Frans Meijers

Chapter 9 provides a review of VET reforms in the Netherlands, including many of the issues dealt with by other authors in preceding chapters. It is a story of trying to learn from the past while looking across borders. It is also a story where structural change and pedagogical innovation come together in the growing understanding that the role of the school, as an institution, needs to change fundamentally from being an industrial education factory towards becoming a career centre.

Such a change implies that learning to change as a result of instruction must become a process of knowledge construction. It also implies a change from making available standard one-size-fits-all programmes towards developing personal competences based on the capacities and interests of learners. Support for these developments that are currently transforming the Dutch VET system are also found in so-called new-learning theories that are based on constructive instead of traditional behaviourist or cognitivist approaches.

III.10 Facilitating Policy-Learning: Active Learning and the Reform of Education Systems in Transition Countries, by Peter Grootings

Grootings argues that statements regarding local ownership and fit-for-context have become more and more popular in the donor community, but that in practice traditional policy transfer or policy copy of presumed best practice and conditional assistance have continued to dominate.

He explores the opportunities for applying active or constructivist learning principles for educational reforms in transition countries. There are four aspects to be considered: (a) the question of 'why' these new principles have any relevance at all; (b) the implications of new learning for 'what' education reforms should cover; (c) the process of educational reform itself and in particular 'how' reform policies are developed and implemented; and (d) (typical for all active-learning approaches) the tensions and contradictions between the 'how' and the 'what' when trying to implement active learning.

Seeing policy-makers as (policy-)learners, international policy advisers should consider themselves as facilitators of policy-learning processes, similar to the new roles that teachers are developing as facilitators of learning processes. The current debates about learning processes, learners and new teacher roles, therefore, are also of immediate concern for policy-makers and their advisers. Policy reform is a learning process for the simple reason that no blueprints exist.

Reference

Carnoy, M. 1999. *Globalization and educational reform: what planners need to know.* Paris: UNESCO-IIEP.

Chapter III.2
Latin America's Efforts
in the Vocational Training of Young People
from Poor Backgrounds

Claudia Jacinto

1 Introduction

Many of the social programmes developed within the framework of the struggle against poverty and/or unemployment in Latin America since the 1990s were focused on improving the entry of young people from low-income and low-education households into the workforce. The method most often used was to offer short vocational training courses, hoping that this would help place these young people in an occupation at a basic level.

There is currently an extensive debate regarding the focus of these programmes and their contribution to the social integration of young people. Many people are asking themselves whether: (a) it would be better to include these young people into the formal education system so that they can have at least twelve years of education; (b) vocational training alone can create an opportunity for these young people to find a decent job and lead lives with enough income to pull themselves out of poverty; (c) the initiatives have been adequately linked to a range of public policies; and (d) it has been possible to overcome the tendency to create 'supply side' courses, which do not take into account the actual demands of the labour market, etc.

This chapter intends to contribute to this debate by summarizing the approaches of the programmes that began in the 1990s, their strengths and weaknesses, and some recently created models attempting to provide new answers to the difficult question of how to introduce young people from impoverished backgrounds into the labour market.[1] We look at training models and their links to the job market (particularly their focus on formal employment or the informal sector, including the creation of micro-enterprises); their generally poor links to formal education; the association mechanisms they propose between public and private institutions; the profiles of the targeted population; and achievements in cases where sufficient information is available.

The central question we intend to clarify is to what extent and by which means these initiatives can contribute to generating a valuable 'second opportunity' for young people from low-income backgrounds, taking into account the process of devaluation in qualifications which is happening simultaneously, changes in the content and types of employment, and the scarcity of the latter.

R. Maclean, D. Wilson (eds.), *International Handbook of Education for the Changing World of Work*, DOI 10.1007/978-1-4020-5281-1_III.2,
© Springer Science+Business Media B.V. 2009

2 Inserting Young People into the Workforce

Differences in educational and employment opportunities, as well as an unbalanced income distribution, are clear structural phenomena in the region. Globalization, the opening of markets and the structural adjustments initiated in the 1990s add to this background of exclusion and have reinforced a productive heterogeneity. Although a certain technological and organizational modernization has taken place inside the leading productive sectors in recent decades, productivity in informal small and micro-enterprises still remains stagnant and, in many cases, outdated forms of production persist.

Between 1990 and 2004, economic growth could be considered deficient and erratic, and gave rise to growing unemployment, an increase in low-quality jobs and widespread emigration (CEPAL, 2005). The proportion of the informal sector in the urban job market jumped from 42.8% in 1990 to 46.7% in 2003. At the same time, differences between the average income in the formal sector and the informal sector increased from 59% to 72% (CEPAL, 2005). While the formal salaried employment sector varies according to annual economic growth, there is clearly a duality in the self-employment sector: one part survives under precarious, low-income conditions; while the other, less important, is composed of more efficient productive units— in many cases small businesses profiting from certain jobs outsourced by large companies.

This job-market decline and increase in segmentation did not impact equally on every population group. One of the most affected was certainly young first-job seekers.

As a matter of fact, demographic tendencies, as well as the expansion of schooling towards universality of primary education and large, but nationally very different, increases in secondary education, led many to believe that the relative position of young people in the workforce would improve during the 1990s. A range of developments, however, contributed to prevent that belief from becoming reality.

On the one hand, secondary education enrolment rates meant that participation in the educational process is still falling short of universality. Even in the countries of the southern region of Latin America (*el Cono Sur*), with high rates of schooling for children, more than half of young people do not graduate from the secondary level. The most critical problems still existing include high rates of repetition and drop-out, and in many cases a poor quality of educational supply. Simultaneously, the basic qualifications required to obtain quality jobs drift upwards towards completion of secondary education, whereas the region shows a devaluation of degrees, certificates or diplomas as the average educational level of young people rises.

On the other hand, erratic economic growth coupled with increasing unemployment affected young people particularly, since first-job seekers and employees with a high turnover are mostly young. Compared to the total workforce, the unemployment rates for the young are double. For example, while at the end of the 1990s the general urban unemployment rate was 10.2%, the average unemployment rate for young people aged 15 to 24 was 19.5% (Weller, 2003). These figures add to deteriorating recruitment conditions and low salaries.

Whereas the position of young people in general is difficult, the situation for those from poor backgrounds and/or with low educational attainment is still worse. Unemployment rates increase notably among those who are poor and as educational levels drop. Women, especially those with low formal educational levels, encounter the biggest problems to enter the job market. In fact, among the low qualified, young women show unemployment rates surpassing by more than 50% those of their male counterparts, while in the group with the highest educational level (thirteen years or more) this gap is 'only' 20% (Weller, 2006).

In an environment demanding completion of secondary education as a necessary but not sufficient requisite to obtain a good job—or even just *a* job—what can be expected from learning programmes focused on specific vocational training and immediate placement in the job market? Very often the limited effects of 'one time' training programmes have been questioned and the need is emphasized for projects targeted to the most disadvantaged—i.e. the young—to surpass the purely assistance approach and to be linked with integral policies of development and social integration (CINTERFOR/ILO, 1998; Jacinto, 1999; Gallart, 2000). The specific training approach, however, has been a model followed by many programmes, and this still continues to be the case.

3 The 1990s: Traditional Approaches and New Training Models

In a context of structural transformations, whose effects on the labour market have just been summarized, social expenditures—with financing by the co-operation agencies—tended during the 1990s to be oriented toward compensatory measures, placement and vocational training programmes, many of them intended for young people who had dropped out early from secondary (or even primary) school. These programmes adopted various forms of management. Among the outstanding ones, three are predominant within collective procedures focused on the training of disadvantaged young people:

1. There are still some *vocational training measures based on regular, public training establishments,* managed by tripartite authorities of professional training or departments/ministries of education;
2. *New types of supply through ad hoc programmes* were implemented, delegating training to diverse institutional agents, many of whom are private non-profit organizations (known as *organizaciones de la sociedad civil*—OSCs) or private training institutes. These new types of supply through ad hoc programmes include:
    2.a) Programmes adopting *competitive 'open-market' models* through bidding for the selection of training institutions and courses;
    2.b) Programmes granting *subsidies to organizations* working with disadvantaged groups.

However, both inside the regular supply of vocational education and training, as well as with the new models, certain common tendencies can be observed, such as the establishment of public/private alliances and a profound decentralization favouring regional organizations and local governance. Below, we will analyse in detail these different types of occupational training for unemployed young people, especially those from poor backgrounds with low levels of education.

3.1 The Traditional Supply of Vocational Training

In the regions, the supply of vocational training for young people not completing secondary education has since the 1950s been under the responsibility of the tripartite institutes of vocational training or the training institutions dependent on the relevant departments/ministries of education. Programmes bearing the name 'apprenticeship' constituted the first public policy for training and employment directed specifically at young people (Casanova, 2004).[2] The groups being enrolled in many of these conventional centres were not, however, generally the most disadvantaged, but learners who—at least potentially—could find places in the formal sectors of the economy. It was only at the beginning of the 1970s that programmes started to be implemented specifically for the informal sector; for instance the SENA of Colombia, the POCET in Honduras and the *talleres públicos de capacitación-producción* (public learning and production workshops) in Costa Rica. Financed and maintained by public funds and with instructors employed as civil servants, these institutions implemented a valuable know-how and provided a low-resource population with vocational training, counselling and, sometimes, loans to start up micro-enterprises (Gallart, 2004). Under these circumstances, timetables tended to be flexible and the training programmes adapted to the perceived needs. Very often, these training centres maintained a close relationship with community associations and diverse OSCs offering parallel services locally. Within the participating population, young people received training to start work in specific jobs (generally in traditional occupations) under self-employment conditions or, in some cases, as entrepreneurs. As will be discussed later, the general lack of work experience among young people weakens their possibilities to establish themselves as micro-entrepreneurs.[3]

3.2 Ad Hoc Occupational Training Programmes

As already mentioned, beyond these offers of traditional institutions, the 1990s witnessed the frequent implementation of social programmes and ad hoc measures against poverty, oriented towards providing vocational training to disadvantaged young people who did not normally have access to institutions of formal training. Many of these programmes were designed by the State, with a great deal of financing from co-operation agencies and multilateral banks, and were implemented by many different institutions and organizations.

The two predominant models (see above) within these ad hoc programmes will be examined next.

3.2.1 The 'Open-Market' Model

The most important programme model was developed principally by the ministries of labour and/or employment, and financed by the Inter-American Development Bank (IADB) and, in some cases, by the World Bank. The 'open market' model adopted consisted in the outsourcing of courses to what were basically private institutions (there were also some public ones) by means of bids. The institutions supplied flexible, work-based training oriented to the formal labour market, including placements in companies, and were responsible for course design and for finding placements for the young people. Another method corresponding to the open-market model is the system of 'vouchers' allowing workers to select their own training courses according to their needs.

Inside this training model, a range of training courses in various occupations were sub-contracted to a wide range of institutions and organizations, both public and private, such as trade unions, technical OSCs (some with an extensive experience in the field, and others recently created) and private training centres. One example of implementation of this open-market model is the national training programmes for disadvantaged youth carried out in several Latin American countries (Argentina, Chile, Colombia, Panama, Peru, Uruguay), known as the *Chile Joven* ('young Chile') model. Some traditional vocational training institutions also participated in public bidding for training courses of this type, for example, the SENAI, SENAC and SENAR of Brazil.

These programmes exemplify a short and reasonably inexpensive training, combined with stages of training 'at work' through placements. In some cases, these programmes have reached better labour market entry results, slightly superior to those of other agencies, because their courses were more oriented toward concrete opportunities in the labour market. It was clear, however, that their positive impact was closely dependent on the general buoyancy of the labour market and the individual size and design of the programme. In Argentina, for instance, a grand-scale programme (its goal was to train 200,000 young people under age 30) was conducted during a period coinciding with a massive increase in unemployment figures. Consequently, its effects on the entry of these young people into the labour market were almost nil (Devia, 2003). In Uruguay, by contrast, where the programme operated on a much smaller scale and with various designs adjusted to different sub-groups of young people, the relative results for the young participants were satisfactory (Lasida, 2004).

One weakness in this category of programmes was its poor contribution to enhancing training institutions. Many of the participating training centres in these short-term programmes for the disadvantaged developed more flexible approaches than the traditional institutions, but lasted only a short time and were hardly sustainable.[4] The desire to develop an alternative model to the traditional institutions, capable of overcoming bureaucracy and to avoid providing training courses not related to the actual demands of the labour market, seem to have affected the sustainability and promotion of institutional learning. One of the dilemmas for vocational training supply is still how to create outsourcing conditions that stimulate experimentation, generate stable technical teams and institutional sustainability, at the same time establishing links with the labour market and leading to acceptable results after completion of the training (Jacinto & Bessega, 2001; Lasida & Berrutti, 2002). The bidding approach for courses specifically focused on the needs of unemployed young people continues to be the model implemented during the last ten years in countries like Peru and Uruguay, and also Colombia where SENA is still active as the national vocational training authority.

3.2.2 Subsidized Programmes for Organizations Working with Disadvantaged Groups

Another type of ad hoc programme was developed within the framework of the Ministries of Social Development and/or institutes for young people, and financed in many cases by multilateral agencies. Under this scheme, OSCs, foundations, churches (particularly the Catholic Church), national training institutions, local governments, etc., received subsidies from the State to provide the learning programmes. The training in these cases is geared toward the informal sector, self-employment and/or the creation of micro-enterprises.

Usually, these social programmes encourage alliances between different public organizations, including health services, education and training institutions and private agencies enhancing social well-being, such as banks awarding micro-credits, youth centres, etc. Subsidizing organizations working with poor populations often allows the adoption of more flexible strategies, adjusted to the individual characteristics and expectations of the young people themselves, and for longer periods. In many cases, these programmes tend to develop a more complete approximation of training and combine the learning of technical skills with social competences (also in the broad sense; for example, training for citizenship), skills in seeking work and work guidance. These programmes, however, showed low concern for the technical quality of the courses and lacked clarity regarding the expected results (Jacinto, 2002). There was little emphasis in the placement of learners and little guidance toward concrete occupational opportunities, even in the informal sector.

Occasionally, these training courses were oriented to the development of entrepreneurial capabilities in general, without having any link with the learning of particular technical skills, nor specific follow-up to a business sector. They did not take into account whether or not the selected young people had the experience and the personal characteristics to manage their own enterprises (Jacinto, 2002).

Nevertheless, another relatively significant part of these social programmes focusing on young people promoted the setting up of micro-enterprises, using a more specific and complex approach. In these cases, mechanisms of selection, training and post-training guidance were included. However, these programmes were more demanding (sometimes including micro-credits) and frequently excluded the poorest, as the enrolment conditions required the participants to already possess a business and/or a secondary qualification (Jaramillo Baanante, 2004). To be successful, some evidence was required that the young people had a certain level of business initiative, either experience in salaried work, entrepreneurial skills or an idea for a business plan (Lasida, 2004).

3.3 Achievements and Limitations of the Strategies from the 1990s

To sum up the general procedures developed in the 1990s within the framework of programmes targeting the inclusion of young people from poor backgrounds into the labour market, the following features can be noted:

- More flexible training approaches were adopted, as the implementation of courses and projects was carried out by sub-contracting public and private agencies offering various types of training, rather than traditional vocational training institutions. Whereas a certain consensus can be observed about the need to start modifying the State's preference to organize social policies (i.e. its institutions, human resources, equipment and infrastructure) from the supply side, the adopted mechanisms, both the 'open market' model and the subsidized programmes, did not lead to efficient vocational training corresponding to the needs of the young people, the demands of the job market or socio-economic developments. Instead, they resulted in haphazard action with more or less quality and efficacy, according to individual cases.
- In spite of its diversification and flexibility, the training organizations experienced difficulties with the design and implementation of the learning. First, they had to confront new duties related to curricular design, institutional management, interaction with other institutions and with the labour market, and they did not necessarily know how to respond to these challenges. Secondly, many organizations revealed their weaknesses in administrative and financial management. They also showed knowledge deficiencies about strategies for institutional planning and internal communication (Jacinto, 2001).
- One weakness was that almost none of the actions taken established links with existing formal education. The certificates that were awarded did not imply any recognition or equivalencies in formal education or regular vocational training, even though the majority of the young people enrolled did not possess a secondary qualification, and although one of the outcomes of enrolment was that almost 30% of these young people returned to formal education (Jacinto, 2004).
- As mentioned earlier, considering how difficult it was for young people, particularly the most economically and socially disadvantaged, to find quality employment, the programmes tended to foresee entry into the formal (salaried) labour market. However, programmes that promoted the creation of micro-enterprises and/or self-employment also played a relevant role. In his analysis of thirty-seven programmes, for example, Jaramillo (2004) identifies twenty-two that were exclusively oriented toward self-employment and another fifteen that included measures for salaried employment and self-employment at the same time. While the impact of the programmes, measured by access to formal employment, differs

among countries, in most cases it can be said to be very limited and only produced slight improvements in some sub-groups (Jacinto, 2004). Concerning the
results of the programmes that might have promoted micro-industry and self-
employment, these also tended to be very sparse, considering the small percentage of new companies that were able to survive their first year. In addition, the
programmes with the highest potential (i.e. including training, follow-up and
micro-credits) tended to exclude young people from the most disadvantaged sectors (Jaramillo, 2004).[5]

- Although training has sometimes been linked with other formative and cultural
  actions, these links do not seem to be vital in the selection or evaluation of
  courses by the central management of programmes. The broadest approaches,
  linking the training programmes to other local or sector development projects
  and to the social integration of young people, remained generally restricted to
  small-scale experiences with little coverage (Jacinto, 1999).

Generally speaking, these measures reveal an attempt to provide greater opportunities to young people confronting increasingly exclusive social contexts and more
complex labour markets. Its most relevant aspects are precisely the fact that they
express the urgent need for a programme and the permanent improvement of its
strategies, increasingly emphasizing the use of concrete job opportunities.

Many of the initiatives, however, proved to over-simplify the problem of young
people entering the labour market, particularly those belonging to the most disadvantaged groups. On the one side, they emphasized the question of low skill
levels without sufficiently taking into account the role formal education plays in
the job-market selection, and the exclusion tendencies of the labour market itself. In
addition, the basic view of young people tends to be short-sighted if it fails to cover
the social and cultural issues than constitute the fact of 'being young/adolescent',
nor taking into account the heterogeneity of social and educational situations that
characterize disadvantaged young people within geographic, local and family contexts. In fact, it turns out that the situations of the young people targeted are very
diverse: from groups very marginal and isolated (indigenous people, homeless children, etc.), to those from poor urban districts or rural young people.

Finally, beyond the diversity of the measures, we should not lose sight of the
fact that these initiatives covered only a small fraction of the potential population
composing all of the young people who dropped out of school without any qualifications. Indeed, in Argentina, Brazil, Chile, Costa Rica, El Salvador and Honduras,
most young people aged 18 to 25 do not complete secondary education. In recent
years, only in Argentina and Chile did a majority of the young population complete secondary education. Meanwhile, in Brazil, Paraguay and El Salvador, more
than 60% of young people did not complete secondary education; this percentage
is more than 75% in Costa Rica and Honduras. In all of these countries there are
significant inter-regional differences, with young people living in large metropolitan
areas being the ones most likely to complete secondary education (SITEAL, 2005).

4 Testing New Ways

The expansion of formal schooling and the introduction of new technologies, particularly in the information and communication sector, affect not only working practices but also everyday life. It is also clear that an occupational strategy for the disadvantaged based exclusively on vocational training for traditional jobs has its limitations, as has been shown in most of the experiences mentioned. Despite these limitations, many of the measures have followed those same patterns. More recent programmes are now trying new models as a response to some of the limitations or weaknesses of the traditional approaches. One aspect that has received particular emphasis is to achieve a better integration of the formative and inter-sectoral approaches. We can differentiate the following strategies in this field:

4.1 Initiatives Promoting Alternative Educational Paths

During recent years some social and employment programmes have encouraged young people and adults to finalize their basic and/or secondary education through learning strategies (in many cases, part-time schooling) that attempt to respond in a more pertinent way to their needs and interests more than traditional educational services. Some initiatives of this type in Argentina, Brazil and Chile have gained momentum in recent years, as well as in other countries.

Among the experiences of this type, the example of Chile is probably the one that has been most systematically implemented and evaluated. The flexible and free method of promoting training forms part of *Chile Califica* (Chile Qualifies), a programme under the auspices of the ministries of education, labour and economy/finance. The World Bank finances 50% of the loans and State contributions cover the other 50%.

This pattern is structured in learning blocks and envisages both classroom and self-learning activities. It works with cost-free books supplied by the Ministry of Education. The State also evaluates the students' progress and awards certificates.

Between 2002 and 2004, using this system, 42,000 persons acquired a basic education certificate and 74,000 a secondary education certificate. An interesting aspect of this programme is that it achieves better completion rates than those of traditional educational paths for adults (Letelier, 2005). Some studies have reported positive results in income and occupational level, especially among women and young people.

4.2 Integral Experiences Linking Training with Job Integration

One example of a recent programme that decided to focus on training and job-entry for occupations in new technologies is the so-called ENTRA-21 (2005). This programme supports training developed by OSCs and youth employment projects in ICTs with a fund of US$20 million, co-financed by Fundación Internacional para la Juventud (FIJ) and the Fondo Multilateral de Inversiones (FOMIN) from the Inter-American Development Bank. The programme subsidizes projects of approximately US$375,000 for up to three years. Until July 2005, ENTRA-21 had carried out twenty-four projects in sixteen countries, reaching 11,227 disadvantaged young people.

Some interesting aspects concerning the design and execution of this programme are worth mentioning. First, its focus was on occupations using new technologies with a broad approach to training that included not only learning about technical abilities but also personal and social skills, as well as job placement. It also emphasized public/private co-operation in design and implementation, in order to join resources and facilitate job integration after training. This last aspect represents the most outstanding point of the programme: its commitment to job entry from its very inception. Consequently, mechanisms to assist young people during the job-entry process were put into place. It intends to be not just another VET programme, but a job-integration programme including training. The job-placement results for young people have been satisfactory, achieving rates between 40% and 68% of entry into the job market within six months after training.

4.3 Programmes Using 'Positive Discrimination' Mechanisms

These practices include:

- Programmes that stimulate the enrolment of young people facing the greatest difficulties, such as first-job seekers in Brazil;
- Other programmes in other communities have created 'sheltered' job opportunities in the public sector. This means reserving jobs or activities for young unemployed people who otherwise would not have the opportunity to enter the labour market if it were not for this strategy, as in the case of the city of Montevideo. This practice demonstrates an interesting strategy of positive discrimination that focuses on creating job opportunities for the most disadvantaged young people. Obviously, this strategy is not without controversy: critics point out deficiencies in the services; trade unions argue that the young are taking jobs away from other workers.

5 Some Reflections on the Future Course of Action

Obviously, the problem has multiple facets, tied to national development and growth strategies in a broad sense. Within a region where social inequalities are extreme and poverty has increased, these hard-fought programmes have made progress in consolidating a system of education, training and social guidance for those young people with minimal opportunities. Some strategies attempt to go beyond the more limited visions of vocational training by creating better links to formal education, promoting entry into the labour market and a more equitable distribution of employment opportunities.

Some points must be outlined regarding opportunities for young people in disadvantaged situations:

- Since the period of formal schooling has expanded, and a long period of education continues to be the best option in terms of finding a job, becoming part of society and conducting a career, we can draw at least three major conclusions about formal education:

  - Young people dropping out of school face increasingly disadvantaged situations in a labour market where secondary education may not be entirely sufficient, but is absolutely necessary for entry into the labour market. There is a need to reinforce incentives for young people to remain in school and promote the return of drop-outs into the education system.
  - During their time in school, all young people should acquire the general basics and fundamental skills for work and social integration. In this respect, the pathetic results of formal basic and secondary schooling and the differences among socio-economic groups clearly indicate the need for change.
  - Bridges between and within different educational paths and learning environments (formal schooling, vocational training, workplace) need to be created and/or reinforced to encourage the social significance of education for young people entering the labour market.

- Concerning programmes and/or measures specifically designed to improve the entry of young people into the job market, it should be noted that there is no evidence of positive results from unselective mass programmes. Consequently, it seems advisable for these programmes to be specific, directed at specifically-selected categories of young people, carefully evaluated and adjusted to specific niches or sectors of the economy. Inevitably, the broad heterogeneity of young people in the region must be taken into account. Their problems are different according to socio-economic levels, gender, educational level, ethnicity, etc. Therefore, it is necessary to identify this diversity in order to formulate proper solutions. More generally, it can be recommended that vocational training programmes in this region should:

  - be dual, that is to say, they should include components of school training as well as on-the-job learning (internship/placements, etc.);
  - have an integral design, apt for promoting the development of not only technical, but also personal and social skills;
  - be able to follow-up the integration of persons into the labour market; and
  - only for some carefully selected groups of a population, promote self-employment and the creation of small enterprises, supporting them with financial services, training and counselling.

As evidence shows, account must be taken of the fact that these measures will reflect general trends in employment closely. One remaining issue is to profoundly reinforce the links between the various educational services and programmes. In Latin America, formal education and vocational training represent two distinct paths that co-ordinate neither their functions nor their resources. They depend on different sectors of public administration, or operate even on a private basis, and are far removed from constituting a unified system (Jacinto, 2002). One of the greatest current challenges seems to be the design of a strategy leading the population to qualifications. The strategic objective would be the implementation of national systems that could link education, vocational training and diverse mechanisms of learning and entry into the labour market. Better links are not only needed to increase efficacy and efficiency; they also drive the broader field of equity, prophesying in this way a wider system of lifelong education, able to cope with social, cultural, economic and technical changes and offering access to diverse training options.

Acknowledgments I am grateful to Victoria González for her assistance in researching and to Veronica Diyarian for her collaboration in writing this text.

Notes

1. Based on the results of regional research covering five in-depth case studies of training programmes for young people in various Latin American countries undertaken in 1999/2000 (Jacinto, 2002). Comments on the most recent developments come from data compiled on several case studies of programmes in recent years, available online at: <www.redetis.iipe-ides.org.ar>
2. Training programmes leading to a qualification, usually lasting two years, and including work placement in industry.
3. Moreover, training supply for micro-entrepreneurs tends not to recognize their internal heterogeneity: from subsidized micro-enterprises with little viability in the market place to self-employment with a potential to grow, or even competitive micro-enterprises in certain market niches. According to Gallart (2004), the programmes focused on disadvantaged populations trying to make the weakest micro-enterprises more competitive, even though most of the time this is just not feasible.
4. Many were created just to participate in the programmes (Jacinto, 1999).
5. The promotion of self-employment experiences and/or micro-enterprise opportunities for young people from low socio-educational backgrounds seems to require extensive follow-up, including measures like: support in the selection of viable niches for products or services; training in management, marketing and skills related to the activity; access to loans; and technical assistance for an extensive period, including psycho-social support (Ruétalo, Lasida & Berrutti, 1998).

References

Casanova, F. 2004. *Desarrollo local, tejidos productivos y formación: abordajes alternativos para la formación y el trabajo de los jóvenes.* Montevideo: CINTERFOR. (Herramientas para la transformación, no. 22)

Comisión Economica para América Latina. 2005. *Estudio económico de América Latina y el Caribe 2004–2005.* Santiago: CEPAL. <www.eclac.cl/publicaciones/DesarrolloEconomico/9/LCG2279PE/LCG2279_e_RE.pdf>

CINTERFOR/OIT. 1998. *Juventud, educación y empleo.* Montevideo: CINTERFOR.

Devia, S. 2003. *¿Éxito o fracaso de las políticas públicas de capacitación laboral a jóvenes? Evaluación del programa testigo 'Proyecto Joven' de Argentina (1993–2000).* Buenos Aires: UBA.

ENTRA-21. 2005. *Informe de gestión.* <www.iyfnet.org>

Gallart, M.A. 2000. El desafío de la formación para el trabajo de los jóvenes en situación de pobreza: el caso argentino. *In:* Gallart, M.A., ed. *Formación, pobreza y exclusión,* pp. 241–302. Montevideo: CINTERFOR.

Gallart, M.A. 2004. Habilidades y competencias para el sector informal en América Latina: una revisión de la literatura sobre programas y metodologías de formación. *CINTERFOR boletín,* no. 155. <www.cinterfor.org.uy/public/spanish/region/ampro/cinterfor/publ/boletin/155/ pdf/gallart.pdf>

Jacinto, C. 1999. *Programas de educación para jóvenes desfavorecidos: enfoques y tendencias en América Latina.* Paris: UNESCO-IIEP.

Jacinto, C. 2001. Contextos y actores sociales en la evaluación de los programas de capacitación de jóvenes. *In:* Pieck, E., ed. *Los jóvenes y el trabajo: la educación frente a la exclusión social.* Mexico: CINTERFOR. <www.cinterfor.org.uy/public/spanish/region/ampro/cinterfor/ temas/youth/doc/not/libro273/epieck7.pdf>

Jacinto, C. 2002. *Nuevas alianzas y estrategias en la formación para el trabajo de jóvenes desfavorecidos: estudios de caso en América Latina.* Paris: UNESCO-IIEP.

Jacinto, C. 2004. Ante la polarización de oportunidades laborales de los jóvenes de América Latina: un análisis de algunas propuestas recientes en la formación para el trabajo. *In:* Jacinto, C., ed. *¿Educar para que trabajo? Discutiendo rumbos en América Latina,* pp. 187–200. Buenos Aires: La Crujía.

Jacinto, C.; Bessega, C. 2001. *Fortalecimiento institucional de entidades de capacitación para jóvenes desfavorecidos.* Paris: UNESCO-IIEP.

Jaramillo Baanante, M. 2004. *Los emprendimientos juveniles en America Latina: ¿Una respuesta ante las dificultades de empleo?* Buenos Aires: IIPE-IDES. <www.redetis.org.ar/ media/document/id522_fieldfile1.pdf>

Lasida, J. 2004. *Estrategias para acercar a los jóvenes al trabajo.* Buenos Aires: IIPE-IDES. <www.redetis.org.ar/media/document/id521_fieldfile1.pdf>

Lasida, J.; Berrutti, E. 2002. Foro Juvenil, ensayos y aprendizajes para las políticas de educación y trabajo. *In:* Jacinto, C. et al., eds. *Nuevas alianzas y estrategias en la formación para el trabajo de jóvenes desfavorecidos: estudios de caso en América Latina.* Paris: UNESCO-IIEP.

Letelier, M.E. 2005. *El programa de nivelación de estudios de Chile: estrategias educativas y formativas para la inclusión social y productive.* (Paper presented at the workshop 'Estrategias educativas y formativas para la inclusión social y productiva de todos', Instituto Nacional para la Educación de Adultos, Mexico D.F., 14–15 November 2005.)

Ruétalo, J.; Lasida, J.; Berrutti, E. 1998. Formación para el trabajo de jóvenes de sectores de pobreza en América Latina. ¿Qué desafíos y qué estrategias? *In:* Jacinto, C.; Gallart, M.A., eds. *Por una segunda oportunidad: la formación para el trabajo de jóvenes vulnerable,* pp. 7–32. Montevideo: CINTERFOR/OIT. (Herramientas para la transformación, no. 6). <www.cinterfor.org.uy/public/spanish/region/ampro/cinterfor/publ/jacinto/pdf/jacint2.pdf>

SITEAL. 2005. *Tendencias interregionales en el porcentaje de jóvenes que no completó la secundaria.* <www.siteal.iipe-oei.org>

Weller, J. 2003. La problemática inserción laboral de los y las jóvenes. *Serie macroeconomía del desarrollo,* no. 28.

Weller, J. 2006. Inserción laboral de jóvenes: expectativas, demanda laboral y trayectorias. *Boletín redEtis,* no. 5. <www.redetis.org.ar>

Chapter III.3
Accountability and Career Technical Education (CTE) Policy: A Brief Review of Six States of the United States

Joshua D. Hawley and Alexandra de Montrichard

1 Introduction

Accountability concerns are at the top of the list of issues that career technical education (CTE) administrators are currently forced to deal with. As it has evolved in the United States, state CTE policy is trying to juggle missions that include preparation for careers with current efforts to improve the academic achievement of youth. This focuses attention at the state level on the articulation of public policies that 'thread the needle'—allowing students to master both occupational content and academic skills.

The United States Federal Department of Education's (DOE) web-site for CTE reflects the three themes CTE is trying to balance for career and technical education:

- Increasing academic achievement;
- Fostering post-secondary transitions; and
- Preparing students for high-skill, high-wage careers.

This emphasis on a variety of outcomes for CTE is reflected in the academic and policy literature. One recent report from the Association for Career and Technical Education stresses the critical role that academic skills play in current CTE practice. The policy paper lays out a framework for CTE in the twenty-first century suggesting that CTE programmes offer both rigorous academic and vocational content. The authors described the issue as follows: 'we believe that CTE courses and instructional methodologies have a place in the high-school environment, and that there should not be an artificial split between academic coursework and vocational studies' (Association for Career and Technical Education, 2006, p. 3).

Additionally, the long-standing programme from the Southern Regional Education Board emphasizes the importance of academic skills for improvements in the quality of CTE coursework. The recent empirical work done by High Schools that Work illustrates the gains when students in CTE achieve high levels of academic as well as vocational content. Bottoms and Young (2005) provide data that if students take at least four credits of maths or college preparatory English as part of a CTE programme, 80 to 90% did not need remedial coursework in college.

R. Maclean, D. Wilson (eds.), *International Handbook of Education for the Changing World of Work*, DOI 10.1007/978-1-4020-5281-1_III.3,
© Springer Science+Business Media B.V. 2009

This focus on accountability has come to a head while the Federal Government's main policy on education, the No Child Left Behind Act (NCLB), faces continued resistance from states. They continue to object to the appearance of unfunded mandates within the legislation.

The difficulty persists when developing performance measures related to curriculum standards. A 1999 report on state-level accountability strategies asserts that:

> most of the measurement issues related to the conflicting purposes of vocational education (school reform versus workforce development) and governance/system delivery (centralized versus decentralized) are quite complex. All states are working on parts of the system or systems. It is hoped that the parts eventually sum to a whole (Rahn, O'Driscoll & Hudecki, 1999).

Nevertheless, states have historically developed strategies to measure and assess the performance of high-school vocational education in each of these areas. The current debate centres on expanding the accountability systems defined by NCLB, but balancing those accountability demands that are unique to CTE programmes.

2 Accountability and Federal Policy

Accountability is the practice of holding schools, districts and teachers responsible for providing quality education and holding students responsible for their own performance. As part of the push to hold school systems accountable, standards and, to varying degrees, accountability systems were developed both at the state and federal levels. As of the 2003/2004 school year, with the exception of Iowa, all states have developed standards for all their core subjects (English/language arts, mathematics, science and social studies/history), as well as school report cards available to the public (The Editors, 2004).

The 1990 and 1998 Carl D. Perkins Vocational-Technical Acts (Perkins II & III) required states to set up accountability systems for their local vocational programmes. Perkins III also added incentive performance funds for states. These frameworks have guided contemporary accountability systems in the sample states, but the debate at the federal level threatens to derail this progress. The various proposals from the White House, Senate and House of Representatives offered very different visions of career and technical education accountability systems. The Council of Chief State School Officers reported that President Bush's 2005 Budget Request expanded achievement and accountability goals from the Elementary and Secondary Education Act (ESEA)—renamed the No Child Left Behind Act—to CTE. This movement, if it occurred, would emphasize achievement of academic outcomes, but still require states to demonstrate workplace preparedness.

The Senate and House of Representatives versions of the current Perkins' Legislation do not extend the accountability goals to CTE in a wholesale manner, but focus on allowing states to define the accountability system that CTE programmes must meet. This legislation at the secondary level focuses on defining the types of indicators that states must meet and requires continuous improvement in educational progress of career-focused students (Association for Career and Technical Education, 2005).

The future of CTE accountability is therefore in question, but only in terms of emphasis. The key question is: will CTE accountability remain divided between labour-market outcomes and academic success, or focus narrowly on the academic outcomes?

3 What is an Accountability System?

Before reviewing state-level accountability, we focus on describing the definitional issues behind accountability systems. The following paragraphs describe the current literature/focus on accountability at the state level.

The National Association of State Boards of Education (NASBE) did a review of state accountability and large-scale assessments in 2001 and outlined the essential elements shared by state assessment systems (National Association of State Boards of Education, 2001). According to NASBE, effective assessments systems:

- have rigorous and detailed standards that are specific enough to determine what needs to be evaluated;
- are designed to address specific goals and purposes (such as student remediation or school district assessment);
- balance validity, reliability and efficiency;
- inform instruction and have consequences;
- have mechanisms to encourage schools and districts to align their instruction and evaluation with the standards; and
- have a clearly articulated relationship with national measures of student performance.

Most scholarly literature on accountability evolved in recent years to focus attention on this broad interpretation of accountability to include standards systems, testing and curriculum frameworks, as well as numerical standards for achievement. In the context of CTE, the research on accountability varies considerably.

4 Issues Raised in the Literature on Accountability and CTE

Our literature review identified three key areas of concern: the integration of vocational education and general education accountability, the quality of CTE programmes and the integration of federal, state and local accountability.

4.1 Accountability of Vocational Education and General Education

CTE is affected by both school reforms, such as No Child Left Behind, and workforce development reforms such as the Workforce Investment Act. In their report on state-level accountability strategies, Rahn, O'Driscoll and Hudecki (1999) argue that this creates a tension in purpose, standards, accountability systems and governance structures, which plays itself out differently in various states. Measures that might be called 'school reform' items and are used by many states include the percentage of students scoring at below a specific level on an academic test, or the percentage of students enrolled in college preparatory coursework. Secondly, measures that might be called workforce development are represented by other indicators, such as the percentage of students passing certifications/licensure exams or the percentage placed in a job related to the training.

School reforms have spurred the development of accountability standards and systems for general education focused on core subjects (English/language arts, mathematics, science, and social studies/history). However, the degree to which vocational education accountability standards are integrated into more general educational standards varies. As of 1999 this had only happened in a few states (Rahn et al., 1999; Stasz & Bodilly, 2004).

4.2 Quality CTE Programmes

The 2004 National Assessment of Vocational Education (NAVE) report focuses on the priorities set out by Perkins III and identified strategies that would help improve secondary vocational programme performance. These include strategies for academic achievement, increased occupational and technical skills and workforce outcomes. To enhance academic achievement the report suggested making this a more explicit focus in Perkins, supporting curriculum development to strengthen the academic content of vocational courses, integrating academic and vocational education, focusing funding to programmes with proven academic content, and investment in focused teacher training to improve teacher quality.

The report quotes a study not yet released that indicates: 'states have begun to reference or encourage academic content in vocational course guidelines [. . .] States spend the highest share of state leadership funds—nearly 20 per cent nationally—to promote integration' (White et al., 2004). However, at the school level integration is still not widespread and the report lists a series of barriers to this integration.

To raise occupational and technical skills in high schools the authors suggest that challenging content and performance standards are required for vocational courses, linked with end-of-course technical assessments and that rewards and sanctions be in place for programmes based on performance. Finally, to improve employment and earnings, particularly for non-college-bound students, the recommendations are to encourage implementation of vocational programme course sequences and promote work-experience programmes.

Other areas identified as key to programme quality and improvement include the linkages between secondary and post-secondary education, which NAVE finds are strong among CTE faculty, enhancing the use of technology and employer involvement.

4.3 Integration of Federal, State and Local Accountability

In accountability there is a potential conflict between federal, state and local needs. Federal requirements tend to focus more on programmatic accountability and aggregated measures that allow cross-state comparisons. Local accountability systems may be more useful to schools for programme improvement, whereas more standardized data collection facilitates comparisons across schools and districts at the state level. 'The result is a patchwork of "systems" at the local and state levels, each moving toward accountability with different data and reporting requirements' (Rahn et al., 1999).

One early report argues that:

> vocational education is particularly susceptible to ineffective, high-level policy-making because local conditions play such a large role in program planning and performance. Programs are planned with an eye toward local economic needs, and program performance is measured in terms of placements, which are found primarily in the local area (Stecher & Hanser, 1992).

This report thus focused on the need to 'understand local accountability mechanisms and their relationship to more highly aggregated state policymaking'. The authors found that 'local accountability systems exist, although they are often informal and unsystematic' (Stecher & Hanser, 1992). They identified four key components that account for much of the variation in the quality of local accountability systems: measures, information, feedback loops and change mechanisms

The level at which accountability data is collected at the state also varies depending on whether they have centralized or decentralized governance structures and/or delivery systems (Rahn et al., 1999).

5 Methodology

5.1 Sample

The six states studied and visited included Illinois, Massachusetts, Michigan, New Jersey, New York and Ohio.

The states selected for this study are different from each other. The population size, labour-market composition and unemployment rates vary. All but two of the states are governed by the State Board of Education; in the other two cases it is the Higher Education Board that has legislative responsibility for CTE.

Table 1 shows that the states vary from smaller north-eastern states, such as Massachusetts, to larger mid-western states like Illinois. All of the states have designated CTE systems.

Table 2 shows that the states have a variety of mechanisms for implementing vocational education. In the case of Illinois, for example, of the 665 public high schools in the state, there were only twenty-six schools offering CTE, and these were

Table 1 Basic information on state education

	Year	IL	MA	MI	NJ	NY	OH
Total enrolment	2002	2,084,187	982,989	1,785,160	1,367,438	2,888,233	1,838,285
in public	2000	2,048,792	975,150	1,720,626	1,313,405	2,882,188	1,835,049
schools	1995	1,943,623	915,007	1,641,456	1,197,381	2,813,230	1,836,015
(Student numbers)	1990	1,821,407	834,314	1,584,431	1,089,646	2,598,337	1,771,089
Diploma	2002	116,657	55,272	95,001	77,664	153,879	110,608
recipients	2000	111,835	52,950	97,679	74,420	141,731	111,668
(Student	1995	105,164	47,679	86,180	67,403	136,234	109,418
numbers)	1990	108,119	55,941	100,522	69,824	146,307	114,513
Total state	2000	18,441	9,515	16,701	16,323	34,837	16,024
expenditures	1995	—	6,524	—	—	—	—
for education ($ millions)	1990	9,867	5,024	9,623	9,208	—	9,206

Sources:
1. National Center for Education Statistics: <nces.ed.gov/ccd/>
2. National Association of State Directors of Career Technical Education Consortia: <www.careertech.org/reference/states/stateInfo.asp>

Table 2 School information on career technical education in six states (number of schools)

	IL	MA	MI	NJ	NY	OH
All public high schools	665	280	763	311	852	826
Public schools offering CTE	26	–	–	–	98	–
– Comprehensive high schools	–				60	
– Vocational high schools	–				–	
– Regional/area vocational/career-technical centres	26				38	
Public schools offering solely vocational instruction according to the National Association of State Directors	26	45	29	50	25	76
Public vocational education schools in 2001–2002 according the NCES	0	43	12	38	25	68

Sources:
1. National Association of State Directors of Career Technical Education Consortia: <www.careertech.org/reference/states/stateInfo.asp>
2. State sources:

- Illinois: <www.isbe.net/career/pdf/avc_directory.pdf>, <www.isbe.net/research/pdfs/quick_stats03.pdf>
- Illinois and New York internal state documents.
- Correspondence with state director's office in January 2004.

3. Hoffman, 2003.

organized as regional vocational technical centres. In contrast, New York had 852 public high schools, ninety-eight of which were offering CTE. Within New York's system, however, sixty high schools were comprehensive in nature and offered vocational schooling as a part of their programme while thirty-eight were regional vocational technical centres.

Table 3 shows both the number of secondary and post-secondary students enrolled in CTE in the six states. The proportion of students in CTE at the secondary level varies from a low of 18% in Ohio, to a high of 55% in Illinois. While 79% of post-secondary students in Illinois are classified as CTE students, in Massachusetts only 39% of students are focused on vocational areas.

Table 3 Student information on career technical education in six states

	IL	MA	MI	NJ	NY	OH
Students in public high schools	550,301	233,179	471,950	310,010	708,456	534,536
Secondary students enrolled in CTE	302,631	46,071	205,020	79,838	256,295	95,253
% of secondary students enrolled in CTE	55.0%	19.8%	43.4%	25.8%	36.2%	17.8%
Students at public community colleges	339,151	80,070	186,847	132,808	245,842	179,077
Post-secondary students enrolled in CTE	268,604	31,842	151,459	65,710	143,397	165,839
% of post-secondary students enrolled in CTE	79.2%	39.8%	81.1%	49.5%	58.3%	92.6%

Source: National Association of States Directory of Career Technical Education Consortia: <www.careertech.org/reference/states/stateInfo.asp>

Several contextual issues surround the issues of accountability and curriculum in these states. Firstly, both Perkins' legislation and state implementation leave an enormous range of variation in how programmes are established and how a vocational completer/concentrator is established. These are important contextual issues, because they govern the scope of a vocational programme. In most cases the interviews show us that states have very inconsistent views on the definition of a CTE programme or the designation of a vocational completer. Current efforts by the federal Department of Education Office of Vocational and Adult Education (OVAE) and others to better define these categories go to the heart of decisions about what unit to assess in vocational education.

5.2 Data Collection

Every state except one was visited by a researcher. An interview protocol was developed by staff familiar with career and technical education and state policy. It was reviewed by key members of the research team and served as the basis for the discussions with the respondents. At one site the respondents were interviewed by telephone.

The focus of this study was a comparison of accountability systems for CTE programmes. The study documents the basic characteristics of accountability systems in each state by determining:

- What are the standards for CTE programmes?
- How are these standards measured?
- What types of tests are used to measure CTE student performance?
- How are the results of these tests used?

Additionally, we focused on documenting state by state:

- the level of CTE and academic curriculum and accountability integration;
- the effects of school reform legislation, specifically No Child Left Behind, on CTE programmes.

Respondents from six states were interviewed individually or in groups for about $1^1/_2$ hours each. A total of sixteen people participated in the interviews. Additionally, the states supplied us with copies of their accountability plans, the current state plan for CTE, and other studies that helped inform our data collection efforts. Each interview was taped and transcribed. The transcription was imported into a computer analysis programme—N'Vivo. These files were the main source of data for the analysis.

5.3 Data Analysis

From the transcripts generated for this study the researchers developed a set of initial codes using N'Vivo software. These codes were based on the interview protocol, producing an initial list of twenty-three codes. These twenty-three codes were grouped into five folders, representing data collected on the following key categories of information: CTE administration; CTE programme requirements and definitions; measures and assessment systems; CTE links with occupations and industry; curriculum; and current legislation. A coding report was printed from N'Vivo software for each of these categories. The codes were applied to specific sets of text on the basis of a reading of the transcripts and subsequent analysis.

6 Results

6.1 CTE Organization and Administration

Overall, CTE forms an important component of the state secondary education systems across our six states. While the country has a federal Department of Education, constitutionally the education systems are state level responsibilities (Fowler, 2003;

Table 4 Basic information on career technical education

		IL	MA	MI	NJ	NY	OH
Type of governance structure	State Board Authority		■	■	■		■
	Post-Secondary Governing Board.	■				■	
Funding strategy	Funding based on student participation		▲			▲	
	Cost reimbursement						
	Instructional units			▲			
	Student weights	▲					▲
	State Foundation grants				▲		
States with dual enrolment policy			●	●	●	●	●
High-school graduation requirements	Graduation contingent on performance on state-wide exit or end-of-course exams		♦		♦	♦	♦
	Curriculum requirements	*	*	*	*	*	*

Note: Ohio states that it will carry out graduation testing requirements and curriculum requirements connected with the Ohio diploma; students must meet both requirements in order to earn an Ohio diploma after 15 September 2006.

Sources: Karp et al., 2004.; Klein, 2001, p. 13.; Krueger, 2004; Silverberg et al., 2004; National Assessment of Vocational Education, 2004; The Editors, 2004, p. 109.

Stasz & Bodilly, 2004). This implies that the provision and co-ordination of vocational education is the responsibility of the states. The states we studied vary in a wide range of governance and administrative responsibilities (Table 4).

In terms of overall state-level co-ordination of CTE, there are effectively two major models: control through the K-12 education system; or the post-secondary system. In the case of our six states, all but two are administered through the traditional K-12 education system. Only New York and Illinois are controlled through the post-secondary system. This difference is crucial, illustrating the bias towards secondary-level vocational schooling. In recent years, however, other states, such as Alabama and Kentucky, outside of our sample, have retooled their vocational education systems to integrate economic development into the administration of vocational schooling (Grubb et al., 1999).

Moreover, state funding of vocational schooling varies considerably. As described in a recent study of vocational funding, there are markedly different funding mechanisms that states have in place to provide for vocational services (Klein, 2001). The amount of money states have available from the federal government for state-level accountability has declined as a percentage of Perkins' funds, and there is some evidence that this has affected the ability of states to shift accountability systems (Stasz & Bodilly, 2004). In our six states, there is no predominant model of funding, with some operating on a per pupil basis and others on a state grant basis.

In all cases, the state administration extends its control to curriculum frameworks and in many of them this includes matched tests to assess student performance.

What this implies in the national context is a core curriculum requirement that needs to be met by all secondary school students regardless of curricular focus, as well as specific vocational competencies that are typically industry or field specific. The long-term outcome of the push for accountability, however, has driven more and more states to require a high-stakes test during high school as a mechanism to ensure that all students attain a minimum level of skills. Of our sample states, Massachusetts, New Jersey and Ohio all require CTE students to pass a graduation test, while New York also requires the Regents Tests (Bishop & Mane, 1998).

The following section examines the perspectives on accreditation and programme design in the six states participating in qualitative interviews. It then moves on to a consideration of how states define CTE completion.

6.2 Programme Accreditation/Approval

As described in the definitional section, CTE requires detailed understanding of school-level performance, as well as a focus on student achievement. Schools are to be judged as systems under the NCLB Act.

In each of the six states, CTE systems are governed by a local legislative system that defines the CTE programme and student, and in some cases specifies the accountability provisions that the programmes must meet in order to remain in compliance. Of the six states, the state of New York and the state of Illinois provide for interesting contrast in contemporary programme approval processes. In the case of New York the programme approval process for CTE includes the following:

1. An internal review that takes into account the opinions of the teachers, as well as employers in the locality;
2. An external review that includes both employers and community or post-secondary education partners;
3. Articulation agreements;
4. A defined work-based learning programme; and
5. Identification of industry-based tests.

The New York programme process seems distinctive for two reasons. First and foremost, it includes a state mandate for articulation. Second, the state is focusing on encouraging work-based learning. While most CTE programmes will include work-based learning, it is usually left to instructors and schools to decide how best to carry it out. Moreover, the interview with the state director's staff stressed the positive role that businesses play in determining demand for the programme by actively engaging in the programme design and proposal process.

The Illinois programme approval process is different, but offers an alternative vision of how CTE programmes should be developed. As defined by the state leaders in CTE, the programme approval process is as follows:

1. Programmes are defined and proposed based on the local labour market (Employment Regional Delivery Systems), which allows programmes to reflect local labour-market demand.
2. Schools outline the potential post-secondary careers for individual students (both career and educational).
3. Programmes describe the industry certifications or tests; and
4. Provide course descriptions.

There are some striking differences when the Illinois programmes are compared to New York. The Illinois programme focuses on assessing demand in the labour market, but the specific employer role is quite difficult to discern. In contrast, the New York programme appears to require more detailed external review. Moreover, the Illinois programme still includes an emphasis on CTE that connects to secondary-only programmes, while the New York criteria appears to require some linkage with post-secondary education.

6.3 Other Programme Criteria

State programme criteria for CTE programmes appear to be quite similar. States all have criteria for curriculum and staffing. What varies is the current move in some states towards providing more specificity around the type and level of employer involvement. The New York criteria, in particular, offer some hope that states are recognizing that the role of an advisory committee needs to include requirements for employer assessment of programmes, rather than leaving this decision up to the local administrators or teachers.

6.4 Definition of a CTE Concentrator

The definition of a CTE concentrator is not common across the states. There is a wide variation in state regulation about the types of criteria that go into a concentrator definition. Firstly, as the description shows, some states define concentrator by the number of credits or hours they have taken in CTE, while others focus on the level of schooling (11th or 12th grade). A third strategy is to designate all those who reach the last level of vocational schooling as concentrators. The following example comes from Michigan and represents one of the most specific attempts to define concentration in CTE coursework:

> Concentrator: A secondary student that has successfully completed 60% of a state-approved career and technical education program must have a minimum of 7,200 minutes per year, except for trade and industry programs that must have a minimum of 14,400 minutes per year. The threshold level would vary depending upon the sequence of courses and number of courses and number of minutes for each individual occupational program.

Moreover, there are differences in the ways states characterize students who complete CTE coursework—or completers. The most common characteristics of completers include the following: finishing an approved sequence of courses in a CTE concentration; completion of a set of courses as defined by state regulations to satisfy Perkins' requirements; or enrolment in a programme for at least two years that meets the common criteria set by the state for career and technical education. The following definition comes from Ohio and clearly represents one of the most elaborate completer frameworks:

> Completer: Secondary program completer—a student who has enrolled in and completed an approved workforce development program (typically 450 hours) AND has demonstrated sufficient mastery of their vocational and academic subject matter to prepare them for their career and lifelong learning goals as set forth in their individual career plan AND is no longer enrolled in secondary school.

Recent work carried out on the definition of a secondary vocational education concentrator leaves no doubt that the states intend to come up with a firm definition that can be applied nationwide (<www.edcountabilty.org>, Summer 2005 Workshop). Some of the most contentious issues are the following:

- *State or local role in determining sequence of courses:* Should there continue to be a state-mandated sequence of courses that determine attainment of a vocational concentrator, or should this be a locally determined set of courses?
- *Threshold for deciding when someone is a concentrator*: As revealed in the interviews, states use different cut-off points (number of credits completed, entrance into last class in sequence) on when to decide if someone has become a concentrator.

7 CTE Standards

Following the discussion of accountability and CTE in the background section, we studied individual state implementation of CTE standards in six states. The basic issues that we see in this section are the standards that states use to measure the quality of CTE, the trend in terms of performance on the current federal standards, and the current debates around federal CTE standards.

7.1 State CTE Measures

Interviews and a review of the basic legislation confirm that states utilize the same system, called the CARS (Consolidated Annual Report) measures, to evaluate the performance of CTE. These measures are divided into four core indicators: student attainment; credential attainment; placement and retention; and participation in and completion of non-traditional programmes. Table 5 lists these standards and includes both somewhat traditional measures of student success, such as academic achievement, as well as more difficult-to-measure items, such as post-secondary placement and retention.

Table 5 Core indicators and sub-indicators: career and technical education

---

Core Indicator 1. Student attainment

This indicator seeks to assess student attainment of the challenging state-established academic and vocational and technical skill proficiencies at both the secondary and post-secondary levels.

1S1—Secondary Academic Attainment;
1S2—Secondary Vocational and Technical Skill Attainment;
1P1—Post-secondary Academic Attainment;
1P2—Post-secondary Vocational and Technical Skill Attainment.

Core Indicator 2. Credential attainment

This indicator seeks to assess student attainment of a secondary school diploma or its recognized equivalent, a proficiency credential in conjunction with a secondary school diploma, or a post-secondary degree or credential.

2S1—Secondary Completion;
2S2—Proficiency Credential with Secondary Diploma (Not required for 2000/2001);
2P1—Post-secondary Degree or Credential.

Core Indicator 3. Placement and retention

This indicator seeks to assess vocational and technical education student placement in, retention in, and completion of post-secondary education or advanced training, placement in military service, or placement or retention in employment.

3S1—Secondary Placement;
3S2—Secondary Retention;
3P1—Post-secondary Placement;
3P2—Post-secondary Retention (Not required for 2000/2001).

Core Indicator 4. Participation in and completion of non-traditional programmes

This indicator seeks to assess student participation in and completion of vocational and technical education programmes that lead to non-traditional training and employment.

4S1—Participation in Secondary Non-Traditional Programmes;
4S2—Completion of Secondary Non-Traditional Programmes;
4P1—Participation in Post-secondary Non-Traditional Programmes;
4P2—Completion of Post-secondary Non-Traditional Programmes.

States are currently allowed the authorities to decide which indicators will be used to assess the achievement of these measures.

The approaches states take to determine which indicators are appropriate to measure success vary substantially. In terms of the academic achievement measures, state-level definitions of CTE academic achievement suffer from the same problems as the achievement measures for secondary education overall. For example, Michigan, New Jersey, Ohio and Massachusetts use their state-generated tests as a way of determining if CTE graduates are meeting academic achievement goals. New York uses the Regents Exams as a measure. In contrast, Illinois uses graduation or completion of schooling as the academic measure.

The indicators used to assess the vocational achievement measure vary more substantially. While New Jersey and Illinois continue to utilize the same indicators of graduation or course completion, programmes in Ohio and Massachusetts use achievement of specific vocational competencies, such as a state-specific test for vocational subjects, to show achievement of vocational subjects. Michigan and New

York based the state indicator of achievement of a specific grade-point average in vocational subjects. New York measures the percentage of CTE completers who attain a high-school diploma.

Finally, states assess the effectiveness of post-secondary completion through various strategies which currently vary substantially, from use of student surveys conducted by local schools in Massachusetts or Michigan, to use of state-level administrative records to determine employment or educational status of students after graduation in New Jersey or Illinois.

7.2 State CTE Performance

Given the variation in the measurement systems adopted by the states, it is no wonder that a review of the most recent data shows such a wide variation in achievement. Table 6 shows the current achievement levels for the six states. It is remarkable that some states maintained a 95% or better measure in any of the indicators.

The variation in the achievement of academic measures ranges from a low of 68.12% in Michigan to a high of 95% in Illinois. Interestingly, the results in Table 6 do not correspond to the most stringent measures. For example, while New York's Regent Exams present a substantial challenge to high-school students, and having 77% of CTE graduates pass those tests seems significant, it is more difficult to judge why only 68.2% of Michigan youth in CTE in the 11th grade reach the state-defined threshold level of career and technical education. This measure is a less rigorous one than the Regents Exams.

Secondly, it is interesting to note that states that use unemployment insurance data to measure the placement rate reported fewer students with successful placement rates. Illinois and New Jersey have lower placement rates, while states that use locally-generated surveys, such as Ohio or Massachusetts, have close to 95% of CTE students reported with successful placement. This result supports the empirical literature that suggests using unemployment insurance data as a way to investigate student outcomes.

Table 6 Achievement of core indicators by state (2003–2004)

	Illinois	Massachusetts	Michigan	New Jersey	New York	Ohio
Academic achievement	95%	70.59%	68.12%	93.05%	76.87%	94.61%
Vocational skills	> 95	92.42%	87.75%	90.52%	81.09%	59.19%
Diploma/equivalent/ degree/credential	> 95	92.42%	> 95	> 95	> 95	> 95
Total placement	76.36%	> 95	94.82%	81.95%	> 95	92.22%

Note: >95 = actual performance of this indicator is greater than 95%.
Source: <www.edcountability.net>

7.3 Perspectives on the Accountability Measures

Interviews with the state staff responsible for CTE showed that states are aware of drawbacks to their current systems. While the state systems currently have helped in terms of understanding the implementation of Perkins, there is a more tenuous linkage to the use of these systems for performance improvement. When asked directly about how the CARS data are used in the state, respondents described that they are used in assessing local programme performance, but indicated that state capacity to judge if local programmes are effective is hampered by the lack of staff to evaluate programmes or the fact that local education systems are accountable to local authorities rather than to state departments.

There are states that are moving towards using data for performance improvement on a more systematic level. One state started doing regional workshops where districts learn about the data that was collected and focus on how to use it.

7.4 Perspectives on Data Quality

There is a widespread understanding that the data used to measure the effectiveness of CTE at the local level needs extensive review before they can be used to assess programmes. The most common system is for states to require that Perkins' data or other state accountability information is entered locally and forwarded to the state department. This situation introduces a lot of potential error into the measurement of student attendance, graduation or testing. In addition, among those states that rely on local authorities to survey graduates, schools potentially can produce inaccurate estimates of student success because of poor knowledge of data collection practices among local school professionals.

8 Other Indicators of Accountability

It is critical for accountability to include data that can improve performance rather than simply assessing programme success or failure. In this light, our qualitative study asked state administrators about the measurement of classroom practices, like work-based learning as well as career counselling. In both cases, the states we surveyed varied considerably on the assessment of work-based learning, but none actually collected data on career counselling centrally. They left open the possibility that this information is potentially available at the local level. However, it reveals that a large part of what might be considered CTE is not documented by the states.

Work-based learning data is available in a number of states, because it is measured as part of the attainment of advanced vocational competency. In one state, for example, the state laws require that students completing a co-operative programme get an assessment at the school level. These assessments, however, are not integrated into the state level accountability system, but are assumed to be available for local teachers and administrators to improve performance.

However, another respondent pointed out that some important changes had been made to the co-operative system, including providing professional standards for co-operative education co-ordinators. This still implies a relatively passive accountability system in this one state, where the state may set broad criteria for professional conduct but does not monitor the operation of work-based learning.

To a certain extent, other states brought up the issue of work-based learning. However, none of the states built work-based learning into their accountability process as far as can be concluded from the interviews. Work-based learning becomes more important, however, as internships and other forms of school and work integration become popular in general and vocational schooling.

8.1 Curriculum Frameworks

Because of the continuing evolution of CTE and, in part, due to the influence of the standards movement, states have often aggressively increased the level of occupational competency required, as well as focusing on formally building academic and vocational integration through curriculum frameworks. This aggressive push has meant increased academic performance among CTE students, and opens the door for better occupational performance through integrated activities.

Sometimes the curriculum frameworks, which are proposed often at the state level, run up against local control of curriculum. For example, states mentioned continued resistance among schools, but noted that this had decreased over time.

9 Conclusion

Accountability and curriculum reform are increasingly impacting state career and technical education systems. The Perkins III legislation focused state-level energy on the larger questions of how to define indicators that will allow them to account for spending of Perkins' funds. This shift in accountability follows decades where vocational schooling has both led other education systems in monitoring the outcomes of schooling, but largely fallen behind the K-12 system in crafting state-level tests.

In part, this is due to the nature of vocational school curriculum and testing, where both academic and vocational skills are integral parts of the educational enterprise. This is also, unfortunately, due to perennial problems with staffing shortages and possibly an implementation problem at the state level. While many staff have left CTE at the state level and have not been replaced, there remain difficulties implementing the new vision of integrated workforce development systems at the state level (Kister, 2001).

A review of the current accountability framework under Perkins and of state indicators revealed some important differences among states in how they approach accountability. It is significant that while a number of states extended the testing from K-12 high schools to vocational programmes, such as New York, a number still use different measures, such as graduation. It is important to note that these measures are not weak in terms of data, but if they are not used consistently this means they cannot be compared effectively against more academic measures.

Similarly, state assessment of occupational knowledge is variable. While a number of states have invested in centralized testing systems, others rely almost solely on teacher-developed tests or industry assessments. While the latter offer some assurance that completers are consistently being evaluated, the former offer no such comfort. Moreover, the data are not comparable between states, and the Data Quality Institute Report in 2005 did not propose a possible solution to this problem.

In terms of curriculum, the current trend is clearly to move to career clusters. While many states have curtailed in-house curriculum development staff, most maintain active staff working with local schools and districts to develop a high-quality curriculum for vocational programmes. The framework adopted by all the states studied in this chapter focuses on career clusters. There are differences, however, as some states (such as Ohio or New Jersey) have moved ahead quickly and use the clusters as the basis for all curriculum, programmes and career counselling.

States and other national governments can gain something from this brief review. The following suggestions follow from the state comparisons:

1. *Academic indicators.* While some states are distinguished by having outcomes based on labour-market performance for employment after graduation, states need to be careful to measure the academic performance of graduates rather than relying upon the graduation rates as indicators of performance. The current strategy of relying on graduation rates or completion rates to compute students' success might be compared against the approach of using a standardized test to measure achievement. Given the labour-market value of basic skills, this would seem to be an important concern.
2. *Vocational competencies:* The potential solutions for vocational competencies are more problematic, but looking at Ohio's home-grown testing system might be useful, as it uses career clusters to define potential outcomes. States often use industry-generated tests, but these are frequently not comparable. One other possibility is simply to use a common test that measures completion of certain general competencies, such as teamwork or technology, which are shared across different vocational fields.

Acknowledgments This study was commissioned as part of a larger review of vocational education by Rutgers University and the State of New Jersey under contract to the Center on Education and Training for Employment at the Ohio State University. We appreciate the generous funding and also the insightful comments from both groups. This manuscript represents the opinions of the authors. Thanks are also due to Dr Christopher Zirkle and Ms Hyo Sun Kim for helping with data collection, preparing the tables and providing feedback on the study design.

References

Association for Career and Technical Education. 2005. *Side-by-side comparison of House and Senate bills with 1998 Perkins Law*. Washington, DC: ACTE.

Association for Career and Technical Education. 2006. *Reinventing the American high school for the 21st century: a position paper.* Washington, DC: ACTE.

Bishop, J.H.; Mane, F. 1998. *The New York state reform strategy: raising the bar above minimum competency.* Ithaca, NY: Cornell University, Center for Advanced Human Resource Studies.

Bottoms, G.; Young, M. 2005. *High schools that work.* Atlanta, GA: Southern Regional Education Board.

Fowler, F.C. 2003. *Policy studies for educational leaders: an introduction,* 2nd ed. New York, NY: Prentice Hall.

Grubb, W.N. et al. 1999. *Toward order from chaos: state efforts to reform workforce development system.* Berkeley, CA: University of California, National Center for Research in Vocational Education.

Hoffman, L.M. 2003. *Overview of public elementary and secondary schools and districts: school year 2001–02.* Washington, DC: U.S. Department of Education, National Center for Education Statistics. (No. NCES 2003-411.)

Karp, M. et al. 2004. *State dual enrollment policies: addressing access and quality.* Washington, DC: U.S. Department of Education.

Kister, J. 2001. *State leadership for career technical education.* Washington, DC: The National Association of State Directors of Career Technical Education Consortium.

Klein, S. 2001. *Financing vocational education: a state policy-makers' guide.* Berkeley, CA: MPR Associates.

Krueger, C. 2004. *Career and technical education: a briefing memo.* Denver, CO: Education Commission of the States.

National Assessment of Vocational Education. 2004. *Final report to Congress.* Washington, DC: U.S. Department of Education, Office of the Under-Secretary.

National Association of State Boards of Education. 1998. *Public accountability for student success: standards for education accountability systems.* Alexandria, VA: NASBE.

Rahn, M.L.; O'Driscoll, P.; Hudecki, P. 1999. *Taking off! Sharing state-level accountability strategies: using academic and vocational accountability strategies to improve student achievement.* Berkeley, CA: National Center for Research in Vocational Education. (No. MDS-1206.)

Silverberg, M. et al. 2004. *National assessment of vocational education: final report to Congress.* Washington, DC: U.S. Department of Education, Office of the Under-Secretary, Policy and Program Studies Service.

Stasz, C.; Bodilly, S. 2004. *Efforts to improve the quality of vocational education in secondary schools: impact of federal and state policies.* Santa Monica, CA: Rand Corporation.

Stecher, B.M.; Hanser, L.M. 1992. *Local accountability in vocational education: a theoretical model and its limitations in practice.* Santa Monica, CA: Rand Corporation.

The Editors. 2004. Quality counts 2004: Count me in. *Education week,* January 8, p. 7.

White, R. et al. 2004. *The structures and challenges of vocational education funding and accountability systems: a report prepared by the academy for educational development for the national assessment of vocational education.* Washington, DC: U.S. Department of Education, Office of the Under-Secretary.

Chapter III.4
The Regional Perspective of Vocational Education and Training

Mike Coles and Tom Leney

1 Introduction

The trading of goods and services is not necessarily constrained by geographical, social, cultural and political differences. Markets are often diverse in nature and goods and services are usually tailored to meet specific needs of the marketplace and of potential customers. There is also a market for people with skills: people engage in training and move to places where they are more likely to sell their skills through work. Vocational education and training (VET) is mostly localized in terms of where people develop their skills, but is generally more wide ranging in the transfer of those skills.

Whatever the specificity of training, a notion has grown everywhere that a person may increase the value of their skills by using opportunities to apply them more broadly. Nowadays, this extends beyond local, regional and national boundaries, so that the supply side of VET is now at least partially responsive to the wider geographical market. On the demand side, there is now better articulation of the skills that are needed in the work place and this is communicated through various markets—some local, some further afield. Thus, it is clear that, through this inter-action with skills markets, VET is an integrating factor with the potential to bring about greater levels of articulation across geographical, social, cultural and political boundaries.

Looking at VET from a different angle, we can see that it is shaped by actions taken to strengthen regional co-operation. Economic factors, such as the availability of natural resources, regional economic strengths and weaknesses, inward invest-ment, and environmental and safety factors, all shape the form of VET. Institutional arrangements have a powerful influence on the quantity and quality of VET. Global markets for goods and services also influence the general level of VET activity. Some factors are within the control of a region or country—others are not. These diverse influences mean that VET systems cannot develop in isolation from other VET systems and some kind of regional integration is inevitable.

A good example of regional co-operation in terms of the supply and demand for VET is in North-Eastern Europe. At first the Nordic Council of Ministers, for whom education, training and labour market issues are an important dimension, was con-cerned only with Finland and the Scandinavian countries. More recently, the Baltic

R. Maclean, D. Wilson (eds.), *International Handbook of Education for the Changing World of Work*, DOI 10.1007/978-1-4020-5281-1_III.4,
© Springer Science+Business Media B.V. 2009

countries have become closely involved, and the network is expanding, perhaps as far as the St Petersburg region in Russia, as well as in Poland. This example clearly shows how zones of mutual trust can grow quite rapidly in continental regions, helping to extend the mobility of labour. Numerous global regions are looking at the possibilities of co-operation of this kind.

A consequence of VET being honed to meet specific needs and used as a tool for regional integration is that it has taken on a wide range of forms. Other chapters in this book will engage with these different forms of VET.

2 Common Challenges

What are the pressures on VET systems that tend to lead to greater unity between regions and countries? Organization for Economic Co-operation and Development studies (2006) and research into progress towards the Lisbon Goal (Leney et al., 2005) identify, not surprisingly, economic pressures as the main driver acting on VET systems. Countries want to strengthen the link between the education system and employment and point to the discrepancies between skills needed in the workplace, job training and qualifications. Economic pressures arise in response to global economic trends, as well as local and national economic situations, such as the need to be responsive to innovation, the development of work organization and of human capital. These generic pressures act as a force for regional integration in VET since they focus attention on responding to common skill-supply issues. Vocational qualifications systems are also believed to have potential for improving the link between education and work, for establishing new pathways from education into employment and for reducing barriers to learning, for example by using new forms of pedagogy and assessment.

Economic needs are perceived to drive innovation in production. Research shows that innovation often takes place via continuous learning on the part of people in the workplace and that forms of learning at work are changing; for example, there is an increasing effort to organize on-the-job learning and utilize self-directed learning. Consequently, learning structures in the workplace are becoming more complex. In particular, the focus is no longer solely on acquisition of technical knowledge, but has widened to include softer skills, new values, new codes of behaviour and the remodelling of past experience. This has resulted in expansion of training provision across regions and greater use of more diverse recognition systems.

Some countries emphasize assessment of vocational ability, recognized through qualifications, as important for employment stability, improved remuneration, and quick and efficient recruitment. Recognition of vocational ability is also expected to reduce risks related to employment, on both the employer's and the employee's side, by preventing mismatches engendered through poor information about workers' skills. Many countries report that rapid economic growth has produced skills shortages and this has exerted pressure to develop the VET system by creating more-efficient and faster responses to changes and emerging needs in the labour market.

Another pressure on VET systems arises from the potential advantages of mobility of labour and the expectation that they should deliver international recognition of skills, including the recognition of formal, informal and non-formal learning that has been carried out in other countries. Among the European Union (EU) countries, there is a commitment to increase mobility of workers and learners across country boundaries. This requires transparency in VET systems and encourages countries to build education and qualification structures that are consistent with other countries in the Union. Recent proposals for a European Qualifications Framework are designed to make it easier for one national qualifications system to articulate with another, without superseding national systems. The European Qualifications Framework will also provide a further means of comparison through the referencing of national qualifications to a single set of levels.

In many countries, low population growth coupled with increased demand for high skills has focused attention on growing skill shortages. This means that older people need to be provided with learning opportunities reflecting change in working practices, a policy challenge to which many countries have been slow to respond. Clearly, the outflow of older skilled workers, resulting in a waste of knowledge and expertise, can also lead to pressures on labour markets, and this is exacerbated in most European countries by recent trends for earlier retirement, particularly among males. The demographic shift has had an impact on the need for (re)training older people, on retirement schemes, pension funding and family life.

Several countries highlight the challenges VET systems face as a result of immigration flows. These pressures include the need to identify skills gained in other countries compared to the national skills recognition system, as well as the need to accept learning that has not been previously recognized through qualifications. There is pressure for more flexible vocational education and training systems for people in disadvantaged situations as a means of improving social inclusion through education and subsequently work.

Social and cultural issues are therefore not divorced from the economic, demographic and immigration issues noted above. At the same time, it is generally recognized that people engage in learning for economic reasons, to improve employment prospects, and for personal development and social reasons—social status, better citizenship and so on. These pressures also include a perception of the need to broaden the current provision of education to include such aspects as values, behaviour and citizenship. There is also a requirement to offer learners more choice and more flexible ways of gaining credit for their learning. The need to give recognition to informal and non-formal learning also falls into this category.

Technological innovations and the global spread of information and communications technologies are creating pressure for countries to be using the most up-to-date methods of production and service provision. The move towards leaner production systems and working organizations—and the risk of rising unemployment rates—brings with it a need for enhanced training and retraining in the use of new technologies. This means that qualifications systems need to adapt to allow the recognition of new knowledge, skills and wider competences related to the use of new technologies.

The pressure to develop learning opportunities means that, in some countries, providers have been required to differentiate course offerings in response to more selective demand. This pressure has had a strong impact on the growing amount of VET provision at post-secondary and higher education levels in many countries over recent years. This demand is expected to grow as lifelong learning provision expands and develops the need for even more learning (Leney et al., 2005). Developing VET as part of lifelong learning requires examination of the structure of provision, including: (a) the links between working life, schools and higher education; (b) the content of programmes; (c) the quality and relevance of provision; (d) resource provision and management; and (e) the roles and responsibilities of different partners and stakeholders. Countries in an OECD study (2006) accept that there is an argument for allowing scope for lifelong learning goals to shape the way the education and training system operates. Stronger linkages are needed between learning at different stages of life and between the formal and the informal structures. Countries suggest that more diverse settings for learning will be needed and different partnerships between funders, providers and qualification bodies will be needed leading to more integrated provision. In future, departures from the existing VET infrastructures are likely to be substantial, at least for some countries.

The fact that all of these pressures on VET systems are common to many countries might be expected to add impetus to their reform agendas. It would probably not be the case, though, that common pressures for reform would lead to common responses. The country or regional context will require bespoke solutions. However, the elements of changing VET infrastructure might be expected to show some commonality and the process of change itself could have features that result from policy-learning about reforms and trials in other countries and regions.

3 Instruments from the EU Experience

The European Commission—working with the member states—has a remit for the development of some policies in the field of education and training. In certain policy areas, member states have transferred responsibility to the EU so that the Union can use 'hard' methods of co-ordination, but for other policy areas, such as lifelong learning, including VET, subsidiarity prevails. This means that member states retain responsibility for legislation, policy development and implementation. In VET, therefore, the European Union cannot mandate but has to find 'softer' policy tools—involving voluntary co-operation. Obviously, this limits the policy instruments available at the European level that have an impact on an area such as VET, for which governments are determined to retain their autonomy. The range of policy levers that could (but may not) be used for the European level development of VET is shown in Table 1.

Table 1 shows that in the case of lifelong learning (including VET) subsidiarity means that mandates and inducements have limited use. The EU can create leverage in some circumstances through *capacity-building* and *systems changing*, as the use

Table 1 Policy levers and the open method of co-ordination (OMC)

Policy instrument	Policy assumptions and expected effects	Lever for EU under the rule of subsidiarity?
Mandates Rules intended to produce compliance.	Capacity to demand compliance. Most will comply but maybe not all.	No
Inducements Transfer of money in return for certain actions.	Sufficient funding provided to generate results; funding drives change, also with unintended outcomes.	No
Capacity-building Transfer of money for purposes of longer-term investments.	Some funding to initiate change: Expect/hope that best practice models produce cascade or 'pump-priming' innovation.	To a limited extent
Systems changing Transfer of authority to alter system of delivery.	New entrants to old institutions that are not producing results generate change or reform.	Indirectly—e.g. in-sector reforms through encouraging social partner activity or Leonardo programmes.
Hortation Use of proclamations, speeches, public relations campaigns to exhort people to take the needed action.	Assumes players are motivated by images, symbols or values.	Yes. The Lisbon process and OMC.
Deliberative change Voluntary and collaborative change processes—bottom-up reform, usually encouraged from higher up.	Relies on collaboration in experimental activity and the identification and voluntary exchange of good practice, etc.	Yes. The Lisbon process and OMC.

of European structural and regional funds demonstrate. The reform of VET and further education in Ireland is a case of EU capacity-building, in that consolidation funding—which is the additional funding made available to Ireland, Spain, Greece and Portugal when they first joined the EU—made a significant contribution to reforms. However, 'hortation' and 'deliberative change' are the main policy instruments used to drive education and training policy at the European level.

The 'soft' method of European co-ordination for VET and several other policy areas is a form of co-operation between governments, social partners and other European stakeholders. It is known as the open method of co-ordination (OMC), which is intended as a means of spreading best practice and encouraging greater convergence towards the main EU goals. The four key stages agreed for the open method of co-ordination, as they apply to education and training, are:

1. identifying priorities and benchmarks;
2. conducting benchmarking exercises to gauge the progress of the EU member states towards the identified benchmarks;

3. identifying instances of good practice and best practice;
4. through peer review, finding effective and practical ways to share best practice.

At the time of writing, the OMC is still a young policy instrument for education and training in the European Union. As a 'bottom up' method for sharing and developing best practice, it is being relied on to generate innovation in VET. This depends on the willingness of the stakeholders to make progress, rather than respond to 'top down' mandates and inducements. In the first two or three years of operation, OMC in education and training has concentrated on the first stages—identifying priorities and benchmarks; conducting benchmarking exercises within the constraints of available data, and beginning to identify good practice, particularly in aspects such as quality assurance, advice and guidance, the recognition of informal and non-formal learning, and developing a European Qualifications Framework as a point of reference. With lifelong learning, including VET, identified as of high importance to the development of a knowledge society and a knowledge economy, the fourth stage of OMC—called variously *peer review, policy-learning* and *bench learning*—now has to play a key role. Such a process across nations and systems is by no means straightforward. Different traditions, drivers and barriers may frustrate the attempt to identify the extent to which good practice can readily transfer from one system to another.

4 Benchmarking to Bench Learning

It is the pressures to change VET systems, and the instruments in place to support the process of creating greater articulation between the systems in different countries and regions, that have created an awareness of the need to move away from comparative performance to a greater focus on understanding the dynamics of system change in different country settings. In the past, the setting out of high-class benchmarks based on the best-known country practice was thought to have the potential to stimulate VET performance in countries with lower performing systems. A respect for the knowledge of local conditions (opportunities and constraints) was probably amongst the motives for such an approach. These local conditions were thought to be the dominant determinant of the shape of reforms. There were probably political pressures too arising from the dangers of explicit interference by European development programmes with the governance of processes within European Union member states or regions.

The focus has shifted to a more mature policy of sharing, co-operation and mutual support for national and regional reforms across borders, as witnessed by the co-operation programmes led by the Education and Training Foundation in the European Union candidate and accession countries. Policy-learning is a well-researched tool that defines a process where the experience gained in different country contexts for reform is of value to outside observers. It is now accepted that the various processes of policy-learning are more likely to lead to stable and effective outcomes of reform processes than the simplistic notion of policy borrowing. Contextual differences in countries and regions are not something that can be controlled as in a scientific experiment. They are powerful, pervasive and valued and are therefore generally non-negotiable. The process of VET reforms can be enhanced by ensuring that key players have *exposure* to the advantages and disadvantages of different models of VET systems and access to experts who can interpret the evidence for policy-making, whilst respecting national infrastructures and resisting over-complex solutions and simplistic, rapid routes to decisions. *Interaction* with managers and policy-makers from other jurisdictions can safeguard and optimize the impact of the exposure phase. Similarly, interactions with models of implementation, such as scenarios (Leney et al., 2004) of VET reform and implementation over different time-scales, are also potentially useful tools. The third stage of policy-learning is *adaptation* of features of other VET models to the national setting. This stage brings the opportunity for consultation and developing of ownership of the emerging model and a first clear sight of major obstacles to implementation. Finally, policy-learning can use the opportunity to conduct *evaluation* of the preferred model by using international experience of VET design. In summary, policy-learning can play a useful role in VET reform by providing a network of external reference points for informing decision-making.

Some writers have suggested that the most fertile ground for policy-learning between countries exists where there are strong similarities between systems. This is not necessarily the case. For example, Finland's education and training systems have 'borrowed' effectively from similar systems (comprehensive schooling, learned substantially for the Swedish model in the 1980s) and from dissimilar systems (competence-based qualifications for adults in the workforce, adapted from a United Kingdom innovation in the 1990s). Rather, it is important to identify the kind of policy-learning that is appropriate to particular problems and challenges. Based on work developed in the Scottish Further Education Unit (McCann & Donald, 2005), which adapted ideas about technology transfer to the world of VET, we can distinguish at least three forms of collaborative innovation for VET. These are:

1. *Knowledge transfer initiation.* This refers to a situation in which activity creates new approaches, services or products that can create innovation. This could take place by way of collaborative research and development, resulting in new solutions to common problems. Long-term development.
2. *Knowledge transfer adoption.* This occurs when an agency engages with an existing knowledge base (perhaps a tool, policy or strategic approach being used in another country) in order to achieve some specific change. This approach may be close to the model envisaged in the European Commission's peer learning pilot. An obvious danger to avoid is the simple trap: 'policy borrowing'. While there are examples of success through policy borrowing, there are many examples of failure. The purpose remains 'policy-learning' in most cases. Medium- and perhaps short-term development.
3. *Knowledge transfer capacity-building.* This refers not to a specific product but to building the capacity for change. Activities in this area emphasize building

the drivers for change, overcoming barriers and building capacity, rather than zooming in on particular initiatives. Medium to long term.

Beyond these formal mechanisms, the reflective outcome of exploring different approaches to similar issues or problems may itself create an environment for innovation.

5 Facilitating and Managing Regional Learning

Having set out the factors that are driving changes to VET (and by implication VET delivery systems), together with a description of the processes in place in Europe for facilitating co-operation, it is useful to examine some case studies of how such processes actually work. Five short case studies follow that are selected to cover the different levels of co-operation that are possible. The Maastricht study provides an opportunity to examine (from a European perspective) national policy goals, progress towards those goals and research evidence that might be useful in shaping future policy responses. The second case study examines the methods used to support national reforms with information and expertise on an on-going basis for countries in the process of VET reform. The third case study examines the ways the infrastructure of the proposed European Qualifications Framework (EQF) can support national reform. Moving to a level closer to the workplace, the fourth case study examines attempts to facilitate policy-learning across enterprises within a sector. Finally, a case study is included highlighting some issues at the level of the individual when mobility of labour across borders is encouraged.

5.1 The Maastricht Study and Communiqué

The Maastricht study (Leney et al., 2005) was the first comprehensive overview of developments and trends in vocational education and training in the thirty-one European countries that agreed to the Copenhagen Declaration on enhanced European co-operation in VET in 2002. The study assessed the contribution of VET to achieving the Lisbon Goal from an economic and social perspective.

The study concluded that initial VET is well developed in most countries and can be seen as contributing to the EU benchmark of young people completing upper secondary education. However, the study suggested that attention must be given to improving the quality and flexibility of initial vocational education and training if it is to continue to attract adequate numbers of young people in the future. Better links to general and higher education are also needed, as well as flexible pathways encouraging young people to improve their range of competences and progress to higher levels.

Continuing vocational training is reported as an area of major concern. Too few Europeans participate and their existing levels of skills and educational attainment are lower than their counterparts in competing countries. Continuing vocational training should support the competitiveness of the European economy by upgrading the competences of the whole workforce, and especially the low skilled, who currently receive very little training. Continuing vocational training also needs to address the problem of the ageing European workforce, and the training of older workers so as to encourage them to remain longer in employment. Immigrants will also need training to take their places in communities. Facilitating learning at the workplace itself is essential in all of this.

Finally, the report suggests that innovation in teaching and learning needs to become a major action. This important aspect has been omitted from European co-operation in VET thus far, and reinforced attention should be given to the training and competence development of VET teachers and trainers, and to their fragmented profession. In other respects, the blend of current priorities and actions resulting from the Copenhagen Declaration are found by Member States to be appropriate.

Commenting on the study, EU Commissioner Jan Figel concluded that:

> The findings of this study influenced the Maastricht Communiqué and in particular inspired the priorities set at national level. [...] The study brings to our notice factors that will influence our VET systems profoundly in the coming years. [...] In the spirit of cultivating the Open Method of Co-ordination, this study is rich in examples of good practice, used to illustrate where countries are innovating and doing well (European Commission, 2004)

In 2006, the European Commission organized a follow-up to the Maastricht Study, to coincide with the VET priorities of Finland's presidency of the European Union.

5.2 Institutions for Catalysing Knowledge-Sharing in VET Practices

There are many organizations and networks that facilitate knowledge-sharing between countries. Universities, professional bodies and international businesses are good examples. Research organizations also facilitate exchange, such as the European Centre for Educational Research, the Vocational Education and Training Network and the International Vocational Education and Training Association. However, whilst all of these organizations serve to inform policy directions in one way or another, and offer the possibility of capacity-building, they do not offer direct, on-going practical advice that is relevant to policy-makers. This challenge is taken up in the main by two EU-funded bodies that engage in a co-ordinated way in supporting VET reform.

The European Centre for the Development of Vocational Training (CEDEFOP),[1] established in 1975, is the reference centre for vocational education and training. It does this by providing information on and analyses of vocational education and training systems, policies, research and practice. CEDEFOP's tasks are to:

- compile selected documentation and analyses of data;
- contribute to developing and co-ordinating research;
- exploit and disseminate information;

- encourage joint approaches to vocational education and training problems;
- provide a forum for debate and exchanges of ideas.

The Education and Training Foundation (ETF)[2] works with developing economies (candidate countries, South-Eastern Europe, Eastern Europe and Central Asia, and the Mediterranean region) in promoting knowledge-sharing and expertise development in the belief that education and training can make a fundamental contribution to increasing prosperity, creating sustainable growth and encouraging social inclusion. The ETF has a clear agenda for promoting integration through VET and in promoting integration by means of VET reform and policy-learning. For example, its priorities are to:

- assess progress and future priorities for reform in partner countries in vocational education and training and its links to socio-economic development;
- design, monitor and assess projects at the request of the European Commission;
- build capacity so that policy-makers and practitioners in partner countries play a full role in modernizing their vocational education and training systems;
- contribute actively to international debate on reform in transition countries. In particular, it may draw on relevant experience in the EU to pilot innovative approaches to reform in partner countries;
- facilitate dialogue amongst stakeholders by developing international, national and local networks.

It is difficult to describe the impact of these two bodies because their span of activities is large and the networks associated with them are vast. The time-scales over which knowledge capital develops also vary enormously, making impact difficult to measure. However, the authors believe that these two bodies make a substantial impact on European and national policy development and implementation, research knowledge, skills capacity, workplace development and European co-ordination and integration. Both centres offer serious levels of support to VET professionals, the infrastructures of enterprises, and training and policy planners. Working in the field of VET over the last twenty years has created a knowledge base that can support policy-learning through making available resources (expertise) and helping with the management of projects and reforms. Thus, CEDEFOP has built up expertise in areas such as cross-country sectoral development and e-learning, while the ETF provides expert analytical and developmental support in forging links between VET and labour-market reform.

5.3 The European Qualifications Framework—EQF

The interface between one VET system and another is most obvious when the qualifications of trained people are compared. If skilled people are to be able to move to new positions in different systems to fill vacancies, and if recruiters are to look outside their 'home' market, it is essential that qualifications systems can articulate one with another. The existence of a translation device, such as the proposed European Qualifications Framework (EQF), makes this articulation possible.[3] The EQF also sets out a series of progressive steps in qualifications that cross the boundaries between schooling, higher education and work-based education and training. In this way the EQF is a framework for lifelong learning.

The EQF is a meta framework—it works on the basis that each country, region or employment sector has its own qualifications framework or frameworks. These local frameworks are the means of recognizing qualifications that support local people and enterprises because they are built to play a part in a training infrastructure. It is possible for all VET systems to link qualifications frameworks to the EQF and, therefore, by using the EQF levels, it becomes possible to compare one framework with another. The market for skills and jobs is potentially larger as a result. Thus, the EQF is at the same time respectful of local qualifications systems and opens up frameworks for use outside countries, regions and sectors.

The EQF proposals have been developed through close scrutiny of current practice in countries, regions and sectors. It draws on the strengths of different VET systems and, therefore, is a tool for the exchange of good practice in terms of qualification levels for VET. This is an important dimension for one system to influence another.

The EQF proposals ask questions of countries and sectors. The proposals are constructed on the basis of learning outcomes.[4] In order to compare a framework to the EQF level, it is helpful if the local framework levels are described as outcomes too. This is often not the case and therefore the EQF applies an integrating pressure for all qualifications frameworks to be clear in terms of learning outcomes from the qualification process, instead of simply defining the learning inputs and the infrastructure that makes these inputs possible. This pressure to use learning outcomes is a powerful tool for enabling examination of the qualification systems from the viewpoint of learners (What is it precisely that I will learn? How does this compare to what I have already learned?) and the enterprise (Is this qualification level from country X what I need? Do these learning outcomes equate with the work practice I intend to establish?). The content, supporting infrastructure and the efficiency become more transparent within the country and to outsiders. This brings with it the possibility of evaluation and reforms that will improve the quality of VET and the system that delivers it.

The EQF proposals are based on eight levels (Coles & Oates, 2004). Countries with more or less than eight levels in their frameworks may find pressure to adapt to an eight-level approach so that articulation with the EQF and, consequently, the frameworks in other countries is more straightforward. In this way, the EQF is not likely to be an entirely neutral translation device. The EQF proposals make it clear that, in addition to all else, it is a means of fostering change. This change is in the direction of the Lisbon Goal of a better market for skills that will offer more and better jobs for European citizens. The EQF is potentially a powerful integrating influence, not just within Europe but also in its articulation with markets and qualifications systems around the world.

5.4 Sectoral Development

The sectoral dimension is a key focus for co-operation at the European level. Some sectors have been quick to take initiatives in this respect. European co-operation taking up the theme of ICT penetration and sectoral convergence serves as a good example.

ICT penetration and sectoral convergence is an important driver for a European sectoral approach to skills and qualifications. In a sector like manufacturing, which is highly regulated with clear occupational profiles, technological changes—and especially ICTs as a driver of change—are eroding existing qualification profiles. In services, developments such as e-commerce also impact on jobs at all levels. In sectors such as ICTs a perceived slow response level in public education and training systems has spurred sectoral initiatives. In 2002/2003 CEDEFOP commissioned a series of studies on innovation of qualification profiles and curricula in Europe in ICT-user industries.

The European Monitoring Centre on Change has also recently commissioned a number of studies in fields such as finance, fishing, media and graphics, textiles and the automobile industry, all of which show the same tendencies. Similarly, the Leonardo da Vinci programme has initiated a number of projects to develop sectoral training modules, assessment standards, and certificates and diplomas.

5.5 Mobility across Borders

The 1990s saw immigration trends and patterns emerge with new flows coming from the countries of Eastern Europe and movements resulting from social instability in the Balkans. Migratory flows today are composed of various categories of persons: asylum seekers, displaced persons, persons requiring temporary protection, members of the family of an immigrant already established in the European Union, migrant workers and persons involved in business migration (of whom the numbers are growing) or tertiary/higher education.

In 2004, the EU embarked upon a further round of enlargement, accepting ten new member states, predominantly from Central and Eastern Europe. Only the United Kingdom, Ireland and Sweden did not set up temporary arrangements for restricting labour market migration, thus allowing free movement of workers from the new EU Member States.

Current research has broadly confirmed this movement as making a positive contribution to those labour markets open to workers from the wider EU, although there is a developing trend of failure to recognize the full value of qualification of migrant workers in many sectors (Anderson et al., 2006). However, sectoral co-operation and EU-funded programmes are likely to place emphasis upon improving recognition.

Successful introduction (and further development) of measures such as the European Qualifications Framework, the European Credit System for VET (ECVET), the European Credit Transfer System (ECTS) and EU mobility schemes have played an important role in the EU's Integrated Programme for Lifelong Learning. Schemes such as Europass aim to increase transparency between the education systems of the EU countries by providing a single structure for the recognition of qualifications and competences across Europe. It seeks to aid mobility in education and will incorporate five already-existing recognition-based initiatives into one coherent framework. It demonstrates a commitment to lifelong learning and new technologies by placing Europass on the Internet where users can update it as and when they gain new qualifications. The five existing programmes that will be absorbed into Europass are: the European CV; the European Language Portfolio; the MobiliPass; the Certificate Supplement; and the Diploma Supplement. Other similar instruments may be added to Europass in future.

Regionalization of VET structures also facilitates cross-border mobility by capitalizing on the trust that develops between all partners in education and training systems that are common and therefore more fully understood.

6 Towards Lifelong Learning Policies

In 2005, the education and labour ministries of thirty-two European countries, including the twenty-five EU member states, submitted national reports to the European Commission on the state of development and implementation of their lifelong learning policies. The resulting Communication, ratified by the European Parliament and Council, and the accompanying report provide a careful stocktaking analysis of the state of development across six major aspects of lifelong learning, including the comprehensiveness of lifelong learning policies in the EU member states, funding, VET and higher education. The Communication makes clear recommendations for further progress at European and national levels.

For VET, the following conclusions are reached:

> The implementation of the instruments and tools developed under the Copenhagen process is at too early a stage for countries to be able to present concrete results, but countries have established priorities for implementation at national level. In most countries, improving the attractiveness of VET is a key concern and a range of policies and measures are being actively implemented to improve the infrastructures and funding, to put in place or consolidate pathways and reduce obstacles to transfers from one type of provision to another, to modernise the curricula and create flexibility in its delivery and to adapt teacher training. A second crucial approach, which is receiving substantial attention, concerns strengthening links with the stakeholders, social partners and enterprises. Guidance and counseling systems are undergoing development in some countries, but this issue still needs more concerted attention.
>
> It is clear from the reports that a large majority of the countries express concerns with the needs of low-skilled citizens and disadvantaged groups and are implementing a range of policy approaches. However there is a lack of information on the non-formal and informal sectors, which makes it difficult to assess the full range of measures in all the countries. The European Inventory on validation of non-formal learning should help alleviate this problem.
>
> The participation of older workers in training is not showing marked improvements. However, an increasing number of countries are putting in place measures for the validation of prior learning and experience and for non-formal and informal learning. In order to achieve the Lisbon goals in this respect, more consideration and a higher priority level

will be necessary. Increasing the relevance of VET by reforming and improving the links of VET with the labour market, the social partners and other stakeholders is of core concern for a large majority of countries. In most of the countries, there is an ongoing process of reviewing and adapting procedures and structures, which includes setting up tripartite or sectoral mechanisms to underpin the process of developing and updating qualifications.

The early identification of skills and needs raises challenges for vocational education and training which are difficult, complex, costly and of longstanding. Overall the reports do not provide sufficient information to make it possible to determine the extent to which countries are developing mechanisms for anticipating skills shortages, gaps and deficiencies.

In relation to the major challenge of increasing the access to training and professional development for VET professionals, measures which are being taken for VET teachers should be adapted and extended to trainers who currently seem to be the group most in need of attention (European Commission, 2005, p. 51).

As we have indicated, lifelong learning is accorded a key role in Europe's agenda for competitiveness, employment growth and social inclusion/cohesion as part of the Lisbon Goals, and VET is a major component of lifelong learning in many European countries. Therefore, it is worth noting the key conclusions that the report and communication reach about the current state of development and implementation of lifelong learning policies at the national level across Europe. Progress has been made towards the agreed goal that lifelong learning strategies should be put in place in all Member States by 2006. Many—but by no means all—countries have now developed lifelong learning policy statements; for example, strategy documents or national action plans. Others have put in place framework legislation. It is still the case, however, that strategies remain imbalanced. There is a tendency either to focus on employability or on re-engaging those who have become alienated from education. It is encouraging that some countries, like Sweden, Denmark, Finland and Norway, are well on their way to achieving a national approach which is coherent and comprehensive, and are making strong progress on implementation. Even so, many countries still have much to do to achieve the agreed benchmarks for education and training.

7 Conclusion

Vocational education and training has been traditionally viewed as most relevant to the micro setting—where workers engage with specific tasks in enterprises and services. The internationalization of markets has gradually transformed VET into a system with a much stronger dependence on interacting with markets outside local communities and beyond national boundaries. This has led to a greater level of regional co-operation in developing people with the skills needed in this wider market. Recruitment has also stretched across boundaries and has been another factor for regional co-operation. Within the European Union, political, financial and social structures have developed which are designed to optimize the value of VET from the regional perspective.

Notes

1. <www.cedefop.eu.int>
2. <www.etf.eu.int>
3. <www.europa.eu.int/comm/education/policies/educ/eqf/>
4. Learning outcomes are statements of what a learner is expected to know, understand and/or be able to demonstrate after completion of a process of learning

References

Anderson, B. et al. 2006. *Fair enough? Central and East European migrants in low-wage employment in the UK*. York, UK: Joseph Rowntree Foundation.

Coles, M.; Oates, T, 2004. *European reference levels for education and training: an important parameter for promoting credit transfer and mutual trust*. Thessaloniki, Greece: CEDEFOP.

European Commission. 2004. *The future priorities of enhanced European cooperation in vocational education and training (VET)*. Brussels: European Commision. (The Maastricht Communiqué.) <ec.europa.eu/education/news/ip/docs/maastricht_com_en.pdf>

European Commission. 2005. *Communication from the Commission: modernising education and training: a vital contribution to prosperity and social cohesion in Europe*. Brussels: European Commission. (10.11.05.COM(2005) final.)

Leney, T. et al. 2004. *Scenarios toolkit*. Thessaloniki, Greece: CEDEFOP. (Dossier series 8.)

Leney, T. et al. 2005. *Achieving the Lisbon Goal: the contribution of VET*. Brussels: European Commission.

McCann, J.; Donald, G. 2005. *Initiating, adopting and building knowledge transfer in Scotland's colleges*. Stirling, UK: SFEU.

Organization for Economic Co-operation and Development. 2006. *Qualifications systems: bridges to lifelong learning*. Paris: OECD.

Chapter III.5
Vocational Education, Training Reform and Regional Integration in the Middle East

Munther Wassef Masri

1 Introduction

With the onset of globalization and escalating technological developments, combined with local, regional and international networks and interconnections, mainly in the economic and technical fields, pressure is increasing on VET systems in the Arab Region to better respond to or even to anticipate in some respects, new socio-economic requirements and labour market needs (Lasonen, 1999).

Increasing competitiveness on the local, regional and international levels has already resulted in growing demands for improving qualification standards in the workforce. But labour markets and vocational education and training systems are ill-prepared to respond to these challenges. On the labour market, we witness a relatively high rate of youth unemployment and low participation rates of women, side-by-side with increasing regional labour mobility. Prevailing VET systems still need to be transformed from predominantly supply-driven into balanced supply-demand-driven systems. VET systems are relatively expensive and overall funding and efficiency remain problematic. There are also still weak linkages and channels with higher education within the concept of lifelong learning. Finally, the role of the private sector in the planning and implementation of VET programmes, as well as human resources and development (HRD) programmes in general, is very weak (Wallenborn et al., 2003).

A regional approach to VET in the Arab region has been going on for a long time, although at a modest level. Until recently, such regional efforts took place either on a bilateral basis or through regional organizations (UNESCO-UNEVOC, 1998). Organizations playing an active role in the field of HRD in general and VET in particular included the Arab Labour Organization (ALO), the Arab League Educational, Cultural and Scientific Organization (ALECSO), the Arab Union for Technician Education, and the Arab Universities Union. More recently, international organizations became more active in their regional approach to VET issues and needs. Such organizations also included UNESCO-UNEVOC, the International Labour Organization (ILO), the European Training Foundation (ETF), the Deutsche Gesellschaft für technische Zusammenarbeit (GTZ) and other bilateral donor agencies. The overall impact, however, has been limited and very uneven in individual countries.

R. Maclean, D. Wilson (eds.), *International Handbook of Education for the Changing World of Work*, DOI 10.1007/978-1-4020-5281-1_III.5,
© Springer Science+Business Media B.V. 2009

More emphasis on regional co-operation and exchange therefore would undoubtedly help individual countries in the region to develop appropriate responses to the challenges they are facing. There are some lessons to be learned, however, from regional projects that have been implemented so far.

2 Regional Priorities

It is worthwhile emphasizing here that many of the issues, fields and challenges of VET benefit well from a regional approach with the possibility of high potential returns—both technically and economically. The areas that can benefit most from such approaches, while maintaining the diversity and specificity of offerings, include practically all key areas of vocational education and training.

- *Occupational classifications and standards:* The regional feasibility of this area is further supported by the need for regional, as well as international, compatibility of such classifications and standards.
- *Testing, certification and qualification frameworks and standards:* This is becoming more and more important from a regional perspective due to increasing labour mobility, as well as the pressures of competitiveness and globalization.
- *Curriculum development:* Regional efforts in this area would deal mainly with methodologies, the exchange of experience, standards and labour-market relevance criteria. This does not exclude the utilization of common curricula and education/training material, as was the case for some efforts in the past.
- *Teacher education and training:* This area is concerned with pre-service systems for the preparation of VET instructors, as well as their in-service training. It can also be concerned with the in-service training of enterprise supervisors, who are expected to undertake some training functions for trainees, apprentices, new recruits, etc. The training of trainers is another relevant area of concern that warrants the availability of regional and excellence centres to offer services to the concerned countries (Grootings & Nielsen, 2005).
- *Career guidance, counselling and employment services:* The importance and general nature of such services would warrant a regional approach, especially with the introduction of on-line systems.
- *System development:* This area would deal with such topics as governance, funding sources, legislative tools, school-based versus co-operative (dual) systems, etc. The fact that there are great similarities among Arab VET systems renders credibility to any regional approaches to VET system development.
- *Publications:* the importance of this area stems from the fact that, apart from textbooks and formal training material, publication efforts in the field of VET in Arabic language are relatively modest. Needless to say, a pool of such publications for the use of learners, instructors and researchers would be beneficial in supporting the VET mission, locally and regionally.

3 Principles and Criteria

To ensure relevance and credibility to a regional approach to the development of VET, activities and programmes should be carefully designed and implemented. A number of principles and criteria should guide regional co-operation.

First of all, there has to be real commitment in individual countries at the policy level by the relevant governmental and private agencies. There also has to be involvement of experts and/or agencies from the various member countries in the planning, implementation and utilization stages. This should secure sufficient levels of ownership by the relevant national agencies in the public and private sectors. Regional projects and programmes also need to be relevant to the countries' needs and the latter should clearly see the benefit and added value of engaging in regional projects. Finally, an important dimension of any regional project has to be the sustainability of outcomes through the continuous availability of human and material resources to ensure impact and follow-up on developments.

To be successful, VET projects should be designed using a regional approach. This means that the dimension of 'regionality' at the planning, implementation and utilization stages of the relevant activities should be defined and highlighted. This can be ensured by identifying issues that are of common interest to the member countries, and from which regionally relevant activities and specific projects can be derived. Experts and officials from the participating countries should be involved in this process in order to ensure commitment at the implementation stage later on. This should happen both at the operational and policy level with a view to securing sustainability and continuity. After all, the aim of regional projects is to assist in national-level changes.

To be adequately utilized, regional VET projects should be owned and sustained by the relevant agency or agencies in each country. After a regional project has come to an end, focal institutions in each country should therefore follow-up on the utilization of the outputs of projects and submit assessment reports accordingly. They should also undertake studies to evaluate the degree of utilization and the impact of project outputs in individual countries. By establishing networking capacities among the national institutions, the sharing of experiences at the regional level could have an additional positive impact on developments in national systems.

The nature and objectives of VET—essentially preparing learners for employment in private as well as public enterprises—make it of prime importance that public/private partnership be enhanced and adopted as one of the criteria for choosing projects. Such partnerships can be enhanced at the planning, implementation and utilization stages (Gill, Fluitman & Dar, 2000).

At the planning stage, public/private partnership can be enhanced through the active participation of employers' representatives in all planning activities at the policy and management levels. On the other hand, public/private partnership should have an impact in the objectives set for the chosen activities and projects. This is mainly ensured through the relevance of projects to labour-market needs. Furthermore, employers would be expected to participate in the funding, governance and sustainability of projects after implementation.

At the implementation stage, public/private partnership can be enhanced through the same channels and activities referred to at the planning stage. In addition, employers' representatives should participate extensively in expert groups involved in the implementation of activities and projects (e.g. designing curricula, setting standards, etc.).

At the utilization stage, enterprises should display ownership as well as involvement in making use of the outputs of projects. Follow-up and evaluation efforts, including impact studies, help to assess the level of private-sector ownership and involvement.

3.1 Evaluation and Assessment Considerations

The design of any activity or project should, at the planning stage, identify the evaluation and assessment processes and techniques to be carried out during and after implementation. For this purpose, a number of factors should be taken into consideration.

Evaluation and assessment activities should, as far as possible, be undertaken by neutral experts or agencies to ensure credibility and accuracy. They should cover outputs, outcomes and, as much as possible, the impact of projects. External evaluation does not exclude the need for internal or self-evaluation, which should clearly be shown in the design of projects. Some activities and projects, by their nature, benefit more if external evaluation is not left to the final stages of implementation. Evaluation efforts during implementation help to introduce any necessary and useful amendments at the appropriate time.

3.2 The Economics of Activities and Projects

The economics of implementation and operation is one of the important dimensions that should be taken into consideration when choosing and designing projects (Masri, 1994). All the relevant financial and funding aspects should thus be carefully assessed with the objective of maximizing outcomes and impact. There are also some other factors that should be taken into consideration. Funding should, of course, be appropriate to the aims of the project, but should also be available in a balanced way to all the countries involved, possibly and preferably matched with counterpart funding, either in cash or in kind. The contracting international experts and consultants should be kept to a minimum. This has the double advantage of economizing on expenditures and enhancing capacity-building efforts in the partner countries.

3.3 Securing Impact for System Development

System development can, in general, be realized by catering for one or more of the three groups of components that characterize education systems. These are the inputs, the processes and the outputs.

In the case of VET systems, as in other education systems, the inputs include such sub-components as curricula, instructors, administrators, learners, physical facilities, governance, legislative tools, evaluation, etc. The processes, on the other hand, comprise such sub-components as teaching/training methodologies, administrative styles, learners' out-of-class activities, etc. The outputs and outcomes include such sub-components as the level of knowledge, skills and attitudes attained by the learners, as well as the relevance to national developmental needs and to life in general, including the labour market.

4 Regional and International Organizations: Roles and Efforts

In what follows, a number of international organizations that are relevant to regional efforts and projects in the field of VET are briefly explored. These organizations all share similar aims that are of benefit to individual countries. They provide external assessment of VET systems and policies from the perspective of other regional and international experts and organizations. By doing so, they also improve mutual knowledge and understanding of VET systems, reforms and issues in other countries. All of them also establish channels and linkages that facilitate the exchange of experiences on the regional and international levels and promote co-operation and linkages at regional and international levels.

We shall present the key regional and international organizations that are currently active in the region and follow this up with a brief case study of a bi-lateral co-operation project in vocational education and training.

4.1 Regional Organizations

4.1.1 Arab Labour Organization

The Arab Labour Organization (ALO) has its headquarters in Cairo. It is concerned with labour issues, including skill and human resources development, mainly at the informal occupational levels that comprise skilled workers and craftsmen. Activities and projects in the field of skills and HRD development are undertaken through the ALO technical arm, the Arab Centre for Human Resources Development (ACHRD) which is located in Tripoli (Libya).

To promote the TVET mission through a regional approach, the ACHRD undertakes such activities as:

- Regional conferences, workshops and seminars.
- Issuing publications on VET issues in the Arabic language, authored by writers from different Arab countries. About thirty such publications have been issued since 1990.
- Training workshops for teacher-trainers and officials involved in the implementation and governance of TVET systems.

- Networking among stakeholders in the Arab Region, through on-line and off-line material and contacts.

4.1.2 Arab League Educational, Cultural and Scientific Organization

ALECSO, which is the Arab counterpart of UNESCO, is an Arab League organization that is concerned with education, culture and science. It has its headquarters in Tunis, and although its mandate in VET is not markedly different from that of the ALO, the diversification of its mandate leaves limited room for VET, with emphasis on the formal systems that are usually school-based and institutionalized.

4.1.3 Arab Union for Technician Education

AUTE is mainly concerned with technical and vocational education, with most of its activities directed towards intermediate university education that is usually offered by post-secondary institutes and community colleges. It has its headquarters at present in Tripoli (Libya). While the mandates of ALO and ACHRD are concerned with the basic occupational levels in VET, that of AUTE deals more with intermediate occupational levels for the preparation of technicians and sub-professionals. The scope and type of activities are, nevertheless, similar for both organizations.

4.1.4 Union of Arab Universities

As its name implies, the Union of Arab Universities (UAU) is mainly concerned with university education. It has its headquarters in Amman (Jordan), and the UAU role in VET is manifested in three areas: (a) scientific research and studies that deal with the various VET issues, including post-graduate studies and theses; (b) pre-service and in-service education and training for VET instructors; and (iii) design of university admission standards and criteria for graduates of VET institutions and programmes.

4.2 International Organizations

4.2.1 UNESCO-UNEVOC Network and International Centre for TVET

The UNEVOC Network covers the world and comprises specialized institutions in technical and vocational education and training (TVET). These institutions are called UNEVOC centres. The general objective of the network is to support developments in national TVET systems through:

- Enhancing regional and international co-operation through the diffusion and sharing of information and best practices;
- Promoting experimentation and innovation; and

- Supporting a dialogue among researchers, policy-makers and practitioners who work in the field of technical and vocational education and training.

UNEVOC was established in 1992 by UNESCO to act as a platform for regional and international co-operation in the field of TVET. At present there are more than 220 UNEVOC centres in more than 155 UNESCO Member States. In 2002, the UNESCO-UNEVOC International Centre for Technical and Vocational Education and Training was inaugurated to strengthen the UNEVOC network. It is based in Bonn, Germany.

Although the UNEVOC network is international in scope, the great majority of its activities are of a regional nature, implemented under the umbrella of UNESCO's regional and field offices. In the Arab Region, such offices exist in Beirut (Lebanon), Cairo (Egypt), Amman (Jordan), the Gulf, etc. UNEVOC centres can be found in some Arab countries.

More recently, a UNESCO-UNEVOC e-Forum was established, providing a free-of-charge e-mail list service to those joining the forum: (a) to help them to connect with experts in TVET from around the world; (b) to identify partners for regional and international co-operation in research and development that targets TVET issues and topics; (c) to pose questions on TVET and obtain authoritative answers from experts in the field; (d) to obtain essential information on TVET development in such fields as curriculum, instructor training, etc.; and (e) to share thoughts and gain access to useful information about TVET.

4.2.2 The European Training Foundation

The ETF is an agency of the European Union that started its operations in Turin (Italy) in 1994 with a mission to assist partner countries in developing quality education and training systems and to enable them to reform their VET systems. The ETF partner countries include many in the Arab Region, mainly along the south and east coasts of the Mediterranean, through the MEDA programme.

ETF shares expertise and advice on policies in education and training across regions and cultures. Each year, its work programme comprises a group of projects that are implemented in the partner countries to facilitate the reform of VET and employment systems. A regional approach is frequently utilized in such programmes and projects. Such an approach, when deemed feasible, helps to spread experience in the development of VET systems, in addition to maximizing outcomes and returns on the relevant projects.

The areas of concern of ETF up until the present cover many themes that are relevant to VET, such as VET policies, teacher and trainer training, training for poverty alleviation, adult and lifelong learning, employment and the labour market, national qualifications frameworks, etc. In addition to its annual *Yearbook*, ETF publications cover a wide variety of topics that reflect national and regional developments and experiences in the field of VET. On the regional level, expert meetings, peer reviews, seminars, etc., help to exchange experiences and establish contacts and channels of communication that assist practitioners, decision-makers and policy-makers in their plans to develop the various aspects of VET systems (Grootings & Nielsen, 2004).

In the Arab Region, ETF projects helped some countries to benefit from the experiences of other countries in such areas as human resources information systems, VET indicators, etc.

5 Case Study: Arab-German Co-operation in VET

This project which was launched and funded by GTZ and was planned from the outset to support the development of VET systems in five Arab countries—Egypt, Jordan, Lebanon, Palestine and Syria—through regional co-operative efforts and involvement. Thus, it was originally planned with a regional perspective at the policy, management and operational levels.

This project is in many respects an interesting one from a regional perspective. First, the regional approach to VET development was comprehensively and institutionally adopted and incorporated at the planning stage with the explicit objective of developing national VET systems with major involvement from regional sources. This approach was formalized through agreements between GTZ and each of the concerned countries. Finally, the structure and governance of the project ensured relevance and provided the utilization of the resulting benefits to be maximized by national VET systems.

Below we list some of the key characteristics of the project that have contributed to its positive impact on the development of TVET systems from a national and regional perspective.

- The relatively long duration of the project, spanning the period 2003–2011, helps to secure the sustainability, impact and credibility of monitoring and evaluation efforts.
- The project has been designed to facilitate the identification and choice of sub-projects that are considered by policy-makers and practitioners as priority areas and are of common interest to member countries.
- Although the scope of the project covered five Arab countries, the outcomes of sub-projects are potentially relevant to all other Arab countries, especially taking into consideration the great similarities in their VET systems and the common language background. It is worthwhile noting here that some VET areas are language sensitive and socially influenced, such as classification systems, glossaries, etc.
- Networking among VET institutions and experts is a major feature of the project, thus facilitating the exchange of experiences to the benefit of national VET systems. The structure and governance of the project, as described below, shows how such networking is secured.
- At the operational level, a relevant focal point is chosen in each country to be responsible for the implementation or supervision of the relevant activities and sub-projects at the national level. Focal points varied in their nature from

one country to another. Autonomous VET agencies or VET departments in the Ministries of Education or Labour are examples of such focal points.

- A regional office in one of the concerned countries (Jordan) with a project office manager, hosted by a national institution, provided the secretariat for the project, undertaking the co-ordinating and networking functions.
- The continuous contacts and communications among focal points in the implementation of sub-projects provided useful channels and frameworks whereby experts and decision-makers in the concerned countries benefited to develop their own VET systems.
- At the middle-management level, project governance is taken care of by a Regional Management Committee (RMC) composed of two senior officials, one from the public sector and one from the private sector from each country. The RMC holds its meetings in turn in one of the five countries twice annually to choose sub-projects from among a pool of project proposals submitted by the focal points in the concerned countries. The RMC submits its recommendations on the choice of projects to a Regional Higher Council, referred to below, in addition to undertaking the function of following up procedures for the implementation of decisions taken by the Council.
- At the policy (macro) level, project governance is taken care of by a Regional Higher Council (RHC) composed of three senior officials—two from the public sector and one from the private sector—from each country. The RHC holds its meetings in turn in one of the five countries as it is required to take decisions on the final choice of sub-projects, to assess their implementation and utilization, and to discuss policies and strategies for the regional project.
- As in the case of the Regional Management Committee, the Regional Higher Council, through its meetings and functions, provides a forum for policy-makers and senior officials to exchange views and experiences on national VET issues and developments on the one hand, and on identifying areas for further regional co-operation and common approaches in the field of VET on the other.
- The way in which sub-projects are implemented depends upon their nature and other practical considerations, such as the availability of expertise and technical resources. Two such models have already been utilized in this project and are described below.

Model 1

The project is implemented exclusively by an institution or group of experts in one country. In this case, regionality is ensured through one or more of the following procedures: (a) establishing a regional steering committee that meets periodically to follow-up and guide the stages of implementation; (b) choosing a counterpart institution or group of experts in each of the other countries not involved in implementation, to be consulted frequently at the various stages of implementation; and

(c) holding periodical regional workshops to discuss and approve the work at the different stages of implementation.

Model 2

The activity or project is divided into parts, and each part is implemented by an institution or group of experts in one country, thus paving the way for more than one country to participate in the implementation. Although the regional dimension is thus assured, homogeneous outputs of the various parts are difficult to guarantee. To minimize such shortcomings, co-ordination efforts are needed through the following measures: (a) periodical meetings/workshops of the expert groups; and/or (b) establishing a regional steering committee that meets periodically to follow-up and guide the stages of implementation.

6 Conclusion

One major conclusion of the review presented here is that efforts directed at regional co-operation and integration can promote and stimulate changes and developments in national TVET systems through channels and venues of co-ordination, peer-reviewing, policy-learning and exchange of experiences. Needless to say, co-operation in VET issues can facilitate similar co-operation in other areas.

Furthermore, national developments in VET are expected to face the need for regional co-operation due to such factors as worker and student mobility, recognition of qualifications, lack of capacities, etc. In other words, national reforms in VET can pragmatically lead to regional co-operation and integration.

References–English

Gill, I.; Fluitman, F.; Dar, A., eds. 2000. *Vocational education and training and training reform: matching skills to markets and budgets.* New York, NY: Oxford University Press.

Grootings, P.; Nielsen, S., eds. 2004. *ETF Yearbook 2004: learning matters.* Turin, Italy: ETF.

Grootings P.; Nielsen, S., eds. 2005. *ETF Yearbook 2005: teachers and trainers: professionals and stakeholders in the reform of vocational education and training.* Luxembourg: European Communities.

Lasonen, J., ed. 1999. *Workforce preparation in a global context.* Jyväskylä, Finland: Institute for Educational Research-University of Jyväskylä.

Masri, M.W. 1994. *Vocational education: the way ahead.* London: Macmillan.

UNESCO-UNEVOC. 1998. *Vocational education and training in Europe on the threshold of the 21st century.* Paris: UNESCO.

Wallenborn, M. et al. 2003. *Human resources development in school-based and company-based technical and vocational education and training (TVET)-Egypt and selected MEDA/MENA countries.* Mannheim, Germany: Internationale Weiterbildung und Entwicklung GmbH.

References–Arabic

باسل البستاني (2003). التعليم، اكتساب المهارات وأسواق العمل في أقطار مجلس التعاون الخليجي-تجربة الامارات العربية المتحدة. (نيويورك: الأمم المتحدة-اللجنة الاقتصادية والاجتماعية لغربي آسيا).

أحمد مصطفى عبدالله (2000). مخرجات التدريب المهني وسوق العمل في الأقطار العربية. (طرابلس-ليبيا: المركز العربي لتنمية الموارد البشرية-منظمة العمل العربية).

طارق علي العاني ونصير احمد السامرائي وعلي خليل التميمي (2001). الشراكة بين مؤسسات التدريب والاعداد وسوق العمل. (طرابلس-ليبيا: المركز العربي لتنمية الموارد البشرية- منظمة العمل العربية).

علي محمد نصرالله وأحمد مديمغ (1998).المواءمة بين مخرجات التدريب والتعليم الفني واحتياجات سوق العمل في الأردن وتونس. (طرابلس-ليبيا: المركز العربي لتنمية الموارد البشرية- منظمة العمل العربية).

المشروع الدولي للتعليم التقني والمهني (UNEVOC). دور التعليم الفني والمهني ضمن نظم التعليم العربية: دراسة حالة ودراسة توليفيه. (عمّان-الأردن: مكتب اليونسكو الإقليمي للتربية في الدول العربية (يوندباس).

منذر واصف المصري (2003). اقتصاديات التعليم والتدريب المهني. (طرابلس-ليبيا: المركز العربي لتنمية الموارد البشرية-منظمة العمل العربية).

Chapter III.6
The Influence of Qualifications Frameworks on the Infrastructure of VET

Mike Coles and Patrick Werquin

1 Introduction

It is likely that most vocational learning resulting from formal schooling is not officially recognized in qualifications. Informal and non-formal learning are probably the dominant forms of vocational education and training (VET). However, the recognition of learning through qualifications is probably dominant in shaping the formal VET system because qualifications are one of the most tangible outcomes of VET for people and enterprises. The financial and social returns to qualification levels are also widely appreciated. It is not surprising, therefore, that the ways in which qualifications are organized exert a powerful influence on the vocational learning system. In this chapter we examine the ways in which the existence of a qualifications framework influences several structural aspects of VET. These structural aspects include the management of the supply and demand for skills, the institutional arrangements, the financing of VET and the way the VET system interfaces with other learning systems and VET in other countries. Before this analysis begins, the diverse nature of qualifications frameworks is examined.

2 The Nature of Qualifications Frameworks

The idea of a qualifications framework that shows how qualifications relate to one another is not new. For many centuries the trade organizations in many countries have exercised control over the right to practice a trade and control how progression in skills is defined and managed. Before this, universities had set down common patterns of recognizing progress within higher academic learning. What is new is the interest of governments in developing overarching frameworks that incorporate qualifications representing the learning outcomes from school, work and higher education. Importantly, the new frameworks are often linked to lifelong learning policy and are intended to capture learning from experience that the learner wishes to have recognized.

A qualifications framework is a classification of qualifications according to a set of criteria reflecting the levels of learning achieved. This set of criteria may

R. Maclean, D. Wilson (eds.), *International Handbook of Education for the Changing World of Work*, DOI 10.1007/978-1-4020-5281-1_III.6,
© Springer Science+Business Media B.V. 2009

be an implicit characteristic of the qualifications themselves or made explicit in the form of a set of level descriptors. In the simplest form of classification the qualifications themselves are arranged in a hierarchy of demand or standard, the lowest level of qualifications rises through a series of steps to the highest level. The qualifications in these hierarchies are sometimes further classified into qualification types (e.g. higher-education qualifications, school qualifications, work-based qualifications). The second kind of classification uses explicit levels that are each defined by criteria—these are often termed level descriptors or level indicators.

The scope of frameworks may be comprehensive for all learning achievement and pathways or it may be confined to a particular sector, for example initial education, adult learning or an occupational area such as agriculture. Some frameworks may have more design elements and a tighter structure than others; some may have a legal basis, whereas others represent a consensus of views among social partners. However, all qualifications frameworks establish a basis for improving the linkages between qualifications and the quality, accessibility and public or labour-market recognition of qualifications within a country and internationally.

Some countries established comparative levels for qualifications in the 1960s (e.g. France) and others more recently (e.g. New Zealand). In Scotland the qualification framework has evolved over the last twenty years or so. It was not until 1985 that the first significant attempt to develop an international framework appeared. CEDEFOP developed a five-level framework (CEDEFOP, 2001) for vocational qualifications to facilitate the comparability of qualifications in the context of an anticipated growth in the mobility of labour. These levels had little impact and European Union (EU) countries made little effort to align their vocational qualifications systems with these levels. More recently, the European Commission has proposed a European Qualifications Framework (EQF)[1] that is intended to operate as a meta-framework.[2] The EQF proposal suggests that the most effective way for nations to articulate with the European framework is through a national qualifications framework (NQF). Evidence suggests that this request is receiving a positive response from the majority of European countries (Bjørnåvold & Coles, 2006). See Coles (2006) for a full review of national qualifications frameworks.

NQFs have various forms and functions, but all have four generic aims:

- to establish national standards for learning outcomes (competences);
- to promote through regulation the quality of education and training provision;
- to act as a way of relating qualifications to each other; and
- to promote access to learning, transfer of learning and progression in learning.

It is often the case that NQFs have policy purposes that go beyond these four aims. The development of an NQF can be used to integrate parts of the qualifications system (for example, professional education delivered via further and higher education) or to modernize parts of the education and training system (for example, to change the regulation of the quality of qualification processes or to change the way public funds are used to support education and training). These wider effects of qualifications frameworks on the infrastructure of VET are the principal focus of this chapter and in the following sections some of these effects are discussed in more detail.

3 Managing the Supply of Skills

Vocational education and training arrangements in a country are always complex because of: (a) the many forms of learning that are considered as VET; (b) the wide range of institutions that deliver VET; and (c) the interaction and overlap of sectors, occupations and enterprises. The complexity of the system can make it difficult to adjust programmes so that training leads to the competences that are required in the workplace, particularly when work practices and technology are leading to changes in competence requirements. It is generally the case that VET competences are defined, delivered and evaluated by means of collaboration between stakeholder groups (usually governments, providers, enterprises and employee organizations). It can be argued that the better the collaboration between stakeholders, the better the modernization process is likely to be. One way in which the collaboration process can be supported is to make sure that labour-market information and information about the qualification process (such as pedagogic methods) are freely available for analysis. Qualification frameworks can make this information easier to use, for example by:

- classifying the levels of qualifications in a commonly understood way;
- requiring the expression of qualification in terms of learning outcomes;
- showing how qualification structures relate to the needs of sectors by defining categories of the content of qualifications;
- quality assuring the qualification process through the use of regulation and accreditation criteria; and
- making transparent the way qualifications at one level can lead to the next level.

There are other ways in which a national set of benchmarks in terms of levels can be used to make statistical analysis of skills requirements easier to express and use across a wide range of sectors.

Qualifications frameworks act as a classification device. This function is important, but it is increasingly common for a framework of levels to be considered as the basis for a classification of units of qualifications (partial qualification), as well as for whole qualifications. By breaking down whole qualifications into units it is possible to modernize a qualification relatively easily by developing a new unit to replace an out-of-date unit. Whilst this can be achieved without a framework, it is usually the case that a unitized system of qualification can become unwieldy and opaque without a classification system. Thus, through the location of units of different content at different levels, it is easy for collaborators defining skills needs to identify the required competences and to provide institutions to deliver them to learners.

These unitized approaches also offer the advantage of easier transfer of credit from one sector to another, particularly in the case of transversal skills, such as communications, team management and health and safety. Thus, modernization of these transversal units of qualifications can improve the quality of training across many sectors.

Qualifications frameworks generally classify qualifications that arise from dedicated training programmes. However, because levels and content are often defined more clearly for qualifications in a framework, usually through learning outcomes, it is easier for an individual to appreciate that they have competences that have developed non-formally (e.g. through work) or informally (e.g. through managing a family) that can meet the requirements of a formal qualification. Recognition of non-formal and informal learning can be facilitated and can go some way to meet skills needs in a region or an enterprise.

All of these examples are specific ways a framework can lead to better articulation of knowledge, skill and wider competence requirements. In addition to improving this articulation, it is possible for frameworks to modernize the supply side of VET, for example by improving the efficiency of delivery.

4 Articulating the Demand for Skills

If VET is 'education and training that aims at equipping people with the knowledge, skills and competences that can be used in the labour market'[3] then qualifications frameworks will impact on the infrastructure of VET whenever they impact on the skills and competences produced by VET that are or can be used in the labour market. There are many reasons to believe that this is going to be the case on the demand side of VET competences because qualifications frameworks:

- can bring transparency;
- can be durable and provide stability;
- can provide consistency;
- can bring confidence;
- can allow for a coherent statistical monitoring by qualification level; and
- are essentially based on learning outcomes.

All these arguments are linked to each other to a large extent. For example, confidence in qualifications may grow because there is transparency of the qualifications system and they therefore reflect a widely recognized system (backed up by main qualifications authorities, such as the ministry of education). Thus, users of qualifications, such as employers, know exactly which competence(s) they are about to hire. Confidence may also arise because there is stability over time making investment in the system—learning how to use it and for improving it—worthwhile in the medium and long term. As a consequence, employers may be more motivated to hire graduates from the VET system and to promote VET itself since they can be sure exactly what recruits know and can do. Greater transparency of VET systems will lead to a more effective use of VET by employers that will waste less time in recruiting due to a more effective search for appropriate skills.

In some countries, such as Spain, Greece, the Czech Republic or Japan, qualifications frameworks are associated primarily with VET (OECD, 2007). As a classification device, a qualifications framework organizes all the qualifications that are delivered in a particular country. Thanks to the concepts of levels and descriptors, qualifications frameworks provide a planning tool for employers who are constantly demanding [new] skills. This additional transparency, brought about by qualifications frameworks, helps employers to identify the skills that they need for the good functioning of the enterprise leading to a better economic performance. What a framework does that did not exist so clearly before is to put a clear label on a qualification and to position this qualification in the big picture by relating qualifications to one another in terms of level. As a consequence, recruiters or people having a demand for skills are better informed about what they are looking for and what is available. They can better compare existing qualifications and therefore better organize their demand for skills.

Beyond that, qualifications frameworks help to articulate the demand for skills with that of supply. This will happen because individuals (typically workers or applicants for a job) will eventually receive strong signals about the skills that are most in demand. This will happen whatever the recruiting scenario the employer decides to opt for: (a) they may look for the competences internally and organize the move/promotion of insiders if adequate competences are available internally; or (b) whether the competences are available internally or not, they may decide to recruit externally.

In both cases, whether using internal mobility or external recruitment, employers may realise that the skills they demand are not available or not available at the expected level. As a consequence, they may organize their own training strategy to promote insiders or send a strong signal to the training authority for them to provide the appropriate training. Individuals themselves will receive all of these signals through more-or-less formal circulation of information within the enterprise or, for outsiders, through using the public employment service for example, or any other usual channel—including, probably, word of mouth. As a result, supply and demand of skills are likely to reach a better match if a framework exists providing transparent information regarding qualifications and qualification levels. In turn, this mechanism is likely to impact back on the infrastructure of VET, which will have to adjust to meet the needs of a better informed demand.

A typical consequence one might anticipate is that VET will have to evolve at a faster pace than before since the labour market and the demand for skills are also evolving ever faster as a result of technological changes. Another possible consequence is that this impacts on curricula in the formal VET sector; so that they are formulated to describe what student should know or should be able to do at the end of their training to better match with the concept or learning outcomes widely associated with the concept of qualifications frameworks. In addition, to allow for the demand for skills to be appropriately planned, whether using external recruitment or internal mobility and/or promotion, qualifications frameworks will improve the confidence of the actors demanding skills toward the VET system.

By the same token, since qualifications frameworks can be heavily based on learning outcomes rather than input (duration of the course, for example) and since, again, many VET competences are not produced in the formal system, qualifications frameworks will help recruiters to appreciate the skills available and to plan their future utilization of VET competences.

Making obvious the demand for skills through the use of levels and qualification types is a clear added value of qualifications framework. Beyond, and thanks to, transparency, confidence will be built so that the main actors in the demand for skills will have greater trust in VET competences that appear clearly in the qualifications framework.

The French qualifications levels represent an attempt to use qualifications levels for economic planning and for better organizing the supply and demand of skills. This system was created as part of French economic planning and went beyond forecasting skills needs by enabling the education and training system to meet business needs by supplying sufficient numbers of people skilled to appropriate levels in appropriate occupations. It was a tool for developing active educational policies directed at increasing and standardizing vocational training in order to guide and promote French economic development (Bouder, 2003). The classifications system led to the setting up a qualifications agency (*Commission technique d'homologation*) that is responsible for positioning all diplomas and maintaining an up-to date classification according to labour-market innovations. One aspect of the classification system is that it is deeply embedded in social hierarchies and goes beyond a simple classification of diplomas and training programmes. However, in the case of France, it did not really work because the form of manpower planning that it was based on did not take into account the practice of enterprises that may have promoted or retrained workers internally. In that sense, the French qualifications levels, despite being deeply embedded in social hierarchies and going beyond a simple classification of diplomas and training programmes, do not constitute a framework. This is probably because it was too heavily based on qualifications delivered by the formal system where a qualifications framework is closely linked to the concept of learning outcomes. The new classification system, introduced in 1994, attempts to classify any training programme regardless of its level, mode of learning, field of application or social use, including personal development activities and leisure programmes. Like other frameworks, this initiative aims to de-compartmentalize the education and training system and form links between formal education, vocational education, university education and professional education.

5 Frameworks and Institutions

Education and training systems often evolve into complex networks with differences between institutions that include:

- dependence on public or private funding;
- licences to operate in an occupational sector;

- licences to operate across a specified number of levels of qualification;
- the nature of enterprises in a catchment area;
- the geography and transportation in an area;
- the type of governance employed; and
- size and the capacity to offer programmes.

There are many more dimensions of difference, and from a consumer point of view both for individuals and enterprises. These differences can lead to confusion and wasted investment of time and money. For example, a qualification programme offered in one institution can differ markedly from that provided in another and yet they can lead the learner to the same state of readiness for employment. How can a choice me made? How can the most efficient use of prior learning be accommodated? Qualification frameworks have the capacity to reduce complexity. This happens not simply by means of the classification of qualifications but also by requiring that every qualification in a framework is described in terms of what a learner is expected to know and do at the end of a programme of learning. Thus, we see a common requirement of transparency for every qualification that is not dependent on any institutional factors.

A consequence of this is that qualification programmes across different types of institution (e.g. initial VET and general education; professional education and higher education) become comparable and points of overlap are evident. This can have the effect of encouraging helpful differentiation between programmes and in facilitating co-operative arrangements to deliver certain programme content. For some time, policy-makers have been concerned with the potential overlap between higher education programmes and high-level VET. The concern stems from the belief that higher education programmes have the potential to deliver programmes that meet the needs of enterprises better than VET.

Thus, institutions (schools, colleges and universities) can both define a qualification framework and be defined by one. By means of making the purposes, structure and content of qualifications explicit through associating them with learning outcomes, it is possible to see opportunities for one kind of institution being able to make contributions to the traditional territory of others. This is not to suggest that the traditional patterns of qualifications programmes are faulty in some way—it simply opens up the possibilities for making more dynamic links between parts of the system which could render decision-making by learners a little easier, thus increasing the efficiency of the system. With increasing use of information and communications technologies in educational development (e.g. distance learning, knowledge management) the potential for these kinds of inter-institutional links are likely to increase.

The institutions that have mainly management roles in the qualifications system can also be affected by qualifications framework development. These institutions include government departments (education, labour and sectoral ministries, such as a ministry of agriculture), qualifications awarding bodies, quality assurance agencies and funding bodies. It is often the case that social partners have important roles. The manner in which the processes are agreed for setting up and managing a NQF can increase or decrease the influence of different types of stakeholder groups on the education and training system. Two rather obvious examples are worth consideration since they are commonly found in increasing numbers in countries where frameworks are being developed. The first example is the tightening of control by government of the qualifications system so that it can be more easily used in government-led reforms. Countries where centralized control is increasing might want to use the framework to introduce new qualifications routes that provide access to qualification for those social groups who are often excluded (or exclude themselves). The second example is where there is an intentional shift of the balance from the supply side of training to the demand side for competences. The role of employers, employees and their representative bodies could be given a stronger role in system management, while that of the providing institutions becomes weaker.

Providing institutions can also be directly influenced by the introduction of a qualifications framework. It can have some associated operational characteristics. A good example is quality-assurance arrangements. Whilst not evident in any framework diagram, the framework may only allow qualifications to be registered on it if the qualifications—and the providers that deliver it—meet certain criteria. So the framework becomes a powerful regulatory tool and a benchmark for national standards. These criteria can require institutions providing programmes and qualifications to change their practices to conform to standard protocols.

It is now clear how frameworks can influence institutions and therefore can be used to drive VET reforms. Frameworks can also be powerful co-ordinating tools capable of changing the VET landscape so that specific reforms can flourish.

6 Financing VET Provision

The existence of qualifications frameworks is likely to have a strong impact on the way VET provision is financed. Framework developments can be expensive. Clearly the scope of the NQFs and their intended purposes directly affect the costs of implementation and on-going maintenance. This distinction between implementation costs and maintenance costs is important. Whilst it is common for NQFs to be established in order to bring co-ordination to existing structures and qualifications, the development of the basis for agreement on an NQF requires:

- policy analysis;
- consideration of experience elsewhere;
- development of options;
- modelling of the favoured option(s);
- engagement of leaders of stakeholder groups;
- specialist task groups;
- consultation; and
- communication with main institutions and the general public.

The implementation phase could also involve piloting technical procedures and full-scale trials. As discussed above, a national body is often established to manage the implementation phase and the on-going maintenance. Making estimates of costs therefore requires anticipating large-scale systemic change that includes these elements and others.

The central administration costs related to the NQF can be relatively small. Even in countries where large agencies are responsible for the NQF, the costs (mainly staff costs) associated only with the NQF can be low. However, where such things as quality assurance procedures, curriculum and assessment monitoring, reviews of employment standards and establishing benchmarks corresponding to other national or international qualification frameworks are involved the costs can rise steeply.

NQFs take the place of informal structures and co-ordinate existing VET provision. It is likely, though difficult to quantify, that there will be some cost savings through this process. It is also likely that in a co-ordinated qualifications system there will be co-financing of some procedures such as the development of employment standards.

Some NQFs are explicitly quality assurance mechanisms and the title *national qualification* is reserved for those qualifications accredited to the NQF. Quality controls on these qualifications can be extensive and therefore expensive. They are intended to develop maximum confidence in users of the qualifications. Where education and training is funded by governments, there is a good case for seeking a return on the investment in quality assurance of national qualifications and consequently public funding favours these qualifications above others.

Another characteristic that has a direct impact on cost and therefore financing is the fact again that qualifications frameworks are essentially based on learning outcomes and also because most of vocational education and training competences are learned outside the formal system. As a consequence, the burden of the cost may move from learning to assessing the real competences of the individuals. The financing will need to be carefully reviewed.

Given the international context, with the existence of meta-frameworks—such as the European Qualifications Framework—and international benchmarks, qualifications frameworks may also have an impact on the way governments and policy-makers communicate about the destination of public money, and therefore on all spending. All countries have national benchmarks and quality standards and policymakers need to show that their financing practice for qualifications and learning programmes is prudent. Therefore, they may use the international benchmarks as a way of showing that they met the international standards in their own countries or even that they have done better, justifying at once the use of public money.

From the point of view of quality assurance, the international context also sets some forms of benchmark because all processes leading to a qualification usually receive scrutiny in a country and all the major international developments, especially at the European level, have quality assurance processes associated with them (higher education framework in the Bologna process; the Copenhagen process common principles for quality assurance).

More generally, all the elements that the existence of qualifications frameworks has brought into the picture are important in terms of financing because they always intrinsically lead to cost-effectiveness analysis. In many countries, the world of qualifications is subject to debates about the over-supply, for instance, of very similar qualifications—which is inefficient. A qualifications framework is a very useful tool to eliminate duplication if it shows that several qualifications are at the same level. The possibility of removing redundancy has just been given to countries such as Poland, for instance, where the number of qualifications has been reduced from 1,000 to 400. A qualifications framework is therefore an important tool for effective financing practice and updating of the qualifications pool.

Using qualifications frameworks can also be useful to bring private investments to the world of qualifications because they represent a mechanism for involving employers. The reason for that is because qualifications frameworks are based on learning outcomes in essence and learning outcomes bring visibility. Therefore, employers will be less keen on formulating their most frequently heard complaint about the lack of transparency and the confusion in the qualifications system.

As a consequence, there must be a role for sponsors, but this role has to be clear or they will not embark on financing qualifications; especially if they feel this is the duty of the government in the first place. To that extent, it is useful to take an international perspective and look for good practice to spot the possible role of private investors in qualifications. Russia is an example of a country where pilot projects and experimentation with the basis of a qualifications framework is privately sponsored. This has arisen because employers in the hotels and catering sector in Russia believe the qualifications system is not delivering the skills entrepreneurs need. It does not necessarily mean that they want to be involved in the delivery processes themselves (teaching, etc.), but they want to be involved in setting standards beforehand. There is a cost to that and this why employers find it acceptable to put money into the system.

Finally, it should not be forgotten that the major reforms likely to occur in the infrastructure of VET due to the implementation of qualifications frameworks will take time. Therefore, financing ought to be carefully planned in the medium or long term.

7 More Flexible Credit-Transfer System

Overcoming compartmentalization of the education and training system has been a goal in many countries. In the late 1980s in New Zealand various independent reports signalled the need for a radical overhaul of the qualifications system that it was felt was hampering participation, achievement and New Zealand's competitiveness. After a series of reforms to various parts of the education and training system, an NQF and a formal system of establishing recognition of qualifications based on unit standards (learning outcomes) were established. A national validating authority (the New Zealand Qualifications Authority) was also set up requiring the assessment of learning programmes to be drawn up against unit standards and to be subject to a series of quality-assurance procedures, including the accreditation of providers. The NQF was both a product of the need for widespread reform and a tool for maintaining a reformed system. The NQF regulatory requirements are a means for bringing increased commonality to different parts of the education and training system, whilst preserving the integrity of those separate systems and the roles of key agencies within them. So employment sector bodies, schools, community groups, private providers and higher education all have separate procedures for developing unit standards and maintaining the quality assurance requirements of the NQF. Universities are not part of this process and there are qualifications that are not sufficiently based on unit standards to be part of the NQF. A comprehensive register of qualifications has been set up to include all qualifications—the NQF qualifications are a subset in this listing.

The Scottish Credit and Qualifications Framework (SCQF) also developed in a way that reduced barriers between parts of the education and training system. However, it also has taken on the task of sustaining systematic transfer of credit at the level of units of qualifications. The SCQF developed as a result of a series of innovations in the education and training systems covering school, vocational and higher education. Each innovation reinforced the SCQF as a means of securing greater coherence in the qualifications system. At the same time as these substantial changes were being implemented, knowledge of system-wide features was shared. Credit transfer was seen as a means of increasing the flexibility of qualifications and the SCQF was identified by its partners as having the potential to accommodate the common principles necessary for its implementation. One of the functions of the SCQF is the credit rating of units of qualifications. The rules for good practice can be agreed centrally, but a prerequisite for credit transfer is that the units of assessment in learning programmes have to be rated in terms of the volume of learning. Making judgements about learning volumes involves close scrutiny of the curriculum and some attention being paid to pedagogy and resource provision. Thus, the providers closest to the programmes are enabled to carry out this process and the influence of the SCQF is extended deep into the education and training process.

8 A Tool for Reform

Policy-making for lifelong learning in the arena of qualifications systems is difficult, underdeveloped and possibly undervalued. Establishing a qualifications framework, in the same way as providing credit transfer, optimizing stakeholder involvement in the qualifications system, recognizing non-formal and informal learning and creating new routes to qualifications for example, seems to be a powerful mechanism to trigger more and better lifelong learning from within the qualifications system (OECD, 2007). This chapter suggests that it is useful to consider the role qualifications frameworks may have on the infrastructure of VET in particular.

An example of a framework being used for purposes that lie outside the education and training system is given by the EQF, having as its principal aim a strong link to the Lisbon Goal of more and better jobs for all European citizens and the creation of Europe as a top-performing knowledge economy. The Maastricht Communiqué (European Commission, 2004) states that the EQF:

> will improve permeability within education and training, provide a reference for the valida-
> tion of informally acquired competences and support the smooth and effective functioning
> of the European, national and sectoral labour markets [...] and should facilitate the vol-
> untary development of competence-based solutions at the European level enabling sectors
> to address the new education and training challenges caused by the internationalisation of
> trade and technology.

The EQF design, which is essentially based on learning outcomes and a set of levels aimed at corresponding with the labour-market job structures, should facilitate this aim. The EQF also has an objective to support and promote change in national qualifications systems. This is a clear signal that the reforming power of national qualifications frameworks can be enabled by the existence of a high-status overarching framework that is respected by trading partners, even if the European Qualifications Framework is by no mean a template and remains a meta-framework.

More generally, countries have made attempts to reform education and training systems in order to bring about more and better lifelong learning. Some of these policy responses bear directly on qualifications systems (cf. OECD, 2004). This is the case for the following points:

- to increase the flexibility and responsiveness of the qualifications system;
- to motivate young people to learn for qualifications;
- to link education and work through qualifications;
- to facilitate open access to qualifications;
- to make qualifications progressive;
- to make the qualifications system transparent;
- to review funding and increase efficiency of the qualifications system; and
- to better manage the qualifications system.

For VET in particular, it is possible to use qualifications frameworks as a policy tool and to review present and future policy on qualifications and qualifications systems, to test the robustness of the latter and see if the benefits they promised have been delivered. For instance, there seems to be reasons to believe that qualifications frameworks can change the landscape because they impact on:

- the provision of VET;
- curricula in the formal VET system;
- barriers to the development of VET;
- the link between VET and the labour market; and
- benefits for VET graduates and participation in, and access to, VET.

They impact on the provision of VET because a close look at all qualifications at their respective level within the qualifications framework provides a clear picture of the qualifications available in a country and therefore will help spot the gap in provision at a given level or for a given qualification.

They impact on curricula through the simple fact that qualifications frameworks are often linked to the concept of learning outcomes and, therefore, the formal VET system will not be able to avoid the discussion about defining the curricula in terms of what learners can do and not about how long they have been studying a subject. This may well be one of the biggest challenges for reforming VET programmes in the years to come.

VET has traditionally suffered from low esteem and, in some countries, is even regarded as the only solution for those students that cannot follow the academic tracks. The development of VET has therefore been hampered by issues not directly linked to the programmes it provided but to the way they are seen in the wider public and, sometimes, among employers. The creation of a qualifications framework may help lift some of the barriers by providing transparency, encouraging employers to hire individuals leaving the VET system and removing dead ends—therefore always offering the possibility for reaching a higher level qualification from within the VET system.

Another typical example about how qualifications frameworks may help improve participation, self-esteem and remove some inequities is by breaking the 'glass ceiling' that seems to exist between the regular VET system and the higher VET system; meaning that individual learners often cannot continue to higher education when they graduate from the initial VET system. A good example is given by Romania where the scheme put in place with levels did not seem to work as transition between levels 3 and 4 was regarded as too great a jump for graduates of the VET system at level 3. Soon after the system was implemented, it was necessary to create a level 3+, in between levels 3 and 4, to accommodate VET graduates.

For all the reasons given above, the existence of a qualifications framework may help more adequately—and therefore more effectively—in linking the VET system and the labour market. In addition, some feedback can be organized so that pieces of information about what employers need are brought into the organization of the VET system. For the same reasons, it will also bring more and better benefits to the VET graduates and may end up in more people choosing this path.

9 Concluding Remarks

Research needs to be carried out into the impact of qualifications frameworks on the infrastructure of VET. More work remains to be done also to link the levels in the framework to the labour market issues or occupations (OECD, 2004).

Qualifications frameworks make explicit the relationship between qualifications. They aim at increasing transparency and showing potential progression routes; they can become the basis of credit transfer systems. They are overarching tools that can be used to engage all stakeholders in developing and co-ordinating the qualifications system. Often they are used as tools for regulation, financing and quality assurance.

At the same time, a qualifications framework can open up opportunities to potential learners, because it makes progression routes clear and can offer the opportunity to rationalize qualifications by reducing the overlap between them. In all of these ways, frameworks create an environment where the whole qualifications system can be reviewed. This means that the management of the qualifications framework can be used as a tool to enhance many policy responses that countries are adopting to react to the lifelong learning agenda, of which VET is a very important component—rather decisive when it comes to global economic performance and coping with emerging issues.

Notes

1. <ec.europa.eu/education/policies/educ/eqf/index_en.html>
2. A meta-qualifications framework is a classification system for levels of qualification where the criteria for levels are written in a highly generalized form. This enables the meta-framework to relate to all more specific (national or sectoral) qualifications frameworks. The EQF is thus a meta-framework that will act as a translation device between different national qualifications systems. As a meta-framework the EQF does not take over any of the established roles of national systems.
3.

References

Bjørnåvold, J.; Coles, M. 2006. *The development of qualifications frameworks in European countries*. (Paper presented to the European Commission Conference on the European Qualifications Framework, Budapest, 27–28 February 2006.)

Bouder, A. 2003. Qualifications in France: towards a national framework? *Journal of education and work*, vol. 16, no. 3, September.

Coles, M. 2006. *A review of international and national developments in the use of qualifications frameworks*. Turin, Italy: European Training Foundation.

CEDEFOP. 2001. *European structures of qualification levels*, vols 1, 2 and 3. Thessaloniki, Greece: CEDEFOP.

European Commission. 2004. *The future priorities of enhanced European cooperation in vocational education and training (VET)*. Brussels: European Commission. (The Maastricht Communiqué.)

Organization for Economic Co-operation and Development. 2004. The development and use of 'qualifications frameworks' as a means of reforming and managing qualifications systems. *In:* Mernagh, E.; Murphy, A.; Simota, T., eds. *Final report of the Thematic Group 1 of the OECD activity on The Role of National Qualifications Systems in Promoting Lifelong Learning*. Paris: OECD. <www.oecd.org/edu/lifelonglearning/nqs>

Organization for Economic Co-operation and Development. 2007. *Qualifications systems: bridges to lifelong learning*. Paris: OECD.

Chapter III.7
Reforming Skills Development, Transforming the Nation: South African Vocational Education and Training Reforms, 1994–2005

Simon McGrath

1 Introduction

In an era where vocational education and training (VET) reform is common, South Africa provides one of the most striking national case studies of the complex interplay between international discourses of both economic change and VET reform, and historical and contemporary forces at the national level. Moreover, the twin imperative of economic and social focus for VET is made particularly complex and challenging by the legacy of *apartheid.*

In particular, the new, democratic South Africa has been faced with abnormally high levels of inequality and unemployment, and the pressing need to break down racial inequities in education, skills and work.

In this chapter I will consider first some of the detail of the *apartheid* legacy in skills development before turning to a consideration of policy developments since 1994. I will finish with an analysis of key tensions that continue to play at the heart of South African VET policy.

2 South African VET before 1994[1]

Internationally, skills development systems tend to reflect and reinforce broader domestic power dynamics. This is particularly apparent in terms of class and gender, which are powerful organizing principles for access to particular programmes and for the resourcing and status of such programmes.

Since the beginnings of formal vocational education and training in South Africa in the second half of the nineteenth century, these forces have been powerfully overlaid with the effects of race, and, to a lesser extent, supporting dynamics of migration and ethnicity.

In its early involvement with the Industrial Revolution, during the late nineteenth century, South Africa obtained skilled labour largely from the United Kingdom, as immigrant miners and other artisans came into the country. As a formal vocational education and training system began to emerge, it was largely English- rather than Afrikaner-dominated, reflecting the continued industrial predominance of the English-speaking community.

Whilst this reliance on imported skilled labour declined (though never disappeared) during the twentieth century, the South African system of skills formation became increasingly distorted by the political economy of race. For most of that century, there was a legally enshrined bifurcation of work and skill (and, of course, income, residency, enfranchisement, etc.) between white and black.[2] White workers were skilled by the colour of their skin, whilst blacks remained largely incapable of skilled status until 1981, regardless of their levels of knowledge and experience.

This bifurcation had massive implications for the system of skills development. White workers were socialized into a powerful vision of their right to be either a labour aristocracy or professionals. Over time, growing prosperity led to a strong upward shift of white employment into service and professional activities, but there was no mechanism to allow public VET institutions or trades to respond by inducting a new wave of black artisans prior to the 1980s.

African workers were treated as eternally unskilled. Moreover, their official status as migrants, either from neighbouring countries or from the system of homelands within South Africa, encouraged the sense of them as interchangeable, homogenized labour.

Thus, there was no real impetus towards VET for Africans as participants in a modern industrial economy. Instead, VET for Africans was seen as a blend of 'appropriate' education for those deemed incapable of benefiting from an academic schooling and equally low-level practical skills development for local needs in the homelands.

By the 1970s, this model was beginning to fall apart. Even under a system of import substitution, many employers were becoming increasingly concerned that technological change at the international level required South Africa to upskill. The early 1970s also saw the beginning of a new and persistent wave of African trade-union activism and a growing worker drive for skills upgrading as part of a move for higher wages and better conditions. To this mix was added a serious drain on white skill through the increasingly hot war South Africa was fighting with many of its neighbours, and the apparently urgent need for a new political approach after the bloody response to student protests in Soweto in 1976.

All of this led the *apartheid* regime to attempt to reform VET as a key strand of its search for a workable strategy that could maintain and entrench white power. In 1979, the Wiehahn Commission began developing a new approach to training that would lead to Africans being indentured as apprentices (Wiehahn, 1981). The following year, the de Lange Commission sought to propose a new education system that would go some distance towards de-racialization of education, but which saw the most appropriate route for African learners as lying in vocational education (Human Sciences Research Council, 1981).

It quickly became apparent that a new bifurcation between the approaches to skills in the workplace and in schools and colleges was being enacted. Although with much contestation and taking more than a decade to come to real fruition, there was a fumbling towards a new consensus between elements of capital and labour about the needs for a de-racialized model of skill that would improve productivity, efficiency and competitiveness, on the one hand, and pay and conditions, on the other. This model would necessarily be largely built on the capabilities of black South Africans. Thus, both employers and unions began to focus strongly on the upskilling of the already employed, addressing the functional competencies necessary for performing existing jobs and beginning to develop a way of looking at career paths for these workers as they became more skilled.

Reforms in education were harder to push forward, particularly where they appeared to threaten the segregation of facilities and undermine white privilege. Thus, what happened in practice was the growth of separate VET facilities for different racial groups, although whites-only facilities still remained in the majority and were far better resourced.

Moreover, the quality and relevance of public VET was undermined by the growing delinking of colleges from employers. As in the United Kingdom, technical colleges had emerged as a means of providing part-time theoretical training for those who were already employed as apprentices. However, by the start of the 1990s, the apprenticeship system was in decline, whilst the new black colleges were often situated far from industrial centres and lacking in links to employers.

Thus, by the early 1990s, there was a relatively powerful coalition for change in workplace skills development, but colleges lacked champions. Never linked to non-racialized trade unionism, they were increasingly seen as an irrelevance by employers. Moreover, the low status of colleges within the education system and their limited political significance meant that the State had little real passion for driving radical change in the sector.

On assuming power in 1994, the incoming government was faced with a divided and divergent system that was in radical need of overhaul in order to respond to a triple challenge: (a) racial integration was a socio-political imperative; (b) the legacy of *apartheid* also meant that there was a pressing need to respond to poverty and inequality; and (c) the global environment into which the new South Africa was entering meant that VET also needed to provide part of an economic response to rapid liberalization and insertion into the global economy.

3 Policy Responses, 1994–2005

African National Congress (ANC) policy on education and training at the time of the 1994 elections called for an integrative response to the legacy of the past. The de-racialization of institutions and systems was an indisputable part of the ANC vision. However, the integrative notion was taken further to include a commitment to an Integrated Department of Education and Labour and a National Qualifications Framework (NQF). Both were seen as essential to ensuring that the progress that had been made by the trade-union movement in the field of training would be carried over into the education system and to expanding the training vision itself to make it more oriented towards developing citizens and not just workers.

However, due to higher strategic considerations related to the composition of a new Government of National Unity, it was decided to keep the two departments separate. This was unanticipated by ANC education and training officials. However, the notion of the NQF still remained and would have to assume greater responsibility as the glue that would stick together the policies of the two departments (Badroodien & McGrath, 2005).

3.1 The National Qualifications Framework

The importance of this role for the NQF was given further symbolic weight when the South African Qualifications Authority Act (Republic of South Africa, 1995) became the first new piece of legislation to emerge in the post-*apartheid* period. This set up a South African Qualifications Authority (SAQA) to oversee the translation of all qualifications into awards according to a new NQF. SAQA was to report to both ministers, although it was seen as primarily under the authority of the Minister of Education, one of the first fault lines to emerge in the new system.

SAQA was to have a relatively small staff that would work with and oversee a large number of (largely) new standard-setting and quality-assurance bodies. It was to be governed by a council representing a wide range of relevant stakeholders. Through this mechanism, and stakeholder membership of the range of new committees, it was intended that the system would become far more responsive to demand (McGrath, 1996; Kraak & Young, 2001; Allais, 2003). Table 1 shows what the NQF looked like.

Table 1 The National Qualifications Framework

NQF level	Sector	Qualification type
8	Higher education and training (HET)	Post-doctoral research degrees
7		Doctorates
6		Masters degrees
5		Professional qualifications
		Honours degrees
		National first degrees
		Higher diplomas
		National diplomas
		National certificates
Further Education and Training Certificate (FETC)		
4	Further education and training (FET)	National certificates (the level 4 certificates would
3		be the terminal qualifications of both schools
2		and colleges)
General Education and Training Certificate (GETC)		
1	General education and training (GET)	Grade 9/Adult Basic Education and Training
		Level 4
		National certificates

3.2 The Department of Education's Policies[3]

3.2.1 The Further Education and Training Act, 1998

Beginning in 1996, the Department of Education embarked on a process leading to a new act governing public and private colleges, now designated as further education and training (FET) colleges, in line with the NQF structure.

The Further Education and Training Act (Republic of South Africa, 1998a) sought to find a balance between an emphasis on the economic importance of FET and the social, cultural and humanistic elements. It sought to address boundary issues between FET colleges and universities by proposing a joint committee to examine these issues involving the Council for Higher Education and the National Board for Further Education and Training. Colleges had long been involved in programmes that were now defined as higher education by the NQF, which, typically, provided education below the university level. Nonetheless, the White Paper was very clear about its opposition to 'mission drift' and the need for FET institutions to focus primarily on their 'core business' of FET provision.

The relationship with schools remained difficult for the White Paper to address. However, in its conceptualization of the implementation trajectory for the new policy, it went into far more detail about an integrated vision of the FET level than had previously been attempted. It suggested a phased approach spreading out from colleges eventually to encompass the whole FET sector. It was stated that, by the end of the third year after the adoption of the act, a framework for incorporating senior secondary schools into the FET system would have been developed. By the end of the fourth year, a decision on the future of senior secondary schooling would have been taken and, from the fifth year, incorporation, if agreed upon, would begin.

Regarding linkages with the Department of Labour's programmes, it was clearly stated that steps should be taken 'to fast-track the introduction of learnerships in FET colleges' (Republic of South Africa, 1998a, p. 26).

The act also introduced procedures for the establishment of the new colleges, focusing particularly on the legislative process leading to mergers of existing institutions. It set out new governance and financial arrangements; and stressed the role of quality assurance. It also considered the place of private providers.

3.2.2 The National Strategy for Further Education and Training, 1999

Once the FET Act was passed, the FET Branch of the Department of Education turned its attention to a strategy for its implementation. This was completed in 1999 (Department of Education, 1999). Central to this process was a set of proposals about funding. It argued that a new funding system should be introduced over time. This should include a core of programme-based funding with additional special-purpose funding. The programme-based element should itself be largely based on the notion of full-time equivalents (FTEs), but it was recommended that there should also be an outcomes-related component to encourage efficiency. It was envisaged that special-purpose funding should be directed at the development of management, staff and learner-support systems, and for the development of new learning support materials. It was recommended that fees would be progressive, but it was made clear that there would be no public funds for student financial aid, unlike higher education. It was strongly expected that FET institutions would have access to significant amounts of funding out of the new levy system established by the Department of Labour (see below).

3.2.3 The New Institutional Landscape, 2001

It was clear to the Department of Education throughout this process that the current number of colleges, and the disparities between them, were untenable. In 2001 the department published its strategy for responding to this challenge after a series of provincial analyses, overseen by a national task team. *A new institutional landscape for public further education and training colleges* (Department of Education, 2001) envisaged a series of fifty large institutions grounded on nine attributes:

- large, multi-site institutions;
- increased autonomy;
- a mixture of specialization and multi-purpose institutions;
- a new quality-assurance framework;
- an increased focus on open and distance learning;
- a greater focus on access for learners with special needs;
- better articulation and collaboration with higher education;
- a commitment to improved student support services; and
- a stress on partnerships with government and the private sector (Department of Education, 2001, pp. 16–20)

The report reinforced the requirement for the staffing of colleges to be more representative. It reiterated the need for curricular reform and for a wider range of programme offerings, supported by a new funding mechanism. It envisaged a transition over time in the degree of autonomy as colleges developed sufficient capacity to manage themselves, and stressed the need for a capacity development effort to support such a growth in powers.

3.2.4 Overviewing FET Policy Development and Implementation

Important elements of the FET policy recommendations of the last decade have been realized in a set of practices, including the transformation of the institutional landscape through the merger process. However, it is striking that a number of policy recommendations remain at best partially acted upon. These include the areas of finance, curriculum, articulation (with schools, higher education and skills development) and addressing both social and economic needs.

3.3 The Department of Labour's Skills Development Strategy[4]

Meanwhile, in 1997 the Department of Labour published the *Green Paper on a skills development strategy* (Department of Labour, 1997). This has formed the basis for subsequent skills policies. The Green Paper called for: (a) a levy-grant system aimed at increasing the investment and involvement of employers in the training of their workforce; (b) new sector education and training authorities; and (c) the introduction of learnerships (the model to succeed and extend the apprenticeship system). These recommendations led to the Skills Development Act (Republic of South Africa, 1998b) and the Skills Development Levies Act (Republic of South Africa, 1999a).

3.3.1 Skills Development Act, 1998

The act created a new institutional framework for skills development in which there is a high level of co-ordination at the national level (via the National Skills Authority—NSA) and at a sectoral level (via the twenty-five Sector Education and Training Authorities—SETAs).[5] The new SETAs' role includes the evaluation of workplace skills plans (WSPs) and the development of sector skills plans; developing and registering learnerships; quality assuring training provision; and managing and administering the grants received through the training levy (legislated by the Skills Development Levies Act). At the national level, the NSA is responsible for developing a macro-skills development policy for the Minister of Labour on a four-yearly cycle.

At the programme core of the new system is the new notion of learnership. Learnerships are legislated by the Skills Development Act to include complex contractual agreements for a fixed period between the learner, the provider and the employer. The contractual agreement provides a framework for formalizing the relationship between these three parties in carrying out the qualification. Beyond the formality of the agreement, this relationship requires high levels of co-operation to ensure the smooth planning and operation of the learnership. Learnerships are located at the core of the Department of Labour's macro-strategy for skills development. They are intended to move beyond the narrow confines of conventional apprenticeships and seek to build learners from disparate levels of prior learning to a situation of competence necessary for meaningful social and economic participation. This requires high levels of investment of resources to provide sufficient support to learners, both within the theory provider and within the workplace (Akoojee, Gewer & McGrath, 2005a).

Learnerships are not just for those who are already employed. There is also a strong commitment to learnerships for the pre- or unemployed. In this model, the employer commits to a period of employment during the time-span of the learnership, but not to subsequent employment.

In addition to establishing the legal framework for learnerships, the Skills Development Act also made provision for the development of skills programmes, which would comprise an occupationally-directed learning programme leading to a credit towards a qualification rather than a full qualification. The purpose of the skills programmes is to allow learners access to short programmes that could be combined towards a complete qualification, thus allowing more flexibility and mobility.

3.3.2 The Skills Development Levies Act, 1999

The funding regime for this radical new approach was legislated in the Skills Development Levies Act (Republic of South Africa, 1999a). Beyond a certain size, all enterprises were required to pay 1% of payroll (0.5% in the first year) as a skills development levy.

Some 80% of these funds would flow through the South African Revenue Service to the relevant SETA. A range of criteria were developed governing how enterprises could claim back the majority of these funds through evidence of training activities linked to their WSPs.

The remaining 20% of the total levy income was set aside for strategic and developmental interventions, including a specific focus on skills development for small, medium and micro-enterprises. These moneys are managed by the National Skills Fund, located within the Department of Labour.

3.3.3 The National Skills Development Strategy, 2001 and 2005

In the National Skills Development Strategy of 2001, the Department of Labour set twelve targets for the skills-development system, with three cross-cutting equity targets, to be met by March 2005 (Department of Labour, 2001). Most of the indicators have been reached, and it is clear that the department has achieved much in its attempted skills revolution (McGrath & Paterson, 2006). However, there are still concerns about the performance of the system in terms of equity and broader impact. A new National Skills Development Strategy was launched in March 2005, which largely seeks to continue along the path of the first strategy (Department of Labour, 2005).

3.4 The Human Resources Development Strategy, 2001

As a further way of building intra-departmental coherence between education and labour, in 2001 the two departments jointly produced a Human Resources Development Strategy—HRDS (Department of Education/Department of Labour, 2001) (Fig. 1).

The first element of the Human Resources Development Strategy, 'building the base', is concerned with early-childhood development, which is the responsibility of various departments, most obviously those concerned with health and education. The second element, the 'supply side', is seen largely as the role of the Department

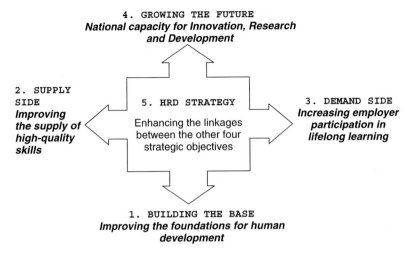

Fig. 1 Visualizing the Human Resources Development Strategy
Source: Department of Education/Department of Labour, 2001.

of Education, albeit with the involvement of other departments, most notably those concerned with labour and (at the higher education level) science and technology. The third element, 'demand side', is primarily the responsibility of the Department of Labour, although here the work of trade and industry in encouraging a high-skills approach is particularly relevant. The fourth element, 'growing the future', is an overlapping responsibility of the Departments of Education, Science and Technology and Trade and Industry in particular.

The strategy itself and the continued enhancement of linkages between the other elements of the approach is driven by the Departments of Education and Labour, who jointly own the HRDS and who jointly convene the national Human Resources Development Co-ordinating Committee.

4 Analysing the Policy Transformation Process and the Remaining Tensions

In the second half of this chapter I will consider the dynamics inherent in the policy process outlined above and the tensions that remain unresolved. I will do so under three headings. First, I will consider the ways in which the principles of coherence and integration have been interpreted in the development of a new South African approach to education and training. Second, I will explore how tensions in this regard relate to other unresolved issues regarding the nature of responsiveness. Third, I will deepen this discussion by shifting into an examination of the way that the institutional logics of departments and conflicting visions of responsiveness relate to differing and inconsistent models of the relative roles of the State, market and people in the decision-making process.

4.1 Coherence

Earlier in this chapter I recounted how the original ANC plan to have an integrated Department of Education and Labour had been abandoned. Of course, SAQA and the NQF were supposed to be the mechanisms for ensuring a common vision between education and training. However, it quickly became apparent that the two departments' institutional logics, and the ways that these intersected with overall government policy, meant that there was a complex set of forces preventing integration. At times, the two departments appeared to have genuine common visions and interests and be pulling together. However, there were clear examples from early in the process that their different interests could also serve to pull the system apart (McGrath, 1996; Akoojee, Gewer & McGrath, 2005a; Badroodien & McGrath, 2005).

As in many other national contexts, Department of Education officials tended to stress the educational and social aspects of VET's role and to downplay the economic ones. Equally typically, Department of Labour officials, on the other hand, tended to focus on what could be agreed upon by employers and trade unions and showed a willingness to dilute educational considerations when these appeared to get in the way of agreement on training reforms.

In spite of a range of working groups and public protestations about collaboration between the two departments, it remained clear that there was little real agreement between them beneath the most general level when it came to the rules of the new game. Thus, learnerships began to develop largely with private providers whilst college qualifications were still predominantly education/supply-led. Education has not yet managed to really access any of the funding 'owned' by labour; whilst labour lacks the set of provider institutions 'owned' by education.

The limits of coherence were also made apparent by the process of reviewing the NQF and SAQA, which began in 2001. Responding to an independent review of the system (Department of Education/Department of Labour, 2002), the two departments spent eighteen months in arriving at a workable compromise (Department of Education/Department of Labour, 2003), which essentially allowed the two departments to strengthen control of 'their' segments of the system, whilst maintaining a weakened SAQA as a largely symbolic point of articulation between the different parts (Akoojee, Gewer & McGrath, 2005a). After a consultation period ending in October 2003, which resulted in widespread external criticism of the compromise, the two departments continued to seek a revised model that could satisfy everyone. However, this has still not been achieved at the time of writing—more than two years later. In the meantime, SAQA is left weakened by inadequate funding and uncertainty about its future, and is not in a position to drive integration without serious departmental and ministerial support.

4.2 Responsiveness

All education is supposed to be responsive to broader individual, community and societal needs. Moreover, it is argued that this is particularly true for VET. Recent international work on VET systems has shown, however, that there are multiple versions of responsiveness to which these systems are supposed to react (Ashton & Green, 1996; Crouch, Finegold & Sako, 1999; Brown, Green & Lauder, 2001; King & McGrath, 2002; Wolf, 2002; Cosser et al., 2003; Akoojee, Gewer & McGrath, 2005b).

The experience of South African VET since 1994 highlights a set of tensions regarding responsiveness. In the public FET college system, it is apparent that there are internal tensions within the Department of Education's position regarding their responsiveness. The FET Act sought to make it clear that social responsiveness and a focus on equity and redress were more important than a focus on preparation for the economy. However, the HRDS, jointly developed with the Department of Labour, places emphasis on the need for colleges to respond to shortages in certain areas of skills. The latter argument is clearly the dominant one in the government's most recent Programme of Action (Republic of South Africa, 2004).

Moreover, the Department of Education's own practices appear to go beyond the language of its policies in stressing the primacy of economic factors. Although the *New institutional landscape* (2001) reflected the department's vision for the sector, its implementation came to be dominated by the funding and technical support given by the corporate sector through the National Business Initiative. Thus, the key support given to colleges in the vital period of mergers was from a highly market-oriented think tank, which stressed the need for colleges to become more efficient and focused on business partnerships. Moreover, this process was given significant support by a series of initiatives from the British Council, which resulted in a strong influence at the institutional level from a managerial reading of the reforms that the British college system had undergone since 1992. To use Argyris and Schön's (1978) useful concepts, it appeared in the early part of the current decade that the Department of Education's theory-in-use of responsiveness was at some variance from its espoused theory.

I have argued elsewhere (McGrath, 2000, 2005a, 2005b) that the Department of Education has a very weak view of what economic responsiveness really means. Whilst the HRDS stressed the importance of targeting older learners who were already employed and of focusing on scarce skills, FET policy appears to be more concerned in practice with the 'problem' of what to do with those 14–19-year-olds who are not deemed suitable for higher education. This has led the department to plan to expand the size of the system massively and, at the same time, to reduce the target-learner age-group.

Moreover, the department has proved very reluctant to address the challenge of the informal economy. In spite of approximately one-third of the economically-active population being engaged in informal work (International Labour Office, 2002), it is difficult to find anything but the most passing mention of the need to support skills development for the informal economy in departmental policies.

At the level of practice, there are examples of colleges that are trying to develop localized and nuanced readings of the challenge of responsiveness. However, there is also evidence that many colleges are developing strategies that threaten to undermine access and educational worth in the search for economic advantage.

The Department of Labour too has faced problems in trying to develop its own account of responsiveness. Although emerging largely out of compromise between organized business and the trade unions, the department's policy attempts to balance a focus on economic growth and competitiveness with a concern for social inclusion and redress. Some sense of the tensions that the department has been trying to manage can be seen in the subtitle of the first National Skills Development Strategy: 'Productive citizenship for all' (Department of Labour, 2001) and in the vision statement for the second strategy: 'Skills for sustainable growth, development and equity' (Department of Labour, 2005).

In spite of its stated concern to balance these different considerations, the department has been criticized for its failure to do enough to support the skills development needs of the smallest and most informal enterprises (King, 1998; King & McGrath, 2002; McGrath, 2005a, 2005b) and for its performance on supporting equity (Badroodien, 2003; McGrath & Paterson, 2006).

Although responsiveness has been seen as a vital part of the new system, it appears that the notion remains too vague and inconsistent to be of much practical use. In the FET sector, the vacuum created by State vagueness in this area has led to the major practical influence of the views of business and the alleged example of the British college sector. In skills development, some progress has been made in broadening access, but the system remains hugely shaped by the particular dynamics of various industrial sectors (McGrath & Paterson, 2006).

4.3 State, Markets and People

Internationally, VET systems have been encouraged to move away from State control and towards responsiveness both to market forces and to the wishes of local people. In developing countries, both of these dynamics have been heavily driven by international development co-operation agencies.

In response to and largely driven by the policies of international co-operation agencies, VET systems have adopted new modes of governance, including national training agencies and institutional governing bodies (Johanson & Adams, 2004; Akoojee, Gewer & McGrath, 2005b; McGrath, forthcoming). Examples of this can be seen in South Africa in new public FET college councils and in the establishment of SAQA and the National Skills Authority.

However, it is important to ask whether a set of global policy certainties necessarily work in the ways intended in a context as unique as that of South Africa.

The case of FET college reform in South Africa provides little support for the argument that decentralization of policy, governance and management necessarily brings about meaningful and sustainable benefits. Rather, the South African case may be one in which the ability of a legitimate State to effect necessary social change has been undermined by a diffusion of power and capacity across nine provinces and, increasingly, fifty institutions.

The national department has taken the view that institutional autonomy can only be developed over time and cannot simply be granted on grounds of ideology. This is an important point to bear in mind in other national contexts. However, the South

African case also emphasizes the need to be consistent both in public statements and in developmental activities in supporting the eventual development of institutional capacities if this is indeed a policy goal.

The South African college sector also provides an important lesson in terms of the need to approach public-sector reform as a particular area of expertise distinct from private sector management. In spite of the Public Finance Management Act (Republic of South Africa, 1999b) and the attempts to adapt the King principles for corporate governance for the public sector (McGrath, forthcoming), there has been too little practical support to the college sector regarding what good governance means for a public institution. Instead, there has been too much advice given by large international management consultancy firms, lacking a real grounding in public sector issues.

Work on school democracy in South Africa (e.g. Sayed, 1999; Karlsson, 2002; Bush & Heystek, 2003) has shown that local-level democracy does not simply come into existence because it is legislated for. Although there was a degree of genuine democratization of decisions about schooling, there have been three difficulties that are likely to affect colleges too. First, more equitable access to membership of governance structures does not mean that old and new power imbalances in society are overthrown. Second, it also does not mean that the new governors are receiving support to develop the necessary tools for good governance. Third, as Karlsson (2002) notes, school governance reform has 'over-reached' in terms of what was expected of governing bodies.

There are also grounds for caution in judging the impact of stakeholderism at the national level. The National Board for Further Education and Training has been almost entirely ineffectual. The SAQA Council has not proved a sufficiently robust and influential body to ensure that the National Skills Authority itself has had the resources to do its job and sufficient autonomy from ministerial interference. Finally, the National Skills Authority has struggled to develop capacity, to get beyond the sectional interests of its stakeholders and to construct a working relationship with the department's officials.

The role of the market in the reformed system is also less than clear. Whilst there has been a language of responsiveness and the favouring of a demand-led approach, it is clear that the South African State takes a rather sceptical view of the primacy of the market, both in the skills field and more generally. As regards skills, the State takes a strong view of the need to overcome the market's failure to produce the right quantity and quality of skills for the right people. Essentially, it has been attempting an institutional approach to transforming the market for skills in terms of both equity and effectiveness.

This view is mirrored at the overall policy level by the increasing tendency of the State to espouse developmentalist positions that seek to intervene strategically in bringing about better outcomes than would happen if left to the market alone (Southall, 2005).

There are grounds for questioning the consistency and detail of the State's vision, but there is fairly widespread acceptance in South Africa that the market cannot be left to decide on skills or on policy areas more generally. However, the greatest concern about a more development approach concerns the State's capacity to deliver on its aspirations (Southall, 2005; Paterson, 2005).

5 Conclusion

It is easy to argue from today's vantage point that the first decade of VET in democratic South Africa saw far too much change, delivered at a pace that outstripped the capacity of new officials and institutions to adapt to a hugely ambitious vision. However, such an argument fails to acknowledge the massive and multiple pressures that there were at the outset for a transformation that was both radical and rapid.

What is clear is that the transformation has proved far more complex than was realized at the point of departure. Developing new institutions, creating a workable NQF, transforming funding and delivering new programmes have all been attempted at the same time as expanding the system and radically reforming access. Inevitably, too, South Africa has found itself faced with many of the tensions that affect VET systems globally, most particularly the difficulty of balancing social and economic imperatives and of ensuring that the Departments of Education and Labour work together effectively.

There have been many successes along the way, but the greatest challenge in the second decade may be in managing a review process that: (a) allows the key successes to continue; (b) identifies the elements of the system that need radical overhaul or abandonment; and (c) which combines honest self-reflection with maintenance of public support for the system. If such a process can be successfully negotiated, then the South African skill revolution may reach a truly successful conclusion.

Notes

1. A more detailed discussion of this history can be found in McGrath et al., 2004.
2. I follow the official South African practice of using racial classifications as a means of understanding how the effects of race continue to shape people's lives without subscribing to any view of the essential nature of racial classifications. In keeping with South African practice, I use 'black' as a collective term to refer to African, Indian and coloured people.
3. This sub-section on FET policy draws extensively on my previous writings, especially McGrath, 2000, 2004 and Forthcoming.
4. This section draws on King & McGrath, 2002; McGrath, 2005a and Forthcoming, as well as Kraak, 2004a and 2004b.
5. The list of SETAs is under revision at the time of writing, with some mergers identified and other changes under consideration.

References

Akoojee, S.; Gewer, A.; McGrath, S. 2005a. South Africa: the unfinished revolution in intermediate skills development. *In:* Akoojee, S.; Gewer, A.; McGrath, S., eds. *Vocational education and training in Southern Africa.* Cape Town, South Africa: HSRC Press.

Akoojee, S.; Gewer, A.; McGrath, S., eds. 2005b. *Vocational education and training in Southern Africa*. Cape Town, South Africa: HSRC Press.

Allais, M. 2003. The National Qualifications Framework in South Africa: a democratic project trapped in a neo-liberal paradigm? *Journal of education and work,* vol. 16, no. 3, pp. 309–23.

Argyris, C.; Schön, D. 1978. *Organisational learning*. London: Addison-Wesley.

Ashton, D.; Green, F. 1996. *Education, training and the global economy*. Cheltenham, UK: Edward Elgar.

Badroodien, A. 2003. Enterprise training. *In:* Human Sciences Research Council, ed. *Human resources development review, 2003*. Cape Town, South Africa: HSRC Press.

Badroodien, A.; McGrath, S. 2005. *International influences on the evolution of South Africa's National Skills Development Strategy, 1989–2004*. Eschborn, Germany: GTZ.

Brown, P.; Green, A.; Lauder, H. 2001. *High skills*. Oxford, UK: Oxford University Press.

Bush, T.; Heystek, J. 2003. School governance in the new South Africa. *Compare,* vol. 33, no. 2, pp. 127–38.

Cosser, M. et al., eds. 2003. *Technical college responsiveness*. Cape Town, South Africa: HSRC Press.

Crouch, C.; Finegold, D.; Sako, M. 1999. *Are skills the answer?* Oxford, UK: Oxford University Press.

Department of Education. 1999. *National Strategy for Further Education and Training*. Pretoria: Government Printer.

Department of Education. 2001. *A new institutional landscape for public further education and training colleges*. Pretoria: Government Printer.

Department of Education/Department of Labour. 2001. *Human Resources Development Strategy for South Africa*. Pretoria: Government Printer.

Department of Education/Department of Labour. 2002. *The report of the Study Team on the Implementation of the National Qualifications Framework*. Pretoria: Government Printer.

Department of Education/Department of Labour. 2003. *An interdependent qualification framework system*. Pretoria: Government Printer.

Department of Labour. 1997. *Green Paper on a skills development strategy for economic and employment growth in South Africa*. Pretoria: Government Printer.

Department of Labour. 2001. *National Skills Development Strategy, 2001-2005*. Pretoria: Department of Labour.

Department of Labour. 2005. *National Skills Development Strategy, 2005–2010*. Pretoria: Department of Labour.

Human Sciences Research Council. 1981. *Report of the main committee of the HSRC investigation into education*. Pretoria: HSRC. (The de Lange Report.)

International Labour Office. 2002. *Women and men in the informal economy*. Geneva, Switzerland: ILO.

Johanson, R.; Adams, A.V. 2004. *Skills development in Sub-Saharan Africa*. Washington, DC: World Bank.

Karlsson, J. 2002. The role of democratic governing bodies in South African schools. *Comparative education,* vol. 38, no. 3, pp. 327–36.

King, K. 1998. Policy coherence in education, training and enterprise development in South Africa. *In:* Morrow, W.; King, K., eds. *Vision and reality*. Cape Town, South Africa: University of Cape Town Press.

King, K.; McGrath, S. 2002. *Globalisation, enterprise and knowledge*. Oxford, UK: Symposium.

Kraak, A. 2004a. The National Skills Development Strategy: a new institutional regime for skills formation in post-apartheid South Africa. *In:* McGrath, S. et al., eds. *Shifting understandings of skill: moving beyond low skills in post-apartheid South Africa*. Cape Town, South Africa: HSRC Press.

Kraak, A. 2004b. Rethinking the high skills thesis in South Africa. *In:* McGrath, S. et al., eds. *Shifting understandings of skill: moving beyond low skills in post-apartheid South Africa*. Cape Town, South Africa: HSRC Press.

Kraak, A.; Young, M., eds. 2001. *Education in transition*. Pretoria: HSRC.

McGrath, S. 1996. *Learning to work: changing discourses on South African education and training, 1976–96*. Edinburgh, UK: University of Edinburgh. [Unpublished Ph.D. thesis.]

McGrath, S. 2000. Coming in from the cold: further education and training in South Africa. *Compare,* vol. 30, no. 1, pp. 65–84.

McGrath, S. 2004. Reviewing the development of the South African further education and training college sector ten years after the end of apartheid. *Journal of vocational education and training,* vol. 56, no. 1, pp. 133–53.

McGrath, S. 2005a. 'Skills for productive citizenship for all': the place of skills development for micro and small enterprises in South Africa. *Journal of education and work,* vol. 18, no. 1, pp. 111–24.

McGrath, S., ed. 2005b. *Skills development in South African very small and micro enterprises.* Pretoria: Department of Labour; Cape Town: HSRC Press.

McGrath, S. Forthcoming. *Transforming the governance of South African public further education and training colleges.* Paris: UNESCO-IIEP.

McGrath, S.; Paterson, A. 2006. Enterprise training. *In:* Human Sciences Research Council, ed. *Human resources development review, 2006.* Cape Town, South Africa: HSRC Press.

McGrath, S. et al., eds. 2004. *Shifting understandings of skill: moving beyond low skills in post-apartheid South Africa.* Cape Town, South Africa: HSRC Press.

Paterson, A. 2005. Public sector training: a 'blind' spot in the 1998 South African national levy-grant policy. *Journal of vocational education and training,* vol. 57, no. 4, pp. 519–36.

Republic of South Africa. 1995. *South African Qualifications Authority Act.* Pretoria: Government Printer.

Republic of South Africa. 1998a. *Further Education and Training Act.* Pretoria: Government Printer.

Republic of South Africa. 1998b. *Skills Development Act.* Pretoria: Government Printer.

Republic of South Africa. 1999a. *Skills Development Levies Act.* Pretoria: Government Printer.

Republic of South Africa. 1999b. *Public Finance Management Act.* Pretoria: Government Printer.

Republic of South Africa. 2004. *Programme of Action.* Pretoria: Government Printer.

Sayed, Y. 1999. Discourses of the policy of educational decentralization in South Africa since 1994: an examination of the South African Schools Act. *Compare,* vol. 29, no. 2, pp. 141–52.

Southall, R. 2005. Introduction: can South Africa be a developmental state? *In:* Buhlungu, S. et al., eds. *State of the nation, 2005-2006.* Cape Town, South Africa: HSRC Press.

Wiehahn, N. 1981. *The complete Wiehahn Report.* Johannesburg, South Africa: Lex Patria.

Wolf, A. 2002. *Does education matter?* London: Penguin.

Chapter III.8
Reform of Vocational Education in the Russian Federation

Olga Oleynikova and Anna Muravyeva

1 Background

The reform processes for Russian vocational education and training (VET) started in the early 1990s when the former USSR split into independent states, and the Russian Federation became a nation consisting of eighty-nine regions, each with a considerable degree of autonomy. In the field of education this autonomy was reflected by the rapid adoption of regional legislation on education, even if based on the Federal Law on Education.

The Federal Law on Education reflects the provisions of the Constitution of the Russian Federation, laying down in Article 42 universal access to free-of-charge pre-school, general and vocational education. The same Article (paragraph 5) also stipulates that national education standards are set by the Federal State. In Section II, Article 9, vocational education and training is subdivided into two levels—initial and secondary VET.[1] Access to both levels of VET is open for general secondary (nine-year compulsory education) and complete or full secondary school-leavers (eleven years). For school-leavers who do not possess a full general secondary education certificate, vocational curricula at both levels are supplemented by a curriculum of complete general secondary education. Thus, in principle both levels of VET provide open access to higher education (Russian Federation. Ministry of Education, 1996)

VET, and especially initial VET, has always played a two-fold role, namely that of preparation for work and of providing some kind of a social security net for children from disadvantaged families (as of now, about 70% of initial VET students come from low-income and single-parent families) (Russian Federation. Ministry of Education and Science, 2005). The social support role of VET that goes back to the Soviet days has, obviously, been transformed by the new market economy conditions, although VET has tended to retain this important social function. However, it has clearly been weakened by insufficient financial support for education from the State. In Russia the share of GDP spent on education amounts to only 3.6% (as against France 5.8% and Germany 4.5%) (National Observatory for VET, 2003). Tensions between the qualifying role and the social protection role of vocational education and training institutions remain one of the big challenges yet to be overcome.

R. Maclean, D. Wilson (eds.), *International Handbook of Education for the Changing World of Work*, DOI 10.1007/978-1-4020-5281-1_III.8,
© Springer Science+Business Media B.V. 2009

2 Processes of VET Reform and Modernization

2.1 The Initial Years of Transition

VET reform in Russia has passed through two stages: an initial one that can be broadly termed *liberalization* lasted until 2002, when it was followed up by attempts to introduce *modernization*.

Modernization has been accompanied by a structural change in the organization of the VET system (National Observatory for VET, 2004). During the administrative reform of the federal and regional governing bodies in 2004, the Ministry of Education, responsible for vocational education, was transformed into the Ministry of Education and Science of the Russian Federation. This ministry is in charge of both VET segments, as well as of the system of so-called supplementary education, which is in fact a prototype of what is usually referred to as continuing vocational education and training (CVET).

Thus, vocational education and training delivered by VET schools, VET centres attached to enterprises and State providers of supplementary education is currently under the jurisdiction of the Ministry of Education and Science and its two affiliated agencies, namely of the Federal Education Agency and the Federal Inspection Service. Vocational training of the unemployed, however, is the responsibility of the Federal Employment Service. This agency either contracts training courses with VET schools or provides labour-market training at its own training centres. The latter issue their own certificates which are recognized by employers.

In initial VET, worker training takes place either directly at enterprises or within the State-run initial VET schools or lyceums. Unfortunately, since 1993 there have been no official figures made available on the in-service training of workers. Secondary VET programmes are available at *technicums* and colleges (Russian Federation. Ministry of Education, 1999). Within each level of VET differences between types of schools depend on the type of programmes—either basic or advanced—and differ in the content and composition of curricula and qualifications.

To fully perceive the scale, scope and problems of the reform and modernization effort in Russia, it is worthwhile bearing in mind that we are talking about a VET system embracing around 3,790 initial VET schools and lyceums (with about 1,649,300 students), 2,600 State-run and municipal secondary VET institutions (with about 2.5 million students), and over 200 private colleges (Russian Federation. Ministry of Education and Science, 2005). These VET institutions are scattered all over the country's eighty-eight regions[2] that differ not only geographically, but also in terms of the level of economic development. Regions are subdivided into 'donor' regions, considered to be doing relatively well economically, and 'recipients' who benefit from additional equalizing subsidies from the federal government.

The overhaul of relations between education and production in the country in the early 1990s resulted in VET schools severing their former links with enterprises. Traditionally, these links included mandatory provision of work-experience placements for VET students, jobs for VET graduates and other forms of support. Given that the only form of ownership of enterprises in Soviet times was State ownership, and given the planned character of the national economy at that time, matching demand with supply used to be part of the overall VET administrative system. The introduction of labour markets has also changed this aspect of the system.

In the early days of the transition period (accompanied by an economic crisis), the VET reform effort was—besides trying to preserve institutions—directed largely at overcoming the 'rigidity' of the system and at liberalizing content and regulations. Hence, the catchwords of those days were diversification of curricular content and increased autonomy of VET schools at all levels. The biggest achievement of this stage was the first generation of VET standards that, for the first time in Russian history, introduced a differentiation between a federal and a regional component. This was meant to provide the regional levels with a certain degree of autonomy that would allow them to address local specificities, including the structure of their labour markets. These VET standards still had to be approved by sector ministries and the Ministry of Labour before their final adoption by the government, but in itself this was a major step forward.

During this period private colleges of secondary VET also emerged, and contract-based training was permitted. This opened up an opportunity for VET schools to raise money to supplement the meagre budgets provided by the State and to broaden their services to embrace different target groups of learners—in particular unemployed and employed adults.

It is noteworthy that contract-based training has served as 'litmus paper' revealing the entrepreneurial spirit of some schools—and its absence in others. Proactive 'entrepreneurial' schools managed to re-establish links with enterprises and receive money that they have used for research and development, as well as to support teachers' salaries. Unfortunately, at the federal level no notice has been taken of this development and of the crucial factors behind it. A proper analysis of the motives, actions and contexts of proactive schools could have resulted in models that would have been beneficial for the whole VET system.

2.2 Revision of Strategies and Priorities

With the gradual development of the national economy and under the influence of globalization, the emerging goals of the knowledge-based economy and discussions about European integration, the constraints of the initial reform efforts became obvious and have led to the strategy and priorities being revised. This was reflected in a number of policy documents, including the 'National Doctrine of Education' (Russian Federation. Ministry of Education, 2000), the 'Concept of Modernization of Education in the Russian Federation' (Russian Federation. Ministry of Education, 2002), and the most recent document 'Priorities for the Development of Education in the Russian Federation' (Russian Federation. Ministry of Education, 2004).

From then on, VET modernization has addressed the following new issues: (a) development of a new generation of VET standards; (b) establishment of an independent quality assessment and certification system; (c) development of a methodology and infrastructure for the identification of the current and future demand for labour; and (d) development of social partnerships in the sphere of VET. These objectives were further specified in 2004 in the 'Priorities for the Development of Education in the Russian Federation'. This document sets down the strategic goals of the country's educational development, which include: (a) improvement of the well-being of its citizens; (b) the promotion of social stability, security of the State and its citizens; (c) the development of civil society institutions; (d) the maintenance of the social and cultural integrity and civil identity of Russian society; (e) the provision of a qualified work force for the labour market; and (f) the development of a national innovation system enhancing the competitiveness of the Russian economy (Russian Federation. Ministry of Education, 2002, 2004).

For VET the main goals are: (a) the development of an up-to-date system of continuing vocational and higher education; (b) enhancing the quality of VET and higher education; and (c) making the education system more attractive for investors. In order to develop an up-to-date system of continuing vocational education and training, it was deemed necessary to: increase the number of VET providers; to establish a system of external assessment and accreditation of programmes and competences; and to facilitate the academic mobility of students. To enhance the quality of VET it was necessary to restructure the system of initial and secondary VET, to create conditions for the innovation-based development of VET, and to better integrate education and training, research and practice. Finally, in order to make the education system more attractive for private investments it was suggested: to increase the financial autonomy of schools by promoting wider diversity in their organizational and legal status; to reduce investment risks for educational investors by promoting stakeholder involvement in the governance of educational establishments; and to introduce new principles for the financing of VET schools.

As of the time of writing, tangible outputs can be observed along two axes of modernization. Firstly, the second generation of VET standards developed in 2002 has seen a broader participation on the part of social partners. And secondly, social dialogue has begun to develop, reflecting both the internal processes at work in the regions, as well as the impact of international projects implemented in Russia, such as those supported by the European Commission and the European Training Foundation.

However, due to the absence of occupational standards in most of the economic sectors, VET standards have not taken full account of employers' perspectives and remain largely based on educational inputs instead of the outcomes. Nevertheless, in the preparation for the third generation of VET standards now under way, employers' needs are receiving more attention. There is also a growing interest on the part of employers in developing sector-wide occupational standards. Such intentions have been clearly voiced by the Russian Union of Industrialists and Entrepreneurs, the biggest association of employers in the Russian Federation. To add weight to its intentions, this union has established a National Agency for Promotion of Qualifications bringing together all relevant stakeholders to create common ground for enhancing the quality of the workforce by expressing their viewpoints in order to reach a consensus. In 2006 the Government of the Russian Federation approved an action-plan addressed to the Ministry of Education and Science, the Ministry of Economy and the Ministry of Health and Social Development setting out concrete measures to develop a national qualifications framework, competence-based VET curricula, occupational standards and VET standards based on the latter. This action-plan is a breakthrough in terms of the conceptual perspective underlying the modernization effort.

Since 2002, the rhetoric of VET policymakers has also visibly shifted towards quality—in terms of relevance to the labour market—regarded both as an objective and outcome of social partnership. Thus, since that time, the VET discourse has been enriched by such notions as social partnership in VET, multi-level multi-purpose VET schools, optimization of the network of VET schools, decentralization of VET governance, per capita financing of schools, lifelong learning and continuing education and training. Furthermore, the discussion about the Bologna and Copenhagen processes has put additional pressure on the system and, in a way, has acted as a catalyst for further modernization efforts (Oleynikova, 2005).

While the preceding overview offers a somewhat static picture of VET modernization effort in Russia, below we take a look at active on-going processes involving various interest groups and stakeholders. Finally, we summarize the main achievements and list some of the remaining challenges.

2.3 Contract-Based Training

The first event was the development of contract-based training. For example, in initial VET schools about half a million adults are trained under contracts with enterprises, employment agencies or under individual contracts. It is interesting to note that the largest number of contracts is signed with individual citizens (around 60% as against 40% in both of the other groups taken together) (Russian Federation. Ministry of Education and Science, 2005), which indicates a high level of interest in education and training among individuals and recognition that education is the key to a successful career and self-fulfilment. On the other hand, paid tuition is distorting the VET system, often tempting schools to launch programmes that may be attractive to individuals, but have little relevance to the labour market. The most typical examples are programmes in law, economics and accounting that can be found even at initial VET schools.

2.4 Competence-Based Curricula

The second process that is currently coming to the fore is the introduction of the competence-based approach to VET curricula. This implies a further transition to new quality-assurance mechanisms and streamlined institutional mechanisms of social partnership in VET.

The development of competence-based VET has been largely triggered by international projects, including the 'VET reform in the North-West of Russia' Project and the recent European Union-funded Delphi II project that ended in 2005 with the publication of a set of manuals on the development and delivery of competence-based modular curricula. These have been approved by the federal Ministry of Education and Science and are currently being piloted in a number of VET schools. In one region that is very development oriented (Sverdlovsk Oblast), the regional VET standard component has been developed based on learning outcomes (competences). It is therefore unfortunate that an independent system of quality assessment has not yet been put in place and assessment remains within the jurisdiction of VET schools. Clearly, until the outcome-based approach has fully taken root, an independent assessment and certification institution has little chance of succeeding.

2.5 Quality Assurance

Nevertheless, certain processes towards improving quality assurance can be observed. Some VET schools have taken the initiative into their own hands. They have opted for ISO certificates in quality management and others have piloted the self-assessment model developed by the Copenhagen Technical Working Group. The second group of schools are working together with a view to submitting proposals to the federal Ministry of Education and Science on the relevance of this model for the Russian VET system. Some VET schools—though few in number—have adopted a modified total quality management model that serves as the basis for the National and Regional Competitions for the Quality Award, initiated by both the federal and regional governments.

2.6 Continuing Vocational Education and Training

Another important process at work in the VET system is the spread of continuing vocational education and training (CVET), despite the fact that the CVET sector is not yet officially institutionalized. However, at the conceptual level, steps have been taken towards integrating all forms of post-initial VET and adult education, ensuring coherence of qualifications, and enhancing the diversity of pathways to extend access to education and training for all age-groups. Under the Delphi II project, a planning model for CVET at the regional level has been developed that has been recommended for use by all regional VET administrations (Muravyeva, 2005). VET schools are increasingly involved in CVET delivery and will be even more so in the near future, with young cohorts dramatically decreasing due to demographic ageing of the population.

There is also a growing need for up-skilling and retraining of the workforce as a result of rapid technological change. It should be stressed that the demographic aging[3] of the population creates new challenges for the VET system in terms of knowledge updating, as it is the young generation, namely recent graduates from the education system, who are familiar with and use up-to-date knowledge and technologies. With the ageing of the population, the inflow of young people into the work force is slowing down and the age structure of the population group that is most active economically and socially (aged 20 to 60) is undergoing dramatic changes.

2.7 Optimization of the School Network

Another on-going process concerns the optimization of the network of VET schools. This reflects other processes, such as the decentralization of VET governance and the need to increase the cost-effectiveness of VET systems (Butko, 2004). Priorities established by the federal Ministry of Education and Science for the reform of the network of VET schools envisage a systemic integration of schools of different levels in establishing larger complexes, including those based on universities, as well as multi-level multi-purpose VET schools/centres. In addition, organizational and curricular continuity between levels of VET and professional education should be established, and qualification profiles and volumes of training should better match the requirements of the labour markets.

The Concept of Optimization of VET Schools, adopted by the federal Ministry of Education and Science foresees (St. Petersburg Department of Education, 2005):

- Choosing a selected number of VET schools to form multi-level and multi-purpose centres of excellence that will remain under federal jurisdiction and deliver training in occupations of importance for the national economy (high-tech sectors, defence industry). These schools will pilot innovations, both technological and methodological. Geographically, such federal centres of excellence will be located in smaller cities having few VET schools. By the end of 2008 about 300 schools of this type will have been established implementing initial (IVET), secondary (SVET) and continuing (CVET) curricula in occupational profiles relevant for each region;
- Modifying IVET and SVET schools into multi-profile and multi-level VET centres under the regional jurisdiction will concern about 40% of the total amount of these schools. Already most SVET colleges have introduced training for two or three new occupations on top of the traditional ones to address the changing needs of the labour market and are implementing IVET and CVET programmes;
- Establishing the so-called resource centres on the basis of the best regional VET schools. Many regions have opted for this model in order to restructure their school networks. The concept of a resource centre, which is quite complex and requires further development, has been thoroughly analysed and piloted in a number of regions in the World Bank financed Education Reform Project. There is a danger that a resource centre becomes just a better-equipped VET school or a methodological and research 'repository', but is not a training centre with advanced technology and equipment that can be used collectively by all regional and inter-regional customers for the practical training of students.

The first outcomes of restructuring the VET schools network are witness to the reorganization of 130 VET schools of different levels into twenty-four university complexes and nineteen multi-profile colleges. This move has reduced the number of legal entities—recipients of public funding—and contributed to the elimination of redundancy in training profiles within a region, streamlining the governance and procedures and resulting in an improvement in cost-effectiveness.

It is expected that the restructuring of school networks will require new organizational and legal formats for VET schools. The rationale behind these proposals is that a new legal status will promote employer involvement in VET school governance, and will thus improve financial support for VET schools.

2.8 Decentralization

The federal policy on the decentralization of VET governance aims at better addressing the regional and local needs of the economy and the population. It also aims at involving regional administrations in VET development as well as activating the participation of employers and professional associations in VET governance. Decentralization means the transfer of VET schools into regional jurisdictions with a redistribution of decision-making powers between the federal and regional authorities. As of January 2005, the responsibilities of VET management and financing for most IVET schools were devolved from the federal to the regional level. The SVET schools are also being gradually transferred to regional jurisdictions. To date, about 92% of IVET schools and about 460 SVET schools have been transferred to the regional jurisdiction. In spite of the fact that decentralization, as such, is a very positive development, the financial situation of VET schools may deteriorate, primarily due to the constraints resulting from very different regional priorities. Plans to streamline regional disparities through targeted federal subsidies for VET schools are under discussion. The transfer of IVET and SVET schools to the regional jurisdiction would require the development of a legal framework empowering the federal ministry to maintain control over the quality of VET, while the infrastructure is devolved to the regional jurisdiction. Thus, a model of VET governance is to be created that would delineate powers and competences, functions and responsibilities of schools and local governments between the regional and the federal authorities.

In preparation for such optimization, the regions of the Russian Federation are modernizing their VET infrastructure by setting up regional centres for labour-market monitoring, for quality assurance and integrated systems for up-skilling (CVET). Some have also started to improve vocational guidance and counselling systems. In certain regions (e.g. in Samara Oblast), stipends and additional benefits have been introduced for students to stimulate training in occupations that are needed by the economy but are not popular. Some regions have started establishing regional centres for the certification of qualifications using international experience. Without the co-ordination and guidance of federal authorities, such issues as the transfer of certificates across regions and the lack of nationally agreed standards may undermine the viability of centres and thus affect their survival.

Regional VET systems are also involved in maximizing the regional element in VET standards so as to improve the labour-market relevance of education and training. To this end, various forms of councils have been set up with the participation of social partners. In some regions VET schools' licenses are reconfirmed only if their training profiles address the regional labour market needs. Employers, regional employment service agencies and students must also speak out positively about the school.

2.9 New Financing Mechanisms

Alongside the decentralization and optimization processes, new financing mechanisms have been devised, including per capita financing of IVET and SVET schools differentiated according to the profile of training (in terms of its relevance for the economy) and the costs of the programme. The development of per capita financing (often referred to as norm-based financing) has been under way for quite a few years but no final model has yet been approved. The decentralization process has also engendered a model of co-financing of VET schools under medium-term target programmes from both federal and regional budgets.

The development of decentralization and optimization mechanisms has revealed a number of bottlenecks in the VET system, including the lack of capacity to analyse demand and the need for a legal framework for CVET, including new organizational forms and their financing. Experience so far has also shown that there are problems motivating VET school principals to become actively engaged in the modernization process. Most principals are baffled or even scared by the on-going changes and fail to react. Only a very few of them are able to be pro-active and anticipate changes. Management and leadership skills of VET administrators and managers at all levels have to be further developed to cope with all the challenges of decentralization.

3 Main Reform Achievements and Remaining Challenges

Summing up this short history of VET reform and modernization in Russia, it can be concluded that some progress has been made:

- The State has recognized the importance of vocational education and training as a prerequisite for the country's economic growth and competitiveness, and is committed to its development and support.
- Measures have been devised and implemented to improve the network of VET institutions and set up multi-level and multi-purpose integrated VET schools and VET centres of excellence.
- VET schools are increasingly involved in training the adult population, including the unemployed.
- There is an increased awareness both among VET policy-makers and practitioners of the need to develop outcomes-based VET standards and programmes.

- VET schools are adopting a methodology of skill-needs analysis that is conducive to enhancing social partnership in VET, alongside other mechanisms of social partnership instituted on the regional and municipal level.

At the same time, the development of the VET system in general has been slowed down by a number of unresolved issues that have not received sufficient attention, even though they have been known about for many years by VET partners and stakeholders. What has been achieved has mainly been stimulated by international projects and has therefore been largely restricted to the community that has been involved in such projects.

Social dialogue on VET remains underdeveloped. As such, social partnership is recognized and practised by pro-active schools, largely by those that have been exposed to international projects. On the system level, there are various councils set up to co-ordinate the efforts of the VET system and social partners, however it is too early to speak about their impact, given that they have primarily focused on intake figures and profiles of training. The major recent development is the setting up of sector skills councils initiated by the international Delphi II project that focuses on competence standards for VET graduates, effective work placements for students, as well as on updating the contents of programmes and the assessment of competences.

On the whole, however, it should be stressed that, in spite of the modernization efforts, there is a pronounced lack of a culture of social partnership on both sides. There remains great reluctance on the side of employers to interact with vocational education (partially because of a lack of appropriate incentives for enterprises). There is also little recognition on the side of regional administrations of a possible role for vocational education as an agent in economic development.

Skill mismatches continue to exist. According to employers—supported by unemployment figures—the competences of VET graduates are irrelevant for the labour market. About 20.7% of the unemployed population have a secondary VET diploma and about 16.4% have initial VET diplomas. Among the economically active population, 7.7% of SVET diploma holders and 6.2% IVET diploma holders remain unemployed (Federal Statistics Service, 2005). Unemployed VET graduates have to make contact with the employment services to receive re-training which, apart from negative social and psychological implications, entails extra costs for the State.

Vocational education programmes also remain largely input-based. There is still an absence of updated occupational standards and the existing classification of labour-market occupations has not yet been revised. In practice, this means that outdated and obsolete occupational profiles are still used as a basis for many programmes provided by VET schools. At the same time, there is no generally accepted methodology and communication system for anticipating skills demand. VET institutions have no guidelines on which they could base new initiatives and often follow the most recent fashion. One of the outcomes of this process is the so-called 'qualification loop'. New occupations on the labour market requiring different or higher qualifications in a new market segment (i.e. finance) remain vacant due to the lack of school graduates having the required knowledge and skills. The rigid dependence in awarding diplomas and qualifications on duration and type of programmes in formal education is paralleled by the absence of mechanisms and instruments to recognize prior learning from non-formal and informal settings.

Drop-out from VET schools remains high as well. It is highest in agricultural and fishery occupations, reaching about 35%; in natural sciences occupations it amounts to 25% and in teaching occupations about 15%. There is a mix of factors that may explain high drop-out rates, including perceived lack of relevance of programmes for obtaining employment, traditional emphasis on general subjects at the cost of practical vocational education, overloaded curricula and old-fashioned teaching approaches. The quality of teaching is also deteriorating rapidly, amongst others things due to an increasing shortage of qualified teachers and practical training instructors. The shortage of instructors amounts to more than 40%, with about 14% of practical training instructors having qualifications that are lower than the qualifications awarded to VET school graduates. This development can be accounted for by the low social prestige of teaching and instruction jobs in vocational education and to the miserably low salaries. The prospective introduction of outcomes-based VET may in fact further aggravate the shortage of VET teachers and instructors, as those who are still working in schools may not be motivated enough to adjust to on-going changes. The situation is made even worse by the rapid ageing of the teaching force.

Translating these weaknesses into practical steps that would be in line with the goals and objectives set down in the Priorities for the Development of Education in the Russian Federation, it would seem first of all necessary to clarify the division of power and responsibility between the federal and regional levels in the system of vocational education and training. Some of the measures currently being discussed will be presented below.

In general terms, the improvement of VET governance should aim at transforming regional VET systems into a resource for social and economic development. Thus, the regional level should become responsible for:

- providing access to VET for all population groups, with special regard to the disadvantaged and individuals with special needs;
- the development and updating of VET standards;
- the organization of in-service training of teachers and practical training instructors; and
- the development of a legal framework for social partnership in VET.

The central government should be responsible for:

- creating the conditions for the free development of the market of VET providers;
- an overall quality assurance system;
- setting the financial mechanisms for the VET systems, including a legal framework for student loans and the participation of employers in co-financing of student loans; and
- initiating measures to encourage employers to participate in VET (e.g. tax benefits for enterprises investing in VET).

Increasingly, there is an awareness of the need for structural changes in the overall VET system and in particular for better integrating the different levels, types and forms of vocational education and training, such as initial and secondary VET, and supplementary and adult training, including training of the unemployed. This would also make it necessary to develop an independent system of quality assessment, ensuring an integrated national education space and enhanced objectivity in the assessment of learning outcomes. Such a system could be based on autonomous not-for-profit organizations authorized to carry out examinations and the certification of learning. At the same time, they could also be responsible for the accreditation of programmes and the issuing of certificates.

Finally, there is also an understanding of the need to change financing mechanisms and their principles. Schools should become more financially autonomous. This would imply a radical change of existing itemized funding principles. It would also require increased accountability for the results that schools achieve. Therefore, financing of VET schools should be based on outcomes that have been clearly identified, formulated and agreed. To enhance overall efficiency of financial schemes it is proposed to introduce new mechanisms that include target figures, educational credits and medium-term programmes. Under the latter programmes, priority financing will be provided for developing up-to-date teaching and learning infrastructures, such as computer networks, education databases, e-libraries, teaching and learning materials, systems of quality assessment and a system of certification and accreditation of curricula, as well as software packages in educational management and governance.

In October 2006 the federal government expanded the National Priority Project on Education to support innovations in VET. In years to come tens of millions of dollars will be granted to VET schools to upgrade their equipment, facilities and to modernize training programmes. It is important to analyse and learn from the experience accumulated in international projects with a view to ensuring that these new investments will complement what the regions are already doing. The beneficiary institutions will receive incentives to work and share the results with other institutions. Past experience suggests that equipping and supporting individual schools does not represent a sustainable long-term solution to the problems of the VET system. Before moving ahead with this initiative, the government would need to develop a long-term vision for the development of the VET sector that takes into account the rapid changes taking place in the workplace as a result of the introduction of ever-more sophisticated technologies and the demand by entrepreneurs for graduates with flexible skills and the capacity to learn fast.

As can be seen from our review, there is a long list of needs and suggestions. The key challenge is to implement some of them. Given the wealth of good practices existing in individual VET schools that could serve as a resource for developing modern and effective models of VET in the country, networking of VET schools should be encouraged to enhance information exchange and the sharing of good practices. This seems to be the only feasible way to envisage a continuation of on-going reforms and modernization efforts.

Notes

1. These titles may be confusing. The term 'initial vocational education' in the Russian tradition refers to education for basic, i.e. lower, levels of occupations. However, as workers used to be able to upgrade their qualifications through courses, 'initial vocational education' also provided a basis for continuing vocational education and training. The term 'secondary vocational education' should not be associated with the secondary level of the education system but refers to post-secondary education and is aimed at training medium-level specialists for all sectors of the economy.
2. In 2005, two regions of the Russian Federation were merged into one, thus bringing the overall number of regions down from eighty-nine to eighty-eight.
3. In some regions of the Russian Federation the average age of the working population is around 50. The current demographic development in Russia is a combination of low birth rates and low average life expectancies, resulting in the *ageing of the population*. According to the State Statistics Committee, the size of the population decreased from 148.3 million in 1992 to 144 in 2004. This trend is expected to continue in the coming years.

References

Butko, E. 2004. *Education and economic strategies of IVET schools in contemporary conditions.* Moscow: Ministry of Education.

Federal Statistics Service. 2005. *Education in the Russian Federation: annual statistics.* Moscow.

Muravyeva, A. 2005. Competence-based VET. *Journal 'Specialist'*, no. 5.

National Observatory for VET. 2003. *VET stocktaking report.* Moscow.

National Observatory for VET. 2004. *VET update.* Moscow.

Oleynikova, O. 2005. Outcomes of the Delphi II project. *Journal 'Specialist'*, no. 11.

Russian Federation. Ministry of Education. 1996. *Law of the Russian Federation on Education.* Edition of January 13, no. 12.

Russian Federation. Ministry of Education. 1999. *Programme of Development of Secondary VET.* Moscow.

Russian Federation. Ministry of Education. 2000. *National Doctrine of Education in the Russian Federation.* (Papers from the conference of education workers.) Moscow.

Russian Federation. Ministry of Education. 2002. *Concept of Modernisation of Education in the Russian Federation.* Moscow.

Russian Federation. Ministry of Education. 2004. *Priorities for the Development of Education in the Russian Federation.* Moscow.

Russian Federation. Ministry of Education and Science. 2005. *Education in the Russian Federation: annual collection of statistics.* Moscow: Federal Statistics Service, Federal Education Agency.

St. Petersburg Department of Education. 2005. Papers from the Conference 'Decentralization of VET Governance'.

Chapter III.9
Vocational Education in the Netherlands: In Search of a New Identity

Jan Geurts and Frans Meijers

1 Introduction

Students' motivational problems in combination with new occupational demands (which resulted from the transition from a primarily industrial to a more service- and knowledge-oriented economy) triggered an identity crisis in vocational education in the 1990s. The search for this new identity will be analysed in this chapter. First of all, we will evaluate the urgency of the problem. In the first section we will show that increasing amounts of criticism were directed at the functioning of the vocational education system during the 1990s. The national qualifications structure was the primary object of criticism, the response to which was the development of competence-based vocational education. In section 3, we will describe the main characteristics of this kind of education, and we will connect this to the concept of the vocational education school as a career development centre. Even though this concept was mainly developed outside the vocational education system (i.e. by academics, social partners and the government), a centrally directed national innovation policy has not really been the preferred option, for political as well as substantive reasons.

Instead, it was agreed that competence-based vocational education should be realized through a variety of regional innovations, managed by the schools themselves. In other words, a 'bottom-up' approach to innovation has been chosen. In section 4, we will critically review this approach taking on the role of a 'critical friend'. Recent research into the development of competence-based learning will receive special attention in section 5. In the sixth section, we will conclude our chapter with a look into the future. In our opinion, vocational education has to focus its search for a new identity through an increase of its own 'professionalism', as a basis for self-direction. The central government can support the growth of personal professionalism and the professionalization of vocational schools by stimulating opportunities for locally initiated experimentation. One way to do this could be by creating a national innovation fund with agreed key goals for innovation. However, proper support for the self-direction of schools requires adequate steering by the government.

R. Maclean, D. Wilson (eds.), *International Handbook of Education for the Changing World of Work*, DOI 10.1007/978-1-4020-5281-1_III.9,
© Springer Science+Business Media B.V. 2009

2 The Qualification's Structure Under Fire

The qualification's structure that was developed during the late 1980s for non-university vocational education had four levels. Every level is associated with a vocational education programme with two major variants: one school-based, whereby the amount of practical training is between 20% and 60%, and one work-based, where this percentage is greater than 60%. The lowest qualification level is one for simple operational tasks, with the associated assistant-level training. The highest level is for autonomous task implementation, with either broad areas of application or specialization, with an associated intermediate- or specialist-level training.

The keys to the qualification structure are the so-called learning outcomes, or 'end-results', that are determined by 'knowledge centres vocational education business', that exist for each sector or branch. In a first step, the social partners (employers and union representatives) establish occupational profiles for key occupations in their industry or branch. They describe—per occupation—the core tasks and the necessary knowledge and skills, taking future developments into account. The social partners then formulate the qualifications and the corresponding 'end results', derived from one or more occupational profiles. They also determine which training variant can be offered, whether the training must be fee-based or free of charge, and to what extent qualifications need to be legitimized by an external, independent institution. At this point, the Advisory Commission on the Education-Labour Market (ACOA), established by the Minister of Education, will be asked to advise whether the qualifications and end results adhere to the legal requirements. After acceptance by ACOA, the Minister of Education ratifies the end-results and the approved education and training variant will be entered in the vocational education central register (the CREBO). From that moment on, educational institutions are allowed to develop—on the basis of the ratified end terms—curricula for the programmes that they are willing and able to offer. Educational publishers translate—sometimes in co-operation with educational institutions—the end results into practical training material. Finally, arrangements are made with enterprises concerning the scope and implementation of the practical training parts. The entire procedure (from end-results to training materials) is regulated by the Educational and Vocational Training Act (WEB).

During the 1990s, there were increasing concerns about the effectiveness and efficiency of the WEB. In Table 1, derived from Geurts (2001), we present the conclusions of a number of studies concerning the functioning of the WEB. In terms of effectiveness, there now exists a plethora of strongly differentiated and narrow-function profiles. Efficiency also has room for improvement. A bureaucracy has been developed to maintain the qualification structure and—as a result—there is again limited responsiveness to the labour market. Moreover, the qualification structure insufficiently stimulates increases in knowledge production, because the WEB allows all parties (schools, knowledge centres and support institutions) to simply implement the WEB without reflecting on ways for improvement. Especially, little thought has been given on relating the agreed qualifications to pedagogic goals. The WEB does not stimulate schools and other parties to actively consider

Table 1 Remarks concerning the effectiveness and efficiency of the qualifications structure

Effective: doing the right things	Efficient: doing things well
• too one-sided attention to the demand side;	• bureaucratic procedures with (too) long durations;
• structure not up-to-date: obsolete occupational profiles;	• insufficient connection with initial- and tertiary levels of vocational education and training, leading to unnecessary delays;
• qualifications not broad and durable enough: too narrow function profiles;	• too little involvement and communication between interested parties;
• much overlapping in qualifications;	
• too many, too differentiated qualifications (approx. 700): not transparent;	• qualification structure is developed in relative isolation;
• blind spots: new occupations are not given enough attention;	• too rigid role distribution between interested parties;
• confusion in the demarcation between initial and post-initial education;	• lack of clarity in description of end-terms;
• deterioration of educational goals.	• actors use their own opportunities for improving interfaces insufficiently.

and apply the qualification structure, possibly offering modifications and improvements from their own perspective. Because they see little opportunity to utilize their own experience, educational institutions have generally not developed a positive relation with the qualification structure. They have, in fact, never viewed it as an instrument to improve the quality of their own work. As a result, the qualification structure is generally used in a defensive manner, namely as an instrument to legitimatize themselves towards government, the inspectorate, businesses and their own teachers.

The quality of vocational education became a subject of increasing contention between employer organizations and the government, certainly after the European Council agreed in Lisbon in 2000 that the European economy needed to transform itself within ten years into the world's most competitive and dynamic knowledge economy. The transition to a service/knowledge economy requires qualifications other than those currently provided and a more responsive system of vocational education. The rise of a service/knowledge economy is accompanied by three megatrends (Korbijn, 2003, p. 45 ff):

1. The market is becoming increasingly demand-driven: customers want (at the lowest possible price) custom-made products, i.e. products tailored to their own specific wishes and needs. Customers are increasingly demanding that producers take all aspects of the products' life cycle into account. This implies that the importance of 'absolute quality' (i.e. quality according to industrial criteria) is decreasing, and the importance of the relative quality is increasing. Durability is becoming less important than functionality and usability.
2. The speed of globalization is increasing: customers, partners and competitors are spread over the entire globe. This trend also accentuates the importance of

relative quality, while time-to-market is becoming decisive. For companies to remain competitive, the time between product development and the moment of actually placing it in the market place has to become shorter and shorter.
3. The world is also becoming increasingly dynamic: technology becomes obsolete more quickly and marketplace demands are changing just as rapidly. This increasing dynamism forces producers to place new products in the marketplace at an increasing tempo.

The effect of these mega-trends is that the market is changing continuously in an unpredictable manner, the ability to innovate is becoming an increasingly important competitive factor and knowledge is becoming of key importance. To survive in this hectic environment, businesses have to innovate constantly and at the same time apply 'concurrent engineering'. The organization of their production processes has to be structured in such a way that employees can work on various different product innovations and, at the same time, work in multidisciplinary teams, applying integrated design for specific innovations. This means that the organization of an enterprise has to become less hierarchical and to utilize all of the knowledge and skills available from its employees.

3 The School as a Career Development Centre

Businesses are under pressure to become flexible 'learning' organizations, which means that they not only have to invest in knowledge management, but also that their employees must become entrepreneurial themselves: they have to be able to be 'self-directing', that is able to manage their own work, take initiatives and make appropriate decisions when needed. The solution for generating self-direction is primarily sought through continuing education and training for experienced employees, and by broadening the qualification structure for new employees. The key idea in current educational innovation is 'competence-based education and training'. This, however, turns out to be an extremely vague concept and includes not only occupational skills but also attitudinal and behavioural characteristics (Thijssen & Lankhuijzen, 2000). In practice, this results in more attention being given to the development of occupational skills—mainly in the form of experiential learning by means of problem-driven training—often to the detriment of abstract and theoretical knowledge. In a certain sense, therefore, the generalization of vocational education during the 1950s is being reversed, without reverting to the narrow industrial-oriented training of that era. In modern competence-based education, as opposed to vocational education and training of the 1950s, attention is paid to self-direction on the basis of reflection, thus to the formation of a reflective practitioner (Schön, 1983).

In the meantime, it has become clear that it is extraordinarily difficult within existing training and educational structures to motivate young people and employees to become self-directing. Existing structures force schools, as well as their support institutions, to define self-direction in terms of knowledge that can, in turn, be validated by means of the qualification structure and can be transmitted to students. For this reason, self-direction is usually defined in terms of meta-cognitive and information-processing skills, and in terms of emotion and affective regulation (Meijers & Wardekker, 2001). It is undeniably true that these competences are important for surviving in a turbulent environment. However, when these are used with an emphasis on technical-instrumental skills, the very essence of self-direction is missed, namely, the competence to identify oneself with (i.e. to voluntarily and durably commit to) society or at least parts if it, such as the work situation (Meijers & Geurts, 2002). Becoming self-directed in the area of work and employment means attaching meaning to one's own work, thereby developing a work-identity (Meijers & Wardekker, 2002).

From this perspective, in the scientific and policy discussion over (the future of) vocational education, as well as in concrete innovation projects, competence-based learning has recently been explicitly understood to be authentic as well as self-directed (Collins, Brown & Newman, 1989; Brown, Collins & Duguid, 1989). By authentic we mean that an explicit and well-thought-out connection between theory and practice has to be made during training, in order for students to develop the competences to become a professional. In the traditional, subject-based education and training model, traineeships were intended for this purpose. Research has shown, however, that there is little connection between theory and practice in traineeships, and there is certainly no systematic development of a work-identity (Meijers, 2004). Therefore, modern competence-based education attempts to create a learning environment in as realistic a manner as possible. Students learn, during their training, to act as professionals and thereby experience the relationship between occupational practice and vocational theory.

Learning must be self-directed as well as authentic if it hopes to produce competent practitioners in a service/knowledge-based economy, according to the constructivist school in educational psychology (e.g. Duffy & Cunningham, 1996; Simons, Van der Linden & Duffy, 2000). Constructivism assumes that individuals actively construct knowledge by interpreting new information on the basis of pre-existing knowledge and experience. Knowledge transfer—at least in the manner that people have always assumed—is therefore impossible. Students can only construct knowledge when the information presented to them can be transformed into something personal (Wardekker, Biesta & Miedema, 1998). This explains why 'knowledge transfer'—as intended by the school system—often achieves only limited success. Constructivist learning approaches argue that students must be activated as much as possible to enable them to construct their own knowledge. Students do not always have to construct knowledge on their own; co-operation with other students can also play an important role because it forces students to be active. For example, students may have to explain something to others, or to compare their ideas with those of others (see e.g. Simons et al., 2000). Teaching then becomes the creation of an environment whereby learners are stimulated, helped and supported in their personal construction (possibly together with the help of others) of valuable knowledge-content and skills. This is expressed in the well-known saying: the teacher shouldn't transfer knowledge, but rather coach the learning process. Traditional educational innovations, such as those based on the theories of Montessori and Dalton, are also based on this idea. It is interesting, however, to note the zeal with which these ideas have been grasped by Dutch vocational education in recent years.

Geurts (2001) has integrated the educational developments around authentic and self-directed learning in a model that attempts to illustrate the process of re-designing traditional, content-oriented education in the direction of a system more concerned with personal, competence-development, and based upon constructivist learning-theory (see Fig. 1). Re-designing of VET proceeds, according to Geurts, along two dimensions: the what and the how.

The what-dimension primarily concerns the contents of VET programmes. Are we concerned with a standard programme or are we more interested in flexible, tailored-made programmes? Questions about narrow and/or broad training arise at the level of school organization. Schools may choose to develop programmes not as a funnel, but rather as a (hand-held) fan. With respect to the 'fan' metaphor, the student doesn't have to explicitly choose a specific occupational specialization at the beginning. Rather, it is important that the student has the opportunity to become familiar with many aspects of the occupational reality, and during the course of their training—and depending upon their own interests and ambitions—they can 'fan out' over the various (work-relevant) specializations. Of course, this fan metaphor does not preclude participants from immediately choosing a narrow education if they wish to do so. In any case, multi-sectoral skill development—as opposed to mono-sectoral—is given priority. For the individual, it is important that, in organizing the curriculum, emphasis is placed upon offering students a training trajectory with

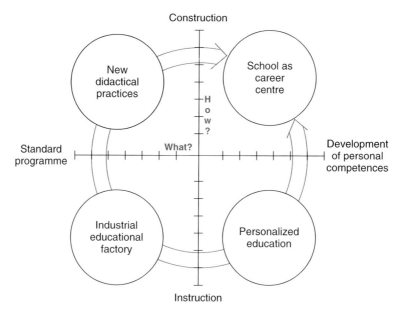

Fig. 1 From training factory to career centre: two main dimensions for re-design
Source: Guerts, 2001.

optimal career guidance. The school becomes then more of an organization that offers individual learning trajectories, instead of standardized courses.

Didactics are the primary concern of the how-dimension. The main thrust here is that vocational education has to make the transition from learning-from-instruction to learning-by-construction. The learning cycle has to be inverted: theory must not precede practice any longer, but practice must guide theory (which then has to be presented just-in-time and just-enough). This idea is being implemented on a larger scale at this moment via various forms of problem-driven education, whereby occupational work-related problems are presented by companies which then need to be solved by students. In this way, there is a guarantee that the occupational problems to be solved are relevant and realistic. Problem-driven learning (and certainly in its most developed form, also known as practice-driven learning) gives vocational education the possibility to develop its own pedagogical methods, with learning-by-doing and constructive learning as important didactical principles. It is clear that the division between learning and working, and between school and business, has to become less pronounced. In this new didactical vision of learning, there is more interaction between the three parties: student, school and business. Each party has a responsibility for their own, active contribution to occupational training seen as part of professionalization. It is assumed that this process will become more efficient, effective and pleasant when the three essential actors optimally co-operate. This requires, at the very least, committed (regional) co-operation with the purpose of optimizing individual careers.

In the lower left of Fig. 1, traditional vocational education is characterized as an industrial training factory. We see a standardized programme with clear diploma requirements, with instruction as the primary learning method. Opposite to the school as factory, upper right, we see the school as a centre for optimal career development. The starting point for achieving a recognized qualification is the interests and capacities of the students. Students develop their own unique set of abilities via a flexible programme, with individual, customized training as the terminus. Construction as opposed to instruction is the primary form of learning. Upper left and lower right, we see intermediate forms of education. New didactical practices such as problem-driven education are to the upper left. At this moment, new practices are almost always placed within traditional, standardized programmes. Lower right refers to the modular organization of existing educational programmes. This *à la carte* education is similar to custom-made education, but is not innovative in the didactical sense.

4 Bottom-up Innovation

The transition from an industrial diploma factory to a career centre is something schools will have to navigate on their own. Since the end of the 1980s, the educational policy of the government—in reaction to the visible boundaries of the welfare state—has been deregulation and decentralization. As opposed to the industrial era, during which the national government (i.e. the Ministry of Education) almost completely determined daily affairs in the classroom, nowadays schools are granted more autonomy. The main reason for this radical shift is—at least with respect to educational policy—the recognition of the fact that the educational innovations for a service/knowledge economy cannot be developed on a drawing board and subsequently implemented—top-down. The 'school as career centre' can only be the result of inside-out innovation, if only for the reason that teachers and school managers need to develop their own new professional identity (Geijsel & Meijers, 2005). The central government limits itself to providing framework legislation directed toward quality requirements and enforcement.

This process of deregulation and decentralization will, of course, take place over a number of years; there will naturally be a period of inconsistencies and confusion. In addition, decennia of 'industrial educational policy' have resulted in the disappearance of almost all innovative ability in the schools today. During the last few decades, innovation has rarely meant the development of new didactical practices on the part of teachers, but rather almost always the incorporation of new scientific knowledge into the teaching materials. School managers used to have primarily an administrative task, and not an innovative one. In short, schools have difficulties in making the transition from being an executor of government policy to that of a developer of their own policy. The result is that they tend to fall between the two roles.

Schools experience the disadvantage of a larger distance to the government without being fully able to harvest the fruits of their own, new-found autonomy (Engberts & Geurts, 1994). Geurts (2001) believes that inspirational school leadership can strike the correct balance between external demand and internal ambitions and competences. It is, however, a problem that this leadership is often lacking; one has to make do with a bureaucratic leadership culture. Apparently, school managers are still mainly pre-occupied with implementing existing legislation and regulations. According to Van Emst (2002), there is a real possibility that schools will even express a growing need for new rules and regulations. Turbulence increases the craving of the school management for even more control. This results in a great deal of 'paper' and red tape: detailed descriptions of tasks, privileges, responsibilities, rights, rules, regulations and organizational schemes, so that everyone knows what his/her place is. In practice, however, hardly anyone pays much attention to such arrangements. In response, school management then enforces the rules even more rigorously. It is not uncommon that the desired control actually leads to stagnation. No one is any longer interested in investing energy in school innovation and renewal.

In governmental policy aimed at increasing school autonomy, 'lump sum' financing plays a large role. A decreasing portion of resources are explicitly reserved for specific purposes. This means that schools have to develop their own policy-making ability so as to make good use of their increasing autonomy. In order to strengthen this ability, the government has decided to implement its innovation policies in the form of projects. For educational innovation that the government considers to be important, an amount of money is made available administered by a (often specially created) non-governmental organization (NGO). This NGO then invites interested parties to submit proposals for innovative projects, which are then evaluated by independent experts. The idea is that the most promising proposals (and thereby also the most innovative contexts) may be identified and rewarded.

After funds are granted for an innovation project, a cycle of research and evaluation begins, conducted under the supervision of the NGO involved. In this cycle, 'good practices' assume an important role, in addition to traditional evaluation research. The idea behind this is that an evaluation procedure can only be viewed as truly meaningful when the assumptions—as well as the approach—are intended to promote the continuous improvement of the knowledge development process within the school itself. The innovation projects are therefore considered based on the principles of the 'learning organization': the projects are viewed as 'learning projects' that are inherently, continuously concerned with improving their own quality (Geurts & Pouwels, 2001). Learning organizations require that parties involved utilize the experience derived from quality-assurance systems, such as the International Standard Operating Procedures (ISOP) and the European Foundation of Quality Management (EFQM). Such quality-assurance systems attach great importance to a systematic approach to monitoring project progress and quality control. They also utilize principles of self-evaluation, such as internal auditing and self-direction and correction. From the viewpoint of the philosophy of self-evaluation, a (continuous) process of quality improvement must be seen as a joint responsibility of all parties involved (the NGO, the school, and the external researcher/evaluator contracted by the NGO).

Thus, the evaluation of an innovation project has to be a co-production of all parties involved, and be characterized by an open and communicative (and thereby a 'learning') policy style. This co-production can be realized by requiring schools to reflect on the project's progress on the basis of a template developed by the involved NGO. In this manner, Axis, for example, an NGO that was founded in 1998 to stimulate students to enrol in technical and science studies, required schools to write so-called 'good practices' that were to be subsequently published on a website. Writing a 'good practice' forces the project to go into 'slow motion' and to clarify (mainly for themselves): (a) which 'practical theory' they adhere to; (b) what people have done (as inspired by this practical theory) in terms of product or process development; (c) whether they have achieved the results predicted by the practical theory; and (d) what can be learned from the project results up to that moment (Geurts & Oosthoek, 2004). The 'good practice' descriptions give the external researchers an opportunity to monitor the quality and progress of the projects in such a manner that the evaluation process also contributes to the development of knowledge. In other words, the evaluation is not based on abstract criteria from scientific discourse but rather on the 'good practices' written by the school itself.

The reports from the Axis project evaluators (Geurts, 2004; Meijers, 2003a; Onstenk, 2004; Sanden, 2004) demonstrate that a 'learning' evaluation style could not easily be realized. A number of different reasons were found. First of all, there exists an educational culture in which evaluation has never been connected with learning. The consequence is that many project leaders began their projects with enthusiastic support of an active, learning evaluation but were rather hesitant about someone 'looking over their shoulder'. In other words, people were hardly prepared to admit that mistakes may have been made. A second reason involves a culture of innovation in which people are accustomed to initiating short-term projects that usually are not integrated in a long-term innovation, but are carried out because external funding happened to be available. All too often, the fortuitous availability of funding determines innovations. Thirdly, most projects function in an environment with a poor history of reflection—something which is associated with the previous two points. People are not used to examining their own actions and have therefore not developed a tradition of doing so. Due to all this, it was very difficult to obtain hard evaluative data for any of the projects. The data were simply not available; all energy was expended in the development of new products and processes. However, during the course of monitoring and evaluation of these projects, due to active co-operation between researchers and project leaders, trust between the two groups developed. It became increasingly clear during this process that writing up good practices had a demonstrable positive added-value for the progress of these projects. Due to these developments, the willingness to invest in good practices increased and in a number of cases there has actually been an effort made to obtain hard data concerning the innovation.

5 Between Dream and Reality

Bruijn, Leeman & Overmaat, (2006) recently published the results of eleven case studies of strong learning environments in vocational education. A strong learning environment is defined as having: (a) constructivist programme characteristics (career identity is the basic principle of the programme; it is oriented towards authentic learning; and there is an integrated thematic and subject-based approach); (b) students participate in cognitive processing activities (mainly construction and reflection), (c) teacher guidance activities (adaptive instruction, coaching and the promotion of self-regulating skills); and (d) evaluation (functional testing of knowledge, insight and skills, as well as assessment of broad competences in situated action). In Table 2 we present the results of this analysis.

Table 2 includes averages of the eleven investigated training programmes for the ten characteristics of a powerful learning environment in decreasing order of implementation. In addition to the means, the number of programmes having a score greater than or equal to 2.5 (a neutral score) are also indicated. As can be seen, the characteristics 'adaptive instruction' and 'professional identity' were relatively strongly developed in a large number of programmes. This is probably due to the fact that those characteristics are easily combined with traditional educational concepts, yet are not at odds with competence-oriented education. More innovative characteristics, such as 'authentic/functional learning' and 'assessment of broad competences', are less prominently present. The level of a programme's authenticity remains limited and seems to be dependent upon fortuitous events, such as the commitment of the instructor. Relatively few programmes demonstrate systematic reflection by the students upon their own results and learning processes and a coaching style by the instructors.

Table 2 Implementation of strong learning environments

Ten characteristics of strong learning environments in order of decreasing implementation

N=11	mean	2.5 or more
Adaptive instruction	2.48	N=8
Professional identity as basic principle	2.32	N=6
Integrated thematic/subject-based education	2.30	N=3
Constructive learning	2.18	N=5
Functional tests	2.07	N=4
Promotion of self-regulating skills	2.05	N=4
Authentic/functional learning	1.98	N=4
Assessment of broad competences	1.93	N=4
Coaching by exploratory learning	1.84	N=2
Reflective learning	1.81	N=1
Total score: strong learning environment	2.10	N=3

1 = weak; 2 = more weak than strong; 3 = more strong than weak; 4 = strong

Other research confirms the picture that, until now, schools have been mainly investing in structural change as opposed to cultural change (see e.g. Meijers, 2003b; Severiens & Joukes, 2001; Boer, Mittendorff & Sjenitzer, 2004). Specifically, there has been little change in the manner in which people communicate within a school (i.e. between students and teachers, between teachers themselves, and between teachers and management), as well as between the school and its environment. Within the school, there remains a situation in which students may contribute little or nothing to the content, the progress or the evaluation of their learning process. 'Construction', in other words, remains a foreign concept. The relation between schools and their environment (and especially local businesses) usually reflects a divided rather than a shared responsibility (Meijers, 2004).

Even though the principles of competence-oriented education (i.e. involving an authentic learning environment and self-directed learning) have achieved broad support during recent years, the implementation of those principles seems to be more difficult. This resulted in extensive criticism of 'new learning' in the Dutch media in 2005. The criticism has focused on two arguments: the ideological character of the proposed educational renewal; and the idea that 'new learning' would threaten the quality of education, because self-directed learning would demand too little of students. Both criticisms are not without their faults (Volman, 2006). The main point is that the opponents of 'new learning' ignore the problems presently confronting vocational education, namely, too little motivation, high drop-out rates and the limited transfer of theory to actual practice. The criticism is perhaps better understood as an attempt of the middle class to retain the selective function of education in which their offspring optimally profit in terms of status, income and power (Bernstein, 1975). Geurts (2005) argues, therefore, in favour of filling up the present pedagogical vacuum surrounding the future of vocational education. If one wants the relevant parties to become interested in innovation, there will have to be more discussion and debate about pedagogical principles, about vocational education's rich societal responsibility, and about how the parties involved can together ensure real improvements. This debate about the essence of this societal responsibility and how it may be best achieved is presently hardly taking place at all.

6 The Future

The vitality and achievements of schools will, in the future, increasingly depend on the extent to which school management is able to develop and utilize the skills and ambitions of their staff in order to satisfy the wishes and needs of their students and local businesses (the demand side). Until now, all parties have assumed—probably as an automatic reaction to vocational education being supply-oriented—that achieving a more demand-driven education required that schools would retain a passive role. In recent years, therefore, there have been many discussions—in and outside educational circles—concerning how students and social partners could take an active role. More recently, there has been a swell of opinions arguing that schools should take a more pro-active stance (WRR, 2004; Van den Brinke et al., 2005).

The proponents of this pro-active stance argue that allowing the content of education to be solely determined by the needs and wishes of students and regional employers would only lead to a qualitatively emaciated supply. First of all, most students and many employers are not able to articulate their intermediate-term wishes and needs. Secondly, some of the interests of employers and students may not coincide. And, thirdly, neither students nor employers are homogeneous with respect to their needs and wishes. The wishes and needs of students and social partners can therefore only partially determine what a good educational 'supply' would be. For a good balance between supply and demand, the professionalism of the school itself has assumed a central role. The school should not only react to external wishes and needs but also take a more pro-active attitude in the development of qualitatively good vocational education. This conclusion, according to Zee (1997), places the reflective competence of the school management and staff at centre stage.

Whether schools for vocational education ever succeed in becoming career centres will primarily depend on the degree to which school managers and staff get the opportunity to develop a new professional identity, based on reflective competence. In the Netherlands, there exists no stimulating innovation structure or culture with respect to the renewal of vocational education. The main reason for this is that the withdrawal of the central government does not in itself create room for educational innovation. The opposite seems to be more likely the case. Whereas before, power used to be clearly concentrated at the Ministry of Education, those wanting to rejuvenate education are now confronted with various, rapidly changing power cliques, inside as well as outside their school (Geurts, 2004). Inside the schools, those desiring innovation are in the minority and they are confronted with a school management that displays little educational leadership. The project-based innovation policy of the government in such a situation often results in 'educational isolation'. Meijers and Reuling (1999) and Meijers (2001) demonstrated that innovation-oriented teachers were merely tolerated to implement innovative mentoring projects because they were subsidized by the Ministry of Education. The school management was, in those cases, not inspired by a clear vision of the future. That, however, was also not necessary because such a vision was not required in order to be eligible for project funding. Moreover, project subsidies were in addition to regular funding, so that the school was not required to make substantive choices. The consequence was that the innovations implemented by the projects slowly dried up after termination of the funding, because—in addition to the absence of a clear vision—there was hardly any attention devoted to letting those achievements 'sink in' to the rest of the regular educational organization.

Geurts & Corstjens (2007) demonstrate that, in technical and vocational education, some lessons have been drawn from these experiences. In the context of the renewal of higher technical vocational education, an innovation programme has been developed in which a direct connection is made between innovatory activities and school policy. Innovation is seen as an institutional choice and the programme supports this when it contributes to goals determined at the national level. In this particular case, that would be an increase in the number of engineers in the country.

Those interested in educational innovation are also confronted with a battle-ground outside the school walls on which the various interest groups articulate their wishes, without having to relate them to the wishes and desires of others. Because the central government has (partially) withdrawn from this arena, these interest groups have increased their relative influence, such that they cannot easily be ignored. In addition, school managers have never really learned to manifest themselves as a pressure group and to negotiate on that basis. One of the consequences is that school management (and the individual teacher) is confronted with contradictory imperatives. In such a situation, it is understandable that schools generally assume a passive role.

In order to resolve this stalemate, two conditions need to be met: (a) more active support from the central government for the needed structural renewal of vocational education; and (b) the replacement of the incidental project-based policy by the establishment of structural innovation funds. Government support should not take the form of (compulsory) rules and regulations, but rather the (temporary) suspension of rules and regulations so that more opportunity is created for schools to attempt real experimentation. Schools must have the opportunity to generate creative solutions for the most important problems that vocational education is presently facing. The government must, in turn, exercise some patience and not immediately strive for standardization. The structural innovation funds, initially championed by Geurts & Van Oosterom (2000), must not only be financially supported by the government but also by employer organizations and unions. The purpose of this public/private co-operation is to force all interested parties to reach a common agenda with respect to the educational innovations deemed necessary and to subsequently invest in the choices made. The funds must be constructed in such a way that a virtuous cycle of knowledge development can be reinforced. Investments are not only needed for the development and implementation of educational innovations but also for their evaluation, so that all parties can contribute to improved designs in the following phases of innovation.

References

Bernstein, B. 1975. *Class, codes and control*, vol. 3: *Towards a theory of educational transmissions*. London: Routledge & Kegan Paul.

Boer, P. den; Mittendorff, K.; Sjenitzer, T. 2004. *Beter kiezen in het (v)mbo. Een onderzoek naar keuzeprocessen van leerlingen in herontwerpprojecten Techniek in VMBO en MBO*. Wageningen, Netherlands: Stoas.

Brinke, G. van den, et al. eds. 2005. *Beroepszeer: Waarom Nederland niet goed werkt*. Amsterdam: Boom.

Brown, J.S.; Collins, A.; Duguid, P. 1989. Situated cognition and the culture of learning. *Educational researcher,* vol. 18, pp. 32–43.

Bruijn, E. de; Leeman, Y.; Overmaat, M. 2006. Authentiek en zelfgestuurd leren in het mbo. *Pedagogiek,* vol. 26, no. 1.

Collins, A.; Brown, J.S.; Newman, S.E. 1989. Cognitive apprenticeship: teaching the craft of reading, writing and mathematics. *In:* Resnick, L.B., ed. *Knowing, learning and instruction,* pp. 347–61. Hillsdale, NJ: Lawrence Erlbaum.

Duffy, T.M.; Cunningham, D.J. 1996. Constructivism: implications for the design and delivery of instruction. *In:* Jonassen D., ed. *Handbook of research for educational communications and technology,* pp. 170–98. New York, NY: Simon & Schuster Macmillan.

Emst, A. van. 2002. *Koop een auto op de sloop: paradigmashift in het onderwijs.* Utrecht, Netherlands: APS.

Engberts, J.; Geurts, J. 1994. Deregulering en kwaliteit in het BVE-veld. *Mesomagazine,* no. 72, pp. 70–78.

Geijsel, F.; Meijers, F. 2005. Identity learning: the core process of educational change. *Educational studies,* vol. 31, no. 4, pp. 419–30.

Geurts, J. 2001. Herontwerp: een onmisbaar onderdeel van kwalificatiestructuur. *In:* Blokhuis, F.; Visser, K., eds. *Jaarboek kwalificatiestructuur 2001.* Den Bosch, Netherlands: Cinop.

Geurts, J. 2004. Herontwerp beroepsonderwijs: een strijdtoneel. *In:* Breebaart, W.; Geurts, J.; Meijers, F., eds. *Beroepsonderwijs: van opleidingenfabriek naar loopbaancentrum,* pp. 77–121. 's-Gravenhage, Netherlands: Haagse Hogeschool.

Geurts, J. 2005. Zonder engagement geen innovatie. *Profiel,* no. 14, pp. 18–20.

Geurts, J.; Corstjens, H. 2007. Resultaatgericht innoveren: een beloftevol en krachtig vernieuwingsconcept. *Tijdschrift voor hoger onderwijs en management,* no. 4, September.

Geurts, J.; Oosthoek, R. 2004. *Bèta/Techniek verbeteren en vernieuwen: 250 good practices.* Delft, Netherlands: Axis.

Geurts, J.; Pouwels, J. 2001. Naar een gereedschapskist bèta/techniek. *In:* Geurts J., ed. *De menselijke kant van bèta/techniek,* pp. 39–58. Delft, Netherlands: Axis.

Geurts, J.; Van Oosterom, W. 2000. Technisch beroepsonderwijs en unieke competenties: pleidooi voor een leer- en leerlinggerichte transformatie. *Mesomagazine,* no. 112.

Korbijn, A. 2003. *Vernieuwing in productontwikkeling.* 's-Gravenhage, Netherlands: Stichting Toekomstbeeld der Techniek.

Meijers, F. 2001. *Mentoring: van jenne naar jutte: mogelijkheden en onmogelijkheden van mentoring binnen onderwijsleerprocessen.* 's-Hertogenbosch, Netherlands: Cinop.

Meijers, F. 2003a. *Bèta/Techniek in ontwikkeling: de Axisverbeterprojecten bekeken.* Delft, Netherlands: Axis.

Meijers, F. 2003b. *Leren in de praktijk: een onderzoek naar de mogelijkheden tot beroepsvorming.* Zoetermeer, Netherlands: Colo.

Meijers, F. 2004. Het verantwoordelijkheidsdilemma in het beroepsonderwijs. *In:* Breebaart, W.; Geurts, J.; Meijers, F., eds. *Beroepsonderwijs: van opleidingenfabriek naar loopbaancentrum,* pp. 5–77. 's-Gravenhage, Netherlands: Haagse Hogeschool.

Meijers, F.; Geurts, J. 2002. Auf dem Weg zu einem neuen pädagogischen Schwung in der niederländischen Berufsausbildung. *Recht der Jugend und des Bildungswesens,* vol. 49, no. 4, pp. 492–513.

Meijers, F.; Reuling, M. 1999. Schoolloopbaanbegeleiding in een turbulente samenleving. *In:* Lacante, M.; De Boeck, P.; Vander Steene, G., eds. *Meer kansen creëren voor het hoger onderwijs*, pp. 11–34. Diegem, Belgium: Kluwer Editorial.

Meijers, F.; Wardekker, W. 2001. Ontwikkelen van een arbeidsidentiteit. *In:* Kessels J.; Poell, R., eds. *Human resource development: organiseren van het leren,* pp. 301–19. Alphen a/d Rijn, Netherlands: Samsom.

Meijers, F.; Wardekker, W. 2002. Career learning in a changing world: the role of emotions. *International journal for the advancement of counselling,* vol. 24, no. 3, pp. 149–67.

Onstenk, J. 2004. *Herontwerp techniek in het middelbaar beroepsonderwijs.* Delft, Netherlands: Axis.

Sanden, J. van der, et al. 2004. *Naar aantrekkelijk technisch vmbo: resultaten van drie jaar herontwerp.* Delft, Netherlands: Axis.

Schön, D.A. 1983. *The reflective practitioner: how professionals think in action.* Aldershot, UK: Arena.

Severiens, S.; Joukes, G. 2001. *Studenten in het HTO. Verschillen in leerstrategieën, motivatie en positie.* Delft, Netherlands: Axis.

Simons, R.J.; Linden, J. van der; Duffy, T., eds. 2000. *New learning.* Dordrecht, Netherlands: Kluwer Academic Publishers.

Thijssen, J.; Lankhuijzen, E. 2000. Competentiemanagement en employabilitystrategie: een kader voor beleidskeuzes. *In:* Glastra, F.; Meijers, F., eds. *Een leven lang leren; competentieontwikkeling in de informatiesamenleving,* pp. 125–52. 's-Gravenhage, Netherlands: Elsevier.

Volman, M. 2006. Het 'nieuwe leren': oplossing of nieuw probleem? *Pedagogiek,* vol. 26, no. 1.

Wardekker, W.; Biesta, G.; Miedema, S. 1998. Heeft de school een pedagogische opdracht? *In:* Bekker-Ketelaars, N. de; Miedema, S.; Wardekker, W., eds. *Vormende lerarenopleidingen,* pp. 57–67. Utrecht, Netherlands: Uitgeverij SWP.

WRR. 2004. *Bewijzen van goede dienstverlening.* Amsterdam: Amsterdam University Press.

Zee, H. van der. 1997. *Denken over dienstverlening.* Deventer, Netherlands: Kluwer. [Ph.D. thesis.]

Chapter III.10
Facilitating Policy-Learning: Active Learning and the Reform of Education Systems in Transition Countries

Peter Grootings

1 Introduction

Multilateral and bilateral donor agencies increasingly issue declarations that refer to the need to contextualize knowledge and secure ownership of development policies by involving local policy-makers and other stakeholders in policy development and implementation. Yet, policy transfer through imposing or copying (selective knowledge about) policies and models taken from other contexts still dominates the day-to-day operational practices of the donor community (King, 2005; King & McGrath, 2004; Grootings, 2004; Ellerman, 2005).

Development agencies and their staff often act as classical school-teachers who have the right knowledge and know best what has to be done. True knowledge just needs to be transferred to (or made accessible for) partners who do not know the truth (yet) and partners should implement measures that are presented to them as best practice. Local policy-makers and local stakeholders are regarded as passive receivers of knowledge and instruction, who do not possess any relevant prior knowledge and experience. Development or reform is seen as a process of social engineering that will be successful, if properly managed technically. In reality, most reform projects are short-lived because they do not fit in context and there is no local ownership. Reforms are often not sustainable. On the contrary, they tend to come and go with the donors and their agencies.

One reason for the gap between declaration and actual behaviour is a particular—some would say erroneous—understanding, often only implicit, of why and how people learn and develop new knowledge and expertise. There are many other reasons, of course, and some of them may be even more important—at least in the short term—such as the fact that policy assistance is usually part of a large financial aid package and accepting and implementing policy advice are part of the conditions for receiving these funds. But even when conditions disappear, the policy transfer approach is likely to remain dominant.

The standard assumption underlying most traditional learning approaches is that someone (of course, the donor representative) possesses the right knowledge and learners who do not have this knowledge (of course, the local policy-makers and other stakeholders) should simply listen carefully and then do what they are told. Carrots and sticks are available in many variations to provide the incentives to make learners listen and do what their teachers tell them to do. However, carrots and sticks often fail to motivate. The donor's truth has not necessarily been heard (or not properly understood, as the donor would argue), nor has it led to the desired and foreseen action (due to lack of 'political will' or—more positively—insufficient capacities as donors would conclude). New learning theories, instead, argue that learners are more successful in acquiring, digesting, applying and retrieving new knowledge when they have been actively engaged in these processes. Facilitating active policy-learning rather than policy transfer may therefore have better chances to contribute to sustainable reformed systems.[1]

Section 2 below will summarize briefly what active or new learning is about. It will also indicate wider implications of active learning for formal education systems, informal learning and the roles and responsibilities of the main stakeholders, in particular teachers and learners. Section 3 will present the systemic nature of educational reforms in transition countries and the role that international donors play in assisting such reforms. Section 4 will introduce the concept of policy-learning as a translation of the principles of active learning to the field of reform policy assistance. Section 5 will present some practical implications and contradictions of the policy-learning concept. It will argue for a different role for donor agencies and consultants based on similarities between the roles of teachers and policy advisers in facilitating learning. Section 6 will suggest that knowledge-sharing should be an integral aspect of policy-learning.

2 Active Learning

Engaging students in successful learning has always been a key problem for educationalists since the development of formal education systems providing standardized obligatory school-based educational programmes. Some teachers manage to survive the system and some students as well, but many do not. There has been talk about bad systems, bad schools, bad teachers, bad learning environments and bad students. Sometimes attention was simply focused on the good students, while the bad ones were left to their own devices or were given shelter in special lower-rated forms of education and training. In many countries vocational education and training has been the second—or last—choice for students who failed *'la route royale'*. Hence, there have always been debates about causes, consequences and possible solutions. In looking for solutions, countries have increasingly tried to borrow from more successful countries.

The policy debates have been coloured by the dominant understanding of why, what, where and how people learn and how people can be motivated to learn at all. The traditional behaviourist and cognitive approaches on which much of standardized (formal and non-formal) education has been based have assumed that learning is basically a steady accumulation of discrete entities of knowledge and skills that can be presented to learners as if filling empty vessels.[2] Hager (2004, p. 411) has pointed at five further assumptions that follow from this understanding of learning:

- There is one best way of learning;
- Learning is essentially an individual activity;
- Learning which is non-transparent is inferior;
- Learning centres on the stable and the enduring;
- Learning is replicable.

In contrast, by seeing learning as a continuous—and highly selective—process of exchange between individuals and their environment, constructivist approaches argue that people give their own meaning to information. They do so based on what they already know and framed by how they have become accustomed to see the world around them. They select and retain what is relevant for them. In so doing they construct their own understanding of reality as a basis to intervene and act. Different people therefore may give different interpretations to the same thing, may retain different aspects and may act differently on the basis of the same information. Constructivists also argue that: (a) there are many ways through which people can learn, apart from someone else passing on pieces of expert knowledge (Verloop & Lowyck, 2003); (b) learning is foremost a social activity (Lave & Wenger, 1991; Wenger, 1998); (c) there is a lot of tacit learning taking place which is not easy to categorize and demonstrate, but which is there when needed (Schön, 1983); (d) learning is dynamic and very much context-bound; and (e) good learning therefore depends on meaningful learning environments (Kolb, 1984; Simons, van der Linden & Duffy, 2000). In combination, these insights are now known as new learning or active learning. While there are currently many attempts to introduce—often on an ad-hoc basis—active learning techniques in traditional educational settings, a more holistic active learning approach has developed into something like a new paradigm. Based on the principles of active learning, several countries, including the Netherlands, are now reforming parts of their public education systems.

Obviously, much of what is now receiving attention as new learning has been around for decennia in the writings of school innovators, such as Dewey, Montessori, Froebel, Steiner, Freinet and others, and has been practised in schools that follow their pedagogical approaches. Until recently, attempts that combined different learning outcomes and alternative ways of learning have remained marginal to mainstream education and training. Most public education became characterized by the single model of expert teachers and trainers passing on bit-by-bit their knowledge and skills to pupils and students who knew nothing or at least not enough. The emergence of an increased interest for the new learning paradigm during the 1990s is the combined result of fundamental changes occurring in the labour market, which have done away with employment security and created a need for lifelong learning (OECD, 1996). Moreover, declining public budgets have also contributed to attempts to make education more efficient and effective. Neo-liberal policy agendas on the left and the right have placed the responsible and autonomous citizen back on stage again. Changes in organization of work within companies also build on responsible workers able to foresee and prevent rather than to react ex-post or too late. The overall economic and political climate of the 1990s has been very receptive for active learning insights. Active learning is more than a scientific approach to learning.

New insights and research results from a whole range of disciplines that are dealing with the question of how people learn and retain new information have provided scientific support for a different understanding of learning.[3] These developments coincide on the importance given to specific criteria for learning outcomes, attention for alternative ways of achieving these learning outcomes and developing instructional models that teachers and trainers may apply when organizing learning processes. The new learning approaches give a more active role to learners in managing and shaping their own learning processes based on the understanding that good learning cannot be achieved when learners remain passive receivers of information and instructions.

The active learning paradigm stresses the need for new criteria for and new kinds of learning outcomes. For reasons of employability in a world characterized by fast-changing job requirements and growing insecurity, learning outcomes should not just be more relevant at a given moment, but they should be durable, flexible, meaningful, generalizable and application-oriented (Simons et al., 2000, pp. 1-2). These criteria could also easily refer to traditional kinds of learning outcomes, in particular if one is concerned about propositional knowledge and technical skills and their transferability in time and context.

New kinds of learning outcomes have become important as well. These include the ability to learn, think, collaborate and control. People should be able to adapt quickly to changing situations, be able to cope well with continuing uncertainty, and know where and how to find the information that they need to deal with the challenges of their work and life situation.[4] Such regulative or meta-learning outcomes have also become important given the sheer amount of new information that is becoming available at ever-faster speeds with new generations of information and communication technologies. This makes it more relevant to consider what people can do with information instead of just having the information available as such (Simons et al., 2000). The need to cope with new (social or key) competences has been a major driving force behind curriculum and educational reform in many countries since the early 1990s. But while initially these reforms have concentrated on the new 'what' as additions to existing curricula and standard approaches, it is now increasingly understood that traditional ways of organizing learning are unable to deal with these new learning insights and requirements.[5] Therefore, the key issues in current educational discussions are not so much about the 'what' but about the 'how' questions: how can new learning outcomes be achieved and how to secure that learning outcomes comply with the new criteria?

From the point of view of the educational sciences, attention paid to new learning outcomes follows from a better understanding about how experience and information are represented in memory and about the kind of learning activities that learners apply. Three different ways of representation are normally distinguished:

- *Episodic* representations are based on personal, situated and affective experiences.
- *Conceptual or semantic* representations refer to concepts and principles and their definitions.

- *Action* representations refer to what can be done with episodic and semantic information.

People differ in terms of their preferred modes of representations. Because conceptual and semantic forms of representation have traditionally been regarded of a higher (intellectual) order, theoretical knowledge has been seen as more important than practical knowledge—learning with the head being superior to learning with the hands. The traditional curriculum therefore consisted of (unrelated) theoretical subjects plus—in vocational streams—practice periods to apply such theoretical knowledge. For modern educationalists, however, good learning outcomes mean rich and complex memory representations whereby there are strong interrelated connections between the different ways of representation. They also argue that these connections can start from any of the three different modes of representation. Some people master theory by starting with practical problems, while others may be more successful when learning the other way around (Simons et al., 2000, p. 3; Driscoll, 2000, ch. 8; Pieters & Verschaffel, 2003).

As mentioned earlier, a reformulation of expected learning outcomes is only part of the story. For educational professionals, the key question is how they can promote new learning outcomes through organizing appropriate learning processes and developing instructional strategies. The new learning theories argue that learners are more successful in acquiring, digesting, applying and retrieving new knowledge, skills and attitudes when they have been actively engaged in these processes. Active involvement, co-operation with other learners and real-life contexts also help to increase the motivation to learn, which in turn makes it easier for people to take responsibility for their learning into their own hands. In combining all this, active learning therefore provides strong learning environments and produces good learning outcomes. The search is now to develop operational approaches to make active learning principles work in practice.[6]

Active learning also implies considerable changes in the roles that teachers and students play in education. With growing attention to active learning, there is a shift of responsibility from the teacher to the learner. The teacher becomes more of an organizer and facilitator of learning processes than the transmitter of expert knowledge or skills, whereas the learner is asked to actively participate in identifying learning needs and in managing the process of acquiring new knowledge. Teachers and trainers still need good knowledge and skills in technical domains, but the ways in which to make these accessible for learners change. Teachers have to be able to identify what learners already know and how they learn best and then to guide them to find the information that can increase their knowledge further. In terms of structure of the education system, active learning insights give strong arguments for creating open and flexible pathways in education, providing a rich variety of learning environments, and recognizing prior and informal learning outcomes (Kok, 2003; Simons et al., 2000; Driscoll, 2000; Verloop & Lowyck, 2003; Grootings & Nielsen, 2005; OECD, 2005).

This new understanding of learning has considerable implications for the organization of formal education (structures and contents), for informal and non-formal learning (recognition and validation) and the role of policy-makers, teachers, students and other stakeholders in education. The active learning paradigm is of relevance for any learning situation where people seek to acquire new knowledge and understanding in order to be able to act competently in a changing context. In the following section I will explore what active learning means for policy-makers in transition countries when faced with reforming their education and training systems.

3 Educational Reforms in Transition Countries

Transition countries are very diverse but all have in common that they are undergoing a fundamental change in their main societal institutions, including the education system. They are seeking to change from centralized authoritarian societies with some form of State-planned economy towards more democratic societies with a market-based economy. For that reason they can be called 'transition' countries. However, contrary to the way the term transition has often been used, nobody really knows where the transition will lead to. One might, for instance, be seeking the general characteristics of democratic market-based economies, but there are no blueprints that countries can simply apply. All modern market economies differ in important aspects from each other and none of them resembles the textbook case. What will come out of the reform process in each transition country will depend to a large extent on how local policy-makers and other stakeholders manage to use the resources that their countries have built up in the past, including the inherited physical and human infrastructures of their education systems (Grootings, 2004).

Transition countries differ from developing countries in the sense that they used to have well-established and—in the recent past—effective and successful education systems. These have become impoverished as a result of continued underfunding and have increasingly lost relevance for a new labour market context: the issue here is reforming and transforming obsolete systems rather than building new ones from scratch.

The reforms in transition countries are *systemic,* as they imply changes that are both *system-wide* and *system-deep*. Reforms are system-wide, in the sense that they require changes in all aspects of the institutional arrangements of the countries. For education and training this means that all the building blocks of the education system need to be reviewed and revised: from delivery, provision, assessment, funding, quality assurance, administration and governance up to research and development. But changes are also system-deep since they require the development of new relations between education and training on the one hand, and other evolving institutions in society on the other. In transition countries these are, in particular, the relations between schools, the labour market and private enterprises. This asks for fundamentally new definitions of the roles of the main stakeholders in education and training, as well as for changes in established working procedures for education and training organizations. These are complicated processes as all these other institutions are also undergoing systemic changes. Vocational schools, for example, have now to educate and train for open and uncertain labour markets and no longer for agreed numbers and assured jobs in hosting companies that were basically interested in hoarding labour.

However, in most countries labour markets are still under development and private sectors are only gradually emerging. Teachers who have always been told how many students they would have and what they should teach them are suddenly in a situation where there is nobody anymore to tell them anything. Developing new roles and relationships is for individuals essentially a process of learning new knowledge, skills and attitudes in order to become competent in a changing context. Reforming a national education system is a collective learning process for all stakeholders (Grootings, 1993).

A major challenge for transition countries facing systemic reforms of their vocational education and training systems is to build up and strengthen their own capacities to formulate reform policies, and not just the capacity to implement imposed or borrowed policies. Reforms of vocational education and training in transition countries (and indeed any kind of major reform in any country) will only be successful and sustainable if policy development, formulation and implementation are firmly based on broad ownership and fit within existing institutions. The concept of policy-learning reflects this understanding. Policy-learning emphasizes not just involvement but the active engagement of national stakeholders in developing their own policy solutions. It is based on the understanding that there are no universally valid models that can simply be transferred or copied from one context into another. At most there is a wealth of international but context-specific experience in dealing with similar policy issues that can be shared.

The discussions about new learning are relevant for education and training reforms in transition countries. They provide key criteria for successful reform and reform assistance. Educational reform can only be sustainable if reform policies are owned by local stakeholders and are embedded in the context of the country. Educational reform is really about stakeholders being motivated to learn new ways of how to organize education and training systems—system wide and system deep. Learning is about developing new roles for all stakeholders at all levels in all the building blocks of the system. The challenge for donors and aid agencies, therefore, is not to sell prefabricated 'what' solutions but to find the appropriate answer to the question 'how to help people help themselves?' (Ellerman, 2004, 2005).[7]

4 Policy Reform is Policy-Learning[8]

Applying active learning insights to a review of vocational education and training (VET) reform experiences in transition countries further supports the need to think in terms of policy-learning.

Such a review indicates first of all that VET reforms in transition countries have often depended heavily on the presence and contribution of international donors.

There is a mix of positive and less-positive experiences. Especially in the initial phases of transition (but sometimes also long after), donors have played a key role in developing awareness of the need for VET reforms, influencing the reform policy agenda and providing resources for strategy development and implementation. Often, however, donors or their experts in the field have showed little familiarity with specific national transition contexts and no understanding for the knowledge, experience, views and expectations of people involved in education and training. Very often also, they have entered partner countries with standardized one-size-fits-all packages of assistance. Capacity-building was usually focused on developing appropriate capacities to implement what donors thought would be necessary.

In turn, many national policy-makers, certainly in the initial stages of transition (but sometimes also long afterwards), were more interested in receiving funding than in policy-making. They were convinced that the key problem was the impoverished state of their educational infrastructures. Moreover, they have often been unable to assess the fitness of donors' proposals for best practice for the institutional context of their own VET systems.

This combination of donor and recipient expectations and behaviour has created problems of sustainability for many donor-supported reform initiatives. With the departure of the donor the reform usually came to a halt. With the limited resources that donors can make available, practically nowhere have system-wide changes been started. Much of the earlier assistance to VET reform in the partner countries was guided by principles of policy-copying. The guiding principle on the donor side seems to have often been: we know your future—and your past is irrelevant. Because international assistance has underestimated the relevance of institutional context, policy-copying has not contributed to system-deep VET reforms either. Stakeholders and policy-makers in transition countries have not been able to learn much about their new roles in a changing VET system—although they may sometimes have become experts on the systems of other countries.

We may not know the details of future VET systems in partner countries, but from international experience some of the basic characteristics that modern VET systems should develop have become increasingly clear. They should be: (a) decentralized; (b) responsive to labour markets and learner needs; (c) transparent; (d) well-resourced (e) providing flexible and open pathways for young and adults; and (f) have a capacity to innovate and adapt to changing conditions. All modern VET systems around the world are trying to become like that! But there is no best practice of how to organize such systems, neither in developed market economies nor in transition countries. There are many good—and perhaps also a couple of bad—context-bound practical examples. Moreover, such examples not only refer to what countries wanted to achieve in their reforms but also to how they have tried to change their systems. How do you make good use of such knowledge and experience about policy objectives and strategies if policy-copying does not work?

The following example may further illustrate the challenges. The policy-learning approach requires an intensified focus on how to organize policy-learning platforms and environments in the countries so that a critical mass of key actors and stakeholders gradually develop VET reform policy understanding and competence. So far, since policy transfer and policy-copying approaches have been dominant in the reform debates in most countries, the concept of stakeholders has been very much influenced by the model—and indeed the ideology—that was taken to be transferred or copied. In vocational education and training reform, a key issue is the involvement of employers, private industry, or—in EU language—social partners. The view is that in a market-based economy governments cannot continue to be the sole responsible authorities for vocational education and training. The essence of systemic reform—adaptation of vocational education and training to free educational choice, private enterprise and labour markets—requires involvement of the enterprises where the graduates will have to find employment.

The reality of the reform process in many transition countries, however, has created a whole series of interesting contradictions. Whereas private sector or social partner involvement was presented as a *conditio sine qua non* for any market-based vocational education and training system, in practice governments have faced a huge problem of disinterest on the side of the private sector (employers and unions alike) to be involved at all. There are many reasons that can explain this situation, but one is the lack of representative organizations at the national level. Another is the absence of any professional capacity among social partners to deal with vocational education and training matters in a reform context. The result was, and often still is, that enlightened governments have to include the interests of the private sector into their own policy thinking. Thus, reform policy remains dependent on a few political reform champions. Another problem is the absence of a professional civil servant community inside or an educational support infrastructure outside the ministry apparatus.

Public educational authorities in transition countries therefore remain the driving force behind vocational education and training reform—certainly at the national level. The involvement of stakeholders representing industry is not something that can be built on from the start, but has to be developed as part of the reform process itself. Interestingly enough, if trade unions have been involved at all in national education reform policy debates, these have often been the teachers unions and understandably—given the state of public budgets and mounting pressures to decrease public spending on education in many transition countries—they have been more interested in defending the social and material status of their membership than in discussing the contents of educational reform. As a result, teachers, also through their unions' behaviour, have become generally regarded as major obstacles to reform. This, in turn, may sometimes even have led to the development of policies that sought to break the power of the teacher and trainer community instead of engaging them more positively.[9]

More recently, however, there is an increasing awareness that teachers and trainers must be included among the critical mass of stakeholders in the reform. This is, most of all, the result of a better understanding of why so many educational reforms all over the world have gone wrong in the past. Exclusion of teachers as stakeholders from the reform process has frequently led to national reform policies failing to trigger any changes at all inside educational institutions and classrooms. Teachers and trainers have now become recognized as crucial agents in making reforms work in their professional capacity of organizers of learning. It has also been understood that involving teachers is not just a matter of informing them so that they know what is expected of them. Nor is it only a matter of training so that they are taught how the new policies must be implemented. As professionals, teachers principally know best what will work in the specific context of their own school and classroom environment, including responding to the particular learning needs of the student population that they have to cater for. Their expertise therefore is an important source for translating general policy initiatives into very divergent real-life contexts. A better understanding of why many educational reforms have not worked has therefore not only implications for the implementation of reform policies, but impacts on the very process of policy development and formulation.

This, in turn, reflects the fact that the current reforms in vocational education and training are very complex development processes that hardly compare to the traditional reform conceptions with their clear stages of preparation, formulation, implementation and evaluation. This is especially true of reforms in transition countries that seek to combine systemic reforms with structural changes and modernization of contents and approaches. Such reforms are not one-off social engineering events designed by external experts but on-going change processes set within a broadly agreed reform agenda. The reform agenda can be quite radical but requires further operational detailing, based on local innovation processes. Reform strategies have to build on the commitment of teachers and trainers working inside their school organizations. It is because of this that teachers who are actively engaged in local innovation and experimentation are an important source of expertise for national policy-makers. Such an understanding of reform puts policy-learning, capacity-building and policy advice at both national and school-levels in a new perspective and, at the same time, with considerable more urgency than before.[10] Traditional top-down or bottom-up strategies have become too simplistic and are insufficient to make reforms work. Policy-learning as a process requires a continuous interaction and dialogue between national and local partners—vertically, as well as among the various local initiatives horizontally.

5 Facilitating Policy-Learning in Practice

A policy-learning approach may be the appropriate response to some of the key challenges related to the VET reform processes in transition countries. Policy-makers and other key stakeholders should be enabled to learn to develop their own policies. But, in practice, there are considerable obstacles to facilitating policy-learning. These stem from the many tensions between 'what' and 'how' in the relationship between experts and novices. Several of these obstacles are known from the search for operational approaches to make active learning work in classical education settings. The key issue remains how a learning situation can be established where the expert acts as a learning process facilitator and the novice can be stimulated to engage actively in learning. However, others obstacles pertain to the field of reform policy development.

Understanding the context limits or institutional fit is not easy and it is a challenge that both local policy-makers and international advisers share. While donors usually do not have a good understanding of the local context (and often do not even speak the language), it can also not simply be assumed that local policy-makers understand the characteristics of their own VET system. It is difficult to question what has always been normal and the rule. Moreover, international consultants do not always understand that the advice they provide is perhaps firmly rooted in the institutional context that they come from themselves; they are often not well informed about policies and systems in other countries. How can local policy-makers assess the fitness of what is sold to them as the latest international trend? How can international advisers properly assess prior knowledge and contextualization of new knowledge? Policy-makers are also under stress to come up with quick solutions. Their political mandate does not leave them much time. Advisers are bound by the financial and time resources that the donors have reserved for their projects. Also, the ownership issue raises some problems, especially when this is restricted to a few co-operative national policy-makers and—simply because of the design of the donor project—leaves out the vast majority of teachers and trainers in schools (Grootings & Nielsen, 2005). How can international advisers facilitate learning under such conditions?

The basic assumption underlying the concept of policy-learning is not so much that policies can be learned but that actual policies are learned policies. Learning is not simply the transfer of expert knowledge or behaviour from one person to another, but rather the acquisition of understanding and competence through participation in learning processes. However, policy-makers are not only policy-learners. They also have to act, and acting on the political scene, especially in environments that are undergoing radical change such as in transition countries, does not always leave a lot of space and time for careful and gradual learning. They have to engage in daily political decision-making and, depending on their position in the system, may often have to give priority to active participation in political power struggles.

On the other hand, policy-makers engaged in systemic reforms are in need of new knowledge which very often contradicts established knowledge and routines. For policy-makers, therefore, because they are under pressure to act, learning is more than merely a cognitive process: learning is practice. Their learning is situated learning as it is an integral and inseparable aspect of their social practice. Lave & Wenger (1991) argue that all learning is situated learning and, more particularly, 'legitimate peripheral participation in communities of practice'. Novice learners learn best when they are engaged in a community of more expert learners; during the learning process they become more competent themselves and move from the margin to the centre. Policy-makers in transition countries can be regarded as highly motivated novice learners and policy-learning can be facilitated by letting them participate in relevant communities of practice (Wenger, 1998). Such communities of practice could be created by bringing together policy-makers from different countries that have gone through or are undergoing reforms of their education systems. International and local policy analysts, researchers, advisers and other practitioners could be part of such communities as well.

However, policy-makers in transition countries may be seen as 'novices' in terms of knowledge and expertise concerning the development of modern education systems in market economies, but they are also 'experts' as far as their own country context is concerned. Similarly, international policy advisers may perhaps be the 'experts' with respect to educational policy-making in developed economies, but they are often 'novices' in terms of knowledge about the particular context of the partner country. Neither local stakeholders nor international advisers really know what 'fits' with regard to modern education policy in a partner country's context. The community of practice concept therefore needs to be further developed to take these differences properly into account in learning experience with high levels of uncertainty. Since old and new knowledge relate to different contexts, there are different peripheries and centres and even those who are closer to the centre remain learners themselves.

6 Policy-Learning through Knowledge Sharing

Reforming education and training systems in transition countries implies combining old and new knowledge in changing contexts for both local stakeholders and international advisers. Policy-learning is not just about learning the policies that other countries have developed, but rather about learning which policies can be developed locally by reflecting on the relevance of other countries' policies. Policy-learning in this sense can only happen when there is information and knowledge available and shared. The principal role of donors would be to facilitate a reform policy-learning process by providing access to such information and experience and by enabling a critical reflection on their relevance. However, donors and their staff cannot do their learning facilitation role well if they do not recognize that they themselves are also learners in the same policy-learning process.

VET reform policy development, seen as VET policy-learning, would have to use knowledge-sharing to enable decision-makers from partner countries to learn from—and not simply about—VET reform experiences from elsewhere for the formulation and the implementation of their own reform objectives. Knowledge-sharing would also enable donors and international advisers to better understand the institutional context and history of the partner country. For them, in becoming familiar with local knowledge, it will also be easier to appreciate and value the expertise that partners bring into the reform process.

International donors and their policy advisers would have to play a role similar to the one a modern teacher is supposed to play: not that of the expert who knows it all and simply passes it on; rather the one who recognizes problems, does not know the solutions yet, but organizes and guides knowledge-sharing and in so doing develops new knowledge for all involved in the learning process. Policy-learning therefore can only happen in partnership.

In policy-learning partnerships, the timing and sequencing of knowledge sharing is of major importance if donor assistance is to have a real impact on local ownership and contextual fit, and if it is to create the necessary motivation, commitment and capacities to sustain reforms. This would ask specific competences from policy advisers as they have to be able to judge where they themselves and their partners are in moving from the periphery to the centre of the community of practice. It would also require a rethinking of the classical development instruments, such as workshops, study visits, technical assistance, pilot projects and so on, with a view to developing strong learning environments for policy-learning to happen.

Policy-learning is sharing experience from the past to develop knowledge for the future. It is also about sharing knowledge from abroad and knowledge that is locally produced. Therefore, it is about developing new knowledge as well. It contributes not only to creating more coherent system-wide reforms that fit, but also facilitates system-deep reforms of VET systems as it enables all stakeholders to learn new roles and develop new working routines. It will be a challenging task to develop concrete approaches that can make policy-learning, which is based on principles of active learning theory, work in practice.

Notes

1. Others would argue that good governance, the participation of civil society, the fight against corruption and sound legal frameworks are more important. This chapter will simply pay attention to the learning aspect that has been neglected so far.
2. See, for a critical presentation of these various learning theories, Driscoll, 2000.
3. These include, besides psychology and educational science (Driscoll, 2000), also brain research (OECD, 2002).
4. These are also called social or key competences.
5. In many English-speaking countries educational reform has in fact taken the form of establishing an assessment system that could measure learning outcomes, assuming that these could be the result of very different learning processes and arguing subsequently that the nature of these learning processes therefore would not be relevant at all. The 'black box' approach to learning has been a typical characteristic of economist approaches to education and training.
6. See the various contributions in Simons et al. (2000) for an account of experiences from different domains.
7. Ellerman, 2005, has summarized this challenge into three 'dos' (starting from present institutions; seeing the world through the eyes of the client; respect autonomy of the doers) and two 'don'ts' (don't override self-help capacity with social engineering and don't undercut self-help capacity with benevolent aid).
8. What follows is a summary of more detailed reviews in Grootings, 2004.
9. Such as through moving from so-called input control (based, amongst other things, on teacher qualifications) towards output control mechanisms based on occupational and educational standards with neglect of the educational and learning processes that would lead to achieving the standards. In such cases, the assessment of standard attainment has frequently replaced education and training as such.
10. Experience from some countries, such as the Netherlands, also points at the need to have additional co-ordinating and support institutions at the sector, regional or school-type level. Such is the role that associations of secondary and higher vocational schools, and sector-based expertise centres are playing. Specialized local, regional and national research and development institutions in turn support these. In other words, reform, innovation or development infrastructures require more than national stakeholders and teachers in schools.

References

Driscoll, M.P. 2000. *Psychology of learning for instruction*, 2nd ed. Boston, MA: Allyn & Bacon.

Ellerman, D. 2004. Autonomy in education and development. *Journal of international co-operation in education*, vol. 7, no. 1, April.

Ellerman, D. 2005. *Helping people help themselves; from the World Bank to an alternative philosophy of development assistance.* Ann Arbor, MI: The University of Michigan Press.

Grootings, P. 1993. VET in transition: an overview of changes in three East European countries. *European journal of education*, vol. 28, no. 2, pp. 229–40.

Grootings, P., ed. 2004. *Learning matters: ETF yearbook 2004.* Turin, Italy: ETF.

Grootings, P.; Nielsen, S., eds. 2005. *The role of teachers in VET reforms: professionals and stakeholders—ETF Yearbook 2005.* Turin, Italy: ETF.

Hager, P. 2004. The competence affair, or why vocational education and training urgently needs a new understanding of learning. *Journal of vocational education and training*, vol. 56, no. 3, pp. 409–33.

King, K. 2005. *Development knowledge and the global policy agenda. Whose knowledge? Whose policy?* Edinburgh, UK: University of Edinburgh, Centre of African Studies.

King, K.; McGrath, S. 2004. *Knowledge for development? Comparing British, Japanese, Swedish and World Bank aid.* London: Zed Books.

Kolb, D.A. 1984. *Experiential learning: experience as the source of learning and development.* Englewood Cliffs, NJ: Prentice Hall.

Kok, J.J.M. 2003. *Talenten transformeren: over het nieuwe leren en nieuwe leerarrangementen.* Tilburg, Netherlands: Fontys Hogescholen.

Lave, J.; Wenger, E. 1991. *Situated learning: legitimate peripheral participation.* Cambridge, UK: Cambridge University Press.

Organization for Economic Co-operation and Development. 1996. *Lifelong learning for all.* Paris: OECD.

Organization for Economic Co-operation and Development. 2002. *Understanding the brain: towards a new learning science.* Paris: OECD.

Organization for Economic Co-operation and Development. 2005. *Teachers matter: attracting, developing and retaining effective teachers.* Paris: OECD.

Pieters, J.M.; Verschaffel, L. 2003. Beinvloeden van leerprocessen. *In:* Verloop, N.; Lowyck, J., eds. *Onderwijskunde: een kennisbasis voor professionals*, pp. 251–84. Groningen/Houten, Netherlands: Wolters-Noordhof.

Schön, D. 1983. *The reflective practitioner: how professionals think in action.* New York, NY: Basic Books.

Simons, R.J.;, van der Linden, J.; Duffy, T., eds. 2000. *New learning.* Dordrecht/Boston/London: Kluwer Academic Publishers.

Verloop, N.; Lowyck, J., eds. 2003. *Onderwijskunde: een kennisbasis voor professionals.* Groningen/Houten, Netherlands: Wolters-Noordhof.

Wenger, E. 1998. *Communities of practice: learning, meaning and identity.* Cambridge, UK: Cambridge University Press.

Section 4
National Initiatives for Reengineering Education for the New Economy

Joshua D. Hawley

College of Education and Human Ecology, Ohio State University,
Columbus, United States of America

Chapter IV.1
Overview: Regional Reviews of TVET

Joshua D. Hawley

1 Introduction

Technical and vocational education and training (TVET) is often a national or even a local issue, much more so than other sub-sectors of the education system. Unlike primary and secondary education, there are few large United Nations' interventions that concentrate on technical and vocational education. Moreover, because TVET serves employers and the labour market, schools and teachers are often more concerned with student completion and placement in work than movement into higher education.

The current United Nations' efforts (the Millennium Development Goals—MDG) to support primary and secondary education are numerous, and are designed to dramatically improve enrolment, the completion rate and the quality of basic education. While the United Nations development goals have implications for schooling after lower secondary education, the degree to which they require government action for upper secondary in general and TVET in particular remains in debate. In the MDG report for 2006, for example, the authors reported that all countries, with the exception of Sub-Saharan Africa, were making substantial progress towards attaining basic education for all.

However, the point remains that for countries to compete in the world economy their young people must be trained beyond basic education, and that technical and vocational schooling needs to play an important role in this process (Lewin, 2004; United Nations, 2006).

The modest efforts that the United Nations have undertaken to support TVET, such as the UNESCO-UNEVOC International Centre, are less operational in focus, in comparison to the Millennium Development Goals. UNESCO's recent work in chronicling the enrolment statistics for TVET are commendable, but there are no major international efforts to support improvements to TVET that I know of and that work on a global basis.

There remain, however, significant regional efforts. The Asian Development Bank has maintained a substantial lending practice in Central and South-East Asia, in particular concerning TVET (Asian Development Bank, 2002). Europe's CEDEFOP and ETF have consistently worked across countries to support their vocational education sectors. The Latin American emphasis on technical and vocational education

R. Maclean, D. Wilson (eds.), *International Handbook of Education for the Changing World of Work*, DOI 10.1007/978-1-4020-5281-1_IV.1,
© Springer Science+Business Media B.V. 2009

continues to be an important part of the conversation about the school-to-work transition (Castro, Schaack & Tippelt, 2000; CINTERFOR/ILO, 2001). A number of agencies, most importantly the World Bank, have supported substantial analysis of the experience in Sub-Saharan Africa in recent years, leading to a renewed interest in investments in TVET in this region (Johanson & Adams, 2004; Ziderman, 2003).

This section reviews the current work on TVET regionally, offering a discussion of a number of critical empirical issues that the sub-sector faces. We begin with a discussion of the role of the international organizations that often deal with TVET, continue with a discussion of regional political engagement with TVET, and end with a critical review of the findings from the chapters in this section.

2 The Status of TVET and the Role of International Organizations

Over the years, the literature on international development and comparative education has shone a spotlight on the critical role that development institutions play. In a 1994 paper, McGinn (1994) pointed out the increasing importance of multinational organizations and companies in national development. Castro (2002) describes the particular role of the Inter-American Development Bank (IADB) and the World Bank in terms of educational policies, focusing specifically on presenting the trade-off between support for educational reform and the use of measures to target changes in education locally. Studies by Karen Mundy have refined both our understanding of the role of these institutions and the specific place they have in the policy-making process (Mundy, 1998; Mundy, 2002; Mundy & Murphy, 2001).

The roles of other international institutions, such as UNESCO and the ILO, or even the European Union's Leonardo da Vinci Programme, have received less attention in the academic literature. While we know that regional development banks, such as the African Development Bank and the Asian Development Bank, have critical roles in lending to vocational education and training, there are relatively few academic studies tracking their involvement and reflecting on their impact on national systems in developing countries. An exception is the study by Chabbott (2002), which describes the specific role of organizations such as UNESCO in establishing the World Conference on Education for All. Additionally, in a paper for the Asian Development Bank, Adams (2002) describes the evolving role of that agency in the international development field, focusing on the development of new policy directions in education.

While those who study the evolution and functioning of the international agencies do not often deal specifically with vocational education and training, the international organizations themselves have frequently focused on this topic, and vocational education and training has long been a critical area for debate about the relative importance of education for employment in national development (Middleton, Ziderman & Adams, 1993).

As mentioned earlier, four agencies (the IADB, the World Bank, the ILO and UNESCO) have recently developed documents outlining policy options for the future of vocational education and training. These papers vary in their stage of production and the formality of the policy directions they explore. The ILO/UNESCO document, 'Revised Recommendation Concerning Technical and Vocational Education', offers the most formal statement, providing recommendations about the structure and function of technical and vocational education (ILO/UNESCO, 2001). It was formally adopted by the governing councils of UNESCO and ILO in 2001. The IADB strategy paper, 'Vocational and technical training: a strategy for the IDB' was approved by the IADB Board of Governors in 2000. Finally, the World Bank has issued a number of studies on the future of vocational education and training in Africa. The summary document, 'Vocational skills development in Sub-Saharan Africa' was produced in 2002 and summarizes the results of a number of reports from consultants on various aspects of vocational education and training in Africa. This paper, unlike some others, is not a formal policy document issued by the World Bank (Johanson & Adams, 2004).

The reports vary in their level of detail. All agencies review current research on vocational and technical education internationally and make recommendations for the larger community of policy-makers. All of the reports reflect current trends in public policy for international vocational education and training, although the IADB and the World Bank's reports are primarily concerned with Latin America and Africa respectively. They each deal with the larger issues of secondary vocational education, privatization and the role of training within enterprises.

2.1 Secondary Vocational Education

Research on the role of development banks has frequently become heated, particularly around policy questions that have special relevance to the vocational education and training sector. For example, in the aftermath of the 1995 and 1999 Education Sector papers from the World Bank, the *International journal of educational development* published special issues discussing the implications of the policy provisions emphasized. In the area of vocational and technical education, for instance, the 1995 Education Strategy reiterated the general distrust of secondary level vocational education as a strategy to support sustained development (World Bank, 1995). In the original 1991 study, the World Bank advocated moving away from secondary vocational schooling (World Bank, 1991). However, scholars like Jon Lauglo and Kenneth King have questioned this wholesale abandonment of secondary-level preparation. Based on studies of individual countries, they state that secondary vocational schooling has its place, provided it is adapted to the needs of the labour market (King & Martin, 2002; Lauglo, 1996). Indeed, secondary vocational education is still the predominant form of vocational skills training in most developing countries. Lauglo & Maclean's (2005) recent book on the topic contains some important information on the continuing debate around which form of vocational schooling to invest in, focusing particularly on matching the level of economic development with the form of vocational schooling.

International agencies are moving slowly away from a commitment to secondary vocational education and towards the broader goal of workforce or human capital development. Except for the UNESCO/ILO policy statement, the specific documents that the organizations produce stay away from vocational education as preparation within the classic French/American model of school-based vocational education (Castro, Schaack & Tippelt, 2000). The UNESCO/ILO statement reminds us that vocational education and training is intended for young people over 15 years of age and concerns 'all forms and aspects of education that are technical and vocational in nature'. This broad statement includes occupational preparation in its vision, but is also linked explicitly to larger social and economic goals, such as poverty alleviation and sustainable development. Likewise, vocational education and training is supposed to facilitate lifelong learning. The ILO/UNESCO statement is probably most similar to the view of 'career and technical education' in the United States, stating that technical skills and vocational competencies should be taught within the context of general education.

The policy statements by the World Bank and the IADB differ from those proposed by ILO/UNESCO. For instance, the IADB states that 'well-focused training is investment in human capital' and offers a 'balance between general and vocational skills.' Unlike those proposed by ILO/UNESCO, the IADB does not define at what age training should begin to be offered by governments, nor does it take a stand relative to the occupational orientation of the vocational and technical education. In fact, there seems to be a general pattern in the review of country-level experiences in IADB documents away from a form of secondary-level vocational education that is explicitly occupational in nature. The IADB, however, remains committed to supporting vocational education and training, as recent lending in Belize and other countries has shown.

The World Bank statement is more formal, offering up definitions for technical education, vocational training and skills development. As the report states: *technical education* is training for technicians; *vocational training* is provision of crafts; and *skills development* is practical competencies, know-how and attitudes (Johanson & Adams, 2004). The emphasis on skills development echoes the larger push in the educational community to provide individuals with basic skills, particularly training in the 'new basic skills' (Murnane & Levy, 1996). The particular goals that the World Bank report outlines include a focus on using vocational education in the public sector, but only when the private sector is unable to provide these services or there are insufficient incentives to support training for disadvantaged groups. This fits into the broader emphasis in World Bank policy to promote private-sector involvement.

2.2 Privatization and the Relationship with Industry

One of the core issues for development agencies is the emphasis on privatization of public services. As Klees (2002) has discussed, the Washington Consensus in the 1980s led to a general focus in World Bank lending on supporting the movement of public goods to the private sector. There is, as Klees discusses in detail, a belief that the private sector can and should take over any State services that they are able to run efficiently; the role of the government should be seen as the provider of services only as a last resort, and only in situations where such services cannot operate efficiently. Moreover, there is a general view that government needs to encourage cost-sharing through user fees. For example, even if services are provided through governmental institutions, they need to share the costs of service provision with the parents and students.

The issue of privatization as applied to vocational education and training is particularly complex. Economic justification for supporting education draws a sharp line between general skills training and specific skills training (Becker, 1993; Johanson, 2002). Right from the start, scholars of human capital theory supported compulsory schooling with the view that students should master skills that are generalizable and that lead to higher education or potential employment in many fields. In contrast, training is often in specific technical areas, and therefore is not considered appropriate for government investment. This dichotomy is debated frequently by scholars in vocational education, as well as more broadly in the economics of education. In practice, it is exceedingly difficult to decide where to draw the line. Many governments do support training at the corporate level in significant ways and, indeed, scholars have shown that this commitment to training has led to sustained economic growth in developing Asian countries (Ashton et al., 1999). In a recent study, we see that, on average, the returns to education in Asia are higher than those in Latin America, although it is difficult to conclude that this is because of differences in the allocation of resources at the secondary education level (Sakellariou, 2005).

One of the critical design issues for leaders in vocational education and training is how to relate to the other educational sectors. The classic dilemma for a large ministry of education in a developing country, for example, is whether vocational education and training needs to be governed through the secondary education system or can be established as a separate department. As Herschbach & Gasskov (2000) point out, these kinds of questions are located at the 'macro-level' of educational planning and raise issues that are social and political, as well as technical in nature. This is not simply an administrative issue, and the larger question of partnerships with other educational organizations, businesses and social partners receives a lot of attention from development agencies. For example, the most important distinguishing characteristic of high-profile systems in Europe is the relationships established by business and other social partners in education and training (Culpepper, 2003; Lasonen & Rauhala, 2000). The quality, as well as the social acceptance, of vocational education and training in Germany is largely due to the substantial relationships with business associations and industry.

International agencies have long supported the German, or dual system, model of vocational education and training in principle, but support at the project level has varied. Many of the projects from the Asian Development Bank in recent years have emphasized supporting secondary-level vocational education and training systems, while the support in African nations has shifted more towards enterprise-based training (Asian Development Bank, 2002; Johanson, 2002). In general, international agencies are continuing to support the position that vocational education and training comes after basic or primary schooling. Only one report—ILO/UNESCO—supported keeping vocational education and training at the secondary level outright.

It is offered as an option for secondary education students at the upper secondary level. The World Bank report by Johanson seems to favour keeping an option of secondary level vocational education and training, but restates the opinion that 'regular vocational schools have to be redirected to areas that are in greater need of skilled labor' (Johanson, 2002).

One area of general agreement concerns the relationship with industry. All of the reports emphasize the importance of including vocational education and training as an option within employment. The agencies differ on the direction of the policy advice, however. For instance, UNESCO/ILO supports co-operative training through employers, while the World Bank and the IADB emphasize employers subsidizing training through training levies. One area of increasing importance is the use of vocational education and training aimed at adults working within the informal sector. This approach to training is particularly critical as labour markets evolve within developing countries. Many nations have established training programmes in entrepreneurship (Johanson, 2002; King & McGrath, 1999).

A third policy issue raised by the development agencies with special relevance to vocational schooling is the continuing effort to encourage enterprise-level training through government policy. Recent studies from Gill, Fluitman & Dar (2000) and Johanson & Adams (2004) provide some basis for stating that governments have increasingly used incentives, such as tax levies, to promote training. As Ziderman (2001) describes, as firms (especially small and medium-sized firms) under-train, governments need to play an increasingly active role in promoting training. However, Ziderman goes on to show that national training funds need to be carefully monitored for sustainability of financing and proper controls should be in place to ensure that funds are spent on appropriate training activities. Ziderman also reports that training levies have become increasingly important in financing training within firms. While there are problems with the use of levies, they give the government a strong role in directing training among firms. These programmes are used in the United States as well, often combined with reductions in unemployment insurance taxes (United States of America. Government Accounting Office, 2004).

Unlike the traditional German system of apprenticeships, current models rely on market mechanisms to increase the skills levels of out-of-work youth, informal sector workers or in-service workers needing re-tooling. Firms are given State funds through tax systems that collect a portion of payroll taxes. Firms can then carry out training interventions (Herschbach & Gasskov, 2000). This model could be problematic from a theoretical perspective. As Ziderman (2001) points out, for large firms the strategy often pays off, but does not necessarily benefit small or medium-sized companies. Moreover, if firms are simply using the funds to provide specific skills training, the State is then subsidizing activities that firms could undertake on their own. To address this concern, many countries (and states in the United States) carefully monitor spending under these levy systems (Moore et al., 2003). However, the tax levies are subject to intense political conflict over the allocation of resources (United States of America. Government Accounting Office, 2004).

Many of the loans granted by agencies are focused on upgrading workers' skills or improving training quality, rather than providing entry level vocational education and training. For example, Johanson (2002) points out that 93% of on-going World Bank projects included informal sector training—a major increase over projects carried out in the 1990s. Moreover, in 43% of the current World Bank projects, they have emphasized training funds. In general, international agencies are continuing to support the position that vocational education and training comes after basic or primary schooling. The IADB, similarly, stresses that model training must include enterprise-based schooling. These increasing connections with firms are seen as a way to remove rigidities in vocational education systems. Interestingly, the three organizations emphasize national vocational qualifications as a strategy to improve the curriculum and training within firms.

2.3 Curricular Focus of Vocational Education and Training

The reports also describe the role of national government in certifying the curriculum according to international agencies. The agencies generally refocused vocational education and training from occupational training to a hybrid of academic and vocational instruction. As the ILO/UNESCO report described, the curriculum for vocational education should lead to interdisciplinary skills that can be used in several occupations. This focus on generalizable skills is largely in response to the evidence that employment and occupational training are often not strongly related (Hawley, 2003; Neuman & Ziderman, 1999). Moreover, the World Bank and IADB reports emphasize the importance of integrating basic skills training and vocational preparation. The emphasis on basic skills seems to be grounded in the perception that vocational education and training is best suited to individuals who have completed primary and secondary education. Certainly in the United States, vocational education reform has resulted in fewer occupational courses in high school and more focus on academic training (Silverberg et al., 2004). Furthermore, curricula must be integrated with business needs and offer competency-based instruction.

There is similarly a restatement of the growing importance of competency-based training. While individuals are supposed to master technical skills, these skills are intended to be embedded within national vocational qualifications or other standards which are certified through industry. As the World Bank report describes, national vocational qualifications help to remove the rigidity of the skills training systems because they allow training to be connected more formally with employers' skills demands (Johanson & Adams, 2004). National qualifications frameworks allow countries to integrate training within firms, leaving government to focus on certifying the competencies that individuals master. These systems are modularized, enabling more flexibility in the delivery of training, and can be designed to meet short-term as well as long-term skills needs (Johanson & Adams, 2004).

3 Regional Strategic Efforts in TVET

Despite the largely scattered scholarship on the role of vocational education internationally, there has been a continuing interest in using TVET to solve strategic economic and equity issues. While countries have undeniably moved students from vocational to general secondary schooling, TVET as a whole remains a critical part of the infrastructure that educational planners use to meet labour shortages. TVET is simultaneously seen as a tool to enable poorer and marginalized youth and young adults receive skills training that will allow them to pursue productive employment. Because of these dimensions, TVET has remained on the agenda of regional and national government agencies. The regional agencies have played a surprisingly important role in places like Europe, where funding from successive programmes has contributed to national investment in TVET within both member and non-member States of the European Union.

4 Overview of the Contributions

The chapters in this section are quite varied in their emphases and the depth in which they deal with TVET issues globally. They represent an important catalogue of largely government-led interventions in this often neglected area. The chapters are summarized by three frames: the truly regional studies that compare TVET across a geographical area; the country level studies that attempt to connect with the regional approach to TVET; and finally a few global studies that were completed as part of this review of regional aspects of TVET. The more in-depth chapters in the first section deal with a review of the reaction by Baltic States to the dissolution of the Soviet system and an important piece on the changes in TVET policy from the European Union.

The second group of studies in this review includes a range of chapters that really are single country-level studies, but have strong regional implications. These are interesting to a more limited audience of TVET scholars and practitioners with specific geographical interests.

Lastly, there are several studies that take a decidedly global look at TVET policy. They include studies of the relationship between TVET and the agricultural sector, and a cross-national paper exploring the possibility of extending the International Baccalaureate Organization curriculum to TVET at the upper secondary level. Finally, there is a study of how the larger TVET systems have shifted in recent years.

We start with the regional studies. The chapters in this sub-section deal with a range of TVET issues, from traditional studies of the evolution and current capacity of vocational education in Africa and Asia, to a look at how the regional policies from the EU government have changed from the da Vinci Programme to the current Lifelong Learning Programme.

IV.2 To Vocationalize or Not to Vocationalize? Perspectives on Current Trends and Issues on TVET in Africa, by Moses O. Oketch

The study by Oketch, which is based on document analysis and interviews/data collection in seven African nations, paints a broad-based view of TVET. The pattern that emerges is one of fractured TVET systems on this continent.

IV.3 TVET in the Asian Region: Issues, Concerns and Prospects, by P.P.G. Lionel Siriwardene and Muhammad Ashraf Qureshi

Similarly, Siriwardene and Qureshi provide a limited view of the state of TVET in Asian countries, reviewing basic problems with the economic transition to services and the burden that overcoming these challenges places upon the State.

IV.4 Transforming TVET Systems with the CPSC in the Asia and Pacific Region, by Man-Gon Park

Park offers an analysis of regional TVET in the Asia and Pacific region. It provides some details about the changing context for TVET in Asia and the Pacific and the challenges facing governments.

IV.5 European Action Programmes for Lifelong Learning, by Johanna Lasonen

Lasonen provides a welcome review of the state of TVET policy under European Union (EU) governance. Going back to the Leonardo da Vinci Programme, the author describes the goals of the programme, and the broad engagement with EU member states. The paper offers a glimpse also at the new TVET policy, the Lifelong Learning Programme, illustrating the integration of financial assistance for higher and vocational education into traditional TVET fields.

IV.6 VET in the Baltic States: Analysis of Commonalities and Differences of Reforms in Estonia, Latvia and Lithuania, by Frank Bünning and Berit Graubner

Bünning and Graubner provide a review of VET in the Baltic States after the collapse of the USSR. The most important discussion is of how the different nations responded in unique ways to the dissolution of the Soviet system, and put in place a similar array of youth, business and adult training services. It is particularly important to note that Lithuania was ahead of the trend on re-organizing its VET systems.

IV.7 Education and Training Needs of Rural Communities: A Situational Analysis of Selected Villages in Fourteen Provinces of Fiji, by Paula Cavu, Isimeli W. Tagicakiverata, Seveci Naisilisili and Viliame Rabici

The first study in the country-level cases by Cavu et al. describes a survey they completed of the training needs for adults in rural areas of the Fiji Islands. Using a standardized protocol, they offer a descriptive analysis of the kinds of training that men and women are interested in following.

IV.8 Social Partnership in Vocational Education and Training in Lithuania: Challenges and Perspectives, by Lina Kaminskienė

Moving from the Pacific Islands to Europe, Kaminskienė offers a study of the evolution of social partnerships in Lithuania, and more generally what steps the government has taken to strengthen TVET since 1990. The paper offers a clear statement of the differences between Soviet labour-driven relations with TVET institutions and the current push to create a structure of social partnerships to develop vocational and technical schools.

IV.9 Integrating Education and Work: The Status of Vocational Education in Brazil by Lucília Regina Machado and Carlos Roberto Jamil Cury

Interestingly, Machado and Cury provide a brief review of the legal and institutional framework for TVET in the largest nation in the Latin American region—Brazil. This study provides some orientation to the legal foundation for technical and vocational education and reviews the size and composition of the institutional structures that make up the TVET system. This is useful for readers who need a quick review of the structure of this important TVET system, but does not answer the larger question about how the legislative changes in the 1990s led to steep declines in TVET enrolments, nor what the evaluation evidence shows about the impact of these changes on Brazil.

IV.10 China's Higher Technical and Vocational Education: Development and Reform, by Jing Mi and Aihua Wu

Jing Mi and Aihua Wu offer a summary of China's TVET system, and an up-to-date review of the changes facing this large country with its rapidly growing economy. The review lacks an evaluative focus, and instead focuses fairly broadly on describing the institutional structure, legal framework and enrolments.

IV.11 The Adoption and Adaptation of the Work-Team Concept in Urban Thai Workplaces, by Chitrlada Burapharat

Burapharat offers a theory-based view from the perspective of adult education on the use of work teams within Thai organizations. This is a strong study in that it places the use of work teams in the context of Thai culture. It is one of the few studies based on data collection from firms in this section.

IV.12 Globalization of the Labour Culture in the Republic of Korea: What 'Tripartite Relations' Mean for Workers, by Phoebe Moore

Moore offers a theoretically rich discussion of the impact of globalization and the problems brought by the East Asian economic crisis on labour relations in the Republic of Korea, and to an extent on TVET in this country. Through textual and socio-cultural studies, she provides some analysis. The result is a rich study for TVET scholars, as it brings out a theoretical literature that is only infrequently related to vocational subjects.

IV.13 Involvement of Labour-Market Partners in TVET in the Russian Federation, by Olga Oleynikova

Oleynikova offers a glimpse at the state of post-Soviet relations between employers and TVET. She uses illustrative cases from a range of locations around the Russian Federation to describe and analyse the current state of work on Russian employer involvement in TVET.

IV.14 Strengthening TVET to Achieve Lifelong Learning for All: Historical Snapshots and Recent Initiatives in Myanmar, by Naing Yee Mar

Mar's essay is an excellent example of a good country case study placed in a regional context. The chapter provides a history of Myanmar's education sector, an update of the current TVET priorities and reforms, and places these in the larger regional context. The major issue with this study is the relatively superficial treatment of the issues that Myanmar is dealing with in trying to provide TVET in a country where the economy has stagnated since the late 1980s.

IV.15 Technical and Vocational Education and Training and Rural Development, by Lavinia Gasperini

Gasperini makes a strong restatement of the traditional connections between TVET and the agricultural sector. The primary contribution of the paper is to raise the important point that TVET is often biased towards the service and manufacturing sectors. The primary problem with this perspective is that both adult education and vocational education have often developed targeted programmes. However, assuming that the rhetoric of TVET is geared away from rural development does not mean that all countries focus on this dimension.

IV.16 An International TVET Programme Development by the International Baccalaureate Organization, by Monique Conn

Conn offers an extremely interesting study which expands the important IBO programmes into TVET. Using case studies of programmes in Finland and Canada, the author shows how students in upper secondary schooling can incorporate TVET and a regular college preparatory curriculum. This is one of the first efforts I have seen that favours fundamentally improving the academic outcomes of vocational students, rather than focusing more on the occupational outcomes.

IV.17 A Profile of TVET in the Asia and Pacific Region: A Survey of Progress, Innovations and Promising Practices, by Chris Chinien, Elspeth McOmish, Mohan Perera and Alex Chinien

Finally, Chinien, McOmish, Perera and Chinien offer a review of a global survey of TVET systems. Using data from responses in a national basis, they are able to illustrate how the structure and focus of TVET has shifted under a globalized world.

5 Conclusion

The topic of regionalism in TVET is an important one. In recent years, TVET overall has been facing a major shift as governments reinvest in many regions, and are faced with the broad need to restructure their education systems to meet the needs of new economic and social realities. The chapters in this section offer a somewhat scattered view of regionalism in TVET, but in several cases begin what might be seen as a trend towards cross-national research. In that light, I would offer several important research ideas for the future that come in part out of a reading of these chapters.

5.1 Regional Political Entities and TVET

Regional political entities, such as ASEAN or the European Union, play markedly different roles in education policy overall, and in TVET specifically. The EU is a very active player and the scholarship in this section shows the marked evolution of EU-sponsored TVET activities. However, we know relatively little about other regional entities such as ASEAN. This is unfortunate as the regional political organizations play an increasingly important role in structuring intergovernmental policies and programmes.

5.2 TVET and Secondary Education

In general, there is a bias toward using TVET in secondary schooling. This results from generations of technically skilled workers being trained in this manner. The traditional view that TVET should be focused at the level of secondary schooling needs to be rethought. There are some policies, such as those of the Millennium Development Goals, that require governments to expand secondary education and potentially offer new vocational options. However, as economies have changed, the importance of TVET at the post-secondary and enterprise levels has come to the fore. The role of secondary-level TVET should be the subject of more research.

5.3 Diversification and TVET

One of the most productive areas of TVET scholarship are studies that explicitly raise the academic mission of TVET, offering to use vocational schooling as a way to build the capacity to teach both academic and vocational skills. I found some of the scholarship in this section avoided this important issue. Therefore, one of the pressing scholarly avenues should focus on the divide between vocational and academic instruction. How can they be integrated? What changes in the curriculum can be made to increase the quality of academic schooling in vocational education?

References

Adams, D. 2002. *Education and national development: priorities, policies, and planning.* Manila: ADB. (Education in developing Asia, vol. 1.)

Ashton, D. et al. 1999. *Education and training for development in East Asia: the political economy of skill formation in newly industrialized economies.* London: Routledge.

Asian Development Bank. 2002. *Policy on education.* Manila: ADB.

Becker, G.S. 1993. *Human capital.* New York, NY: Columbia University Press.

Castro, C.d.M. 2002. The World Bank policies: damned if you do, damned if you don't. *Comparative education,* vol. 38, no. 4, pp. 387–99.

Castro, C.d.M.; Schaack, K.; Tippelt, R., eds. 2000. *Vocational training at the turn of the century.* Frankfurt am Main, Germany: Peter Lang.

Chabbott, C. 2002. *Constructing educational development: international development organizations and the World Conference on Education for All.* New York, NY: Routledge Falmer.

CINTERFOR/ILO. 2001. *Modernization in vocational education and training in the Latin American and the Caribbean Region.* Montevideo: CINTERFOR/ILO.

Culpepper, P.D. 2003. *Creating co-operation: how states develop human capital in Europe.* Ithaca, NY: Cornell University Press.

Gill, I.S.; Fluitman, F.; Dar, A. 2000. *Vocational education and training reform: matching skills to markets and budgets.* New York, NY: Oxford University Press.

Hawley, J.D. 2003. Vocational-technical schooling and occupational matching in Thailand: differences between men and women. *In:* Osman-Gani, A.; Akaraborworn, C.T., eds. *Second International Conference on Human Resource Development in Asia: national policy perspectives.* Bangkok: National Institute of Development Administration.

Herschbach, D.R.; Gasskov, V. 2000. Financing workforce preparation programs. *In:* Herschbach, D.R.; Campbell, C.P., eds. *Workforce preparation: an international perspective,* pp. 74–88. Ann Arbor, MI: Prakken Publications.

International Labour Organization; UNESCO. 2001. *Revised Recommendation concerning technical and vocational education.* Geneva, Switzerland: ILO; Paris: UNESCO.

Johanson, R. 2002. *Sub-Saharan Africa: regional response to Bank TVET policy in the 1990s.* Washington, DC: World Bank.

Johanson, R.K.; Adams, A.V. 2004. *Skills development in Sub-Saharan Africa.* Washington, DC: World Bank.

King, K.; Martin, C. 2002. The vocational school fallacy revisited: education, aspiration and work in Ghana 1959-2000. *International journal of educational development,* vol. 22, no. 1, pp. 5–26.

King, K.; McGrath, S., eds. 1999. *Enterprise in Africa: between poverty and growth.* London: Intermediate Technology Publications.

Klees, S.J. 2002. World Bank education policy: new rhetoric, old ideology. *International journal of educational development,* vol. 22, pp. 451–74.

Lasonen, J.; Rauhala, P. 2000. Vocational education and training in the Nordic Countries. *In:* Herschbach, D.R.; Campbell, C.P., eds. *Workforce preparation: an international perspective,* pp. 96–102. Ann Arbor, MI: Prakken Publications.

Lauglo, J. 1996. Banking on education and the uses of research: a critique of World Bank priorities and strategies for education. *International journal of educational development,* vol. 16, no. 3, pp. 221–33.

Lauglo, J.; Maclean, R., eds. 2005. *Vocationalization of secondary education revisited.* Dordrecht, Netherlands: Springer.

Lewin, K.M. 2004. *Beyond primary education for all: planning and financing secondary education in Africa.* (Paper presented at the Donor Conference on Secondary Education in Africa, Vrije Universiteit Amsterdam, Centre for International Co-operation.)

McGinn, N.F. 1994. The impact of supranational organizations on public education. *International journal of educational development,* vol. 14, no. 3, pp. 289–98.

Middleton, J.; Ziderman, A.; Adams, A.V. 1993. *Skills for productivity: vocational education and training in developing countries.* New York, NY: Oxford University Press.

Moore, R.W. et al. 2003. *Training that works: lessons from California's Employment Training Panel Program.* Kalamazoo, MI: W.E. Upjohn Institute for Employment Research.

Mundy, K. 1998. Educational multilateralism and world (dis)order. *Comparative education review,* vol. 42, no. 4, pp. 448–78.

Mundy, K. 2002. Retrospect and prospect: education in a reforming World Bank. *International journal of educational development,* vol. 22, no. 5, pp. 483–508.

Mundy, K.; Murphy, L. 2001. Transnational advocacy, global civil society? Emerging evidence from the field of education. *Comparative education review,* vol. 45, no. 1, pp. 85–126.

Murnane, R.; Levy, F. 1996. *Teaching the new basic skills.* New York, NY: The Free Press.

Neuman, S.; Ziderman, A. 1999. Vocational education in Israel: wage effects of the VOCED-occupation match. *Journal of human resources,* vol. 34, no. 2, pp. 907–32.

Sakellariou, C. 2005. *Heterogeneity in the returns to education: multi-country evidence from Latin America and East Asia.* Washington, DC: World Bank.

Silverberg, M. et al. 2004. *National Assessment of Vocational Education: final report to Congress.* Washington, DC: U.S. Department of Education.

United Nations. 2006. *The Millennium Development Goals report, 2006.* New York, NY: United Nations.

United States of America. Government Accounting Office. 2004. *Almost half of states fund employment placement and training through employer taxes and most coordinate with federally funded programs.* Washington, DC: GAO.

World Bank. 1991. *Vocational and technical education and training.* Washington, DC: World Bank.

World Bank. 1995. *Priorities and strategies for education: a World Bank review.* Washington, DC: World Bank.

Ziderman, A. 2001. *Financing vocational training to meet policy objectives: Sub-Saharan Africa.* Washington, DC: World Bank. (Africa Region Human Development Series.)

Ziderman, A. 2003. *Financing vocational training in Latin America.* Washington, DC: World Bank.

Chapter IV.2
To Vocationalize or Not to Vocationalize? Perspectives on Current Trends and Issues on TVET in Africa[1]

Moses O. Oketch

1 Introduction

Forty years ago, Philip Foster exploded the vocational school myth in Africa. He argued that 'it might be more fruitful to encourage small-scale vocational training schemes closely associated with the actual ongoing developments and quite divorced from the formal educational system' (Foster, 1965, p. 154). He even recommended that 'the burdens of vocational training should be shifted to those groups who are actually demanding skilled labour of various types' (p. 158). Many writers have continued to address the issue of vocationalization in various contexts (see e.g. Heyneman, 1979, 1986, 1987, 1997; Neuman & Ziderman, 2003; Gill & Leigh, 2004; Hawley, 2003; Middleton, Ziderman & Adams, 1993; Blaug, 1973; Pscharopoulos, 1997; Green, 1998; Ngome, 1992; King & Martin, 2002; Wilson, 2001, 2005; Wolf, 2002) and many of the arguments in support of technical and vocational education and training continue to be based on the assumption that vocational training is more useful for job entry than general education. This assumption may correspond to the vocational education curriculum of twenty years ago, but it is wrong today. Nowadays, vocational education is seen as training for future training; not as a way to facilitate job entry, but as a way to facilitate vocational-specific skills over a lifetime. Essentially, the content and organization have changed. But has it in Africa? In this chapter, I reflect on this issue.

2 A Brief History of TVET Policy in Africa

Psacharopoulos (1997) argued that TVET has been called upon to solve a multitude of problems, some of which he advises would have 'better been dealt with by other types of policies, completely unrelated to education and training' (p. 386). He identifies the following as the most common of these objectives that have driven TVET policies (and, it can be added here, not least in African countries):

1. Vocational education and training can overcome youth unemployment.
2. Instilling technological knowledge, based on what happened during the British industrial revolution, followed by Germany and Japan. It is a common belief that

R. Maclean, D. Wilson (eds.), *International Handbook of Education for the Changing World of Work*, DOI 10.1007/978-1-4020-5281-1_IV.2,
© Springer Science+Business Media B.V. 2009

economic progress depends heavily on technological know-how. It therefore logically follows that the first step is to expand vocational and technical education.

3. Vocational education and training offer some hope to the academically less-able students who are not able to progress through the general education system.
4. As everyone cannot be trained for top-level jobs, vocational education and training can provide the much-needed middle-level technicians and artisans.
5. In its role in equipping young people with skills needed in the labour market, vocational education and training can reduce unemployment leading to higher incomes and reduced poverty.
6. Vocational education can provide the skills needed in an increasingly globalized world where manufacturers outsource production to countries with lower labour costs.

Middleton et al. (1993, p. 54) summed up these factors in a way much more relevant to contemporary African experience when they argued that general opinion still favours the idea that 'vocational education and training improves attitudes toward skilled, manual work, and thus diverts at least some young people from seeking the white-collar jobs that are in increasingly short supply'. The problem, however, is that most of these objectives connected to TVET policy indicate that it is primarily aimed at occupational education and is terminal in nature. Initially, it was associated with colonial educational policy in colonized parts of the world, not least, in Africa (Wilson, 2005). It became undesirable in post-independence Africa once Africans were in charge of educational policy. What had been viewed as suitable for Africans by colonial education authorities on the basis of Africa's economic production structure was not viewed the same way by Africans themselves. They (the Africans) considered it as a 'second-class' education (Wilson, 2005). Not surprisingly, the first conference of African States on education held in Addis Ababa in 1961 clearly set the tone in placing priority not on TVET but on expanding (academic) secondary and tertiary education (UNESCO, 1961), with a view to quickly developing the African manpower needed to replace colonial personnel and other expatriates in the civil service.

However, less than a decade after gaining independence many governments reverted to supporting vocational education and training on the basis of the shrinking number of civil-service jobs and to encourage young people to remain in the rural areas where they could contribute to the economy by participating in agriculture. A sudden surge in the numbers of young people completing primary education and the unmet demand for secondary education left TVET as a viable response by governments to solving what was considered a mismatch between education and the labour market. Massive support from international assistance agencies, particularly the World Bank, was also directed towards establishing and expanding public vocational education and training systems, and to legitimize pre-employment training as an important component of public education and manpower needs (Middleton et al., 1993, p. 4; Psacharopoulos, 2006, p. 330). Yet, despite its subsequent appeal to policy-makers, who in 1961 had had little enthusiasm for it, and the momentum gained by arguments in support of TVET both nationally and internationally, Philip Foster raised a 'warning flag' as early as the 1960s over government involvement in massive expansion of TVET. The evidence from field research did not match the assumptions about the benefits anticipated of TVET. Young people did not want TVET and when they joined TVET, they expected it to be an avenue to higher levels of education. Moreover, using vocational and agricultural labour to punish students who did not perform well in (academic) class activities or for misbehaviour within African schools only worsened their perceptions about TVET (Wilson, 2005). Furthermore, those who had undergone TVET were not only less well paid, but often stayed un-employed much longer than their counterparts who had gone through general education. Foster's work added international controversy to what was already a dilemma and a subject of political debate within the circles of African Ministers of Education.

Mark Blaug followed later in 1973 with the argument that vocationalization cannot be a remedy for educated unemployment. It cannot prepare students for specific occupations and reduce the mismatch between education and the labour market. He went on to observe that, in general, individuals could tell that academic streams promised higher wages and a better livelihood than vocational education (Tilak, 2002). For those opposed to TVET, it was an opportunity to brand it as 'useless' education, associated with those with less aspiration for higher education and better paying jobs, clearly reflecting the misgivings expressed by Psacharopou-los (1997). In the villages of Africa, parents did not feel much pride—if any—when their children only managed to enter a TVET stream. Yet, such strong arguments against full acceptance of vocational education and training have to date not deterred African governments from pursuing vocational education and training programmes in public education systems. Some countries may have momentarily slowed down their emphasis on elaborate training systems following these debates but, going by the evidence of subsequent years, vocational education and training seem to have maintained their inherently powerful, but also paradoxical, appeal in Africa's edu-cation systems.

3 Current Trends and Issues in TVET in Africa

Research evidence and analysis coming from Africa show that TVET in Africa has failed if measured by the key objectives mentioned by Pscharopoulos (1997) and which have underpinned TVET policies in the continent. If anything, the demand for academic and higher levels of education has risen in spite of growing unemploy-ment and under-employment among the educated in several African countries (see e.g. Atchoarena & Delluc, 2001; King & Martin, 2002; Oketch, 2000, 2004). Yet, governments still maintain faith in TVET, even when there is compelling evidence that it can be a wasteful public investment. Psacharopoulos (1997) has argued that

TVET has failed because it is a simple solution to a complex set of problems, with too much weight placed on intuitive logic rather than empirical evidence. Here, I follow up this argument, but ask what has changed? The following questions guide the inquiry.

- How is TVET defined and what is the TVET framework today?
- At what level does TVET start in formal education?
- What is the purpose of TVET and has that purpose changed over the past twenty years?
- Who are the providers of TVET?

3.1 Procedure

An opportunity to respond to some of these questions presented itself in the summer of 2004. The UNESCO Institute for Statistics (hereafter UIS) commissioned a small study undertaken by myself and two colleagues at the Institute of Education, University of London, whose main aim was to assess the extent and limitations of the data and knowledge about global provision of TVET and, based on the findings, to identify steps that could be taken to improve international data (Green et al., 2004). Initial and background investigations were undertaken based primarily on the analysis of UIS data in the *Global education digest, 2004* (GED) and other data sets supplied to the team in raw form by UIS, but a number of issues needed follow up with representatives in selected countries in order to obtain clarification. The UIS data, however, enabled the research team to purposefully identify countries for follow-up interviews (UNESCO Institute for Statistics, 2005).

3.2 Sample

Thirty countries were selected for follow-up via telephone interviews. These countries represented a range of types: (a) of regions (eight countries in South and East Asia; three countries in Central Asia; nine countries in Africa; five countries in Latin America; three Arab States; and two Pacific States); (b) of levels of economic/industrial development; (c) of population size; and (d) of the degree of comprehensiveness identified by the team in the GED country data returns. Once the selection was agreed by UIS, relevant individuals within each of the selected countries were contacted through e-mail. The exchanges introduced the team, explained the nature of the investigation and requested telephone interviews. An interview guide questionnaire with forty-two items, some requiring short yes/no answers and others prompting discussion/explanation, was attached.

Seventeen countries responded positively. The following seven African countries were among them: Botswana, Egypt, Ghana, Senegal, Seychelles, Tunisia and

Zimbabwe. The telephone interview sessions lasted roughly an hour and, while based on items on the questionnaire, generally addressed issues related to the four questions stated above. Where further clarity was needed, e-mail exchange was used.

3.3 How is TVET Defined and what is the TVET Framework Today?

In the seven African countries, technical and vocational education and training included and referred to a range of learning experiences that were viewed as relevant to the world of work and which occurred in a variety of learning contexts, including educational institutions and the workplace. It includes learning designed to develop the skills for practising particular occupations, as well as learning designed to prepare for entry into the world of work in general (Green et al., 2004). There was no mention, however, of training designed for re-entry into the world of work. Much of the learning is occupational and terminal. TVET is not purposefully provided to act as a foundation for entry into further education either. TVET is mostly initial vocational training (IVT) undertaken by young people in diversified secondary schools and viewed as preparation for employment. Where there is any continuous vocational training (CVT) undertaken by adults, it only relates to specialized government ministries or departments needing such skills. Not surprisingly, there is a lack of schemes aimed at *re-skilling* and *up-skilling* as a prerequisite to engage in global manufacturing and/or respond to economic globalization.

3.4 Levels of Entry into TVET

In general, the education systems in Africa are divided into four levels as follows (Atchoarena & Delluc, 2001):

1. Primary education, lasting six to eight years;
2. Lower-secondary education, lasting three to four years;
3. Upper-secondary education, lasting two to three years;
4. Higher education lasting about four years.

The emphasis placed on TVET at each of these levels varies from country to country depending on the importance that each country assigns to it. In some cases, TVET forms a separate system that parallels the general education system with its own institutions, teachers, programmes and curriculum (Atchoarena & Delluc, 2001). In such cases, the issue is mostly on the proportion of academic content in the courses offered and the level of specificity in the vocational courses on offer, what Wilson (2005) refers to as 'convergence between academic and vocational education'. In many cases, however, TVET is offered alongside general education in integrated schools forming a dual-tracked school system. Table 1 provides a summary

Table 1 The features of TVET in selected African countries

Country	TVET features
Botswana	• TVET starts from senior secondary school but TVET proper is offered at post-secondary institutions for those who graduate from senior secondary; • There is less clarity on the level of specificity or distinction between TVET and general education at the secondary level.
Egypt	• TVET is offered from junior secondary level but TVET proper begins at senior secondary; • TVET forms a separate system that parallels general education with its own teachers, programmes and curriculum.
Senegal	• TVET begins at senior secondary level upwards, but there are problems deciding levels of specificity in the TVET and general curriculum.
Seychelles	• TVET courses are offered at post-secondary level only. Both junior and senior secondary provide general courses.
Tunisia	• TVET is offered at junior secondary, but there is also TVET at senior secondary and at tertiary levels.
Zimbabwe	• TVET is offered at post-secondary level for those who do not qualify for higher education admission. However, 12% of the content at the secondary level has vocational content
Eritrea, Ethiopia, Malawi, Namibia, Niger, South Africa	• TVET provision in secondary level is over 2% of the total enrolment.
Botswana, Côte d'Ivoire, Burkina Faso, Morocco, Togo, Tunisia, Uganda	• TVET provision at secondary school level is between 5 and 9% of the total enrolment. In these countries, TVET now includes reasonable levels of general content (i.e. a balanced level of specificity).
Egypt, Cameroon, Congo, Gabon, Mali	• TVET's share of secondary total enrolment is over 10%.
Algeria, Côte d'Ivoire, Mali, Morocco, Senegal, Tunisia	• TVET retains a fairly large amount of general content.
Botswana, Egypt, Ghana, South Africa, Zimbabwe	• TVET retains a fairly large amount of specificity.

Source: Author's interviews with representatives of selected countries, supplemented with information obtained from Atchoarena & Delluc, 2001.

of some of the key features of TVET in the countries studied, as well as in some other African countries.

3.5 Levels of Participation in TVET

TVET generally occupies a small and marginal position in the school systems of most African countries. While in some cases specialized ministries have been created with the aim of strengthening and/or streamlining the development of TVET throughout the entire education system, for the most part, it does not receive the same emphasis that general education does. At the secondary level, where much of TVET specificity is meant to develop, only a tiny percentage of those enrolled can be classified as pursuing TVET streams. However, problems of data collection at national level and lack of consistency across countries make comparative analysis difficult (also see Atchoarena & Delluc, 2001). There are generally problems resulting both from data collection and classification that make it difficult to analyse the precise nature of TVET provision in different countries. However, broad differences between French-speaking and English-speaking systems are more easily observable than the finer distinctions in countries within each of these groupings.

A further problem results from the fact that much of the private provision and, indeed, some of the public TVET provision are not captured by the national data-gathering exercises. Overall, there seems to be a decline in the share of TVET as a percentage of enrolments in secondary education (Table 2). One explanation offered by Atchoarena & Delluc (2001, p. 39) for this is uncertainties about the effectiveness of TVET in matching the requirements of the labour market. An alternative explanation is an expanded secondary education that is offering general education. Still, it is unclear in those cases where secondary education has not expanded whether more young people are opting to join post-primary but non-secondary institutions, such as community polytechnics or family apprenticeships.

Despite the problems with data collection, Atchoarena and Delluc have grouped countries into three categories. First are those countries where the provision of TVET in secondary enrolments is less than 2%. Among these countries are Eritrea, Ethiopia, Malawi, Namibia, Niger and South Africa. Second are those countries where the proportion of TVET enrolment in general secondary education over the past few years has been between 5 and 9%. Examples in this category include Botswana, Burkina Faso, Côte d'Ivoire, Morocco, Mozambique, Togo, Tunisia and Uganda. Third are countries where the share of TVET enrolment in secondary education is over 10%. Examples include Cameroon, Mali, Gabon, Congo and Egypt.

In the English-speaking countries, TVET retains a high level of specificity, whereas in the French-speaking countries elements of modernization of their TVET programmes have led to a reasonable balance between general and vocational content. This makes it easier for those who opt for one reason or another to join TVET to progress to higher levels of education or come back to general programmes without much difficulty.

Table 2 Percentage of TVE enrolments in secondary technical and vocational education

Year	1970	1975	1980	1985	1990	1995	2000	2001	2002	2003
Benin	2.7	2.7	6.7	6.1	7.5	n/a	9.0	9.0	8.0	9.0
Botswana	20.5	12.3	8.9	8.0	5.8	6.3	4.0	3.0	3.0	3.0
Burkina Faso	15.2	16.9	14.2	8.0	7.0	n/a	8.0	9.0	9.0	8.0
Cameroon	23.7	25.4	27.0	24.5	18.0	n/a	21.0	19.0	18.0	n/a
Chad	10.1	4.5	n/a	6.3	4.9	2.3	2.2	2.0	2.0	2.0
Congo	9.9	7.0	9.1	10.6	6.7	11.7	n/a	10	10	n/a
Côte d'Ivoire	7.5	13.3	9.7	8.1	7.6	n/a	n/a	–	–	n/a
Eritrea	–	–	–	–	0.6	n/a	1.0	1.0	1.0	1.0
Ethiopia	4.5	n/a	n/a	0.8	0.4	0.3	1.0	1.0	2.0	4.0
Gabon	16.3	11.1	21.7	23.1	n/a	9.4	7.0	7.0	7.0	n/a
Guinea	3.3	1.8		5.8	9.8	3.5	n/a	n/a	n/a	n/a
Lesotho	9.3	3.4	5.0	3.4	3.3	1.1	2.0	2.0	2.0	1.0
Malawi	1.8	2.8	2.7	1.5	1.3	0.8	n/a	n/a	n/a	n/a
Mali	10.2	9.4	n/a	n/a	12.6	11.9	11.0	n/a	n/a	11.0
Mauritania	n/a	n/a	4.7	5.3	2.2	2.8	3.0	2.0	2.0	4.0
Mozambique	3.6	n/a	n/a	7.9	6.4	8.1	9.0	5.0	5.0	5.0
Namibia	1.0	1.2	0.9	0.6	0.1	n/a	n/a	2.0	n/a	n/a
Niger	2.9	1.73	1.4	1.2	1.1	0.9	6.0	n/a	2.0	1.0
Senegal	9.3	10.5	10.6	6.8	3.6	2.6	n/a	n/a	n/a	n/a
South Africa	n/a	n/a	n/a	n/a	1.5	n/a	4	5.0	5.0	5.0
Togo	9.6	8.0	5.2	5.7	6.7	4.6	7	n/a	n/a	n/a
Uganda	14.6	12.1	7.1	6.0	4.6	5.0	13	7	5.0	5.0

Source: Atchoarena & Delluc, 2001, p. 40.

Generally speaking, there is a low and declining proportion of TVET in secondary education, which can be partly attributed to the public's attitude towards this type of education. For the most part, that attitude has been shaped or influenced by lack of progression to higher levels of education and the low skills that TVET offers those who pursue it. There is also a gender aspect to this as well. Where the picture seems improved in terms of female participation, TVET becomes an even less prestigious branch of education.

3.6 What is the Purpose of TVET and has that Purpose Changed over the Past Twenty Years?

In these seven countries the purpose of TVET remains tied to solving the mismatch between educational expansion and the labour market. Not surprisingly, most of the provision is terminal and leads directly to entry into the labour market, where often many young people join the pool of the unemployed. Unfortunately, it is those from the lower socio-economic strata that still dominate in TVET because they cannot afford the general and higher levels of education. This has contributed to the perceptions that people hold about TVET. In Egypt, however, it is reported that the attitudes of young people towards TVET are now becoming increasingly positive, although TVET is still dominated by socio-economic factors and those from working-class families are more likely to enrol compared to those from the middle class.

In Ghana, people in general place low value on TVET. Their attitude to this type of education is that it is inferior to academic education, still reflecting what Philip Foster discovered there four decades ago. As a result of this attitude, it has been the less bright pupils who have often opted for TVET courses. Like all the other countries in the study, Ghana proclaims the idea that TVET leads to direct entry into the labour market and is therefore useful in responding to unemployment and poverty problems. Similar responses were obtained for Senegal, Seychelles, Tunisia and Zimbabwe. In general, the traditional objectives mentioned earlier have continued to guide national policy on TVET, while individuals prefer academic streams with the promise of higher wages. Going by the responses obtained through these interviews, it can be concluded that the purpose of TVET has not changed much over the decades.

3.7 Patterns of Delivery

Aside from the differences discussed above, there is an obvious difference in the way TVET is organized in French-speaking and English-speaking countries. This, as noted earlier, is attributable to the colonial influences that have largely been retained to date with minimal modifications. In Algeria, Morocco, Senegal and Tunisia, which are all Francophone, TVET retains a fairly large amount of general content as has been the case with TVET in France. However, lack of specificity towards vocational content has the disadvantage of delinking the TVET courses from the mostly informal labour-market skills. Atchoarena & Delluc (2001) found this to be the case in their study of TVET in Côte d'Ivoire, Madagascar, Mali and Senegal, where the informal sector, especially micro-enterprises, is totally ignored by the programmes and patterns of TVET delivery. Originally modelled on the French school system, TVET in these countries has often not fully taken into account the possibilities of traditional apprenticeship for meeting the needs of the artisanal sector, which provides jobs but often stands in need of improvement. In contrast, Anglophone countries display a much stronger experience, both in dual forms of public-sector training and in the provision of training for the artisanal sector (Atchoarena & Delluc, 2001). In the case of these English-speaking countries, the vocational content is generally high and the academic content is extremely limited. While this has the advantage of reflecting specificity in terms of the skills needed in the informal sector, where more jobs continue to be created, it has the disadvantage of limiting progression to higher levels of education or movement between vocational and general institutions. This high level of specificity leads to narrowness, an issue that often makes TVET less appealing, relegating it to a type of education only capable of leading to what many refer to as 'dead-end' jobs. But, there are some emerging trends in countries such as Botswana, Ghana and South Africa, where TVET has been 'modernized' from the traditional apprenticeship schemes to programmes that permit movement into the national training system. The aim of this approach is to include a balanced proportion of general and vocational content that would enable participants to move both laterally within the TVET programmes and vertically to general or advanced education institutions. This progression within and between TVET and general education, when fully implemented, can create a breathing space whereby the education system responds to the types of skills demanded for the labour force at different periods.

3.8 Who are the Providers?

For many years, State provision dominated the field of education in many African countries. However, over the past twenty years, private provision has been steadily growing. This has happened as State provision has either found it increasingly difficult to expand and cope with increased demand for education or simply because the State's capacity to monopolize provision of education has generally deteriorated and become unattainable. This can also be said of the TVET sector. Atchoarena and Esquieu (2002, pp. 21–22) conducted research on this phenomenon and documented patterns of provision and policy issues with reference to private technical and vocational education in sub-Saharan Africa. They conclude that:

1. Private provision of TVET is growing rapidly and even dominates in some countries, such as Mali.
2. There is heterogeneity in private provision with key aspects, such as legal status, ownership, objectives and financing, most difficult to establish clearly.
3. The majority of private TVET institutions enrol students from low socio-economic backgrounds.
4. A sizeable number of private institutions cannot be properly traced in government registrations records, implying that they operate illegally.
5. Many of the private providers offer courses with a high concentration in commercial trades, although there are also a few cases such as in Mali where 21% of the offerings are in technical areas (such as light industrial skills).
6. Given their private nature, tuition fees are the main source of operational resources for these institutions.
7. The private sector has the benefit of tailoring the courses to the labour-market demands and seems to be flexible in adapting to demand.
8. There is little evidence to indicate a close working relationship between enterprises and the private institutions. In most cases, it is up to the students to choose what they would like to specialize in by themselves. The degree to which they respond to the actual needs of the enterprises is thus less known.

The good news, however, is that private providers tend to provide programmes which, on average, appear to be better prepared compared to State institutions, although there is also great variation in terms of quality within the private provision.

In all the seven countries in this study, data on private provision were reported as being difficult to obtain. Interviews with the respondents revealed similar concerns or features, as summed up above in the Atchoarena and Delluc (2001) study. Some key issues and contrasts are worth mentioning. In Botswana the provision is still predominantly offered by the State in six vocational institutions and forty-one brigades (vocational institutions training at craft level). There were some private providers, especially in Gaborone, but the Ministry of Education does not have full details of how many there are and the nature of their operations. Similar responses were obtained from the six other countries, although the State monopoly was noted as sometimes being in doubt. In Senegal, the respondent reported that data on private institutions were difficult to obtain but acknowledged that they exist and in visible numbers. Similarly, in Zimbabwe, there are several data collection problems to be faced when dealing with private institutions, but the respondent acknowledged that most of these institutions provided TVET to those who had completed secondary-level education. It was thought that there are over 350 such private institutions in the country, most of which are offering commercial-based programmes. In Ghana, there are 160 technical and vocational institutions run by government agencies and 250 registered private institutions. It is thought, however, that there could be approximately another 700 unregistered private providers. Private technical and vocational institutions run a variety of courses in Ghana which last an average of three years. Their students take either the City and Guilds of London Institute or the Ghana Education Service Craft examination or the National Vocational Training Institute (NVIT) Craftsman or Tradesman Grade examination.

4 Recent Concerns over TVET in Africa

Aside from the early criticisms by Philip Foster (1965) and Mark Blaug (1973), numerous concerns have been voiced over the past decade. Atchoarena and Delluc (2001, p. 38) summarize them in Africa in terms of:

- poor quality;
- very high cost;
- training not suited to actual socio-economic conditions;
- disregard of the informal sector's needs;
- disregard of the labour market and of the high unemployment rate among graduates.

In view of the changes in the labour market, the objectives of technical and vocational education have become more diverse: they are no longer simply economic but also social, including the fight against poverty and the integration of young people into the working world, all in line with the articulations in the Millennium Development Goals (Atchoarena & Delluc, 2001), and the present day demands of globalization. Given the prevailing economic trend, two other major objectives have

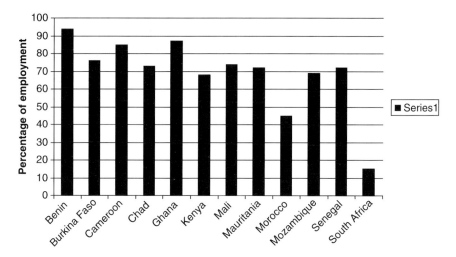

Fig. 1 Informal sector employment as a share of non-agricultural employment, selected African countries (1990s)
Source: Johanson & Adams, 2004, p. 52.

been identified and which must now be pursued: (a) to train the workforce for self-employment; and (b) to raise the productivity of the informal sector (Caillods, 1994, in Atchoarena & Delluc, 2001). Figure 1 reveals the growing importance of the informal sector in terms of providing employment outside the agricultural sector, but lack of resources is seen as a hindrance to pursuing these new critical objectives. This is all the more so given that TVET is an expensive form of education and expanding it without necessary and adequate facilities and equipment does not lead to increasing productivity in the long run. Yet, at the same time, criticisms of TVET have led to cuts in the volume of training provided in public institutions and a call for the mostly family-run informal enterprises to take on more responsibility for providing TVET.

A look at the funding of TVET can shed light on the contradiction between the emphasis for skills and the limited funding that governments are willing to commit to it. Moreover, the international pressure on countries to meet their Education for All goals by 2015 has meant that more resources have been shifted, both within national budgets and by international aid assistance, to realizing universal primary education—and yet the rhetoric over skills and the value of TVET continues.

4.1 Financing of TVET

As is the case with provision, delivery patterns and levels of participation, the financing of TVET as a percentage of public education expenditures varies considerably from country to country. It ranges from as low as 0.9% a decade ago in Ethiopia to 12.7% in Gabon at the same period (ILO, 1998/1999, cited in Atchoarena & Delluc, 2001). In all the seven countries in the UIS study, it was noted that obtaining the financial breakdown for TVET is difficult because allocation is made for the entire education sector rather than by programme. It is therefore hard to provide accurate expenditure on TVET. Difficulties in specifying spending on TVET are compounded by the fact that provision in the private sector is hardly covered by the data. Interviews with respondents in all seven countries revealed that many of the private providers do not want to co-operate in providing their financial information and, in cases where they do, the figures are often inaccurate. Nevertheless, Table 3 can shed some light on the levels of financial allocation to TVET in selected countries in the 1990s.

Table 3 Percentage of technical and vocational education expenditures in total education expenditures

Country	%	Year	Country	%	Year
Benin	3.3	1995	Guinea	7.5	1993
Botswana	5.5	1991	Lesotho	3.3	1994
Chad	2.0	1994	Malawi	1.1	1992
Congo	4.9	1980	Mali	9.1	1995
Côte d'Ivoire	4.8	1994	Mauritania	2.3	1995
Eritrea	1.6	1994	Mozambique	6.2	1990
Ethiopia	0.9	1993	Namibia	2.0	1995
Gabon	12.7	1992	Senegal	2.7	1990
Ghana	4.9	1990	Togo	3.7	1994

Source: ILO, 1998/1999 cited in Atchoarena and Delluc, 2002, p. 45.

4.2 Conclusion

Based on the information gleaned from other studies and interviews with representatives in the seven countries, it can be concluded that:

1. Business has been as usual over the past two decades—TVET is still driven by the traditional objectives identified earlier in all of these countries.
2. TVET mostly begins at lower secondary and/or junior secondary level in a majority of African countries.
3. Excellent institutions offering TVET at post-secondary level, such as national polytechnics, are under pressure to convert into degree-granting institutions allowing wider diversity of courses and a large mix of general education programmes in addition to their technical and vocational courses.
4. TVET is not attractive to families and is seen as a last resort by those who cannot access general education.
5. There are countries, such as Egypt, with a dual-track system, the problem with which is the danger of tracking students into ability groupings.
6. There is a tremendous growth in private providers, especially for business-related skills.

5 The Way Forward and Some Perspectives

There is no doubt that TVET is important in Africa's development and, from the analysis of trends and issues in the region, the key point is to transform it so that what is offered can reflect the prevailing reality in the labour market and the global economy. This transformation must partly begin with TVET policy casting off its traditional mould, and taking as its objective the need to provide convergence with academic education (Wilson, 2005), in addition to establishing links to the informal sector. More importantly, private providers who are more flexible should be encouraged but carefully monitored to ensure that the courses they offer are of acceptable standards and quality. Where government provision has proven wasteful, inflexible and inefficient, alternative provision through employers should be sought and encouraged. In addition, more and accurate data should be collected to monitor patterns of provision in both government institutions and private provision in order to provide a basis for a new TVET framework in many African countries. Under present-day skills, TVET should reflect the development of 'high-skills' as well as 're-skilling' rather than being a mere means of addressing 'runaway' unemployment in formal sectors. Specifically, the following are recommended:

1. Increased specificity within TVET programmes where general educational content has dominated with the result that these programmes are less useful to the informal sector.
2. Lateral and vertical movement should be allowed.
3. TVET should be de-linked from having to provide a solution to manpower and unemployment problems.
4. There should be increased proportions of TVET content in general programmes and increased general content in TVET programmes.
5. Encourage high skills rather than low skills in TVET programmes.
6. Promote re-skilling and up-skilling to cope with technological changes.
7. In some instances, it may be right for the public sector to withdraw from vocational schooling altogether, especially where waste has been so serious, the needs for general education so compelling and labour-market growth so sluggish.

Note

1. This chapter is a modification of the original version appearing as an article in the *International journal of educational development*, 2007, vol. 27, pp. 220–34.

References

Atchoarena, D.; Delluc, A. 2001. *Revisiting technical and vocational education in Sub-Saharan Africa: an update on trends, innovations and challenges.* Paris: UNESCO-IIEP.

Atchoarena, D.; Esquieu, P. 2002. *Private technical and vocational education in Sub-Saharan Africa: provision patterns and policy issues.* Paris: UNESCO-IIEP.

Blaug, M. 1973. *Education and the employment problem in developing countries.* Geneva, Switzerland: ILO.

Foster, P.J. 1965. The vocational school fallacy in development planning. *In:* Anderson, C.A.; Bowman, M.J., eds. *Education and economic development.* Chicago, IL: Aldine.

Gill, A.M.; Leigh, D.E. 2004. *Evaluating academic programs in California's community colleges.* San Francisco, CA: Public Policy Institute of California.

Green, A. 1998. Core skills, key skills and general culture: in search of the common foundation in vocational education. *Evaluation and research in education,* vol. 12, no. 1, pp. 23–43.

Green, A.; Oketch, M.; Preston, J. 2004. *Global report on technical and vocational education and training: report to UNESCO Institute for Statistics.* London: University of London Institute of Education.

Hawley, J.D. 2003. Comparing the pay-off to vocational and academic credentials in Thailand over time. *International journal of educational development,* vol. 23, no. 6, pp. 607–25.

Heyneman, S.P. 1979. The career education debate: where the difference lies. *Teachers College record,* vol. 80, no. 4, pp. 659–88.

Heyneman, S.P. 1986. The nature of a 'practical curriculum'. *Education with production,* vol. 4, no. 2, pp. 91–103.

Heyneman, S.P. 1987. Curriculum economics in secondary education: an emerging crisis in developing countries. *Prospects,* vol. 17, no. 1. pp. 63–74.

Heyneman, S.P. 1997. Russian vocational and technical education in the transition: tradition, adaptation, unresolved problems. *Institute for the Study of Russian Education newsletter,* vol. 6. no. 1, pp. 22–34.

Johanson, R.K.; Adams, A.V. 2004. *Skills development in Sub-Saharan Africa.* Washington, DC: World Bank.

King, K.; Martin, C. 2002. The vocational school fallacy revisited: education aspiration and work in Ghana, 1959–2000. *International journal of educational development,* vol. 22, no. 1, pp. 5–26.

Middleton, J.; Ziderman, A.; Adams, V.A. 1993. *Skills for productivity: vocational education and training in developing countries.* Washington, DC: World Bank; New York, NY: Oxford University Press.

Neuman, S.; Ziderman, A. 2003. Can vocational education improve the wages of minorities and disadvantaged groups? *Economics of education review,* vol. 22, pp. 421–32.

Ngome, C. 1992. *Vocationalisation of education in Kenya: factors that have influenced policies and practices in the colonial and post-colonial period.* Nairobi: Kenyatta University, Department of Educational Foundations. [Mimeo.]

Oketch, M.O. 2000. Costing and financing higher education for development in Sub-Saharan Africa: Kenya's case. *International education journal,* vol. 3, pp. 1–10.

Oketch, M.O. 2004. The emergence of private university education in Kenya: trends, prospects and challenges. *International journal of educational development,* vol. 24, no. 2, pp. 119–36.

Psacharopoulos, G. 1997. Vocational education and training today: challenges and responses. *Journal of vocational education and training,* vol. 49, no. 3, pp. 385–94.

Psacharopoulos, G. 2006. World Bank policy on education: a personal account. *International journal of educational development,* vol. 26, no. 3, pp. 329–38.

Tilak, J. 2002. Vocational education and training in Asia. *In:* Keeves, P.J.; Watanabe, R., eds. *The handbook on educational research in the Asia-Pacific Region.* Dordrecht, Netherlands: Kluwer Academic Publishers.

UNESCO. 1961. *Conference of African States on the development of education in Africa: final report.* Paris: UNESCO.

UNESCO Institute for Statistics. 2005. *Global education digest, 2005.* Montreal: UNESCO-UIS.

Wilson, D.N. 2001. Reform of TVET for the changing world of work. *Prospects,* vol. 31, no. 1, pp. 21–37.

Wilson, D.N. 2005. Promise and performance in vocationalised secondary education: has the baby been thrown out with the bath water? *In:* Lauglo, J.; Maclean, R., eds. *Vocationalisation of secondary education revisited.* Dordrecht, Netherlands: Springer.

Wolf, A. 2002. *Does education matter? Myths about education and economic growth.* London: Penguin.

Chapter IV.3
TVET in the Asian Region: Issues, Concerns and Prospects

P.P.G. Lionel Siriwardene and Muhammad Ashraf Qureshi

1 Introduction

The twenty-first century is one of emerging challenges and an era of knowledge, information and communication. Globalization and unprecedented advancements in information and communication technologies (ICTs) have already signalled the need for a new human-centred development paradigm. Education, particularly technical and vocational education and training (TVET), has a crucial role to play in this new era for all regions of the world, including Asia and the Pacific. In view of the immense potential of TVET to generate growth, it is emerging as a vital empowering tool for improving living conditions by enhancing the capacities of individuals to be employed, obtain decent work and increase their earnings. Orienting TVET to the needs of the world of work is, therefore, indispensable not only for economic and social development, but also for sustainable development. This calls for a paradigm shift in TVET, such as the one taking place in the Asian Region—as everywhere else in the world. Its philosophy, vision and mission, goals and objectives, policies and practices, content and methodologies are all changing to keep pace with advances in science and technology, industry and business. In spite of the fact that the World Bank, once TVET's staunchest supporter, introduced a radical shift in its policy in 1991, all countries still announce their interest in TVET, especially in the Asian Region where it has come to be regarded as the master key that can transform the economy, alleviate poverty, save the environment and improve the quality of life (Quisumbing, 2005).

2 A New Role for TVET

Thanks to the unprecedented advances in science, technology and communications, the world today is a global village with far greater interdependence between countries. However, the global level of development continues to be distressing in the Asian and Pacific Region, where about two-thirds of the world's population lives. Most of these people are still living in developing countries, if not some of the least developed. While worldwide, one out of five men and one out of three women

R. Maclean, D. Wilson (eds.), *International Handbook of Education for the Changing World of Work*, DOI 10.1007/978-1-4020-5281-1_IV.3,
© Springer Science+Business Media B.V. 2009

are still illiterate, in Asia, particularly South Asia, one out of three men and one out of two women are illiterate (Mehta, 2003). Education for All is still far from a reality in this region. This situation calls for new patterns of education with a catalytic role for TVET in keeping with the changing role of work and its impact on national and international economies and competitiveness. For sixty years, the world has failed to achieve Education for All. It is now time to reconsider the basic options—including the option of TVET—to give to the world, and particularly developing countries, the chance of achieving Education for All (Hughes, 2005). For this to be possible, TVET will have to enable learners completing basic education to enter the labour market with some basic know-how and skills. With work becoming more knowledge- and technologically-based, TVET can play a key role as an entry point to the knowledge society. However, a radical policy reform would need to shift TVET away from heavy investments by the central government in equipment, workshops and instructor training to a pragmatic and meaningful partnership with its major stakeholders in industry, trade and agriculture. Some governments are already embarking on new approaches to providing TVET programmes through improvements in content, teaching methods, models of delivery and teaching/learning processes (Mar, 2005). Two successful examples are provided by the Republic of Korea and China. While the Republic of Korea successfully tailored its TVET system to forecast needs, China almost completely overhauled its antiquated system by encouraging the private sector to provide financing, materials, apprenticeship and guidance to align training with the needs of the market (UNESCO-UNEVOC, 2005).

3 The Present Scenario and Regional Context

In the recent past, there have been some impressive but uneven developments in education. TVET, which consists of a diverse range of courses, is usually offered at the upper secondary level and beyond, with the lower secondary stage being only for general vocational skills for all students (Maclean, 2005a). Globally, almost 50 million students were enrolled in TVET in 2002, 90% at the upper secondary level. At the moment, one in five upper secondary students is enrolled in TVET on a world scale. However, the enrolment rate varies widely: in East Asia, including China, TVET programmes account for 33% of enrolment, while in West Asia its share is less than even 4% (Ellis, 2005).

3.1 Vocational Gross Enrolment Rates

In a global study of TVET by the University of London Institute of Education of the various combinations of students in a number of countries, especially the vocational gross enrolment rates (VGERs), major variations in the public provision of vocational education were noted (Green, Oketch & Preston, 2004). The study showed that the public provision of vocational programmes in East Asia seems to be low, with the highest rate being the Republic of Korea at 16%. In Oceania, Australia stands far above any other country with a VGER of 68%. Other Asian VGERs are generally low, varying from 0.4% for India, 0.5% for Bangladesh and Pakistan, 4.2% Malaysia and about 9% for Thailand. The study indicates that countries are increasingly including both general and vocational content in all secondary programmes as they fine-tune their curricula to meet particular requirements. Although this strategy has resulted in a rise in the status of vocational training in some countries by being included within a broader range of secondary and tertiary programmes, developing countries still regard it as a second-rate option (Ellis, 2005).

3.2 Globalization, Industry Restructuring and TVET

As a result of globalization, the restructuring of industry is now also taking place across the world. As a result, TVET is also undergoing a major reorientation, particularly regarding curriculum revision which is becoming increasingly industry- and market-driven, with an emphasis on new technology, the removal of obsolete subjects and the modernization of equipment and teaching/learning materials. However, TVET frequently exists in complete isolation from industry, which is a major problem requiring immediate attention. For TVET to assist and facilitate industry, strong school/industry linkages are essential. As the financial resources of countries in the Asia and the Pacific Region are limited, it is to be hoped that donor agencies would continue to assist them in their reform of TVET, as in the past. This would enable them to modernize their existing facilities to serve the growing requirements of regionalization and internationalization.

The restructuring of TVET in the region is accordingly emerging as an urgent priority in view of the challenges posed by globalization and the ICT explosion. However, for this restructuring to be meaningful, it must take into account curricula, resources, teachers, assessment and examinations, school/industry links and certification, non-formal options and the involvement of the private sector (Maclean, 2005b).

4 Philosophy and Objectives

At present, preparation of skilled personnel and increases in national productivity and competitiveness seem to be the urgent objectives of TVET in most countries of the region. Nevertheless, many countries are also pursuing objectives unique to their own contexts. While India stresses the need for reducing the aimless pursuit of higher education, there are others that highlight the formative and developmental role of TVET, particularly when it is imparted during the basic cycle of education. Awareness of career paths, career planning and vocational guidance also finds a place in the philosophy of many countries.

In many countries' philosophies of TVET there are concerns not precisely reflected under the statement of its objectives. TVET as an integral component of school education is reflected in the educational objectives of several countries. Some countries also have various kinds of vocational or vocationally-oriented schools (Mishra, 1995). A present policy shift in the region relates to TVET being demand- or industry-cum-market driven, as opposed to supply-driven as in the past. However, the size, population and economies of countries are creating different situations with regard to TVET. Some countries are reconstructing TVET to meet the needs of their changing societies and the free-market economy.

5 Organizational Problems and the Constraints of TVET

Countries in Asia and the Pacific are going through an intensive evolutionary process with regard to TVET. National models continue to emerge to cope with present and future needs, and structures are becoming increasingly relevant to national economic and social requirements. The number of TVET institutions is also increasing. As a result many structures are now providing different entry and exit points and horizontal and vertical mobility.

There are countless ways in which TVET is organized in different countries of the region and even within the same country. Although each country, to some extent, has its own pattern, every country seeks the most cost-effective model that offers efficient instruction (Mishra, 1995).

5.1 Problems and Constraints

The most industrialized countries in Asia are China, India and Japan. In recent decades, countries such as Thailand, Malaysia and the Republic of Korea have enjoyed rapid progress, earning the title of 'newly industrialized countries' (NICs). Thailand's rapid economic growth needed skilled manpower requiring compulsory education to be extended to year 9. Malaysia's economic profile changed from a mainly agricultural and mining nation to a more balanced economy with a growing manufacturing industry. The Republic of Korea's rapid industrialization required skilled manpower in large numbers. These countries have accordingly reformed and developed their TVET systems. Other less-industrialized countries in the region are also improving their systems to meet industrial development needs and growing global competitiveness.

A major problem with TVET is that it is generally three to four times more expensive than general education. As developing countries' resources are limited, they are forced to seek assistance from international agencies, such as the World Bank, the Asian Development Bank and elsewhere, which have often radically changed their policies and strategies (UNESCO-UNEVOC, 2005).

Unemployment is a serious problem in Asian countries and they are reforming their education systems to alleviate this. The Asian region has a big potential for job creation through TVET. Despite the diversity in populations, cultures and levels of development, countries are faced with weak linkages between education and national economic activity. This issue is being addressed by creating, as far as possible, linkages with employers and the job market. However, there is a general shortage of reliable mechanisms to assess job-market demands so as to avoid a mismatch between training and employment.

5.2 The Participation of Women

The participation of women in TVET has been low but is increasing rapidly. As a result, large numbers of women are entering the job market in countries such as Bangladesh, India, Indonesia, Pakistan, Philippines and Thailand. In a number of countries, separate TVET institutions have been created for women, in addition to regular institutions. TVET courses in keeping with women's preferences are also offered to encourage their participation.

5.3 TVET and Rural Uplift

The Asian region is largely rural and agrarian. An increase in TVET in rural areas is planned so that these economies can benefit. However, there is concern that TVET in rural areas is insufficient and irrelevant, even though it has immense usefulness for farm technology, agro-based industry and bio-technologies. There is an urgent need to focus TVET on improving agricultural productivity in the region.

5.4 Image and Status of TVET

A major problem for TVET has been its low status among students and parents. In many countries, it is still considered as 'second-class education' (Maclean, 2005b). This problem is gradually decreasing with the recognition of its usefulness and the key role it plays in national development and employment generation.

5.5 Access, Equity and Participation

Access and equity are both essential for ensuring meaningful participation in TVET, but increasing enrolment is no guarantee of achieving them. Although there has been a three-fold increase in secondary enrolments in the region over the past forty years, there is still unequal access to this level affecting females, the handicapped, members of various social or racial groups and people from remote areas (Maclean, 2005b). There are indications that the proportion of females in secondary education, as well as in TVET, is increasing. However, this is happening more in the relatively industrialized countries of the region, such as Malaysia and the Republic of Korea where it reached about 50% as compared to only 27% in Bangladesh, Myanmar and Mongolia (Maclean, 2005b).

Equity and access can be helped also by reducing drop-outs, which are quite appreciable in many systems. Equity can also be helped by removing the disparities between urban and rural institutions, which are still prevalent in several Asian countries. These disparities are due to poor planning and the shortage of funds. There is an urgent need to improve TVET for rural areas throughout Asia.

Some countries are using new methods of student enrolment to ensure equity and better participation in TVET programmes. It has been observed that some students who qualify and enter TVET institutions have no interest in vocational courses and this constitutes a wastage of resources. Some countries have adopted aptitude and ability tests so as only to admit students who will benefit from these programmes. These measures are likely to help in reducing high drop-out rates.

6 Policy and Planning

The importance placed on TVET is relatively recent. Frequent changes in policy and planning have been made in recent years to meet emergent industrial and economic development needs. There is a growing realization of issues related to the relationship between TVET and the economy, between ecology and social development and the role that TVET can play in improving national productivity and competitiveness. Many countries have also recognized the need for discussion with the labour market, chambers of commerce and other appropriate bodies when planning TVET. This is because labour market demands constantly vary. Planning is also largely dependent on population and demographic trends, literacy rates and the level of primary education, factors that place more pressure on secondary education and hence on TVET.

Co-operation between TVET and industry (i.e. employers) is still weak in many countries. Close links should be maintained with industry to improve student job placement, periodic industrial experience for teachers, the provision of equipment and teachers and, more importantly, representatives of industry sitting on school boards.

6.1 Role of the Private Sector

An important policy issue is the role of the private sector in TVET. With more private sector participation and with more public/private partnerships, not only would the quality of training improve but countries would greatly benefit from additional funds so as to reduce expenditure. In India, the Republic of Korea, Philippines and

Thailand many large industries run their own training departments. In many other Asian countries, TVET is high on the development agenda, as well as collaboration between institutions and industry. A notable example in this regard is that of Japan which encourages practical training in agriculture, business, fisheries, home economics, nursing and society welfare in co-operation with industry (Okada, 1995). Even some less-industrialized countries, such as Bangladesh, Nepal, Pakistan and the Philippines, have recently made major shifts in TVET development strategy in co-operation with industry and trade sectors.

6.2 Institution/Industry Linkages

The issue of linkage between industry and institutions has been a subject of immense interest throughout the world (Mishra, 1995). In many Asian countries, institution/industry linkages are still weak and are taking time to develop due to insufficient knowledge about each others' capability and potential. Industry's lack of interest or its critical attitude towards TVET institutions is also due to the fact that many institutions have been functioning in complete isolation from industry's demands. Institutions can benefit greatly if industry were better informed about their programmes. Industry too needs to collaborate as it would be a major beneficiary if TVET institutions functioned more efficiently. TVET/industry co-operation could also facilitate 'sandwich'-course training and 'day-release' or 'block-release' programmes to meet urgent occupational demands.

7 A National Co-ordinating Mechanism

Several countries in Asia have set up national co-ordinating bodies to oversee the TVET system. As well as educators, these bodies include representatives of State authorities, industry, agriculture and the private sector and meet regularly to identify problems and resolve them. These mechanisms also help in minimizing mismatch between demand and supply of graduates, as well as providing programmes for disadvantaged population groups, such as women. Identification of organizational changes to improve the responsiveness of the systems to market demand is also supervised by these co-ordinating mechanisms. Co-ordination of TVET activities is helping to prevent duplication of efforts and wastage of resources. On the contrary, the pooling of resources is facilitating the task of making the system more cost-effective. Good working examples of these co-ordinating mechanisms exist in Australia with the Vocational Education, Employment and Training Board (VEET) (Wolfensberger, 1995), in the Philippines with the Technical and Skill Development Authority (TESDA) (Lacson & Justimbaste, 1995) and in Pakistan with its National Vocational and Technical Education Commission (NAVTEC) at the federal level and technical education and vocational training authorities (TEVTA) in the provinces.

7.1 Decentralization

A major policy change in some countries is the decentralization of TVET. Large countries with many provinces find these essential, but other countries may find the concept of decentralized planning and implementation a useful strategy. Countries such as Bangladesh, China, India, Indonesia and Pakistan are beginning to benefit from decentralization. The organization and management of the TVET system in a large and diverse country such as India is a formidable task. The need for an effective relationship between education, working life and the community has long been recognized in India and this philosophy has helped the country in its policy of decentralizing to regions, with a National Council for Technical and Vocational Education at the federal level. In Pakistan, the TEVTAs in the provinces and NAVTEC at the central level also provide a workable example of national co-ordination and decentralized management.

7.2 Research on TVET Policy

A significant drawback is that very little research is done on TVET at the national level. Research findings could be of great help to policy-makers and planners, and a big incentive to teachers. A research pool should be developed among national TVET institutions and research competencies urgently developed. Exchange and sharing of information and experiences through regional and international co-operation and networks, such as UNESCO-UNEVOC, could go a long way in assisting countries in this regard.

7.3 Multi-Skilling and Broad-Based Training

In TVET planning, too often institutions do not meet national requirements both in respect of course content and the numbers of students trained. A decrease in manpower demands in some occupational areas due to saturation of job markets, or less manpower being needed due to new technologies and automation, is making the task of planning TVET systems more difficult. Recasting training programmes should enable those trained to fit into more than one job situation, which is becoming more desirable from industry's point of view.

7.4 Selection of Sites for TVET Institutions

Not enough attention is always given to the siting of institutions. In principle, sites should be in proximity of industries so as to facilitate student training and institution/industry linkages. Too often, sites are selected for political expediency.

Feasibility studies can greatly help in this regard. Not enough attention has been given to the design of buildings to make them cost-effective. Quite often 'standard-type plans' made for general purposes are used which may not be suitable every-where. Industry's advice could go a long way to overcome this problem.

7.5 Articulation

Articulation is a major reform in some Asian countries. 'Bridging courses' have helped in providing opportunities to TVET system graduates to enter tertiary educa-tion. The creation of post-secondary TVET institutions has also contributed towards the democratization of education and has helped in raising the status of this form of education. Australia, New Zealand and the Philippines are practising articulation in TVET as a major reform to provide alternative pathways in technical fields with higher technical institutes and junior colleges providing credit points and systems enabling entry into higher education institutions. Bangladesh, Pakistan and India have opened other pathways to higher technical education through the polytechnic system, where places are reserved on engineering degree courses for polytechnic graduates who are admitted on a competitive basis. Degree-level vocational courses are also available in India to better prepare graduates for the world of work. About 100 Indian universities and colleges are involved in degree programmes of this type. Another method in India is the use of open learning and flexible delivery to provide a pathway to those for whom further education might not otherwise be an option.

An innovation in this regard is provided by Bangladesh which attempted to articulate TVET with general education (Rafique, 1995). Pakistan has also launched a Matric (ten years of schooling) technical programme which is similar in nature.

7.6 Structures

TVET structures are being continuously revised and developed to meet the needs of the changing job market. During the 1960s and 1970s a simple three-tiered structure was common. The first tier, the 'certificate' level, was for trade or craft vocational training for skilled workers. The course duration was generally two years and en-try was upon completion of Grade 8 in secondary education. The second tier was the three-year diploma course for technician training with entry after Grade 10 of secondary education. The third level was higher education for engineers. The three tiers still function in many TVET systems, while major reorganizations are taking place. Cross-national comparisons of TVET structures are not easy due to differ-ences in programmes and course specifications, the involvement of different min-istries, diversification within and across the former tiered structure and variations in nomenclature.

7.7 Stage and Level

The upper secondary stage is the most common level for TVET in many countries of Asia, such as China, India, Indonesia, Israel, Japan, Malaysia, the Republic of Korea and Thailand. It is organized in two- or three-year blocks over the final years of schooling and essentially aims to impart pre-employment skills. The programmes may be strongly to lightly vocational, depending on the countries needs and requirements.

7.8 Administration and Management

The efficient management of TVET continues to be a weakness in many countries. This is often due to a lack of people with managerial training and expertise. It is also due to the appointment of people without clear recruitment procedures. The promotion of individuals on the basis of seniority from the education sector as a whole often leads to inefficient and incompetent managers. Poor planning and insufficient time being given to carry out managerial functions are common factors leading to poor management. Management training programmes hardly exist in TVET systems. Management information systems (MIS) are rare and so are the facilities available for inspection, monitoring and evaluation. A few countries, for example Australia, Bangladesh, Pakistan, India, Malaysia, Philippines and the Republic of Korea, have set up MIS facilities. The availability of computer facilities has significantly helped to improve management functions. An efficient management system would help to justify expenditure and prevent wastage by reducing drop-out and repeater rates among students. It can also assist in rationalizing student enrolments, while maintaining teaching and training efficiency, i.e. quality and standards. It can also assist in maintaining information on students, teachers and resources, examinations and awards—as well as finances.

Changing course contents driven by new technologies and new job-market requirements are making new demands on TVET managers, who now require competence in the management of change—a vital need today. Heads of TVET institutions generally lack leadership qualities and tend to follow routine practices. Leadership implies competence, vision, good communication and teamwork, besides being articulate and able to obtain the best from a team.

TVET systems, especially in developing countries, are more prone to administrative delays. These delays adversely affect performance and the quality of training. In a few countries, ministries of education have set up separate units to handle TVET, such as India, Bangladesh, Pakistan and Sri Lanka. Ministries of education are also responsible for the accreditation of non-formal private-sector TVET institutions and for monitoring their progress. Bangladesh, Pakistan and India have autonomous boards established by the Ministries/Departments of Education to accredit the vocational training institutions. These boards are also responsible for providing learning resources, conducting examinations and certification.

8 Curriculum and Training

Most of the problems facing Asian countries are curriculum related. The rising demand for TVET is expanding in both formal and non-formal systems. New programmes and delivery approaches are being developed. The cognitive content of training is increasing because a knowledgeable, broad-based and multi-skilled workforce is required. Countries such as Malaysia, Thailand and the Republic of Korea, where rapid industrial progress has taken place, are now requiring multi-skilled employees with competency to undertake many functions. An innovation in the region is, therefore, the integration of training courses with combinations of specialized training for multi-skilling.

TVET curricula, of necessity, need to be prepared, revised and developed continuously so that they continue to be relevant. Many countries lack competence in curriculum development and some of them have set up curriculum development units. The mismatch between what students learn and the needs of the job market is a major concern in most TVET systems. A major shortcoming is a mechanism for obtaining information about current job-market demands and future needs. Some countries carry out tracer studies to obtain the views of past graduates and employers on improving the curriculum and the employment of graduates. Practical courses in industry for students are a concern in many countries that are not sufficiently industrialized.

8.1 Monitoring and Evaluation

The upgrading of the teaching/learning process is also a matter of growing concern as is the maintenance of quality and standards. Many developments are taking place in this regard. Monitoring and evaluation of TVET programmes are being developed using computer facilities. There have been serious shortcomings in monitoring and evaluating TVET and, indeed, there is insufficient assessment of teaching methods and student performance in education systems in general. Establishing TVET monitoring and evaluation units within departments of education is an urgently needed reform in many countries.

8.2 Competency-Based Training

A major innovation in some countries is competency-based training where achievement of competency is the basis of measuring progress in training. Standards of performance for this purpose are specified by industry. Australia, Bangladesh and New Zealand have developed occupational competency standards in co-operation with industry. TESDA in the Philippines and TEVTA in Pakistan are in the process of developing competency-based training standards.

8.3 The Dual Model

The German Dual Model has influenced many countries, such as China, Indonesia, the Republic of Korea, Thailand and Viet Nam. This programme is provided according to the needs of industry, which establishes contracts with industry providing skills training and practical experience while the institution provides the theoretical component of the training (Timmermann, 1995).

8.4 Modular Training

Modular training is proving useful for both initial training and continuing education. It is also useful for upgrading skills of the employed and for those changing jobs. It is also helpful in meeting lifelong learning of skills.

8.5 Flexible Delivery

Countries are taking initiatives to introduce flexible delivery and learning approaches. Australia, China, India, New Zealand, Philippines, Thailand and Viet Nam are among countries that have developed open learning, distance education, self-paced and continuing education methods to reach school drop-outs, working people and populations in remote areas. Flexible delivery is also helping in making lifelong learning attainable in the future. The future of TVET greatly depends on flexible learning for more non-formal, more part-time, more private-sector, more industry-oriented and more market-driven programmes.

8.6 Entrepreneurial Skills

TVET curricula in many Asian countries include entrepreneurial skills for business and industry imparting concepts such as self-employment and small-scale management. The poor interest in such activity by TVET graduates has been a major concern. Australia and New Zealand have been pioneers in this regard. Entrepreneurial skill development is now being actively pursued in many other countries, such as Bangladesh, India, Pakistan, Philippines and Thailand. Other countries are also helping young entrepreneurs with small business loans, material incentives, financial support and tax exemptions.

8.7 Teacher Training

The recruitment and retention of competent teachers, especially those with industrial experience, has been a major problem for TVET systems in many countries.

Frequently, salaries are insufficient compared to those in industry. Teachers who join TVET systems often leave to take up jobs in industry. Sometimes the causes of leaving are lack of satisfactory career prospects and unsatisfactory working conditions. Some systems, however, do offer career building to teachers through teacher education and industrial experience programmes, as well as incentives through merit-based promotion schemes—and sometimes even by providing housing and assistance with children's education. The shortage of teachers has necessitated the use of part-time teachers or trainers seconded from industry. The shortage of teachers in many countries is making it difficult for serving teachers to be released for further training. Teacher up-grading is an urgent priority for every country so that TVET can be continually improved.

8.8 Vocationalization of Curricula

A major concern of countries is the extent to which general lower secondary education could be vocationalized. The consensus has been that it should create an awareness of the world of work and provide an appreciation of hands-on skills. Outcomes would be a healthy attitude towards practical work and mental preparation for taking up a career involving the use of practical skills. One dilemma is that vocational training at this level is not adequate for work purposes, so questions are asked as to whether the effort and expenditure are justified. However, some South Asian countries, including Bangladesh, India and Pakistan, are increasing the vocational content of education at the secondary level.

8.9 Assessment of Training Quality

Maintaining the high quality of training is generally hampered by funding difficulties for the acquisition of physical resources and the recruitment of competent teachers. Many systems do not have the procedures and facilities in place for the systematic assessment of training quality and standards. For these systems to be effective and efficient, quality and standards are absolutely necessary. Australia and New Zealand provide good examples of industry/institution linkages that can assist and facilitate TVET systems in this regard.

8.10 Vocational Guidance and Counselling

The social and financial background of most TVET students in the Asian Region makes vocational guidance and counselling absolutely necessary. Many TVET systems have set up the required facilities, including 'vocational guidance centres', in their institutions. Working teachers are generally associated with this work and they do advise students on a day-to-day basis. Some TVET institutions provide training for those appointed to conduct vocational guidance and have facilities for maintaining student records, as well as regularly updated employment and job-market information.

Vocational guidance and counselling helps students with the selection of TVET courses that suit their interests and potential, and provides advice on career prospects and employment possibilities. Counselling work is also useful to help students who are having personal difficulties. It is important to mention that vocational guidance and counselling not only help students but also teachers—both directly and indirectly—in teaching their students.

9 Costs and Funding

A major issue facing TVET is its comparatively high cost. Governmental budgets are generally inadequate and many Asian countries are forced to seek the assistance of international agencies, such as the World Bank, the Asian Development Bank and bilateral donors. It should be noted that many of these agencies have gone through a radical shift in their policies after, in some cases, being the staunchest supporter of TVET for decades (UNESCO-UNEVOC, 2005). The high unit cost of TVET is placing a limitation on the numbers that can be trained and the extent to which training can be provided. It is also affecting the quality of training. The physical and teaching resources, such as the recruitment of teachers, the modernization of equipment and the purchase of consumable and other training materials, are the hardest hit. The quality and employability of the TVET graduates is also suffering and inadequate training courses and trainee numbers in many cases do not justify the expenditure on institutions. For developing countries this really is a dilemma and they need urgently to reconsider the strategies of donor agencies so that they can reform their institutions—often established with the assistance of these donor agencies. A matter to be considered by donor agencies could be provision of seeding grants for technical support for particular purposes (Maclean, 2005a). The comparisons of cost per graduate rather than cost per enrolled student make the costs look even higher due to the high drop-out and repeater rates in many TVET institutions.

9.1 Cost-Effectiveness

Cost-effectiveness is extremely important since it is a useful indicator of productivity within the institution. If an institution uses the resources efficiently then it can be cost-effective. Cost-effectiveness has not been given much consideration in TVET systems in many Asian countries. They are mostly engaged in quantitative expansion without any regard to the quality of the graduates. There is an imperative need to assess and demonstrate quality and cost-effectiveness so that these institutions can contribute to improving national production and competitiveness.

9.2 Public/Private Partnership

Public/private sector partnerships are increasing in many countries and have been instrumental in providing both training and funding. However, developing countries are still finding it difficult to exploit this potential due to the fact that their TVET institutions have been working in complete isolation from industry. Private-sector involvement can help governments to augment funding for TVET while making the optimum use of resources for national development.

9.3 Project Work

Some TVET institutions use their workshops to produce saleable items, mainly for other schools, and thereby generate funding. Combining training with production is an innovation in many Asian countries that has been responsible for improving the quality of training and providing additional funding. There is a need to exploit this potential source of revenue for improving the quality of TVET. China provides a very good example in this regard, where technical schools are encouraged to run factories or enterprises to generate funding.

9.4 Industrial Funding

A major funding agency available to TVET is industry itself. Industry can help institutions with the provision of equipment, setting up workshops, paying for teaching posts and helping with training. Levies and assistance from industry are only possible when TVET institutions function efficiently and produce the graduates that industry requires. Several countries in Asia have enforced levies on industries, usually those with a certain number of employees, on the basis that industry is the main beneficiary of TVET. The Republic of Korea's in-plant training through the enterprise's own facilities is a case in point. Many other countries could benefit from such examples.

9.5 Diversifying Funding

Diversifying TVET funding sources is a major development in some countries in the region. Revolving funds with public and private-sector contributions have been established in some countries encouraging enterprises to provide training. Private institutions have also been established through this funding. Thailand placed a skills-development levy on industry, a major beneficiary of TVET, so as to establish a skills-development fund to support innovative schemes.

Governments need to reassess their budgeting for TVET in the light of the growing need for the national economies to improve their productivity and competitiveness. There is also a need on the part of many governments in the region to encourage the private sector to invest in TVET and then to support these initiatives so that these efforts could eventually lead to more training places.

10 Regional Co-operation

Regional co-operation has been encouraged over a long period, but shows little progress. It can help countries especially when problems are similar and resources are limited. It is mutually beneficial in areas such as the exchange of information and experiences, identifying common problems and seeking solutions, the use of teachers and equipment, curriculum development and improving the quality of training. Regional co-operation can assist the development of TVET structures, teacher upgrading, the maintenance of skill standards, the movement of students on a credit transfer basis, and even assist in providing employment possibilities. A regional information exchange system can be of much benefit. Regional co-operation can be made effective through the use of regional co-operation mechanisms, such as the Association of South-East Asian Nations (ASEAN) and Asia-Pacific Economic Co-operation (APEC), amongst others.

While regional and international co-operation are useful, countries in Asia can benefit greatly through mutual collaborative efforts among their national TVET institutions. The UNESCO-UNEVOC Network has been assisting countries in the region in the exchange of information and experiences, the development of infrastructures and the establishment of regional and national databases. There is an urgent need, both on the part of the countries and of UNESCO-UNEVOC, to accelerate this co-operation through the establishment of regional centres and national nodal points so that this potential can be fully utilized.

11 Conclusion

In spite of the fact that TVET is regarded as a priority for development in the region, there is still much to be done to achieve the vibrant, rich, high-quality education desired by all countries to restructure industry and enhance national production and competitiveness in this age of globalization and information. On the other hand, in the minds of most parents and students, TVET still remains a second-class education, suffering from a a lack of status. The present need is to reform TVET so as to equip its learners with skills of the future as opposed to the obsolete skills and know-how of the past. In this way, they can contribute to providing a competitive edge to national economies. This huge task is both urgent and imperative and calls for bold innovations in philosophy, objectives and practice. Nowhere is the need for economic, social and sustainable development greater than in the vast, diverse and still developing region of Asia and the Pacific. The biggest challenge in the region, which is mostly rural and agrarian, is to facilitate rural transformation and to alleviate poverty. For this purpose there is an urgent need to mobilize innovative and alternative approaches. Improvements are required in content, teaching practices, modes of delivery and teaching/learning processes with a bold shift from a supply-driven approach to the market-driven philosophy, objectives, practices and approaches of the future. There is also an urgent necessity to improve the delivery and outreach of TVET systems in the region using ICTs to optimize and maximize the results.

Asia and Pacific as a region has a big resource in the form of an abundance of manpower. However, this resource is also the region's greatest liability. For TVET, this challenge is the biggest opportunity in view of its huge potential to increase the region's productivity and competitiveness through reform and modernization in this age of information and globalization. In view of its huge magnitude, this task is beyond the capacities of most of the developing countries in the region. This matter therefore requires the urgent assistance of donors to provide support to these countries in their new and bold reform initiatives. New donor orientation, support and strategies can enable countries to produce the needed technical manpower for economic and social uplift. These approaches can also assist in achieving a competitive edge in their bids to derive optimum benefits from global and regional trade and mobility in this age of unprecedented technological advancement. The urgent challenge for TVET is to bridge the gap between the demands for jobs and the actual needs of society for economic, social and sustainable development. There is also an urgent need on the part of countries and donors for substantial investments in the skills of the future, particularly future generations, which for many governments in the region could be bold initiatives.

References

Ellis, S. 2005. Current international data for TVET and their limitations. *Prospects,* vol. 35, no. 3, pp. 367–80.

Green, A.; Oketch, M.; Preston, J. 2004. *Global report on technical and vocational education and training: report to UNESCO Institute for Statistics.* London: University of London Institute of Education.

Hughes, P. 2005. Why access to TVET for All is essential if EFA is to be achieved? *Prospects,* vol. 35, no. 3, pp. 253–67.

Lacson, J.D.; Justimbaste, B.S. 1995. *Philippine country paper.* (Paper presented at the International Workshop on Organisational and Management Alternatives for Vocational Education within the Educational System, 1995, Bhopal, India.)

Maclean, R. 2005a. Orientating TVET for sustainable development. *Prospects,* vol. 35, no. 3, pp. 269–72.

Maclean, R. 2005b. Setting the context: an overview of secondary education reform with particular reference to the Asia-Pacific Region. *In:* Lauglo, J.; Maclean, R., eds. *Vocationalisation of secondary education revisited.* Dordrecht, Netherlands: Springer.

Mar, Naing Yee. 2005. Approaches and concerns in TVET in Myanmar. *Prospects,* vol. 35, no. 3, pp. 331–42.

Mehta, A.C. 2003. *Progress of literacy in India: what the Census 2001 reveals.* New Delhi: NIEPA.

Mishra, A.K. 1995. Organizational alternatives in vocational education. *In:* Central Institute of Vocational Education of India, ed. *Vocational education: organizational and management alternatives.* Bhopal, India: Pundit Sunderlal Sharma Central Institute of Vocational Education.

Okada, S. 1995. *Country paper on Japan.* (Paper presented at the International Workshop on Organisational and Management Alternatives for Vocational Education within the Educational System, 1995, Bhopal, India.)

Quisumbing, L.R. 2005. Education for the world of work and citizenship: towards sustainable future societies. *Prospects,* vol. 35, no. 3, pp. 289–301.

Rafique, A. 1995. *Country paper on Bangladesh.* (Paper presented at the International Workshop on Organisational and Management Alternatives for Vocational Education within the Educational System, 1995, Bhopal, India.)

Timmermann, D. 1995. Dual training in Germany: is it a model for other countries? *In:* Central Institute of Vocational Education of India, ed. *Vocational education, organisational and management alternatives,* pp. 68–87. Bhopal, India: Pundit Sunderlal Sharma Central Institute of Vocational Education.

UNESCO-UNEVOC. 2005. Vocational education: the come-back? *Education today,* no. 13, April–June.

Wolfensberger, J. 1995. *Organizational structure of vocational education and training in Australia.* (Paper presented at the International Workshop on Organisational and Management Alternatives for Vocational Education within the Educational System, 1995, Bhopal, India.)

Chapter IV.4
Transforming TVET Systems with the CPSC in the Asia and Pacific Region

Man-Gon Park

1 Introduction

The Asia and Pacific Region extends from Mongolia in the north to New Zealand in the south and from the Cook Islands in the east to Iran in the west. It embraces the world's largest ocean, the Pacific (165 million square km.), as well as its third largest ocean, the Indian (73 million square km.) and a range of important seas. It contains three of the largest and most populous countries in the world (China, India and Indonesia), several mountainous and land-locked States (such as Bhutan and Nepal), and twenty-two small archipelagic States, territories and protectorates. With only 23% of the world's total land area, the region is home to about 58% of its population.

Twenty-four of the Colombo Plan Staff College (CPSC) member countries in the region are situated in the following geographical areas: North-East Asia (Japan, Mongolia and the Republic of Korea); South-East Asia (Indonesia, Malaysia, Myanmar, Philippines, Singapore, Thailand and Viet Nam); South Asia (Afghanistan, Bangladesh, Bhutan, India, Iran, Maldives, Nepal, Pakistan and Sri Lanka); and the Pacific (Australia, Fiji, New Zealand, Palau and Papua New Guinea). These countries are diverse in terms of socio-economic status and this has significant implications for the development of technical and vocational education systems.

Sustainable human resource development (HRD) through technical and vocational education and training (TVET) is an ambition for every country in the world. But rapid population growth and intensification in the exploitation of natural resources is making the Earth more fragile environmentally—and we are now aware that its capacity is not unlimited. This sustainable HRD concept was realized during the 1992 Earth Summit held in Rio de Janeiro in which heads of State and government adopted Agenda 21 and stressed the link between the sustainable use of natural resources and human development. The concept of sustainable development emphasized that economic development should enable present generations to meet the present needs without depriving the following and future generations of the same opportunities.

In order to put Agenda 21 into practice, a special programme known as Capacity 21 was launched by the United Nations Development Programme (UNDP) to aid countries in the development and implementation of capacity-building programmes.

R. Maclean, D. Wilson (eds.), *International Handbook of Education for the Changing World of Work*, DOI 10.1007/978-1-4020-5281-1_IV.4,
© Springer Science+Business Media B.V. 2009

The realization and importance of sustainable human resource development has been actively pursued since then.

Investment in human resource development is the key to the development process of any country. It requires linkages and an integrated multidisciplinary framework to bridge the traditional gap between sectors, as well as new innovative approaches to ensure sustainability and the optimum use of scarce resources. The latest information and communication technologies (ICTs) are also playing a greater role in the enhancement of individuals' capabilities to perform better in their work place and, at the same time, to ensure the sustainability of scarce resources.

The CPSC, a specialized agency for human resource development in TVET for its member countries in the Asia-Pacific Region, has been undertaking programmes and courses of further professional development in technical and vocational education over the past thirty-two years. It has thus accumulated a wealth of resources on all major aspects of technical and vocational education and sustainable HRD that need to be disseminated across the globe. CPSC, directly and indirectly, has been contributing towards HRD in this region with an emphasis on sustainability.

This chapter highlights some of the contemporary issues in TVET for HRD in the region, some programmes initiated by international and regional agencies to solve the pressing problems in sustainable HRD, the dilemmas and implications in sustainable HRD, the catalytic role of CPSC in the Asia-Pacific Region and the challenges for sustainable human resource development.

2 Regional Issues for Human Resource Development

Human resource development through TVET is actually a cycle of investment in human resources to enhance productive capabilities, the utilization of those resources to produce higher output, and the consumption by those human resources of the benefits arising from the increased output, thereby leading to an enhanced quality of life (UNESCO, 1999).

The Asia and Pacific Region contains countries of great diversity in terms of the size of their economies, demographic trends (population growth), ageing of the population, international migration, urbanization, the concentration of the population in rural areas, poverty, workforce mobility with the opening up of labour markets, the technology divide, etc. These diversities pose great challenges for international and regional organizations to successfully implement sustainable human resource development programmes.

Several CPSC member countries have witnessed marked improvements in the areas of health, nutrition and education over the past five years. However, some of them continue to grapple with low per capita income, rapid urbanization, inadequate access to ICTs, brain drain, an ageing population, rapid population growth, etc. Some of the most urgent issues are presented here with statistics taken from the World Bank and the United Nations Economic and Social Commission for Asia and the Pacific (ESCAP) data sources (World Bank, 2003).

2.1 Demographic Trends

The countries of the Asia and Pacific Region are heavily populated and are home to almost 3 billion people. The region includes some of the world's most populous countries, like China with 1.28 billion people, followed by India with 1 billion, Indonesia with over 210 million, Bangladesh and Pakistan with around 140 million people each.

Young people (under 25 years of age) constitute a sizeable and growing proportion of the population and their reproductive health concerns are a major issue, especially in view of the spreading HIV/AIDS pandemic. On the other hand, large ageing populations are emerging as an area of concern in countries all over the world. This is mainly connected with declining fertility and increased longevity. The proportion of older people is thus getting larger relative to the working population.

It is interesting to note that the number of people aged 60 and above in less-developed regions is more (393 million) than those in more-developed regions (235 million). The growth of the ageing population (by the year 2050), as estimated in World Bank documents, is five times more for the less-developed regions than for the developed regions (World Bank, 2003).

Table 1 gives the total population, the older population, population density and population growth rate for CPSC member countries.

Table 1 Population, population density and population growth rate: selected Asian countries

No.	Country	Total population in millions	Population aged 60 years or older (in 000)	Population density (people per sq. km.)	Population growth rate (% per annum)
1	Afghanistan	22	1,100	33	1.8
2	Bangladesh	135	7,210	912	1.3
3	Bhutan	2	144	48	3.2
4	Fiji	0.83	NA	45	0.7
5	India	1,068	81,089	325	1.5
6	Indonesia	214	17,169	113	1.4
7	Iran	66	3,922	40	1.4
8	Japan	128	31,027	342	0.5
9	Republic of Korea	48	5,532	481	0.6
10	Malaysia	25	1,561	76	2.1
11	Maldives	0.29	16	956	1.6
12	Myanmar	53	3,389	81	2.0
13	Nepal	24	1,438	164	2.1
14	Pakistan	148	8,611	185	1.9
15	Papua New Guinea	6	NA	12	1.8
16	Philippines	81	4,513	270	2.0
17	Singapore	4	463	6,134	0.5
18	Sri Lanka	19	1,857	307	1.3
19	Palau	0.02	NA	46	1.5

Source: World Bank, 2003.

The percentage growth rate of the population in most of the CPSC member countries has not changed considerably over recent years. However, when comparing the countries of the ESCAP region, Japan, the Republic of Korea, Singapore and Thailand are the CPSC member countries with the lowest population growth rate, while Bhutan and Fiji are the countries with the highest rate (Fig. 1). Put simply, the more developed countries have lower population growth rates while the less-developed countries have higher population growth rates (Fig. 2).

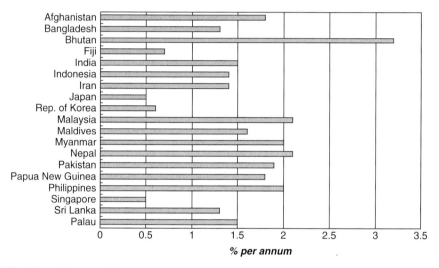

Fig. 1 Population growth rates

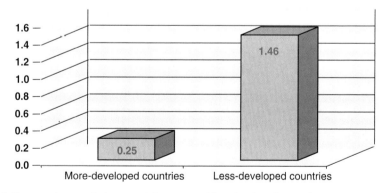

Fig. 2 Comparative population growth in more- and less-developed countries

Due to the limited geographical area, the population density is highest in Singapore and Maldives (Fig. 3). In the case of Bangladesh, the population is mostly concentrated in big cities.

The number of ageing people is growing as a result of lower fertility rates and better health conditions (Table 2). This increase in the aged population is an area

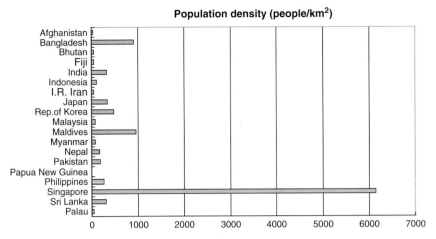

Fig. 3 Population density in the Asia and Pacific Region

Table 2 Percentage of the older population by region in 2000, 2015 and 2030

Region	Year	65 years or older	80 years or older
Asia	2000	5.9	0.9
	2015	7.8	1.4
	2030	12.0	2.3
Europe	2000	14.7	3.0
	2015	17.6	4.7
	2030	23.5	6.4
Latin America/Caribbean	2000	5.6	1.0
	2015	7.6	1.5
	2030	11.5	2.5
Middle East/North Africa	2000	4.4	0.6
	2015	5.5	0.9
	2030	8.4	1.4
North America	2000	12.4	3.3
	2015	14.7	3.9
	2030	20.0	5.4
Oceania	2000	10.1	2.3
	2015	12.4	3.1
	2030	16.3	4.4
Sub-Saharan Africa	2000	2.9	0.3
	2015	3.1	0.4
	2030	3.6	0.5

Source: <www.census.gov/ipc/www/idb/>; <www. unescap.org>

for concern for less-developed countries (United Nations Population Fund, 2002; Hermalin et al., 2002).

The publication *Global aging: the challenge of success* (Kinsella & Phillips, 2005) points out that people aged 65 or above already make up nearly one-fifth

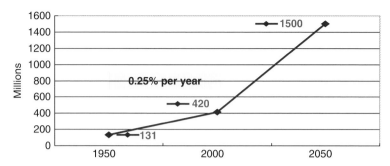

Fig. 4 Growth of the ageing population (60 years and above)

of the population in many European countries—and this proportion is rising. And less-developed countries are also seeing their populations growing older, ushering in new social problems for societies that already have few public support systems. By 2050, nearly 1.5 billion people aged 65 or older will reside in less-developed countries increasing at the rate of 0.25% per year (Fig. 4).

2.2 The Brain Drain through International Migration

Since the 1970s, Asia has been largely a region of out-migration, much of which is intra-regional. Today, out of the 179 million people who are outside their countries of birth, an estimated 50 million are in Asia. Of the many forms of international migration in the region, the movement of labour across borders has been most significant. Contrary to the intent of governments to regard migration as a temporary phenomenon, it has been sustained over the past thirty years. Asia, like other regions before it (North America, North-West Europe, the oil-rich Gulf countries), has not escaped the need to import labour to sustain the development processes. One report painted the following picture of Asian region migrants (Asis, 2005).

> In the 1980s, the high performing economies of Japan, Hong Kong, Singapore, and later on in the decade, Malaysia and Thailand, had to import migrant workers. The construction sector, plantations, fishing and rice mill industries and factories in these countries experienced labour shortage, as locals moved on to better job prospects. The demand for female migrant workers increased, but the demand was limited to domestic work (Hong Kong, Singapore, Malaysia) and entertainers (Japan). On the other hand, the Middle East continued to draw migrants, although not in the same scale as in the previous decade. A remarkable development was the opening of the labour market to women migrants to fill jobs in the service (mostly domestic workers), sales and professional (e.g. medical personnel) sectors. The Philippines, Indonesia and Sri Lanka became the major source countries of domestic workers. Female migration from the latter two countries, in particular, is heavily directed to the Middle East countries. While domestic workers also dominate female migration from the Philippines to the Middle East, a sizable number are professionals (mostly nurses and other medical personnel). The concentration of women migrants in domestic work and entertainment (also in caring professions such as nurses) highlights the gendering of the labour market. In Asia, male labour migration has specialized in addressing the labour needs in the formal/productive sectors, while female labour migration is responding to the domestic work force.

In view of some of the above trends and associated immediate problems and issues in labour force migration, we can summarize that:

- Mobilization of the workforce across national borders would continue with migration from less-developed countries to more-developed countries.
- The disparity of skills and competencies with regard to the optimum qualifications required remains a matter of concern both for employers and migrants.
- The demand to standardize and harmonize TVET systems through accreditation and certification would grow.

2.3 Massive and Rapid Urbanization

Urbanization has taken on a new dimension and become a matter of concern in the Asia-Pacific Region. In an article published by the United Nations, it says that in 1999 47% of the world's population (2.9 billion people) lived in urban areas. By 2030, it projects that this proportion will reach 60%, totalling 4.9 billion people. Roughly 95% of this massive urban growth will occur in less-developed countries.

More than 60% of the increase in the world's urban population over the next three decades will occur in Asia, particularly in China and India, but also in Pakistan, Bangladesh, Philippines and Viet Nam. According to World Bank indicators, Asia will have a lower overall urbanization rate in 2030 (53%) than any other region. Africa will be slightly higher at 55%, while Latin America is projected to reach 83%. However, Asia's total urban population will exceed 2.6 billion in 2030, compared with 604 million in Latin America and 766 million in Africa. Such huge flows of human resources to urban areas will put pressure on governments to take measures and allocate funds for better health, education and accommodation (World Bank, 2003; Mendes, 2005).

2.4 Poverty Alleviation

Poverty is a serious issue all over the globe. The severity of the issue can be judged from the fact that the first goal under the UN Millennium Development Goals (MDGs) is related to the commitment to eradicate poverty and hunger: <www.un.org/milleniumgoals/>.

The 2005 report on the MDGs has given an improved picture of poverty reduction in the Asian region. Even with an overall population growth of more than 800 million since 1990 in developing regions, the number of people living in extreme poverty has fallen by 130 million worldwide. The situation in some African countries where poverty persists is still not good; extreme poverty has risen in that region from 227 million in 1990 to 313 million in 2001, i.e. one in five people in the developing world still lives below the extreme poverty line of $1 per day income. The statistics are given in Fig. 5.

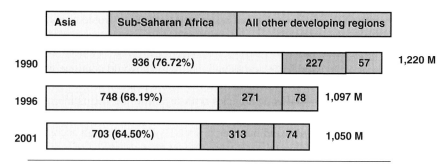

Fig. 5 The number of people living on less than $1 per day, 1990, 1996 and 2001 (millions)

2.5 The Technology Divide

The digital divide is often described as the disparity that has emerged between the 'haves' and the 'have-nots' in a society grounded on ICTs. Generally, the 'haves' are the well-educated with the financial means to invest time and effort to acquire skills that will enable them to flourish in an information society. The 'have-nots', mainly from the lower-income groups, are the ones who lack affordable access to ICTs, thus being disadvantaged in terms of employability and learning opportunities. This digital disparity can be seen in Table 3, which gives the number of Internet users in CPSC member countries:

Table 3 Number of Internet users in CPSC member countries

No.	Country	Literacy rate (%)	Number of Internet users per 100 people
1	Afghanistan	NA	NA
2	Bangladesh	50	2.04
3	Bhutan	56	1.75
4	Fiji	94	6.7
5	India	68.36	1.75
6	Indonesia	92	3.76
7	Iran	83	7.24
8	Japan	99	48.27
9	Republic of Korea	98	60.97
10	Malaysia	92	34.41
11	Maldives	97	5.34
12	Myanmar	89	0.05
13	Nepal	59	0.34
14	Pakistan	60	1.03
15	Papua New Guinea	65	1.37
16	Philippines	93	4.40
17	Singapore	97	50.87
18	Sri Lanka	95	1.17
19	Palau	92	NA

It can be seen that, although most countries have access to Internet technology, there is a considerable disparity between Japan, the Republic of Korea, Malaysia and Singapore and the rest. This emerging divide is no longer between the traditional haves and have-nots, but between those nations that are wired and those that are not. Of course, the developed countries already have the edge. For example, in the Republic of Korea high-speed Internet access is available to the majority of the people, as compared to Afghanistan and Bhutan which have minimal Internet facilities in work places and homes.

3 Dilemmas and Implications for Sustainable Human Resource Development

Nowhere in the world can we appreciate the enigma of social, economic, scientific-technological, politico-cultural disparity than in the Asia-Pacific Region. In spite of the significant achievements made during past years, these imbalances are still conspicuous. Japan, the Republic of Korea and Singapore not only exceed world averages on many development indicators, but are also considered the precursors of technology. On the other hand, South Asia, which includes Afghanistan, Bhutan, India, Nepal and Pakistan, was described by Churton (2004) as 'the poorest region, the most illiterate, the most malnourished, the region with the highest human deprivation and the most militarized region in the world'.

Indeed, the widening inequality of opportunities, wealth and empowerment continues hounding the region resulting in a negative impact in the pursuit of sustainable human resource development. These dilemmas therefore need serious consideration.

3.1 Poverty

A UNDP *Human development report* presented a comparative analysis among Asia-Pacific countries: the poverty indices of Singapore and Brunei are negligible while those of Myanmar and Lao PDR (38.9 and 32.3, respectively) are quite high. The same report cited the poverty indices of Malaysia (14.2), Philippines (16.5) and Thailand (18.7), which are within the same range as Singapore, while those of Indonesia (27.7) and Viet Nam (28.7) are moderate (UNDP, 2003).

The unequal distribution of wealth leads to unsustainability—both for the 'haves' and 'have-nots'. The 'have-nots', whose ratio still stands high at one in three Asians, are trapped in the vicious cycle of deprivation and vulnerability. Since they can hardly cope with survival, security and enabling needs, they inevitably become unsustainable. They are unable to participate in governance, which is necessary for peaceful development.

On the other hand, the 'haves' can afford a higher level of sustainability since they can choose which actions to pursue. But more often than not, they are reluctant to adopt sustainable patterns of development and stubbornly adhere to malpractices of over-production and over-consumption.

3.2 Disparity in Educational Access and Quality

Education constitutes the core of strategies that promote values and could transform the well-being of the individual, society and the environment. Although the right to education is decreed in the constitution of most—if not all—countries, it remains disproportionately accessible. For a long time, the rare opportunity of attending schools has belonged to the 'privileged few', leaving the 'insignificant many' to the dark side of ignorance and illiteracy. The World Bank (2003) reported that over 1 billion children under the age of 15 require improved primary and secondary services, while 400 million young people between the ages of 17 and 24 require tertiary, vocational education and skills development. In rural areas, the number of children who do not go to school, the number of adult illiterates and gender inequality in education are high. The drop-out rate after primary level is also high because the impoverished farmer can no longer meet the cost of his children's further education. And even if he can just afford the government's school system, his children do not receive a good education. Families with a higher economic status benefit from higher potential and better opportunities in gaining access to education.

The quality of education is also a factor to consider because it is the very instrument to create new relations for sustainable human resource development. Today, many institutions mushroom every year and there have been minimal checks on the quality of services that these offer. Most countries lack accreditation and certification systems to benchmark educational and training standards, to serve as a licenser by quantitatively and qualitatively evaluating them, to support workforce mobilization and to establish a clearinghouse of information and co-operation agencies (UNESCO-UNEVOC, 2004).

3.3 Population and Migration from Rural to Urban Areas

Although, remarkably, the population growth rate in the region is decelerating, the actual population continues to increase. Such a condition will intensify land use, thereby generating further pressure on natural resources. Mendes (2005) refers to a UN estimate that by 2015 fifteen conurbations in the region will become mega-cities with a population of at least 10 million each. In particular, South Asia already has mega-cities like Dhaka, Karachi, Kolkata and Mumbai that are expected to experience further sharp population increases due to migration as well as natural growth.

Urbanization and rural/urban migration are some of the most pressing dilemmas thwarting a sustainable human resource development system. They have changed the economic structure leading to a remarkable decline in the agricultural sector and a shift to industrial and service sectors (Kaosa-ard & Rerkasem, 2000). This led to the intensification of the rural/urban gap and eventually the inequitable distribution of income and production assets. Moreover, it resulted in problems of uncontrolled growth, inappropriate waste disposal practices, lack of adequate drinking water supply and sanitation facilities, and flooding. The urban poor, who are most affected by these problems, contented themselves in the slums by constructing clusters of shanties wherever and however they could. In the Asia-Pacific Region, these slums are typically temporary structures made of cardboard or jute sacks lacking basic infrastructures and services such as water supply, sewage, drainage, roads, health care and education (WHO/UNICEF, 2001). Demolition of these shanties is common but not successful, since the slums either move to another place or come back again.

3.4 Lawlessness

To live in an environment of peace and security is fundamental to human dignity. Countries in the Asia-Pacific Region are riddled with insecurities and armed conflicts, which have resulted in a significant number of human tragedies, displaced people, refugees and wars. Characteristically, corruption has debased fair and efficient economic transactions, undermined governmental legitimacy, threatened political stability and jeopardized socio-economic development in most Asia-Pacific countries. According to the Transparency International Corruption Perceptions Index (www.transparency.org), some countries in the region are high on this global list. Indeed, governance structures are highly militarized, devoid of transparency, and freedom of expression and debate do not exist.

In another vein, there is an upsurge of crime and lawlessness related to juvenile delinquency as a result of drugs and alcoholism, unwanted pregnancies, etc.

3.5 Environmental, Health and Safety Hazards

Health is wealth. A healthy population breeds a healthy nation. On the other hand, ill-health breeds a sick nation. It hampers economic and social development, triggering a vicious cycle that contributes to unsustainable resource use and environmental degradation. The tsunami-stricken developing countries of Sri Lanka, India, Indonesia and Maldives have shown that they are vulnerable to natural hazards and disasters. Other countries of the region suffer from limited natural resources, heavy dependence on imports and limited commodities.

Hunger, malnutrition, malaria, water-borne diseases, bird-flu, dengue fever, drug and alcohol abuse, violence and injury, HIV/AIDS and other sexually transmitted diseases are common scenarios. According to the 2003 UNDP *Human development report* (UNDP, 2003), inadequate water supply and poor sanitation cause more than 500,000 infant deaths a year, as well as bringing a huge burden of illness and disability in the region. Cholera is prevalent in many countries, particularly those where sanitation facilities are poor, such as Afghanistan, China and India. Only an estimated 48% of the Asian population has access to proper sanitation—less than in any other region of the world. The situation is worse in rural areas, where only 31% of the population have improved sanitation, compared to 78% in urban areas.

3.6 Non-availability of a Labour-Market Information System

Occupational forecasting is extremely important and is an essential tool for address-ing the occupational imbalances in the labour market. Recognizing the uncertainty of projection about the growth in employment demand and the need to develop an appropriate supply-side framework stands at the core of priorities in the area of labour-market information management system (LMIS). This would make the TVET sector responsive to labour-market needs. Making such predictions requires expertise in the application of economic analysis, modelling and forecasting.

3.7 Widening of the Digital Gap

The issue of the digital divide, the lack of sustainability in efforts and the tech-nical knowledge gap reflect the present-day scenario in the Asia-Pacific Region. During the past two decades, the world has witnessed a technological revolution that has provided mankind with totally new communications media. Through the use of networks, information in all forms is disseminated throughout the world. E-applications have created the potential to bring benefits to society, the economy and the State. In particular, e-government, e-health, e-education and e-commerce have been identified as services enhancing not only economic growth, but also pro-moting democratic and social progress and bringing sustainability. The dilemma is that in most of the developing countries of the CPSC the availability of ICT services is still at a very low level. The issue of the digital divide persists between the urban and rural areas of any one country and as well as between countries of the region. For example, access to the Internet by households in Afghanistan is below 5%, while in the Republic of Korea high-speed Internet connections are available to almost 80% of the population.

4 The Important Role of the CPSC as a Catalyst

4.1 CPSC Emergence

The Colombo Plan Staff College was born on 5 December 1973 after twenty-six member countries agreed to establish a regional centre for TVET, through a reso-lution signed and agreed by the Colombo Plan member countries. The college was created as a specialized agency of the Colombo Plan to address issues in TVET with the following main functions (Park, 2004):

- Providing courses of further professional education and training;
- Conducting conferences on various aspects of TVET;
- Assisting in the conduct of projects in TVET;
- Promoting and co-ordinating research;
- Advising and assisting member countries in developing TVET; and
- Collecting and disseminating information on TVET.

The CPSC activities thus focus on human resource development through training, consultancy work on major projects in the member countries, research and development in major areas of TVET and processing and dissemination of information in technical education and training.

4.2 Major Thrust Areas of CPSC

Over the past more than thirty years, CPSC has accumulated a wealth of resources in various fields of technical and vocational education. Table 4 gives a glimpse of programmes conducted by CPSC over recent years in eight major thrust areas known as the 'CPSC-RING'.

The table only includes the CPSC regular in-country and regional programmes. It does not include consultancy work and other research and development activities conducted in that particular area. The programmes are prepared taking in to consideration regional trends, while the in-country programmes are prepared according to the specific demands of each member country.

It is evident from Table 4 that there has been an attempt on the part of CPSC to cover all major thrust areas over the past five years. The ICT component is the most popular area among all the member countries of the region. This popularity laid the foundation for the development of the CPSC's web-based teaching and learning system and the integration of information and communication technology in all programmes of the Colombo Plan Staff College.

The second most popular thrust area is the project, programmes and the institutional management focusing on total quality management, knowledge management, ISO and accreditation and certification systems, and project preparation

Table 4 CPSC-RING for technology transfer, education and training services

Major thrust area	2000/2001	2001/2002	2002/2003	2003/2004	2004/2005
Computer and Internet technologies	7	7	8	7	6
Projects and institutional management	5	5	5	5	4
Sustainable development and poverty alleviation	2	1	1	1	1
Curriculum development	3	1	3	1	2
Research and development	2	2	1	2	1
Industry-institution linkages				2	
Non-technical skills	1	2		1	2
Global partnership	1			1	2

implementation and monitoring. The trainee group that this area focuses on is the top and middle-level management of TVET systems.

4.3 CPSC Strategies over the Recent Past

Human resource development itself is a challenging task. In order to bridge the technological gap and make its programmes sustainable, while meeting the challenges of sustainable human resource development, the CPSC has launched several initiatives under its Corporate Strategic Plan over recent years. In 2003, the CPSC launched the '4Rs Strategy':

- Refocusing programmes, projects and activities to provide demand-driven, sustainable and innovative services for HRD;
- Repositioning for a lead role in the advancement of HRD in the Asia-Pacific Region so as to obtain the full benefits of emerging global trends and using cutting-edge technologies;
- Restructuring the organizational system through a quality management system, effective delivery of services, networking, global partnership and expansion of membership; and
- Reengineering for production of creative, practical, pioneering and technology oriented outputs in TVET responding to national, regional and international demands.

In 2004, the CPSC decided on even more proactive services through the '3As Approach':

- Accelerated services to clienteles to transform amidst environmental changes;
- Advanced systems and best practices in HRD;
- Aggressive mind-set with determined actions for continual improvement.

In 2005, the two previous approaches were combined for a more focused, improved and specialized service through the 'STELAH Services':

- Supporting national and regional HRD programmes, projects and activities;
- Technology transfers to member countries;
- Expanding a web-based teaching and learning system;
- Labour-market information services;
- Accreditation and certification services; and
- Higher education service in technology education.

4.4 CPSC Innovative Web-Based E-Teaching/Learning System

The web-based and e-teaching/learning system (CPSC WB TLS) is an innovative, flexible and lifelong learning system that has been developed with all in-house capabilities and resources. The system not only introduces technological awareness

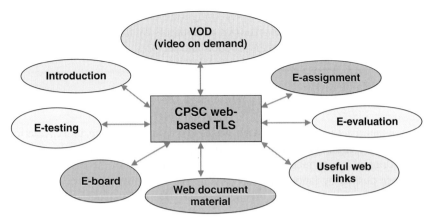

Fig. 6 Components of the CPSC web-based teaching/learning system (WB TLS)

and benefits to its participants as a by-product, but also exemplifies knowledge-management, economizing the cost of programmes and introducing the latest trends in teaching and learning.

So far, CPSC has launched more than a dozen web-based teaching and learning programmes on different topics utilizing its in-house facilities and resources. The overall structure and design of the programme can be understood from Fig. 6.

All CPSC programmes are becoming web-based to provide continuous learning, to make learning easy and interactive and accessible anywhere anytime. The interactivity of these programmes is one of its unique features that makes them an outstanding and unique form for common e-learning programmes.

5 Challenges for Sustainable Human Resource Development

5.1 Globalization

One major challenge for sustainable HRD is globalization. This process is fostered not only by technological change and the continually falling costs of ICTs, but also by the decisions of developing countries in Asia and the Pacific and elsewhere to embrace market-oriented development strategies and to open up their countries increasingly to the world economy. The world is thus fast becoming one interdependent global market-place with rising competitiveness.

A key contributor in the success of the competitive global market is the knowledge and skills of the workforce within national boundaries and within enterprises. Thus, compared to the past, nations and organizations will need to update much more regularly the skills mix of their workforce and employees to respond to the opportunities or threats created by globalization and rapid technological change.

Indeed, intense global competition is reconfiguring the market-place and each enterprise must differentiate itself from its competitors by the quality of the human systems and processes behind their products and services.

5.2 Cross-Border Workforce Flow and Investment

The Asia and Pacific Region has seen waves of investment by Japanese, American and European companies. It has also seen cross-border investments by the four Asian 'dragon' economies of Hong Kong, the Republic of Korea, Taiwan and Singapore pushed by labour shortages, rising wages and stronger exchange rates. The three 'tiger' economies of Indonesia, Malaysia and Thailand are also investing overseas. As other Asian countries industrialize successfully, they will also undertake cross-border investments. There has also been an increase in regional co-operation zones in the Association of South-East Asian Nations (ASEAN). With this scenario, synergies among the regional and international human resource development organizations like CPSC need to develop strategies and plans to cope with challenges of cross-border workforce mobility with standard skills (Park, 2005b).

5.3 Technological Environmental Changes

The convergence of ICTs has ushered in a big revolution in every facet of human life. Given the magnitude of the environmental changes that these ICTs have the potential to induce, it is vitally important that we understand how this revolution has changed, is changing and will continue to change our primitive community to an e-community—and now the u-world. Technology leaders should be aware of the need to improve existing common and special infrastructures in support of pervasive computing, digital convergence and stronger bandwidth. The next generation of Internet communication services, infrastructures and growth engines will see wireless broadband service, radio frequency identification, system-on-chip, embedded SW, DMB and others. Moreover, faculty and staff need re-training and up-training so as to be responsive to the calls of the new technology in TVET institutions (Park, 2005a).

5.4 Enhancing International Networks

The development of sustainable human resources requires concerted efforts and approaches from all national, regional and international training organizations. With the globalization of markets and economies, the challenges are not specific to any one country or institution. Hence, strong networks and partnerships among regional and international organizations and institutions are required for the development of sustainable human resources.

5.5 *Increasing Cross-Cultural Communication and Experiences*

The Colombo Plan Staff College, with its nineteen member countries, is a cross-cultural organization with varied internalized values, attitudes and behaviours, communication media, etc. The joint programmes and ventures, integrated, flexible and interactive teaching/learning activities provide opportunities for increased cross-cultural communication and sharing of experiences. The challenge is to meet the expectations of all stakeholders with varied levels of needs and demands (Mahmood, Kim & Park, 2004).

6 Concluding Remarks

Human resource development is a concerted process. No single department at the national level and no single agency at the regional or international level can do the HRD job successfully alone. To make the HRD programmes and projects successful and sustainable, ICTs play a very important role and provide the potential to make them flexible. However, it needs to be ensured that the majority of people in developing countries obtain access to the Internet and the digital divide is minimized to the maximum possible extent. The idea of e-communities and e-textbooks is gathering momentum and their careful planning and implementation would bring promising results. The international agencies, like UNESCO-UNEVOC, ILO, ADB, CPSC and others, should jointly undertake collaborative programmes utilizing their resources.

In sustainable development, the three key areas that need to be taken into consideration are: economic sustainability; environmental sustainability; and social sustainability. For economic sustainability, the TVET system, including all of its essential elements, should ensure that learners/participants develop a wider set of economically-related knowledge skills and attitudes. For environmental sustainability, the TVET system must raise the participants' and the course developers' awareness of the use of scarce resources and minimize wastage. It should thus include areas like environmental concepts, personal values and life-styles and skills for critical thinking and practical action in HRD programmes. Social sustainability means that the basic needs of all participants are satisfied, regardless of their gender, ethnicity or location (Peng Boo Tan, 1997). It provides an equal opportunity to all to develop and utilize their talents.

References

Asis, M.M.B. 2005. *When men and women migrate: comparing gendered migration in Asia.* Quezon City, Philippines: Scalabrini Migration Center.

Churton, M. 2004. *ICT implications for culture and development for learning.* Bangkok: SEAMEO-UNESCO.

Hermalin, A.I. et al. 2002. *The well-being of the elderly in Asia: a four-country comparative study.* Ann Arbor, MI: University of Michigan Press.

Kaosa-ard, M.S.; Rerkasem, B. 2000. *The growth and sustainability of agriculture in Asia.* Manila: ADB.

Kinsella, K.; Phillips, D.R. 2005. Global aging: the challenge of success. *Population bulletin,* vol. 60, no. 1.

Mahmood, T.; Kim Myong Hee; Park, M.-G. 2004. *A short method for building web-based teaching and learning systems: the CPSC experience.* (Paper presented at the International Conference on 'New Challenges in Technology Education for HRD in Asia and the Pacific Region', 20–21 September 2004, Kolkata, India.)

Mendes, M.R. 2005. *Urban environmental management challenges in Asia.* Kanagawa, Japan: Institute for Global Environmental Strategies.

Park M.-G. 2004. *CPSC as a catalyst for regional accreditation and certification of TVET institutions: prospects and challenges.*(Paper presented at the International Conference on Accreditation and Certification for TVET Institutions, 2–3 December 2004, Seoul, Republic of Korea.)

Park, M.-G. 2005a. *Transforming TVET systems with CPSC in Asia and the Pacific Region.* (Paper presented at the International Conference on 'New Challenges in Technology Education for HRD in Asia and the Pacific Region', 20–21 September 2004, Kolkata, India.)

Park M.-G. 2005b. *Environmental changes through ICT from e-Community to U-World.* (Paper presented at the International Conference on 'Developing e-Community Centers', Agra, India, 2–6 May 2005.)

Peng Boo Tan. 1997. *Human resources development in Asia and the Pacific in the 21st Century: issues and challenges for employers and their organizations.* (Paper presented at the ILO Workshop on Employers' Organizations in Asia-Pacific in the Twenty-First Century, Turin, Italy, 1997.)

UNESCO. 1999. *Second International Conference on Technical and Vocational Education: final report.* Paris: UNESCO.

UNESCO-UNEVOC. 2004. TVET for sustainable development. *UNESCO-UNEVOC Bulletin,* no. 8, April.

United Nations Development Programme. 2003. *Human development report, 2003.* New York, NY: UNDP.

United Nations Population Fund. 2002. *World population ageing 1950-2050.* New York, NY: UNFPA.

World Bank. 2003. *World development indicators, 2002.* Washington, DC: World Bank. <www.worldbank.org/data/wdi2005/index.html>

World Health Organization/United Nations Children's Fund. 2001. *Global water supply and sanitation assessment 2000 report.* Geneva, Switzerland: WHO; New York, NY: UNICEF.

Chapter IV.5
European Action Programmes for Lifelong Learning

Johanna Lasonen

1 Introduction

Vocational education and training has been a part of the process of creating a European community since the 1950s. The European training programmes Erasmus and Comett were launched in the 1980s. After the Maastricht Treaty, agreed in 1992, such training programmes were expanded further at the same time as emphasizing their importance to the internationalization of education. With a view to promoting and intensifying educational co-operation, in 1995 the European Commission created two new educational programmes called Socrates and Leonardo da Vinci. Both are umbrella schemes that brought together previously separate action programmes in the field of education. Leonardo da Vinci has been a European Union (EU) action programme in the field of vocational education and training that replaced earlier schemes such as Comett, Eurotechnet, Petra, Force and a part of Lingua. Leonardo I ran from 1995 to 1999, while Leonardo II covered the years 2000 to 2006. Socrates has been the EU umbrella programme for co-operation in school and higher education. Socrates I (1995–1999) was followed by Socrates II (2000–2006). Since 2007, the European education and training programmes were further merged under the title Lifelong Learning Programme (LLP), being a successor to the Socrates, Leornardo da Vinci and e-Learning programmes. The LLP covers the period 2007 to 2013 with a budget of about 7 billion Euros. The overarching LLP initiative consists of learning opportunities from childhood to old age.

The purpose of these programmes has been to promote the international mobility of students, teachers and educational administrators, develop educational practices, and make European education systems more transparent through mutual learning. The target group of these programmes has been individuals in schools, colleges, universities and companies. The motives behind internationalization include sustainable economic growth, competitiveness, a need for an educated workforce and social cohesion. This chapter describes the development of European education and training programmes, especially in TVET, and assesses their effectiveness.

R. Maclean, D. Wilson (eds.), *International Handbook of Education for the Changing World of Work*, DOI 10.1007/978-1-4020-5281-1_IV.5,
© Springer Science+Business Media B.V. 2009

2 The Socrates[1] Programme

The European Economic Community, after its foundation in the 1950s, initially ad-dressed educational matters only in the areas of vocational training and the transition from education to employment. When higher education became part of the European agenda in the 1970s, one of the first activities was to promote student mobility. Joint Study Programmes were established in 1976 and remained in operation for about a decade. They provided financial support for networks of departments that exchanged students for a period of up to one year and also included some funds—though on a modest scale.

Subsequently, in 1987, the Erasmus programme was inaugurated. Its name not only reminded one of the Dutch humanist and theologian Desiderius Erasmus Roterodamus (1466–1536), but also served as an acronym for the European Com-munity Action Scheme for the Mobility of University Students. Erasmus was in-tended to increase the quantity of European higher education activities and to broaden their scope. It rapidly became the most visible of the various newly emerg-ing European educational programmes. Though its financial resources did not reach the amount needed to pursue the ambitious aim initially set by the European Com-munity of supporting a temporary study period in another European country for 10% of higher education students, Erasmus became the largest student mobility programme hitherto established.

A new chapter in the history of European support for temporary student mobility and trans-border co-operation between higher education institutions was expected to begin when the Socrates and Leonardo da Vinci programmes were established in 1995. Socrates integrated more than a dozen educational programmes which had been set up in the late 1980s and early 1990s. They were revised or supplemented to form two new large European programmes: Socrates for the different sectors of general education and Leonardo da Vinci for vocational education. Socrates ab-sorbed Erasmus and Lingua, which became two of a total of five sub-programmes. The adult education sub-programme was the result of the restructuring of an already existing programme. The amount of funds available for adult education was sub-stantially increased. Comenius was introduced as a sub-programme for the school sector, while open and distance learning were the most noteworthy additions to al-ready existing programmes.

The Socrates Institutional Contracts have covered a broad range of possible co-operation activities: organization of student mobility; teaching staff mobility; intro-duction of the European Credit Transfer System (ECTS); curriculum development, including curricula at initial or intermediate level; programmes at advanced level; and modules focusing on the history, society, culture, politics or economies of other European countries, as well as integrated language courses.

Student and teacher visits to universities in Europe have been among the most popular of the activities funded under the Socrates programme. Between 1997 and 2000 European universities, acting within the framework of the Socrates pro-gramme, entered into a total of 4,823 co-operation agreements (Lanzendorf & Teichler, 2002, p. 34).

The first phase of Socrates, the European education programme, lasted five years. The figures covering this time (1996–2000) indicate that 500,000 students undertook a period of study in another European university, 10,000 schools formed European partnerships and thousands of projects were developed to promote European languages (European Commission, 2005).

When Erasmus became a sub-programme of Socrates, support for student mobility and co-operation in higher education was substantially increased. In addition, the mobility of teaching staff and curricular innovation were now also promoted in the context of a special emphasis on a broad development of the European dimension in higher education and efforts to make the non-mobile students also benefit from European exchange activities.

The second phase of the Socrates programme started in January 2000 and ran for seven years until 2006 (European Commission, 2000). The programme budget for this seven-year period was 1,850 million Euros. The second phase has continued along the same path as the first one while also introducing some new features. Two key ideas were emphasized: the promotion of lifelong learning and the building of a Europe of knowledge. The aims of the programme have been:

- to strengthen the European dimension of education at all levels;
- to improve knowledge of European languages;
- to promote co-operation and mobility throughout education;
- to encourage innovation in education; and
- to promote equal opportunities in all sectors of education.

The Socrates programme has consisted of eight actions: (1) *Comenius* on general school education; (2) *Erasmus* on higher education; (3) *Grundtvig* on adult education and other educational pathways; (4) *Lingua* on the learning of European languages; (5) *Minerva* on information and communication technologies (ICTs) in education; (6) observation on and innovation in education systems and policies; (7) joint actions with other European programmes; and (8) accompanying measures that bring flexibility, synergies and horizontal priorities. The first three actions have corresponded to the three stages that constitute milestones of education throughout life: school, university and adult education. The other five actions have been horizontal. All eight have had common priorities.

Socrates has taken account of all types of learning, whether formal or informal, and all levels of education from nursery school to university and adult education, which is becoming increasingly important. Socrates has been relevant to all those involved in education: teachers, educational staff, administrative and management staff, pupils and students, all playing an increasingly active part in European co-operation projects. Until 2006, there have been a total of thirty-one countries taking part:

- Twenty-five European Union member states: Austria, Belgium, Czech Republic, Cyprus, Denmark, Finland, Estonia, France, Germany, Greece, Hungary, Ireland, Italy, Latvia, Lithuania, Luxembourg, Malta, Netherlands, Poland, Portugal, Slovakia, Slovenia, Spain, Sweden and the United Kingdom;

- Three EFTA (European Free Trade Area) countries: Iceland, Liechtenstein and Norway;
- Two associated countries: Bulgaria and Romania—(in due course, Turkey).

Socrates encourages the broad dissemination of information, ideas and good practice, for example through the setting up of networks.

Since 2007, Comenius, Erasmus, Leonardo da Vinci and Grundtvig are the sectoral sub-programmes of the Lifelong Learning Programme—Socrates has been removed as a sub-programme.

3 The Leonardo da Vinci[2] Programme

The Leonardo da Vinci programme has been the first integrated community programme in the field of vocational education. The European Council approved the programme under Article 127 of the Maastricht Treaty, where it was stated that the Community must pursue TVET policies without harming the national legislation and decrees of the member states. The first phase of the Leonardo da Vinci programme was planned under the influence of earlier special programmes:

- Comett I (1986–1989) and Comett II (1990–1994) promoting co-operation between higher education establishments and industry;
- Eurotecnet (1990–1994) promoting innovation in education;
- Force (1991–1994) developing further education, continuing vocational education (CVT);
- Petra I (1987–1991) and Petra II (1990–1994) on vocational training of young people, initial vocational education and training (IVET) and transition from school to work;
- Lingua (1990–1994) on developing language skills.

Among the challenges faced in designing the Leonardo programme was integrating all these previous programmes into a single unified whole with a view to achieving a sharper focus on developing educational policy.

Leonardo da Vinci is a vocational education and training programme whose legal basis was laid down in Article 10, paragraph 4 of Council Decision 94/819/EC taken on 6 December 1994 (European Commission, 1994). It was resolved that the development of educational policy would also be promoted through co-operation across national boundaries and through innovation and exchange activities. This came to form the practical basis for the Leonardo da Vinci programme, whose first phase lasted five years (1995–1999) and which was adopted as the main tool of European educational policy. The programme was allocated a budget of 620 million Euros with nineteen objectives. They included fostering the quality of and innovatory activities in the education systems of EU member states and promoting lifelong learning, the education of disadvantaged target groups, educational access, language education, equal educational opportunities, transparency of qualifications, open education and distance education, vocational guidance, and co-operation between higher education establishments and industry.

The budget of the second phase (2000–2006) of the Leonardo da Vinci Programme was raised to 1,150 million Euros. The objectives of the second phase of the programme were:

- to improve the skills and competencies of people, especially of young people, in vocational training at all levels with a view to facilitating their integration and reintegration into the labour market;
- to improve the quality of and access to continuing vocational training and promote the lifelong acquisition of skills and competencies;
- to promote and reinforce the contribution of vocational training to the process of innovation with a view to improving competitiveness and entrepreneurship, also as a means of creating new employment opportunities.

A central feature and advantage of the Leonardo da Vinci programme has been its cross-national character. Each project was required to have partners from not less than two or three different member states. This has enabled the programme to influence educational practices in Europe through cross-cultural exchanges of experiences. In 2003, the Directorate-General for Education and Culture of the European Commission ordered the external interim evaluation of the Leonardo da Vinci II Programme. Between 2000 and 2002, the programme brought together more than 77,000 partners to work on a shared project idea (European Commission, 2004). Such partnerships have made it possible to establish permanent networks for collaboration across national boundaries and for the exchange of good practices. The programme has become well-known through its promotion of trans-border mobility, which has allowed participants to gain work and study experience abroad. The programme has provided funding for staff and trainee exchanges benefiting nearly 127,000 people in vocational education. Effectiveness improved in 2000–2002 compared to the previous programme period (1995–1999). The number of beneficiaries increased and the quality of mobility projects improved. The number of pilot projects increased between 2000 and 2002 (180 pilot projects in 2000 and 204 in 2001).

The experiences acquired through these exchanges have fostered young people's personal development, helped them to improve their self-confidence and language skills, and to understand different cultures, working methods and organizations. Project outcomes indicate that residence abroad has also had a positive effect on the participants' employability. Further, the Council's decision on the Europass certificate was specifically based on the outcomes of Leonardo da Vinci projects. The Europass certificate lists work experience accumulated in other countries. Similarly, the Green Paper on mobility and other initiatives broadening the opportunities of European students' vocational education emerged mainly as a result of exchanges that took place as a part of the Leonardo Programme. The programme functioned also as a development centre for innovation and experimentation. Pilot projects were a central tool of the programme, with partners from different countries working on a shared project idea and testing it in practice. More than 2,500 innovative trans-border pilot projects generated a great number of different products, such as new curricula, study modules, information materials, manuals, study materials and work tools (European Commission, 2005). Disseminating the innovations identified in these products is a major future challenge. However, the most profound impacts can be achieved when project partners learn from cross-national activities. Intercultural learning in vocational education is a major step towards a citizens' Europe, where exchanging experiences and promoting common goals are a part of daily reality.

The enlargements of the European Union in May 2005 with ten countries and in January 2007 with two more countries have also been a central concern in programme development. A decision in 1997 by the relevant association councils allowed EU candidate countries to take part in the programme. Towards the end of 1999 the programme benefited from the participation of fifteen EU member states, three EFTA countries from the European Economic Area and eleven candidate countries, amounting to a total of twenty-nine countries. In the twenty-first century, some thirty-one countries could participate. In the candidate countries the programme has attracted widespread interest, and it has clearly helped these countries to prepare their education systems for EU membership. The Leonardo da Vinci Programme has been able to make a substantial contribution to the development of cross-national initiatives in the field of TVET and the internationalization of best TVET practices related to teaching quality and teaching contents, innovations and expanding the European dimension.

However, in planning the new Lifelong Learning Programme phase, account has been taken not only of the strengths but also of the weaknesses of the first and second phases of the programmes. The difficulties that arose during the implementation of the first phase were due to the complexity of the centralized administration of the programme. Another weakness was that inadequate attention was paid to designing the programme with a view to complementing other schemes in the fields of education and training. The Commission has ensured that the experiences gained during the first phase were put to use in the second phase by simplifying procedures and continuing with the decentralization of programme administration. The Leonardo da Vinci Programme has been a central tool in the work to evolve lifelong learning strategies generating synergies between the EU's educational and employment policies. Additionally, among the aims of the second phase was that of involving certain agents—particularly labour-market organizations and small and medium enterprises (SMEs)—more closely in vocational education across national boundaries. The Leonardo da Vinci programme has been a central factor in efforts to promote active citizenship encompassing the EU as a whole, at the same time as it has also been used to illustrate what a citizens' Europe should mean.

4 The Lifelong Learning Programme (2007–2013)

Lifelong learning 'refers to all general education, vocational education and training, non-formal education and informal learning undertaken throughout life, resulting in an improvement in knowledge, skills and competences within personal, civic, social and/or employment-related perspectives. It includes the provision of counselling and guidance services' (European Commission, 2006b, p. 6). The Lifelong Learning Programme consists of four sub-programmes:

- the *Comenius Programme* (1,047 million Euros) for pre-school and formal education up to the level of upper secondary education (ISCED-3);
- the *Erasmus Programme* (3,114 million Euros) for higher vocational and academic education, including trans-national student placement in enterprises;
- the *Leonardo da Vinci Programme* (1,725 million Euros) for vocational education and training in schools or enterprises; and
- the *Grundtvig Programme* (358 million Euros) for adult education.

Additionally, the LLP includes the *transversal programme* (369 million Euros) linking the four sub-programmes. The four key transversal activities consist of: (a) policy co-operation and innovation in lifelong learning; (b) promotion of language learning; (c) development of innovative ICT-based content, services, pedagogies and practice for lifelong learning; and (d) dissemination and exploitation of the results and exchange of good practices. Finally, the new *Jean Monnet Programme* (170 million Euros) supports institutions, mainly higher education institutions, in European integration (European Commission 2006a, 2006b). During the Leonardo da Vinci Programme, some 50,000 funding receivers in 2006 will be increased to 80,000 receivers in 2013. Each European Member State has a chance to increase trans-national activities in vocational education and training,

The funding and activities of the LLP Programme are available to twenty-seven European Union member states, to Iceland, Liechtenstein, Norway—and to Turkey. The programme period is seven years. The share of the Leonardo da Vinci Programme in the LLP budget (some 7 billion Euros) is about 25%.

The Leonardo da Vinci Programme addresses the teaching and learning needs of all persons in vocational education and training, other than at tertiary level, as well as institutions and organizations that provide TVET. The difference between the previous and new programme period is the exclusion of tertiary education. The actions of the Leonardo da Vinci Programme comprise mobility of individuals, multilateral projects in development and transfer of innovations, networks and accompanying measures, such as dissemination and valorization activities.

5 Impact of the Leonardo da Vinci Programme on Enhancement of TVET

The Leonardo da Vinci and other European education programmes have focused on countering social exclusion and under-achievement at school through the provision of support targeting disadvantaged groups and the promotion of equal opportunities for women and men. Special attention has been paid to language learning, particularly to the learning of those languages that are less widely used and taught. There has also been an emphasis on the importance of studying in a multicultural environment as one of the cornerstones of European citizenship. The new information and communication technologies (ICTs) have permeated the whole programme.

The status of vocational education rose considerably in the 1990s; it was seen as a central means of responding to the increasingly rapid changes in society and the economy and of promoting employment, social cohesion and competitiveness. There was also a broadening awareness of the importance of lifelong learning in terms of knowledge, skills and qualifications. Lifelong learning has gained a central role also in vocational education because it made it possible to improve employment and adaptability as a part of efforts to formulate a European employment strategy. The European educational policy was articulated in two White Papers (European Commission, 2001, 1995).

5.1 The Effect on the Internationalization of Education Systems

According to an external evaluation report and national reports, as well as reports by labour-market parties, the Leonardo Programme exerted important and substantial influence on, in particular, the people and organizations who actually took part in it and their immediate environment (European Commission, 2005). The effects involved primarily the internationalization of education systems, which also improved the external image of vocational education systems. As many of the applicants saw it, the innovations sought in the programme referred to the integration into vocational education of a European dimension or co-operation across national boundaries. The trade unions that took part in the projects considered that the programme promoted learning from other countries in the area of innovation and quality. Many reports make a particular mention of the positive effects that the programme had had on learning processes, such as the evolution of cross-national collaboration into networks and collaboration groups. As regards the contents of vocational education, the programme affected the scheduling of study modules, language education and the introduction of new technology in education. According to the evaluations, it was the effects of the mobility-promoting aspects of the programme that were felt most strongly; moreover, they were highly positive from the perspective of individual beneficiaries. Nearly all reports state that mobility projects across national boundaries succeeded in equipping students with new social and intercultural skills, enhancing their self-confidence, improving their access to the labour market, and making them more familiar with new working methods. Those students who were given a Leonardo da Vinci grant for a stay abroad described innumerable positive work and learning experiences. Some of their accounts point out that, through the experience gained by the programme participants, mobility has a highly important long-term effect on the quality of education. Simultaneously, this increases demand for mobility. Taking part in pilot projects affected learning in collaboration processes across country boundaries, while participation in mobility projects generated intercultural education and provided European young people with work experience. The success stems from the efforts made in the programme to base supra-national activities on a uniform approach. The fields where the effects of the programme were felt indicate that it was able to foster the development of European citizenship (European Commission, 2004, 2005).

5.2 The Effect on National Education Systems and Esteem for TVET

In the EU candidate countries, the effect of the programme on education systems was quite clear. As described in the reports submitted by these countries, the areas affected most strongly by the programme were the modernization of their education systems and—possibly most importantly—their EU membership process. In Romania, for example, the programme was explicitly associated with a reform of initial vocational education and recently issued draft legislation on further and supplementary education.

In this context, an external evaluation credited the programme with having initiated change in the economic systems of these countries. In 2001, the European Union could look back on twenty-five years of promoting student mobility and co-operation in higher education, including vocational higher education. Within this quarter of a century the activities supported had expanded from involving about 100 departments and about 1,000 students to almost 1,800 higher education institutions and about 100,000 students spending a period of study in another European country each year. Though certain core functions have remained the same since the beginning, the nature of the activities and the organizational context of the programme changed in many respects over the years (Teichler, Gordon & Maiworm, 2001).

Kämäräinen and Fischer (2008), who have studied the impact of the European programmes through research on knowledge accumulation of TVET, indicated that a section of 'Surveys and Analyses' of the Leonardo da Vinci Programme has produced the research results dealing with the issue of parity of esteem between vocational and general education pathways in Europe (see also Lasonen, 1996; Lasonen & Young, 1998). The issues of attractiveness of TVET and parity of esteem are still the priorities of European education and training policies (European Commission, 2006a).

5.3 Transparency of Qualifications

The internationalization and multiculturalization of work and learning environments have contributed to a conscious attention to cultural competence. The discussions about key qualifications launched in the early 1970s focused on the renewal of occupational competencies and on knowledge and competence structures of a new kind. No particular attention was yet paid to the transparency of competencies across national boundaries, nor was (multi)cultural competence seen as a relevant topic in the then debate.

Since the 1990s, there has been a continued emphasis on the significance of transparent TVET practices and qualifications. The Copenhagen Declaration in 2002 meant the start of a process of intensifying co-operation in the field of TVET in Europe. It is thought to have been stimulated by the Bologna Process in higher education that had been launched in 1999. There has been an endeavour to clarify qualification and competence requirements so as to make qualifications and competencies more readily understandable and more valued on the labour markets of Europe. Every EU/ETA country has named a NPR (national reference point for vocational qualifications) contact point that provides information about the country's vocational qualifications and its recognition of occupational competence acquired in another EU/ETA country. The ENIC[3]/NARIC[4] network is responsible for degrees and matters pertaining to their recognition. The activities of ENIC are co-ordinated by the Council of Europe and UNESCO (ENIC/NARIC Network, 2005).

As a part of and as concrete measures stemming from the Copenhagen and Bologna processes, a supra-national credit transfer system is being developed, both in higher education and in TVET. A start has been made on setting up a supporting system—the European Qualifications Framework (EQF)—for initial vocational education and training. Efforts to find out how the transparency, comparability and mutual recognition of qualifications across different countries and different levels of education systems can be promoted by developing common principles and indicators for assuring the standard of qualifications and study credits. These date from 2002, when the EU appointed a working group for the purpose.

The Europass certificate was created in 1999 for use in the EU/ETA countries. In 2000–2003 the eighteen participating countries issued some 50,000 Europasses. For example, about 2,000 Finnish students have earned a Europass. Upper secondary students are an overwhelming majority (93.3%) among those who have completed study modules meant to qualify them for a Europass. To its holder, a Europass is a document certifying their working and educational career in a form that is identical in all EU/ETA countries. To education providers, it is a tool for organizing international study modules (Opetushallitus, 2005).

5.4 Towards a Multicultural Society

Internationalization and multicultural co-operation are no new phenomena in national education systems. What is new is that in the last few decades internationalization has increasingly become an option available to everyone, including those teaching and studying in vocational education establishments. The Leonardo da Vinci Programme is an excellent example of internationalization in this area. Traditionally, vocational education provision has been local and national. This is because the contents of vocational competence are more mutable than those of, for example, general education. The ways in which expert workers are trained tend to change in response to shifts in national occupational structures, technological development, changing natural resources and economic factors, and the current employment situation.

The factors that have led to the internationalization of vocational education and training provision include both trends towards democracy and equality and globalization itself—the internationalization of the economy. There is an indirect link between globalization and how the structures of vocational training and qualification requirements have been developed at national level. Workforce preparation is shaped by an increasingly international labour market, the exchange of consumer goods and services, and multinational commerce.

European and national educational and exchange programmes designed with a view to boosting international co-operation, mobility and transparency have led to a substantial expansion in student and teacher exchanges and in multinational joint projects between educational establishments.

The aim of multicultural education is to foster students' cultural identity and offer every student a high standard of education. A meeting between different cultures is a meeting also between different world pictures, life-styles and practices.

Unconsciously or consciously, education involves beliefs about and explanations of how we should handle otherness and value diversity, how we should treat a stranger who thinks differently from ourselves, and what we should teach future workers about the creation of a more just society and world. At its best, the diversity surrounding us exerts a benign influence on individuals' and groups' experiences, consumption patterns, life-styles and identity. Interculturality is seen as an opportunity to reform education and pedagogical strategies.

Cultural competence is an occupational core competence. The effectiveness of intercultural co-operation depends on professional expertise and adaptation and interaction skills. It may be assumed that cultural competence emerges when intercultural awareness develops into the understanding and the knowledge and skills needed to operate smoothly in diverse environments, together with different people. Multicultural competence refers to attitudes, knowledge and skills and the social and cultural awareness required if one is to cope in intercultural situations.

As regards the nature of multicultural competence, we may ask whether it is a separate field of expertise or whether it should be seen as an essential component of practical competence. It might be argued that cultural competence should be considered an internal element of every type of domain-specific expertise. Understood in a broad sense, competence covers personal characteristics, core competence and domain-specific skills.

Occupational competence includes basic domain-specific skills, specialized competencies, technical and social rationality, interaction skills, and the ability to live with diversity and understand it in the context of production systems. Interculturality is an essential constituent of every field of occupational competence. As regards the qualifications of an expert, the various constituent elements of competence are integrated into an aggregate of knowledge and skills rather than representing separate and distinct catalogues of features. Multicultural competence is an inbuilt element of the given occupational domain and its practices and functions, rather than an external addition. This entails also an awareness of one's occupational domain and job as a part of the global economy. In short, multicultural competence is competence of a high standard to operate effectively in multicultural work environments and learn there. However, the European education and training programmes have potential to contribute more to the development of coherent multicultural societies.

6 Conclusions

The internationalization of education is a process shaped by political, economic and cultural relations. Its political motives are linked—directly or indirectly—with foreign and security policies, the promotion of peace and mutual understanding, and the strengthening of national and regional identities. The aim of the EU action programmes in education and training has been to create links between various areas of education and stimulate co-operation in European matters across different education systems. As large umbrella programmes, they symbolize the extension, since the 1992 Maastricht Treaty, of the responsibility of the European Union to all areas of education.

Education, training and learning make it possible to promote interculturality and social pluralism. At the global level, education contributes to the success of individuals, nations and economies. European and national educational programmes designed with a view to boosting international co-operation and mobility have led to a substantial expansion in student and teacher exchanges and in multinational joint projects between educational establishments. New contexts require a better understanding of multiculturalism, more interaction skills and more conflict resolution and problem-solving skills. Multicultural competence is a natural component of expertise and professional identity. The internationalization of education should involve as its by-product the fostering of students' and teachers' intercultural competence.

A problem facing these efforts is the circumstance that internationalization at the system level, the multiculturalization of societies and the curriculum-level implementation of intercultural learning do not necessarily support each other; instead, they are handled as separate issues. Education for intercultural understanding is intended to train people to work as intermediaries between, as interpreters of and as fully empowered members of different cultures. Multiculturalism, anti-racism, the fostering of ethnic equality, intercultural understanding, globalization education, new forms of communication and sustainable development pose new challenges to education and training and to their exchange programmes.

Notes

1. Socrates was a Greek philosopher who believed in a humanist vision of the world and rejected dogmatism. His maxim 'Know thyself' is a fundamental basis for self-knowledge and respect for self and other people.
2. The programme was named to commemorate an Italian genius, Leonardo da Vinci, born in 1452 in Vinci in the Republic of Florence, who epitomized the Renaissance humanist ideal. He was a painter, sculptor, architect and engineer.
3. ENIC—Network of National Information Centres.
4. NARIC—Network of National Academic Recognition Centres.

References

ENIC-NARIC Network. 2005. *The European gateway to recognition of academic and professional qualifications.* <www.enic-naric.net>

European Commission. 1994. Council Decision No 94/819/EC of 6 December 1994, Article 10, paragraph 4 on a European Union programme on vocational education and training. *Official journal of the European Union L 340, 29.12.1994/8–24.* <europa.eu.int/comm/education/doc/official/index_en.html>

European Commission. 1995. *Teaching and learning: towards a cognitive society.* <europa.eu.int/comm/education/doc/official/keydoc/lb-en.pdf>

European Commission. 2000. Decision No 253/2000/EC of the European Parliament and of the Council of 24 January 2000 establishing the second phase of the Community action programme in the field of education 'Socrates'. *Official journal of the European Communities 3.2.2000 L28/1–15.* <europa.eu.int/comm/education/doc/official/index_en.html>

European Commission. 2001. *European Commission White Paper: a new impetus for European youth.* <europa.eu.int/eur-lex/lex/LexUriServ/site/en/com/2001/com2001_0681en01.pdf>

European Commission. 2004. *Report from the Commission: interim report on the implementation of the second phase of the Leonardo da Vinci Programme.* <europa.eu.int/comm/education/programmes/evaluation/evaluation_en.html>

European Commission. 2005. *Evaluation of programmes and initiatives in the field of education and training.* <europa.eu.int/comm/education/programmes/evaluation/evaluation_en.html>

European Commission. 2006a. Decision No 1720/2006/EC of the European Parliament and of the Council of 15 November 2006 establishing an action programme in the field of lifelong learning. *Official journal of the European Union, 24.11.2006 L327/45.* <europa.eu.int/comm/education/doc/official/index_en.html>

European Commission. 2006b. *The Lifelong Learning Programme, 2007–2013.* <europa.eu.int/comm/education/programmes/llp/index_en.html>

Kämäräinen, P.; Fischer, M. 2008. Research on technical and vocational education and training (TVET) in the context of European co-operation. *In:* Rauner, F.; Maclean, R., eds. *Handbook of technical and vocational education and training research.* Dordrecht, Netherlands: Springer.

Lanzendorf, U.; Teichler, U. 2002. The policies of higher education institutions. *In:* Teichler, U., ed. *Erasmus in the Socrates Programme,* pp. 13–28. Bonn, Germany: Lemmens. (ACA Papers on International Co-operation in Education.)

Lasonen, J. 1996. *Reforming upper secondary education in Europe: surveys of strategies for post-16 education to improve parity of esteem for initial vocational education in eight European educational systems.* Jyväskylä, Finland: University of Jyväskylä, Institute for Educational Research. (Publication Series B: Theory into Practice, no. 92).

Lasonen, J.; Young, M. 1998. *Strategies for achieving parity of esteem in European upper secondary education.* Jyväskylä, Finland: University of Jyväskylä, Institute for Educational Research.

Opetushallitus. 2005. *Europass.* <www.oph.fi>

Teichler, U.; Gordon, J.; Maiworm, F. 2001. *Socrates 2000 evaluation study.* Brussels: European Commission. <europa.eu.int/comm/dgs/education_culture/evalreports/education/2001/soci-expost/soc1xpsum_en.pdf>

Chapter IV.6
VET in the Baltic States: Analysis of Commonalities and Differences of Reforms in Estonia, Latvia and Lithuania

Frank Bünning and Berit Graubner

1 Introduction

The development of vocational education and training (VET) is a major concern of the Lisbon strategy for the prosperity of Europe in the twenty-first century. As the Baltic States have been one of the focuses of attention for European VET policy after their application for accession to the European Union, reforms in VET have enjoyed special attention there.

The enlargement of the European Union and related challenges have been key drivers for European policy. Since the Lisbon Council met in 2000, the development of VET has been high on the European political agenda. The Copenhagen Declaration of 2002 endorsed the commitment to intensify European co-operation in this area. The newest member states of the EU—among them the Baltic States—are now involved in the implementation of the Copenhagen Declaration and can be seen as a source of enormous (human) potential which will contribute significantly to the objective of greater co-operation.

Estonia, Latvia and Lithuania are three neighbouring countries that have shared a recent common history. It seems of particular interest to analyse the attempts to reform their (vocational) education systems, since the dynamic and speed of reform is a significant impetus for the development of a common European era. This chapter describes approaches to reform of VET in the Baltic States. The socio-economic background of the Baltic States, aspects of lifelong learning and their correlation with European education policy form the backdrop to the outline of essential steps for VET reform in Estonia, Latvia and Lithuania.

Despite the commonalities that the Baltic States share, it would be a sweeping generalization to speak about the 'Baltic VET' reform. The three countries have launched their very own reforms to develop VET systems that meet the demands of twenty-first-century Europe. This chapter describes the reforms of the individual states, noting the diversity and commonality of approaches to reform.

R. Maclean, D. Wilson (eds.), *International Handbook of Education for the Changing World of Work*, DOI 10.1007/978-1-4020-5281-1_IV.6,
© Springer Science+Business Media B.V. 2009

2 VET in the Light of the Socio-Economic and Political Situation

Despite their status as independent states, their individual historical development, language and traditions, Estonia, Latvia and Lithuania share much in terms of political, economic and social life. Their development in the twentieth century was very much determined by independence after the First World War followed by Soviet (and for a short time German) occupation during and after the Second World War. As a result of the latter, the three Baltic neighbours share a significant history resulting in similar political, economic and social structures. Consequently, the education systems, including VET, have, in the past, shown a general congruence.

After more than forty years of Soviet occupation, however, they regained sovereignty and independence in 1990 (Lithuania) and 1991 (Estonia and Latvia), which allowed them to rethink and reshape themselves into democratic republics. All three set themselves the goal of accession to the European Union (EU). After all preconditions had been fulfilled, the three states were formally declared full members of the EU on 1 May 2004, a crucial cornerstone in the Baltic States' history. Being now equal partners, they have been enjoying special attention in European policy. During the process of application for accession to the EU, each of the Baltic countries harmonized its legislation according to EU norms and principles.

After regaining their sovereignty, the three countries started their development independently of each other. In each of the Baltic States decentralization has been one of the most urgent items on the agendas throughout society. This also applied to the education system in general and the vocational educational and training sector in particular. However, as the goal of ensuring mobility among students and the workforce gained importance, co-operation in VET became indispensable. In 1998, the agreement on the creation of a common educational space in general upper secondary education and vocational (up to higher education level) education within the Baltic States was signed.

Like the political system, similarities can also be found in the countries' economic development. Transformational processes from centrally-planned to a market-driven economy began to establish themselves after the political changes and, in general, economic activity has increased steadily since the end of the 1990s. Surveys state that: 'the hitherto consequent reforms have solidified the foundation of a market economy, created a stable macro-economic environment and garnered the trust of investors' (Ramina, Hodireva & Silina, 2002, p. 9).

Nevertheless, large-scale problems had to be overcome: inflation, which temporarily increased to a dramatic peak (e.g. 1,021% in Lithuania in 1992 compared to the previous year), had largely been fostered by the internal and external price convergence that accompanied price liberalization (Hamburgisches Welt-Wirtschafts-Archiv, 2006). Large-scale privatization programmes and policy strategies to support small and medium-sized enterprises have helped to considerably increase gross domestic product (GDP) in recent years.

The economy at the turn of the millennium was characterized by a considerable growth in exports and a favourable economic situation: the moderate domestic inflation and the strong US dollar, coupled with expanding industries due to co-operation with international neighbours, increased activities in the oil sector and therefore the use of Baltic Sea terminals (e.g. Riga, Ventspils, Klaipeda, etc.) and this rapid diversification and dynamism had encouraging impacts on Baltic economies. In recent years, the focus of economic growth has shifted slightly from the domestic market towards an increase in exports to Western European countries. Owing to small domestic markets, exports—and thus international economic co-operation—have become more dominating. After successfully reorienting its export flow towards Western European countries, Lithuania, for example, increased its GDP by as much as 5.9% in 2002 and Estonia 6% in the same year (Statistics Lithuania, 2002; Annus, Jõgi & Tilmanis, 2006, p. 26).

Preparations for the common EU market and efforts towards free-market competitiveness proved to be key drivers for positive economic development. In order to reach market economy competitiveness, companies and enterprises were challenged to restructure their business activities, to reorganize business processes and adapt them to market demands.

Governmental programmes and foreign (especially EU) investment are still important sources of support for the Baltic economies, e.g. more than 50% of Latvia's direct foreign investment comes from EU countries. Inflation still remains comparatively high today in Latvia, with 6.2% in 2004, whereas Estonia's inflation rate has fallen steadily in recent years to 3.0% in 2004 and is expected to further converge towards the EU average of 2.1%. Lithuania's inflation rate at 1.1% was even below the EU average (2004). Differences in GDP (data referring to GDP per head) are equally spread among the Baltic States: Estonia is ahead with 6,700 Euros, followed by Lithuania with 5,200 Euros and Latvia with 4,800 Euros, in comparison with the EU-25 average of 22,400 Euros (EDS-Europäischer Datenservice, n.d.).

One consequence of the developments outlined above is far-reaching changes in the employment situation. Some economic sectors have experienced enormous declines, among them agriculture, construction and processing industries, while others, most of all the service sector, transport and communications, have benefited. Thus, employment figures in the declining sectors have shrunk drastically, while the developing branches have faced and are still facing the growing need for qualified workers. Technological progress has also contributed to some extent to the rise in unemployment figures. Despite various attempts and a number of successfully implemented strategies and programmes to reform and optimize the VET and labour-market training structures, one of the greatest problems still to be solved is the imbalance between supply and demand. While there are high unemployment rates, with a considerable number of youth, women and long-term unemployed, enterprises report a lack of sufficiently qualified labour. Alarmingly, the highest number of unemployed, especially in Latvia, is among young secondary vocational education graduates (41.8% according to the Central Statistical Bureau of Latvia, 2001). This clearly highlights the mismatch between skills, experience and qualifications gained within education and training and the actual demands of the labour market.

To this should be added a large socio-economic discrepancy between economic centres and larger cities, on the one hand, and rural regions, smaller towns and peripheral areas, on the other, in terms of investment, economic development, demography and employment.

While education already plays a significant role in the organization of a society, it becomes even more important in the fundamental changes affecting the Baltic States. VET, as the educational sector that prepares young people for their professional lives and that guides employees throughout their working lives, must be given special attention. It is influenced by political, social and economic factors, but has itself social and economic roles and responsibilities. The current employment situation, present labour-market demands and the growing social and regional anomalies have an extensive impact on the further development of the vocational education and training system in all three of the Baltic States, as is shown in the following section.

3 Educational Reform Movements

3.1 Estonia

Estonia's education system has experienced significant changes since the beginning of the 1990s. The current education policy reflects liberal economic and political developments. Much attention is being paid to such issues as privatization and community responsibility for schools and cost efficiency in education. A number of initiatives in recent years (Learning Estonia, Education Scenarios 2010, Tiger Leap Programme and Education Forum) foster the new approaches of the post-Soviet era.

In 1999/2000, the education strategy Learning Estonia was set up, developed by the Estonian Ministry of Education and the Education Forum Task Force (involving social partners and non-governmental organizations—NGOs). The draft of Learning Estonia had been the subject of discussion for two years (2000–2001) before it was adopted by the government.

In 2001, the development strategy Knowledge-based Estonia, the Action Plan for the Development of Vocational Education, the Higher Education Reform Strategy and the National Development Strategy on Youth Work were approved and put into practice (Annus et al., 2001).

The Action Plan for the Development of Vocational Education, 2001–2004, summarizes wide-ranging measures to improve the quality of vocational education. Much attention is paid to labour-market relevance and the broadening of access for all age groups. The Action Plan puts special emphasis on the development of regional training centres providing primary training for students, retraining for adults, pre-training for students in general secondary education, and vocational education and training for people with special needs.

Detailed targets for the reform of the VET system were set in the Action Plan for Developing the Estonian VET System, 2001–2004. It defined a total of twenty-three tasks linked to specific targets to be achieved in the period 2001–2004:

- to increase the number of VET students by 8% per year;
- to decrease the drop-out rate from 13% (in 2000) to 8% by 2004;

- to privatize approximately 30% of VET schools and providers by 2004;
- to change the student/teacher ratio from 12:1 in 2000 to 16:1;
- to increase the number of teachers with university degrees from 75% (2000) to 100% in 2004;
- to double the amount of foreign-language classes in all programmes;
- to increase the focus of VET programmes on vocational standards;
- to achieve more with public funding.

The implementation of this Action Plan and the extent to which the targets have been met is questionable (Annus, Jõgi & Tilmanis, 2006, p. 33).

3.2 Latvia

After the national independence of Latvia in 1991, major changes were initiated in the education system. As part of the changes and reforms, the weaknesses of VET were addressed and objectives were identified.

In 1997, the report on *Vocational education and training reform in Latvia* (Bernan Associates, 1997) identified the main weaknesses of the current vocational education and training system. In summary, they were as follows:

- Unsatisfactory legal foundation. The Law on Education, adopted in 1991, regulates only the administration of initial VET and stipulates its structure. The legislation does not integrate the social partners in VET curriculum development.
- Insufficient structure for the provision of initial VET, continuing vocational training (CVT) and retraining.
- An inadequate network of institutions (VET providers, research centres, etc.).

This analysis of weaknesses served as an impetus for the reform process. In particular, the co-operation of VET providers and employers was sought. In doing so, the Tripartite Co-operation Sub-Council for Vocational Education and Training Reform and Employment was established in 2000. This is a subdivision of the National Tripartite Co-operation Council, an institution aiming to foster co-operation between governmental bodies, employers and unions, as well as institutions concerned by national VET policy.

Despite far-reaching reforms to strengthen VET in Latvia, it would appear that further restructuring would be beneficial to a coherent strategy. In particular, the management of VET under the jurisdiction of different ministries results in fragmented provision, 'since, of course, the ministries, first of all, take into consideration the interests of their branch and then solve the VET administrative issues independently from other ministries: plan the network of educational establishments, enrolment of students, financial resources and, in co-operation with the educational support institutions under their jurisdiction, they plan curriculum and provide education quality control' (Lanka & Mūrnieks, 2006, p. 66). This approach does not encourage coherent provision and could arguably be reviewed.

3.3 Lithuania

The reform of vocational education in Lithuania was initiated very soon after independence in 1990. The first steps in the reform were the development of a vocational education policy and strategy. The endorsement of international co-operation was encouraged. However, the early years in the reform had very limited impact on political decisions concerning VET. In the middle of the 1990s, reforms focusing on the principle of decentralization were launched. Much attention was paid to the modernization of the teaching curriculum and social partnership development. Furthermore, in the mid-1990s, increased attention was given to involving the participation of educational institutions in the reform of vocational education policies, strategies and the development of curricula.

The Law on Vocational Education and Training was adopted in 1997. It provided the legal foundation for the current structure and administration of the vocational education and training system of Lithuania. The law fosters the co-operation of governmental institutions and social partners. It defines the provision of initial VET (oriented towards the continuous education of young people) and labour-market vocational training (oriented towards adult continuous and, in some cases, initial vocational training).

The 1999 White Paper on Vocational Education and Training in the Republic of Lithuania set out the direction for the development of vocational education and training. One of the White Paper's objectives is to ensure compatibility of education and qualifications with relevant recommendations within the EU, while at the same time retaining national identity.

One of the challenges in the reform of the Lithuanian VET system has been the involvement of social partners. The lack of employers' interest in VET has been addressed elsewhere and is not the focus of this chapter.

Additional weaknesses are vocational counselling and the low esteem of VET in Lithuania. Prior to the reform, a vocational orientation system had been in practice. One deficit of the prior system was that it tended to advise only the weaker students to follow a career pathway in VET. In doing so, VET in Lithuania suffered from the reputation of being a pathway for the less academically privileged. The current problems are under-developed vocational counselling systems in general education schools, the lack of qualified counsellors, the lack of a vocational counselling strategy and methodology (Laužackas & Danilevičius, 2006, p. 76).

Closely linked with the efforts to reform the VET systems are the approaches to strengthen lifelong learning processes in the Baltic States as part of the transition to a market economy, while continuing technological progress has changed employment and occupational structures fundamentally.

4 The Lifelong Learning Perspective of VET in the Baltic States

Recent discussions on VET policy and strategies show that its definition has changed considerably from the original narrow concept of 'preparing young people for a fixed profession, a specific working place' to the broader understanding of VET as a process that is not finished when a person obtains his or her certificate on successful completion of initial training. As outlined above, economic development in the Baltic States, as in any other modern society, is subject to constant evolution. The challenges of a modern market economy and technological progress have had substantial impacts on employment and occupational structures. VET graduates starting their professional career cannot expect to fill the same workplace all their lives, i.e. to be trained for one particular field of occupation that is going to secure their job for a lifetime. Reality shows that the constant changes in market demands, technology and employment structures, even in professions, set the agenda for different demands on today's working population. VET needs to be reorganized and restructured in order to meet changing labour-market demands on the current and future workforce.

As economic trends tend to change rapidly, it is difficult at each stage to predict what kinds of professions are needed and how many employees will be required for what field. That is why employers need workers who show a high degree of flexibility and mobility, the capacity to work with modern equipment and who keep themselves up to date with new technologies. They should also have a good command of their first and at least one or two foreign languages and possess skills in various occupational fields and profiles. VET must no longer provide only basic professional knowledge and skills, but it is even more essential to impart the capacity to learn, to teach learning strategies and to be able quickly to learn how to use new technology. People should be aware that school and vocational education only set the foundations for each individual's further development. Education that clearly evokes an awareness of the need and that provides the necessary preconditions for lifelong learning is high on European political agendas. Thus, implementing policies to develop lifelong learning strategies is also one of the major goals in the Baltic States.

4.1 Latvia

Latvia has developed the Lifelong Learning Memorandum, where the most important basic skills needed are listed, e.g. the ability to work with information and communication technologies (ICTs), the capacity to acquire, analyse and share information, knowledge of foreign languages, etc. (Ramina, Hodireva & Silina, 2002, p. 17). Continuing vocational training (CVT) has been given special attention since the Law on Vocational Education, which came into force on 1 September 2001. This includes a broadened focus on further education and training.

There is no secure statistical data on the number of people who participated in CVT courses, but as far as businesses are concerned, the motivation and capability to invest in personnel training appears to be slightly higher in large enterprises, where the potential increase in profit acts as a stimulus. The Latvian Government has established the State Employment Service, an institution that organizes training and retraining for the unemployed aiming at improvement of employability and fast re-entry into the labour market. Responsibility for adult education has been transferred to the regional governments. Since investment in the adult education sector is within the remit of local government, large regional differences occur—at best there exist well-organized and functioning, local government-funded adult education centres.

4.2 Estonia

Similar to Latvia, Estonia, too, embodied continuing vocational training (CVT) in its legislation and worked out an Action Plan for Developing the Estonian VET System, 2001–2004, in which the main principles for restructuring were defined. However, as some experts have stated, its implementation 'has been less than optimal. A coherent strategic and policy framework on CVT is still not in place' (Annus, Jõgi & Tilmanis, 2006, p. 33).

In order to foster adult education, several more programmes were adopted (e.g. Estonian National Development Plan, 2003–2006, or the National Employment Plans) all of which stressed the necessity for improving CVT and lifelong learning policies in order to improve qualification and employability of the country's workforce. The necessary steps towards improved CVT demanded by these documents (e.g. favourable tax regulations, development of an adult education financing model according to those in other European countries, establishing a State-financed institution to co-ordinate adult education systems and co-operation among institutions and social partners, development of regulations for licensing and accrediting trainers, etc.) have either not been sufficiently implemented up to the present or have not yet had the anticipated effects—partly due to a lack of participation and motivation on the part of those concerned.

Like Latvia, Estonia has also invested in the establishment of regional training centres that have already been mentioned before. CVT is one of these centres' responsibilities.

4.3 Lithuania

In Lithuania, the governmental body responsible for CVT and lifelong learning is the Ministry of Social Security and Labour (MSSL). The legal basis for its functions are the Law on Vocational Education and Training (1997) and the Law on the Support of the Unemployed (1990), both of which are implemented by the Lithuanian Labour Market Training Authority and the network of labour exchanges. This system's main objective is support of the unemployed by means of training, counselling and guidance, as well as labour-market research. Although these institutions focus mainly on training and re-training programmes for unemployed adults and disabled people, a network of fourteen labour-market training centres and six labour-market training services also provides courses for CVT and lifelong learning for the employed, e.g. short courses for employees whose current qualification is in low demand or non-formal vocational training programmes. The criticism is often made that, instead of developing effective co-operation, these programmes are rather seen as direct competition for existing vocational educational institutes. An interesting innovation seems to be the labour exchange. This institution provides co-ordination between employers' needs and potential employees. The main activities of the network of forty-six labour exchange offices throughout the country include the registration of unemployed citizens and job openings, labour-market forecasts, efficiency studies of training programmes and, not least, the disposal of finance from the State Employment Fund. However, since those involved complain about the low interest in their services, it is estimated that only about half of job seekers make use of it. Another weakness of the system appears to be the fact that the provision of appropriate training programmes is to a large extent subject to the availability of finance, and does not depend on urgent local needs.

In order to overcome structural and content-related difficulties, foreign (mainly EU) expertise is used in all three Baltic countries, for example via the Leonardo da Vinci, PHARE, Comenius or Socrates programmes, as is illustrated in the following section.

5 The European Dimension

Estonia's VET development was backed up by several European programmes. PHARE offered substantial support for the reform of the (vocational) education system. The extent of the support for the significant PHARE initiatives can be il-lustrated as follows:

- PHARE 2000: Project enhancing human resource development in the Ida-Viru (North-East) region. This initiative offered financial support of approximately 1.3 million Euros, including Estonian co-financing of 300,000 Euros.
- PHARE 2000: Project enhancing human resource development in the southern Estonian region. The project involved a budget of some 2.4 million Euros, in-cluding Estonian co-financing of 650,000 Euros.
- PHARE 2001: Project enhancing human resource development in the islands region, with a budget of approximately 1.2 million Euros, including Estonian co-financing of 24,000 Euros, providing essential financial support for the edu-cational reform.

Similarly to Estonia, Latvia's reform process of its education system was supported by European initiatives. Recent examples of PHARE 2000 projects in Latvia are the Qualification Infrastructure and Development of College Study Programmes.

In Lithuania, the European Union has supported VET reform through the PHARE programme since 1993. A recent example for a PHARE initiative is the programme Vocational Training for Economic and Social Cohesion. The overall objective of this programme is to support Lithuania's economic and social cohesion. The programme focuses on employment growth. The budget of 4.23 million Euros, including 1.19 million Euros of national co-financing, illustrates the priority paid to VET, continu-ing vocational training and lifelong learning.

Here, the influence of the European Union was exemplified by PHARE initiatives. However, other initiatives, such as the Comenius, Socrates and Leonardo da Vinci Programmes, have also to be mentioned in this context. Furthermore, the European Training Foundation (ETF) and other national European research institutions provided significant expertise for the reform processes. The European Training Foundation developed a network of national observatories (watch-dog committees) in the countries concerned. Its analytic work culminated in a set of publications identifying key indicators of labour-market developments and progress reports of the reform movements.

In summary, the reform of VET systems in the Baltic States started in the early 1990s and took into consideration EU standards. The development of VET systems in accordance with European standards has resulted in a favourable position for these countries' vocational qualifications, compared to other European VET systems, which evolved more traditionally and appear to be at a disadvantage. For example, German vocational qualifications are particularly disadvantaged. According to the European-Level System, Dual Vocational Education Qualifications awarded in Germany after three years of training are classified as Level 2.

Despite these reforms, the three Baltic States still face a number of problems in the area of VET. In particular, the perception of VET as a lower-status career option is an impediment to further development. As vocational education and training do not generally enjoy high esteem, it is not surprising that Estonia, Latvia and Lithuania are lacking qualified VET teaching and management staff.

In 1990, the acceding countries for EU membership (of the former Eastern European Soviet bloc) launched significant reforms to restructure their VET systems. The results of this reform movement have been impressive, particularly when one considers that the starting date was only 1989. Lithuania, Latvia and Estonia have enjoyed special attention because geographically they occupy an important strategic position. Since the enlargement of the EU (European Commission, 2004), they are now serving as 'outposts' towards the east. This shared experience provided the foundation for (re-)establishing co-operation on various levels among these countries' vocational education systems. Soon after regaining their independence, it became clear that co-operation in the area of VET was absolutely necessary in order to ensure mobility of the workforce (Neudorf, Krusts & Vincentas, 1999, p. 2). One result of this awareness was the Agreement on the Creation of a Common Educational Space in General Upper Secondary Education and Vocational (up to the Higher Education Level) Education with the Baltic States, which was signed in 1998. In 1999, a further step was taken with the Cesis Agreement. Mutual recognition of school-leaving certificates was agreed upon, as well as co-operation in general education, including VET. A very solid result of this co-operation is a comparative analysis of the different VET systems in the Baltic States. This survey was designed to facilitate co-operation in the field of education.

Despite enormous efforts, mobility between the three Baltic States appears to be rather limited. It can be suspected that the language barrier inhibits cross-Baltic mobility.

The EU has set itself the ambitious goal—set in Lisbon in 2000—of becoming the world's leading 'knowledge society' by 2010. Member states are working towards it by reorienting their VET systems. However, when the Lisbon Council set the goal, the number of EU countries was fifteen. By 2010 it can be expected that this number will grow to twenty-eight. The deadline of 2010 requires a special investment in VET by 'old' and 'new' member states, as well as candidate countries. For a period of time, reform in the new member states has aimed to develop their VET to a standard comparable to that of the 'old' member states. However, little effort was made to truly work together on a common European VET framework. The Lisbon Council has set new priorities. The demand to meet these targets for almost twice as many countries has raised the stakes for VET in current and future member states (de Rooij, 2004).

6 Drawing the Threads Together

Since the reestablishment of their sovereignty, the Baltic States have made enormous efforts to develop their VET systems in line with European standards and to harmonize their (vocational) educational policy with EU requirements. At the same time, while following the guidelines of the European Union, they have been endeavouring to retain their national identity. Thus, they may well serve as an example for a pro-European national VET policy and their expertise can certainly be of service to other EU accession candidates—and especially to transitional (former Soviet) countries (Council of the European Union, 2002).

Estonia, Latvia and Lithuania have initiated their very own reforms to develop their national VET systems, with the result that each has its own varying structure. For example, Estonia and Lithuania have transferred the responsibility of agricultural VET, including the related training institutions, from the Ministries of Agriculture to the Ministries of Education and Science. Consequently, most VET institutions are now under the jurisdiction of one ministry. In Latvia, the VET schools fall under the jurisdiction of different governmental bodies (Cabinet of Ministers, Ministry of Education and Science, especially the Vocational Training and Continuing Education Department, as well as the Professional Education Centre, not to mention the Ministries of Agriculture, Welfare, Culture and the Interior).

Education and training programmes, levels and qualifications show only minor differences due to their orientation towards EU standards. More substantial variability has to be detected in the quality assurance systems. In Lithuania, accreditation and licensing measures function under the responsibility of the Ministry of Education and Science, while in Latvia and Estonia, effective quality assurance systems are yet to be established or will undergo significant improvement.

Besides these differences, there are a number of similarities in the three states. It is significant that European education policy has supported and inspired the reform processes. Some difficulties appear to exist throughout the Baltic States: the very low esteem of VET; the difficulty of involving employers; and the need for qualified labour in the services and communications sectors. Despite far-reaching reforms, the negative image of VET is an impediment to its further development.

References

Annus, T.; Jõgi, K.; Tilmanis, L. 2006. Vocational education and training in Estonia: reform processes and tendencies. *In:* Bünning, F., ed. *The transformation of vocational education and training (VET) in the Baltic States: survey of reforms and developments.* Dordrecht, Netherlands: Springer.

Annus, T. et al. 2001. *Modernization of vocational education and training in Estonia.* Tallinn: National Observatory of Estonia.

Bernan Associates. 1997. *Vocational education and training reform in Latvia.* Turin, Italy: ETF.

Council of the European Union. 2002. *Draft council resolution on the promotion of enhanced European cooperation in vocational education and training.* Brussels: European Union.

de Rooij, P. 2004. *EU enlargement and education for the labour market.* <www.etf.eu.int/ WebSite.nsf/0/CB6DB14948F21151C1256E6E00363870?OpenDocument>

EDS-Europäischer Datenservice. N.d. <www.eds-destatis.de/de/database>

European Commission. 2004. Education & Training 2010: The success of the Lisbon strategy hinges on urgent reforms. Joint interim report on the implementation of the detailed work programme on the follow-up of the objectives of education and training systems in Europe. *Official journal of the European Union C,* 104/5,

Hamburgisches Welt-Wirtschafts-Archiv. 2006. <www.hwwa.de/EU-Beitrittslaender/>

Lanka, A.; Mūrnieks, E. 2006. Vocational education and training in Latvia: the problems and solutions. *In:* Bünning, F., ed. *The transformation of vocational education and training (VET) in the Baltic States: survey of reforms and developments.* Dordrecht, Netherlands: Springer.

Laužackas, R.; Danilevičius, E. 2006. Vocational education and training in Lithuania: reform processes and tendencies. *In:* Bünning, F., ed. *The transformation of vocational education and training (VET) in the Baltic States: survey of reforms and developments.* Dordrecht, Netherlands: Springer.

Neudorf, R.; Krusts, G.; Vincentas, D. 1999. *Comparative analysis of VET systems of Estonia.* Turin, Italy: ETF.

Ramina, B.; Hodireva, V.; Silina, S. 2002. *The modernization of vocational education and training in Latvia.* Riga: Latvian National Observatory.

Statistics Lithuania. 2002. *Statistical yearbook of Lithuania.* Vilnius: Statistics Lithuania.

Chapter IV.7
Education and Training Needs of Rural Communities: A Situational Analysis of Selected Villages in Fourteen Provinces of Fiji

Paula Cavu, Isimeli W. Tagicakiverata, Seveci Naisilisili and Viliame Rabici

1 Introduction

The purpose of this research project was to conduct a survey of the training needs of people in rural communities of the fourteen provinces in Fiji. The rationale behind this exercise was to take the Fiji Institute of Technology (FIT), a training and education institution, to the homes of this target group, bearing in mind the advent of distance education and learning. However, it was also found that people in most rural communities did not fully understand the role of FIT, so the researchers had an opportunity to market the institute through awareness-raising in the villages. All the participants were grateful for the opportunity to meet and talk to professionals from FIT on various issues. Even very remote villages were among those visited.

Questionnaires in the Fijian language were administered to 1,807 participants in sixty villages. The survey found that all participants wanted skills-training programmes to be conducted in their villages. It was also found that participants selected training programmes that were relevant and necessary to their immediate and future needs. The choice of training depended mainly on available resources, developmental needs, village and family needs and individual aspirations. This research gave all stakeholders—the government, non-governmental organizations, aid agencies, provincial offices and training institutions—an insight into the training needs in rural communities, as well as their developmental goals and aspirations.

Training-needs assessment (TNA), the basis of this research initiative, is timely especially as communities in rural areas have often been disadvantaged in terms of educational opportunities and development. The most obvious cause for this disadvantage is the great distance from rural communities to educational centres, which in Fiji's case are primarily clustered around towns and cities. Additional obstacles include the lack of transport, poor road conditions and the high cost of travel.

Rural communities, especially Fijian villages, have visible differences in levels of development. However, there is no hard-and-fast rule about the degree of development in rural areas as some villages in outer islands appear to have better living conditions—with flush toilets, regular clean water supply and electricity—than some villages closer to urban centres.

R. Maclean, D. Wilson (eds.), *International Handbook of Education for the Changing World of Work*, DOI 10.1007/978-1-4020-5281-1_IV.7,
© Springer Science+Business Media B.V. 2009

A significant similarity, however, is that both rural and peri-urban Fijian villages are beginning to experience an influx of school-leavers and dropouts, some with educational qualifications up to Form 7 and even tertiary levels. According to village elders, this influx is the result of examination failure and/or lack of employment opportunities. Some youths have, however, turned to farming and other schemes to earn a living, while some have become a burden to their communities through idleness and resorting to crime.

The TNA conducted for this research was aimed at identifying the educational and developmental needs in rural areas, with special consideration for the culture and attitude of the dwellers. Results from this survey would provide stakeholders with significant data on much-needed training to be conducted and a solid base for its effective implementation.

2 Background

Fiji has a population of over 868,000 (2003 estimate) and has a gross domestic product per capita of US$2,060 (2001 estimate). Life expectancy is around 69 years while the literacy rate is around 93.7% (2003 estimate). Major revenue earners are tourism, sugar and the garment industry, but in recent years remittances from Fijian people working abroad have become equally significant (Encarta encyclopaedia, 2004).

According to the Fiji Islands Education Commission report (Fiji. Ministry of Education, 2000; Sharma, 2000; Tavola, 2000), education is well established in Fiji as it has existed for over 160 years. Some of the concerns, however, have been the uneven situation of educational provision between schools. This situation is the result of the diversity of authorities controlling schools, differences between rural or urban location and the resources available in each community. Ministry of Education records show that in 1999 47% of high schools were run by committees, 35% by religious groups and 8% by the government. In addition, relatively more diploma holders and new graduates were teaching in rural schools as compared to a higher number of degree holders with more experience in urban schools.

It has become increasingly clear that rural dwellers are greatly disadvantaged, not only in terms of educational facilities and access to information but also in terms of physical infrastructure, such as housing, sanitation and transport. A result of these disparities reported in the Fiji Islands Education Commission report is that only 40% of students in rural schools passed the Fiji School Leaving Certificate in 1999, as compared to 62.3% in urban schools.

At the national level, in terms of projected socio-economic development, stakeholders are concerned that of 17,000 school-leavers each year, only about 2,000 are able to find employment (Mausio, 2003). But school-leavers in urban centres still have an advantage in that they have easy access to various tertiary training institutions offering a wide range of programmes. School-leavers in urban areas have many options to choose from, whereas those in rural communities often have only their villages to return to.

Institutions such as the University of the South Pacific and the Fiji Institute of Technology have established centres in major towns throughout Fiji, but the problem of access to training programmes by those in remote rural communities still exists. Part of the problem is that many school-leavers in rural areas continue to seek white-collar job opportunities, but fail to recognize the value of working in their local environments. It is for this reason that various organizations, including FIT, are taking time to visit rural communities to introduce local dwellers to ways they can maximize the return from their resources in a sustainable way.

Non-formal education (NFE) or continuing education has been acknowledged as a remedy as it has the potential to empower people by widening and deepening their range of skills and assisting them to increase their marketability and contribution in their community (Schoeffel, 1986). This is supported by Veramu (1997, p. 53; 1992) who says that 'people need to be empowered to control their own destiny and to have a say in the appropriate type of sustainable development that suits them.'

The strength of NFE is its inclusiveness and accessibility. People in rural communities do not have to travel as training and trainers are brought to them. NFE complements formal education very well providing an avenue for everyone, especially school-leavers and drop-outs, to acquire skills relevant for an effective contribution and survival in their community (Hamadache, 1991).

The government has committed itself, through its ministries, NGOs and training institutions, to implement programmes ranging from agriculture and small business administration to community health awareness (Veramu, 1997).

The Fiji Institute of Technology, through its Research and Development Unit, also shares the vision that NFE has a major role to play in Fiji's national prosperity and development. The training-needs assessment initiated by FIT was intended to strengthen the decision-making base for the planned training of communities in rural areas.

3 Methodology

The team consisted of eight researchers who all work under the auspices of the FIT Learning Centre. The initial intention of the team was to conduct a training-needs assessment in mixed communities, but this had to be abandoned due to lack of resources. Instead, it was realised that a TNA survey conducted in Fijian villages would be within the team's budget. A pilot survey to test the questionnaire was carried out in three villages. The results were analysed and the questions were modified to ensure reliability and validity. The pilot was also intended for team members to obtain experience of the real-life situation in villages and to try out methods.

Upon completion of the preparatory stages, members of the team went in groups of two, three and occasionally individually to conduct the survey in the provinces. Prior to and during each visit all important officials and dignitaries were informed, such as elders, village chiefs, school-teachers and church leaders, to facilitate the team members carrying out their survey. All village surveys were conducted in the evenings with most of them ending late at night. Proper protocol was followed with formal presentations, then an explanation by the team leader, followed by filling-in of questionnaire forms and concluding with a long discussion session.

It was observed that during the discussion sessions the elders always spoke first while the other participants took their turn in descending order of age and status. An open discussion among the villagers would only involve the elders; young people were never expected to air their views publicly. Ocitti (1990) calls this 'vertical communication', which expresses the difficulty of direct dialogue between the old and the young in indigenous societies. He also noted a 'horizontal human relationship', which exists primarily among one's peers, where there is freedom to think, talk and act. In Fijian society, it is a sign of respect for the young to remain quiet unless spoken to.

However, during the visits, the researchers managed to get a response from all present by posing direct questions to the elders, then the women and then the youths. All responses were directed back at the researchers. Noticeably, all general comments and suggestions came only from the elders and the chiefs, but none from the youth.

The discussion was always lively and interesting as it was an avenue for people to ask questions on various issues and not just education. There were problems encountered by the research team, such as inadequate time in each village, lack of funds and treacherous road conditions, but the team were not deterred and managed to complete all field work on time.

The researchers were aware that dealing with descriptive data from this survey would involve two general limitations in the form of validity and reliability. Therefore, in the initial stages of research formulation and preparations, key control mechanisms were put in place to ensure a satisfactory degree of validity and reliability.

One of the key mechanisms for controlling validity and reliability was an emphasis on procedures throughout the process. During the initial stages of formulating the theoretical framework, the principal researcher and team made a number of consultation visits to principal stakeholders, which included key officials in various government ministries, training institutions and provincial offices. The visits ensured that research parameters were clear, indicators were defined precisely and all data-collecting instruments would lead to reliable results.

A series of briefings involving all team members ensured that field-work procedures were precisely adhered to by all so that consistency and reliability of results were achieved. This was absolutely necessary as the team members were sent to different parts of Fiji.

Another mechanism used for controlling reliability was the series of checks and reviews of research tools and items. Important decisions had to be made, especially regarding the questionnaire and its suitability for rural indigenous Fijians. After the pilot test and a retest, the final questionnaire was presented in Fijian vernacular and the team were satisfied of its suitability. The team also took into serious consideration issues such as question types, question lengths and time to complete the questionnaire. The clarity of items in terms of font size was reviewed to ensure that all participants were able to read the words clearly. This was necessary as people of all ages were intended as participants in this research.

The researchers were aware that the issue of validity would emerge regarding sampling and representation. The major obstacle and limitation in sampling was the lack of funding to cover a bigger percentage of provincial populations. For this reason, the team had to be content with a target sample of 100 participants per province. This included both genders and all ages.

Other control measures that research assistants had to ensure in all locations were:

- The venue of the research survey must be a village hall or school classroom.
- The atmosphere should be relaxed and casual so that all participants could contribute fully.
- All participants had to be provided with pencils for filling out the questionnaires.
- At least thirty minutes was allowed to fill out the questionnaire.
- Additional time was allowed for open discussions (debriefing after collecting the questionnaires).
- The necessary social protocol was to be adhered to in all villages and provinces.

Despite all the measures taken, the researchers acknowledge that there were limitations, such as intentional and unintentional biases in this research. It was possible that some data may have been inadvertently emphasized more than others and some may have been used to highlight a particular point of view. Additionally, the researchers acknowledge that there is also the possibility that the sample of participants in each province may not be an accurate representation of the entire populace.

It is quite possible that items used in the questionnaire may not be variables of primary interest and may have affected respondents' interests in different ways. Sensitive issues such as educational level and status may have posed problems for some participants. While every possible measure was taken to ensure reliability and validity in this research, the team acknowledges that there are limitations that may have had a bearing on the results.

4 Findings

Thus, sixty villages from fourteen provinces were visited and a total of 1,807 respondents surveyed: 54% of whom or 974 were male; and 46% or 833 were female. Tables 1 and 2 present the training needs identified by respondents, as well as supporting data from the questionnaire. Due to the magnitude of the participation, the priority focus of the analysis was on training needs, ethnography and educational levels, and the logic behind choices

Results identify specific training needs indicated by participants of both genders from each village and province. The villages visited in each province were some distance from each other in order that provincial summaries reflected a reasonable sample of the training needs among the general provincial populations. Analysis

Table 1 Training needs choices by province (female)

Flower arrangement	Sewing/screen printing	Cooking	Tourism/small business administration	Family education/ child-rearing	Basic English
Rewa	Kadavu	Naitasiri	Rewa	Lau	Cakau
Kadavu	Naitasiri	Lomaiviti	Kadavu	Kadavu	
Naitasiri	Lomaiviti	Ba	Naitasiri	Ba	
Lomaiviti	Ba	Tailevu	Ba	Serua	
Nadroga	Namosi	Nadroga	Serua	Tailevu	
Ra	Ra	Bua	Nadroga	Ra	
	Macuata	Namosi		Macuata	
	Bua				
6 (43%)	8 (57%)	7 (50%)	6 (43%)	7 (50%)	1 (7%)

Table 2 Training needs choices by province (male)

Basic machine repair	Basic carpentry/ plumbing	Basic electrical	Tourism/small business ad- ministration	Resource management	Time management
Rewa	Rewa	Rewa	Kadavu	Lau	Macuata
Kadavu	Naitasiri	Naitasiri	Ba	Macuata	
Naitasiri	Lomaiviti	Lomaiviti	Serua	Bua	
Lomaiviti	Tailevu	Namosi	Tailevu		
Ba	Nadro	Ra	Nadro		
Namosi	Bua	Cakau			
Serua					
Ra					
Macuata					
Bua					
Cakau					
11 (79%)	6 (42%)	6 (42%)	5 (36%)	3 (21%)	1 (7%)

by gender, age-groups and educational levels provided significant information for decision-makers. In terms of the differences in training choices, the most significant one was between genders in all provinces. However, comparisons at village and provincial levels displayed an interesting trend—that communities or villages along the coast, including the outer islands, had a different set of choices from communities and villages in the interior regions or mountains. This finding suggests that *geographical location* and *available natural resources* are significant factors that determine training choices.

Other factors that became evident from the study are *income sources* and *development* or *lifestyle needs*. There was no correlation between training choice and educational level, nor between training choice and age. This suggests that choices were not solely based on individual needs but also on community aspirations (Plowman, 1992).

The most popular training choice for men was basic machine repair (Table 2), while women had five popular choices which were: flower arrangement, sewing, cooking, small business administration and family education (Table 1).

Table 3 shows that 327 teenagers (18.1% of total sample) participated in this survey. Of this figure, an alarming 80% or 262 are school-leavers and drop-outs. In the total sample of 1,807, this percentage translates to 14.5%.

Levels of education for both genders vary slightly but a larger percentage of female participants had reached higher secondary and tertiary levels. A significant finding is that 98% of participants are educated above Classes 6–8, which indicates a high level of literacy in rural Fiji (Table 4 and Fig. 1). This suggests that trainers tasked with conducting training in rural communities would have few problems in terms of communication and delivery.

It can be concluded from this survey that basic machine repair (Table 2) came out strongly as the significant/popular choice for men, while women had five choices of comparable significance (Table 1). In terms of age, a clear majority of participants (82%) were above 20 years of age, 25.7% of whom were over 41. This wide range

Table 3 The number of participants by gender and age groups

| Age group | Participants by gender and age-groups | | | | |
	16 – 19	20 – 30	31 – 40	41 +	Total
Number male (%)	192 (20%)	350 (36%)	194 (20%)	238 (24%)	974 (54%)
Number female (%)	135 (16%)	273 (33%)	198 (24%)	227 (27%)	833 (46%)
Total (%)	327 (18.1%)	623 (34.5%)	392 (21.7%)	465 (25.7%)	1807

Table 4 Total participants by educational level

| Classes 1–5 | | Classes 6–8 | | Forms 3–4 | | Forms 5–7 | | Tertiary | |
Male	Female	Male	Female	Male	Female	Male	Female	Male	Female
30	8	292	225	321	267	321	316	10	17
3%	1%	30%	27%	33%	32%	33%	38%	1%	2%
2% of sample		29% of sample		33% of sample		35% of sample		1% of sample	

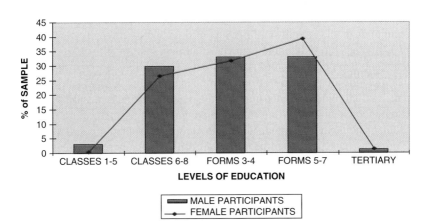

Fig. 1 Comparative levels of education (by gender)

in age groups is indicative of the inclusive nature of non-formal education, coupled with adult education.

5 The Logic Behind the Training Choices in the TNA

The choice of training by participants did not differ with age or educational levels, but reflected and depended upon a combination of the following key factors:

1. Gender.
2. Local natural resources—forest/sea/farming, etc.
3. Current income sources.
4. Geographical location—coast or interior, and distance from urban centres.
5. Developmental/lifestyle and educational needs (Fig. 2).

The major advantages of TNA-based training from the local to the national level can be summed up as follows:

1. Individuals in the village (community) will have an opportunity to acquire new skills that would help them improve their own standard of living and empower them in managing their sources of income.
2. For the community as a whole, this would result in overall improvement in the quality of life in the village, improved productivity and better management of natural resources.
3. For the provinces, this would result in better utilization of development funds, as villagers are now more informed and aware of their potential to implement relevant village projects effectively.

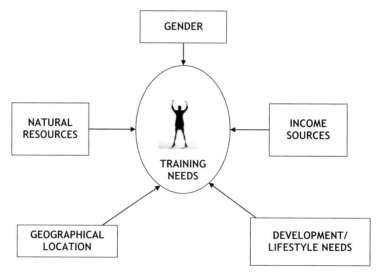

Fig. 2 Factors that determine training choices

4. For Fiji, this would result in skills training in rural communities, effective resource management, reduction in social evils, such as poverty and crime, and opening up further opportunities for growth.

6 Conclusion

Results from this survey would provide useful information to key stakeholders, such as government departments, donor agencies and provincial councils, for decision-making on rural training and education. In addition, the training areas identified by participants have provided FIT, especially the Learning Centre, with specific areas for short courses that may receive accreditation. The most popular choices for courses include, amongst others, basic English, flower arrangement, basic plumbing, basic carpentry and tourism/business studies.

Recommendations and projections discussed in this chapter would function as guidelines for the development and improvement of education and skills training for our rural communities over the next decade.

Researchers from the Learning Centre have established a good working relationship with village elders, chiefs and provincial administrators throughout Fiji, and have inadvertently lifted their expectations of FIT. The onus is on key stakeholders to use the results of this survey as a basis for delivering effective relevant training to rural communities. The vision is that if our rural people were empowered with the necessary skills, they would become more independent and would play a leading role in developing and improving the economies of their own communities.

For institutions, such as the Fiji Institute of Technology, the University of the South Pacific and the Training and Productivity Authority of Fiji, the results of this survey provide ideas for developing relevant courses targeted at school dropouts and rural dwellers. It is hoped that in the next decade more institutions and organizations would share this vision and pursue the delivery of skills training to our rural people.

References

Encarta encyclopaedia. 2004. CD-ROM, Microsoft Corporation.

Fiji. Ministry of Education. 2000. *Learning together: directions for education in the Fiji Islands. Report of the Fiji Islands Education Commission.* Suva: Government Printer.

Hamadache, A. 1991 Non-formal education: a definition of the concept and some examples. *Prospects,* vol. 21, no. 1, pp. 111–24.

Mausio, A. 2003. Melanesia in review: issues and events: Fiji. *The contemporary Pacific,* vol. 15, no. 2, pp. 440–47.

Ocitti, J.P 1990. Is indigenous African pedagogy a real option? *Adult education and development,* vol. 90, no. 35.

Plowman, K. 1992. *Community groups and empowerment: adult education for a democratic culture.* Canberra: Australian Association of Adult and Community Education. (Paper presented at the thirty-second AAACE National Conference, Canberra, 1992.)

Schoeffel, P. 1986. Non-formal education in the Pacific Islands: an overview. *Adult education and development,* vol. 26.

Sharma, A. 2000. Technical and vocational education and training. *In:* Fiji. Ministry of Education. *Learning together: directions for education in the Fiji Islands.* Suva: Government Printer.

Tavola, H. 2000. Education in rural Fiji. *In:* Fiji. Ministry of Education. *Learning together: directions for education in the Fiji Islands.* Suva: Government Printer.

Veramu, J. 1992. *Let's do it our way: a case study of participatory education in a rural Fijian school and community.* Suva: Institute of Pacific Studies, University of the South Pacific.

Veramu, J. 1997. *Adult education and community development in the South Pacific.* Valelevu, Fiji: The Fiji Adult and Community Education Think-Tank Group.

Chapter IV.8
Social Partnership in Vocational Education and Training in Lithuania: Challenges and Perspectives

Lina Kaminskienė

1 Introduction

Social partnership in technical and vocational education and training (TVET)—that is to say co-operation and the interrelationship of functions and responsibilities among the State, employers and employees—has been set as one of the priorities of educational reform and is an important principle for the effective development of the vocational education and training system in Lithuania.

Particularly in recent years, a change of roles has become apparent between the State and non-governmental sectors in the TVET system. According to the International Labour Office (ILO), there are three phases in the sharing of functions and responsibilities between the State and private sector in the vocational education and training system:

- *The first phase:* an unstructured and unregulated TVET system, where professional skills were acquired through the principle of apprenticeship.
- *The second phase:* a supply-driven TVET system (the State-dominated system). This phase describes the situation when the VET system does not adequately react to the needs of the vocational activity system,[1] but decides alone what kind of training is needed for professions and qualifications.
- *The third phase* is characterized by a demand-driven system. This is a situation when a TVET system is directly influenced by the needs of the vocational activity required by the market economy, and thus tries to satisfy those needs by supplying the labour market with appropriate professions and qualifications.

However, today, a new tendency is clearly seen in Lithuania and other post-Soviet Eastern and Central European countries. This is an attempt to strengthen relationships between the TVET system and vocational activity system, while seeking new forms of co-operation.

R. Maclean, D. Wilson (eds.), *International Handbook of Education for the Changing World of Work*, DOI 10.1007/978-1-4020-5281-1_IV.8,
© Springer Science+Business Media B.V. 2009

2 The Theoretical Background of Social Partnership in TVET

2.1 Social Partnerships as an Intermediary between Two Systems

Social partnership in the Lithuanian TVET system is analysed from the perspective of different TVET models. Duties and responsibilities of social partners, as intermediaries between the vocational activity system and the education system are based on the theory of the duality of the vocation, which combines both its subjective and objective aspects.

The subjective aspect of the vocation reflects the individual preferences of a person, i.e. his/her preference for a certain activity on the basis of a human being's inner dispositions, often defining them as a human calling (Laužackas, 1997). The objective aspect of a vocation focuses on work, its structure and the conditions under which it can be carried out.

It is obvious that the interaction of the objective and the subjective aspects of vocation in the TVET system expresses itself on a different level than that of the vocation itself. At this level, the education system is likely to represent the subjective aspect, while the objective aspect is represented by the vocational activity.

2.2 Social Partnership in Supply, Demand or Co-ordination Models

As a rule, the interaction of the educational and vocational activity systems defines the model of the vocational education and training system in a country, as well as the functions delegated to social partners. Three models of the interaction of the educational and vocational activity systems are distinguished: demand, supply and co-ordination (Fig. 1).

The first model describes the situation when the vocational activity system plays a more active part in relation to the education system. The education system (or TVET system in this case) is directly influenced by the changes and needs of the vocational activity system and, thus, is adequately organized to react to these needs. This interaction model is called the 'demand-driven model' (sometimes the term 'manpower-requirement approach' is used) (Georg & Sattel, 1995).

2.2.1 The Supply-Driven Model

The supply-driven model (or 'social-demand approach' according to Georg & Sattel, 1995) exists in a country when the education system is the dominating partner. Vocational education and training is organized and planned without any or without sufficient attention to the needs of the labour market. The supply-driven model characterizes the situation when educational establishments alone decide what kinds of qualification are needed. Such decisions are based not on an analysis of labour-market needs, but on the capacity of the existing TVET system (training classes, teachers, manuals, etc.).

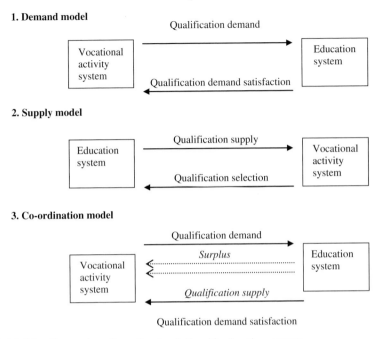

1. Demand model

Qualification demand

Vocational activity system → Education system

Qualification demand satisfaction

2. Supply model

Qualification supply

Education system → Vocational activity system

Qualification selection

3. Co-ordination model

Qualification demand

Surplus

Vocational activity system ← Education system

Qualification supply

Qualification demand satisfaction

Fig. 1 Models of interaction of vocational activity with education systems

The first model seems to be the most attractive one; however, in reality it can only function in a stable economic and political environment. During the transitional period, which has been characteristic of Central and Eastern European countries (including Lithuania), this model could not resolve the existing problems in the vocational education and training system. The reason was that the labour market was not itself stable; companies had to survive in a very hard competitive market. For example, in 1997, the Vocational Education and Training Information Service noted that around 80% of employers were not sure of their future plans for two or three years ahead (VET Informational Service, 1997). For these reasons, neither employers nor their representative organizations participated in the early phases of the reform of the education system in Lithuania.

The supply-driven model, which has been deeply rooted in Lithuania, did not help to solve the problem of unemployment. It gave employers wide possibilities to choose the necessary employees (labour force over-supply was extremely common until 2000–2002) and they provided workers with only minimal social guarantees (low wages, fixed-term contracts, etc.). The biggest drawback of the supply-driven model is that the school became isolated from the real working world and prepared workers and specialists who did not satisfy the new qualification requirements and could not adapt to the requirements, which were evolving rapidly due to changes and innovations following the impact of globalization on the economy, as well as IT development and other factors. The supply model thus isolated social partners from active participation in the vocational education and training system and their participation became fragmententary. Even in 1997, when the TVET Law was passed, it took a year or two for the first real co-ordination activities to start, under the initiative of the Ministry of Education and vocational schools—but not of the social partners themselves.

Both the supply and the demand models have their advantages and disadvantages. Every State tries to balance and to regulate the relationship between its educational and vocational systems and the labour market. The third, 'the co-ordination model', expresses a certain compromise (coherence) between the demand and the supply models. According to Laužackas (1997), this model seems to be the ideal one. However, achieving it requires a very flexible vocational education and training system in the country with the following features: (a) a mechanism to balance and co-ordinate the tasks and functions of the key players in the system; (b) a clear strategy for the TVET system; (c) a well-regulated legal basis; (d) a regular analysis of what is happening in economic sectors; (e) a well-established monitoring system of the labour market, etc. During the period 1991 to 2002, Lithuania tried to re-orient its supply model to align it with the demand one. Nevertheless, because of the changes taking place before and after 2004 (enlargement of the EU), during a period when the Lithuanian labour market lost about 200,000 of its active working-age population (there are no officially confirmed figures yet), discussions about the co-ordination model became more active.

3 Historical Background of Social Partnership in Lithuania

3.1 The Social Partnership Model in Lithuania before the 1990s

During the Soviet era, social dialogue was of an artificial nature and based on the principle of 'supervision', which was organized in a centralized way. Industrial enterprises had a duty to supervise vocational schools, which were their suppliers of labour. Vocational education and training at that time was based on the Soviet labour theory, which said that a human's activity is a link between the subject and the object—through activity a human being affects the surrounding world, as well as changing himself/herself. Actually, social partnership as it is understood today (co-operation and sharing responsibilities between the State, employers and employees) did not really exist in the Soviet period.

During this period the TVET system was unified according to a Soviet model; consequently, very similar vocational education and training systems now exist in all post-Soviet countries. The typical features of the vocational education and training system in Lithuania before the 1990s were as follows:

- A planned economy;
- Centralized management;
- Close relations (based on supervision) with large enterprises;
- Monolithic teaching curriculum;

- Absence of unemployment;
- Low image of vocational education and training (Gurskiene, 2004).

In addition, the old system was associated with low productivity and an unsuccessful economy. 'There was no competition in applying for a job. A person's vocational career depended on both his/her competence and ideological criteria' (Beresneviciene, 1999).

Social dialogue in the Soviet vocational education and training system was artificial because there was no competition in the market; economic relations between enterprises and users were based on the principle of the planned economy—but not on competition. The labour force in Lithuania, as well as in the other Baltic countries, was not oriented to the needs of these countries but to satisfy the demands of the USSR or the other Soviet republics (within COMECOM—the trading bloc).

It is also very important to say that the prestige of vocational education and training was very low, which consequently led to a rather superficial attitude at all levels of society towards the system.

3.2 Social Partnership in TVET from the 1990s until 1997

After regaining independence, most of the previous co-operation between educational establishments and enterprises collapsed because of ineffective organization and/or because many large enterprises went through a long restructuring process. New ways of co-operation had to be established.

The collection of articles 'National school' was the first document, which tried to describe the principles of the educational reform in Lithuania starting from 1990. In 1992 the Lithuanian Educational Concept was prepared. This document was the first to introduce social partnership as part of the vocational education and training system in the country. This document stressed the following problematic and important areas, to which particular attention had to be paid:

- The foundation of private schools;
- The necessity of social dialogue;
- Development of a register of educational programmes;
- Independent evaluation of knowledge and competences (evaluation separate from the educational process) while transferring this function to social partners (employers);
- Ensuring continuity of education;
- Modular teaching (Dienys & Pusvaškis, 1998).

During the first years of independence (1990–1994), Lithuania failed to create and to develop a mechanism in order to ensure a harmonious relationship between the education system and the economy. Only after 1994, when employers' organizations became stronger and started to appreciate their role in the TVET system, did social partnership acquire a more concrete form.

In 1997 social partnership was formalized in the TVET system in Lithuania by the adoption of the law on vocational education and training. Almost in parallel, in 1998 'The White Paper on VET'—a manual for vocational training—was prepared. The idea of publishing such a document was inspired by the experience of the new economy, becoming acquainted with European systems of vocational training through the European Union's PHARE programme, vocational training reform and other projects, as well as new experiments. 'The White Paper' described social partnership as an engine for the continuous renewal of the vocational education and training system. The principle of social partnership was described as co-operation and interrelation of the State, employers and employees, which would result in defining the boundaries of duties and responsibilities for each partner during the planning, organizing, implementing and evaluating of vocational education and training tools and programmes. The main condition for ensuring the quality of these tasks was based on co-ordination and negotiation of different vocational training interests (Lithuania, 1999, p. 19). Based on these strategic documents, social dialogue in Lithuania was organized at three levels: national-political; vocational-political; and vocational-practical. This model of social partnership still exists today.

3.2.1 The National-Political Level

The Lithuanian Vocational Education and Training Council co-operates closely with the Ministry of Education and Science and the Ministry of Social Security and Labour. This council is organized on a tripartite basis: an equal number of representatives of State institutions, employers and employees participate on this board. The Lithuanian Vocational Education and Training Council is a co-ordinating body ensuring that the interests of all social partners are represented. Employers and employees are represented by their organizations (chambers of commerce, confederations of industrialists, trade unions, etc.).

At the regional level, the district vocational education and training councils play an advisory role. They provide expertise and perform consulting and co-ordination functions in regions.

3.2.2 The Vocational-Political Level

Industrial boards (otherwise called expert groups) are also organized on the tripartite principle (TVET institutions, employers and trade unions from different economic branches). The aim of these groups is to develop policy for vocational education and training. Industrial boards form a part of the system for development of vocational education and training standards. Following decisions by the Lithuanian Vocational Education and Training Council and the Central Industrial Institute, a new board is organized in order to analyse the needs, development perspectives and qualification needs for each specific sector/branch. Fourteen industrial boards are established at the methodological centre for VET.

3.2.3 The Vocational-Practical Level

Working groups develop concrete vocational training standards (VET Information Service, 1998). There are two types of working groups: (a) vocational standards groups; and (b) vocational training standards groups. Both groups work on the basis of a contract with the industrial board. The first type (vocational standards groups) makes concrete vocational studies, prepares sectoral analysis, defines developments and trends in vocations and makes forecasts of the future need for specialists (Laužackas, 1997). Vocational training standards groups prepare projects of the necessary vocational and vocational training standards (Fig. 2).

The principle of social partnership is applied not only for the development of vocational training standards but also in the organization of practical training (apprenticeship), curriculum updating and in the final qualifications examinations process.

Nevertheless, in the first years of the educational reform, TVET schools were more active participants in the system than the social partners. The period 1990–1997 was very difficult for companies and business-related organizations. On the other hand, companies did not meet fierce competition, which came later; particularly after the economic crisis in Russia in 1997–1998 and after joining the EU in 2004. One could say that the system of vocational education and training in the first years of the reform was prepared exceptionally by joint efforts of State institutions and schools. Only in 1998 did social partners become more actively involved in the TVET system.

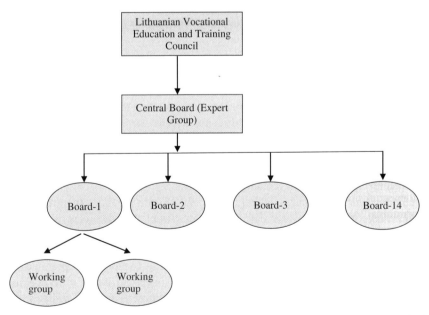

Fig. 2 Model of the social partnership for developing vocational and vocational training standards

4 The Present-Day Social and Economic Developments in Lithuania

4.1 Trends and Developments Influencing TVET

Social partnership in Lithuania, as in other post-Soviet countries, is a rather new phenomenon, compared to such countries as Germany or Austria with long traditions of social dialogue. Today, social partnership development issues are discussed following the bottom-up principle. It is of primary importance to identify the main barriers which prevent successful development of social partnerships in vocational education and training. Employers should be attracted to the TVET system through their representative structures: trade associations, chambers of commerce, confederations, etc.

Increasing competition, more active trade and co-operation in the EU and foreign markets have become the key factors today making employers more interested in TVET. Investments into new technologies, innovations in management and/or production processes increased the need for broader competencies.

In 1998–2000 many Lithuanian companies had to re-orient their export markets from Russia to the EU. It became clear that only high-quality products corresponding to EU standards and directives could be sold in this new market.

Lithuanian companies have experienced the impact of global economic changes, which are manifested by new technologies, the development of a knowledge society, international trade and more active involvement of the labour force. Thus, as rightly noted by the authors of the White Paper: 'qualifications as established by high world standards and continuous learning became an exceptional condition of self-realization for each individual' (Lithuania, 1999).

The first practical steps in trying to co-ordinate the educational and vocational activity systems were implemented in 1998, when the State attributed several concrete functions in TVET to its social partners: the Lithuanian Chambers of Commerce, Industry and Crafts and, a few years later, to the Chamber of Agriculture.

As Pusvaškis (2003) puts it, previously it was the schools themselves that conducted assessment according to general regulations set by the Ministry of Education and Science. This system made it difficult to ensure the comparability of qualifications awarded. To ensure a more consistent approach, the Ministry of Education and Science decided to involve the employers' organizations and, in 1998, a reform in this direction was launched. By 2003 the modified examination system had been implemented throughout the country.

A decree by the Ministry of Education and Science regulates the organization of the final examinations for TVET students, stipulating the responsibilities of chambers of commerce in this process. The chambers of commerce are responsible for monitoring the preparatory phase of final qualifications examinations by involving specialists from enterprises with expertise in vocational programmes and in developing questions for a theory examination. This is carried out in co-operation with vocational schools. In addition, chambers of commerce are responsible for the supervision of practical training in companies in order to ensure that TVET students gain the necessary practical skills. The overall model of the roles and functions of social partners while preparing and organizing final qualification examinations can be illustrated as in Fig. 3.

This new way of conducting assessment has obliged schools to become more committed to meeting the qualification requirements set by the State and to pay more attention to labour-market trends. The participation of all the interested parties—employers, employees and school representatives—in the process stimulates further development through social dialogue.

Within the labour-market training system, the first steps to transfer responsibility for the final assessment to the chambers of commerce have also been taken. The separation of responsibilities for training and final assessment is designed to enhance the effectiveness and quality of vocational education and training. This should help develop a mechanism to recognize and validate informally acquired competencies.

4.2 Key Players in Social Dialogue

In Lithuania vocational education and training schools, which represent State institutions, are the active partners and initiators of social dialogue. According to the

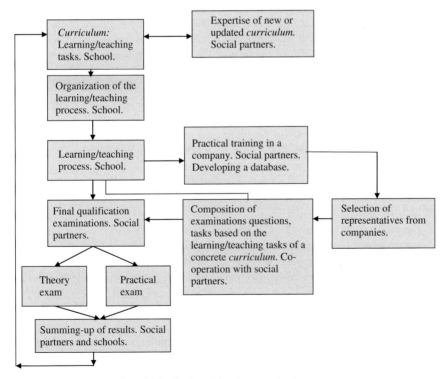

Fig. 3 The organizational model for final qualification examinations

Law on VET (Lithuania, 1997), the following State and State-supervised institutions are responsible for vocational education and training:

- The Ministry of Education and Science;
- the Ministry of Social Security and Labour;
- The Lithuanian Vocational Education and Training Council, composed on a tripartite principle of the State, employers' and employees' organizations;
- Other ministries, departments, district administrations and municipalities;
- The Methodological Centre for Vocational Education and Training under the Ministry of Education and Science;
- Industrial institutes;
- Labour-market training centres;
- The Employment Service under the Ministry of Social Security and Labour;
- Tripartite committees under the Ministry of Social Security and Labour;
- The Experts Council, the Ministry of Social Security and Labour and labour-market training centres.

The number of the institutions and offices listed (which does not include the TVET schools) is evidence that the State is playing an active role in the organization of the TVET system. While this is a positive approach, showing that the State is responsible for education, on the other hand this rather centralized approach may discourage social partners from assuming more functions and responsibilities in the education system. Moreover, the State has the role of co-ordinator or moderator, being responsible for maintaining the balance of the above-mentioned structures. While delegating specific functions and responsibilities to social partners (for example, the organization of final qualification examinations is delegated to chambers of commerce and the chamber of agriculture), the State also has to find the appropriate financial resources.

Employers' organizations in Lithuania are comparatively young, having only been established since the first years of Lithuanian independence. Today, the Lithuanian Chambers of Commerce, Industry and Crafts (1992), the Confederation of Industrialists (1993) and the Confederation of Employers (1999) are the biggest and the most active employers' organizations.

- *The Lithuanian Chambers of Commerce, Industry and Crafts* is the only non-governmental organization in Lithuania benefiting from an individual law. There are five regional chambers of commerce with headquarters in Vilnius. Today chambers of commerce bring together over 1,500 enterprises. In 1999 the Law on Chambers of Commerce was supplemented by several articles allowing TVET schools and other types of training organizations to become members of chambers of commerce.
- *The Lithuanian Confederation of Employers* is a public organization uniting over 500 enterprises and about 100 associated structures. The confederation represents the interests of employers in various governmental committees, commissions, councils, ministries and other State organizations.

- *The Lithuanian Confederation of Industrialists* is a union of associations. The confederation unites about forty trade associations, nine regional associations and about sixty non-associated structures. The confederation plays an active part in the lobbying sphere, as well as delegating experts from different branches to industrial boards working on vocational standards.

Vocational education and training, unfortunately, has not yet become a priority area of activity for social partners. This attitude has been influenced by the transitional period in politics and the economy, as well as a strong preference on the part of business organizations for lobbying and representation.

Employees in Lithuania today are represented by various trade unions, which are united in four associations: the Lithuanian Trade Union Association; the Lithuanian Trade Unions Centre; the Lithuanian Labour Federation; and the Lithuanian Workers' Union.

Similarly, like employers organizations, trade unions have not paid much attention to vocational education and training issues. They are not adequately trained and prepared to participate as equal partners in social dialogue. During the first years of independence their major concern was to represent and to defend TVET as supplied by the State. Nevertheless, such organizations still lack information about their potential, or approach their functions and responsibilities for TVET in a different way. Recent discussions, while developing a new Law on TVET, only confirm this fact. Furthermore, trade unions had no administrative structures that could undertake these roles and functions in the TVET system. Neither did they have any experience of negotiation and participation in social dialogue.

Meanwhile, today, chambers of commerce, confederations of industrialists and the chamber of agriculture are quite experienced and capable of sharing responsibilities.

5 Social Partnership in the Context of the EU Enlargement Process

5.1 Development of the Legal Basis for Social Partnership in Lithuania

Legal conditions have already been created for social partners to participate in initial and labour-market vocational education and training in Lithuania. The first legal document in Lithuania describing the principle of social partnership was the Law on Inhabitants Employment Law, enacted in 1990. This law legitimated the principles of social partnership and functions of tripartite committees in the field of labour-market policy.

Participation of social partners in the vocational education and training system was first defined in the White Paper (Lithuania, 1999) and the Law on VET in

Lithuania (Lithuania, 1997). Social partners have been attributed the following functions:

- to supply proposals to the Lithuanian VET Council, while defining requirements for TVET programmes (modules) and final qualification examinations;
- to organize final qualification examinations;
- to register practical training agreements/contracts between schools, enterprises and individuals;
- to supervise practical training agreements and their implementation.

According to this law, the term 'a competent institution' was introduced into the TVET system. The Lithuanian Chambers of Commerce, the Confederation of Industrialists and the Chamber of Agriculture were granted this status.

In 1999 the supplemented Law on Chambers of Commerce and Industry allowed TVET schools and other training organizations to become members of these business organizations. In 1998 the Law on Non-formal Adult Education also foresaw roles and functions of social partners in continuous vocational education and training.

5.2 The Impact of PHARE, Leonardo da Vinci and Other EU Programmes

Starting from 1994 to 1998, Lithuania, as well as other candidate-countries for European Union membership, benefited from the PHARE programme (this originally meant: Poland and Hungary: Assistance for Restructuring their Economies). The first phase of the PHARE programme was focused on modernization of vocational education and training in post-Soviet countries. Particularly, this reform aimed at:

- Audit/revision of the current curriculum and development of a new curriculum;
- The development of teaching qualifications at all levels of vocational training, including teachers, employers and members of trade unions;
- The modernization of educational equipment;
- Initiation of partnerships with educational institutions in the EU countries;
- The development of TVET strategic documents (Lithuania, 1999; Zimina, 2002).

After the end of the first phase of the PHARE programme (1995) in the candidate countries (Estonia, Lithuania, Romania and Slovenia), new vocational education and training laws were adopted.

The PHARE reform gave impetus to involving social partners in the development of the TVET system in Lithuania and other countries. In almost all of these countries social partners, particularly employers, were involved in the management of vocational education and training through tripartite social partnership agreements at national, regional and local levels. Furthermore, the relationships between vocational schools and local enterprises were determined. In Estonia and Lithuania leading bodies under the Methodological Centre for VET were established fostering the assessment of vocational education and training needs in certain sectors of the economy (Zimina, 2002).

A further reform, which started with the second phase of PHARE and other EU programmes, was mostly oriented towards the national qualifications systems (in Estonia, Lithuania, Poland, Slovenia and Hungary). The problem of more active involvement of social partners still remains a problem for such countries as Bulgaria, the Czech Republic, Latvia and Lithuania—amongst others.

From 1997 other EU programmes (mostly the Leonardo da Vinci Programme) allowed development of various sectors of the TVET system in Lithuania. These programmes contributed to the successful reform of TVET, as well as harmonizing the Lithuanian TVET system with other systems in EU countries. The Leonardo da Vinci Programme particularly contributed to the mobility of students and teachers, social partners in the EU countries, as well as considerably strengthening co-operation between schools and enterprises.

These EU programmes allowed Lithuania to prepare for new challenges that appeared following the integration process resulting from economic and social developments.

6 Challenges for Social Partners in Lithuania

6.1 New Responsibilities for Social Partners

Today, social partners meet with new challenges: increased competencies in TVET schools and enterprises; the appearance of new players in the TVET system; higher quality standards. All of these issues are outcomes of the reform in the TVET system, integration with the EU and more intensive regional and international co-operation.

New tasks and responsibilities for social partners have opened up on three main levels:

1. Co-ordination of roles and functions on the decision-making level (political level);
2. Teaching/learning pathways at the structural level (standardization, qualifications framework);
3. Co-ordination of tasks and responsibilities to optimize the teaching/learning process (organization of practical training, final examinations, etc.).

On the decision-making level it is very important to regulate and to balance supply and demand for the labour market, as well as creating a better mechanism to satisfy the needs of the vocational system. An effective co-ordination on the decision-making level requires fulfilling at least the following conditions:

1. A country should have a TVET regulating institution/board/council, where the interests of the social partners are represented.

2. A country should develop a feedback mechanism in order to monitor quality issues in TVET.
3. Direct contacts and co-operation between enterprises and schools should be encouraged.

At the level of structuring teaching/learning pathways, roles and responsibilities of social partners could cover the following aspects:

- contribution to the development of the National Qualifications Framework;
- contribution to the development of vocational training standards;
- contribution to the certification process (assessing formal, non-formal or informal learning).

On the level of optimizing the teaching/learning process, social partnerships could contribute to a better development of practical training, and new forms and places of teaching/learning. Having evaluated challenges on these three main levels, the following areas of activities for the development of social partnership can be identified:

1. *Participation in the development of initial and continuing vocational education and training policy* through direct relations: enterprise/educational institutions; through educational committees in chambers of commerce; and through TVET councils at national and regional levels. It is of primary importance to make the participation of employers more active in the regions. If on the national level the interests of social partners are more-or-less well-represented in the TVET councils, regional TVET monitoring structures lack the participation and contribution of social partners.
2. *Participation in the work of expert groups* (industrial institutes) for developing vocational standards. Because of the complicated mechanisms, long-term procedures and low financial compensation, employers are unwilling to participate in the development of occupational standards. Similarly, because of low-motivation, employers are rather passive in providing expertise to vocational and labour-market programmes. These areas of activity require a new approach from all sides, both the State and employers. The input of social partners, while developing vocational standards, as well as while reviewing vocational programmes, allows new competences to be introduced in TVET schools and prepares the labour force for the necessary qualifications.
3. *Participation in evaluation* and making new vocational and labour-market training programmes coherent.
4. *Participation in final qualification examinations.* Though the function of organizing final qualification examinations has been delegated to chambers of commerce since 1998, many areas remain problematic. For instance, employers do not participate in preparing final examination questions and not all of them are acquainted with the educational content before the examination. The existing system for the organization of final examinations does not allow the acquired competences to be compared at the national level. This problem highlights the

need to develop a unified system of final examinations. Projects of this type, supported by European structural funds, are taking place in Lithuania today.

5. *Participation in the management of vocational education and training institutions.* The involvement of employers on the boards of vocational education and training institutions is an exception rather than a rule. This is because of the Soviet stereotype of school 'patronage', which functioned before the 1990s. Employers must adopt a new attitude.

6. *Better organization of practical training.* There still exists a problem in ensuring the quality of practical training, as there is no guarantee that a student will gain the necessary skills and knowledge. In order to solve this problem, the Ministry of Education and Science, in co-operation with social partners, develops regulations for enterprises that are willing to accept apprentices. Only those enterprises that meet these regulations will receive students for practical training. A special database of such enterprises will be developed. The Lithuanian chambers of commerce and other business organizations should certify the appropriate enterprises.

The above-mentioned areas of activity for social partners are the main ones—but not all. Changes to be introduced into the new Law on VET should allow a more active involvement of social partners at different levels of the TVET system.

6.2 Changes in the Legal Basis for Social Dialogue

All the key players involved in the TVET system admit that the legal framework for TVET needs updating and improvement. At the end of 2002 the Ministry of Education and Science started preparatory work for amendments to the Law on VET. In 2004 a draft for the new law was confirmed (Lithuania, 2005).

It is expected that the new law will eliminate the contradictions present in the old law. The main contradiction was that initial vocational training is completely separated from labour training, which makes the process of integration very complicated and heavy on the one hand, and, on the other, creates barriers for implementing the idea of lifelong learning.

New changes also appeared because of the integration of Lithuania into the EU. The new law should focus on transparency of qualifications, mobility, the accreditation of qualifications, not only taking into account the Lithuanian education system, but other EU countries too.

7 Conclusions

Although the Lithuanian vocational education and training system is still in a transitional phase from the supply-driven and demand-driven to the co-ordination model, social partners are involved in such activities as the development of vocational standards, the organization of final qualification examinations, supervision of practical training, management of TVET schools, sharing costs in training and re-training, evaluating vocational training programmes, etc.

During an eight-year period, the achievements of social partnership in vocational education and training system have been quite considerable. The following changes can be identified:

- change of the content of social partnership: relations between schools and companies became based not on supervision but on co-operation, which is typical of a market economy;
- changes to the curriculum, based on the needs of the economy, the new requirements; plus more active involvement of experts from companies in the development of vocational training standards;
- updated and expanded new TVET programmes;
- modernized TVET and practical skills formation processes;
- new and flexible teaching/learning methods implemented;
- practical training is organized in modernized schools or directly in companies;
- an independent system of assessment of knowledge and skills implemented;
- experts from companies are involved in this process.

Having evaluated the existing potential of employers and employees, while developing social partnership in vocational education and training system, the following steps should now be taken:

- training of employers and employee representatives in order to ensure their more active participation in the functions and responsibilities of social partners;
- developing local and regional co-operation between educational establishments, regional administrations and social partners;
- developing TVET departments within chambers of commerce, industry and crafts and chambers of agriculture in order to carry out the delegated functions fully;
- promoting social partnership, explaining its aims and tasks in a vocational education and training system;
- involving social partners in different committees, councils and other structures related to vocational education and training issues;
- regularly updating and improving the legal basis for the development of social partnership with the active participation of social partners in this process;
- ensuring financial support for sustaining social partnership;
- involving social partners in various national and EU projects; and
- developing research activities in the field of social partnership for TVET.

A new culture of social partnership has emerged in Lithuania and other Eastern and Central European countries. The involvement of social partners in the vocational education and training system is a logical outcome of the free-market system. Social partnership in Lithuania has already contributed to the overall quality of the vocational education and training system. This process is still going on so that social partners respond to new challenges by trying to co-ordinate the interests of TVET institutions, employees and employers' organizations.

Note

1. The term was first used in Lithuania by R. Laužackas (1997), while speaking about the labour-market system.

References

Beresneviciene, D. 1999. New possibilities for adult education and continuous development in Eastern and Central Europe. *Vocational education: research and reality*, no. 2.

Dienys, V.; Pusvaškis, R. 1998. Changes in Lithuanian vocational training system during the first stage of educational reform. *Vocational education: research and reality*, no. 1.

Georg, W.; Sattel, U. 1995. Arbeitsmarkt, Beschaftigungssystem und Berufsbildung. *In:* Arnold R.; Lipsmeier, A., eds. *Hanndbuch der Berufsbildung*, pp. 123–42. Opladen, Germany: Leske & Budrich.

Gurskiene, O. 2004. Initial vocational education and training policy in Lithuania and the EU. *Vocational education: research and reality*, no. 8, pp. 38–51.

Laužackas, R. 1997. *Reform of the vocational education and training curriculum: didactic features*. Kaunas, Lithuania: Vytautas Magnus University.

Lithuania. 1997. *Law on Vocational Education and Training in Lithuania*. Vilnius.

Lithuania. 2005. *Law on Vocational Education and Training in Lithuania. Draft*. Vilnius.

Lithuania. Ministry of Science and Education; Ministry of Labour and Social Security. 1999. *White Paper: Vocational education and training*. Vilnius: Ministry of Science and Education.

Pusvaškis, R. 2003. The chambers are in charge of the final examinations for students at vocational schools. *CEDEFOP info*, no. 3.

VET Informational Service 1997. *Preliminary report: role of social partners developing VET in Lithuania*. Vilnius: VET Information Service.

VET Information Service. 1998. *Report on VET in Lithuania in the social and economical context*. Vilnius: VET Informational Service.

Zimina, N. 2002. Features of VET development in countries-candidates to European Community. *Vocational education: research and reality*, no. 5, pp. 118–27.

Chapter IV.9
Integrating Education and Work: The Status of Vocational Education in Brazil

Lucília Regina Machado and Carlos Roberto Jamil Cury

1 Introduction

This chapter aims at providing an insight into the implementation of policies that take into account adapting technical and vocational education and training to the technological changes taking place in the Brazilian economy. Here, general statistical data, legal measures and concepts function together in order to tackle the present situation, and make a general statement that may start a dialogue with UNESCO's Member States.

2 Rethinking Formal Education and Training for Work

In the past, formal education and training for work have been linked to each other in order to confirm that both are necessary to enhance the quality of human life and to provide the right circumstances for maintaining the community. This association can also found in legal documents and in speeches by governmental authorities, sometimes to cement this close relationship and, at other times, to break it apart. Examination of actual historical situations will reveal the peculiarities of each particular situation.

Formal education today has its place in the governmental agendas of all countries. At the same time, science and technology are affecting most productive processes, so it is necessary to re-examine the close relationship between formal education and training for work and, whenever applicable, to remove any divergence that may harm preparation for work.

Brazil, an heir to this dualistic tradition, intends to take advantage of the close relationship between the two. It is believed that such an approach will overcome the traditional view of vocational education and make it an integral part of basic education—the right of every citizen.

R. Maclean, D. Wilson (eds.), *International Handbook of Education for the Changing World of Work*, DOI 10.1007/978-1-4020-5281-1_IV.9,
© Springer Science+Business Media B.V. 2009

3 Legal Measures in Favour of Vocational Education

According to the Federal Constitution of Brazil, education of any sort 'aims at the full development of the individual, his training for the exercise of citizenship and his qualification for work' (Federal Constitution, Article 205). This principle appears again in Article 2 of the Basic Directives Act, immediately after acknowledging the importance of the link between school and the world of work. Therefore, vocational education should be regarded as one element in the nation's efforts to provide equal access by all citizens to the full range of social services.

Because vocational education forms part of a world where technological innovations are taking place at an ever-increasing speed, affecting nations, institutions and individuals, there is an urgent need to invest in people's qualifications to become builders of the economic and social wealth of the country. Vocational education cannot be seen as a parallel educational network within a dual system, set apart from basic education. Basic education is a right for all citizens, as is laid down by law. In Brazil, there are three stages of basic education: early childhood education; fundamental (or primary) education lasting eight years; and secondary education lasting three years.

As a minimal requirement for the recognition of oneself as an equal member of society, the Federal Constitution in Article 7, para. 33, prohibits any type of work for young people under the age of 14—except as an apprentice.

The combination of vocational education and primary education represents an achievement that has enjoyed a long history of parallelism, duality—and prejudice. In a society such as Brazil's, still suffering from the residue of a slave culture and a hierarchical class division, vocational education has been viewed as second-class education. Existing social barriers consigned vocational education to the role of a 'network' training labour for menial jobs, subject to stereotypes and even prejudices. The 'other network', on the other hand, was a stronghold of the ruling classes and reserved for an elite.

This perverse tradition of a 'double network' is now forbidden by law.[1] However, we still have a long way to go before we reach a situation where vocational education would be chosen voluntarily by individuals who saw the advantage of its benefits, thus 'enhancing' the value of human work, according to Article 170 of the Federal Constitution.

One of the steps to achieve this situation is the legal obligation to progressively introduce universal secondary education (Article 208, II of the Federal Constitution), as well as lengthening compulsory schooling. For that very reason, a 1996 act gives every citizen the 'possibility of access to vocational education' and further states that 'candidates who have completed secondary education or equivalent' are eligible to admission to higher education. This tends to confirm the present trend that expects vocational education to be a regular route to higher levels of education.

Furthermore, a decree dating from 1997 states clearly that every citizen should receive a secondary education, also clarifying that vocational education courses should be parallel to or follow on from general secondary education.[2] At that time, it was discovered that it was actually illegal to have regular secondary education and vocational education at the secondary level.

Taking into account this irregularity, the government felt obliged to revoke this decree and replace it with another one allowing regular secondary education and TVET to exist at the secondary level, associating education for work with the education of young people and adults.

This new decree clearly conforms to the National Curricular Guidelines for Vocational Education. It is eventually hoped to adopt an Organic Law on Vocational and Technological Education that will represent a 'solid, permanent and coherent body of legislation'. Since 2003, several initiatives have been launched towards adopting such a law, especially a document on public policies for vocational and technical education. This document expressed the need for a policy that combines vocational and technological education with basic education. This integration should consist of an organic, universal and democratic sub-system of this same vocational and technological education in all its levels and forms. Whenever offered by the public sector, these courses should be free of charge. A similar statement contained in the Fundamentals of the Organic Bill reads as follows:

> Vocational and technological education attempts to present technology as a historical and social process; to provide the worker with knowledge so as to inform him about his role as an agent in the transformation of production and of work, providing information on scientific and technological discoveries.
>
> Based on such principles, vocational and technological education will contribute to the complete education of the individual, promote the transition from school education to actual work, and place emphasis on aspects regarding work, technology and innovation, so that the worker will be properly qualified for vocational practice.

Vocational education, as a measure to reduce social inequalities and to promote the economic development of the country, is seen as a responsibility that falls upon public schools under a policy for ensuring good quality. Due to its importance, these measures are the subject of constant debates between members of the government and other stakeholders through forums and public hearings.

Still another project aims to promote educational networks that will transform the present Fundamental Education and Teacher Valorisation Development Fund (FUNDEF) into a Basic Education and Teacher Valorisation Development Fund (FUNDEB) through a constitutional amendment to be followed by proper legislation. The constitutional amendment proposes that vocational education will receive public resources intended to develop educational networks. Besides this broad fund, the bill provides for the creation of a Vocational and Technological Education Development Fund aiming, among other things, to promote the training and qualifications of teachers.

One of the networks that forms a sub-system at the national level is the Federal Network of Technological Education, with its federal centres of technological education, the federal technical schools, the federal agro-technical schools and the decentralized educational institutes. It is also worth mentioning here that there are some vocational schools in the state and municipal networks, as well as schools and foundations maintained by the private sector and by non-governmental organizations.

Concerning the organization of curricula, the Bill of Law states:

> The curricula of vocational education and of vocational technical education at the secondary level will be organized with a view to including scientific, technological, social and humanistic knowledge that will form the common core of general and universal knowledge, in addition to specific knowledge and skills reflecting actual work and production activities.

Since vocational education courses at the higher education level are already provided for, the Bill of Law goes on to say clearly:

> The curricula of vocational technological education at the higher education level involve, in addition to the training of technologists, other modalities of undergraduate and graduate studies linked to the technology area, the licensing of teachers in these subjects, as well as applied research and the extension education.

The teacher-training component is very important since, in order to attain the objectives of the different forms of education, both pre-service and in-service teacher training will be necessary. Pre-service training will always take place at the higher education level and the administrations of the respective systems will be responsible for providing in-service education aimed at teacher updating and improvement.

The Bill of Law also mentions a specific evaluation system. This system foresees the conduct of surveys on vocational education, the compiling of updated information and data, as well as the establishment of quantitative and qualitative indicators for the courses. The evaluation of technological courses, on the other hand, will take place under the provisions of the National System of Higher Education Evaluation Act (SINAES).

Vocational education is therefore called upon to become a full and qualitative element in the education system. According to the law, access to vocational education at the secondary level is an integral part of the process to achieve universal secondary education in all its forms. However, in spite of advances made on the legal aspects, there are still two major obstacles to be overcome: (a) the inadequate numbers of students who actually reach secondary education; and (b) the circumstances and competitive nature of the market place.

It is incumbent on public policies at each level of government to acknowledge the importance of TVET as an instrument both for educating citizens to achieve vocational competence and as a strategic measure contributing to national scientific and technological development so that Brazil is on an equal footing with other countries.

4 Diversified Networks of TVET Institutions

Technical and vocational education and training in Brazil are offered through a wide and diversified network of institutions. Approximately 3,948 institutions were registered in the Vocational Education Census (Brazil. Ministry of Education, 1999). Of these, 2,034 offered courses in initial and continuing training (formerly basic) with 2,045,234 students enrolled and 1,567,888 graduate students (Posthuma, 1999).

The School Census of Technical Courses (Brazil. Ministry of Education, 2003) reported the existence of 2,789 educational institutions offering technical courses.[3] The number of courses totalled 6,446 with an enrolment of approximately 600,000 students. In 2002, 248,000 students graduated from their respective courses.[4] The Higher Education Census (Brazil. Ministry of Education, 2002) counted 636 courses training technicians. The total number of students enrolled in these courses totalled 81,348 with 12,673 successful graduates.[5]

4.1 The Federal Network

Established in 1909 by the then President of the Republic Nilo Peçanha, the federal network has existed for nearly 100 years and is present in twenty-two Brazilian states comprising 139 schools classified as follows:

- thirty-six agro-technical federal schools (EAF)—these independent bodies operate preferentially in agriculture and cattle-raising activities offering technical courses with initial and continuing training as well as secondary education;
- thirty-four federal centres of technological education (CEFETs)—these federal independent bodies offer higher education in technology at undergraduate and graduate levels, as well as training for teachers and specialists in technical and technological education;
- thirty technical schools linked to federal universities (schools without administrative, financial or budgetary autonomy offering technical courses, as well as regular secondary education);
- thirty-eight decentralized educational units (UNED). These are schools with their own sites but dependent, in administrative, pedagogical and financial terms, on the CEFET to which they belong; and
- one federal technical school.

As of October 2004, modifications were introduced in the structure of federal technological education, in order to insert the thirty-four CEFETs into the federal system of higher education that, from now on, comprises colleges (*faculdades*), technology colleges, integrated colleges, institutes and higher education schools, university centres and universities. Thus, the CEFETs now have access to the research and graduate sectoral funds, as well as to greater incentives for the qualification of teachers and for the expansion of higher education courses. This will enhance their role as reference centres for the diffusion of scientific and technological knowledge and encourage local and regional development.

According to the Vocational Education Census (Brazil. Ministry of Education, 1999), 103 of the Brazilian institutions offering initial and continuing training courses (formerly basic) belonged to the federal sphere, corresponding to only 5.1%

of the total number of institutions offering such courses, and to 3.6% (72,966) of the total enrolment with 59,757 graduates.

According to the School Census of Technical Courses (Brazil. Ministry of Education, 2003), these institutions represented 5% of the provision of technical courses in the country. However, in terms of their student body, their participation was more significant representing 13.2% of the 600,000 students enrolled in technical courses in Brazil.

Concerning the offer of higher education technology courses, however, participation of the federal institutions was quantitatively more significant with 143 courses representing 23% of the country's total, according to the Higher Education Census (Brazil. Ministry of Education, 2002). The number of students enrolled in these courses reached 16,895 (20.8% of the country's total). In that year, 1,228 students graduated from federal technician training courses (9.7% of the country's total).

4.2 State Networks

According to the 1999 Vocational Education Census (Brazil. Ministry of Education, 1999), 800 state institutions offered this form of education (20.3% of the total of such institutions in Brazil). Approximately 23.4% of these (187) taught initial and continuing training courses (formerly basic) representing 9.2% of the Brazilian institutions offering such courses. The number of courses reached 889 representing approximately 3.2% of the courses taught in the country. The number of students enrolled totalled 120,999, of which 62,578 completed the course (5.9% and 4.0% of the Brazilians respectively).

The participation of state educational institutions is larger regarding the offer for technical courses. The School Census of Technical Courses (Brazil. Ministry of Education, 2003) showed that this percentage equals 19.8%. The number of students in state schools corresponded to 27.5% of the total of 600,000 enrolled in the country.

As to the courses for training technologists, according to the Higher Education Census (Brazil. Ministry of Education, 2002), enrolment totalled 14,170 corresponding to 17.4% of the total number of students in such courses in the country. Among these students 2,394 graduated (18.9% of the total).

4.3 Municipal Networks

According to the Vocational Education Census (Brazil. Ministry of Education, 1999), of the 3,948 institutions offering vocational education in Brazil only 342 were municipal, representing 8.7% of the total. Among these municipal institutions 199 (58.2%) offered initial and continuing training courses (formerly basic), which means that the municipal networks totalled 9.8% of all the Brazilian institutions offering this type of course. However, this proportion was less significant if examined from other angles: only 3.4% of the courses offered (930 in 27,555), 3.9%

of the total enrolment (79,790 in 2,045,234) and 3.6% of the graduates (56,495 in 1,567,888).

According to the School Census of Technical Courses (Brazil. Ministry of Education, 2003), the participation of the municipalities in the provision of technical courses in relation to the other networks is smaller than that concerning the offer of initial and continuing training courses. Only 4.1% of the educational institutions that offer technical courses in Brazil were municipal. In terms of the number of students, this participation represented only 3.3% of the 600,000 students enrolled in such courses in the whole country.

Even smaller, however, was the participation of this network in the supply of higher education courses in technology. According to the Higher Education Census (Brazil. Ministry of Education, 2002), only eleven courses were available at municipal institutions—1.7% of the Brazilian offer. The enrolment reached 1,296, corresponding to 1.6% of the total and the graduates numbered 130 (1%).

4.4 The Private Network

According to the Vocational Education Census (Brazil. Ministry of Education, 1999), this is the largest network of educational institutions offering vocational education in Brazil, consisting of 2,656 institutions and corresponding to 67.3% of the total.

The greater part of them (56.2% or 1,545) offered initial and continuing training courses (formerly basic). This group represented 76.0% of the educational institutions offering these courses in Brazil. In 1999 the number of courses totalled 24,189, 87.8% of the offer available to the Brazilian population. Consequently, private institutions numbered 1,771,479 students enrolled, corresponding to 86.6% of the enrolments in courses of this type and the number of graduates totalled 1,389,058.

The participation of the private network in the provision of technical courses is also very significant. According to the 2003 School Census of Technical Courses (Brazil. Ministry of Education, 2003), 71.1% of the Brazilian institutions offering this type of education were private, accounting for 55.1% of the 600,000 students enrolled in such courses.

The private network also leads the offer of higher education courses in technology. Data from the Higher Education Census (Brazil. Ministry of Education, 2002) indicate that the number of students enrolled totalled 48,987 (60.2% in relation to the country as a whole), among which 8,921 reached completion.

4.5 The S System

The SENAI network (Serviço Nacional de Aprendizagem Industrial) now comprises 765 operational units (SENAI, 2004). There are 230 vocational education centres,

38 technology centres, 369 mobile units and 128 training centres/agencies. In 2003, SENAI received 1,918,363 enrolments, 69% of which were in vocational improvement courses (specialization and vocational initiation); 36.6% in initial and continuing training (formerly basic); 3% in industrial apprenticeship; 2.4% in technical courses; and 0.3% in higher education courses in technology. The SENAI courses that grew most in relation to previous years were apprenticeship courses (34%) and the higher education technology courses (44%) (www.senai.dn.br).

SENAC (Servicio Nacional de Aprendizaje Comercial) has a national network of 474 institutions, 59 of them mobile, and it received 1,783,294 enrolments in 2003 (SENAC, 2004) (www.senac.br).

In order to ensure the evolution of micro and small enterprises, the SEBRAE (Serviço Brasileiro de Apoio ao Empreendedor e Pequeno Empresário) assigned priority to educational actions that are developed by the Education and Development Section of the Entrepreneurial Culture Unit (UEDCE). These courses are directed towards the development of competence in business management in a continuing education perspective and use diversified educational techniques and different media, including distance education. Other than courses, SEBRAE develops educational projects aiming at the dissemination of an entrepreneurial culture (www.sebrae.com.br).

SENAR (Servicio Nacional de Aprendizagem Rural) develops vocational training in rural areas by means of non-formal approaches in occupational areas such as agriculture, forestry, aquaculture, mining, agro-industry and cattle–raising. The courses are directed exclusively to the rural producers who work in family businesses, to the rural workers and their families (www.senar.org.br).

5 Sources of Funding for TVET

Funding for public vocational education stems from several sources, since the Basic Directives for National Education Act do not provide for the financing of this form of education. It has no exclusive or specific sources of financing, nor does it have a fund of its own. These sources are therefore: public budgets (federal, states and municipalities); financing from international agencies such as the Inter-American Development Bank (IABD); from private enterprises, workers' unions, co-operatives, social movements and non-governmental organizations.

However, the most significant sum comes from a para-fiscal system, a monthly and compulsory social contribution levied by the Department of Social Welfare on the total of the wages paid by the firms from each sector to employees exclusively for the management of the institutions of the so-called S System.

These resources are subject to widely different systems and models of management due to the existence of parallel systems of training, as well as to the fragmentation of public policies resulting from the lack of a single financing policy and from the piecemeal application of resources in programmes and initiatives that in some cases duplicate each other.

In the absence of a public policy for vocational education, several emergency programmes and funds[6] sprang up in order to finance these activities. Among the funds specifically directed to that end are the following: the Expansion of Vocational Education Programme (PROEP)[7] of the Ministry of Education; the National Quali-fication Plan (PNQ)[8] of the Ministry of Labour and Employment; the Vocationaliza-tion of Nursing Workers Project (PROFAE);[9] and FINEP's PROEDUC—Education for Competitiveness Programme.[10]

Other programmes can also be mentioned, whose general scope is not pri-marily the financing of vocational training but which nevertheless reserve part of their resources to that end: the Tourism Project of the National Economic and Social Development Bank (BNDES); the Programme for the Support of Indus-trial Development (Prodesin); the Support to Economic Infrastructure Programme (Proinfra); the Encouragement to Research in the Area of Health Programme fi-nanced by the Sectoral Health Fund; and the Induction of Regional Development Programme of the Ministry of National Integration maintained by the Constitu-tional Fund for Financing the Northern Region (FNO) and the Bank of Amazonia (BASA).

Another important source of resources for vocational capacity-building is the FUST—the Universalization of Telecommunications Services Fund—managed by the Ministry of Communications that receives 1% of the gross revenue of all telecommunications companies with the sum of R$3 billion available for its main task, which is fighting illiteracy and the digital divide.

There is also FUNSET—Fundo Nacional para Segurança e Educação no Trânsito—having, among other sources of financing, 5% of the total of all traffic fines collected, which are used for the application of resources in the formulation and promotion of projects and programmes for training and improving the person-nel in charge of the engineering, education, computerization, policing, supervising, operation and administration of traffic.

With a view to the consolidation of a public policy of expansion, diversification and improvement in the quality of the supply of vocational, technical and technolog-ical education in the country, the federated units (the states and the Federal District) are monitored and oriented by the Ministry of Education. Each one of these units, based on updated analyses of social demand and managerial information, must de-fine its own plan, implement it and revise it periodically.

Due to the size and complexity of the work to be developed, it was deemed nec-essary to promote the institutional and technical strengthening of the state systems as well as the exchange of experiences, one of the reasons for the establishment of the Expansion of Vocational Education Programme (PROEP) of the Ministry of Education. Since 1998 the UNESCO Office in Brazil, by the means of technical co-operation agreements, has been monitoring and participating in these actions, offering advice to several of these federal units through their State Secretariats of Education and/or Science and Technology (UNESCO, 2003).

To that end, the federal units have discussed and adopted diversified legal models of state management in an attempt to solve financial, administrative and educational difficulties that have caused a series of breakdowns and lack of dynamism in the implementation of the guidelines prescribed and in the application of the covenants.

In most of the federal units, with the exception of the more successful ones, there is no solid tradition in the provision of this kind of education. Moreover, the states are not legally obliged to provide it either. For these reasons, the state administrations have no strong motivation to implement vocational education or to provide it with stable and continuous financing. The result is a weak dynamism and precarious administrative and educational structures in the state agencies responsible for the management of these policies and also in the schools created for this purpose. The functioning and maintenance of the vocational schools financed by PROEP must be ensured by the state administrations as a response to the investments in infrastructure, equipment, capacity-building, consultant activities and services made by this programme. Without budgetary provision and/or the creation of specific state funds for vocational education, the educational and administrative problems that affect these school centres cannot be avoided.

A new policy for the financing of vocational, technical and technological education is being discussed by the Federal Administration, which sees it as a fundamental condition for a qualitative leap forward: the establishment in the Brazilian states' legislation of constitutional or legal responsibility for the financing of this form of education, as well as the unification of the different resources financing it into a specific national fund.

Co-ordinated by the Ministry of Education and oriented towards a pluralistic management that is open to negotiation, this fund would seek to ensure the democratic participation of all the representative parties (the various governmental sectors, employers, workers and educators), as well as transparency and the ethical commitment, with a view to the expansion, the fairness and the control of the distribution of resources.

6 Conclusion

The government is faced with unemployment, with the fact that through lack of opportunities workers are being relegated to the informal economy, with finding work for a great number of vocational workers and with finding a solution to the vocational training of future generations. If it is truly concerned about this situation, it cannot reduce vocational education to a mere technical exercise that ignores the competences required by a labour market requiring higher levels of skill and, therefore, the conscious participation of all. Valuing vocational students is necessary for their self-esteem, their self-respect and their future responsibilities within the labour market. The vocational student is also a citizen who is concerned, as a social being, with the future of society. For this reason, vocational education, instead of being divorced from school education, should be integrated into it as a higher form of qualification.

Notes

1. Article 29 of the 1937 Constitution explicitly mentions a double network with parts reserved for different social groups.
2. This decree provided for three levels of vocational education: basic, in the form of separate courses; technical, at secondary education level; and technological, at the higher education level.
3. According to that census, the two richest Brazilian regions, the Southeast and the South, have 84.2% of all these institutions, 67.6% and 16.6% respectively. The State of São Paulo itself has 41.7% of the schools offering technical courses in Brazil. The Northeast represents only 7.9% of the total and the Center-west and the North, 3.8% and 2.1% respectively.
4. According to that census, 95.3% of these courses were located in urban environments, whereas only 4.7% were in rural areas. Health courses are the ones with the largest enrolments, 25.5%, representing 27.3% of the total number of courses. Next come industry and management with 18.6% and 14.8% of the total number of students respectively. The distribution of enrolment according to sex is relatively proportional: 51% of the students are male and 48.9% are female. Women outnumber men in specific vocational areas: health (76.9%), management, arts, communications, social development, leisure and tourism. On the other hand, men outnumber women in the areas of industry (87.6%) and agriculture and cattle-raising (76.3%). This latter area concentrates younger students (68.4% are under 19 years of age). The area of health receives older students (28% were over 30). In the total enrolment, 31.1% of the students belonged to the 20–24 age bracket.
5. According to that census, the courses are distributed in the following areas: 269 courses (42.3%) in sciences, mathematics and computer science; 163 courses (25.6%) in engineering, production and building; 110 courses (17.3%) in social sciences, business and law; 46 courses (7.2%) in services; 20 courses (3.1%) in humanities and arts; 19 courses (3.0%) in health and social welfare; and 9 courses (1.4%) in agriculture and veterinary medicine.
6. The FAT, Assistance to Workers Fund, represents an important reference for the financing of vocational education in Brazil for two basic reasons: (a) the sum of money it collects; and (b) the democratic management model it establishes—the tripartite (government, employers and workers) and equal representation in its Governing Council (CODEFAT).
7. Launched in November 1997 with resources of approximately US$500 million, half of which coming from a loan by IABD, and the rest from the Brazilian counterpart—Ministry of Education and FAT, of the Ministry of Labour budgets. It aims at providing the vocational education centres with infrastructure, equipment and qualified personnel, and also at adapting and updating curricula.
8. Financed by the Assistance to Workers Fund (FAT) with counterpart contributions required from each project. Between 1995 and 2001, it involved 15.3 million workers. The resources invested in this programme grew from R$28 million in 1995 to R$493 million in 2001. In 2002 these resources totalled R$153 million and in 2003 R$186 million.
9. Established in 2000, with a total cost of US$370 million, of which US$185 million come from IABD financing. In 1999 Brazil had 460,000 workers in the nursing area, however, 74% of this total were assistants qualified for clerical tasks only.
10. FINEP—Financiadora de Estudos e Projetos—is a public company linked to the Ministry of Science and Technology. Through the PROEDUC—Promotoria de Justiça de Defesa da Educação—it has financed nineteen projects benefiting over 21,000 student-workers through fundamental and secondary education programmes offered by the firms.

References

Brazil. Ministry of Education. 1999. *Censo da educação professional.* Brasília: Instituto Nacional de Estudos e Pesquisas Educacionais Anísio Teixeira.

Brazil. Ministry of Education. 2002. *Censo da educação superior*. Brasília: Instituto Nacional de Estudos e Pesquisas Educacionais Anísio Teixeira.

Brazil. Ministry of Education. 2003. *Censo escolar dos cursos técnicos, 2003*. Brasília: Instituto Nacional de Estudos e Pesquisas Educacionais Anísio Teixeira.

Posthuma, A.C. 1999. *Qual o rumo da formação profissional no Brasil? Análise do primeiro quadriênio do PLANFOR*. (Paper presented at the twenty-third Annual Meeting of the Associação Nacional de Pós-Graduação e Pesquisa em Ciências Sociais (ANPOCS), Caxambú, Brazil, 1999.)

SENAC. 2004. *Relatório geral do Senac, 2003*. Brasília: SENAC.

SENAI. 2004. *Relatório anual do Sistema SENAI, 2003*. Brasília: SENAI.

UNESCO. 2003. *Atuação da UNESCO na área de educação professional: relatório*. Brasília: UNESCO Office Brazil.

Chapter IV.10
China's Higher Technical and Vocational Education: Development and Reform

Jing Mi and Aihua Wu

1 The System of Chinese Vocational Education and Training

China is a developing country with a population of 1.3 billion and 9.6 million square kilometres of land. In the last twenty years, under its policy of opening up to the outside world, carrying out reforms and developing a socialist market economy, China has made great advances in economic and social development, and in people's standards of living. The economic development of China is constantly accelerating, and vocational education and training (VET) are developing rapidly too.

Chinese children follow nine years of compulsory education starting at the age of 6. Elementary school lasts six years and junior secondary school three years. Senior secondary school (general high school or secondary vocational school) usually lasts three more years. Higher vocational education can continue for two or three years and a bachelor's degree at university is obtained after four years.

VET is an important part of the Chinese education system, since it plays a significant role in the continuing growth of the Chinese economy and society. In China, VET is divided into three streams which take place post-elementary school, post-junior secondary school and post-senior secondary school. The government pays particular attention to the post-junior secondary school level by emphasizing the establishment and spread of the vocational system that covers both vocational formal education and vocational training, and establishing linkages between VET and other educational streams (see Fig. 1).

Formal vocational education leads to the award of academic credentials in junior secondary vocational schools, senior secondary vocational schools and higher vocational schools. Secondary vocational education is carried out in secondary technical schools, secondary vocational schools and skilled worker's schools. Higher vocational education is carried out by higher professional training schools, vocational and technical colleges, professional and general universities.

- Junior secondary vocational education enrols elementary school graduates for three years of study.
- Senior secondary vocational education enrols junior secondary school graduates for three years of study (some schools for four years).

R. Maclean, D. Wilson (eds.), *International Handbook of Education for the Changing World of Work*, DOI 10.1007/978-1-4020-5281-1_IV.10,
© Springer Science+Business Media B.V. 2009

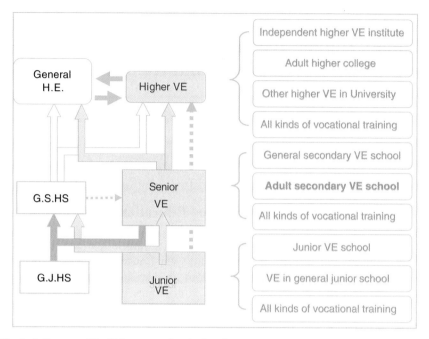

Fig. 1 A diagram of the Chinese vocational education system

- Higher vocational education mainly enrols senior secondary school graduates or those with an equivalent educational level for two or three years of study. It also enrols junior secondary school graduates for five years of study.

The Chinese Government has decided to make senior secondary vocational education the core of its policy to expand higher vocational education, and to leave the management of junior secondary vocational education to the responsibility of local governments.

2 Structure and Scale of Tertiary Vocational Education in China

To meet the need for the practical and skilled workers required by China's modernization process, efforts have been made to develop tertiary vocational education over the past twenty years. At present, there are six streams for tertiary vocational education:

1. Independent, system-reformed adult colleges;
2. The same course at universities;
3. Tertiary vocational education conducted by colleges
4. The same course at ordinary universities;
5. The experimental units of tertiary vocational education in five-year technical colleges; and

6. The new pattern of direct linkage between secondary and tertiary vocational education.

One can note that these courses are mainly at college level at present (two or three years). The aim of tertiary vocational education in China is to serve social and economic development, particularly by guaranteeing students entry to immediate employment after graduation. It is hoped to achieve a satisfactory combination of production, teaching and research.

The objective of tertiary vocational education in China is to train a highly-skilled workforce for jobs in the modern economy. Students graduating from high school should be trained to enter advanced practical employment with a wide-range of competency and aptitudes for occupations on the cutting edge of production, management and service. Tertiary vocational education is an important part of Chinese higher education policy.

There are three kinds of admission to higher vocational education in China:

- The national entrance examination for senior middle-school graduates (pursuing two or three years of college learning);
- The local entrance examination for secondary vocational school graduates (pursuing two or three years of college learning);
- The local entrance examination for junior middle-school graduates (pursuing five years of college learning).

There are five kinds of school systems: full-time, part-time, correspondence/self-study, e-learning and those conducted by regular higher education institutes.

From 1998 to the end of 2005, new student enrolment in vocational and technical colleges increased by more than four times, from 0.54 million to 2.68 million (Fig. 2); total student enrolment increased from 1.17 million to 7.13 million (Fig. 3). By the end of 2005, there were 1,091 independent vocational and technical colleges throughout the country, 921 of these were at tertiary level (Fig. 4). In addition, there were more than 600 regular universities conducting vocational and technical education (Fig. 5). It has been planned that there should be at least one vocational and technical college in each city (prefecture). The number of colleges, new student enrolments and total student enrolments for regular vocational and technical colleges

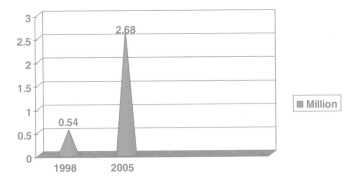

Fig. 2 New student enrolments in technical and vocational education in 1998 and 2005

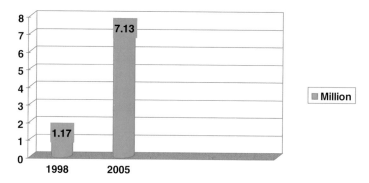

Fig. 3 Total student enrolment in technical and vocational education in 1998 and 2005

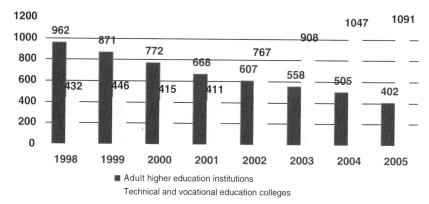

Fig. 4 Numbers of technical and vocational education colleges from 1998 to 2005

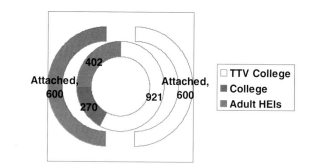

Fig. 5 Structures of technical
and vocational education
providers in 2005
Source:

throughout the country account for 60.8%, 43% and 53% of those of regular colleges and universities respectively. This represents nearly half of the higher education institutions in China.

3 Tertiary Vocational Education Policy in China

The Vocational Education Law of the People's Republic of China (China. Ministry of Education, 1996) was adopted in 1996. In recent years, the Chinese Government has paid much more attention to vocational education than before. In July 2002, the State Council National Conference on Vocational Education pointed out that China should organize a modern vocational education system and expressed some specific requirements. After the National Conference on Vocational Education held in June 2004, authorized by the State Council, the Ministry of Education and seven other ministries and committees printed and distributed the *Several opinions on further strengthening of vocational education* (Ministry of Education and Seven Other Ministries, 2004). After that, the State Council formally authorized the establishment of a Cross-sector Joint Conference on Vocational Education, responsibility for which will be undertaken by the Ministry of Education. These measures laid the foundations for the development of vocational education as a priority system. In November 2005, the State Council National Conference on Vocational Education was held once more. It emphasized that China should make developing vocational education a key factor in economic and social development and the foundation of its educational strategy. Thus, China will make further efforts to set up and improve 'the modern vocational education system conforming to the Chinese approach'. The present policies on higher vocational education that are being carried out by Chinese government are listed below.

3.1 To Strengthen Collectivization, Market-Orientation and Growth

The decision of the State Council to place strong emphasis on the development of VET means that China should: (a) positively promote the reform and innovation of this system; (b) promote the integration and re-structuring of existing public vocational schools; and (c) revise the structure of school management. Profitable co-operation should be encouraged between tertiary vocational institutions, as well as co-operation between colleges and enterprises. Private capital and foreign capital should be used positively to build groupings of vocational education institutions offering a range of training activities. Vocational education groupings should be encouraged to adopt the structure of non-profit organizations, such as the University Alliance, as well as integrating and re-structuring their educational resources in order to take advantage of each other's strengths and to become more efficient through the sharing of resources. Furthermore, groupings of vocational education institutions are encouraged to adopt the methods of a business enterprise, such as a franchise, and to plan the educational provision as a whole, unifying the standards for running schools and employing the latest management methods (State Council of China, 2005). Such groupings of tertiary vocational education institutions will encourage the promotion of higher levels of college/industry collaboration in the interests of resource sharing and synergy. For colleges and enterprises it is a 'win-win' situation. It is also beneficial for the establishment of educational contracts for training in tertiary vocational institutions, for facilitating the employment of graduates, for promoting co-operation between colleges and universities in eastern and western China and the development of both.

3.2 To Develop the Dual Qualification System

Other priorities that would create favourable conditions for employment are the search for an approach that combines national employment standards with professional teaching curricula, improves the training provided, innovates with new training methods, makes teaching correspond to the expectations of the workplace, and ensures the quality and diversity of human skills. This has to be accomplished without prolonging the period of schooling or increasing the teaching hours. At the same time, the supervisory and guidance services of the local education, labour and social security departments are called upon to implement 'dual qualifications' in local tertiary education institutes and ensure that this process is carried out smoothly. The Ministry of Labour and Social Security and the Ministry of Education will disseminate successful innovatory experiences from experimental projects, strengthen research into the classification of occupations and occupational standards, modify employment standards in keeping with developments in science and production techniques, and step-by-step introduce comprehensive vocational qualifications adapted to job-clusters.

3.3 To Strengthen the Combination Production/Teaching/Research

Over several years and on three separate occasions, the Ministry of Education has held a Conference for Exchanging Experience on the Combination Production/ Teaching/Research in tertiary vocational education. These meetings defined the guiding principles for the development of tertiary vocational education as follows: 'the aim of tertiary vocational education in China is to serve social and economic development. Its objective is the students' immediate employment after graduation, and its development will be carried out through the combination production/teaching/research.' Tertiary vocational institutions are expected to use their initiative to satisfy the demands of economic and social development. They are to train people to be highly-skilled in practical abilities and possessing professional ethics, who can meet the immediate demands of the production, construction, management and service industries. These people should also be reliable and functional.

3.4 To Develop Exemplary Tertiary Vocational Institutions

The objective of building exemplary tertiary vocational institutions is to benefit from the enthusiasm of local governments and vocational colleges in promoting policy directives. The plan is to select and build about 100 tertiary vocational institutions, each with distinctive characteristics, that should be well supported by society and correspond to the directions in which tertiary vocational education is expected to develop. They will be important centres providing human resources for local social and economic development and they will be the most important tertiary vocational institutions in China, also having an international impact. They should play a leading role in the building of Chinese tertiary vocational education systems and take the lead in introducing training models combining production/teaching/research. They are equally expected to take the lead in introducing teaching and educational reforms, educational resource sharing and international communications, so that tertiary vocational education in China can reap the benefit.

At the same time, the Ministry of Education will reinforce the preparation of an exemplary curriculum. Over recent years, the Ministry of Education has licensed 415 professions as ministry-level educational reform experimental sites, 62 professions as national projects of excellence and 75 curricula as being of national interest for tertiary vocational institutions.

3.5 To Develop Practical Training for Vocational Education

Economic and social developments in China have raised the urgent need for skilled personnel who have mastered advanced technologies. However, the practical conditions for vocational training in China are unable to satisfy the demand for high-quality skilled workers. It is for this reason that the country has brought together the financial and physical resources to build a series of practical training institutes to accelerate vocational education. The intention is to improve the quality of vocational education, making a greater contribution to economic and social development.

The objective of setting up this infrastructure is ultimately to have some 15,000 vocational institutions in the country (including secondary vocational schools) and to develop college/industry collaboration so as to foster employment. It is hoped that eventually some 200,000 professionals would be available to provide practical training for more than 20 million students. To give full scope to the available educational resources, the planning of local governments will be strengthened, and excellent material and resources made available. The central government will also provide help with the financial input. These national-level practical training institutes for vocational education will be distributed throughout different regions, and incorporate teaching, training, occupational skill tests and technology services under one roof. Building started in 2004 and is designed to be completed in five years. The guidelines for these practical training institutes are: the cost-benefit ratio, orientation, lifelong education and active development.

3.6 To Improve Teaching Staff in Tertiary Vocational Institutions

Each tertiary vocational institution should adopt effective measures to promote timely in-service teacher training so as to improve practical abilities. At the same time, the tertiary vocational institutions should recruit professionals or technicians with wide practical experience in a profession, enterprise or society as part-time teachers (this includes retired people). Local education departments should set up a system for the evaluation and recruitment system of 'dual-mode teachers' in accordance with the needs of tertiary vocational education. They should be able to confer academic titles and recruit teachers, and provide policy support for building teams of 'dual-mode teachers'.

The Ministry of Education has established six teacher-training institutes for tertiary vocational education in the country. The mission of these teacher-training institutes is principally: (a) to provide training that will improve the theoretical level, practical ability and professional skills of tertiary vocational education teachers; (b) to conduct training in modern educational technology; and (c) to award a second bachelor degree and provide graduate education.

4 The Long-range Development Objectives of Tertiary Vocational Education

Now that China is well on the road to industrialization, it may soon be the largest manufacturing country in the world. Its economy is undergoing thorough modernization, and new industries and skills are being developed all the time. It can be seen from the development of higher education in China that the country has passed through the stage of universalizing higher education. Higher education is now changing from society-based, market-based development towards balanced development, from caring about the number of skills to achieving a balance between the supply of higher education graduates and the demands of the labour market. This also means a balance between training a highly skilled workforce and meeting the demands of the majority of young people for access to higher education, as well as the balance between academic education and vocational training.

Up to the year 2020, there will be a major expansion in the scale of TVET, with enrolment eventually accounting for about half of the places in higher education. The TVET system will be optimized through diversification and alignment with the lifelong learning system. Thousands of skills will be inculcated so as to support the industrialization and the transformation of economic growth in China. Further efforts will be made to build an affluent society and to raise quality in the interests of the whole population of China.

References

China. Ministry of Education. 1996. *Vocational Education Law of the People's Republic of China, 1996.* Beijing. (Adopted at the nineteenth Meeting of the Standing Committee of the eighth National People's Congress on 15 May 1996.)

Ministry of Education and Seven Other Ministries. 2004. Several opinions on further strengthening
    vocational education. *Educational newsletter of China*, no. 1, 14 September.
State Council of China. 2005. The decision of State Council on vigorously promoting the develop-
    ment of VET. *People's daily*, 10 November.

Chapter IV.11
The Adoption and Adaptation of the Work-Team Concept in Urban Thai Workplaces

Chitrlada Burapharat

1 Introduction

An organization always seeks the best possible mechanism to implement changes and to improve organizational performance. In this era, where knowledge and learning are the focus of attention, many organizations have begun to realize that their competitive edge depends very much on the knowledge and capacities of their staff. Through their abilities to learn, to apply their knowledge and their work experience, employees possess knowledge that can become organizational wisdom—as well as intellectual property.

Nowadays, the trend towards learning organizations and knowledge-management becomes a very important strategy in business competition. Many Thai enterprises in various professions, such as computers, hospitals, banks, etc., are attempting to turn theory into practice by adopting such strategies in their management.

The usual practice is for organizations to aim at creating web-based communication to help generate learning and information—a minor step in creating a learning organization. The question is how an organization in Thailand can create a working environment to stimulate and sustain sharing and learning abilities. The purpose is to achieve product or management innovation. Many companies are seeking ways in which they can improve their organizational operations. To create such an environment, Thai enterprises require teamwork from every employee. Teamwork is the focus. For instance, it is possible for adults to learn through other means than classroom-based lectures—it was once thought that this was the only way that learning can be delivered. Different strategies, such as informal learning, participation and brain-storming, are now incorporated into the design of group-dynamic training programmes. Individuals also have an opportunity to participate in workshops, to contribute and to share their knowledge in an environment of peer support and egalitarianism (Burapharat, 2003).

R. Maclean, D. Wilson (eds.), *International Handbook of Education for the Changing World of Work*, DOI 10.1007/978-1-4020-5281-1_IV.11,
© Springer Science+Business Media B.V. 2009

2 Learning is Required at All Levels

Generally, the main goal of education and learning is to reduce the educational gaps among people and to reinforce democracy by stimulating the individual's participation in the larger society. Wilson (2003) and Hawley and Paek (2005) suggest that a learning workplace needs knowledge workers and this, in turn, demands the reform of secondary and post-secondary education, especially technical and vocational education and training (TVET). The most recent report from the Asia-Pacific Economic Co-operation (APEC) shows that basic education in Asian countries did not usually prepare employees with entry-level skills, while the labour market demanded technically skilled workers (Hawley and Paek, 2005). This implies that a person recruited into a company still has knowledge and skills gaps—either managerial or technical—compared to the real needs of the organization. Unfortunately, to be able to compete in the global market place, an enterprise cannot wait for changes to take place in governmental policies on secondary and post-secondary education, but must ensure that the employee acquires technical and basic skills using various forms of training, either formal or informal.

The promotion of learning in an organization highlights the theory of adult education—one of the most talked about theories in the world of business management today. Adult education concepts have long been one of the key areas for human resources development (HRD) in Western management studies. In Asia, especially in Thailand, applying this concept in the area of management has been very slow. It has been at Chulalongkorn University (CU), Srinakharintarawirot University (SWU) and Chiang Mai University (CMU) where most adult education theories have been developed, mainly for community development. Perhaps, it is time to become more familiar with the concepts of adult education in order to understand more about value differences between cultures.

Adults require and obtain knowledge through different learning styles, such as experiential learning, self-directed learning, etc. While promoting learning, an organization has to keep in mind these differences, because it is the channel for an individual to take in information, as well as providing it. Knowles' model of adult learning (1973) advocates that education must be learner-centred and constructed to accommodate the diverse needs and interests of learners. Thus, it is the job of managers and others involved to find ways of tapping into this hidden intellectual capital, to find the means to sustain lifelong learning and to create a positive environment for knowledge-sharing. The wisdom of an organization could be hidden anywhere. Sometimes, it is the quiet person, usually good at observing, who can suggest creative answers to problems. Thus, the promotion of learning and sharing at all levels may create learning opportunities in order to cultivate wisdom drawn from people's knowledge and experience.

3 Learning as a Change Strategy

Adult educators believe that education and learning are the means to bring about change because they raise awareness of the self, which empowers individuals to make change (Freire, 1969). Individual learning brings about change because people become aware of what needs to be changed as a result of the education and information they have received. Knowles (1973) stated that most of the time adult learners viewed themselves as non-learners, because they failed to consider themselves as possessing learning potential. On the contrary, an adult will achieve a higher level of intellectual performance because of the experience of life. This can be renewed, if not increased, and thus heighten his/her ability to learn and enquire. Mezirow's (1978) theory of transformative learning stated that 'individuals change their frame of reference by critically reflecting on their assumptions and beliefs. Based on this process of critical reflection, the adult learners then consciously change their behaviours to accommodate their newly defined world.' That is how change begins.

It is fair to say that, nowadays, everyone has the opportunity to access different forms of education and information, either e-learning, web-based learning or group-based learning. In reality, employees at many levels in an organization may have been neglected or may have refused to share information, especially those who are considered as incompetent and different. For example, an individual who cannot comply with performance appraisal criteria may be viewed as incapable.

The concepts of learning and development have also been misunderstood and misinterpreted. The printed form used in performance evaluation is often copied directly from foreign sources. In many cases, it results in bias in the design and implementation of the performance appraisal process. Such bias may cause rifts in labour management and unfairness in justifying an employee's self-development opportunities. On the other hand, managers—in many cases the bosses—often forget about bureaucratic procedures when evaluating their favourite group. In such situations, standard rules of appraisal can be waived. Many people who are not complying with office politics may be excluded from new information and training or may not be invited to participate in brainstorming sessions. Many employees are 'marginalized' in this way. It is time to adopt this word in organizational studies, since this is what it means when people are ignored in a social organization.

To sustain change, learning and sharing are the keys. 'In the complex enterprises of the new millennium, learning has moved from the periphery—from something which prepared people for employment—to the lifeblood which sustains them' (Boud & Garrick, 1997, p. 1). This, in turn, transforms the nature of work in which the employees are engaged to create new working practices and ways of production. The culture of learning is necessary to overcome development barriers. Thus, the construction of an environment supporting various learning styles and various forms of inquiry is very crucial to support lifelong learning in an organization. A team environment can create a culture of knowledge-sharing and synergy.

4 The Team as an Environment for Learning and Knowledge-Sharing

Other than attempting to accomplish business goals and re-skilling their employees, today's modern enterprises may also have higher responsibilities—to foster the development of an individual as a whole person. Regardless of their educational background, employees or adult learners come to work from diverse backgrounds, with different levels of education and literacy, as well as of work and worldly experience (Knowles, 1973). They also come with many strengths embedded in their language, upbringing and culture. It is the manager's job to find ways to tap into their skills and tacit knowledge and to make the most of their learning abilities. One of the channels is through collective means.

Learning alone, however, cannot stimulate change. It has to happen together with sharing to create dynamics of information flow for further knowledge creation. Modern management gives importance to working together (Senge, 1994; Wenger, 2002) as the grounds on which to create such opportunities. That immediately gives importance to the team setting. For example, group participation can enhance the attitudes of employees and their performance (Green, 1998). Participation is a way of encouraging worker involvement in decision-making, which has long been a topic of interest to theorists concerned with enhancing the attitudes of employees and their performance in the workplace. Participation has been associated with motivation and leadership. There are many successful workplaces that actively involve members in participation and decision-making processes throughout the organization.

In a regular hierarchical organization, a team helps build bridges between an individual and organizational performance (Fig. 1). When we look at the transformation taking place in the nature of work, it is noticeable that the trend is increasingly in favour of creating teams. A team is seen as a crucial means to drive changes in larger organizations. Synergy can be achieved through teams when the members join together to create work or accomplished through results that individuals could not have carried out by themselves alone. To create human relationships and participation opportunities, an organization has to improvise because positive relationships are the mechanism for bringing about knowledge-sharing and learning environments.

A team is not merely a group of people who are working together to achieve the group's goals and objectives or produce high-quality work, but the ideal place to start the stimulation of learning for both individuals and organizations (Burapharat, 2003). Working as a team requires many skills since teams are not just the act of bringing individuals together and working on a certain project or task. Team skill is undeniably one of the crucial basic skills needed. It means a healthy

Fig. 1 The team as a bridge

relationship and positive environment in which people can have confidence in each other and support each other. A team today also has the responsibility of creating a culture of knowledge-sharing and learning to build healthy community-of-practice networks. Not only is a trusting environment created and supported, but at the same time positive ground is formed for people to participate.

Working together has always been part of human nature. The question often asked is 'how can one create a better team?'. This is realised in creating and managing the relationship, encouraging cohesive co-operation and lessening communication barriers. To construct a team environment with positive energy, the building of good relationships is of the essence. Developed from group therapy theory, 'group dynamics' offers opportunities to focus on team members' relationships. This adoption and adaptation of the concept includes small-group theory and team learning. They focus on the ability to hold dialogue and skilful discussion that can help enhance the learning and articulation capabilities of an individual. Due to different abilities to express themselves, some individuals in a team need support and encouragement from their colleagues to express their opinions.

5 Dialogue within a Team is Crucial

A team needs an environment that stimulates the learning atmosphere. This has to be generated by the team members—only they can do it. The climate within a team should be such that individuals can express themselves freely and feel in a dynamic relationship with the other members of the group. The greatest emphasis in building a positive environment for learning within teams should be placed on achieving the right atmosphere through communication. Effective communication 'is a prerequisite for every aspect of group functioning' (Johnson & Johnson, 1997, p. 140). Alan Webber adds: 'conversation is the means by which people share and often create what they know' (cited in Isaacs, 1993, p. 1).

Concerning the transfer of knowledge, Senge (1994) wrote that two primary media with which teams build their learning capabilities are 'dialogue' and 'skilful discussion'.

Reflecting the essence of Buddhism, many contemporary thinkers, such as Senge (1994) and Bohm (1996) amongst others, see dialogue as a tool to encourage people to pay more attention to others' ideas that might normally be ignored, especially contradictory ideas. This is because people are usually preoccupied with defending their own ideas—a lack of awareness that encourages confusion and problems. In Metcalf's opinion, our perception of the world comes from an accumulated pool of knowledge which gives us a sense of meaning and individuality passed from one person to another. By creating awareness, an individual can gather relevant information and organize it into a meaningful understanding through such processes as dialogue (Metcalf, 1999). By being more conscious of our own thoughts, we can learn from different opinions to create a setting for a collective learning environment. Dialogue as collective learning and inquiry is defined as: 'A process for transforming the quality of conversation and the thinking that lies beneath it. Dialogue opens a new possibility for shared thinking or exchange thinking' (Isaacs, 1993, p. 2)

Dialogue plays a big part in creating positive relationships and interactions that are at the heart of effective group and team development. Isaacs (1993, p. 3) points out that dialogue requires creating a series of increasingly conscious environments. These environments can develop as a group of people become aware of the requirements and discipline needed to create them. Dialogue is seen as a means to explore the underlying irrationality of thought and action that causes conflict between team members.

Dialogue has been claimed to be the primary aspect that a team should concentrate on improving, as the value of the individual will be recognized through the dialogue process. An environment can be created that is open and encourages individuals to offer opinions and take risks in putting forward ideas and to learn from each other through trust, respect and sharing goals.

When communicating, people will normally defend their own ideas and assumptions against people who have different ideas and point of views (Bohm, 1996). Each individual has different opinions and assumptions—assumptions regarding basic ideas such as the meaning of life, self-interests, the national interest, religious interest, or whatever is deemed important. These assumptions are defended when they are challenged (Bohm, 1996, pp. 2–3), a behaviour that can create conflict between individuals in teams. According to Bohm (1996) and Isaacs (1993), people may over-react when defending their assumptions and opinions in the face of another team member's opinion—even when they know that they are not right. People generally choose to defend their own points of view and do not judge the merit of other's opinions. Such behaviour causes them to lose their grip of certainty about all views, including their own (Isaacs, 1993, p. 3). For example, if an individual hears somebody else who has an assumption that seems outrageous to them, the natural response might be to get angry or to react in some other way. This reaction was triggered only because the other person came up with an opposing opinion (Bohm, 1996, pp. 12–13). This may be due to the fact that 'words can be interpreted in many different ways. And, of course, this is the basis for many misunderstandings' (Johnson & Johnson, 1997, p. 52).

Dialogue can be used to get at the root of different assumptions and provide a means for team members to deal with them openly. 'Dialogue actually involves a willingness not only to suspend defensive exchange, but also to probe into the reasons for it. In this sense, dialogue is a strategy to resolve the problems that arise from the subtle and pervasive fragmentation of thought' (Isaacs, 1993, p. 2). It is suggested that individuals should suspend their assumptions and concentrate on thinking together. What the team members need is to let 'authenticity' flow freely in the belief that, in order for teams to discover insight, free communication should be encouraged in the group. 'Authenticity' is defined as the ability to speak openly without concealing disagreement.

Dialogue is more than just the way people talk, communicate and exchange ideas and information among team members. Isaacs (1993), Bohm (1996) and Senge (1994) emphasize 'dialogue' as an appropriate means of authentic communication among members of a group. By doing so, individuals can learn together, can interact with each other and discover how the team functions. This can accelerate the learning process and lead to the achievement of collective understanding (Senge, 1994). Most informal learning theory stresses the need for an 'authentic' setting to produce genuine communication, which plays a big part in creating the 'basis for rich learning experiences that have the potential to be robust and highly transferable' (Garrick, 1999, p. 19). The main element in team learning thus encompasses communication strategies as being 'authentic' among the team members.

The concept of dialogue can be applied effectively in the workplace, especially in teams. Bohm (1996, p. 14) concludes that people should attempt to suspend their own opinions and to look at the opinions of others: listen to everybody's opinions and try to see what they all mean. If different individuals can understand the scope of the varying opinions, then they are sharing a common content, even if they do not entirely agree. In reality, the opportunities for authentic dialogue mentioned by Bohm (1996), when applied in real situations, could be very difficult because of organizational hierarchy, bureaucracy, personal preferences, etc. At the conversational level, socialization, according to Takeuchi and Nonaka (2004), means sharing and acquiring tacit knowledge through direct experience from individual to individual. In the Thai setting, there are some socialization elements that can enhance the sharing atmosphere.

6 The Thai Setting

Thai educational and vocational institutions produce graduates with skills that are inadequate for the needs of business. The 'twenty-first century requires the education and training of knowledge workers—those who are able to use logical-abstract thinking to diagnose problems, research and apply knowledge, propose solutions, and design and implement those solutions, often as a team members' (Wilson, 2003). It would be wise to find ways in which to support the collectivistic nature of Thai society using team techniques. Many collective mechanisms are already in place, for example, the roles of peer support in the form of the informal third person and pseudo-sibling relationships (Burapharat, 2001). Complementing Thai cultural behaviour will help people feel more able to express themselves. Many Thais admit that they cannot discuss things openly or speak directly to others, particularly Westerners. They also feel uncomfortable communicating in public or with certain people, such as those with a higher level of education than themselves or with a dominating character. The focus then should be on the patterns of dialogue typical of the Thai nature.

The nature of Thai participation is obviously different from participation in other cultures. Hofstede (1994) observed that Thais have a collectivistic nature. He defined collectivism as 'standing for a society in which people from birth onwards are integrated into strong, cohesive in-groups, which throughout people's lifetimes continue to protect them in exchange for unquestioning loyalty' (p. 225). Triandis, McCusker and Hui (1990) described collectivism as: 'A social pattern consisting of closely linked individuals who see themselves as part of one or more collective (family, co-workers, tribe, nation); are primarily motivated by the norms of, and duties imposed by those collectives; are willing to give priority to the goals of these collectives over their own personal goals; and emphasize their connectedness to members of these collectives' (p. 2). Many writers have described the collective characteristics and behaviour of people from East Asia as group or socially oriented, and as promoting the goals of others, with the emphasis on public roles and relations (Hofstede, 1994; Triandis et al., 1990). Generally, collectivism refers to emotional dependence on family, kinship, structure, organization and, finally, on the social system. A highly collectivist culture emphasizes social interdependence, connectedness and mutual deference or compromise as dominant values.

In the workplace, the collective nature also applies. Burapharat (2003) concludes that, after examining many cultural and behavioural mechanisms, urban settings both support and obstruct collective procedures. Upon further investigation of Thai relationships in urban enterprises, it was found that the nature of collectivism and value functioned quite differently from Western individualistic behaviour. Knowledge exchange, Thai style, needs both supportive personal relationships and a supportive environment to create an informal atmosphere in which people feel comfortable enough to share their knowledge and experiences. In order to develop a learning atmosphere in a team, Thais need constructed patterns of mutual interdependency and emotional dependence.

The special characteristic of kinship also plays a part. Burapharat (2001) found that one of the most interesting themes emanating from research is the brotherhood/sisterhood or pseudo-sibling relationship, which acts as the basic relationship among team members. This unique behaviour within the workplace demonstrated that an intimate and interdependent relationship affects the level of authenticity towards one another. By calling each other 'big brother/sister' (*Pii*) and 'little brother/sister' (*Nong*), employees feel very comfortable in assuming one of these two roles and feel part of an intimate, collective group.

The words *Pii* and *Nong* are genderless language, and are usually attached to the pet name or nickname of the person, such as *Pii Paul* or *Nong Ann* rather than simply using the first name. Most Thai people have both a first name and a nickname or pet name. Referring to each other in such a manner creates a warm and friendly atmosphere with an immediate sense of being a family member. This is something that takes place immediately when people start talking. Beyond smiling, it works as an icebreaker strategy when people first meet. Both of these Thai terms, usually determined by ages and job ranks, are used at all levels in organizations. If somebody did not understand the relationship, perhaps mistakenly referring to an older person as *Nong* for instance, no harm is done. There can be some adjustment or it can be left like that. For example, a staff member may mistakenly call a younger person *Pii*, but does not change to *Nong* after learning that person's age. In many cases, the word *Pii* is used to show respect for a person who has greater experience and knowledge.

The brotherhood/sisterhood relationship creates an atmosphere allowing people to be open to each other and communicate the information in their mind. They can communicate when offered the opportunity and when they are close enough to one another. As one staff member mentioned, she felt free to communicate her mind within her department where she was familiar with her colleagues more than in other groups of which she did not form a regular part. The sense of authenticity depends on the level of closeness. Team members can trust one another; here is a secure place to be truthful where ideas are not dismissed. This relationship eases the tension related to losing face and reduces the problem of non-assertiveness.

Such a relationship creates a warm and relaxed atmosphere for people to feel at ease with each other. For dialogue to take place, team members have to be open to the others' opinions and hold back their assumptions, to listen and try to understand while being able to voice their own opinions. Within the brotherhood/sisterhood relationship, a sense of a family is generated in which members can overlook statements that seem to create conflict by looking on the other as their own siblings. Another noticeable aspect of the brotherhood/sisterhood relationship is that when the sibling relationship functions the organizational hierarchy recedes into the background. Managers and staff feel on equal terms and comfortable in assuming their social identity, rather than respecting hierarchical roles. While employing the sibling relationship, team members demonstrate some sensitivity in dealing with the other team members. Caring action is also part of building an authentic and intimate relationship. In a manager's case, the evidence shows that even outside the office, his brother role continued, such as showing an interest in the welfare of his staff-members' families.

In conclusion, the fundamental nature of being a Thai supports working together and is worth taking advantage of to create a positive team environment at work. In practice management needs to be carefully designed to complement the best of the team members' nature, while being aware of many national cultural traits that can obstruct the transfer of information. In the Thai setting, the pseudo-sibling relationship plays a vital part in building an authentic atmosphere. By so doing, learning through sharing and exchanging knowledge and information can be encouraged. Although the relationships are rather informal, they seem to encourage authentic dialogue among those involved. The particular Thai brotherhood/sisterhood inter-relationships are a form of friendship with multiple layers of closeness and trust. Within a team, this enables the team members to communicate with each other through an authentic atmosphere. They feel comfortable to talk to each other. This relationship also concerns the barrier in an organizational hierarchy between the boss and employees, as well as among the employees themselves. In building an authentic setting to enhance learning, the academic literature has rather focused on building dialogue between individuals rather than the characteristics of the interrelationships between them. The prevailing theories need to expand their boundaries to acquire more information about other elements involved in building an authentic atmosphere and dialogue.

7 Designing a Team-Learning Workshop

Most teams have a fundamental problem with encouraging good co-operation among their members. Frequently, they experience bad communication, conflict, no pleasure in working together and prefer working alone, while communication skills have been neglected. Carrying out a short-term group dynamics workshop provides fundamental understanding about the importance of learning in an organization through the use of groups and teams, as well as having adult education applications.

Most workshop and training sessions adopted from Western institutions have often been copied in their totality—imposed on a different cultural environment without modification. Such knowledge transfer has taken the form of teaching that did not help individual development because it merely communicated content. The adoption of Western concepts in different cultural environments is challenging due to the lack of correspondence to the social etiquette embedded in diverse behavioural protocols. For example, research findings show how Thai team members should be approached respecting their cultural style. Team members have built a layer of brotherhood/sisterhood relationships to enhance dialogue during their collective behaviour. They need an authentic atmosphere to exchange information and learn from one another. Western literature on dialogue does not explicitly discuss building informal or other kinds of relationships as a means to pursue an authentic atmosphere. However, the Thai sibling style stresses the importance of building informal relationships as the gateway to having trust in each other. Many management change programmes applied in Thai settings concentrate on working and operational processes, rather than preparing human resources for change. One of the reasons might be that a basic understanding about the theory and practice of adult education has been overlooked.

Individual adult employees need workshops that help stimulate the use of their knowledge and experiences. They need common ground for getting to know each other and a positive environment for discussion. An intervention and change programme has to be designed, researched, planned and evaluated to complement Thai collectivistic characteristics. This workshop attempts to create an informal atmosphere with some humour and to encourage dynamic communication, while adding new skills such as presentation, teamwork, interpersonal relations, leadership, problem-solving, communication, creativity and innovation. However, what skills are to be emphasized depends on the needs of the group. Facilitation skill is also stressed in order to demonstrate different means of communication and knowledge-sharing. Activities are designed for participants to experience different means of learning and to reinforce their relationships with different people with whom they are not familiar.

8 Case Studies

Many teams expressed their initial frustration over the problems of working together. Even though the groups were composed differently, similar problems were repeated: personal conflicts, lack of communication, divisions within the group and low cohesiveness. This was an indication that there was a need to improve relationships among the team members.

To accommodate and facilitate interrelationships among individuals, group dynamic workshops were conducted with several different teams in a financial enterprise. The contents and activities were designed to match the special requirements of each group with different teamwork problems. The main purposes of these group-dynamic workshops were to expand participants' knowledge about the learning organization and the roles of individuals and groups/teams in it. Another purpose was to create an opportunity for every member to get to know their colleagues so as to enhance cohesion. Frequently, there was limited communication between individuals whose work was not related, so many of them never talked or associated with one another at work.

The workshops tried to facilitate communication by using different activities, such as group activities, games and brainstorming. These activities were designed to arrange different group combinations in order to mix individuals together as much as possible. The reasons for this strategy were to make group members work together with people with whom they were not familiar. Individuals learned to know each other better. With the help of ice-breaking and brainstorming sessions, each participant had a chance to talk to other team members he/she had never talked with before, and to share their knowledge. Valuing other people's ideas was also a purpose of the workshop, since the workshop talked about the creation of a positive team environment—but did not create a sibling-like environment.

In one case, a team faced many problems affecting their whole working relationship. Ninety-four members of this department had been transferred from other departments because they were viewed as problematic. Being treated in this manner, these individuals were full of anger and resentment; had low motivation; low morale; there was no communication; they were unhappy; had no pleasure in working; and lacked the will to work with one another. They displayed aggressiveness and procrastination. They felt valueless and failures with no career future, etc. The average age of the whole group was over 45. As a result, many of them kept to themselves and never talked to anybody at work—no smiles, no laughter and no fun. Their educational backgrounds ranged from Grade 4 to bachelor's degree. Antagonism and grievances were omnipresent.

The implementation of the one-day workshop was designed to provide different perspectives towards learning and knowledge-sharing, including team-building. The workshop was also designed to include many strategies to support different learning environments in a flexible timeframe, such as learning through humour, informal learning, learning by doing and learning from experience. It was focused on increasing the participants' motivation and basic soft skills: especially articulation; and communication abilities such as self-expression, presentation, facilitation, public speaking, brainstorming, listening and speaking in combination with applause, compliments and rewards for those who participated in brainstorming sessions. In the brainstorming session, learners' experiences were written on flipcharts. Participants learned the theory and practice of facilitation skills. These ninety-four people were divided into smaller groups of eight or nine—recommended numbers. The assigned facilitators had to write down the knowledge from the rest of the group on the flipcharts, with the idea of bringing out the best of each participant. Individuals have a psychological need for their ideas to be acknowledged and respected. Recording their ideas on the flipchart says that these ideas have been recognized. People had to patiently listen to those who had difficulties in reading and expressing themselves. They all felt more relaxed and involved in such an environment. Individuals were also more open to their colleagues' opinions. Other soft skills, such as presentation skills, were another way to stimulate their self-motivation. The presenter becomes the 'star' and, for a moment, he/she feels proud. Through the workshop, individuals learned more about each other. For example, one group found out that one of their colleagues had a problem with near-sightedness and was so very shy about it that they always hid behind a newspaper and communicated to no one. The group adopted a more understanding attitude, as well as finding a solution to help this person. This fact was communicated to the departmental manager who changed his negative perspective about this individual. It also came to light during the training session that many of the team members were illiterate.

Feedback after the workshop and follow-up upon return to the work settings seemed to indicate some improvements in their relationships. When they returned to their daily work, the participants became less aggressive, opened up to each other's opinion, showed more co-operation and were open to each other's requirements. Individuals were more relaxed around each other and most groups reported that their relationships were getting better. There was more communication, more smiling, motivation and enthusiasm to work with each other. After their adjustment to their new environment, they became more collaborative in working together and showed more confidence in work. They also created a community of practice to learn from each other, such as teaching each other new computer or report-writing skills. On top of these soft skills, this group was very lucky to have a departmental manager who supported their development by adding a variety of informal and formal training sessions. Formal training sessions were for core competencies such as negotiation skills, calculation, legal knowledge, etc. Many teaching and learning programmes arose from learning together. For example, employees who were experts in the Excel programme were asked to teach and to tutor peers who had no such skills. Individuals who knew more about accounting and mathematics were asked to help those who were weak in these skills. Peers were asked to assist each other in writing reports and proposals. Making use of individual expertise, even if that expertise is seen by others as insignificant, is very important to those who need basic knowledge and computer skills. Later on, this department, apparently composed of people stigmatized as 'useless', was able to develop and was rewarded for making a high profit for the enterprise.

The objective to increase soft-skills had been met—socialization skills like speaking and listening to compliment and stimulate Thai collective nature. About 90% of the participants agreed on the usefulness of the programmes in terms of increased positive relationships. Individuals had better relationships and gained positive feelings from sharing learning. From the personal to the team level, positive

relationship-building was very important to cement ties between individuals to foster the transfer and creation of knowledge. Individuals learned to be interdependent
and to share knowledge with the rest of the team. Through hands-on experience,
they received knowledge about facilitation skills. Moreover, the surprising finding
about workplace illiteracy indicated a lack of very fundamental skills for work. This
unexpected finding caused concern about the quality of the formal education system.
Does it produce a workforce with skills to match current requirements and does it
make employees keen to adjust themselves to the real work environment?

9 Conclusion

The case study showed that Western theory, such as group dynamics based upon a
background of adult education theory, can be applied to the Thai environment. The
theories accommodate different learning requirements and encourage self-directed
learning, rather than forcing people to learn and change. Different aspects of the
theory complement the Thai collectivistic nature, perhaps because they were close
to Buddhist philosophy, the key determining factor in Thai cultural development
(Blanchard, 1958; Klausner, 1987; Mole, 1973). Programmes and activities designed to complement the collectivistic nature and self-expression in the Thai setting
need to include group-dynamic concepts, together with adult education and team
concepts. The workshop had to allow everyone to be themselves as much as possible while socializing. It focused on learning and sharing while adding soft skills and
practising team working.

An organization can create such a change by creating more positive opportunities
for people to talk. While an organization can create plans and policies, this does not
guarantee moving ahead as one big team to promote change. Many firms focus on
profit-sharing, rather than their human resource development. An enterprise has to
rethink its management directions and commitments to human resource training
and development so as to support both the organization's performance development
and profit-making. An enterprise has to have some way to balance profit-sharing
and development of its human resources. This is very important since, in practice,
a training programme may reach the bottom-line workers whom the organization
had neglected to ask about their development needs. It is time for a Thai enterprise
to review its management strategies for tapping into the tacit pool of knowledge its
workers possess, and support its employees to become the source of knowledge for
the organization. The experience of the people working as front-line employees and
the learning capabilities of an individual can guarantee change in an organization,
if the management encourages the building of a learning culture. The workshop
provided an example of an open learning environment where the team can be the
grounds for positive and supportive mechanisms.

It can be concluded that individuals need a positive opportunity for ideas to flow.
This calls for good communication skills, such as speaking and listening to each
other's ideas. Skills, such as being aware of local social etiquette, help improve

the interrelationships among the team members and that is the way to bring out tacit knowledge. At the same time, a team is the best place to start practising those skills.

The concepts and practices discussed in this chapter might make it feasible for human resource developers in other cultural milieux to adopt—and adapt—the approach pioneered in Thailand. One caveat is that 'Western' and even Japanese notions of work teams will not work well unless tailored to local cultures.

References

Blanchard, W. 1958. *Thailand: its people, its society, its culture*. New Haven, CT: Hraf Press.

Bohm, D. 1996. *David Bohm: on dialogue*. London: Routledge.

Boud, D.; Garrick, J. 1997. *Understanding learning at work*. London: Routledge.

Burapharat, C. 2001. *The importance of sibling relationships in developing an authentic setting in Thai workteam*. (Paper presented at the fifth International Workshop on Teamworking (IWOT-5) organized by the Catholic University Leuven, Belgium, 10-11 September 2001.)

Burapharat, C. 2003. *Patterns of learning and knowledge exchange in Thai work teams: a study of team members communication and relationships etiquettes*. (Unpublished Ph.D., Ontario Institute for Studies in Education, University of Toronto, Canada.)

Freire, P. 1969. *Pedagogy of the oppressed*. New York, NY: Continuum.

Garrick, J. 1999. Informal learning in the workplace. *Asia-Pacific journal of human resources*, vol. 37, pp. 118–20.

Green, M. 1998. *Organizational participation: myth and reality*. Oxford, UK: Oxford University Press.

Hawley, J.D.; Paek, J. 2005. Developing human resources for the technical workforce: a comparative study of Korea and Thailand. *International journal of training and development*, vol. 9, no. 1, pp. 79–94.

Hofstede, G. 1994. Business cultures: every organization has its symbols, rituals and heroes. *UNESCO courier*, vol. 12, no. 5.

Isaacs, W.N. 1993. Dialogue: the power of collective thinking. *The systems thinker*, vol. 4, no. 3.

Johnson, D.W.; Johnson, F.P. 1997. *Joining together: group theory and group skills*. Toronto, Canada: Allyn & Bacon.

Klausner, W.J. 1987. *Reflections on Thai culture*. Bangkok: Amarin.

Knowles, M.S. 1973. *The adult learner: a neglected species*. Houston, TX: Gulf Publishing.

Metcalf, G.S. 1999. *A critique of social systems theory*. <hypernews.ngdc.noaa.gov/hnxtra/Metcalf_paper.html>

Mezirow, J. 1978. Perspective transformation. *Adult education*, vol. 27, no. 2, pp. 100–10.

Mole, R.L. 1973. *Thai values and behaviour patterns*. Rutland, VT: Charles E. Tuttle Company.

Senge, P. 1994. *The fifth discipline fieldbook: strategies and tools for building a learning organization*. New York, NY: Bantan Doubleday Dell.

Takeuchi, H.; Nonaka, I. 2004. *Hitotsubashi on knowledge management*. Weinheim, Germany: John Wiley.

Triandis, H.C.; McCusker, C.; Hui, C.H. 1990. Multimethod probes of individualism and collectivism. *Journal of personality and social psychology*, vol. 59, no. 5, pp. 1006–20.

Wenger, E. 2002. *Communities of practice: learning, meaning, and identity*. Cambridge, UK: Cambridge University Press.

Wilson, D. 2003. *Knowledge workers and knowledge management in the workplace*. (Paper presented at the Symposium on Adult Education: Learning Opportunities for the Future, Canadian Defence Academy, Kingston, Ontario.)

Chapter IV.12
Globalization of the Labour Culture in the Republic of Korea: What 'Tripartite Relations' Mean for Workers

Phoebe Moore

1 Introduction

The economic crisis of East and South-East Asia in 1997 had a rapid and significant impact on the security of the 'culture' of labour forces, which includes relations between management, government and workers; and the stability of workers' employability and re-employability. This was particularly relevant for the Republic of Korea (hereafter 'Korea') where workers suffered a drastic rise in unemployment, which rose from 2.0% in 1996; to 7.7% in 1998; to 8.1% in the fourth quarter of 1998 (UNDP, 1999, p. 40). More than 3 million Korean people were unemployed in 1998 (Amnesty International, 1998), which is a significant number in a country with a population of 48 million (Deen, 2003). Whilst layoffs have not been scarce in the Korean labour force over time, the *reason* for the layoffs changed as a result of the economic crisis. Prior to the crisis, job loss was usually attributed to the situation of the national economy, but following the crisis, individual workers were blamed for not having the necessary skills and attitudes required in the new global economic landscape to either retain or regain employment in the 'new labour culture'.

The leaders' passion to promote the globalization of this 'tiger' knowledge economy has begun to alter the idea of employability itself, as though it were an immutable requirement for the transformation of an entire culture. In fact, the culture of tripartite relations between management/government/worker has not actually been altered, but merely involves a worker-mandate shift that places the responsibility of 'self-improvement' into the hands of workers, thus saving the government from the need to pursue its welfare-state role. Instead, workers have been blamed for their lack of preparedness for the future of the labour culture. The crisis of 1997 across Asia inspired reform-driven restructuring of vocational education and training (VET) to become part of a Ministry of Labour (MOL) manufactured 'labour culture', which has come about in partnerships with international organizations that advocate Korea's globalized stance. New requirements for training and workplace norms were expected to give workers the tools to adopt new forms of learning for renewed employability. In this way, VET to adapt to the new labour culture is conceptualized as a mechanism of the concept of *trasformismo* as defined within the neo-Gramscian literature.

R. Maclean, D. Wilson (eds.), *International Handbook of Education for the Changing World of Work*, DOI 10.1007/978-1-4020-5281-1_IV.12,
© Springer Science+Business Media B.V. 2009

This chapter looks at a specific project designed by the Korean MOL just after the economic crisis, entitled the 'new labour culture', in which leaders have attempted to restructure knowledge through an imposed cultural shift. The third section focuses on transnational relations between VET specialists through looking at international educational strategies, and notes that employability has become based on workers' 'knowledge' of specific and newly introduced skills, due to the transition from manufacturing to a knowledge- and information-based economy. The chapter goes on to investigate exactly which skills for learning and work attitudes have become employable in the culture of the changing job market, as employment has become increasing unstable. The crisis recovery period following 1997 thus marks Korea's decision to unabashedly enter the global 'knowledge economy' as a competitive player but, unfortunately, the Korean culture of work has *not* been transformed, and continues to demonstrate a culture of continuous power struggles with little improvement in workers' position on the political landscape.

2 The 'New Labour Culture'

The following discussion of the 'new labour culture' (hereafter NLC), introduced by the MOL, includes information obtained during a semi-structured interview held by the present author in December 1999 with the then Vice-Director of the Korean Labour Management Co-operation Division. The reason for conducting the interview was to gain a greater understanding regarding this proposed new form of culture publicized in the Korean media after the crisis. An NLC can be seen as a project attempting to display unions' and management's needs for cultural restructuring and the internationalization of work norms. This process requires workers' strict co-operation with the government, and despite the construction of a Tripartite Commission which still meets regularly in 2005,[1] the project aims potentially to converge a multitude of voices, and to provide limited concessions within an age of uncertainty—but ultimately is designed to circumvent workers' upheavals.

The MOL introduced the idea of the NLC in July 1999, and companies were given two months to respond according to the 'three phases' printed in the *Korea Herald* (Kim, 1999, p. 18) (see Fig. 1).

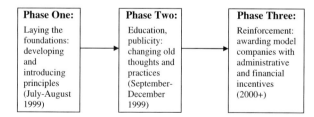

Phase One:	**Phase Two:**	**Phase Three:**
Laying the foundations: developing and introducing principles (July–August 1999)	Education, publicity: changing old thoughts and practices (September–December 1999)	Reinforcement: awarding model companies with administrative and financial incentives (2000+)

Fig. 1 Three phases for the creation of a new labour-management culture

Companies were given a matter of months to educate workers and to 'change old thoughts and practices', and were expected to receive awards given to model companies after the millennium. A sudden adoption of a globalized labour culture, modelled after Japan and the United States (according to the Vice-Director), was the MOL's prescription for business survival in what he called the 'IMF age': an age of reform that would prevent future upheavals.

The Minister presented the three principles of the NLC:

- *Trust and esteem*: the basic level to facilitate easy relations between labour, management and government.
- *Co-operation and engagement*: the action programme.
- *Autonomy and respect*: the goal to be achieved between management and labour to eliminate the need and/or possibility for the government to intervene into business affairs by establishing a worker/management relationship.

The principles of the labour culture require a shift in traditional power relations between the three agents: workers, management and the government. The *Korea Herald* article (Kim, 1999) quotes a Minister of Labour: 'Korea must observe a new paradigm of labour relations in which employers and workers are partners in every sense of the word'. The Minister also stressed that 'increased [...] aggressive employee training' is a prerequisite to healthy labour relations. As the MOL is a government body, the composition of this proposal is from its origins embedded in unequal relations but, ultimately, the ministry wants to encourage management and workers to find ways of negotiation and resolution between themselves.

So, bi-partite relations are a distinct indication of how the 'culture' of labour would progress. The Vice-Director offered a more complete explanation of his use of the term 'culture' by first listing the basic activities of labour relations, including collective bargaining and strikes, and human resource management. He claimed that companies should invest in labour culture training with the intention of 'making trade unions co-operate'. A 12.2% decrease in trade union membership in 1998 may have indicated a higher level of co-operation, or that union members are learning to co-operate with policy-makers. Alternatively, perhaps workers are choosing not to join unions, despite the notion that it is their only chance to enjoy legitimate representation. To achieve autonomy, as the third principle of the above list indicates, perhaps workers need labour unions as a tool to negotiate with the government if they feel that their autonomy is being challenged. The Vice-Director stated that the autonomy supposition is a *goal*, not *reality*. He mentioned that labour leaders do not respect union laws, and often use violence to pass their message, which is 'intolerable'.

As a solution, The Vice-Director said that union members would have to change their 'minds'[2] and become more flexible toward leaders' decisions that were, admittedly, made in haste and with international consultancy. The most significant change, he stressed, would be union members' co-operation with laws and government policy. Trade unions are learning; they have gradually started to conform to labour laws and to realise that violence will not help. The Minister referred to percentages of trade union membership, company investment and the models of modernization (Fig. 2) for the NLC.

Because Korea's labour history is considerably shorter than that of the United States and Japan, Korea would have to accelerate its development of 'modern' labour relations. The final outcome of the labour culture project was intended to cultivate 'modern' labour relations. The Vice-Director presented the model, 'Composition of the future-oriented labour-management community' which was also published in the *Korea Herald* in late 1999. The question now is whether workers can quickly adapt to new institutional requirements, and whether their way of thinking and culture can or will easily incorporate the new 'education' and 'training' of work habits—the relatively ambiguous terminology that represents the 'new labour culture'. Companies must invest in new forms of VET if they wish to remain competitive and stable. There is 'no choice', and the minister claimed that Korea faced few choices as a result of the economic crisis and IMF restructuring. But the crisis was the main reason for the need for a transformation of labour relations.

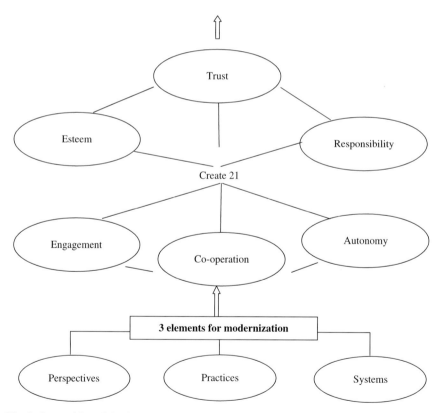

Fig. 2 Composition of the future-oriented labour/management community
Source: Kim, 1999, p. 18.

What quality marks the beginning of co-operation? *Trust*, according to the model prepared by the MOL. As a result of on-going tensions over many years, there has been very little trust between workers, management and policy-makers in Korea. Since 1987, co-operation has been attempted but without trust there can be no success in labour relations. Trust will take time, but someone should make the first move and 'management' was the target. Management should learn to trust the government's economic policy and implement policies within their companies.

Labour flexibility became a core theme in the restructuring of labour and remains a priority for policy-makers. Lay-offs are usually justified as a temporary remedy for economic difficulties in Korea and on-going restructuring of labour is a crucial element for the continuation of capitalism. The possibility of being laid off, however, makes people work harder, and while they feel stress and fatigue now, the recognition of necessary changes within VET will stabilize their positions, the Vice-Director stated. One change within the post-crisis era is that workers must become more cognisant of the significance of their behaviour for company survival. In the past, workers and management alike were not as concerned about keeping their companies alive, partly because the government propped up lagging companies, and partly because there was less dependence on foreign investment. In the contemporary age, workers will have to take on increased responsibilities for their own employability, as well as the well-being of their companies.

Unions must be government *partners* in the NLC. But would new laws implemented in the crisis-restructuring era reflect the needs and desires of workers? The Minister stated that *institutions* must change before laws can be made. The Tripartite Commission exists to facilitate policy changes; legal changes will be considered within the infrastructure of the Commission. It will take time for changes to truly affect relations. The interviewer reminded him of the *lack* of time that he had emphasized previously, of the urgency to change the labour culture to meet the standards of the United States and Japan. But with the same vision, he said, practices can be changed, since change depends on people's *minds*.

If workers do not follow the lead of management, and management neglects to follow the lead of the MOL's NLC mandates, then businesses, especially those that are foreign-invested, will fail and workers will lose their jobs. That was the message from this prominent civil servant. Perhaps the reality is a reminder to workers and management of who is still in control: the Korean Government and the leading managerial class, and workers are excluded from development dialogue.

3 The Restructuring of Ideas

In the mid-1990s, in order to accommodate the State's objectives for globalization, the Korean MOL began accelerating relations with international organizations with a goal to model Korean VET programmes to those seen within the culture of the 'convergence club'[3] (Magariños, 2001). Korean President Kim Dae Jung (1997–2003) reasoned that 'the ideas and the modus operandi of the industrial society of the past will not prepare us for adaptation and adjustment [. . .] the time has come for us to positively transform our consciousness to fit the coming century' (Kim, 1997, p. 205).

The knowledge society comes about through becoming a 'learning society'. Everybody (researchers, managers, workers) contributes to that process through sharing their distinctive insights and know-how in building institutions and social systems capable of holding/memorizing, mediating and continuously constructing new knowledge (Nyhan, 2002, p. 20).

The need for new forms of knowledge within the workforce arises with changes in production. During the age of Fordism, workers were trained to work on mass assembly-line production. Nyhan (2002) states that the crisis of European industry in the 1970s and 1980s was due to a lack of appropriate knowledge for the changes that technology began to have upon work expectations. Enhanced interest in 'knowledge' in education systems is a 'timely reminder of some of the fundamentals that have been lost' (p. 30), which involves out-of-date assumptions that adaptation will occur outside of clearly defined training.

The World Bank and OECD's (2001) review of Korean progress since the economic crisis shows that some amount of reform of education has been implemented, but more was needed to guarantee an appropriately skilled workforce for the growing knowledge economy. Recommendations include the integration of skills instruction such as 'communication skills, capability to utilize ICTs, as well as increased possibilities for gaining field experience' (World Bank/OECD, 2001, p. xv). These international organizations also advise partnerships between universities and industry, the enhancement of pedagogical training with an emphasis on new knowledge and information and communication technologies (ICTs), the development of performance-based pay systems, knowledge sharing systems, and the expansion of exchange programmes between Korean and foreign educational institutions. At this ideational level, these powerful institutions recommend several actions to improve Korea's chances of composing the work force needed and to 'provide better co-ordination between needs of the labour market and industry, and the supply of education' (p. xv).

With this in mind, the Korean Government sought to build on international partnerships. In partnership with UNESCO-UNEVOC and other international organizations, the MOL aimed to standardize and reform VET programmes to give them a more globally competitive edge (ROK, 2001, pp. 61–62).

Korea's greatest resource for development is manpower, according to experts at UNESCO, but it is unrefined in its potential. The Asia-Pacific coalition of UNESCO-UNEVOC emphasizes 'innovativeness, creativity, adaptability, and self-learning' as the most attractive performance indicators for workers in the knowledge economy, and holds meetings for educators to discuss implementation. The first principal strategy for training is 'entrepreneurship skills development'— one of the primary components of neo-liberal economic growth, as entrepreneurs are often the strongest negotiators of capital and the 'brains' behind the system.

OECD emphasizes that knowledge and information as 'assets' are becoming increasingly valuable for nations to position themselves as competitive players in the global knowledge economy (OECD, 2000, pp. 12–13). As the value of assets has shifted from tangible to intangible, workers' supposed 'lag' in adjustment to expectations of what knowledge *is*, appears to require government-led strategies to provide training that can quickly train capability and efficiently (Leadbeater, 1999, p. iv). The implications of a knowledge-based economy or the 'new capitalism' (Leadbeater, 1998, p. 384) are that very specific types of worker knowledge and behaviour are expected for effective utilization of human capital for development, and will enhance national economies' competitiveness.

> The new capitalism, that of the Knowledge Economy, will be driven by the discovery and distribution of rival intangible goods—information and knowledge—created by largely intangible assets—human and social capital. These knowledge-intensive goods are best produced through collaboration and competition, partnerships and networks, which bring together public and private (Leadbeater, 1998, p. 384).

In this context, the Korean government has adjusted investment strategies, and has restructured VET programmes, requesting that workers and civil society co-operate with its incentives (ROK, 2001, pp. 12–13).

Industry in Korea has been changing, the 'Republic of Korea' states in one of its government booklets and, therefore, the government is changing investment strategies to prioritize research and development surrounding this issue. 'Until now', the booklet continues, Korea has 'focused on research and development in medium-high tech industries, such as electronics, automobile, machinery and ship-building, in which it retains relatively high competitiveness' (ROK, 2001, p. 7). 'Recently,' however, the government has changed its strategic investment into 'fields of new technology, such as IT'. When the share percentage of ownership of the total market by 'foreigners', or non-Korean investors, rose from 2.24% in 1983 to 9.11% in 1997, jumping to 18.6% by late 1998 (the highest percentage since 1983),[4] the 'market' required a critical overview of the workforce. This influx of foreign capital is located in the knowledge industry more predominantly than in any other sector and this has created an increase in demand for skilled 'knowledge workers' (ROK, 2001; Lee, 2001), thus changing the nature of what it means to be 'employable' in Korea.

In response to these changes in industry-specific investment, new demands have been made of the labour market, and the very concept of employability and what constituted re-employability has been quickly thrown into disarray. If workers could not keep jobs in the insecure post-crisis situation, they were expected to join VET programmes that would make them 'employable'. If workers were privileged to remain in positions of employment, they were expected to attend developmental VET that would aid in maintaining their 'employability'. The government's hegemonic project intended to involve the workers by providing the means for them 'to help themselves'.

A senior researcher at KRIVET focused on the workers' situation with regard to training and how the researcher, in an 'elite' position conducting government-sponsored research, understood *employability*. She stated that management had developed different expectations and needs for training than the workers in the post-crisis period. Workers were expected to seek qualifications and training for life-long learning, which would increase their mobility. Management in the restructuring scenario sought workers who could prove that they had gained training in what were called 'international skills'. This expert reflected on a July 2002 newspaper article about the end-of-the-contract system for labour, which stated that the average age to leave a job had become 38. Thus workers may want to gain new skills in order to keep up with changing expectations occurring in the increasingly flexible labour market with a high rate of worker turnover.

The KRIVET researcher mentioned that people in the automobile and computer industries were more likely to keep their jobs. However, the reasons for layoffs had changed, she stressed. During the economic crisis, many educated people lost their jobs due to external forces. Unemployment subsequently became the result of actual *unemployability* of individuals. Unemployed workers after the economic crisis were forced to accept their own 'unemployability' in the face of new skill requirements, and had to enter VET programmes that taught internationally accepted knowledge and ideas for self-improvement and skills development.

Post-economic crisis Korean VET programmes were designed to prepare work-ers to play an active role in integration into certain fields of technology that are seen to require flexible workers who commit to a lifelong plan of learning in order to re-main employable. Knowledge itself thus has become a commodity in post-industrial society, and would be provided by the public sector *to* the private (Leadbeater, 1998, p. 379). State guidance for this process became increasingly important due to 'its [the State's] role in producing knowledge, through the education system' (p. 379). Jessop (2001, p. 63) notes that knowledge becomes a commodity when it is artifi-cially made scarce, as opposed to the commodification of labour power that occurs when it enters the labour market and becomes submerged in the labour process. The commodification of knowledge brings about an unprecedented role for the State, if it is to inspire a 'profound social reorganization [. . .] required to turn it [knowledge] into something valuable' (Schiller, 1988, p. 32).

In 1997, 13,888 firms were entitled to offer a 'Vocational Competency Development Programme' to employees (KOILAF, 1999a, p. 109). This programme involved training workers for new work styles of individual performance and 'com-petence' (p. 109). However, the increase in demand for knowledge workers drasti-cally exceeds the demand for the 'unskilled' (ROK, 2001, p. 14). Furthermore, 'the wage gap between production workers and managerial/white-collar employees has begun to widen since 1998, because production workers suffered more severe pay cuts' (Katz, Lee & Lee, 2001, p. 232).

Thus, restructuring of knowledge and skills in Korea involved the government establishing relations with international agencies whose intentions focus on the con-vergence of production relations, including employable skills.

4 Restructuring the Content of VET Programmes

The promotions of new characteristics of labour performance include several ele-ments that contrast with the Korean cultural expectations of workers. Rowley and

Bae (2002) observe how core ideologies of human resource flows, work systems, evaluation and reward systems, and employee influence can be systematically contrasted to new characteristics. Traditional Korean work practices include: the prioritization of an affiliate organization over the individual him/herself; emphasis on collective equality; and community orientation over individual equity and market principal orientations. Kim and Briscoe (1997) note that traditional human resource management in South Korea is based on an emphasis of group harmony (*in hwa*). Incentives and bonuses were based not on individual performance but on that of the group. Team spirit was the formula for excellence in the traditional workplace—cultural norms that were bound to change with the MOL's NLC.

The major changes introduced by VET programmes are in the areas of performance appraisal and payments systems, lifelong learning and individualization of work. These cultural shifts are reflective of the post-Fordist age wherein modes of control over the process of work have been rewritten. In the post-Fordist production age, the stipulation for manual skills has become nearly *completely replaced* by the demand for individuals' 'knowledge' (Aronowitz & DiFazio, 1994, p. 83). New work styles have changed promotion and compensation techniques to fit individual performance, which were to be appraised by managers who were equally inexperienced in the new standards (Kim and Briscoe, 1997).

4.1 Performance Appraisal and Payment Systems

Perhaps the two most difficult requests made by the government for labour discussed by the first Tripartite Commission in negotiation for restructuring of culture were labour flexibility and changes to the traditional payment system toward a *performance*-based system.

People with intelligence, skills, creativity and willingness—the knowledgeable—are critical for sharpening the competitive edge in the era of infinite competition. It is becoming increasingly important to lay a solid ground for economic recovery through remodelling corporate infrastructure and creating an atmosphere where workers of ability are valued (KOILAF, 1999b, p. 11).

In November 1997, just as the economy began its dangerous slide toward a crisis, the MOL took a renewed interest in vocational programmes designed to achieve the above competences. The Vocational Training Promotion Act of 24 December 1997 began a trend by changing the titles of the VET facilities to vocational *ability development* training facilities, and the term 'vocational training' became vocational *ability development* training (ROK/MOL, 1999, 2005). 'Ability', a relatively ambiguous term used repeatedly in the emerging training institutions, refers to a particular work ethic included as part of training procedures. Workers were increasingly expected to assume new responsibilities and skills for the international work standard, regardless of their rupture with the past work culture in Korean corporations and businesses.

A KOILAF publication recommends some 'basic directions' for the implementation of a performance-based wage system. Guidelines are:

- Help workers and employers to find common ground for the introduction and operation of a performance-based system.

- Ensure that the procedures for adopting a new wage system comply with the law and any counter-productive effect is averted.
- Induce a simplified wage system (KOILAF, 2002, p. 11).

Employers and workers were encouraged to introduce a profit-sharing system wherein profits exceeding targets could be shared equally. Management was requested to run business openly and with transparency, so that workers could easily identify what types of performance would be expected of them. These suggestions aimed to democratize the performance-based system, requiring an entirely new set of performance requirements that expect individuals to take responsibility in the restructured economy.

4.2 Individualism and Lifelong Learning

After the crisis, individualism and lifelong learning became crucial worker qualities that are sought in the knowledge economy, and workers were expected to demonstrate those skills. Korean workers have historically not been judged according to individual performance evaluations, which are a new requirement in many restructured companies. Traditional Korean culture is said to be more community-oriented than individual-oriented. However, workers are struggling to adopt individualistic attitudes. Korea has no time to account for cultural work styles, or for its Korean 'spirit'. Koreans will have no choice in the matter because of unlimited competition around the world.

Nonetheless, individualism was to be emphasized in the workplace. A higher quality of education would be offered to the younger generation so as to distinguish the workforce of the future. Employees increasingly need to be 'creative, and they will also need to be able to adapt to rapid changes in society [. . .] employees should be given various opportunities to study continuously in order to adopt self-directed learning methods for absorbing new information' (Lee, 2001, p. 4).

Twenty experts and officials at the Korea Labour Institute (KLI) were brought together in 2003 to form a research team under the Qualification System Reforms Task Force (KLI, 2003). The research team intended to come up with visions and innovations for the qualification system and to review changes to VET since restructuring in 1997 and beyond. The study notes the shift towards learning for life and work, which is centred on the individual and states that 'decent work underpins individuals' independence, self-respect and well-being, and, therefore, is a key to their overall quality of life'. The study notes that every individual has a right to VET and compares Korea to several other nations, including Argentina, Bolivia, Brazil, Chile, Germany, Guatemala, Italy, Mexico and Spain, whose national constitutions accommodate this. This right is also acknowledged at the international level, for example in the Universal Declaration of Human Rights (1948) and the American Declaration of Human Rights and Obligations (1948). In the most recent phase of VET in Korea, researchers at the KLI have decided that education is the right of citizens and is a crucial way to find access to employment, reducing the likelihood of unemployment and with significant increases in life-cycle earnings.

The study claims that economic, social and technological factors cumulatively account for the growing emphasis on the individual in Korean VET. The production of goods and services in *any* contemporary economy has begun to rely on human, rather than physical, capital, or 'on its workers' individual and collective endowment of knowledge and skills'. The 'individual' is the new citizen of society and has been granted a central place in statements of learning and training objectives. So the process of formal education and training in 2003 was no longer limited to the passing on of information, but envisions a society that prioritizes a scenario of 'individuals learning to learn so that they can find out for themselves'. Factual knowledge itself is no longer enough, but individuals are encouraged to learn how to analyse, access and exploit information and in turn to devise and create new knowledge. Taking charge of one's own learning and ability to learn is the only way to survive or to 'live and work in the knowledge and information society'. VET makes individuals employable and productive and helps them escape poverty through mobility and choice. These statements, perhaps, do not sound controversial at first reading. But who decides what VET curricula should be provided and to whom? Who decided that 'individuals' were to become the primary producers in Korea?

'Individuality' was not only part of a new concept of the culture of employability, but was concretely associated with 'citizenship'. According to the EU Memorandum on lifelong learning, active citizenship refers to how 'people participate in all spheres of economic and social life, the chances and risks they face in trying to do so, and the extent to which they feel that they belong to, and have a fair say in, the society in which they live'. This incorporates ideas of participation as well as replacing ownership, similar to the ownership that is increasingly expected of nations' development (see Cammack, 2001, 2002a, 2002b).

So individuals are now expected to take responsibility for their own employability and the government has declared that VET is an important factor in this process. 'Lifelong learning' is the way in which workers can adapt to rapidly changing economies over time, and the government (ROK, 2001, p. 42) suggested a widespread series of facilities to support and incorporate lifelong learning into the very core of Korean culture. National and regional lifelong education centres and lifelong learning halls were to be developed. Libraries, self-governance centres, social welfare halls, women's halls and citizens' centres were to be strengthened. A pilot project entitled 'learning clubs for turning local culture into lifelong learning' was suggested. An information network was intended to result from this campaign, as well as a database to organize information on professors, lecturers and education programmes of lifelong learning institutions. One booklet, 'Occupational World of the Future', offered workers access to available VET and other forms of education so that they, as citizens, could prepare themselves for new employability requirements in the knowledge economy.

4.3 Incentive Structure

But in a nation with such a tumultuous history of unrest, how would workers react to drastic changes and reform in the employment structure and labour market? The government quickly homed in on aspects of employment that would prove to be the most volatile, and tried to create an incentive structure to circumvent uprisings. Through framing the government-required training programmes as positive incentives for personal development, and in the post-crisis era as a means to remain or to become 'employable' after the enormous amount of lay-offs, the government applied a 'strategy on the part of the dominant power to gradually co-opt elements of the opposition forces—a strategy known in Italian politics as *trasformismo*' (Cox, 1999, p. 25). '*Trasformismo* can serve as a strategy of assimilating and domesticating potentially dangerous ideas by adjusting them to the policies of the dominant coalition and can thereby obstruct the formation of class-based organized opposition' (Cox, 1983, pp. 166–67). The Korean government sidelined potentially dissident groups by providing a social safety net taking the form of VET programmes to appease laid-off workers who were most likely to oppose elite-led accumulation strategies.

About half of the employers surveyed (Park, Park & Yu, 2001, pp. 144–45) stated that the most difficult subject for firms undergoing employment adjustment was to convince workers of the necessity for employment adjustment.

The following matters were ranked as the second, third, and fourth most difficult things in the implementation of employment adjustment: 'consultation about the criteria to select who are to lose their jobs'; 'consultation about the compensatory package for workers to be adjusted'; and 'consultation about the number to be adjusted'. These were not favourable signs for the application, ease or effectiveness of 'adjustment'. Management realized that sudden layoffs are not easily accepted by workers, and sought ways to appease and help prevent backlash and resistance to what they had been told was a market-driven inevitability. Employment adjustment includes attrition, 'honourable' retirement, dismissal and 'others'—which refers to spin-offs or early retirement (Park et al., 2001, p. 128).

Management created regulations that introduced the idea of *voluntary* participation with incentives for involvement in training schemes, which in some cases provided a rare option to secure employment in the midst of the crisis. New incentives were introduced under the Employment Insurance System (EIS), a system designed to reduce the risk of job loss after the lifetime employment laws had been revised (KOILAF, 1999c, p. 112). The EIS 'purports to popularize vocational training and enhance firms' competitiveness [...] provides incentives such as subsidies and financial assistance to encourage individual firms to invest in the internal labour force, thereby improving labour productivity, employment stability and the firms' competitive edge in international markets' (p. 58).

But the 'hottest issue' was how to encourage workers to participate voluntarily in the vocational competency development programme (KOILAF, 1999c, p. 110). To encourage voluntary participation, the government offered businesses two alternatives: (a) support for implementation of the subsidization for implementation costs to employers; and (b) paid leave for training (p. 110). One KRIVET report shows that workers who do not attend the training programmes stated that they did not do so simply out of lack of desire, and out of deliberate resistance to require- ments for attendance. The study shows that 47.4% of attendees of training went due to mandate, whereas 14.9% attended training programmes voluntarily. The study 'Educational and training program situation in Korea' (KRIVET, 2000) also shows 15.9% of companies have taken part in internationalization strategies via vocational training programmes. There are 191 new types of programmes being implemented and the number of companies that now require participation in these is increasing every year. Laid-off workers were opposed to forced training programmes because of unwillingness or because of a suspicion of the limited short-term benefits— demonstrating the lack of consensus for these initiatives.

This study has claimed that Korea's VET reform has been managed by a govern- ment that was not immediately able to consolidate hegemonic consensus or com- monsense, but led a programme of passive revolution. The government has shown that, once again, it is almost completely unswervingly taking unilateral charge of recovery at the guidance of the IMF. Its introduction of an NLC involves an explicit request for workers' co-operation with management and the government, and for an adaptation to the knowledge economy VET-taught employable skills.

5 Conclusion

'The twenty-first century', the Korean MOL website reads, 'is the era of knowledge and information! In this era, superior human resources are the basis of individual, corporate, and national competitiveness' (ROK/MOL, 2005). Vocational 'ability development' is 'preparation for productivity increase, employment stability and a prosperous future'. The NLC, a framework for tripartite relational changes, was intended to reverse a history of intense labour conflict and to ultimately achieve 'superior human resources'. Simultaneously, it introduced globalization of expec- tations in the workplace, introduced through 'voluntary' training programmes that employees were required to attend, in order to maintain or to rediscover individual employability in the impending knowledge economy. Has this strategy been effec- tive, ultimately? Has the government's strategy resolved the issues of unemployment and labour struggles that it set out to address?

In late December 2004, the Korea Employer's Federation held a survey with eighty-eight human resources management officers. This survey predicted unstable labour-management relations by 2005 (KOILAF, 2004a). Some 60% of officials indicated that they expected industrial relations to be less stable by 2005, and only 11% predicted improvements. The survey also showed that the primary difficulty in resolving on-going labour-management strife was due to 'the struggle-oriented ten- dency of unions' (28%), 'influence from higher-level labour organizations' (25%) and 'irrational laws and systems' (19%). From these comments, it seems as though the intentions of the NLC have not been completely realized. In terms of unemploy- ment, in October 2004, Korea suffered a three-year high as farms and non-service industry sectors continued to dismiss workers (KOILAF, 2004b). Is this because workers have failed to become employable? Or has the economic crisis reached new levels of magnitude?

While the NLC was implemented to encourage tripartite communication between involved parties, it does not appear to have promoted harmony of social dialogue within the Tripartite Commission. In 2001 at the meetings of the third Tripartite Commission, which had been reformulated after a series of failed attempts to complete negotiations since its first meetings in 1998, leaders discussed the issue of vocational training. The 'government' promised to 'look for ways of enhancing the efficiency of operation of systems, including efforts made for stabilization of insurance for projects of job-skill development, [and] rationalization of the system' (ROK/Tripartite Commission, 2001). 'Management' promised to cultivate an environment that would encourage workers' voluntary education and training, with the recognition that 'such education and training will form the basis of the nation's industrial competitiveness in the future'. These statements demonstrate the on-going impulse to expect workers to meet the challenge of maintaining individual employability for the sake of their nation's sustained development. But while the government and management have been clearly represented at the commission's meetings, unions have not demonstrated the same appearance. One of the two most prominent umbrella labour unions, the Korean Confederation of Trade Unions (KCTU) has not rejoined the commission after withdrawal in 1999 due to members' disapproval of its decisions at the first meetings.

In 2005, the leader of the KCTU resigned after confrontations at a special meeting called to discuss whether this important organization should rejoin the Tripartite Commission—despite its history of disappointment and the paralysis of union representation. The leader sought 'agreement or disagreement' from union members, but in protest some members poured flammable liquid on the floor. These members perhaps feel that the KCTU's membership of the commission will turn out to be a double-edged sword and will not promote worker representation, but will represent complacency toward the passive revolution of changes taking place in the Korean 'labour culture'. The failure to include worker representation in restructuring and development plans, through the promotion of their employability but without inclusive and representative union involvement, demonstrates an on-going hegemonic crisis. Several pressures have contributed to ruining these relations, including the impulse to globalize and to become increasingly competitive within the knowledge economy. Nonetheless, without hegemonic resolution, attempts to locate an inclusive forum for negotiation of globalized development strategies will continue, and ideally may play a role in the formation of true democracy in this small but volatile nation.

Notes

1. The First Tripartite Commission was established on 15 January 1998. Management, government and union leaders met to negotiate the restructuring of the Korean economy at that time. Issues brought to the table included wage stabilization and the promotion of labour-management

co-operation, enhancement of 'basic labour rights' and also the enhancement of 'labour market flexibility'.
2. In 'Kunglish', or Korean inspired English, 'mind' means 'way of thinking'.
3. The notion of convergence, or nations' abilities to replicate industrialized countries' development trajectories, was both implicitly and explicitly a part of IMF restructuring schemes such as that applied to the Republic of Korea in 1998 and onward. Members of the 'convergence club' are advanced industrial countries, and the benchmarking of best practices for the creation of wealth emanate from them.
4. Statistics provided during an interview the author conducted with a senior researcher at the KRIVET Asia-Pacific regional headquarters in Seoul, 9 August 2002.

References

Amnesty International. 1998. *Republic of Korea (South Korea) arrests of trade-union leaders.* 21 July 1998. <web.amnesty.org/library/Index/ENGASA250241998?open&of=ENG-KOR>

Aronowitz, S.; DiFazio, W. 1994. The new knowledge work. *In:* Ahier, J.; Esland, G., eds. *Education, training and the future of work-1: social, political and economic contexts of policy development,* pp. 76–96. London: Routledge.

Cammack, P. 2001. Making the poor work for globalization? *New political economy,* vol. 6, no. 3, pp. 397–408.

Cammack, P. 2002a. The mother of all governments: The World Bank's matrix for global governance. *In:* Wilkinson, R.; Hughes, S., eds. *Global governance: critical perspectives,* pp. 36–53. London: Routledge.

Cammack, P. 2002b. Attacking the poor. *New Left review,* vol. 2, no. 13, pp. 125–34.

Cox, R.W. 1983. Gramsci, hegemony and international relations: an essay in method. *Millennium: journal of international studies,* vol. 12, no. 2, pp. 162–75.

Cox, R.W. 1999. Civil society at the turn of the millennium: prospects for an alternative world order. *Review of international studies,* vol. 25, no. 1, pp. 3–28.

Deen, T. 2003. United Nations: Advocates 'social safety net' in Third World. *Third World Network, 2003.* <www.twnside.org.sg/title/safety-cn.htm>

Jessop, B. 2001. The state and the contradictions of the knowledge-driven economy. *In:* Bryson, J.R. et al., eds. *Knowledge, space, economy,* pp. 63–78. London: Routledge.

Katz, H.; Lee, W.; Lee, J., eds. 2001. *The changing nature of labour-management interactions and tripartism: is co-ordinated decentralization the answer?* Seoul: Korea Labour Institute.

Kim, D.J. 1997. Address to the Nation, 19 December 1997, Article 6 #2. *In:* Sohn, C.-H.; Yang, J., eds. *Korea's economic reform measures under the IMF Program: government measures in the critical first six months of the Korean economic crisis,* pp. 203-10. Seoul: Korea Institute for International Economic Policy. (Translated by the Blue House.)

Kim, M.H. 1999. Employers and workers are partners: new labour culture seeks co-prosperity through coexistence. *Korea Herald,* Wednesday, 24 November, p. 18.

Kim, S.S.; Briscoe, D. 1997. Globalization and a new human resource policy in Korea: transformation to a performance-based HRM. *Employee relations,* vol. 19, no. 4, pp. 298–308.

Korea International Labour Foundation. 1999a. *Changes in the employment structure: recent developments, current labour situation in Korea.* Seoul: KOILAF. <www.koilaf.org/publication/link16.htm#4>

Korea International Labour Foundation. 1999b. *1999 guidelines for collective bargaining: labor, management and the government.* Seoul: KOILAF.

Korea International Labour Foundation. 1999c. *Labour relations in Korea.* Seoul: KOILAF.

Korea International Labour Foundation. 2002. *2002 collective guidelines for collective bargaining: labour, management and the government.* Seoul: KOILAF.

Korea International Labour Foundation. 2004a. 61% of personnel or HRM managers predict unstable labor-management relations for 2005. *Labor today,* no. 239, 31 December 2004. <www.koilaf.org/index2.htm>

Korea International Labour Foundation. 2004b. *Unemployment unchanged at 3.5%.* <www.koilaf.org/index2.htm>

Korea Labour Institute. 2003. *Learning and training for work in the knowledge society.* <www.logos-net.net/ilo/150_base/en/report/rep_toc.htm>

Korea Research Institute for Vocational Education and Training. 2000. *Educational and training program situation in Korea.* Seoul: KRIVET.

Leadbeater, C. 1998. Who will own the knowledge economy? *Political quarterly,* vol. 69, no. 4, pp. 375–85.

Leadbeater, C. 1999. It's not just the economy, stupid. *New Statesman,* 27 September, pp. iv–vi.

Lee, K. 2001. *New direction of Korea's vocational education and training policy.* (Paper presented at the International Conference on TVET, Adelaide, Australia, 2001.)

Magariños, C.A. 2001. *Managing UN reform: UNIDO's need-driven approach.* (Paper presented by the Director-General of the United Nations Industrial Development Organization at the Royal Institute for International Affairs, Chatham House, London, 21 September 2001.)

Nyhan, B., ed. 2002. *Taking steps towards the knowledge society: reflections on the process of knowledge development.* Luxembourg : Office for Official Publications of the European Communities.

Organization for Economic Co-operation and Development. 2000. *Knowledge management in the learning society: education and skills.* Paris: OECD.

Park, D.J.; Park, J.; Yu, G.-C. 2001. Assessment of labour market response to the labour law changes introduced in 1998. *In:* Park, F. et al., eds. *Labour market reforms in Korea: policy options for the future,* pp. 125–50. Seoul: World Bank and Korea Labour Institute.

Republic of Korea. 2001. *Human resources development strategies for Korea: human resources knowledge new take-off.* Seoul: Republic of Korea.

Republic of Korea. Ministry of Labour. 1999. *Labour sector reforms gaining speed: MOL decides to operate the second-term Labour Reform Task Force.* Seoul: International Co-operation Division. <www.molab.go.kr/English/English.html>

Republic of Korea. Ministry of Labour. 2005. *Vocational ability development overview.* <www.molab.go.kr:8787/labor/labor_06_01_01.jsp>

Republic of Korea. The Tripartite Commission. 2001. *National initiatives concerning social dialogue on training.* <www.logosnet.net/ilo/150_base/en/topic_n/t23_kor.htm>

Rowley, C.; Bae, J.S. 2002. Globalization and transformation of human resource management in South Korea. *International journal of human resource management,* vol. 13, no. 1, pp. 522–49.

Schiller, D. 1988. How to think about information. *In:* Mosco, V.; Wasko, J., eds. *The political economy of information,* pp. 27–44. Madison, WI: University of Wisconsin Press.

United Nations Development Programme. 1999. *Social safety net for the most vulnerable groups in the Republic of Korea.* Seoul: UNDP.

World Bank; Organisation for Economic Co-operation and Development. 2001. *Korea and the knowledge-based economy: making the transition.* Washington, DC: World Bank/OECD.

Chapter IV.13
Involvement of Labour-Market Partners in TVET in the Russian Federation

Olga Oleynikova

1 Introduction

The present chapter is based on a number of independent surveys and reports of international projects implemented in the Russian Federation (henceforth Russia) in the field of VET, as well as the author's personal experience. To date, no analysis of the problems mentioned in the title has been performed in Russia.

The vocational education and training (VET) sector in Russia is made up of two major types of institutions, initial VET schools[1] and *lyceums* (ISCED, level 4) and VET colleges and *technicums* (ISCED, level 5B). VET schools are all State schools that serve both to provide young people with basic technical skills making them employable on the labour market, and to accommodate the social-support needs of youngsters from disadvantaged families. Both levels provide access to higher education.

To obtain a coherent picture of VET/enterprise interaction in contemporary Russia, it may prove worthwhile to take a retrospective look at the interaction between the VET sector and labour-market partners in the days of the planned economy within what used to be called the 'command-administrative system' characterized by tight control on the part of the State of all spheres of life and subsystems of society, including education and training. It was mandatory at that time for all State enterprises—and there were no other ones—to co-operate with and support schools at all levels of the education system (including kindergartens, general schools, initial VET schools and *technicums*), including universities.

All enterprises were twinned with a number of local general and VET schools and offered schoolchildren vocational orientation and training in basic skills. VET students were provided with work experience during the course of study and jobs upon graduation. Enterprises were also obliged to have instructors on their staff who would supervise the practical training periods conducted in the enterprise. Apart from these arrangements, enterprises were supposed to support VET school workshops with machines, tools and other equipment, and provide materials and supplies.

Almost all big enterprises had affiliated to them technical/vocational schools or institutes of higher education that provided pre-service and in-service training for their workers.

R. Maclean, D. Wilson (eds.), *International Handbook of Education for the Changing World of Work*, DOI 10.1007/978-1-4020-5281-1_IV.13,
© Springer Science+Business Media B.V. 2009

This streamlined interaction worked practically without a hitch aimed at both training the workforce for the labour market, and at providing a social security net for children and youth from disadvantaged families, or those with learning problems or deviant behaviour. The above situation mirrored both the social and economic system in place in the country, and the needs of the industrial economy in which one would acquire one occupation that lasted a lifetime, with in-built trajectories of in-service training and promotion.

2 The Changing Context

With the collapse of the socialist economy, the repercussions immediately rico-cheted off onto education and training. On the one hand, the State relaxed its grip on the economy and new processes in the society and economy evolved—particularly chaos and instability. New forms of ownership emerged and enterprises changed hands and ownership. On the other hand, a large number of enterprises either had to close down or opt for conversion from producing one type of goods to another. Transition from total State ownership to multiple forms of ownership plunged the economy into uncertainty that reshaped the system of labour relations, entailing new roles for employers, employees and the State, as well as their interaction.

The overarching uncertainty diverted enterprises, preoccupied largely with sur-vival and staying afloat, from the priorities of education and training. Confusion was omnipresent and it took about ten years for the economy to settle down. Dur-ing these ten years the culture of the VET/labour-market dialogue was very much diluted and new mechanisms were very slow to take shape. The situation was ex-acerbated in 1998 when a major financial crisis broke out that further distanced most enterprises from education and training. However, new private enterprises that managed to recover from the crisis more quickly than others were the first to give the lead in addressing education and training needs and began to include training in their development strategies, relying on their goodwill and common-sense, as well as learning from best international practices. However, there was no standard model of co-operation with the system of education in place (National Observatory for Professional Education, 2004).

As of 2000 the economic situation began to stabilize and grow, with the result that employers were showing once again interest in the qualifications of the work-force. In this improving context enterprises began to be more selective in their hiring practices and developed an awareness of the added value of in-service training and upskilling.

It should be pointed out, however, that the above refers to the 'average' tendency. There were enormous variations due to the size of the country and regional differ-ences that are conditioned by geographic, social and economic factors. Also, due to the level of development and awareness of their social responsibility, marked differences were observed between different sectors in addressing education and training issues (Analytical Centre 'Expert', 2005a).

More advanced and development-oriented companies from both traditional and new sectors that were well established on the market (about 5 to 8% of the total number of enterprises in the country) began to build close links with VET schools and colleges. These, as a rule, are large companies or corporations consisting of dozens of enterprises (Analytical Centre 'Expert', 2005b). Smaller companies simply cannot afford to spend time and effort on interacting with colleges and universities and they make do with the workforce available on the labour market. VET schools, for their part, try to keep up links with enterprises established in the 'old' days, often without due regard to the changed situation—and sometimes governed by the paternalistic thinking that enterprises 'owe' them something.

3 The Degree of Involvement of Labour-Market Partners

Certain sectors and companies are more outspoken about their requirements regarding the workforce, and proactively interact with the external environment to change it for the better. Others are traditionally 'introvert' and remain focused on their internal processes. The first category is actively exploring the concept of a learning organization and considers education and training as an investment. It is common for the more advanced companies in this group to accuse the VET system of inability to produce adequately trained specialists and they rely on their own training schemes, including in-service staff training.

Generally, the following types of employer/company/VET co-operation can be identified (Analytical Centre 'Expert', 2005b):

1. Close co-operation, resulting in graduates meeting most of the employer's skill requirements. This concerns such sectors as finance and insurance, the production of high-tech equipment, the fuel industry and metallurgy, where there is new recruitment of personnel and a high demand for skills. This type of co-operation is observed in big companies that can afford to invest in education.
2. Weak co-operation: graduates often failing to meet the employers' requirements. This affects rapidly developing sectors involving a wide range of employers. However, the latter are not in a position to invest in education (construction, media, parts of the IT sector, trade, marketing and consulting, tourism, hospitality, etc.).
3. Fairly close co-operation: graduates meeting company skills requirements up to 50%. This particularly concerns sectors with monopolies: telecommunications, railways, air transport, etc. This group differs from the first group in that the market is not developing as rapidly due to the monopoly of companies.
4. Very weak co-operation: skills of graduates failing to meet requirements of the world of work. The sectors concerned are often facing stagnation or uncertainty: most of industrial production requiring engineers, including the chemical sector, machine-making, forestry, etc. As a rule, these sectors are made up of numerous enterprises with only limited financial resources and lacking a culture of networking. VET schools and colleges training specialists for these sectors are not

particularly aware of the work-market requirements but, as a rule, are confident that they know what the sector needs better than the people in the sector themselves. Employers can neither invest in education, nor offer competitive salaries, which is a demotivating factor for both schools and graduates.

It should be pointed out that, apart from factors indicated earlier, the reluctance of enterprises—with a few exceptions—to become involved with education and training is also due to other reasons: (a) a lack of legal provisions for enterprises to participate in the distribution of funds allocated for VET at all levels; and (b) a lack of tax benefits for enterprises that invest in education and training, including support for VET schools and colleges. Another factor having a negative impact on VET/enterprise co-operation relates to the structure of the labour market in the country, and specifically to the high rate of unemployment among college and university graduates that allows employers to be able to pick and choose from this 'surplus'. The result is that college and even university graduates often fill jobs requiring lower levels of education and training. It should be added that the graduate's education and training qualifications are not taken into account in terms of the salary offered in such cases.

According to the State Statistics Committee, in recent years about 30 to 40% of the total number of unemployed consists of university or college degree holders, while about 5% of the total unemployed population are young graduates from all levels of vocational education. As of end of 2005, of the 5.7 million unemployed, one-third represented higher education graduates (State Statistics Committee, 2005).

4 Communication or Discourse?

The discussion that follows is aimed at showing that it is too early to speak about a discourse between the VET system and the world of work. At this point in time we can only speak of initial steps towards establishing communication channels between the two systems taken by the most proactive players on both sides.

Both systems—that of employment and VET—have not developed a co-ordinated and informed interpretation of the concept of social partnership/social dialogue that would lay the foundation for articulated and coherent communication. For the most part, VET schools interpret social partnership narrowly as links with enterprises and, occasionally, with employment agencies. Links with enterprises are often limited to inviting employer representatives to sit as members of examining boards, and organizing work placement of students in companies.

It is only very recently that VET schools have begun to ask enterprises about their requirements concerning the skills and competences of workers and specialists. However, these attempts have not yet been supported by VET standards, which remain largely shaped by the VET system itself. Furthermore, there are neither legislative nor institutional mechanisms to support VET/enterprise links, which has a negative impact on the situation.

As such, both sides lack a culture of co-operation. The recovery and gradual growth of the socio-economic environment, with urban areas taking the lead, shows signs of the business community organizing itself. Umbrella or branch organizations have been formed covering self-employed, small, medium or large businesses. Practically all of them show interest in initiating co-operation with education and training.

One positive example is the Russian Union of Entrepreneurs and Industrialists,[2] embracing 328,000 physical and legal entities from all sectors of the economy and all regions of Russia. Spurred by its members, in 2005 the union instituted two committees, one for the development of occupational and VET standards, and the other for enhancing quality in VET. Both committees aim at fostering links between industry and the VET sector. It can be expected that the joint efforts of employers and VET in developing outcomes-based VET standards will contribute to dealing with the most acute problem, namely that of overcoming the skills mismatch in the labour market.

The lead given by the Union of Entrepreneurs and Industrialists has been followed by the Union of VET Principals, representing about one-half of Russia's 2,800 VET colleges, which is actively involved in both committees.

Other major employers' associations, such as the Co-ordinating Council of Associations of Employers of Russia (uniting thirty-two Russian companies, sectoral and inter-sectoral employer organizations and NGOs) and about eighty smaller associations of entrepreneurs and industrialists, do not have education and training issues on their agendas, nor does the Tripartite Commission—a traditional social partnership body representing the government, employers and employees (represented by the Federation of Independent Trade Unions). The Tripartite Agreement for 2005–2007 does not mention education and training issues (Komarovsky & Blasum, 2005).

In two sectors, employer associations, being dissatisfied with the quality of training, have initiated a movement towards VET. One is the catering sector, where the Federation of Restaurant Owners and Hoteliers developed occupational standards as early as the end of the 1990s with the support of the Ministry of Labour. The other—the Association of Construction Workers initiated by the German construction company Knauf, an active player of the Russian market—undertook to develop occupational standards for a number of building trades. Unfortunately, both occupational standards have failed to have any impact on standards, but are widely used by VET schools that have accommodated the employment needs in their training programmes.

The Federation of Restaurant Owners and Hoteliers is currently launching another project in conjunction with the NGO Centre for VET Studies to update the standards and pilot the catalogue of occupations and qualifications for this sector, to be further complemented by a catalogue of training modules.

It is interesting to note that on the sector level employers are more aware of an urgent need of a shift towards market-oriented competence-based VET system than the VET system itself. However, at the grassroots level, the first steps towards social dialogue are often made by proactive VET schools and colleges.

The above endeavours are well in line with the policy declarations of the federal government urging closer links between education and training and the labour market as a pre-requisite for making the Russian economy more competitive and the welfare of society more comprehensive. These declarations are contained in such policy documents as the National Doctrine of Education, the Strategy of Educational Modernization, the Strategy of Social and Economic Development of the Russian Federation for the medium-term period, and the Priorities for the Development of Education in the Russian Federation (Lomonosov Moscow State University, 2002).

The first practical steps to bridge the gap between the world of work and VET have been taken only recently when the federal government adopted an Action Plan for VET Development that envisaged the setting of basic occupational standards.

It has to be noted, with a degree of regret, that before the restructuring of the federal ministries in 2004, the former Ministries of Education and Labour had started a dialogue about the relevance of VET for the labour market. However, as a result of the restructuring that took place in 2004, the Ministry of Labour was abolished, leaving behind only a Federal Employment Service and a division within the Ministry of Health and Social Development to address labour-market issues. As it is, the Federal Employment Service is dealing mostly with unemployment, while the above-mentioned division has not yet shown visible signs of activity in areas relating to occupational standards.

Apart from emerging attempts by employers to co-operate with education and training, and by the government to regulate this co-operation, a certain movement is observed on the VET side under the impact of international projects, especially those supported by the European Community (the Tacis Programme). Among major multi-national projects, some have in real terms contributed to fostering VET/labour-market links:

- the Tacis project 'VET Reform in the North-West of Russia' supported by donors from different European countries and co-ordinated by the European Training Foundation;
- the Tacis DELPHI-I and DELPHI-II projects;
- the Tacis Institution Building Partnership Programme (IBPP) Russian-Finnish project 'Social dialogue in VET';
- the Tacis IBPP Russian-Irish project 'Adult education' (European Commission, 2005a, 2005b, 2005c).

Due to these projects' input:

- labour-market orientation of VET institutions has grown by means of piloting skills, needs analysis procedures and competence-based VET curricula;
- VET content has been reviewed in a number of occupations;
- employers' motivation and involvement has grown for the logistical, information, personnel and social support of VET schools;
- employers began to be more actively involved in the governance of VET institutions and in accreditation procedures;

- skills councils have been established in a number of regions in such sectors as catering, construction, the clothes industry, the chemical industry and machine-building to address the issue of supply and demand of skills, assessment of competences and content of VET. At this stage the councils unite small and medium enterprises, employment services, trade unions and VET schools and, in a few cases, officials from the regional administrations (departments of labour). These councils have been made possible by the DELPHI-II project. The first year has proved a success and led to the assumption that, once employers see the benefits and returns of co-operating with VET, they will respond by investing their time and resources. It can be expected that, with time, these councils may lead to the establishment of sector councils on the federal level that would institutionalize the dialogue mechanism of enterprises/VET co-operation.[3] More and more VET schools are involving employers in their governing bodies (boards of trustees, advisory boards).

As has been indicated earlier, there is no legal framework for the involvement of labour-market partners in VET, except for an internal regulation of the Ministry of Education, 'On social partnership at secondary VET schools (colleges)', stipulating that colleges develop social partner mechanisms and conclude agreements with enterprises to ensure the provision of work experience placements for students, as well as some other issues.

On the regional level, some attempts have been made to institute joint bodies that would assist in bridging the gap between the supply of and demand for skills and promote education and training, including on-the-job training. As a rule they are affiliated to the office of the regional governor or to the regional administration. These bodies, bearing a variety of names (co-ordinating council, council for the framework policy, consultative councils, regional sector councils for employment policies, initial VET councils, etc.) in different regions, unite companies, local administrations and VET and higher education institutions.

However, whatever organisms have been put in place locally or regionally, for the most part they do not address fundamental issues of VET—co-operation with enterprises (i.e. building a dialogue between the two systems)—limiting themselves to identifying the quantitative demand for occupations and jobs and translating them into target intake figures for VET schools. This is in most cases largely a 'hit and miss' undertaking as, first, there are no reliable methodologies to anticipate labour-market developments and, second, enterprises themselves are, for the most part, unable either to articulate their vision of the future or to anticipate changes in the demand for skills.

One of a few exceptions is the Co-ordinating Council in Kemerovskaya Oblast, which is involved in planning and organizing the training of workers and specialists for the coal-mining enterprises of the region (coal-mining being the key sector regionally).

Other examples of communication between the labour market and VET players are the various agreements concluded regionally or at the municipal level between employment service agencies and VET administration bodies,[4] or tripartite and sector agreements (e.g. in the Moscow region) to promote the training of unemployed youth in an occupation relevant for the local labour market. There are also direct agreements between individual VET schools and employer enterprises (on internships for students, staff (re)training, the supply of materials and shared use of equipment, etc.). About 60% of VET colleges have agreements with employment agencies and enterprises. These and other forms of effective enterprise/VET co-operation are explored in more detail below.

5 Samples of Best Practice

As has been indicated above, one format of VET/enterprise co-operation is the so-called 'training under contracts with enterprises' that can take a number of forms: one is training of students in specific occupations established by the enterprise. The advantage of such training is that enterprises can in this case 'dictate' their requirements on the content of training (of course, within the limits of the present VET standard), or they can initiate training for a new occupation relevant for the enterprise or courses meeting specific company needs. Under agreements with VET schools, companies are known to have introduced courses into the curriculum aimed at familiarizing students with the functioning of the enterprise and its corporate culture, with a subsequent certification of students by the enterprise. Students studying under contracts with enterprises usually begin working for the company during their final years of training.

Sometimes agreements for training target groups for the enterprise are concluded between local authorities on whose territory the company is situated and the VET school/college. In this case tuition as such is free of charge. However, the enterprise may offer some sort of financial support, both to students and to the school, especially if the enterprise wants a new course to be introduced.

This form, attractive as it may look, has one major weakness: contracts signed between the enterprise, the VET school and the student are legally binding only for the enterprise and the VET school in the part relating to financial obligations, while having no legal obligations for the student whose tuition has been paid for by the enterprise. Hence, if upon completion graduates refuse to work for the enterprise, they cannot be made to repay the costs of training. This is the way the law currently functions and, naturally, attempts are being made to amend it, under pressure from major corporations who invest heavily in VET and higher education contracts.

Contracts are also signed for in-service training of the staff of the enterprise at VET schools and for upskilling VET teachers at the enterprise. Unfortunately, the latter has not become common practice and is not mandatory. However schools practising this model have appreciated its added value. It should be stressed that such training contracts emerge only when a sustainable zone of trust between the school and the enterprise has been formed.

It is common for VET schools and enterprises to jointly perform vocational orientation measures for schoolchildren and first-year students. However, these measures mostly envisage visits by representatives from the enterprise to general secondary schools and study visits by schoolchildren and young students to the enterprise. Only a few enterprises provide extensive information support for vocational orientation, except for large developing enterprises that are committed to a systemic approach in attracting candidates to VET schools that are part of the corporate infrastructure (such as the Norkickel Company, or RUSAL (Russian Aluminium) Company, for example) (Analytical Centre 'Expert', 2005a).

Well-established developing companies are becoming increasingly aware of their social responsibility and initiate innovative actions to interact with regional administrations in support of VET and higher education. For example, in 2004 the government of St Petersburg adopted a regulation 'On measures to develop the system of secondary VET in St Petersburg for the years 2004-2007' aimed at enhancing the market orientation of VET schools and colleges. The regulation has resulted in co-operation agreements concluded by a number of leading companies with the regional government aimed at shared financial support of a number of VET schools and colleges (on a 50/50 basis).

Proactive companies are also known to equip special workshops at their enterprises for the practical training of VET students or to modernize workshops in VET schools—as most VET schools cannot afford new equipment, materials or supplies themselves.

On the whole, both proactive enterprises and VET schools are very serious about the work placement periods for students, as the companies take advantage of these periods to pick the best candidates for employment at the enterprise, and thus minimize the adaptation period that may take from one to three years, depending on the company. We may contrast this with companies that have failed to perceive the added value of co-operating with VET schools and who may even charge for accepting students for work experience.

Some companies and VET schools agree to share the responsibility for training specialists: VET schools deliver theoretical training and all practical training is covered by the enterprise. During the first two years costs of practical training are met by the VET school as students do not yet have qualifications of use to the enterprise, while during years three and four the costs of practical training are covered by the company. A number of companies—though not many—pay VET schools for every graduate who has worked at the enterprise for over six months.

Attempts are made, for example by the RUSAL Company, to establish their own corporate universities that would embrace programmes at five levels:

- level 1: vocational orientation;
- level 2: VET (to train workers and line managers, and upskill them);
- level 3: higher education;
- level 4: in-service education;
- level 5: individual training for top managers/executives (State Statistics Committee, 2005).

The company is currently devising standards for all levels of training. Such efforts can only be commended. However, they arouse certain concerns relating to the compatibility of these standards with the State education and training standards and, hence, the future mobility of the workforce may be in jeopardy.

It should be stressed that proactive companies often choose to set up training centres of their own affiliated to the company, having little trust in State VET schools. Such training centres would offer training in most occupations of initial VET and may also commission training from VET schools in those occupations that these schools are known to deliver to the standard acceptable by the company. Such training centres may be launched in locations where there are no State VET schools, providing training in occupations required by companies based there.

Other types of communication between VET and labour-market players can be summed up as follows:

- to motivate students to stick with their occupation of training, big companies (such as, for example, RUSAL, Sibneft, Vneshtorgbank and others) establish scholarship schemes for students who commit themselves to working for the company upon graduation;[5]
- competitions of student projects (grant competitions) initiated by companies to pick the best undergraduates as prospective job candidates;
- to ensure high standards of teaching, companies may offer grants to teachers, arrange study visits and training for the faculty at enterprises, or send their specialists to teach at educational establishments;
- joint projects carried out by students for the benefit of the company;
- companies may provide temporary summer jobs for students to replace workers/employees while the latter are on vacation, and organize visits to the company on a regular basis.

Summing up the emerging labour market/VET communication channels, it can be concluded with a certain amount of confidence that signals coming from both ends of the scale are numerous and diversified—and sometimes contradictory! It is obvious, though, that the zone of trust between VET and labour-market partners is not yet adequate. The key reasons for this are input-based standards and lack of awareness of its added value by both parties. The initiative of proactive companies taking the responsibility for training (complementary as it may be) carries a latent threat to the State VET system, undermining its credibility. Also, such companies can by no means meet the country's education and training needs. Corporate education and training puts a huge number of small and medium enterprises at a disadvantage because they cannot afford to invest in VET and have to rely on the State system.

In this situation, the VET system should pay more heed to the signals coming from proactive enterprises and respond to them flexibly.

6 Signals from Enterprises

Independent surveys tell us that companies are more often dissatisfied, not so much with the occupational/technical competences of VET and higher education graduates, but with their soft skills/competences. Advanced and sustainable companies are more concerned with the candidate's 'potential' and personal qualities, than with technical skills and knowledge, especially if the company has a training centre of its own where candidates can be brought up to company standards.

Another 'gap' identified by employers is the graduates' lack of knowledge and understanding of the way companies function. This is often a result of the fact that VET schools and colleges are either unaware of these issues, for lack of communication with the world of work, or do not bother to find out how companies operate in terms of major business processes and the roles of qualified specialists within the hierarchy. It is an open secret that teachers delivering theoretical subjects have often not worked at enterprises for more than a dozen years—if at all—and hence teaching and learning are organized in a way that is little related to the real world.

Many VET schools would claim, however, that their graduates are doing well on the labour market as they do not receive any direct complaints from companies. Such VET schools overlook the fact that employers in most cases simply have no choice and have to make the best of the available graduates in a situation of fairly low labour mobility in the country. As it is, VET schools lack systemic tracer studies and hence have no data about how well their graduates fare on the labour market.

Dissatisfied with educational modernization, leading Russian companies are implementing their own models of personnel development that may or may not involve VET schools. These models embrace company training centres, corporate universities, continuing training and adaptation schemes and aim at addressing training needs of companies that are often more dynamic than the supply provided by the State or private providers.

Education and training schemes taken on board by companies and implemented through their training centres primarily focus on developing such skills as personal efficiency and management skills that VET schools have failed to equip their students with. Big companies that can afford it extensively resort to distance learning and multi-media courses that the individual can master at the work place, or at a university/college where he/she is doing a course of study. Contrary to the VET system, companies commonly opt for modular training schemes.

Practically all companies complain about the VET standards, as does the VET sector itself. Most companies claim that businesses should dictate their requirements to the State system of education, and the latter should match these requirements.

Companies that use their profits to invest in training complain about a lack of tax incentives and suggest that the State and business should share education and training costs, explaining that they have, apart from other things, to re-train VET graduates before the latter can be effectively employed in the company. Both the VET sector and companies are affected by:

- the low-prestige of qualified workers and a shortage of the workforce in such occupations as machine operators, welders, metalworkers, blacksmiths, and some others that benefit from low demand;
- a lack or shortage of VET schools and curricula in certain occupations (e.g. ichthyology);

- an outflow of young people from rural areas into bigger cities;
- a lack of labour-market forecasting tools.

In the context of the labour-market players' growing concern about the quality of VET graduates, the VET sector has to be more proactive in proving its relevance for enterprises by:

- changing its approach to VET standards, making them market-oriented and flexible and introducing competence-based VET;
- institutionalizing and supporting best models of VET—enterprise co-operation building on the best practices already available across Russia and 'products' yielded by international projects;[6]
- taking on board practical tools to engage and motivate employers and their associations;
- matching and updating VET content to the regional labour markets' demand in terms of occupations for training and the quality of outcomes;
- initiating measures to support training specialists in occupations enjoying low popular demand (possibly by sharing costs between the State and companies).

It is also in the interests of the VET system to actively lobby for amendments to the Tax Code relating to tax benefits for enterprises involved and investing in VET. However, it may well be expected that companies and corporations are better-placed to do this themselves. Nevertheless, if the VET system fails to contribute to the process, the eventual amendments are likely to be of benefit only to large companies, leaving small and medium enterprises (SMEs) on the 'outskirts'. Thus, the cleavage between large proactive and profitable companies and smaller ones that are supposed to constitute the bulk of the market economy would be widened, with ensuing negative consequences for the economy, society and citizens.

Today is the right time for the VET system to consolidate and show its role, with the modernization processes well under way, including the optimization of the network of VET schools and the decentralization of governance.

7 Conclusions

Despite objective economic and psychological problems that account for differences between sectors, regions, VET schools and companies, there is a fundamental problem that impedes adequate skills supply by the system of education, namely a lack of a national qualifications framework (NFQ) that would assign uniform requirements to every level of qualifications of the work force, and would be linked to awards at every level of education. The NFQ would assist in identifying generic requirements to skills and competences of VET and university graduates as needed by employers and could be used to formulate educational standards, thus bringing the two societal systems nearer together.

It is also obvious that teaching and learning should be brought closer to the working environment, which can be achieved by intensifying and streamlining practical training periods/work assignments of students, as is already done by proactive companies and VET schools.

Another issue is teacher qualifications that have to be enhanced. Incentives have to be devised to attract younger generations to work for VET. More company employees and executives should be involved in teaching. This is not feasible for SMEs that would not have enough staff to release for these purposes. However, SMEs should promote networking and closer links with big companies that have already demonstrated examples of best practices in addressing this issue.

On the whole, business/educational co-operation is an issue directly related to the social responsibility of both parties, and the sooner they develop an awareness of it, the better it will be both for education and for companies. To this end, more information support should be provided highlighting this perspective on the co-operation and disseminating of best practices both from Russia and abroad.

Notes

1. VET school is the generic name for various types and levels of VET institutions in Russia that will be used in the chapter, unless otherwise specified.
2. The Union was set up in 1990 to unite companies and enterprises from most sectors of the economy, including industrial, financial, business, insurance and leasing ones. It includes about 100 branch offices and corporate associations.
3. It should be stressed though that chambers of commerce are practically uninvolved in the promotion of enterprise involvement with education and training. The only positive example can be attributed to the outputs of the Delphi-I project in Samarskaya Oblast (the Volga Region), where the local Chamber of Commerce and Industry initiated the regional law on 'Participation of Enterprises of Different Types of Ownership in Training, Re-training and Upskilling Workers and Specialists in VET Schools' (European Commission, 2005a).
4. Employment services purchase training from about 3,000 VET schools across Russia, selected through a tender (National Observatory for Professional Education, 2004).
5. The percentage of graduates taking jobs in occupations other than their occupation of training remains high and, in some periods (e.g. end of the 1990s), reached up to 80%.
6. The most effective instruments for 'catching the eye' of employers, as shown by the international VET projects, include the following:

   - skill-needs analysis (regular skill-needs analysis has proved to establish improved links between education and the business community);
   - involvement of enterprises in the development of the content of training;
   - participation of enterprise staff as part-time teachers at VET schools;
   - involvement of employers in assessing student competence;
   - internships of VET teachers and trainers at enterprises.

References

Analytical Centre 'Expert'. 2005a. *Curricula and education and training technologies of Russian corporations.* Moscow.

Analytical Centre 'Expert'. 2005b. *Universities and employers on graduates and reform of education.* Moscow.

European Commission. 2005a. *Final report of the TACIS IBPP project 'Adult Education'*. Brussels.

European Commission. 2005b. *Final report of the TACIS IBPP project 'Social dialogue in VET'*. Brussels.

European Commission. 2005c. *Recommendations of Delphi II project 'Development of education links and initiatives in VET and higher education'*. Brussels.

Komarovsky, V.; Blasum, E. 2005. *The role of Russian employers in promoting social dialogue.* Moscow: Analytical Centre for Developing Social Partnership.

Lomonosov Moscow State University. 2002. *Modernisation of Russian education.* Moscow: Lomonosov Moscow State University, Higher School of Economics.

National Observatory for Professional Education. 2004. *VET update: stocktaking report.* Moscow.

State Statistics Committee. 2005. *Labour market data, 2000-2005.* Moscow: Official Publications.

Chapter IV.14
Strengthening TVET to Achieve Lifelong Learning for All: Historical Snapshots and Recent Initiatives in Myanmar

Naing Yee Mar

1 Introduction

In order to keep pace with developments in the world, there are currently moves to make TVET a vehicle for meeting emerging needs in the livelihoods of young people and adults. To some extent, this will also benefit the national social and economic situation. Countries often hope that the potential of TVET and the impact of its contributions in achieving these aims can be fully realized not only by improving the quality of TVET programmes but also by promoting lifelong learning opportunities for every individual. This chapter therefore examines the importance of TVET in promoting vocational competencies as part of the lifelong learning process for all, and explores its dynamic in developing countries, with particular reference to the situation in Myanmar.

The TVET system in Myanmar is based on shared responsibility by different ministries through a variety of forms of delivery, with the result that its curricula are highly diverse. Not many empirical studies have been conducted as yet to evaluate the effectiveness of TVET in Myanmar. As a result, there is very limited documentation on issues relevant to vocational policies and practices that focus on a competency-based lifelong-learning oriented approach.

This implies that the availability of statistical information in the field of technical, agriculture and vocational education is a limiting factor. Therefore, the scope of this study focuses rather on secondary and post-secondary school-based vocational education and training programmes offered in the areas of technical, agricultural and vocational education by the different specialized ministries in Myanmar. These programmes aim to enable learners to cope with the emerging challenges relating to job opportunities in the various economic sectors. They also encourage lifelong learning for all through the creation of flexibility and accessibility to TVET.

2 Why TVET?

Traditionally, technical and vocational education carries the principal responsibility of developing the labour force in a country. This, in turn, improves productivity. Notwithstanding, current changes in technological, socio-economic and cultural

R. Maclean, D. Wilson (eds.), *International Handbook of Education for the Changing World of Work*, DOI 10.1007/978-1-4020-5281-1_IV.14,
© Springer Science+Business Media B.V. 2009

environments, including profound changes due to the impact of information and communication technologies (ICTs) and the computerization of society, have stimulated the role of TVET to go beyond traditional approaches and practices. This is particularly true in relation to policy formulation and implementation, and the relevant strategies and structures (UNESCO, 1999, p. 61).

In reviewing the issues of TVET on aspects of lifelong learning, the Dakar Framework for Action on Education for All (EFA) consists of six goals stressing the importance of both accessibility to learning opportunity and continuous learning possibilities for all young people and adults beyond primary school. Along with the Dakar Framework for Action on EFA, the Millennium Goals (UNESCO, 2000) encapsulate eight main ways of assisting developing countries in achieving economic and social development. Those that are particularly important relate directly to the quality of education.

2.1 TVET in Relation to Environmental Variables

What the concept of promoting TVET as part of the lifelong learning process actually means for a community or an individual differs from one country to another. Each country has its own unique set of environmental forces—socio-cultural, political-legal, technological, economic—which have a strong impact on the educational environment. These variables in the societal environments may not constitute national educational activities in the short term, but can, and often do, affect the long-term development of education. In addition to these societal considerations, governments, local communities, educational suppliers and learners, as well as trends in labour markets, directly influence the effectiveness of education and, in turn, are affected by it.

In essence, countries apply different approaches to reform and promote TVET as an essential component of the total educational process. To give some examples: countries like Singapore, Thailand, Taiwan, India and Myanmar provide more TVET opportunities at the secondary and post-secondary levels, compared to the importance placed on expanding compulsory education in countries such as Cambodia, Viet Nam and Laos (Cheng, 2005; Mar, 2004). Countries such as Ghana, Senegal and Swaziland have decided to incorporate a measure of vocational content into general education programmes at the primary or lower secondary level, in order to prepare young people for wage employment or self-employment, if they do not continue with their schooling (Atchoarena cited in Wilson, 2005, p. 76). In Ghana, Kenya and Botswana, the drive for vocationalization has been strongest at the junior secondary level (Lauglo, 2005).

Since countries have expressed great concern about the future development of their TVET systems, it is important that these systems are able to meet the needs of both adults and young people, and secure the basis for future development. These concerns relate to: (a) how individuals can be encouraged (and assisted) to fully participate in the digital age; (b) what efforts can be made to reach individuals who are often 'hidden away' from view in different corners of their country, mainly in rural areas; and (c) to what extent they can retain young people in the education system for as long as possible and offer flexibility of learning.

Overall, TVET needs to evolve through the educational process by initiating a future-oriented policy and strategic educational planning to foster the all-round development of nations. It should also provide a sound foundation with further opportunities in education for those individuals who may wish to profit from lifelong education.

Whether 'education and training' are delivered through formal, non-formal or informal means, they aim to develop human resources in the interests of employability and better citizenship. They will also inculcate a continuum of improvements concerning initiatives for each individual's livelihood and will encourage them to live and work harmoniously with others.

2.2 TVET in Relation to Vocational Competencies

The broad concept of vocational competency is concerned with an individual's ability to cope with, and capitalize on, the unique challenges and opportunities demanded by the working environment. Vocational competency is an important characteristic of human capacities that TVET can provide exceedingly well. It is a key strength that can be embedded in any individual and may be carefully built on and accumulated over time. It may also be called a core capability, because it includes a number of constituent skills (Wheelen & Hunger, 1998, p. 160) that can be a means of securing the necessities of life.

What is classed as vocational competency is also, at least in part, context-specific, in that the competencies required by an individual to function effectively in his or her society depend upon the social and economic context of that society. In reviewing vocational competencies in the context of developing countries, trends in the economic sector of society can have an obvious impact on the vocational competencies of individuals, especially in a country like Myanmar. It is, therefore, important to develop both understandings, not only based on what is expected of individuals in their various working environments, but also the individuals' capacity to extend their capabilities.

3 TVET and Its Implications for Lifelong Learning in Myanmar

3.1 Societal Considerations

The size of Myanmar's population[1] was 40.76 million in 1990 and had increased to 53 million by 2004. Geographically, Myanmar, with an area of 676,553 square kilometres, is divided into fourteen administrative areas—seven states and seven divisions. Broadly speaking, the seven different states are each dominated by a major ethnic group, whereas the seven divisions are dominated by the largest group—the Barmar.

Myanmar is a country with enormous indigenous ethnic diversity, consisting of over 135 ethnic groups. Some 73.4% of the population lives in remote and rural areas. Thus, one of the matters of increasing concern in the Myanmar education sector is to focus on how such a diverse population can be motivated to take increased responsibility for its own effective lifelong learning. This is particularly important in the perspective of developing sustainable economic livelihoods. Gender wise, women in Myanmar account for 51% of the total population and are taking more and more initiatives. They are playing an active role in society to better their own living conditions in parallel with the continual evolution of socio-economic conditions.

It is estimated that 64.1% of the population is engaged in the agricultural sector, while Myanmar's industrial workers account for just 8.4% of the population. The service sector involves 18% of the population. This structure has remained largely unchanged over the past two decades. Traditionally, the Myanmar economy relies on the primary sector: agriculture, livestock, fishing and forestry.

The structural characteristics of the labour force, presenting the employed population by industrial groups as reported in the '1990 Labour Force Survey', showed that almost 60% of the total labour force is engaged in the primary sector. This sector is the main contributor to gross domestic product (59.9%). With the population growing at about 2% per annum, this translates into a per capita income increase of about 4% per year. Public expenditure has been restricted by a low and declining rate of revenue collection, which, at 5.1% of gross domestic product (GDP) in 1999–2000, was among the lowest in the world.

The structure of the economy has not evolved much since market reforms began and led to an average annual growth rate of 5.1%. As a consequence, public revenue has been insufficient to allocate public expenditure to important public services, in particular, education and health.

In turn, the demand for specific levels of investment in skills, knowledge and education may directly affect the growth or decline of productivity in these different sectors. During the Four-Year Economic Development Plan Period (1992–1996), the productivity of the different sectors in GDP—namely, production, services and trade—was approximately 60%, 18% and 22% respectively (Myanmar. Ministry of National Planning and Economic Development, 1998). The agricultural sector has contributed approximately 38% of total GDP in that period, whilst the manufacturing sector generates only 9%.

To accompany these figures, statistical information, such as members of the working population who have completed a vocational course to at least secondary vocational training level, or employment/unemployment by educational level, is still not available.

In an agro-based country like Myanmar, the role of self-employed family workers is of particular importance. This is most critical where agricultural holdings are operated on a household basis and where self-employed labour in various agricultural activities is most common. Most of these self-employed family workers reside in rural areas.

A new economic policy and development situation has been introduced since 1988 through a series of reforms. As a result, Myanmar has increasingly turned its attention to raising productivity, as well as modernizing and upgrading skills, especially in the primary sector. This is important not only because the country needs to improve its levels of productivity by making the best use of the available resources, but also because the problems of limited access to knowledge and skills are making it more difficult to respond appropriately to changes resulting from the information age.

3.2 Prospects and Concerns in Myanmar Education

3.2.1 Structure of the School and Reforms

Following the 1998 educational reforms, by 2004 schooling in Myanmar had been changed from ten to eleven grades in basic education. This now consists of five years of primary and six years of secondary schooling (lower secondary consists of grades six to nine, and upper secondary of grades ten and eleven). These are followed by several types of higher education institutions.

The Ministry of Education (MOE) is functionally the main sponsor of education and training, especially in the areas of basic education and teacher training. The major higher education institutions, which numbered sixty-four in 2004, also fall under the responsibility of the MOE. Ninety-nine other institutions are currently under eleven different ministries and the Public Services Selection and Training Board.

Although the activities of these higher education institutions are decentralized and administered by thirteen different ministries, academic and administrative policy relating to higher education is centralized and managed by two councils: the Universities' Central Council; and the Council of University Academic Bodies.

Traditionally, the administrative process throughout the education sector has been centralized, but in recent times there have been moves to decentralize management and responsibility. This is also designed to promote active community participation. However, educational decisions and initiatives remain largely the province of central ministerial departments.

In order to lay the foundation for an education system that is well co-ordinated and equitable, the Myanmar Naing-ngan Education Committee was established in 1991. This committee has overall responsibility for major policy matters, establishing budget priorities and general supervision of the whole educational process.

The underlying goal of educational reform was to create an education system that would generate a learning society capable of facing the challenges of the 'Knowledge Age' (Myanmar. MOE, 2004). This was initiated by holding annual seminars in both basic and higher education sectors attended by administrators, teachers and educational specialists. Overall, the objectives of the various educational promotion programmes (EPP) stress not only bringing about quality education at all levels and for all, but also improving the accessibility of a range of educational options for all individuals. Within the framework of these EPP, the MOE has also developed the long-term plan for the education sector (2001–2031) with the aim of transforming the whole of Myanmar society into a lifelong learning society.

3.2.2 Myanmar EFA

Through innovative actions, such as various literacy campaigns and the Myanmar EFA National Action Plan, the literacy rate in Myanmar continues to increase steadily—from 89.7% in 1999 to 93.3% in 2004. Literacy partly contributes to increased output per worker. Thus, attempts to achieve improvements in literacy and EFA may be one of the best efforts a country can make to promote its future economic growth and sustainable development. For example, 'farmers with four years of primary education produce about 13% more than those without such education' (*Financial Times*, 1980, quoted in Stonier, 1983).

The results and recommendations of the EFA Forum, EFA Task Forces and EFA Working Groups have all contributed to an upgrading of basic education. Primary school enrolments have increased from 91% of the cohort (1998–2000) to 96.56% (2004–2005). As all individuals are entitled to access to learning on a lifelong basis, it is notable that post-primary schools, over-aged-children-to-primary-education programmes, and the one-school-in-one-village objectives have been initiated since 2001–2002. These initiatives have addressed situations where access to public schools is difficult.

The quality of basic education is being promoted through curriculum reforms. Since 1998, pre-vocational education and the MOE's newly introduced life-skills curriculum have been redesigned and expanded, particularly in lower and upper secondary formal (general) education. To guarantee a broad view of competencies during the basic system, co-curricular activities are primarily focused on the three main areas—basic communication skills; expansion of knowledge and skill; and attitudinal development—in both the lower and upper secondary school systems.

Monastic education in Myanmar, which follows the official curriculum under the supervision of the Ministry of Religious Affairs, traditionally plays a major role in primary education, as well as in civil society. It is a means of helping individuals to learn social competencies, underpinning Myanmar's attempts to introduce social sustainability.

Evidence shows that Myanmar's EFA strategic activities and policies reflect preventive, reactive and remedial approaches to facilitate and promote lifelong learning. These are under the supervision of the MOE, in collaboration with nine related ministries.

For example, the present retention and completion rates indicate that less than 60% of children complete the full five-year primary cycle (Myanmar. MOE, 2003a). As shown in Fig. 1, for many years drop-outs have been highest in the first grade (KG) and this number has declined from 23% in 1989/1990 to about 18% in 2000/2001. However, dropouts continue to be highest in the first grade.

However, a positive sign is that the drop-out rate in lower secondary level (by the end of grade nine) is decreasing and the education sector review (Myanmar. MOE, 2003a) cited that between 97 and 98% of pupils graduate from lower secondary schools. In addition, 83–84% of those who pass examinations continue their studies at upper secondary level. It also stated that the remaining 15% who left the school should not be considered as drop-outs.

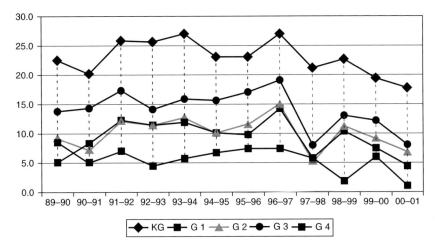

Fig. 1 Drop-out rates in primary schools
Source: Myanmar. MOE, 2003b.

Questions have been raised about these school-leavers. Are they joining TVET schools or not? This underlines the importance of integrating the pre-vocational curriculum into general education, which could be seen as useful for all school-leavers.

Notwithstanding such considerations, and as is the case with other developing countries, unfortunately in Myanmar there are still pockets of out-of-school primary, secondary and post-secondary school-aged youths, who cannot be accommodated by the existing education system. This occurs for a variety of reasons, including poverty, language problems due to membership of different ethnic minority groups, and hardships associated with living in rural areas or in isolated locations with no ready access to education.

These are fundamental issues that must be addressed if the overall quality of EFA activities is to be improved so that all primary education leavers are able to engage in income-generating livelihoods. As a result, non-formal education has become one of the four main EFA goals in Myanmar.

3.2.3 Efforts in Non-Formal Education

One of the main challenges in strengthening TVET as part of the lifelong learning process is its relationship with non-formal education (NFE). NFE in Myanmar focuses on basic educational services for all children, youth and adults who, for various reasons, have not been reached by the formal school system. This includes those who could not afford schooling or have dropped out of school, as well as those who completed primary school but could not continue further. The Myanmar Educational Research Bureau (MERB), which is one of the departments within the MOE, is the focal point for NFE in Myanmar.

In co-operation with the Myanmar Literary Resource Centre (MLRC), MERB is also responsible for training volunteer adult facilitators by conducting a series of national workshops, such as: the National Workshop on Preparation of Vocational Learning Materials; the National Workshop on Preparation of Literacy Learning Materials on Agriculture; and the National Workshop on Development of Strategies for Continuing Education in Myanmar.

NFE programmes include: functional literacy; income generation and quality-of-life improvement programmes; skills-development programmes; individual interest improvement programmes; and future-oriented programmes through continuing education. Learning materials for these continuing education programmes have been developed by MERB through its own facilities.

Alongside the traditional mode, since 2002, MERB has been experimenting with using distance education methods to provide NFE programmes for its facilitators using data broadcasting systems. These programmes are delivered not only through the 640 e-education learning centres, but also through the 750 community learning centres and multimedia classrooms situated in basic education schools in every township. There are 324 townships in the country.

Emphasis still needs to be placed on the necessity of upgrading training opportunities to improve the quality of NFE facilitators. It is also important to enhance the flexibility and effectiveness of existing programmes with regard to the skill development programmes. Viewing NFE at grassroots level, it is one of the crucial factors in realising the goals of TVET for out-of-school youth and adults as part of EFA. Qualified training instructors and ICT learning-support materials are in great demand.

3.3 Approaches to Strengthening TVET in Myanmar

3.3.1 TVET Structure and Reforms

TVET in Myanmar first dates from 1950, shortly after achieving independence from the British (1948). At that time, Myanmar was among the fastest-growing Asian economies since it was well-endowed with natural resources in the 1950s and had a highly literate population. The State was expected to play a leading role in industrializing the economy, while fulfilling the manpower needs of the country was a major concern. However, the current structure of TVET in Myanmar originates in the early period of Burmese Socialism (1972), when the government launched the Twenty-Year Plan. According to this plan, within the framework of Burmese Socialism (1962–88), various reform measures were adopted in a priority shift from heavy industry back to agriculture and the commercialization of State enterprises.

In 1998, to intensify educational reforms, the sixty-five technical, agricultural and vocational institutes and schools (plus one technical teacher-training institute) under the Department of Technical, Agricultural and Vocational Education (DTAVE) were transferred to the other relevant ministries, such as: the Ministry of Science and Technology; the Ministry of Agriculture; the Ministry of Co-operative Affairs; the Ministry of Social Welfare; and the Ministry of Livestock Breeding and Fisheries. The original DTAVE remained, but was renamed the Department of Technical and Vocational Education (DTVE) under the Ministry of Science and Technology, which had been established in 1996. In order to accommodate changes occurring in the economy, currently fifty-six higher-level institutions exist under this ministry, including five technological universities, two computer universities, nine governmental technical institutes (GTIs), twenty-six governmental technical colleges (GTCs) and twenty-four computer colleges. The ministry also has responsibilities in vocational training.

Like some other developing countries (for example, Singapore and Taiwan), Myanmar provides the majority of its vocational and technical training opportunities at the secondary and post-secondary level. If young people are unable or unwilling to continue onto higher education, there are opportunities for them to join various vocational schools and institutes after leaving the general school system, having completed primary and secondary levels. After the educational reform in Myanmar, the formal (general) school cycle has been changed so that students who pass the matriculation examination at the end of the secondary level can join different universities or TVET institutes providing various professional qualifications beyond basic competencies and skills.

3.3.2 TVET Initiatives in Myanmar

Pre-Vocational Education

Some key TVET initiatives in Myanmar are worthy of mention. At the secondary level, the school curriculum has been redesigned and expanded to include pre-vocational subjects (at least 13% of class time is allotted to these subjects per week). However, effective vocationalization in general education has yet to be fully implemented in most of the country's middle and high schools. Even when practical subjects are offered, in some schools these are often constrained or are less effective than anticipated due to limited facilities or a lack of interest on the part of students. Nevertheless, creating opportunities for pre-vocational and vocational education at all levels of basic education is one of the focal points in the Myanmar Long-Term Thirty-Year Education Development Plan (2001–2031) for the basic education sector (Myanmar. MOE, 2004). Relating to curriculum reform, vocational subjects such as industrial arts, agriculture, home economics and fine arts (painting and music) were introduced at the lower secondary level, aimed at providing a foundation for the future. To ensure that a broad range of competencies are covered, co-curriculum subjects at the primary and secondary levels concentrate on three main areas: basic communication skills; expansion of knowledge; and skill and attitudinal development. The desirability of including ICT skills in the curriculum is also becoming increasingly accepted.

Life-skills education at both the primary and secondary levels, as part of the core curriculum, has also been introduced to promote social skills. This includes problem-solving, creative thinking, critical thinking, decision-making, communications, self-awareness, interpersonal skills, empathy and the ability to cope with emotions and stress. Myanmar monastic education has traditionally played a major role in equipping individuals with desirable social competencies.

Since 1998, national centres for human resource development (NCHRD) have been introduced under the MOE. The NCHRDs aim at facilitating the satisfaction of community needs by launching vocational, professional and technology-based courses that are in demand. These centres provide a number of courses in partnership with foreign and local private enterprises.

The NCHRD are located at universities, educational institutes, degree colleges and colleges under the MOE. These centres offer a wide variety of options in the form of certificate, diploma or degree courses in the fields of foreign languages, computer science, computer engineering, accountancy, business management, environmental studies, multi-media arts, gemmology, cosmetic technology, law and teaching—all with a strong emphasis on promoting vocational skills. These are income-generating courses that enable the institutes involved to provide supplementary remuneration for their staff. These courses are undertaken by students in addition to their regular courses at these institutions. They develop more options and consequently more career choices for the young people of Myanmar.

Technical Education

Currently, nine governmental technical institutes (GTIs) under the Ministry of Science and Technology offer two-year courses to gain the GTI certificate, replacing the three-year courses that were offered before the reforms. The number of courses provided in these institutions has been expanded from eight in 1987/1988 to fifteen since 2003/2004. This represents a significant increase in enrolments compared to 1987/1988 (Table 2).

After the reforms, all the technical high schools were upgraded into governmental technical colleges (GTCs) to meet the needs of those students who have graduated from lower secondary schools but who did not continue their education at upper secondary schools. Twenty-six GTCs have gradually been introduced in all states and divisions throughout Myanmar to provide technical education. In the decade following 1987, the rapid establishment of industrialized zones in many states and divisions has brought about a noticeable increase of enrolment in these institutes and colleges (Myanmar. MOE, 2001).

The curricula of the GTIs and GTCs are designed with a theory/practical ratio of 40:60. The curriculum, syllabus and instructional materials have been updated, and students have been encouraged to carry out more practical exercises related to their chosen subjects. It is evident that existing courses do not adequately provide the knowledge and skills needed for employment and, therefore, re-training is often required once the individuals involved have found employment.

The breakdown of the intake by type of courses offered in GTIs in 2003/2004 is shown in Table 1. Although trends cannot be readily discerned in the choice of each subject from a single year, nevertheless current statistics indicate a significant increase in the number of students studying technical subjects. The average numbers

Table 1 Intake by type of course in the government technical institutes (GTIs) in 2003/2004

Type of course	Intake			
	Male	Female	Total	Total (%)
Civil engineering	797	892	1,689	16.1
Electrical engineering (power)	1,353	809	2,162	20.6
Electrical engineering (electrical & communications)	794	694	1,488	14.7
Mechanical engineering (power)	1,632	303	1935	18.5
Mining engineering	22	–	22	0.2
Mechatronic	382	156	538	5.1
Information technology	207	424	631	6.0
Food and chemical	19	56	75	0.7
Plastic and rubber	28	36	64	0.6
Architect	33	115	148	1.4
Textile	33	48	81	0.8
Petroleum	86	–	86	0.8
Metallurgy	48	24	72	0.7
Bio Gas	119	54	173	1.7
		264	1,316	12.6

Source: Prepared by the Myanmar UNEVOC Centre/MERB, 2004.

Table 2 Teaching staff and students in the government technical institutes (GTIs) and government technical colleges (GTCs)

Academic year	No. of GTIs & GTCs	Teaching staff	Enrolment	Average no. of students	No. of teachers	Teacher/ student ratio
1984/85	7	202	4,374	625	29	1:22
1985/86	8	288	4,819	602	36	1:17
1986/87	10	424	5,721	572	42	1:13
1987/88	10	426	6,493	649	43	1:15
2003/04	35	3,378	23,225	664	96	1:7

Source: Prepared by the Myanmar UNEVOC Centre/MERB, 2004.

of teaching/learning hours per week prescribed by DTAVE are thirty-two for a student and eighteen for a teacher in the GTIs. Table 2 also shows the average number of students and teachers per GTI/GTC and teacher/student ratios. These were favourable over the 1984–2004 period in comparison with the higher-education average of 1:20.

Agricultural Education

Since Myanmar is basically an agricultural country, there is a great demand for middle-range technicians in that sector. To fulfil this need, in 1954 the Myanmar Government, with assistance from the Ford Foundation, established a State Agricultural Institute offering a three-year diploma course in agricultural technology. There is also a great need for skilled workers in the agriculture sector. Consequently, the Myanmar Government has opened agricultural high schools (AHSs) and State agricultural institutes (SAIs).

A series of interviews conducted by the author of this chapter with key stakeholders in the Ministry of Agriculture, as well as with students, revealed that the major reason for students not being interested in joining the SAIs was: 'no opportunity to get a proper job after completion of the training period'. It is no doubt for this reason that between 1984 and 1988 enrolment levels decreased dramatically—though enrolment in 2003/2004 has improved (Table 3). The seven SAIs under the Ministry of Agriculture offer three-year courses in agriculture and animal husbandry, granting a diploma in agriculture after the successful completion of the course. The curriculum and instructional materials used in the SAIs are based mainly on traditional methods of cultivation and are highly theoretical, rather than reflecting advanced techniques in agriculture. Concerning the quality of skills development in the agricultural sector, the curriculum of the SAI programmes is designed with a theory/practical ratio of 40:60.

Table 3 also shows the average number of students and teachers per SAI. Teacher/student ratios were favourable over the period 1984–1989 in comparison with an average ratio in higher education of 1:20. The average numbers of teaching/learning hours per week prescribed by DTAVE in the SAIs are forty-four for a student and twenty-two for a teacher.

The subject 'rural education', which includes farm management and agricultural extension, accounts for only 9% of the total teaching time. Graduates receiving a diploma in agriculture are eligible for employment in the Myanmar Agriculture Service as extension agents at the level of the Deputy Township Manager. However, experience has shown that graduates lack many of the practical skills actually required to carry out the job.

Recent statistical information on the AHSs is not readily available. Nevertheless, it is known that enrolments in these schools have been declining, from 1,216 in 1996/1997 to 648 in 1997/1998. A key assumption concerning decreasing enrolments in agricultural schools and institutes includes the massive introduction of ICTs elsewhere in the education system through the involvement of computer companies. As was pointed out earlier, the agricultural certificate awarded does not adequately qualify graduates to find reasonable jobs and, of course, most jobs are necessarily available in rural areas.

Table 3 Teaching staff and student relationship in the State agricultural institutes (SAIs)

Academic year	No. of SAIs	Teaching staff	Enrolment	Avge. of students	No. of teachers/SAI	Teacher/student ratio
1984/85	6	96	1,152	192	16	1:12
1985/86	6	140	907	151	23	1:6
1986/87	7	155	790	113	22	1:5
1987/88	7	170	695	99	24	1:4
2003/04	7	193	2,972	Not yet available	Not yet available	Not yet available

Source: Prepared by the Myanmar UNEVOC Centre/MERB, 2004.

A persistent criticism of the agricultural education provided is that the facilities of the programmes and schools are not attractive to the younger generation, with particular reference to the lack of practical exercises provided by schools. An ICT-based learning environment might encourage learners and teachers to achieve better performance levels. However, computer-based teaching/learning is still very limited in the agricultural sector compared to technical education, and teaching methods are less advanced.

Vocational Education

Non-industrial training, including commercial training, is carried out either on-the-job or in vocational schools that follow a very practical non-academic type of course that does not correspond to the traditional academic years. For the last ten years the number of vocational schools has tripled, while total enrolment has increased by four times. Except for commercial schools, the semi-skilled training provided by DTAVE falls into two basic categories:

- Post-primary schools offering vocational training to those young people who have completed part or all of their primary education; and
- Post-middle schools for students who have obtained a middle-school certificate. These schools offer an artisan type of training.

In 1997, to intensify educational reforms, the vocational training schools formerly under the Ministry of Education were also transferred to the relevant ministries. Table 4 shows the number of graduates who have successfully completed these respective TVET institutions (diploma level) and schools existing during the reporting period under various government ministries.

Table 4 Skills training in TVET institutions under various government ministries

Institution	1997/98	1998/99	1999/00	2000/01	2001/02	2002/03
Ministry of Co-operatives						
Commercial schools	749	1490	555	881	578	420
Myanmar Lacquer-ware Institute	39	37	49	36	27	25
Weaving schools	137	129	89	353	233	212
Co-operative colleges	–	511	369	541	620	714
Co-operative training schools	699	832	685	846	541	573
Ministry of Science and Technology						
Handicraft schools	1244	556	984	707	566	519
Machinery repair and maintenance schools	180	85	80	102	72	62
Ministry of Social Welfare, Relief and Resettlement						
School of Home Science	1900	1424	1287	1619	1883	1367

Source: Myanmar. Ministry of Labour, 2005.

4 Lessons Learnt from the Myanmar Experience

During the educational reform process, the decentralization of responsibilities for technical, agriculture and vocational schools, training centres and institutes under different ministries represents an attempt to achieve a more cost-effective, practical and applied way of teaching and learning through TVET. The ministries have been steadily playing a greater role in the planning phase. This process is continuing and ministries are now more able to embrace a systematic alignment of overall management, education policies and processes, mindset and culture, organizational structure, technology and budgets. As a recent education sector review mission (Myanmar. MOE, 2003a) reported: 'this—the 1998 education reform—is considered a turning point in Myanmar educational history'.

With the implementation of plans for the promotion of education, TVET institutions have undertaken vast reforms in areas such as curricula, teaching methods, facilities, research and management. Teaching methodologies, like problem-based learning encouraging critical thinking, analytical, creative and research skills, are being promoted. The assessment system has also been reviewed and replaced with a credit system so as to be in line with international practice and to give students more flexibility. This also facilitates entry and re-entry into TVET institutions.

Special attention has been given to meeting the needs of those who live in remote regions, in particular to improving literacy among the various ethnic groups (up to 93.3% in 2004). Myanmar acknowledges the need to lay a proper foundation for populations who are mainly involved in the primary sector of the economy. Under the supervision of the MOE and in collaboration with related ministries, Myanmar EFA strategic activities and policies have therefore been adjusted to reflect preventive, reactive and remedial approaches to education in order to facilitate and promote lifelong learning and skills development, especially for out-of-school youth and adults.

Concerning the ICT infrastructure in education, since 2001 a Satellite Data Broadcasting System has been introduced in collaboration with the Ministry of Information, so that, by 2004, 619 e-education learning centres had been developed. The MOE is increasingly using e-learning and multi-media facilities to provide short-term training and education programmes for teachers working under the MOE. One of the main challenges in strengthening TVET in Myanmar is the importance of non-formal education which promotes a continuing education concept in the context of lifelong learning. This concept focuses on young people who have not participated in the regular school system, or who have dropped out of the regular school system before completion for various reasons. Those who could and should take advantage of the new opportunities for TVET are not only dependent on their own initiative, but are actively stimulated and directed by local communities.

A number of lessons and best practices that emerge from the Myanmar experience may be of value to other developing countries at similar levels of development. Among the lessons learned, it is clear that evaluation and assessment practices related to competence-based education are critical to achieving successful TVET for all in the information age. A transformation to TVET is not implemented overnight, and there are many challenges and potential pitfalls which must be addressed to achieve successful lifelong learning. The study identified the following key lessons from the Myanmar experience:

1. *TVET for all:* TVET in support of lifelong learning in Myanmar is an important ongoing process (for all), whether through formal or non-formal means. The various TVET programmes can therefore improve the range of skills and knowledge of underprivileged groups, young people and adults who are not able to continue their general education opportunities, or who want to undertake an alternative learning possibility. Greater emphasis still needs to be placed on the necessity of upgrading training possibilities, the provision of qualified instructors and advanced teaching materials in order to strengthen the quality of TVET education in a geographically large country like Myanmar.

2. *The selection of TVET programmes:* Differences in the levels of enrolment in TVET schools and institutes in Myanmar suggest that the location and type of schools and the educational facilities offered by the programmes, the availability and competence of qualified teachers, the interest and social composition of students, current economic trends and the opportunities available for further education, either locally or abroad, are all important considerations for students when they select a TVET programme.

3. *Continuing support for student-centred learning in TVET:* The approaches adopted by Myanmar educational programmes are increasingly favouring student-centred learning. However, the resources available for practical classes (within schools or those linked to the business environment), which are of special interest to learners, are still rather limited. Consequently, the system of final assessment gives more emphasis to theory than to practical activities. This relative lack of emphasis for on-the-job learning is said to have a negative impact on the livelihoods of youth and adults. Evidence from this study suggests that one of the best ways of creating on-the-job learning is to achieve effective partnerships between education and the business sector.

4. *Learning interaction combining practical experiences from the field and theoretical studies:* From a learner's and a teacher's point of view, in general one of the main reasons for choosing technical and vocational education is a wish to learn more about practical subjects and to acquire skills based on practical, hands-on experience through education. However, the dominant learning and teaching culture in Myanmar is still one where learners and teachers learn from books rather than from practical activities.

5. *The digital divide needs to be bridged:* It is important to take into account the accessibility of appropriate learning resources, in terms of both the available technology and sufficiently qualified trainers to support the lifelong learning process of an individual. On the other hand, Myanmar has learnt that familiarity with technology can also become a barrier to developing vocational skills effectively, and that the digital divide needs to be bridged in order to allow traditional learners to become involved with technology-supported learning environments.

6. *Monitoring of the labour market:* Evidence presented here suggests that an accurate monitoring of labour-market demand and opportunities should be one of

the top priorities for all TVET providers. The TVET system should promote efficiency in supply for the labour market.

7. *Financial implication for TVET:* Myanmar's experience shows that learning beyond the basic competencies should increasingly be the responsibility of learners and employers. Given the rising demand for lifelong learning processes and skill improvement, several principles should therefore guide future educational financing.

8. *Absence of empirical studies:* It is regrettable that few, if any, empirical studies have been conducted to evaluate the effectiveness and impact of TVET in Myanmar. As a result, there is an absence of reliable hard data to help improve the less effective elements in the training offered, or to help better focus the TVET offered to meet those training needs that are already particularly well served.

5 Conclusions Drawn

It may be said that TVET initiatives in the educational process are not new to Myanmar, although, as a result of recent educational developments and reforms, it is new to some teachers and learners, both in terms of the curriculum and modes of delivery. The TVET system is firmly established in Myanmar in both the formal and non-formal modes of delivery. Nevertheless, the country has to cope with the fact that it has enormous indigenous ethnic diversity, with a high proportion of the population living in remote and rural areas. Therefore, one of the growing concerns in the Myanmar education sector concerns how these individuals can be provided with an opportunity to take an increased responsibility for their own learning throughout their lifetime, so that they are equipped to earn their living effectively. The concepts of continuing education, community involvement and technological assistance all play crucial roles in the Myanmar education system. Furthermore, there is the issue of adopting a more methodical approach throughout the implementation process, which includes basic financial planning and learner-based planning, both of which are essential if TVET is to be an important vehicle for achieving lifelong learning for all. However, more attention needs to be given to how technical and vocational education is perceived in relation to promoting continuous learning opportunities in a way that is appropriate and attractive to the individuals.

Note

1. The population statistics presented in this section are based on the 1973 and 1983 censuses.

References

Cheng, Y.C. 2005. *New paradigm for re-engineering education: globalization, location and individualization.* Dordrecht, Netherlands: Springer. (Education in the Asia-Pacific Region Series.)

Lauglo, J. 2005. Vocationalised secondary education revisited. *In*: Lauglo, J.; Maclean, R., eds. *Vocationalisation of secondary education revisited*. Dordrecht, Netherlands: Springer.

Myanmar. Ministry of Education. 2001. *Thirty-Year Long-Term Education Development Plan, 2001-2030*. Yangon.

Myanmar. Ministry of Education. 2003a. *Education Sector review*. Yangon.

Myanmar. Ministry of Education. 2003b. *Education for All: national action plan*. Yangon.

Myanmar. Ministry of Education. 2004. *Development of education in Myanmar*. Yangon.

Myanmar. Ministry of Labour. 2005. *Handbook on human resources development indicators, 2004*. Yangon: Department of Labour/UNFPA.

Myanmar. Ministry of National Planning and Economic Development. 1998. *Review of financial, economic, and social conditions for 1997–98*. Yangon: Printing and Publications Distribution Enterprise.

Mar, N.Y. 2004. Utilizing ICTs to achieve lifelong education for all: a case study of Myanmar. *Educational research for policy and practice*, vol. 3, no. 2, pp. 141–66.

Stonier, T. 1983. *The wealth of information: a profile of the post-industry economy*. London: Methuen.

UNESCO. 1999. *Final Report, Second International Conference on Technical and Vocational Education*. Paris: UNESCO.

UNESCO. 2000. *The Dakar Framework for Action*. Paris: UNESCO.

Wheelen, T.; Hunger, D.J. 1998. *Entering 21st century global society: strategic management and business policy*. Addison Wesley Longman, Inc.

Wilson, D. 2005. Promise and performance. *In*: Lauglo, J.; Maclean, R., eds. *Vocationalisation of secondary education revisited*. Dordrecht, Netherlands: Springer.

Chapter IV.15
Technical and Vocational Education and Training and Rural Development

Lavinia Gasperini

1 Introduction

Poverty is mainly a rural phenomenon since 70% of the world's poor are rural (IFAD, 2001). Rural/urban inequalities are also a major obstacle to sustainable development. Unless they are addressed as key development actors, requiring appropriate competencies and skills to play a role in national socio-economic and cultural development, rural people are most likely to be among those who are not reached by the drive towards the Millennium Development Goals (MDGs).

Skills development for rural youth and adults is a lifelong learning process which plays an important role not only in increasing economic returns, but also in social outcomes, such as enhanced representativeness of rural livelihoods in the national arena, social cohesion, health or peace-building.

Most of the labour force in least-developed countries (LDCs) is in the agricultural and rural sector. The dimension of rural poverty and the mutually reinforcing relationship among improved skills for rural people and food security and poverty reduction (Burchi & De Muro, 2007) are driving a change in technical and vocational agricultural education and training (TVAET) towards a clear focus on contributing to reaching the MDGs. Rethinking TVAET and rural development in a way that is consistent with the challenge of poverty reduction, as well as the magnitude of the challenge, will require new responses by governments and donors, since simply scaling up existing provision patterns would be neither affordable nor cost/effective.

2 Rural Stigma, Urban Bias

The concern for technical and vocational education and training (TVET) and rural development is not new. For decades many authors have pointed out the urban bias of education systems and the urgency to address the basic learning needs of rural people (Lê Thanh Khoi, 1974; Ahmed & Coombs, 1975; Dumont, 1976). At the same time, rural development specialists have been insisting on the need to address rural people, not as a marginal group but as a neglected majority, whose contribution to national and international food security and economic and social development is critical.

R. Maclean, D. Wilson (eds.), *International Handbook of Education for the Changing World of Work*, DOI 10.1007/978-1-4020-5281-1_IV.15,
© Springer Science+Business Media B.V. 2009

In former colonial countries, TVET had usually been offered by the government as the second-best opportunity of a two-track system, targeting mainly indigenous people. Such people were stigmatized as more apt to undertake manual work. Therefore, skills development in agriculture was mainly directed at them.

After the independence processes during the 1960s and 1970s, TVET was considered by many countries as an important aspect of modernization, catalyzing a significant share of national education budgets and international aid. Many countries, however, displayed a contradiction between the declared education policy—emphasizing equity and the universalization of primary education—and a development paradigm that placed priority on investments in industrialization, industrial TVET and higher education, which were considered as more likely to speed up growth and modernization.

Concurrently, the inadequate resource allocation for agricultural and rural development accentuated the decline in this sector. This coincided with an important reduction of investments for TVAET, which became more evident during the 1980s and 1990s. Several other interacting factors contributed to aggravate the crisis for TVEAT, the most important being the overall decline in public spending for TVET as a consequence of the structural adjustment policies of the World Bank sector policy paper (World Bank, 1991). In addition, a common misunderstanding of the aims and strategies of the 1990 World Conference on Education for All and its Declaration emphasized investments in primary education and overlooked basic non-formal education, including skill training for youth and adults.

In the following years, the increasing educational gap between urban and rural people, for whom formal and non-formal agriculture courses were often the only education available, contributed to increasing rural poverty and to overall national food insecurity.

Today agricultural education and training suffers a crisis that in many ways reflects the general crisis of TVET public providers. Similarly, the main interacting obstacles to efficiency and effectiveness have been: (a) unequal access to TVAET for urban and rural students; (b) a predominantly male student clientele; (c) poor infrastructures, poor training quality and low staff capacity; (d) lack of market-relevant courses; (e) weak linkages with employers and off-campus situations; (f) outmoded curricula; (g) weak experiential learning; (h) a supply-driven orientation; and (i) overall, inadequate funding.

In addition to these aspects, TVAET is also affected by a low level of collaboration between education, research and extension institutions, farmers and rural communities in promoting mutual learning. This particularly concerns generating, sharing and utilizing agricultural and rural development-related technology, as well as knowledge and information in seeking solutions for rural poverty. This is reflected in the lack of interaction among different providers of TVEAT, such as Ministries of Education, Labour and Agriculture, as well as between technical schools, vocational training centres, post-secondary education, non-formal education, extension programmes, farmers' associations and agricultural and rural development research institutions (FAO & World Bank, 2000).

3 Poverty and the Rural Challenge

Rural poverty is prevalent among small farmers and landless families. Much of the poverty found in urban areas is a consequence of rural deprivation and rural economic decline, which trigger migration to cities (United Nations, 2005, p. 34). In the poorest developing countries, the population will continue to be predominantly rural for decades to come.

Agriculture is still the world's largest employer, involving about half of its workforce (about 1.2 billion people). In developing countries the overall agricultural workforce is much higher in percentages: in Africa, for example, agriculture employs two-thirds of the total workforce. Women alone account for 20 to 30% of the global wage agricultural workforce. Considering that half of the people of the world are under 25 years of age and that the majority of the world's youth is rural, making farming more productive, profitable and rewarding and life in rural areas more attractive for young people, and especially for women, is a crucial step towards reducing poverty. At the same time, it would curtail the large-scale migration of young people to urban areas. Policies that favour urban investment would need to be reviewed, given that most of the world's poor will continue to be rural over several of the coming decades.

The change that TVAET is undergoing can be better understood in relation to the role of rural people in agriculture, rural development and sustainable livelihoods. This reflects an important shift aiming to make a more effective contribution to poverty reduction and food security—and to the MDGs in general. Defining a few key terms helps to better understand the predominant TVAET reform processes, as well as their aims, target groups, main problems and strategies.

By common definition, *rural areas* are dominated by farms, forests, water, mountains and/or desert. Typically, *rural people* have agriculture as their main occupation; they are farmers, nomads, pastoralists or fishermen; they deal with animal production, transformation and marketing of food and non-food products and services. Rural communities are diverse culturally, socially and economically. By and large, their labour is cheap because gainful employment options are limited, and many rural groups are marginalized. Rural people often lack access to adequate basic social services because rural areas have low national priority, because rural people do not have political voice, especially the poor, and because providing services to them is more expensive. This happens despite the fact that they are the majority of the population in developing countries and despite their critical role in determining food security and environmental sustainability, agriculture being the primary interface between people and the environment. Although rural people play a crucial role in national survival—food and raw materials for clothing and shelter—for themselves and for urban people, their social status and standard of living are lower and their self-identity is affected by discrimination.

Disadvantage in rural communities is magnified by other characteristics of life in the countryside, such as geographic isolation affecting education and the provision of health services. High rates of poverty and scarcity of resources often result in a lack of appropriate services—including education and training—and qualified providers. These are some of the reasons explaining the fact that more than 80% of the world's out-of-school children live in rural areas, as well as the vicious circle that exists between poverty and illiteracy. Some 70% of existing child-labour is to be found in agriculture with many children engaged in hazardous work. Among rural dwellers are millions of children and adolescents exploited as workers on cocoa, tobacco or banana plantations, sometimes forced to work more than twelve hours a day in conditions bordering on slavery. Skills training can prevent these children from joining the ever-growing ranks of illiterate adult farmers. Rural people's disadvantage in access to, retention in and completion of basic education is one of the main reasons why they rarely proceed to agricultural and rural development-related post-primary and higher education courses, which are mainly attended by urban students. Ensuring that the needs of all rural young people and adults are met through appropriate learning and skills development programmes—not necessarily requesting a formal qualification to access them— would contribute to achieving the MDGs, as well as the Dakar Framework for Action goals.

The sustainable agriculture and rural development approach, as developed from the Earth Summit to the World Summit on Sustainable Development, has four pillars: cultural, social, economic and environmental. *Sustainable*[1] *agriculture and rural development* (SARD) is understood as a process of constant change and transformation of rural areas. It encompasses a wide range of long-term processes and programmes, expanding beyond agriculture and based on empowering the poor, such as:

- Enhancement of governance at the local, district and provincial levels, including linkages with the private sector, civil society and governmental agencies.
- Development of productive sectors: agriculture,[2] non-agricultural industry, mining, tourism, natural resources, environmental management, etc.
- Development of institutions and their capacities in key areas, i.e. education and training, health, research and extension, marketing, savings and credit, environment, transportation, etc.
- Development of rural infrastructures for roads, electricity, telecommunications, housing, water, sanitation, etc. (Avila & Gasperini, 2005).

SARD, as opposed to other production-driven approaches, is centred on people and focuses on improving livelihoods in terms of satisfying the cultural, social, economic and environmental needs and aspirations of present generations without endangering the ability of future generations to do the same. Such definitions recognize the primary importance of local stakeholders in rural development and poverty alleviation strategies. As in all people-centred approaches, there is broad agreement about the need for fostering the knowledge and skills of the rural population—the key actors in development efforts.

Improved access to education and skills development for rural people has a critical role also in the *sustainable livelihood* approach, as a critical step in placing people at the centre of their own development. Livelihoods are defined as comprising the capabilities, assets and activities required for a means of living. They are considered sustainable when they can cope with and recover from stresses and shocks and maintain or enhance their capabilities and assets (Chambers & Conway, 1991).

4 From TVAET to Skills for Rural Development

While the impact of globalization on the rural labour market has led to a diversification of employment patterns, characterized by the decline of wage employment and the expansion of self- and non-farm employment, the sustainable livelihood approach has contributed to broadening the conventional TVAET approach. A change process is thus going on in several countries to broaden traditional TVAET (see Atchoarena et al., 2003), focused mainly on agricultural production, to include a wide range of skills needed to promote SARD, and to embrace all those living in rural areas and involved in farm and off-farm employment, such as extension personnel, the staff of rural institutions, farmers' and women's associations and civil society organizations.

In spite of many setbacks in rural development, as well as in the TVET agendas, three international events shaped a policy environment that contributed to relate the TVAET change process to the global agenda of poverty reduction. These were the World Food Summits (Rome, 1996 and 2002) and the Earth Summit (Rio de Janeiro, 1992), which closely connected the food security challenge[3] and the need to increase agricultural productivity with environmental, economic and social challenges. These events addressed the economic growth and international competitiveness of the agricultural sector, not in isolation, but to be addressed together with soils, forests, coastal areas and sustainable natural resources management, as well as with employment generation, poverty reduction and building social capital. Within such a framework, the World Summit on Sustainable Development (Johannesburg, 2002) developed the SARD approach. The pro-poor Millennium Development Summit (2000) development framework, the MDGs and the Millennium Project (2005) reiterated and reinforced the main message of previous events. The Millennium Project explicitly addressed skills for rural development within the chapter 'Launch a global human resource training effort for the Millennium Development Goals', where the training of 'village specialist in health, soil nutrients, irrigation, land reclamation, drinking water, sanitation, electricity, vehicle repair, road maintenance and forest management' are addressed as a first priority (UNDP, 2005, p. 235).

The awareness that the skills needed by rural people can only partially be addressed by traditional secondary and tertiary education and training has led several countries to consider that Goal 3 of the 2000 Dakar Framework for Action on EFA—focusing on 'ensuring that the learning needs of all young people and adults are met through appropriate learning and life-skills'—should give priority to basic education and skill-training needs for all those who live in rural areas through a multiplicity of delivery systems, formal and non-formal, including extension, literacy and post literacy.[4]

Vocational education and training are often dealt with by urban education and training specialists, who frequently declare themselves unfamiliar with the agricultural and rural development context and prefer to work on TVET for industry and services, targeting mainly urban people. Conversely, agricultural trainers dealing with basic skills for rural development are often unaware of the latest debate on TVET reform and have limited pedagogical knowledge and skills. This dichotomy is mirrored by the lack of collaboration between formal and non-formal education courses run, for instance, by the Ministry of Education and those run by the Ministry of Agriculture, more often denominated as extension courses. This results in the duplication of cost and a lack of efficiency for countries. Agricultural extension is the 'function of providing need- and demand-based knowledge and skills to rural men, women and youth in a non-formal, participatory manner, with the objective of improving their quality of life' (Qamar, 2005). Considering that 'extension' is the expression adopted by agricultural institutions for denominating their non-formal delivery system of education and training for rural people, inter-sectoral collaboration with other providers, such as the Ministry of Education and civil society, would allow savings for the country and lead to overall greater efficiency and effectiveness of skills development for rural people.

So as to contribute to address through inter-sectoral collaboration the complexity and the challenges of the rural environment and provide some promising experience, FAO and the International Institute for Educational Planning (UNESCO-IIEP) co-published the study 'Education for rural development: towards new policy responses' (Atchoarena & Gasperini, 2003). The study provides the research base for the Education for All flagship partnership on 'Education for Rural People' coordinated by FAO and implemented in collaboration with UNESCO[5] and 270 other partners, which promotes collaboration among the education, agricultural and rural development sectors to ensure basic education and skills training to all rural people. The initiative focuses on research, capacity-building and the sharing of good practices. An on-line 'tool kit'[6] with teaching and learning materials for formal and non-formal TVAET for teachers and instructors, farmers, extension personnel and the vast public was made available. The issues addressed are at the core of the basic skills in demand among rural people, such as: plant biology and forestry; water; soil and land rights; animals and pastoralism; biodiversity; rural finance; agro-business and marketing; book-keeping; fishery; food and nutrition; as well as other aspect important for sustainable livelihoods, such as HIV/AIDS, gender and peace education and training for conflict management and communication.

5 Diversified Skills for Sustainable Agriculture and Rural Development

Skills development needs and consequent policies differ substantially within a country, but also between industrialized and developing countries. The post-industrial human resources requirements are predominant in the countries of the Organisation for Economic Co-operation and Development, where the transition from the industrial age to the information age is now underway. The situation is quite different in developing countries where the boundaries between manual and mental work are not fading away so quickly, and where the information and knowledge society is still far from being a shared reality. In such countries, rural people are faced with the challenges imposed on their livelihoods by the 'global village', which marginalizes and neglects them and requires the adoption of new technologies to ensure competitiveness, efficiency and access to markets. To overcome the process of marginalization, however, rural livelihoods need to ensure that natural resources are managed in a sustainable way, and that their local, diverse, traditional, agro-industrial knowledge, competencies and skills are cross-fertilized by universal knowledge and modern science and technology.

In a world that changes very rapidly and requires resilient citizens, a diversified and constantly updated curriculum is thus a response to the variety of knowledge and skills in demand among rural people from different agro-ecological systems and socio-economic and cultural backgrounds. Participatory curriculum planning and updating exercises have been promoted in TVAET, based on a methodology involving the key actors living in the rural environment, and includes a range of skills and competencies far beyond the traditional ones (FAO, 1998).

Acknowledgment of the importance of including diversified skills in TVAET and of the complexity of the challenge of rural development have also led to complementing the traditional core agriculture-related technical skills with a range of additional skills that are increasingly in demand, such as communication, facilitation, negotiation and leadership skills. These are critical for forging non-formal education practitioners (such as extension and literacy staff), rural youth and community leaders and, overall, for empowering rural people. Other essential skills are necessary for fostering innovation and change and developing effective participation citizenship and welfare, such as: entrepreneurship skills; income-generating, micro-finance and other business skills needed for self-employment; population education, gender issues; HIV/AIDS prevention; and mitigation or critical thinking and awareness about social, political and legal institutions and basic rights. The participatory curriculum development methodology, favoured by decentralization processes, allows a selection to be made among a range of these skills, as well as of a number of core basic competencies and skills for agriculture, food security and sustainable rural development on the basis of the demand and characteristics of the training needs required by rural livelihoods and the labour-market context.

6 Some Examples of TVAET Basic Competencies and Skills

Since this chapter is intended mainly for educators, who are less familiar with agricultural and rural development issues, the following paragraphs provide some examples of issues addressed by TVAET core competencies and skills. These are related to crop and livestock production, forestry, fishery and aquaculture, water control, food quality, food processing and food storage, rural infrastructure and marketing information.

- Basic skills training and extension on *crop production* addresses a large spectrum of activities aimed at improving land productivity in a sustainable way, allowing the farmer to obtain the maximum profit by producing plants, feed and cereals which provide nutrients for humans and good forage for herbivores. Teachers and students are faced with issues that are politically sensitive and critical for health, the environment and food safety, such as ensuring adequate and balanced crop nutrition, applying fertilizers and replacing nutrients lost by extraction through harvesting and by soil erosion, by leaching below the root zone and emissions to the air. In addressing insect infestations, knowledge of traditional methods of plant protection and the use of pesticides is complemented by integrated pest-management (IPM) techniques. Farmer field schools (FFS) are community-based, practically-oriented, field-study programmes providing an opportunity for farmers to learn IPM together, using practical, hands-on methods of discovery-based learning, initiated in the IPM domain and subsequently expanded to other agricultural practices. Started around the 1980s, they are rapidly expanding in Asia, Africa and Latin America.[7]
- *Irrigation* can be addressed from an interdisciplinary perspective, cutting across crop production, livestock and water management. Irrigation is an opportunity to reduce the unit cost of growing crops by increasing yields and improving their quality. Students can also learn how to diversify crops and plant selection to improve pastures. Since large herbivores are mainly found in cropping areas where land for pasture is scarce or non-existent, crop residue straw remains a single major resource used for feeding herbivores. Maximizing profit from agriculture and environmental protection will need local adaptation of good agricultural practices, such as crop rotation and integration of crop and animal production. This includes livestock production and household activities such as bee-keeping and rabbit, geese, duck and chicken production, fed with locally available feed resources and by-products. Additional good agricultural practices may include agro-forestry, conservation agriculture and crop association practices.
- *Livestock* provides an appreciating asset, a source of income, food and insurance, as well as important inputs to farming, such as manure and draught power to many poor people in developing countries. Furthermore, it can provide employment and stimulate trade. Small livestock farming is a common practice in rural villages, where large numbers of sheep, ducks, pigs and, above all, chickens surround the houses. They provide their owners with meat, milk, eggs and money. But when animals are of small size, this often means that they are not of a good breed, are poorly fed or that the animals are ill. When an animal has a contagious disease, it will spread to all the others in the village. To address such problems, basic skill training and extension in livestock builds capacities that go from the breeding of animals (cattle and small livestock species, such as goats, etc.) to feeding and nutrition, reproduction, conservation and processing of their own products; to recognizing zoonotic and zoonoses diseases.[8]
- Within the skills-development framework, artisan fishermen and the *small-scale fisheries* sector—producing over one-third of the entire food fish consumed world wide—are often overlooked. In developing countries, there are as many

as 30 million artisan fishermen. This labour-intensive activity is frequently characterized by low individual productivity and high levels of wastage and spoilage, due to limitations on infrastructure, craft, gear and fishery techniques. Most small-scale fishermen lead a precarious existence at or below subsistence level. Often they live in remote areas and lack access to supplies and services for their daily needs—and markets for their products. They lack also access to basic skills training and technical advice and assistance from extension workers that could help them to improve their efficiency and to generate incomes, market their products, as well as feed themselves and their families.

Basic skills training and extension in small-scale fishery include simple techniques such as hand-lining. This apparently simple procedure involves a lot of forethought in order to select the hook, line and sinker that are suitable in size and strength to the fish that one intends to catch. In addition, the fishing technique must be developed to ensure that fish attracted to the bait are actually caught. Trapping is another one of the oldest fishing techniques. Training allows both traditional and modern techniques to be used, since there are many different kinds of traps. Vessels and on-board equipment are essential to operate the traps and to transport the fish back to shore. Fish can also be farmed, and in this case it is necessary to know what is the best place for a pond, how to dig the pond, how to fill it with water, and how to take care, drain and fertilize it. In aquaculture students learn what kind of fish to raise, how to introduce the young fish into the pond, what and how to feed them, how to harvest the fish and how to raise one's own young fish to start the process over again. Basic skills for aquaculture are in the curriculum of some rural primary schools—such as the Colombian Escuela Nueva.

- *Forestry* vocational education and training has a special long-standing tradition in formal and non-formal courses, but it is also experiencing the impact of change. Students of traditional forestry TVET—in many cases of urban origin—were taught to produce, grow, plant, manage and harvest trees and process timber. Graduates would fill positions in forestry research, management, plantation establishment, timber harvesting and industry. The forests were a public good entrusted to, managed and protected by the State. Traditional forestry education included degrees, diplomas, certificates and in-service training. Sub-degree or diploma-level education prepared students for work in forestry and the forestry industry—sawmills, plywood factories, furniture-making, nursery management and machinery operation and maintenance. Certificate training in developing countries prepared forest guards (rangers) hired by the public sector, which was a major employer of graduates. The changing role of the public sector, the demand of civil society and the decentralization and participation approach connected to the sustainable rural development approach has had implications also for forestry education. Its vision and clientele have broadened, ranging from basic to higher education students. Forestry education and training delivery systems have readjusted to better contribute to reducing rural poverty and promoting rural development. They also address basic skills development for all those who live in the rural environment. Rural people in many areas have long been involved in the conservation and cultivation of trees on agricultural land and in forested areas. In many countries, rural people traditionally plant trees for a multiplicity of household uses, above all for cooking and keeping warm. But planting trees means also the possibility to obtain a variety of commercial construction materials, charcoal and fuel wood production, and for many other activities such as pit-sawing, sawmills, woodworking, tree farming, and the gathering and selling of fruits, timber, resins, gums and other forest products for commerce. Environmental degradation and the depletion of tree cover are sometimes symptomatic of poverty and a lack of comprehensive traditional tree and environmental management systems, which can be strengthened by basic forestry education and skills training. The deterioration of forest land leads to the loss of fodder, shade, fruit and other benefits. An understanding and perception of the long-term consequences of deforestation and mastering practices to promote the natural process of re-growth and re-generation of forest and techniques in managing certain types of trees, such as coppicing and pollarding, as well as the ability to identify a large number of species of trees and the role they play in people's lives, are some of the basic knowledge and skills required by people living in forested areas.

- TVAET addresses skill training in *food quality, processing and storage* as important issues for rural livelihoods, as well as for urban consumers. Food and water that urban and rural people consume need not only to be adequate in amount, but also safe and of good quality for the producer to sell as well as the consumer to use. Foods eaten at home or in public eating places may appear to be safe but may also show evidence of contamination. If food, beverages, dishes or utensils are unclean, if the food looks or smells bad, if a food that is meant to be eaten hot is served cold, or if the environment where the food is served has flies, cockroaches or evidence of rodents, or if food servers have dirty hands and clothes, then it is likely that the food being served is unfit. In every household, but especially in those with less than ideal sanitation, some knowledge about food-borne disease is very important. Through basic skills training, rural people can improve the storage techniques associated with different products and climates. For example, in temperate climates much of the production of fruits and vegetables is confined to a relatively short growing season and storage becomes essential for the provision of fresh produce outside of the harvest season. In tropical countries production is often extended, but storage may still be necessary. Products may be stored for a few days or weeks, but some temperate produce may also be stored for periods of up to twelve weeks. Not all fresh products are amenable to storage and some products may require specific post-harvest treatments, such as 'curing' or 'waxing' prior to successful storage. There are various different storage techniques, the choice of which will depend on cost and the produce to be stored. Skill training develops the capacity to master such techniques.

- *Water control* is another critical area where skills are needed to learn the various methods that can be used according to local circumstances to gain the maximum benefit. This requires knowledge on crop-water requirements and yield responses to water, as well as on the correct use of the appropriate equipment for different irrigation techniques. These include a range of options such as: (a) using a watering-can on very small plots of land, such as vegetable gardens that are near to a water source; (b) basin irrigation, commonly used for rice grown on flat lands or terraces on hillsides; (c) furrow irrigation, meaning small channels carrying water down the land slope between crop rows; or (d) sprinkler irrigation, similar to natural rainfall where water is pumped through a pipe system and then sprayed onto the crops. Skill training in water control allows farmers to improve the quality of their lives and their incomes by making informed decisions on the most appropriate use of the different techniques.

- *Rural infrastructures* (roads, telecommunications and reliable market facilities) are poor in rural areas. Improving rural infrastructures is critical for expanding the range of market opportunities available to producers, improving linkages between producers and traders, reducing both input and support services delivery costs. Basic skills training contributes to improving increased access to and use of appropriate low-cost technologies—such as animal power instead of hand power, a well and low-cost treadle pumps to maintain the water supply in villages and techniques of low-cost road maintenance. Basic skill training in the use of ITCs, such as radios, computers or cellular phones, which are very useful to obtain updated market information and other information important to improve rural livelihoods, are often included in skill-training activities for rural people.

- *Marketing information* for rural people is very important to negotiate products and prices with farmers and traders. Basic skill training in marketing enables small farmers to make the calculations necessary to decide whether or not they should plant different crops, or plant existing crops at different times, and how to grow new crops which may attract good market prices. Sometimes rural farmers find difficulties in finding out where to buy seeds for new varieties of crops and information about their profitability. Knowledge and market information on harvesting and post-harvesting costs, as well as out-of-season production of perishable horticultural crops, or farm storage for less-perishable staple crops, such as rice, maize or potatoes, are examples of basic skills training on marketing to help rural farmers to decide whether or not to store in any particular year. This same knowledge can also be used to help them decide whether or not to invest in building a storehouse if they do not already have one. Storing crops without the correct storage facilities is usually a bad idea, as quantity and quality losses may mean the farmer will not be able to benefit fully from higher seasonal prices. This information is essential for rural farmers before going into new, possibly risky, business ventures.

7 Critical Issues and Policy Options

Today's challenge is that of transforming traditional agricultural education and training into a skills development system responsive to rural people's needs, which contributes to poverty reduction, food security and the achievement of the MDGs.

Success depends on how countries will face a combination of critical issues and policy options, which can be synthesized as follows:

- *Privileging the rural poor by broadening the EFA national plans to explicitly focus on skills for rural people,* and specifically on rural youth and adults.
- *Considering basic skills development for rural people as a public good,* which allows communities to reduce their vulnerability and cope with man-made and natural disasters, as well as changing economic and social conditions.
- *Developing synergies between formal and non-formal skills development* run by educational and agricultural institutions, civil society and the private sector (encompassing literacy and basic skills training, extension, agriculture and rural development schools and colleges, polytechnics, universities, etc.) and expanding such collaboration also to health, infrastructure and finance ministries.
- *Reducing* the emphasis on academic pathways and credentials and increasing the recognition of non-formal and informal learning.
- *Collaborating with agricultural research* to promote knowledge, information, competencies, skills and values for better farming and improved livelihoods.
- *Updating the curriculum* to address multiple scenarios and diversified capacities in farm and off-farm skills and technologies, as well as a range of life-skills dealing with interpersonal and social issues.
- *Addressing post-training support.*
- *Shaping new responses, such as improving the training capacity of non-governmental providers* to address the magnitude of the challenge.
- *Promoting positive discrimination measures* to address rural/urban and gender inequalities.
- *Developing a holistic approach to agriculture and rural development skills development.* For example, the training of farmers has implications for higher agricultural education. Conversely, people with university education are needed for curriculum reform in primary, secondary, TVAET and teacher training. Their leadership can reinforce change at the other levels, including skills development.
- *Addressing the vocational education and training needs of rural people within poverty reduction strategies and sector-wide approaches* as the way to address the learning needs of the majority of the world's people who play a key role in global sustainability and food security.
- *Reviewing policies that favour urban investment,* given that most of the world's poor will continue to be rural over several of the coming decades.

However, skills training for rural people and reform processes for greater effectiveness depend also on a supportive surrounding macro-economic environment (remunerative prices to producers, fiscal and monetary policies) and sector polices (enterprise development support, credit, meritocratic access to jobs, infrastructure, etc.), which promote rural development and employment. Acquiring education and skills without the chance to use them can contribute to fostering civil strife and migration to cities. These take us far beyond the world of schools and classrooms, to a partnership between education and agriculture and rural development policy-makers and planners, managers and practitioners. In such an alliance, who can ensure that skills and knowledge acquisition are followed by skills and knowledge utilization?

Acknowledgments Inputs and/or comments to this chapter were kindly provided by David Atchoarena, Caterina Batelo, Daniela Bruni, Riccardo del Castello, Malcolm Hazelman, Annalisa Planera, Maria Grazia Quieti and Marcela Villarreal.

Notes

1. From the Latin *sustinere*: *sus* means 'from below' and *tenere* 'to hold'.
2. Agriculture is broadly defined to include the production, conservation, processing and marketing of crops, livestock, forestry and fish products.
3. National food security is achieved when a sufficiently stable and safe supply of food is available in the country to satisfy: (i) consumption requirements normally filled from on-farm production and home gardens; (ii) market demand; and (iii) relief distribution needs. Household food security is achieved when all household members have sufficient means to obtain all the food they need from some combination of their own production, traded or purchased supplies, and gifts or donations, and when they know about and put into practice the principles of good nutrition. Sustainable food security exists when domestic markets are performing well and households possess sufficient assets and income-earning opportunities to meet all their basic needs from their own resources.
4. See: <www.fao.org/sd/erp/ERPotheractivities_en.htm>
5. See: <www.fao.org/sd/erp/>
6. See: <www.fao.org/sd/erp/ERPtktoolkit_en.htm>
7. FAO introduced the FFS approach in Africa in 1995 and since then it has been taken up by a range of government and development programmes. The impacts range from increased knowledge and uptake of agricultural practices to various forms of demonstrated empowerment, including spontaneous growth of farmer networks and associations.
8. Zoonotic disease can be transmitted to any vertebrate and infection may be naturally transmitted also between animals and humans. Zoonoses are diseases that are transmitted to humans through food or water. All kind of diseases have an impact on human health and on national and household economy because of reduced production.

References

Ahmed, M.; Coombs, P.H. 1975. *Education for rural development: case studies for planners.* New York, NY: Praeger.

Atchoarena, D.; Gasperini, L., eds. 2003. *Education for rural development. towards new policies.* Rome: FAO; Paris: UNESCO/IIEP.

Atchoarena, D. et al. 2003. Strategies and institutions for promoting skills for rural development. *In:* Atchoarena, D.; Gasperini, L., eds. *Education for rural development: towards new policy responses.* Rome: FAO; Paris: UNESCO/IIEP.

Avila, M.; Gasperini, L. 2005. *Skills development for rural people: a renewed challenge.* (Background paper for the Working Group for International Co-operation in Skills Development. 10–11 November 2005, FAO. Rome.)

Burchi, F.; De Muro, P. 2007. *Education for rural people: a neglected key to food security.* Rome: Università degli Studi Tre. (Working paper, no. 78.)

Chambers, R.; Conway, G. 1991. *Sustainable rural livelihoods: practical concepts for the 21st century*. Brighton, UK: Institute of Development Studies. (Discussion paper 296.)

Dumont R. 1976. *Training for agriculture and rural development*. Rome: FAO/UNESCO/ILO.

Food and Agriculture Organization; The World Bank. 2000. *AKIS/RD strategic vision and guiding principles*. Rome: FAO/World Bank.

Food and Agriculture Organization. 1998. *Participatory curriculum development in agricultural education. A training guide*. Rome: FAO.

International Fund for Agricultural Development. 2001. *Rural poverty report 2001: the challenge of ending rural poverty*. Rome: IFAD.

Lê Thanh Khoi. 1974. *Education in rural development*. Paris: UNESCO.

Qamar, K. 2005. *Modernizing national agricultural extension systems: a practical guide for policy makers of developing countries*. Rome: FAO.

United Nations. 2005. *World Youth Report 2005: young people today, and in 2015*. New York, NY: United Nations.

United Nations Development Programme. 2005. *Investing in development: a practical plan to achieve the Millennium Development Goals*. New York, NY: UNDP.

World Bank. 1991. *Vocational and technical education and training*. Washington, DC: World Bank.

Chapter IV.16
An International TVET Programme Development by the International Baccalaureate Organization

Monique Conn

1 Introduction

The success of the curriculum models developed by the International Baccalaureate Organization (IBO), addressing the academic needs of students in the 3 to 19 age range, is now well known. IBO programmes, and specifically the two-year pre-university Diploma Programme, grew out of international schools' efforts to establish a common curriculum and university entry credential for geographically mobile students. International educators were also motivated by an idealistic vision: they hoped that a shared academic experience emphasizing critical thinking and exposure to a variety of points of view would encourage intercultural understanding and acceptance of others by young people.

The IBO has grown rapidly and now provides, through the medium of three working languages (English, French and Spanish), three related programmes that represent an educational continuum for students from 3 to 19 years of age: the Primary Years Programme (PYP, for ages 3 to 11/12), the Middle Years Programme (MYP, for ages 11/12 to 16) and the Diploma Programme (for students aged 16 to 19). The last is designed as a two-year academic preparation for university.

A great deal of interest has recently been raised by those reviewing curricular provision in some national systems, as well as in the private sector, in adapting the IBO's educational models and principles for technical and vocational education, particularly at the upper secondary level. In collaboration with some authorized schools and partner institutions the IBO has now embarked on the development of a framework of international education that will incorporate the vision and educational principles of the IBO into local programmes that address the needs of students engaged in technical and vocational education.

R. Maclean, D. Wilson (eds.), *International Handbook of Education for the Changing World of Work*, DOI 10.1007/978-1-4020-5281-1_IV.16,
© Springer Science+Business Media B.V. 2009

2 What Are the Aims of an IB Technical/Vocational Framework?

2.1 Providing a More Inclusive Provision for Students Aged 16 to 19

In its efforts to develop a coherent educational continuum for young people aged 3–19, the IBO recognizes that there is currently a hiatus between its two programme frameworks, the Primary Years Programme (for 3- to 11/12-year olds) and the Middle Years Programme (for 11/12- to 16-year olds), which are both inclusive, whole-school programmes, and the Diploma Programme which is clearly academic in nature and design and, in some schools, selective. Working in partnership with schools and local authorities to broaden access to the kinds of learning fostered in the Diploma Programme would potentially respond to the needs of many young people who are currently excluded from the experience of the Diploma Programme.

2.2 Responding to the IBO's Mission Statement

As an organization devoted to the development of international education worldwide, the IBO adopted an ambitious mission statement in 2002:

> The International Baccalaureate Organization aims to develop inquiring, knowledgeable and caring young people, who help to create a better and more peaceful world through intercultural understanding and respect.
>
> To this end the IBO works with schools, governments and international organizations to develop challenging programmes of international education and rigorous assessment.
>
> These programmes encourage students across the world to become active, compassionate and lifelong learners who understand that other people, with their differences, can also be right. <www.ibo.org/mission/>

This mission statement echoes the concerns expressed by UNESCO itself in its 1945 constitution, which states: 'The wide diffusion of culture, and the education of humanity for justice and liberty and peace are indispensable to the dignity of man and constitute a sacred duty which all the nations must fulfil in a spirit of mutual assistance and concern' (UNESCO, 1945). It is clear that these ambitious aims should inspire educational programmes for all students—not just those bound for academic university programmes. The strategic plan of the IBO includes the development of new pathways to help more students access an education that responds to these values. In its design and through its implementation in local contexts, the IBO's technical and vocational framework will foster the attributes of the 'IBO learner profile' (Box 1), which defines learner outcomes for all IB programmes.

Box 1. The attributes of the International Baccalaureate learner profile

The aim of all IB programmes is to develop internationally minded people who, recognizing their common humanity and shared guardianship of the planet, help to create a better and more peaceful world.
IB learners strive to be:

Inquirers	They develop their natural curiosity. They acquire the skills necessary to conduct inquiry and research and show independence in learning. They actively enjoy learning and this love of learning will be sustained throughout their lives.
Knowledgeable	They explore concepts, ideas and issues that have local and global significance. In so doing, they acquire in-depth knowledge and develop understanding across a broad and balanced range of disciplines.
Thinkers	They exercise initiative in applying thinking skills critically and creatively to recognize and approach complex problems, and make reasoned, ethical decisions.
Communicators	They understand and express ideas and information confidently and creatively in more than one language and in a variety of modes of communication. They work effectively and willingly in collaboration with others.
Principled	They act with integrity and honesty, with a strong sense of fairness, justice and respect for the dignity of the individual, groups and communities. They take responsibility for their own actions and the consequences that accompany them.
Open-minded	They understand and appreciate their own cultures and personal histories, and are open to the perspectives, values and traditions of other individuals and communities. They are accustomed to seeking and evaluating a range of points of view, and are willing to grow from the experience.
Caring	They show empathy, compassion and respect towards the needs and feelings of others. They have a personal commitment to service, and act to make a positive difference to the lives of others and to the environment.
Risk-takers	They approach unfamiliar situations and uncertainty with courage and forethought, and have the independence of spirit to explore new roles, ideas and strategies. They are brave and articulate in defending their beliefs.
Balanced	They understand the importance of intellectual, physical and emotional balance to achieve personal well-being for themselves and others.
Reflective	They give thoughtful consideration to their own learning and experience. They are able to assess and understand their strengths and limitations in order to support their learning and personal development.

2.3 Filling a Gap in International Education

The OECD (quoted in Vidovich, 2004) defines the internationalization of education as 'an international orientation in content, aimed at preparing students for performing (professionally and socially) in an international and multicultural context, and designed for domestic students as well as foreign students'. Schools also need to rethink the international and intercultural orientation of pedagogy, as well as content knowledge, ensuring an 'open flow of people and ideas between the school and the international arena, using both educational and non-educational (especially business and industry) sources [...] and extensive individualized networks across the globe' (Vidovich, 2004).

While the Primary Years Programme and the Middle Years Programme meet the needs of the whole 3 to 16 age group, the Diploma Programme is designed for the academically oriented students aged 16 to 19. However, even in developed countries, 30 to 70% of this age group opt for vocational studies, therefore being beyond the current reach of international education. In a changing global economy, it is essential that students preparing directly for active employment develop a good understanding of world issues and contexts and an understanding of their responsibilities as global citizens. Several groups (and particularly schools) engaged in international education have already stressed the need for internationally recognized qualifications in areas currently not addressed by an academic programme like the IB Diploma Programme. Several areas of study and activity, such as business and administration, information technology and tourism, are often subject to relatively similar guidelines globally. Consequently, there are numerous internationally recognized diplomas at the polytechnic and university levels that have helped to standardize such studies. There is, however, no international qualification in such areas at the secondary level. While the IBO is not ready at this stage to develop such a range of courses itself, it wishes to explore ways of working in partnership with agencies and schools in order to develop ways of internationalizing local technical and vocational studies at the upper secondary level. Through its experience in developing programmes, assessment and teacher professional development internationally, the IBO is well placed to create these contacts and connections to provide students with a truly international experience.

2.4 Reducing the Academic Versus Vocational Divide

Banking on its experience and reputation in curriculum and assessment development through international collaboration, the IBO can contribute positively to technical and vocational education by challenging the perception (still prevalent in many parts of the world) that technical and vocational education is of lesser status than academic studies. By using and adapting chosen elements of the IBO's Diploma Programme, a carefully designed educational framework will now engage students who have chosen technical and vocational education in challenging learning and rigorous assessment through a programme of international education.

3 What Are the Characteristics of Learning in Such a Framework?

3.1 Preparing for Work in a Knowledge Society

It is increasingly recognized that to prepare students to become effective participants in the rapidly changing twenty-first century society, schools must equip them
with the tools and the learning dispositions to cope with, but also to manage and
influence, change. An IB technical and vocational programme framework will need
to: (a) develop a range of broad work-related competencies as well as deepen understanding in general areas of knowledge; (b) help students develop flexible strategies
for knowledge acquisition and enhancement in varied contexts; (c) prepare students
for effective participation in the changing world of work; (d) foster attitudes and
habits of mind where students become true lifelong learners willing to consider new
perspectives; and (e) involve students in learning that develops the capacity and will
to make a positive difference.

3.2 Technical and Vocational Education

The IBO is working with schools and local authorities to develop a pilot programme
framework for generic, broad-based technical and vocational education, rather than
a specific skills-based vocational training. On successful completion of the course,
students will be able to enter employment directly or to progress to further studies
in higher education. It is important that this programme framework prepares students for flexibility and mobility in a range of employment opportunities, as well as
continuing lifelong learning. This means integrating broad, general learning areas,
as well as specific vocational content in the programme, developing a challenging
programme for high achievers, ensuring that participating schools work in close
collaboration with higher education institutions and the working sector locally and
internationally.

3.3 A Flexible Framework

As technical and vocational education is subject to the pressures, priorities and
requirements of diverse national and local economic contexts, it is important to
achieve an appropriate balance between prescription of common programme elements, national or local requirements and school or student choice. Where there is a
high degree of governmental control through examinations, such a balance is harder
to achieve, but there is a growing trend to allow more local autonomy to schools.
The IBO's experience with government and university recognition of its Diploma
Programme is a positive factor in the development of such locally accredited international programmes in technical and vocational education.

The programme framework will be based on basic qualities of the Diploma Programme:

- a balance of breadth and depth of learning;
- a coherent mix of required elements and school or student options;
- explicit statements for values, aims, orientations and learning outcomes allowing the sustained development of concepts, skills, understandings and attitudes;
- a strong emphasis on learning fostering intercultural understanding;
- the development of critical thinking, inquiry and research skills;
- varied pedagogy, including collaborative learning;
- an exploration of human endeavour, through the school-based experience and work-based learning activities;
- strong student involvement in self-assessment and reflection;
- an encouragement of entrepreneurship, creativity and innovation;
- a sustained experience of community involvement and service;
- rigorous assessment through a blend of external as well as internal assessment methods;
- varied, dynamic pedagogy, supported by appropriate in-service teacher development;
- school/IBO collaboration in programme development and quality assurance supported and enhanced by an international network of like-minded schools and organizations.

4 Who Are the IBO's Partners?

4.1 The Creation of a Programme in Finland

Finland recognizes and promotes English-language education in general, as well as vocational upper-secondary education. In addition, there is in Finland a recognized need for upper secondary technical and vocational education programmes with a wider international focus. The Oulu Business College (OBC) and representatives from the municipality of Oulu (a city located in central Finland), as well as from the Finnish Ministry of Education, met with the IBO in December 2002 to discuss the development of a locally-based international programme in business education in co-operation with the International Baccalaureate Organization. This request was fully supported in principle by Oulun Lyseon lukio, a local IB world school which uses the IB Diploma Programme. Discussions and seminars were held over the next year, while teachers and administrators in the business school were becoming familiarized with the orientations of the Diploma Programme through attendance at IB teacher-training workshops and the study of curriculum materials in collaboration with the IB world school.

A first invitational symposium on vocational education in an international context was held at the IBO's curriculum and assessment office in Cardiff (United Kingdom) at the end of June 2003. This symposium brought together twenty-two participants from the IBO and the OBC, as well as individual educators and specialists in vocational education from Australia, Denmark, Finland, Sweden, the United Kingdom and the United States of America.

In the meetings in Cardiff and, subsequently, Oulu (December 2003) a steering committee was formed and a two-phase pilot project developed:

1. Preparation phase, July 2003–July 2004: The Oulu Business College, in cooperation with the IBO and the Finnish educational authorities, continued the design of an experimental three-year programme, the 'Business and Administration International Programme', which complies with the Finnish requirements for their vocational qualification and contains elements of the academic IB Diploma Programme. The IBO's contribution to this development consisted in encouraging and supporting the local IB world school staff in their participation in planning groups; it also provided OBC staff with access to further IB Diploma teacher-training workshops; it organized curriculum development meetings and started planning the research and evaluation processes associated with this new initiative.

2. Implementation phase, August 2004–August 2007. The pilot programme 'Business and Administration International Programme' is now being taught at OBC in co-operation with Oulun Lyseon lukio, while curriculum development continues in key areas and research is put in place. The OBC offers a three-year course focusing on issues such as customer service and marketing. Students taking this course also study the IB business and management course, English and economics (the latter being an elective for students). These IB courses start in the first year of study, except for economics which starts in the second year. Students also take a course focused on critical thinking in the world of work, a course being developed in collaboration with the IBO. Finally, they are engaged in community service activities, take part in a locally developed course about intercultural communication and complete a final project reflecting on their educational and work-based experience. It is planned that four cohorts of students will follow the pilot programme. A final evaluation of the pilot project will take place in August 2007, when a decision will be made on the continuation, amendments to, and potential expansion of, the agreed framework for this pilot. The first and second cohorts number about twenty students each.

For the full duration of the pilot project, the IBO has authorized the local IB Diploma school to teach IB courses to the OBC students, who are registered as certificate candidates for the IB Diploma and undergo the regular assessment processes associated with their choice of courses. The IBO continues to provide OBC staff with access to teacher-training workshops. It participates in the bi-yearly steering committee meetings and organizes seminars, workshops and curriculum development meetings with teachers involved in the project and other experts.

4.2 Development of a Similar Partnership in Quebec, Canada

The seminars organized within the development described above and another invitational symposium held in 2004 included participants from other IB world schools. Among them, two IB Diploma schools in Quebec declared their interest in launching a similar scheme in collaboration with the IBO and, indeed, with the OBC in Finland, in order to extend the values and the benefits of an IB international education to students engaged in vocational education within their institutions. In the education system in Quebec (which is under the jurisdiction of the provincial ministry of education) students obtain a secondary school leaving certificate at the age of 16/17 and can then continue their studies in a *Collège d'enseignement général et professionnel* (*Cégep*), where they opt for a two-year pre-university academic programme or a three-year 'technical' programme that leads either to direct employment or to a range of programmes in tertiary education.

The Collège François-Xavier Garneau in Quebec City and Collège Laflèche in Trois-Rivières are two such *Cégeps* which, as authorized IB world schools, offer their pre-university academic students the option of taking the IB Diploma instead of the provincial programme. The two schools have developed a very close working relationship and drafted the pilot framework together, with the intention that this framework of studies would eventually become an option for students engaged in any of their many technical programmes. They have based these efforts on the explicit aim of helping their students who choose a technical and vocational programme (the majority of the student population of Quebec's *Cégeps*) to develop an international and intercultural outlook as they prepare themselves to be citizens and professionals in an increasingly pluralist world.

A steering group was formed with representation from the two *Cégeps*, the Quebec Ministry of Education, the IBO and also the local association of IB world schools in the province in order to shape the development of, and support for, the pilot programme framework. The project was facilitated by the fact that both institutions are already authorized IB world schools, very experienced in the teaching of the Diploma Programme, as well as in technical and vocational education, and very confident in the merits of blending elements of both. At the time of writing this text, the project has been approved by the IBO's governing body, is fully supported by the Quebec Ministry of Education, and the two *Cégeps* will start recruiting about forty students each for the first year of implementation of the programme, which was due to begin in September 2006. For the first year, it is planned that the students will come from the following technical and vocational programmes:

- Police technology;
- Correctional and youth services intervention;
- Fashion design and marketing;
- Hotel management; and
- Tourism.

The students' three-year programme will feature all the required elements of their respective technical and vocational options, as well as a common core developed in collaboration with the IBO within the principles of the international framework. They will study the IB's French A1 (mother tongue and literature course) as well as an IB second-language course with the other IB students engaged in the Diploma Programme. They will also follow the critical-thinking course developed in collaboration between the participating schools and the IBO, as well as specially designed local courses on ethics and multiculturalism, sustainable development and physical health. An intercultural experience (living and/or working in a different cultural environment) will be required by the schools (within the programme's community service activities, on-the-job training or as a special project) in order for the students to get a better understanding of the organizational differences, the customs, rules and codes for the practice of their profession in different cultural contexts. Like their Finnish counterparts, the students will also complete a final project at the end of their programme, reflecting on chosen elements of their experience.

5 The IBO's Framework for a Programme of International Education

5.1 Extending the Pilot

The two contexts described above present opportunities for the IBO to deepen its understanding of how an international dimension can be incorporated in technical and vocational studies, and of how the organization can contribute to this process through its experience in international curriculum and programme development, professional development and research. Indeed, the organization's strategic plan states its intention to increase access to the values of the IBO to students who would not normally follow one of its mainstream programmes, particularly the Diploma Programme.

As the two pilot projects progress and benefit from each other's experience through a collaborative process of development, evaluation and research, it will be advantageous to gain insight into the applicability of this experience in other national and cultural contexts through controlled expansion of the pilot. The IBO has therefore developed a generic framework which could be proposed to other interested parties, either IB world schools themselves wishing to extend the benefits of international education to students in technical and vocational studies (as in Quebec), or institutions forming a close formal partnership with IB world schools (as in the Finnish project). These partnerships will involve a range of agencies, including schools, colleges, local or regional education authorities, national education ministries (providing organizations), to develop programmes which combine:

- locally or nationally validated technical and vocational qualifications;
- mainstream subjects from the IBO's Diploma Programme;
- a range of other elements which reflect the values of the IBO.

5.2 Components of a Career-Related Programme

Following approval by the organization, all technical and vocational education programmes (normally spread over two or three years of full-time study) developed in collaboration with the IBO will include the components shown in Box 2.

Box 2. The components of all IBO technical and vocational programmes
Required elements of the local or national qualification.
Mainstream IB Diploma Programme subjects:

- a modern language from group 2 (foreign languages);
- one or more other subjects from any other hexagon group (individuals and societies, experimental sciences, mathematics, the arts).

The Diploma Programme subjects (except for mother tongue and group 2 languages) will be examined in English, French or Spanish.
Other mandatory elements:

- the critical-thinking course developed by the IBO;
- community involvement and service;
- an extended piece of reflective writing or a presentation.

Where appropriate, as agreed with the IBO to fulfil the requirements of the programme framework, school-based elements:

- locally devised units or courses of study developed specially for this programme.

This framework will be developed through the IBO's usual collaborative processes, where schools and teachers contribute to the development, share ideas and resources, participate in international professional development events and engage in regular discussion and debate through technology. It is interesting to note that the pilot project already crosses the language barriers and fosters dialogue and collaboration between Finnish and French-speaking schools and teachers. This is a powerful way to help schools develop and integrate an international dimension into their programmes.

5.3 Assessment and Certification

Due to the combination of locally-determined and IB elements of the programme framework, there will be a blend of direct IB assessment of student learning (for IB mainstream Diploma courses) and of internal assessment performed by the schools themselves: for some elements of the programme (such as the critical-thinking course, community involvement or other locally-developed courses) student work will be authenticated by the school and endorsed by the IBO. The organization will develop common generic criteria for these aspects of the programme and will monitor this internal assessment through the organization of a process of guided peer review of school documentation, within a collaborative form of programme evaluation. The partnership between schools, local authorities and the IBO will be reflected in student certification upon completion of the programme. In addition to the local or national technical and vocational qualification, a student will receive:

- certificates for Diploma Programme subjects taken;
- a certificate of international education with the logo 'In collaboration with the IBO', provided specific conditions are satisfied;
- a record of achievement produced by the school or providing organization summarizing all the activities successfully undertaken by the student during the course of study on the international programme.

5.4 Conditions for School Participation

A set of criteria will form the basis for an authorization process for all future schools or partners requesting authorization to offer this programme framework for their students. In so doing, the IBO aims to ensure that the proposed local programmes are well aligned with the organization's mission statement, learner profile and the Diploma Programme's general aims and objectives. The school or agency will be asked to demonstrate the added value that the programme would bring, and how the IBO's core values would be embedded in student learning.

In this process, the IBO is using its experience in developing collaborative processes of quality assurance through initial programme authorization and evaluation. The school or agency will need to provide evidence of the financial, human and technological resources that will be allocated to the programme, including on-going curriculum development, student support and teacher professional development.

6 What Are the Issues Related to the Development of Such a Framework?

The IBO's motivation in the development of this pilot programme framework is obviously to use the leverage of partnerships with like-minded organizations and experienced IB world schools to understand better how an international dimension can be incorporated in, and influence, technical and vocational studies. This experience will be essential to get an understanding of the ways in which the organization's educational programmes can benefit a broader range of students at the upper end of secondary school.

Several important issues have been identified for study and research, for example:

- How will the teaching and learning styles of the Diploma Programme courses compare with those used in local technical and vocational contexts? Will they form a coherent educational experience for the students?
- What elements of critical thinking will be most adapted to the needs of young people already involved in the world of work?
- What will be the role of problem-based learning in such a context? How can active inquiry and learner involvement be best fostered in both academic and work-related learning?
- Will adult learners in technical and vocational education find the programme meaningful and interesting? How should courses and approaches be adapted for a wide age range?
- How can metacognition and reflection related to work-related learning be fostered? How will students develop learning dispositions that will make them effective lifelong learners in their context?
- How can effective professional development and mechanisms for collaboration be developed for academic and technical and vocational studies teachers?
- How can we reach a balance of valid and reliable school-based and external assessment? How will different national and cultural contexts view this blend of local and international assessment and qualification?
- How can international mindedness be fostered in specific work-related environments, and what should be expected of students?
- More generally, are there specific areas where a truly international curriculum can be developed to help students participate in emerging forms of work in the global arena? How can the IBO contribute to this development?

6.1 Evaluation and Research

At the same time as the development of the pilot project is taking place, the IBO is engaged in establishing the parameters for a thorough evaluation of the course, as well as defining areas of relevant research, in collaboration with the schools themselves and with local universities. There are six evaluative aims, outlined as follows:

- To determine the nature of student learning, together with formative and summative achievements, in the academic and core elements of the programme.
- To monitor the development of student perceptions of international mindedness throughout the period of the programme.
- To identify teacher pedagogy and perceptions of the programme, and their changes over time.
- To explore the administrative, management and organizational issues arising from the implementation of the programme within the institutions.

- To identify patterns and choices for employment/higher education both for students participating in the international programme and for other students.
- To explore employer/higher education expectations of skills, attitudes and knowledge of students recruited from the international programme and to evaluate their achievement in practice.

Research methods will include interviews of different constituent groups, questionnaires, teacher comments on student progress, formative and summative assessment results, and surveys on attitudes regarding elements contributing to international mindedness. The longitudinal research will involve constituent groups within the programme, as well as control groups in all institutions. In addition to English, both Finnish and French will be used in the research, through the collaboration of the schools themselves, as well as local universities.

7 Conclusion: Future Directions

The pilot programme framework described above clearly constitutes an opportunity for the IBO to explore ways of developing new approaches for reaching a large number of young people (and potentially a number of adults as well) engaged in pre-tertiary programmes of study that had not been developed so far by the organization. The time may come when the IBO itself may develop an international technical and vocational qualification in a number of areas of study. However, the current approach of blending local and international elements might well be seen to serve the needs of students better, at least in a large number of areas: it may be the best solution to allow local economic, cultural and educational choices to be made according to the local context. At the same time, such a flexible framework will create a dynamic network of internationally-minded schools sharing a vocabulary and educational aims for lifelong learning and responsible citizenship, collaborating to develop a truly international educational experience for their students.

There is little doubt that with time and experience, this new provision will influence the Diploma Programme itself. The IBO continues to review and develop its programmes to make them suitable for twenty-first century learners. Human endeavour and particularly the world of work are changing realities that students must explore in order to develop a 'range of broad employment-related competencies which [. . .] provide the basis for 1) effective participation in emerging forms of work and work organizations; 2) access to a range of education and training pathways, both initially and subsequent to commencing employment; 3) improved flexibility and mobility in employment; and 4) effective participation in adult life generally' (Munro, 2003). The classic distinction between academic preparation for university and more work-orientated study will likely become increasingly blurred and irrelevant. The IBO's current investigation in collaboration with its partner schools and agencies, therefore, may have wide-ranging implications for the future development of its programmes of international education for the upper secondary school.

References

Munro, J. 2003. *Constructing a core curriculum for vocational education in an IBO Context.* (Paper prepared for the Conference on Vocational Education for an International Context, Cardiff, United Kingdom, 26 June 2003.) (Unpublished.)

UNESCO. 1945. *Constitution of the United Nations Educational, Scientific and Cultural Organization.* Paris: UNESCO.

Vidovich, L. 2004. Towards internationalizing the curriculum in a context of globalization: comparing policy processes in two settings. *Compare,* vol. 34, no. 4, pp. 443–61.

Chapter IV.17
A Profile of TVET in the Asia and Pacific Region: A Survey of Progress, Innovations and Promising Practices

Chris Chinien, Elspeth McOmish, Mohan Perera and Alex Chinien

1 Introduction

Given the importance of human capital and skills development for economic growth and social cohesion and inclusion, in 1999 UNESCO convened a group of experts from around the world to the Seoul Congress for a collective reflection on critical reforms necessary for adapting changing labour market needs and growing public expectations. The recommendation which emerged from the Seoul Congress was used to update UNESCO's standard-setting (normative) instrument for TVET (UNESCO, 1999). This instrument was further updated in 2002 through a collaborative effort between UNESCO and ILO (UNESCO/ILO, 2002). Various initiatives were undertaken to encourage Member States to implement this recommendation. In 2003–2004 UNESCO conducted a survey to assess the extent to which its Member States had implemented the recommendation as part of major reform initiatives to cope with the demands of the new economy. More specifically, the survey attempted to gather information on the extent of policy and programme reforms undertaken since the second International Congress on TVET held in Seoul in 1999. The survey was divided into four sections, each focused on a different set of issues, namely: (a) policy, planning and management of TVET systems; (b) access to TVET; (c) relevance and quality of TVET systems; and (d) monitoring progress with TVET. The survey questionnaire was sent to all Member States. Fifty per cent completed and returned the questionnaire. Results of the survey responses from nineteen countries (representing a response rate of 58%) were used to generate a profile of TVET for the Asia and Pacific Region. The countries included in the analysis were: Australia, Bangladesh, Bhutan, Fiji, India, Indonesia, Iran, Japan, Lao PDR, Malaysia, Nepal, Pakistan, Philippines, Republic of Korea, Solomon Islands, Thailand, Tonga, Vanuatu and Viet Nam.

All responses that could be summarized into frequency counts and percentages were used to make comparative analyses. The open-ended questions that yielded more qualitative information were analysed for recurrent themes, which contribute to the understanding of TVET reform initiatives in the region and numerous

R. Maclean, D. Wilson (eds.), *International Handbook of Education for the Changing World of Work*, DOI 10.1007/978-1-4020-5281-1_IV.17,
© Springer Science+Business Media B.V. 2009

innovative and promising practices being implemented throughout the Asia and Pacific region to improve the efficiency and effectiveness of TVET.

2 An Overview of TVET in the Asia and Pacific Region

Two-thirds of the countries have implemented a national strategy to oversee policy formulation and the planning and management of TVET in the Asia and Pacific Region (Fig. 1). Over half of the countries had established specific initiatives to ensure that TVET was relevant to the world of work and to monitor progress against some established benchmarks. Access to TVET has received the most attention among the four key issues under consideration. This is not surprising in the context of the MDGs and Education for All (EFA).

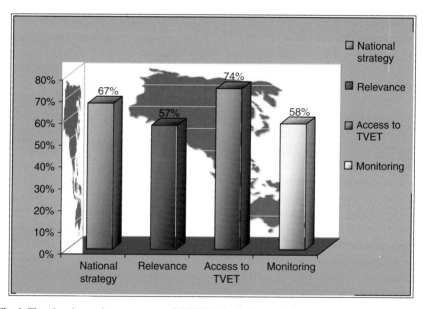

Fig. 1 The planning and management of TVET in the Asia and Pacific Region

As shown in Fig. 2, the monitoring of TVET programmes was the area where there was most significant variation between the developing and least-developed countries. It is noteworthy that less was being done in the least-developed countries for monitoring programme outcomes. Also of significance is the fact that both the developing and least-developed countries were slightly more engaged in various initiatives to increase access to TVET.

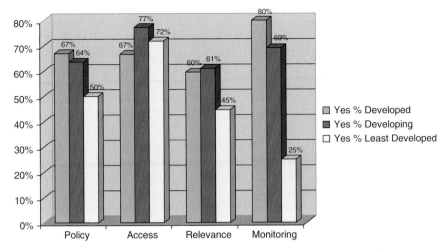

Fig. 2 The involvement of developed, developing and least-developed countries of the Asia and Pacific Region in TVET

3 Policy, Planning and Management of TVET Systems

3.1 Goals of National Strategy/Plan

Human resources development was the theme for the development of a national strategy or master plan for TVET in all countries. In this context, TVET is positioned to contribute to the development of a highly skilled workforce to support a strong performance in the global economy.

3.2 National Strategy/Master Plan for TVET

As shown in Fig. 3, a significant number of countries (78%) have also developed a national development plan for TVET, with the most developed countries of the region more likely to have already completed such a plan. In general, the developing countries were in the process of implementing their plans. All national framework documents for the region also bind TVET to the two major Millennium Development Goals (MDGs): the fight against poverty and discrimination against women.

In some countries the development of the TVET master plan is carried out in collaboration with an economic planning unit under the responsibility of the Prime Minister's office and the plan is based on a national development strategy. Increasingly, TVET is perceived as an enabling instrument on the road to becoming an

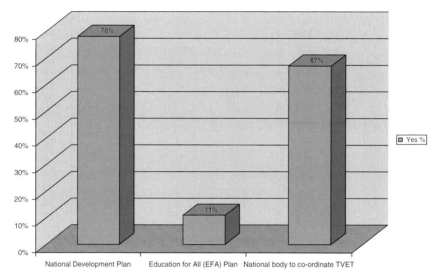

Fig. 3 Countries in the Asia and Pacific Region with various national development plans for TVET

industrialized nation and for improving the living conditions of the poor, especially those from rural areas. TVET is also increasingly being seen as an instrument for promoting environmentally sustainable development.

TVET institutions are being encouraged to use more formal and systematic planning that is in strategic alignment with each country's national development plans. Below are listed some specific goals forming part of the national strategy/plan identified by Member States:

- To address labour turnover, skills shortages and mismatch, changing workplace due to technological innovations, changes in industrial structures, employment security and social valuation of workers;
- To align all agencies strategically to address skills shortages and mismatch;
- To ensure an adequate supply of human resources to support progress in IT and other growing fields;
- To establish a system to support workers' career development and lifelong learning needs;
- To reconcile employers' short- and long-term needs with that of employees' career life-plans.
- To develop vocational awareness among young people

3.3 A National Body for TVET

Some 67% of countries have established a national body for TVET. However, in some countries plans establishing such an entity are still pending government approval. The mandate of this body is to ascertain the availability of a skilled labour force to support economic growth and to ensure social cohesion and inclusion. Such an entity allows countries with decentralized jurisdictions to maintain a national focus on TVET. The establishment of a national body for TVET has resulted in a net increase in public and private skill-training institutions.

The national body can also take the form of a national council chaired by the minister of education and involving many other ministries. When a national body is not in place, it is usually the ministry of education that has the overall responsibility for TVET. In some countries, TVET is administered by the ministry of labour. Countries with no national body were less likely to be engaged in the development of a national plan for TVET. Some international funding agencies are recommending the establishment a national body for TVET as part of strategic development plans.

Under enabling legislation, some national bodies have the mandate to make decisions on strategic policy, establish national objectives and priorities for the training system, co-ordinate programmes, develop and expand TVET, and ensure programme quality on a national basis. Typical responsibilities of the national body include:

- To co-ordinate all TVET activities;
- To develop guidelines for the reform of TVET;
- To provide labour-market information;
- To contribute to policy development;
- The financing of TVET;
- To establish training funds;
- Curriculum development;
- The development of learning materials and other resources;
- To design teacher-training strategies;
- Training and staff development;
- Programme monitoring and evaluation;
- To be responsible for a management information system;
- To liaise with all key stakeholders.

With the support of the Commonwealth of Learning, senior vocational education officers from the Asia-Pacific Region have established the Pacific Association of Technical, Vocational Education and Training (PATVET) as a regional body to support the improvement and development of skills development in the region. A resolution has also been made that a national body should be established on each island State to strengthen TVET.

3.4 The Contribution of TVET to EFA

EFA, with its strong focus on primary education and remedial education for adults, is not universally embraced in the TVET sector and was only included in the national strategy of two small island States (11%). However, all countries were involved in various initiatives to improve access and equity in TVET, which in effect is consistent with the goals of EFA.

4 Facilitating Access: TVET for All

4.1 Funding Expansion

Eighty per cent of the countries indicated that there has been some funding to increase education and training opportunities in general. While in some countries TVET funding has increased, it has generally remained stable in others. No decline in funding was reported. In some countries new facilities were under construction and others were being planned.

Expansion of funding for TVET is clearly related to the health of the economy. The output of TVET is a key consideration which is often overlooked when considering the expansion of TVET. How many TVET graduate can be absorbed by the labour market in a given economic situation? In one instance, the TVET share of the total education system was established at 20% to address this issue. This much was necessary to match TVET output to corresponding growth in business and industry.

Lack of adequate government support and funding for TVET is a major problem for small island States. In some developing countries, especially these small islands, although no substantial national government funding has been appropriated for TVET, financial support from the World Bank, the European Union, the Asian Development Bank and other foreign donors is helping the expansion of TVET. More wealthy countries in the region are also helping smaller States in building the capacity of their human resources in TVET. Many non-governmental organizations (NGOs) and international non-governmental organizations (INGOs) have also launched skill-development programmes, particularly at the community level. A topology of expansion drawn from the survey responses includes the introduction of new courses, renovation, expansion and modernization of existing facilities and establishment of new centres and institutions,

Some TVET institutions are attempting to generate income to cover their basic operational costs. For example, some TVET institutions have introduced a time-sector privatization concept, which allows the public and private sector to utilize TVET facilities to deliver staff training under an agreed payment scheme. Other cost-saving initiatives include: (a) merging institutions into multi-campus facilities to enable the sharing and mobilization of resources; and (b) the fusion of agencies to reduce overlapping in skills development activities.

4.2 Efforts to Change the Image of TVET

Given the general belief that TVET can give a country's economic and socio-economic development a huge upturn, various initiatives are being undertaken to improve the image of TVET and to encourage young people to consider a skilled trade as a career of first choice. In some countries TVET policies are being modified to promote lifelong learning by developing pathways between different educational levels, or the articulation of TVET with higher education. Other initiatives include:

- Using the context learning approach in the teaching of mathematics, science and technology to encourage more students to take these subjects;
- Introducing pre-vocational education in general education to help inculcate a culture of skills development among young people, especially among girls; and
- Offering programmes supporting the school-to-work transition.

4.3 Improving Access and Equity for Designated Target Groups

Although few countries indicated that the goals of EFA were integrated in the national strategy or master plan for TVET, results showed that there were a considerable number of initiatives that have been implemented to increase the participation of designated target groups in TVET, namely: women and girls; poor people from rural areas and remote communities; people with disabilities; people with non-English speaking backgrounds; conflict-affected people; and ethnic minorities—when applicable.

Lack of support for TVET from the public and from politicians has been an obstacle for increasing government assistance for improving access to TVET. Some programmes are being established by training institutions without government support. Fig. 4 shows that considerable efforts were being deployed by countries to increase the participation of disadvantaged target groups in TVET. The level of effort for people affected by war reflects the fact that fewer countries of the region were involved in war or armed conflict, rather than a lack of interest to meet the needs of this target group. Fig. 4 provides a brief overview of these accomplishments related to TVET for All.

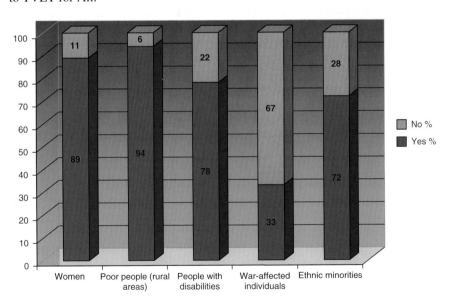

Fig. 4 An overview of the provision of TVET for All for designated groups

4.4 Women and Girls

Eighty-nine per cent of the countries reported having implemented various initiatives to attract women and girls to TVET. The following measures are illustrative of these efforts:

- Committees were formed to promote the participation of women and girls in TVET. In some cases, the policy was built into the national strategy, or became an additional strategy that was added to the national plan;
- Women included in planning and decision-making at all levels; female instructors were encouraged;
- Develop special TVET programmes for girls who have dropped out of schools;
- Offer gender-sensitive training to TVET personnel;
- Implement a gender-friendly training environment in TVET;
- Establish polytechnics for women;
- Provide financial incentives to encourage employers to give women greater access to apprenticeship in non-traditional occupations;
- Introduce female-friendly trades, such as tailoring, hairdressing and weaving, to increase women' participation in TVET; and
- Provide assistance to parents of school-aged children.

4.5 Poor People from Rural Areas and Remote Communities

Almost all countries (94%) had implemented programmes to encourage the participation of poor people from rural and remote communities in TVET. A summary of specific initiatives that have been implemented is as follows:

- Integrating a national poverty eradication programme into the national strategy or master plan;
- Investments to strengthen communities and regions economically and socially disadvantaged through learning and employment;
- More formal programmes, such as apprenticeship training, are often concentrated in urban areas where most businesses and industries are located. Incentives are provided to encourage employers to hire apprentices from rural areas. Incentives are also provided to hire apprentices from rural areas to address skill shortages in these regions;
- Employment facilitation programmes introduced to train disadvantaged target groups, such as small farmers or fishermen, to augment self-support abilities and enhance employability;
- Flexible training delivery and establishment of community-based training centres;
- Taking training to people in rural areas with mobile training units;
- Imparting income-generating skills;
- Annexing skill-training programmes to secondary schools;

- Running campaigns to motivate youth and adults to participate in training programmes;
- Facilitating access to training for people with little or no education;
- Using mobile training teams to train trainers; and
- Agriculture-based programmes for poor people living in rural areas.

4.6 People with Disabilities

In most countries, equity policy is mandated by law and TVET training for people with disabilities is enacted in specific legislations. Seventy-eight per cent of countries have implemented specific programmes to remove barriers that have excluded people with disabilities from involvement in TVET. Some programmes for people with disabilities are run by non-governmental/voluntary organizations. The range of activities implemented to improve access to people with disability to TVET in the region includes:

- Incentives to encourage employers to sponsor apprentices with disabilities;
- Purchasing training places in TVET that are dedicated to people with disabilities;
- Injecting more TVET funding targeted to people with disabilities;
- Established a co-ordinating system to facilitate the routing of people with disabilities from school to TVET and employment; and
- Establishing special skill-development programmes.

4.7 Conflict-Affected People

Given that the great majority of the countries in the region have not been involved recently in war, armed conflict or civil unrest, only 33% reported programmes to address the skill-development needs of people affected by conflict. Only six countries in the region reported having to deal with war-affected individuals. Where applicable, the following provisions were made:

- Establishment of a quota system for admitting war-affected persons in TVET; and
- Establishment of skills-development programmes for people affected by ethnic tension.

4.8 Ethnic Minorities

Eighty-three per cent of the countries were engaged in special initiatives to include ethnic minorities in TVET. However, it appears that in some countries ethnic minorities are more interested in general education rather than TVET. The following inclusion initiatives were reported:

- Making funds available for the provision of inclusion;
- Establishing mechanisms to give minorities a voice in decision-making;
- Establishing employment equity programmes that provide pre-vocational training to job-seekers encountering barriers;
- Incentives to encourage employers to sponsor apprentices from ethnic minority groups;
- Establishing training programmes to enable ethnic minority groups to overcome deficits in literacy, numeracy and language skills; and
- Programmes to integrate foreign workers.

4.9 Equity Policy for TVET

The mandate to address socio-economic needs and labour-market requirements with relatively modest resources places considerable pressure on TVET. Eighty-nine per cent of countries have implemented equity policy to facilitate access to TVET. In many cases, equity policy was encapsulated in the national strategy for TVET. The goal of the equity policy is to combat exclusion and discrimination and to promote inclusion, which is one of the basic axiomatic principles of UNESCO. The equity policies reported aimed at the traditional designated target groups, namely: women and girls, poor people, people with disabilities, war-affected people and ethnic minorities. In addition, other important sources of discrimination were also addressed, such as: learning disability, over-age, cultural differences, language, literacy, numeracy, religion, unemployment, the incarcerated and people living in isolation. Below is a list of specific approaches implemented to address the issues and concerns related to equity:

- Establishment of specialized agencies to oversee the implementation of equity policy;
- Reporting outcomes on a regular basis to ensure accountability; and
- Providing scholarships and financial assistance to allow poor people to participate in TVET.

4.10 PLAR

Only 56% of the countries in the region reported having implemented a system for assessing and recognizing prior learning (PLAR). Again, the health of the economy seems to be a key determinant for offering PLAR services in TVET. Some countries have enacted special legislation incorporating PLAR services in TVET, which is available to applicants upon enrolment. Countries that have successfully established PLAR services have in most cases also established some form of vocational qualifications framework, which has been used as a basis for setting national standards for occupational skills. These standards are used for assessing and recognizing prior learning. PATVET is attempting to introduce a regional qualifications framework for the Pacific islands. It is assumed that this framework will enable workers from small island States to migrate to wealthier countries. This can be an important source of income for countries which rely heavily on remittances. Two other initiatives closely associated with the PLAR system are: (a) career counselling; and (b) providing multiple-entry/exit to TVET programmes.

4.11 Other Initiatives to Increase Access

Other initiatives to increase access to TVET include the following:

- Flexible delivery to accommodate the needs of disadvantaged groups;
- Adopting instructional methods to meet the special needs of designated target groups;
- Providing professional development to equip teachers with the knowledge and skills to work with and teach people with special needs;
- Offering dual-track high-school programmes, which prepare students for both academic and TVET options: school-based apprenticeship programmes;
- Incentives provided to employers in support of the training and hiring of older workers who are welfare recipients, redundant or re-entering the workforce.

5 Relevance

In general, all countries were committed to forging strong links with the world of work so that TVET graduates would be equipped with the skills needed to enter wage employment and self-employment. Most countries (72%) have held some form of national consultation for capturing the input of key stakeholders in order to enhance the relevance of the TVET system and its programmes. Typical consultation formats include: (a) a national forum; (b) a national council; and (c) a ministerial commission. Some countries are establishing sector councils to identify and address current and anticipated challenges for skills and learning, and to implement long-term human resources planning and development strategies for their respective sectors. At least four countries—Australia, Japan, Malaysia and the Philippines—have developed occupational standards as part of their workforce development strategy. These occupational standards are used for developing: (a) a national qualifications framework; (b) training standards; (c) benchmarks for establishing prior learning assessment and recognition of skills acquired on a non-formal and informal basis; and (d) for training provision and certification.

Below are listed some initiatives introduced to increase the relevance of TVET:

- Obtaining industry collaboration in training delivery, such as an advisory input. Curricula are reviewed every five years in collaboration with industry to ensure the authenticity of occupational requirements;
- Promoting cross-industry collaboration;

- Facilitating flexible mixes of skills;
- Predicting and addressing skill shortages;
- Developing skills to support innovation in industry;
- Use of competency-based approaches for learning and learning assessment;
- Paid professional leave enables TVET instructors to participate in industrial training to update their industrial knowledge and skills. They are expected to share the skills acquired with other instructors and students.

5.1 Flexibility in TVET Delivery

In their efforts to increase the flexibility of TVET, at least 50% of countries were offering various scheduling options, such as day and block release and sandwich programming, which allows learners to combine on-the-job training with school-based training. In most of these countries (83%), TVET programmes were available either in the evening or on a part-time basis (Fig. 5). It is noteworthy that in most countries the majority of TVET students study on a part-time basis.

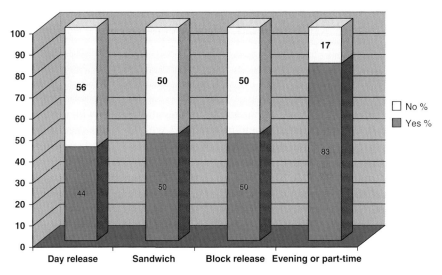

Fig. 5 The availability of TVET courses

5.2 Use of ICTs in TVET

Only one-third of countries were using radio, television, the Internet and other open and distance learning (ODL) modalities, in spite of the potential capacity of ICTs to increase the flexibility of TVET delivery (Fig. 6). Some public and private providers are delivering training content only by distance and others are using a blended strategy. In general, the major emphasis of policies for integrating ICTs in education is

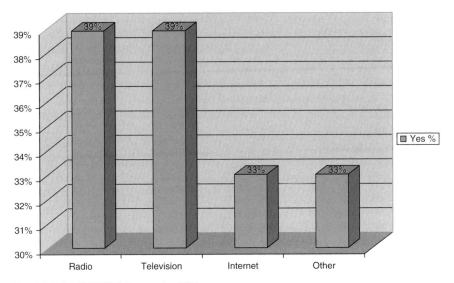

Fig. 6 Mode of TVET delivery using ICTs

very much at the university level. While some countries were planning to introduce ICTs for on-line learning in TVET, others had no provision for making a commitment to more flexible means of delivery.

5.3 Comments on Developing Countries

Small island States were less likely to use ICTs in TVET, but there was a belief that ODL is extremely important for small island States, irrespective of their size.

5.4 New Competencies in TVET

A significant number of countries have introduced specific initiatives to identify and incorporate generic broadly transferable skills in TVET (Fig. 7), such as communication (78%), teamwork (72%) and technology skills (78%).

Other approaches being used to infuse new competencies through TVET include:

1. Collecting, analysing and organizing information;
2. Communicating ideas;
3. Planning and organizing activities;
4. Solving problems;
5. Learning to learn;
6. Innovation skills;
7. Entrepreneurship skills.

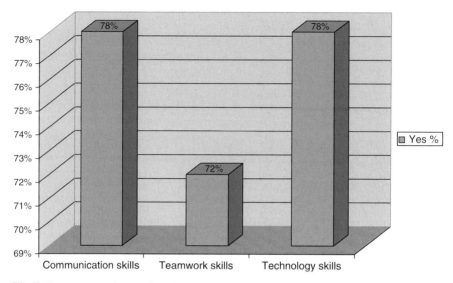

Fig. 7 New competencies acquired through TVET

UNESCO's Asia and Pacific Regional Office in Bangkok has organized capacity-building workshops and professional development to train TVET teachers so as to infuse and facilitate the development of new competencies. Some TVET systems have introduced compulsory courses and extra-curricular activities allowing students to learn new competencies. Efforts are also being made to design and develop curricula for teaching new and emerging technical competencies, such as mechatronics (mechanics and electronics technology) and autotronics (automotive and electronics technology).

5.5 Micro-Business, Farming and Artisan Skills

Approximately two-thirds of the countries have implemented micro-business (61%), as well as farming and artisan skills (67%). These initiatives include community-based training for enterprise development, which aims to prepare TVET graduates for creating enterprises that may provide a livelihood immediately after completing their training programmes. Entrepreneurship, which is central to this approach, is fast becoming an integral part of TVET. Entrepreneurship training is sometimes included in compulsory general foundation courses, which also include rural development and environmental protection, as well as financing and setting up micro-business and artisan trades.

6 Monitoring

A substantial proportion of the countries (61%) have already established national goals or benchmarks against which to measure the provision of TVET. Some coun-

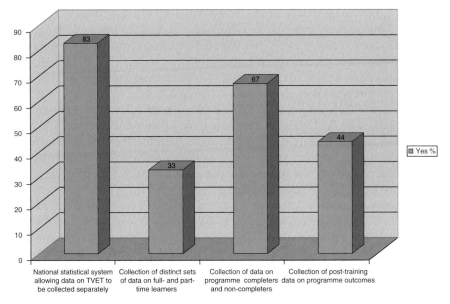

Fig. 8 Measuring TVET

tries have also developed an action plan and key performance measures for assessing the national strategy or plan. Through PATVET, member countries are sharing knowledge, skills, experiences, resources and information on TVET. This will provide useful benchmarks for assessing TVET. Some TVET systems are using ISO 9001 management system certification to ensure quality and effective delivery of services.

As shown in Fig. 8, it is noteworthy that 83% of the countries have a national statistical system that allows data on TVET to be collected separately. Not all countries (33%) were collecting statistical information distinguishing part-time from full-time learners. However, a substantial number of countries (67%) were tracking programme completers and non-completers. Surprisingly, only 44% of the countries were conducting tracer or follow-up studies to determine the rate of placement and graduates' degree of satisfaction with TVET programme.

6.1 Impact of UNESCO's Recommendation for TVET

The purpose of UNESCO's Revised Recommendations for TVET was to assist its Member States in adapting TVET to meet the needs and expectations of a rapidly changing global economic environment (UNESCO/ILO, 2002). There are many similarities between countries' national development plans and UNESCO's recommendations for TVET. The Seoul Congress on TVET (UNESCO, 1999) and UNESCO's recommendations gave some impetus for TVET reform in many countries. Since the recommendations were adopted, all Member States of the Asia-Pacific Region involved in this survey have undertaken major initiatives for policy and programme reforms in TVET. In some countries, especially the developing and least-developed ones, the recommendation had a direct impact on TVET reforms. In more developed countries, the labour-market demands had a stronger influence on TVET development. However, the thrust of UNESCO's recommendations is generally consistent with the reform of TVET systems. Although the nature of the reforms was consistent with the UNESCO's Education for All movement and the UN Millennium Development Goals, there were no indications that these two international benchmarks for development were used as a primary reference for developing national TVET plans. It should be said here that a few countries were unaware of the existence of UNESCO's recommendations.

Experience has demonstrated that a national seminar is an effective way of disseminating major recommendations for TVET reform, as it facilitates consensus-building between government/industry/labour/institutions/educators/administrators and service receivers on key priorities, from educational reform to the establishment of an action plan to address needs.

All the countries that were aware of UNESCO's recommendations for TVET unanimously embraced this standard-setting document. In the developing and least-developed countries, lack of funding and shortage of trained staff are minimizing the impact of the recommendations and slowing the rate of progress in TVET reforms. In spite of these barriers, all countries of the Asia and Pacific Region are making vigorous efforts to strengthen TVET in strategic alignment with their national human-resources development plan and labour-market requirements. UNESCO's recommendations provide a most valuable blueprint for the development and improvement of TVET in its Member States.

References

UNESCO. 1999. *Lifelong learning and training: a bridge to the future; final report of the International Congress on Technical and Vocational Education; Seoul, 1999.* Paris: UNESCO.
UNESCO/ILO. 2002. *Technical and vocational education and training for the twenty-first century.* Paris: UNESCO; Geneva, Switzerland: ILO.

Section 5
Learning for Employment and Citizenship in Post-Conflict Countries

David Johnson and Lyle Kane

Department of Education, University of Oxford, United Kingdom

Chapter V.1
Overview: Vocational Education, Social Participation and Livelihoods in Post-Conflict Countries

David Johnson and Lyle Kane

1 Introduction

The collection of papers in this section is concerned with the well-being[1] of youth in those developing countries that have suffered violent conflict. We know that violent conflict and poverty are inextricably linked (Buckland, 2005), that conflict retards economic and social development and is a key obstacle to achieving Education for All and the Millennium Development Goals (UNDP, 2003; World Bank, 2003). We know too that youth are at once the primary victims and primary actors in conflict[2] and are therefore central to any approach to human development. In its recent *World development report: development and the next generation* (World Bank, 2007), the World Bank explores the importance of 'investing' in young people and argues that the decline in fertility rates in most developing countries means that many will see a larger share of people of working age with fewer children or elderly dependents to support. This raises new challenges, but also, it asserts, provides 'an unprecedented opportunity to accelerate growth and reduce poverty'.

We aim, in this overview, to outline the promises and pitfalls of vocational education aimed at young adults in conflict-affected countries. In so doing, we take the social sciences concept of 'youth transitions'[3] with the aim of examining three critical and overlapping aspects thereof—education, work and citizenship—in those countries with fragile economies and human relationships. The World Bank argues that these transitions are 'critical for poverty reduction and growth because they relate to building, maintaining, using, and reproducing human capital' (2007, p. 40). This notwithstanding, the paper argues that while we know that they are an important source of human capital and vital to economic growth and human development, we have not been able to answer with confidence or precision some crucial questions about the effects of conflict on the participation of youth in education, economics and civil society. Nor have we, as a research community, been able to articulate clear policy choices for governments, aimed at improving learning, work and life opportunities for youth in the developing world. This was confirmed in a conference on Education and Conflict: Theory, Policy and Practice, convened by Oxford University in collaboration with UNICEF in April 2006 (see Johnson & Van Kalmthout, 2006). The conference concluded that we have only rough measures of youth well-being at our disposal. As a consequence, policies and services aimed at

R. Maclean, D. Wilson (eds.), *International Handbook of Education for the Changing World of Work*, DOI 10.1007/978-1-4020-5281-1_V.1,
© Springer Science+Business Media B.V. 2009

young people in conflict-affected countries are crudely targeted and operate on a 'rule of thumb' (Annan, Blattman & Horton, 2006). Those practitioners involved in post-conflict reconstruction were extremely conscious of the limitations of our current knowledge base and the lack of evidence-led approaches to development planning and programming.

2 Equality of Opportunity

Thus, the first theme that we are concerned with in exploring the potential of vocational education is equality of opportunity and the well-being of youth in conflict-affected developing countries. In particular, we are concerned with the opportunities available for youth to continue to learn (in diverse ways) beyond primary school, and the extent to which such learning offers continuities to work and to productive citizenship. Simply put, equality, or rather 'inequality of opportunity', in access to education, to work and earnings, and to participation in civil society, defines the issue. For us, economic growth and human development is more than simply a reduction in absolute deprivation. A sound understanding of relative deprivation or inequity is of critical importance in building human capacity. When inequity becomes deeply entrenched in a society, this threatens stability and the opportunity for human development and economic growth.

The fact of the matter is that inequalities between different groups in society, or 'horizontal inequalities' (Johnson & Stewart, 2007; Mancini, 2005; Østby, 2003; Stewart, 2000) have been shown to be a source of violent conflict (Marshall, 2005). Indeed, horizontal inequalities in educational access are a particularly important form of inequality since they lead to other horizontal inequalities—in income, employment, nutrition and health, as well as political position. Thus, the education sector plays a critical role in conflict-affected or conflict-prone societies: on the one hand, its values and structure can reflect inequalities in power;[4] on the other hand, it is pivotal in affecting these values and inequalities, potentially offering a way of breaking from the past. Education is a powerful influence over identities, both through its content and its structure. Moreover, it is a source of power and of income in contemporary societies. Access to jobs depends on the kind and level of education attained and, similarly, political participation at higher levels, particularly in the civil service, depends on education.

3 Vocational Education

The second theme explored here focuses more directly on vocational education in war-affected countries and the role it might play in bridging horizontal inequalities.

It seems that the educational preparation of youth for work and life is at a very low level in developing countries, particularly among the poor. Many are not learning as much as they should and, specifically, they are not learning what might be relevant to the demands of a rapidly-changing global economy. The outcome is that many begin work too early in low-skills jobs and find that they are unable to make progress along the skills ladder to enhance their earnings. For many governments, development partners and international NGOs, the favoured response is more education and training, especially vocational and skills-based training. Yet, a survey of war-affected youth in Uganda—SWAY (Annan, Blattman & Horton, 2006)— questions the internal logic of this approach. It suggests that:

> While those with vocational training are doing relatively well economically, it is not necessarily the case that an expansion of these programs will lead to more meaningful livelihoods to youth. Rather, the association between economic success and vocational training may be spurious—trained youth may be doing well not because of their training, but because they were more talented and entrepreneurial in the first place. A more rigorous evaluation of programs will be required to assess whether vocational training has any positive impact at all.

This suggests that we would be wise to look beyond supply-side factors alone and consider instead such demand-side factors as human capability and agency, if we are to offer a more considered set of proposals for enhancing young people's well-being in the developing world.

Hence a number of questions arise. These are:

1. What are the continuities between vocational education, work and citizenship in post-conflict societies?
2. What policies have been adopted in a range of conflict-affected countries that might account for differences in the patterns of youth transitions (continuing to learn, engaging in work and exercising citizenship)?
3. What role does individual agency and human capability play for those youths who do and for those who do not participate in vocational education in post-conflict societies?

To understand better these questions, we propose a conceptual model of vocational education as a learning system in fragile, conflict-prone and post-conflict countries. Four main contexts in which vocational education as a holistic learning system might function are identified. We shall return to the questions themselves.

The first context in which vocational education and training might occur is as an educational solution to the impact of on-going, low to high intensity conflict. The classic response here is 'skills development'. An example of this approach is identified by Yarrow (in this section) in the provision of vocational education for refugees or internally displaced persons.

The second context of vocational education and training in countries experiencing conflict can be seen as more future-oriented systems planning and policy work. Here, planning for the return of refugees for example, or ideological concerns about the nature of a future curriculum, the relevance to the world of work and economic growth are all important issues for VET (see Barakat, in this section).

Second, the role of TVET in the study of educational reconstruction and transformation in post-conflict environments is interesting. In practical terms, the provision of vocational education comes as a result of fire-fighting or short-term policy solutions for education and training that are very often ill-defined or only tenuously linked to the search for longer-term economic forecasting (see Barakat, Kane and Inglis in this section) or the rebuilding of identity and the forging of a new democratic citizenship (see Paulson in this section).

The third context in which VET might function is as a strategic driver of human development. In this case, the vocational education response is not an isolated response. Here it is necessary for more 'joined-up thinking' about VET as a learning system, and as a more integrated delivery system. This is not as yet fully appreciated between NGOs and frontline agencies (see Karpinska in this section).

The fourth context in which VET might function is in the re-building of a nation in the aftermath of conflict. There is a growing body of theoretical work on education as a process in rebuilding civil society and TVET's role in this has been identified by some as crucial (see Humphreys & Weinstein, 2004). Because access (or the lack thereof) to education and training gives rise to conflict in the first place, and because of its role in building peace and minimizing the horizontal inequalities discussed above, the role of TVET in securing peace and stability is an important focus of enquiry. We offer, in Fig. 1, a conceptual model of the field of education and conflict studies.

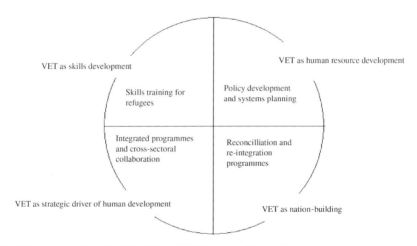

Fig. 1 A conceptual model of the field of TVET and conflict studies

4 Overview of the Contributions

Framed by the conceptual model discussed above, we return to the three questions raised earlier and consider how they are variously addressed in this section.

V.2 From Assessment to Planning: Hope for TVET in Uganda, by Bilal Barakat, Lyle Kane and Alex Inglis

The first of the questions above is explored by Bilal Barakat, Lyle Kane and Alex Inglis. The authors stress the need for improved assessment tools to advise TVET planning in post-conflict situations. Using the case study of Uganda, where the most thorough study of war-affected populations to date has taken place (The Survey for War-Affected Youth or SWAY), this chapter discusses the importance of reliable data and ways in which it has the potential to shape TVET programming in northern Uganda so as to be contextually appropriate in terms of supporting social reintegration and matching opportunities in the economy.

V.3 Linking TVET to Economic Opportunities in Post-Conflict Liberia, by Lyle Kane

The theme is further taken up by Lyle Kane in this chapter. He further explores the need to design TVET programming around the specific economic context of the target population. He explores the problems facing the TVET programmes associated with the United Nations' Disarmament, Demobilization and Reintegration (DDR) initiatives in Liberia, the mismatch between training and economic opportunities, and the way the aid system can bridge that mismatch through more contextually appropriate TVET programming and nurture and create economic opportunities.

V.4 Deepening the Divide: The Differential Impact of Protracted Conflict on TVET Versus Academic Education in Palestine, by Bilal Barakat

Continuing this line of exploration, Bilal Barakat's chapter aims at illustrating the varying impact of conflict on TVET compared to general education. The chapter makes the point that TVET is negatively perceived among Palestinians in terms of both national aspirations and personal emancipation as compared to academic education. In the case of the continuing 'low intensity' Palestinian–Israeli conflict, these issues are of great importance.

V.5 Co-ordinated Programming for Skills Development and Livelihoods in Post-Conflict Societies: What Promise Does TVET Hold for Southern Sudan? by Zuki Karpinska

Karpinska's chapter engages with the second theme. She examines the difficulties of government, external agency and NGO co-ordination in providing cohesive and effective TVET. The chapter uses the region of Southern Sudan as a case study, a context rife with complicated political, economic, physical and social challenges.

While grim in her description of the current state of TVET implementation in the region, Karpinska is hopeful that recent co-ordination efforts have created a setting for improvements in service delivery.

V.6 Vocational Training in Post-War Sierra Leone and Liberia, by **Andrew Benson Greene Jr.**

In his chapter, Andrew Benson Greene further mines this line of enquiry. He discusses the need for TVET programming to take advantage of new technologies, while nurturing and developing traditional craftsmen, such as blacksmiths, to support the agricultural sector. The chapter uses a set of existing programmes to paint a picture of TVET in post-conflict Sierra Leone, emphasizing existing programmatic solutions to the contextual obstacles facing war-affected populations, such as support for amputees in the form of prosthetics, and the need to design programming around local social and cultural structures.

V.7 TVET and Community Re-Integration: Exploring the Connections in Sierra Leone's DDR Process, by **Julia Paulson**

Julia Paulson furthers the discussion of the third theme outlined above. Her chapter discusses the ways in which TVET acts as a tool for reintegration of ex-combatants, using as a lens the DDR initiatives in Sierra Leone. Paulson goes on to pose the question of how TVET can be more effective in the reintegration process.

V.8 TVET, Women and Conflict: Palestinians in the Lebanese Civil War, by **Rachel Yarrow**

The question of individual agency is further taken up in Rachel Yarrow's chapter. This chapter describes and analyses the activities of two NGOs providing TVET to Palestinian women during the Lebanese Civil War. Yarrow discusses the extent to which these two case studies effectively capitalized on the opportunities offered by the post-conflict situation to reshape 'traditional' or 'conservative' gender roles and empower women. The concern is not an academic one. In an informal assessment of a tailoring programme offered to young women from the camps, one NGO came to the conclusion that the girls that passed through the programme were doing worse than those that did not. Those that passed through the programme found little demand for their skills in their home camps. Meanwhile, those that did not pass through the programme found ways to return to formal education.

   Thus, this section offers an overview of the challenges for educational reconstruction in a number of single-country cases. Normally, it would be useful to group countries in respect of the historical stage of conflict and reconstruction (e.g. Angola, Burundi, Sierra Leone and Sri Lanka are examples of countries emerging from conflict, whilst Cambodia, Guatemala, Lebanon and Nicaragua have longer histories of post-conflict reconstruction) and effecting comparisons within the group. However, due to limited space in this section, we have decided to offer simply selected examples of writings on vocational education and the challenges of employment and citizenship.

Notes

1. Well-being is defined here as opportunities for educational, social and economic participation.
2. One of the initial causes of the ethnic conflict between Sinhalese and Tamils in Sri Lanka was the frustration felt by Tamil students, who had been shut out of places in universities and other avenues for civic involvement.
3. Five youth transitions are identified in the literature: learning, going to work, staying healthy, forming families, and exercising citizenship (see World Bank, 2007).
4. Ukiwo (2007) shows how the lack of education among Northerners in Nigeria in the early years of independence debarred Northerners not only from high-level federal civil-service positions, but even from running their own state.

References

Annan, J.; Blattman, C.; Horton, R. 2006. *The state of youth and youth protection in Uganda.* Kampala: UNICEF Uganda.

Buckland, P. 2005 *Reshaping the future: education and post-conflict reconstruction.* Washington, DC: World Bank.

Humphreys, M.; Weinstein, J.M. 2004. *What the fighters say: a survey of ex-combatants in Sierra Leone, June-August 2003.* New York, NY: Columbia University. (Center on Globlization and Sustainable Development, working paper, no. 20.) <www.stanford.edu/~jweinst/docs/manuscripts/humphreys_combatantsurvey.pdf>

Johnson, D.; Stewart, F. 2007. Education, ethnicity and conflict. *International journal of education and development,* vol. 27, no. 3, pp. 247–51

Johnson, D.; Van Kalmthout, E. 2006. Education and conflict: research, policy and practice. *Forced migration review,* supplement, July. <www.fmreview.org/FMRpdfs/EducationSupplement/full.pdf>

Mancini, L. 2005. *Horizontal inequalities and communal violence: evidence from Indonesian districts.* Oxford, UK: Centre for Research on Inequality, Human Security and Ethnicity. (CRISE working paper, 22.) <www.crise.ox.ac.uk>

Marshall, M.G. 2005. *Major episodes of political violence, 1946–2004.* Severn, MD: Centre for Systemic Peace.

Østby, G. 2003. *Horizontal inequalities and civil war.* Oslo: Norwegian University of Science and Technology.

Stewart, F. 2000. Crisis prevention: tackling horizontal inequalities. *Oxford development studies,* vol. 28, no. 3, pp. 245–62.

Ukiwo, U. 2007. *The 'reform' agenda: liberalization, technocracy and democratization in Nigeria, 1999–2007.* Berkeley, CA: University of California.

United Nations Development Programme. 2003. *Millennium Development Goals: a compact amongst nations to end poverty.* New York, NY: UNDP.

World Bank. 2003. *Breaking the conflict trap: civil war and development policy.* Washington, DC: Oxford University Press/World Bank.

World Bank. 2007. *World development report: development and the next generation.* Washington, DC: World Bank.

Chapter V.2
From Assessment to Planning: Hope for TVET in Uganda

Bilal Barakat, Lyle Kane and Alex Inglis

1 Introduction

One of the major obstacles facing the implementation of TVET programming in post-conflict situations is a lack of data on the needs and skills of the target population. In terms of a strict concentration on the ability of TVET programming to improve the skill-set and employability of participants, this lack of data poses the problem of leading to a mismatch between TVET and the contextual economic opportunities. But, in the post-conflict context, where the implementation of a holistic approach to TVET is necessary, with an integrated set of programmes designed to address the challenges specific to a war-affected population, a lack of data poses a much more serious set of problems.

Inappropriate programming can even exacerbate the challenges facing war-affected populations rather than support their recovery. Culturally insensitive psychological therapy exercises, unsuitable housing schemes for displaced persons, ignorance of the physical frailties of injured persons—it is not hard to imagine the ways in which these mistakes could have a negative impact on the experience of programme participants.

The lack of reliable data is a complex problem to overcome. Post-conflict contexts are often defined by a collapsed or weak government and social-service infrastructure. As a result, what data can be collected are often unreliable or potentially manipulated. In addition, in order to be truly effective and avoid a time lag between the end of the conflict and delivery of services, data should be collected during the conflict, posing risks for the safety of data collectors. Access to the potential target population in the midst of war is often tenuous at best.

> One consequence of this state of affairs is that programming is often based on immediate and observable needs, rules of thumb, and possibly erroneous assumptions about what sort of help ought to be provided. With only rough measures of well-being at our disposal, a second consequence is unavoidably crude targeting of services (Annan, Blattman & Horton, 2006, p. iii).

One thing is clear: there is a marked lack of international standards in terms of data collection for war-affected populations. This has the potential to lead to programming that is poorly matched to the needs of the population. In the best-case scenario,

R. Maclean, D. Wilson (eds.), *International Handbook of Education for the Changing World of Work*, DOI 10.1007/978-1-4020-5281-1_V.2,
© Springer Science+Business Media B.V. 2009

such mismatched programming has simply been a waste of time and money. In a worst-case scenario, it has created a new set of challenges for the target population to contend with.

A current example of an attempt to address this problem is the UNICEF Uganda commissioned Survey for War-Affected Youth (SWAY). This project set out to assess the effects of the conflict in northern Uganda on the youth in the region. Utilizing quantitative surveys and qualitative interviews, SWAY seeks to answer the question 'who is suffering, how much and in what ways?' (Annan, Blattman & Horton, 2006, p. iii). While these questions about suffering are relevant, they seem incomplete. As a recent World Bank report points out: 'for education reform and transformation, the post-conflict reconstruction environment is the best of times and the worst of times, an opportunity and a constraint' (Buckland, 2005, p. 25). There are undoubtedly a set of skills and abilities that come out of being actively involved in a conflict that can aid in post-conflict reconstruction.

This chapter aims to examine the relationship between needs/skills assessment and a holistic approach to TVET programming, using northern Uganda as a case-study.

The first section provides a brief overview of the key features of the conflict. The second section describes recent and existing TVET initiatives. The third section discusses the structure of SWAY as an outstanding and timely example of needs assessment during conflict, making some critiques of its limitations. The findings are discussed and the recommendations reviewed. The fourth section looks at the upcoming TVET initiatives in Uganda and the way that SWAY can improve the effectiveness of these initiatives. The concluding remarks include general recommendations for assessment and planning practices that can improve TVET programming in post-conflict situations.

2 A Brief Overview of the Conflict in (Northern) Uganda

In 1962, Uganda gained its independence from British rule. Since that time the country's development has been marked by deep social and political volatility and civil war. The instability seemed to have come to and end in 1986 with the conclusive military victory of the National Resistance Movement (NRM) led by the current president Yoweri Museveni. However, rebels opposed to the NRM reorganized themselves in southern Sudan and later became known as the Lord's Resistance Army (LRA) under the leadership of Joseph Kony. Disappointed by the inability to present a credible military threat to the NRM regime, and particularly with the lack of popular support among the communities of northern Uganda, the LRA turned against the civilian population, brutally terrorizing it with acts of murder, torture and mutilation (WCRWC, 2005)

A particular feature of the conflict in northern Uganda is the wide-scale abduction and recruitment by the LRA of male and female youth into forced labour, sexual slavery and combat roles. Recent evidence suggests that the number of young people abducted during the war is 60,000 or even higher (Blattman, 2006). The capacity of the LRA was strengthened through support from the government of Sudan beginning in 1994 to engage in a proxy war against southern Sudanese rebels who were, in turn, being supported by the Ugandan government (WCRWC, 2001).

Since 1996, much of the population of northern Uganda has been forced by the government to resettle in 'protected villages', which are essentially IDP (internally displaced persons) camps. These camps are not only crowded and unsanitary, but they often fail to offer protection. Their population continues to suffer from attacks, to the extent that large numbers of young people prefer to commute to larger towns at night to avoid forced recruitment (WCRWC, 2005). Moreover, curfews and a prohibition on travel far from the camps have meant that most have lost access to their land. Conflict over land tenure upon return of the IDPs to their communities is a real risk in post-conflict northern Uganda.

Facilitated by the Comprehensive Peace Agreement for southern Sudan, negotiations between the Ugandan government and the LRA have recently moved forward culminating in a cease-fire agreement in August 2006 and the retreat of LRA fighters to assembly zones on the Sudanese side of the border (United Nations, OCHA, 2006). For the first time in decades, an end to the conflict seems feasible—though by no means certain.

3 TVET in (Northern) Uganda

In contrast to many other conflict and post-conflict settings, Uganda maintains an established and relatively stable government. Its managerial capacity and political will appear favourable to effective educational reconstruction (WCRWC, 2001, p. 61), subject to the availability of sufficient funds. Several schemes for complementary basic education of target populations, such as the urban poor, nomads and conflict-affected children, already exist. There is also a strong movement towards decentralization, allowing for some flexibility in addressing the needs created by a conflict that varied in its local intensity. Government investment in education has been high. In the financial year 2001/2002, around 20% of the government budget was spent on education and training (Farstad, 2002). In contrast, public financing for TVET in Uganda is limited and the main responsibility is placed on the private sector for both delivery and financing. The private training providers deliver programming in a variety of areas and at different levels, and issue their own certificates. Private institutions are not obliged to register with the Ministry of Education and Sports (MoES), but are encouraged to do so.

In 2000 TVET was delivered by some twenty-nine government technical and agricultural training centres with a total intake of 3,340 (Farstad, 2002). There were 187 registered private TVET institutions and another 400 that have applied for registration. These private centres follow a national curriculum instituted by the government. Industrial training is delivered by four public vocational training institutes and some 400 private training providers. Both of these streams, in particular the former, have attracted criticism for being too academic. TVET also features prominently as Strategic Objective 2 in Uganda's National Action Plan on Youth, which likewise emphasizes apprenticeship schemes over formal State provision of training (Uganda, MoGLSD, 2002)

Vocational training is a fairly common experience among male youth in northern Uganda: '20 percent of youth over the age of 16 have had some sort of vocational training, primarily in trades like construction, carpentry and joinery, and driving. Such programmes were generally paid for by the youth themselves or their families' (Annan, Blattman & Horton, 2006, p. 32). This is despite the fact that, as in many places, there is a cultural bias, with a stronger orientation towards formal education than towards TVET. Many enrol in TVET because of their poor test results and failure to gain entry into an academic institution.

The economic context for TVET provision in Uganda is one of a dominantly rural and agrarian economy, especially in the north. In the Apaca district in the north, home to over 600,000 people, the largest employer, an engineering firm, has a mere thirty employees. While, in principle, it is possible for a large number of micro-enterprises to offer a substantial number of employed positions when all taken together, the reality in northern Uganda remains that the economy depends on small-scale agriculture according to customary land tenure. This is borne out by urbanization rates, which peak in the Gulu district at around 25%, but are below 5% in several other northern districts. (The national average is 13%.) (See the *Uganda districts information handbook* (Rwabwogo, 2005) for all of the above.)

4 The Survey for War-Affected Youth—SWAY

Until recently, very little reliable information was available on the effects of war in northern Uganda. While psycho-social studies of individual victims existed, there was little hard evidence about community effects or the prevalence of exposure to violence. SWAY has attempted to address this gap. As mentioned above, it applied a mixed methodology of quantitative surveys and qualitative interviews. A detailed survey of 750 male youth from a specific war-affected region was followed by thirty in-depth interviews of randomly selected individuals from the survey group.

One of the primary arguments that SWAY makes in terms of methodology and participant selection is that the Western methods for categorizing youth are poorly matched to local realities. The Western definition of 'child' as anyone under the age of 18 simply does not hold true for much of the world. In many cultures in Uganda, the transition from youth to adult is defined by marriage or ownership of land. SWAY decided upon a more contextually relevant and broad definition of youth as anyone between the ages of 14 and 30. In addition, SWAY argues that categories, such as 'the formerly abducted' or the 'orphaned', are circumstantial:

> Targeting based on these simple categories would appear to miss more than half of the most vulnerable youth: the severely injured, the illiterate, the unemployed, those estranged from their families, or those with severe symptoms of emotional distress. In fact, the proportion of acutely vulnerable youth inside these circumstantial categories only slightly exceeds the

proportion outside of them; hence the predictive power of this method is exceedingly poor (Annan, Blattman & Horton, 2006, p. 80).

While the scope of the project is impressive, the gender dimension is problematic. Motivated by the desire to test and improve the methodology on the presumably easier to research group of male youth, the study of females has been deferred to a second, later, project phase. The problem of the exclusion of females from Phase I—whether the justification is sound or not—is exacerbated by the fact that it has not been sufficiently highlighted. The title of the preliminary report gives no indication of an exclusively male focus, thereby inviting the potentially misleading or inappropriate generalization of the findings—and programmes based on them—to both genders. But there is every reason to suspect that the conflict's impact on its victims differs by gender. The prevalence of sexual and gender-based violence across modern conflicts has also played itself out in the Uganda. Amnesty International reports evidence of widespread sexual violence committed by both sides in the Ugandan conflict (Amnesty International, 2004). Obviously, the effects of this cannot be simply ignored in post-conflict recovery programming. One advantage that Uganda does have over much of the rest of Africa in terms of health issues related to sexual violence is that HIV awareness is relatively high and condom usage is common, although the conflict-affected north fares worse than the national average (Tumushabe, 2006).

However, SWAY did produce some conclusions that run counter to popular perceptions and that are highly relevant to programming for skills development. The survey found that while 35% of males and between 15% and 20% of all females had been abducted for at least a day, all youth, whether abducted or not, have suffered and witnessed tremendous violence. The average survey participant had witnessed or partaken in nine of the thirty-one types of violent experiences that they were questioned about. Nevertheless, it also showed only modest levels of psycho-social trauma and low levels of aggression. Moreover, even traumatized individuals exhibited a high level of social functioning. Uganda is relatively unique in terms of conflict and post-conflict recovery in that social structures remained relatively intact throughout the war. As a result, many of the challenges associated with reintegration have been mitigated by the nature of the existing support structures in the larger community. The key elements to successful social reintegration were found to be family cohesion and peer support. The relative strength of these two support structures in the Ugandan case has led to the surprising lack of emotional distress in youth returning from conflict.

The survey asserts that 'family acceptance is remarkably high. Only 1% of youth report that their family was unhappy or unwelcoming upon their return. Over 94% of the youth report being accepted by their families without insult, blame or physical aggression' (Annan, Blattman & Horton, 2006, p. 66) Reception from the community was 'typically strong and welcoming'. Insults and fear were reported, but are not seen as particularly detrimental to reintegration. In fact, nearly all forced recruits who escaped from the LRA returned to their home communities. This is in spite of the fact that many were forced to commit atrocities against their neighbours, friends or even families. Acceptance of ex-combatants as regular members of the community, however, is coupled with resentment of programmes targeted specifically at them, essentially being perceived as a reward for violent activity. These findings undermine the logic behind the huge investment in reintegration support that has become standard in post-conflict recovery programming. SWAY calls for a shift from broad-based psycho-social programming to targeted support for the minority of returnees actually suffering from severe emotional stress.

In addition to the relatively stable social structures within the communities that the abductees were returning to, reintegration is helped by a very strong local tradition of spiritual cleansing of returnees as a sufficient condition for community acceptance. The cultural interpretation of stress and trauma often plays itself out on a religious plane and is addressed through the structure of religion (Annan, Blattman & Horton, 2006, p. iv).

Currently, few young people have safe access to land (Stites, Mazurana & Carlson, 2006) and therefore to traditional livelihoods. This might change as the 'decongestion' of IDP camps continues, especially if they are dismantled entirely in the near future. The lack of opportunity for agriculture has meant that most youth that are economically active perform casual labour such as collecting firewood, carrying loads, quarrying, hawking and vending, construction, riding a *boda boda* (bicycle taxi), or making bricks and charcoal. Formal employment is rare: 'just fifteen percent of occupations represent more or less regular (and usually high-skilled) employment—operating a repair shop or small business (such as a kiosk), a vocation (including carpentry, tailoring, and driving), or a profession (a teacher, public employee, or health worker)' (Annan, Blattman & Horton, 2006, p. 37).

As a result, the median monthly income of youth in the conflict affected areas is less than US$5 per month. Nevertheless, 'few youth leave the region to look for work—primarily, it seems, because of few contacts, fewer resources, no language skills, and an emotional tie to their homes' (p. 35).

5 Implications for Holistic TVET Programming

As mentioned, SWAY's results suggest that many are abducted for relatively short periods of time and their education is only moderately affected. Those abducted lost an average of one year's schooling. It therefore seems particularly appropriate to aim educational interventions at all youth, because the experience of 'episodic' education 'due to financial pressures arising from poverty, insecurity and lack of family support' does not differentiate former child soldiers from those never abducted.

The major finding of the SWAY study is the need for 'age-appropriate education and income generating activities' (Annan, Blattman & Horton, 2006, p. iii). The average youth surveyed only worked seven days each month earning US$3.85 (p. v). SWAY describes the economy as an 'occupational ladder' where you have increasing opportunities with increasing skills and training (p. v). Unfortunately, given these dire economic circumstances, the opportunity costs to enrolment in TVET and other educational programming often put them out of reach of many returnees.

There are still a set of health-related issues that are interfering with returnees integrating into the labour force. Firstly, war related injuries are a formidable problem. Over 15% of the surveyed youth have been injured or are debilitated in some way that affects their ability to work. Some 2% are 'extremely injured' and in need of urgent treatment (p. vi). Secondly, poverty related nutrition problems are prevalent with 40% of the surveyed youth only eating one meal a day (p. vi). The devastating effects of HIV/AIDS, both direct and indirect in terms of creating children-headed households, add to the problem (Stites, Mazurana & Carlson, 2006).

As the following quotations show, there is much room for improving the provision of TVET as part of the reconstruction process in northern Uganda:

> Current programming has focused primarily on humanitarian needs and psychosocial support (broadly-defined) but has tended to neglect interventions to support war injuries, education, and economic activities (Annan, Blattman & Horton, 2006, p. 72).
>
> The lack of education and the shortage of skilled individuals in most of the study sites constrain livelihood strategies. Many of the schools in and around the camps are barely functioning as educational institutions (Stites, Mazurana & Carlson, 2006, p. 9).
>
> Technical/vocational training exists, but is far too limited in its scope. Apprenticeships and the provision of tools upon graduation would go far to assist graduating students in finding and being able to work (WCRWC, 2005, p. 10).

There is, in fact, some experience in Uganda with TVET as part of the DDR and reconstruction effort following the consolidation of NRM's power in the early 1990s. But the relevance of this for the current situation should not be overstated. The aim then was the formal disarmament, demobilization and reintegration of parts of a regularized guerrilla army. The challenge in northern Uganda, by contrast, involves building sustainable livelihoods for whole communities. Even with regard to ex-combatants, there is little similarity. Abductions and the trickling back of those escaping have been a continuous process over the course of a decade. Only half of those returning ever passed through any kind of reception centre. Some studies of past 'Reintegration through Training' programmes can, and should, provide an important foundation to be built upon. The Gulu Vocational and Community Centre, for example, gathered experience during the 1990s with the integration of vocational training for youth with community outreach, adult literacy and peace education (Muhumuza, 1997).

It is important to note that the expansion of existing training programmes will not necessarily replicate the economic benefits currently evident, because the present self-selection has a bias towards those who are more entrepreneurial to begin with. Indeed NGO-funded youth appear to benefit less from training than self-funded ones. Unfortunately, 'we don't know whether, when and why vocational programs assist youth' (Annan, Blattman & Horton, 2006, p. 34). Accordingly, the actual effect of training is one of the main areas where further research is needed.

Without such research, training interventions might actually do harm as, indeed, such interventions have on previous occasions. Indeed, SWAY reports on a tailoring training programme whose participants fared worse than women left to their own devices (p. 34). Moreover, TVET interventions designed for reconstruction and reintegration need to respect what is an important best practice in non-conflict settings, namely that TVET should not be an academic dead-end. Otherwise what is intended as a remedial measure could in fact end up increasing the disadvantage of conflict-affected youth who might otherwise have found their way back into and succeeded in the formal education sector.

SWAY's findings suggests that 'individuals themselves may be better judges of what skills and opportunities suit their own skill set, interests, and local demands' (Annan, Blattman & Horton, 2006, p. 74) and that it might be more effective to provide vouchers that could be used towards NGO or private training programmes (see WCRWC, 2005, for a list of these). This, however, leaves open the question of what support NGOs should have when setting up programmes.

A liberalized but regulated approach such as the one described above resonates well with government policy. Recent initiatives include the plan to create the Uganda Vocational Education and Training Authority (UVETA). The proposed UVETA is expected to stay away from basic training delivery, but rather focus on promoting financing of and co-ordinating all formal and non-formal training activities (Haan, 2001).

Part of the reform process is a Universal Post-Primary Education and Training (UPPET) policy. It includes the provision of equipment to business, technical, vocational education and training (BTVET) institutions, as well as introducing community polytechnics to all districts, including the conflict-affected north, where grants and bursaries are paid for students in secondary and technical schools (Okecho, 2006). This appears to go some way to meeting SWAY's concern that 'there is an urgent and immediate need to support broad-based secondary and tertiary schooling' (Annan, Blattman & Horton, 2006, p. 71) for the most needy.

The training needs of youth who were actively involved in the conflict are not strikingly different from those of their peers. Their moderate loss of schooling does not present an insurmountable obstacle to entering regular BTVET, because BTVET programming offered is at the intermediate level and only requires primary education to enter. In the IDP camps in northern Uganda, schooling is effective in the basic sense of achieving relatively high primary enrolment and basic literacy. Enrolment is not far below the national average of 90% of the primary school age-group enrolled and the literacy rate is around 70%. However, quality in the IDP camps is highly problematic. In Kitgum, 140 primary schools have been displaced into thirty-four learning centres associated with IDP camps. This has resulted in ludicrous congestion with—arithmetically—up to 300 children per teacher and up to 400 per classroom (WCRWC, 2005).

Mainstreaming seems appropriate for all but the most heavily traumatized who spent many years in the LRA and lost most or all of their schooling opportunities, for whom, in any case, TVET is not the first concern. Notably, high trauma appears to be associated with community rejection more than with the severity of violence experienced or with lack of education or training opportunities. For these cases, educational and training components of rehabilitation interventions need to be part of a holistic approach. Their relatively small number makes it feasible in principle to offer intensive personal support to these hardship cases.

A major source of concern for TVET and livelihood interventions, however, is those who have been disabled as a result of the conflict. Thirteen percent of youth in the SWAY sample were found to possess 'an injury that impeded them from earning a living' (Annan, Blattman & Horton, 2006, p. 46).

Given the traditionally strong social cohesion, community-based rather than individualistic projects appear most promising. An example of a community programme supported effectively by international non-governmental organizations is GUSCO, the Gulu Support the Children Organization (Omona & Matheson, 1998). GUSCO runs reception centres for traumatized children, where they receive vocational training, trauma counselling and family reintegration support. While children only stay in the centres for up to six weeks, reintegration follow-up is conducted regularly until a year after release. On the one hand, GUSCO's approach demonstrates the effectiveness of integrating TVET into a participatory approach based on local traditions; on the other hand, it also confirms that providing even medium-term follow-up requires the dedication of significant resources and is unlikely to be feasible on a mass scale.

The low rate of urbanization means that training in institutional settings runs the risk mentioned in the introduction: it will often run counter to reintegration into home communities for the simple reason that training institutions are geographically located elsewhere and require the trainees' absence from the very communities where they seek integration.

Given the rural economy of northern Uganda, TVET cannot be expected to result in wage employment. If the livelihood options for the majority consist at best of entrepreneurial self-employment (but more realistically of small-scale agriculture or micro-enterprise self-employment), education and training for livelihoods has to reflect this fact (Stavrou & Stewart, 2000; Stites, Mazurana & Carlson, 2006).

In northern Uganda it is argued that 'a return to the land is the only realistic economic option, not just for the long term, but now' (Annan, Blattman & Horton, 2006, p. 75). There are signs that this return is imminent. Despite the uncertainty over whether the conflict will truly end and warnings of the consequences of premature and forced return in particular, the IDP camps have since the end of 2006 been slated to be dismantled (Uganda-CAN, 2006a).

While solving some problems, this promises to create new ones. The prolonged absence and the destruction of traditional boundary markers during the conflict mean that the traditional tenure will be difficult to reinstate. There is also fear of losing land in the face of large-scale commercialization of agriculture. Due to high population growth, there will also be many more people returning to the countryside than originally left it. Land insecurity, therefore, has serious implications both for local livelihoods and the sustainability of peace (Uganda-CAN, 2006b). The promotion of sustainable livelihoods must therefore 'include innovative strategies for increasing access to land in addition to [...] attention on other income-generating activities' (Annan, Blattman & Horton, 2006, p. 71).

6 Concluding Remarks

The Survey for War-Affected Youth (SWAY) was not designed as a needs assessment for TVET. Yet it does carry important implications for TVET's role in mitigating the effects of the conflict. This should not surprise us since skills development needs arise out of the reality of people's lives.

It is instructive to compare SWAY's approach with other examples of the effects of the war in northern Uganda, particularly those conducted by the Women's Commission for Refugee Women and Children (WCRWC) in 2001 and a study by Tuft University's Feinstein International Center in 2006 (Stites, Mazurana & Carlson, 2006). Both are decidedly neither longitudinal nor randomized, but follow a more qualitative approach. Like SWAY, WCRWC produced conclusions of significance to TVET programming, especially the more recent study with its focus on livelihoods. Together, they drive home the importance of multi-methodology, rigorous research to provide the basis for sound programme design.

However, a number of critical questions remain. To begin with, how do environmental factors bear on the feasibility of a 'larger-scale, randomly sampled, longitudinal survey'? Can we expect it to be possible to replicate SWAY's success in tracing youth that had migrated in contexts where social networks have broken down to a much larger extent or where the conflict itself is more chaotic, involving a multitude of armed factions and shifting coalitions? Even if it is possible, it might well take a disproportionate effort.

Time is another important factor. While a time span of less than a year between the start of the project and the presentation of its Phase I results is in itself impressive, the fact that at least two years will have passed until even both genders have been surveyed is an important constraint. While greater resources can no doubt go some way towards speeding up the physical data collection, this is not necessarily what takes the longest. It is a regrettable—but inescapable—fact that in other contexts where there is a well-defined 'end' to the conflict in the form of the signing of a peace treaty, or the collapse of a regime, funds may become available for TVET and other programming that have to be spent more quickly. This is, of course, another reason to conduct assessments while conflict is still on-going, but this in turn risks the situation changing drastically when hostilities cease, because returning refugees and/or demobilized soldiers change the local dynamic, and the labour market in particular.

Either way, the profile of those whose livelihoods are to be supported represents only one kind of assessment that is necessary to determine the appropriate initiatives. Not only the demand for training, but also surveys of the availability of training and skills development, and of the demand for graduates and livelihood opportunities are necessary. Reliable quantitative and qualitative assessments are not only crucial to informed programming, but also to provide a baseline against which programme success can eventually be determined.

Compared to general education, it would seem that effective planning of TVET programmes for reconstruction is, if anything, even more dependent on reliable data on all the dimensions of demand and supply mentioned above. Capital investments for many kinds of TVET are higher than for general education and, in many ways, TVET is inherently more difficult to build up incrementally.

While the physical infrastructure for general education is relatively flexible and can be used for literacy classes and adult education outside school hours, specialized technical or agricultural training institutions lack this generic quality.

This provides yet another reason for focusing on the participatory and community-based promotion of generic skills for livelihoods as 'life-skills' in conflict and

post-conflict contexts, over highly specialized and capital-intensive technical training, at least as an initial response. Such an approach also ties in with the inclusion
of life-skills and the integration of health, civic, livelihood and academic content in
general school curricula, blurring a potentially unhelpful distinction.

References

Amnesty International. 2004. *AI report 2004: Uganda.* <web.amnesty.org/report2004/uga-
summary-eng>

Annan, J.; Blattman, C.; Horton, R. 2006. *The state of youth and youth protection in northern
Uganda: findings from the Survey for War Affected Youth.* Kampala: UNICEF.

Blattman, C. 2006. *The consequences of child soldiering.* Brighton, UK: Institute of Development
Studies, Sussex University. <www.hicn.org/papers/wp22.pdf>

Buckland, P. 2005. *Reshaping the future: education and postconflict reconstruction.* Washington,
DC: World Bank.

Farstad, H. 2002. *Integrated entrepreneurship education in Botswana, Kenya and Uganda.* Oslo:
National Institute of Technology.

Haan, H.C. 2001. *Training for work in the informal sector: evidence from Eastern and Southern
Africa.* Washington, DC: World Bank and ILO.

Muhumuza, R. 1997. *Guns into ox-ploughs: a study on the situation of conflict-affected youth
in Uganda and their reintegration into society through training, employment and life skills
programmes.* Geneva: ILO.

Okecho, C.W. 2006. *Education in the Northern Uganda.* (Paper presented at the Education Sector
Review, 25–27 October 2006, Kampala.) <www.education.go.ug/Northern.htm>

Omona, G.; Matheson, K.E. 1998. Uganda: stolen children, stolen lives. *Lancet,* vol. 351, no. 9100,
p. 442.

Rwabwogo, M.O. 2005. *Uganda districts information handbook: expanded edition 2005–2006.*
Kampala: Fountain Publishers.

Stavrou, S.; Stewart, R. 2000. The reintegration of child soldiers and abducted children: a case
study of Palaro and Pabbo Gulu District, northern Uganda. *In:* Bennett, E.; Gamba, V.; van der
Merwe, D., eds. *ACT against child soldiers in Africa.* Pretoria: Institute of Security Studies.

Stites, E.; Mazurana, D.; Carlson, K. 2006. *Movement on the margins: livelihoods and security in
Kitgum District, northern Uganda.* Medford, MA: Feinstein International Center.

Tumushabe, J. 2006. *The politics of HIV/AIDS in Uganda.* Geneva, Switzerland: United Nations
Research Institute for Social Development. (Social Policy and Development Programme paper,
no. 28.)

Uganda Conflict Action Network—Uganda-CAN. 2006a. *Minister of relief: all northern Uganda
IDP camps to be dismantled by Dec. 31.* <www.ugandacan.org/index.php?catid=7&blogid=1>

Uganda Conflict Action Network—Uganda-CAN. 2006b. *Land in Uganda.* <www.ugandacan.
org/land.php>

Uganda. Ministry of Gender, Labour and Social Development—MoGLSD. 2002. *National Action
Plan on Youth.* Kampala: MoGLSD.

United Nations. Office for the Co-ordination of Humanitarian Affairs—OCHA. 2006. Uganda:
most rebels have left northern Uganda for Sudan. *IRIN news,* 26 September 2006.
<www.irinnews.org/report.asp?ReportID=55722>

Women's Commission for Refugee Women and Children—WCRWC. 2001. *Against all
odds: surviving the war on adolescents. Promoting the protection and capacity of
Ugandan and Sudanese adolescents in northern Uganda.* New York, NY: WCRWC.
<www.womenscommission.org/pdf/ug.pdf>

Women's Commission for Refugee Women and Children—WCRWC. 2005. *Learning in a war
zone: education in northern Uganda.* New York, NY: WCRWC.

Chapter V.3
Linking TVET to Economic Opportunities in Post-Conflict Liberia

Lyle Kane

1 Introduction

Many would argue that the success of a technical and vocational educational and training (TVET) programme should be measured by how it improves the employability of its participants. Assuming that this is correct, it is a complex outcome to measure, as there are a number of factors, other than participation in vocational education programmes, that impact upon an individual's ability to work (as is discussed throughout this section in our argument for a holistic approach to TVET.) Ultimately, however, the goal of TVET is to support participant inclusion into the labour force. Given this fact, the need to link TVET programming to economic opportunities within the local context cannot be over-emphasized.

Post-conflict economies, almost without exception, are fragile and poorly functioning. The effects of extended conflict include the destruction of the physical infrastructure, struggling social services and stagnation across most economic sectors. The *need* for skilled labour in these circumstances is huge, in that the reconstruction process is labour-intensive and requires a skilled labour force. But, the *demand* for labour, in terms of paid employment opportunities, is usually small given the state of the economy. This chapter will be using the case of Liberia to explore the necessity to structure TVET programming around the labour *needs* of the target population, while working within the larger reconstruction strategy to negotiate the gap between the *need* and *demand* for labour.

2 Politics, Conflict and Education in Liberia

On Christmas Day 1989, Charles Taylor's National Patriotic Front of Liberia (NPFL) entered Liberia, marking the beginning of the country's civil war. In 1990, after a year of brutal and intense fighting, a splinter group of the NPFL captured, tortured and assassinated President Samuel Doe. The president's death set up a scramble for power between several armed factions that would continue for the next fourteen years (Ellis, 2001).

R. Maclean, D. Wilson (eds.), *International Handbook of Education for the Changing World of Work*, DOI 10.1007/978-1-4020-5281-1_V.3,
© Springer Science+Business Media B.V. 2009

After a 1994 ceasefire failed to hold, a negotiated truce in 1997 was followed by elections. With a campaign slogan of 'He killed my mother, he killed my father, but I will vote for him', Charles Taylor was elected head of State. President Taylor was accused of widespread corruption, supporting the conflict in Sierra Leone and engaging in hostilities with Guinea. In 2002, the simmering tension between Taylor and his opposition parties within the country boiled over and the civil war resumed. Under increasing pressure from the most dominant opposition faction, Liberians United for Reconciliation and Democracy (LURD), Charles Taylor vacated the presidency and went into exile in Nigeria in August 2003.

On 11 September 2003, the United Nations Mission in Liberia (UNMIL) was established. UNMIL and the Economic Community of West-African States (ECOWAS) supported an interim government until the country was prepared to hold democratic elections. Much of the international community saw the interim government as incompetent or corrupt. A report to the Secretary-General of the United Nations stated: 'The financial administration of the National Transitional Government of Liberia continues to be weak with an archaic internal control system and a virtually non-existent external oversight system' (UN News Centre, 2005). As a result, very little was accomplished over the next two years.

In November 2005, Ellen Johnson-Sirleaf was elected president of Liberia, the first female head of State on the African continent. A former World Bank economist, President Johnson-Sirleaf is well-respected by the international community, and her policies to date have been widely regarded as transparent and sound (see, for example, World Bank, 2006a). While strong in terms of policy, the current government has faced a huge obstacle in terms of access to reliable funding.

Despite continuing economic problems, Liberia has come a long way in the last year: in 2006, the Truth and Reconciliation Commission was established; Charles Taylor was imprisoned by the Special Court for Sierra Leone and is in The Hague awaiting his trial for war crimes scheduled to begin in 2008; and Monrovia has electricity for the first time in over a decade.

3 What Is the Legacy of the Liberian Civil War?

By the time it was over, the Liberian Civil War had claimed the lives of over 250,000 people (USAID, 2006), mostly civilians, and had led to the complete breakdown of social, legal and security services. The complete breakdown of the education system has left a 'lost generation' of youth (World Bank, 2006c). The destruction of infrastructures and the psychological trauma associated with living in a country so steeped in violence for such an extended period of time has had an impact on every Liberian. With over 850,000 externally displaced refugees and much of the remaining population internally displaced, the Liberian conflict was the primary humanitarian crisis in West Africa for much of the 1990s (UNMIL, 2006a). Displaced communities were either relocated to refugee camps, if they were fortunate, or fled to impromptu squatter camps, often in Liberia's capital, Monrovia. The pre-war population in the capital was somewhere in the region of 300,000–350,000; during the conflict the population tripled to approximately 1 million (UNMIL, 2006a). In the vain hope of escaping the war, those who fled to the city ended up caught in the crossfire, as many of the later battles of the war were fought on the streets of Monrovia.

Those fortunate enough to be taken out of Liberia to refugee camps in Nigeria and Ghana, aside from being in a more secure environment, often had access to educational programmes and other support structures. Many of them returned after the war in a much better position than their counterparts who were left behind and, for the most part, did not have access to such support. Still, these populations were often traumatized from the experience of resettlement, and in need of support in terms of recovering their livelihoods after the conflict. They also faced the resentment and stigmatization of being seen as having 'abandoned' their communities.

Those who were displaced within Liberia were often afforded little support. During the final stages of the war, Monrovia had essentially become a large refugee camp. Caught between the various factions, these at-risk populations lived on a battlefield for much of the conflict. Many people were forced to join the fighting to avoid becoming victims themselves:

> And, the war hit in the night. So, everybody went, and nobody see who is who. We just go out in the darkness. I had to find my way to go that side, and I went along with a group. I didn't know where my mother was or my father. So, I just walk alone with a group and when I went, these guys I was walking with, so they took me along. I used to help them, do some things for them. They send me, I go there. And, when … the NPFL came, they say, 'you know you have to be a man too. You can't just be with us.' I went and got … I was forced to take up gun. Because, I didn't know nobody to where I went. I was like … something like I didn't know what I was doing. But, I didn't see nobody that I know. Nobody. No family around. So, I was forced to fight for survival. At that time, if the people come, if you are frightened, you are forced to go and live in the bush. Yeah, because they come in the town, four hundred men with truck and gun and bullet, and they take us. So, this is how I become soldier (W., former NPFL child soldier in interview with author, 12 April 2006).

The number of active combatants who fought during the war is estimated to be well over 100,000. The estimates of children who were actively involved in combat over the course of the war are as high as 50,000–70,000 (Singer, 2001). These young people are now facing a myriad of problems: post-traumatic stress disorder (PTSD), debilitating injuries, drug addiction, alienation from the community, a lack of education and skills, and no stable community to return to.

Women were particularly brutalized during the war. Sexual violence was so prevalent that 60 to 80% of the women who remained in the country were victims of rape or sexual assault (Singer, 2001). This has added to the existence of extremely unhealthy gender dynamics in post-conflict Liberia, including widespread prostitution. The HIV rate is somewhere between 8 and 26%, birth-rates are high at 6.8, infant mortality is almost 16% of live births, the literacy rate for women is at 39% (as opposed to 72% for men) and there is a 32% gap between primary school enrolment rates for boys and girls (UNMIL, 2006a).

4 Post-Conflict Recovery

With the end of the conflict and the establishment of UNMIL in 2003, Liberia has been the recipient of vast amounts of aid over recent years. Virtually every major development agency in the world has an office in the country providing emergency relief, refugee relocation, education, food and nutrition, disarmament, small-scale psychological counselling, reconstruction, and political and economic support. This influx of aid has had positive and negative effects on the situation in the country. While some of the programmes have been successful and have benefited the population, an emerging micro-economy, due to the presence of a large aid-worker population, has raised the cost of living for Liberians. Also, a 'hand-out' culture has been created, with an over-reliance on the temporary scaffolding of aid. In addition, aid packages often come with an agreement that a certain amount of materials and labour will be imported from the donating country. This practice further limits the already scarce employment opportunities for the local population.

Liberia's most recent disarmament, demobilization, reintegration and rehabilitation (DDRR) process began rapidly in December of 2003 and proceeded in three phases, the third and final of which continues in remote areas at the time of writing (UNMIL, 2006b). According to UNMIL, which led the DDRR process, 100,000 former combatants have been disarmed, including 12,000 women and 11,780 children (UNMIL, 2006a). Of the demobilized ex-combatants, 94,000 were given access to rehabilitation and reintegration programmes funded by the UNDP DDRR Trust Fund and by USAID, the European Commission and UNICEF, which often included skills and/or vocational training components. This DDRR process was preceded by earlier attempts in 1994 and 1997, which collapsed when the conflict resumed. Many of the ex-combatants who were demobilized in these earlier processes were re-recruited into fighting forces (United Nations Office of the Special Advisor on Africa, 2005).

In terms of the continuing refugee problem, as of June 2006 there were still 163,880 Liberian refugees in camps in neighbouring countries. About 100,000 refugees were expected to return by the end of 2006. In addition, there are currently over 10,000 refugees from other countries currently living in camps in Liberia. Most of these refugees are from Côte d'Ivoire and Sierra Leone, but others come from as far away as Sudan and Iraq (UNMIL, 2006a).

5 What Role Has TVET Played in the Recovery Process?

Liberia has an incredibly young population with an average life span if 41.5 years and 43% of the population is under the age of 15 (World Bank, 2007). Of the 11,780 children demobilized through DDRR, 6,028 have benefited from educational programmes: 48% of these accessed formal education; 30% were involved in agricultural vocational training; 29% enrolled in other vocational training; 6% joined apprenticeship programmes; and 4% participated in public works (UNMIL, 2006a). That the majority of the 'lost generation' is choosing to access vocational-related training options rather than formal education demonstrates the need to develop sound and effective programming to meet this demand.

Much of the TVET programming in Liberia has exclusively targeted ex-combatants, which has caused a certain amount of resentment among the civilian population. In May 2006, UNMIL reported that 65,893 ex-combatants had completed or were currently participating in training and education programmes; approximately 13,000 of these were women. Much of the vocational training provided by the DDRR has been sub-contracted to local and international non-governmental organizations, including Don Bosco, Catholic Agency for Overseas Development (CAFOD), Liberia Opportunities Industrialization Centres (LOIC) and United Methodist Committee on Relief (UMCOR). The training provided tends to focus on construction skills, including masonry, roof-tiling, general construction and plumbing, but also includes agriculture and business skills. TVET programming geared towards women included cooking, domestic skills and small business management—programming potentially reinforcing stereotypical gender roles.

Much of the programming was implemented through an 'Arms for Training' campaign wherein a collection site was set up and vouchers for training programmes were exchanged for arms. Unfortunately, there seems to have been inadequate planning in most of the phases of this initiative.

> It was crazy, ten times as many people showed up at the collection site as were planned for, so they were sending people away. They were sending people *with guns* away! And then, they had not warned the training centres that people were coming, and had not set up all the funding for them. It was an absolute mess. Even the training programmes themselves were ridiculous. People simply can't find work in the fields they were trained in (M., UNMIL employee, interview with author, 18 April 2006).

While the chaos related to the disarmament stage of the programme is disturbing, of particular concern here is the lack of positive outcomes to the TVET programmes. If participants are not able to employ their learned skills in the marketplace, earn a living and improve their livelihoods, then what is the point of the training? How do you bridge the gap between training and opportunity?

6 What Is Economic and Manpower Forecasting?

There is a dialogical relationship between TVET and economic growth in that growth targets cannot be met without the necessary supply of skilled labour (Parnes, 1962), and the development of a labour force is pointless without existing or future employment opportunities. The question then becomes: how do you plan TVET programming around the expected labour needs within the given economic context? Mentioning the phrases 'economic forecasting' or 'manpower forecasting' naturally arouses feelings of dread in anyone familiar with the unfulfilled hopes and dreams affiliated with the forecasting projects of the 1960s. Despite this, both developments in the field and the curbed enthusiasm of the last several decades have created forecasting models that have the potential to play an integral role in TVET planning in post-conflict reconstruction.

As a result of its early failures, economic forecasting has been relegated to the fringe of academia and practice for much of the last thirty years. A 1994 study showed that only 17% of academic economic programmes offered a course in economic forecasting (Hanke & Weigland, 1994), despite the claim three years earlier that 'more and more companies are recognizing the importance of formal forecasting. At present, the demand for trained forecasters is far greater than the supply' (Jain, 1991, p. 2).

As in most economic fields, forecasting is separated into macro-economic forecasting and micro-economic forecasting. As would be expected, macro-economic forecasting is concerned with government and monetary policy, interest rates, and multipliers within the national context. Micro-economic forecasting focuses on competitive markets, profit maximization, and pricing and costs within a specific institution or sector (Loomis & Cox, 2000, p. 352).

Much of the history of economic forecasting is led by *structural* models, based on the popular economic theory of the day. The problem with this is that when the structural theory becomes unpopular, so too does the corresponding model. *Non-structural* models put themselves forward as not being bound to any particular school of thought, but this is as much a weakness as it is a strength in that it fails to employ the positive aspects of grounded economic theory. Therefore, the norm has become a blending of structural and non-structural approaches to forecasting.

> The hallmark of macroeconomic forecasting over the next 20 years will be a marriage of the best of nonstructural and structural approaches, facilitated by advances in numerical and simulation techniques that will help macroeconomists to solve, estimate, simulate, and yes, *forecast* with rich models (Diebold, 1998, p. 189).

Looking past the theoretical issues, the practical obstacles to creating reliable forecasting models are intimidating, particularly within the confines of the unstable economies of the developing world, and even more so in post-conflict economies. Data collection is often weak in developing countries, and perhaps simply non-existent in post-conflict contexts. It is necessary to factor in the potentialities for technological advances, political and policy changes, and price and market shifts (Ahamad & Scott, 1972); and it is often difficult to accurately estimate start dates of potential projects, and the specific manpower needs for planned projects (Kwak, Garrett & Barone, 1977).

The solution to some of these obstacles has been to accept the fact that, at best, economic forecasting can act as a guide rather than an exact measure of the future of the economy. This can be seen in the popularity of stochastic forecasting models, which leaves room for a number of different potentialities. Economists have even suggested using an uncertainty interval of 50% rather than the standard 95% when applying forecasting models (Granger, 1996), on the understanding that forecasting cannot be an exact science.

Data collection is another matter altogether. Making any kind of estimate about the future of an economy, and linking those estimates to a practical and contextually appropriate set of programmes, requires an enormous amount of data, both quantitative and qualitative. Unfortunately, particularly in post-conflict situations, this need is often not met due to a lack of availability, a lack of effort or to the practical and financial obstacles presented by gathering data. It must be noted that safety concerns for data collectors in times of war are significant. If data is collected once the conflict has come to an end then the implementation of much-needed programming is potentially delayed while the process of data collection, tabulation and analysis is carried out. For example, in 2005, 43,000 demobilized and disarmed ex-combatants were prevented from beginning the vocational education programming phases of the DDRR in Liberia due to poor planning and funding constraints. As a result, UNMIL had to make an international call for increased funding while these at-risk youth waited, creating a potentially volatile situation. The same issues could arise while assessments or data collection exercises are taking place.

Data collection concerning the Liberian economy has been carried out, but in a relatively perfunctory manner. The World Bank and other agencies have collected data and made estimates on the 'big picture' of the Liberian economy: gross domestic product (GDP), international debt, per capita income, etc. But, in terms of assessing the potential of the Liberian marketplace and creating reliable forecasting models that can be used to determine prospective opportunities for Liberians, very little has been done.

7 What Is the State of Liberia's Economy?

According to the latest World Bank data (2007), agriculture makes up 66% of Liberia's US$548.4 million national GDP, industry makes up 15.8%, and services make up the remaining 18.2%. The main products in the agricultural sector are coffee, cocoa, rice, cassava, palm oil, sugarcane, yams and okra. While rice is the main staple of the Liberian diet, it is still being imported in most cases. There are continuing efforts to establish rice farms within the country. Much of the industrial sector is based on the production of iron ore, rubber manufacturing and construction materials. Two of the major profitable exports, diamonds and timber, were sanctioned by the United Nations until they met international standards of transparency. The sanctions put on the diamond sector still remain in place, while reforms in the timber industry have allowed the lifting of sanctions in this sector. There is also a substantial shipping industry that takes advantage of Liberia's sizeable port. Relaxed shipping regulations and low fees have made Liberia a popular destination for importers. Despite a fair amount of economic potential in a number of sectors, unemployment is pervasive at 85% (World Bank, 2006a).

There are several factors that must be considered in any discussion of the economy in Liberia. Much of the physical infrastructure of the country was destroyed during the war, including manufacturing plants, agricultural sites, many of the rubber plantations and the road network. Secondly, the aid industry has deeply impacted the economy by driving up prices on housing and services. In a country where the per-capita income is less than US$2 a day (World Bank, 2006b), a one-bedroom apartment in Monrovia can rent for upwards of $1,500 a month. Thirdly, there is a sizeable immigrant community that has a strong influence across several sectors (including the lucrative rice trade), and at least some of these profits are being shipped abroad. Also, as nearly one-third of the national population has relocated into the capital and away from the agricultural lands, this will drastically affect the nature of the economy in the coming years. Lastly, there is an increasing population of Liberians who are returning home from Europe and the United States to set up businesses.

Until very recently, Liberia was seen as a pariah in terms of international economic assistance. First there was conflict throughout much of the 1990s, then with a former warlord as president, and recently with an interim government that was widely seen as incompetent, Liberia remains in dire financial circumstances, with over US$2.7 billion in international debt. But, with the election of President Johnson-Sirleaf, and her experience working at the World Bank, the international financial institutions are becoming more supportive.

> During his visit to Liberia on 21 and 22 July, the President of the World Bank, Paul Wolfowitz, pledged the Bank's commitment to the economic development of Liberia and agreed to provide assistance for labour-intensive public works schemes aimed at building key infrastructure and generating employment (United Nations. Security Council, 2006).

8 How Has TVET Been Linked to the Economy?

Planned economies tend to have a much higher success rate in terms of economic forecasting, and linking needed-manpower estimates to employment opportunities than market economies (Youdi & Hinchliffe, 1985). This is intuitive given that planned economies are able to predict labour demands in each sector to a greater degree, and given that the size and investment in these sectors are often predetermined and dictated by the State. Post-conflict scenarios offer an opportunity to take advantage of this same concept, given that the post-conflict economy is often initially driven by planned projects funded by international aid.

In 2006, the Liberian Government and the World Bank agreed upon a US$68 million grant focusing on emergency rehabilitation and repair of critical infrastructure, utilities maintenance (roads, water and sewage), and construction of new community facilities (schools and health clinics.) The secondary goal of the grant is to create employment opportunities for Liberians (World Bank, 2006c).

This is not the first attempt by the Liberian government and the aid community to develop employment-generating projects. According to UNMIL, approximately 60,000 of the 65,893 ex-combatants who were trained in their TVET initiatives are said to have participated in short-term employment schemes (World Bank, 2006c). Much of the TVET training linked to employment initiatives is geared towards construction, derived from a vision that the newly trained ex-combatants would be able to rebuild the physical infrastructure of the country destroyed during the war. However, this vision resulted in limited, very short-term opportunities upon completion of vocational training, and many of the participants struggled to use the skills they learned during TVET in the market-place. The problem many face is an overabundance of trained labour in a given field. This becomes particularly problematic when considering the vulnerable state of the trainees who cannot find work upon completion of their training:

> See, many houses don't have toilet, don't have sink. So, it's not easy to find work in plumb-
> ing, you know? . . . Because most of Liberia doesn't have plumbing (K., former LURD child
> soldier, trained as a plumber during DDRR, interview with author, 12 April 2006).

UNMIL initiated some small-scale projects to address unemployment through its 'quick-impact scheme', which commissioned minor building and infrastructure projects that temporarily employed 900 ex-combatants and community members (UNMIL, 2006a). USAID also implemented a public works project, primarily geared towards building roads, which temporarily employed 10,000 ex-combatants and other unemployed Liberians producing 500,000 days of paid work (USAID, 2006). Reception of this project was mixed, due to the low rate of pay offered and, once again, they offered only short-term employment.

Recent initiatives by the new government appear to be attempting to bridge the gap between training and employment through several job-creation strategies. In 2006 two major programmes were introduced with the support to the International Labour Organization (ILO) and the government of the Netherlands: the Liberia Emergency Employment Programme (LEEP), designed to offer temporary employment in infrastructure development, and the Liberia Employment Action Programme (LEAP), aimed at capacity-building with the goal of long-term employment

9 Conclusions

There is no doubt that Liberia has been, and continues to be, in a fragile situation in terms of development. The economy remains in shambles, there are hosts of lingering social problems, and there is a marked under-supply of skilled labour. Properly managed, TVET has the potential to increase the capacity of Liberia to address some of its economic and social woes. But, TVET programming needs to be designed for, and organized around, the contextual economic opportunities. Estimating these prospective opportunities is no small task. Problems of data collection, assessing existing skills, and predicting the future capabilities of various sectors in terms of infrastructural capacity are just a few of the difficulties facing post-conflict societies in general and Liberia in particular. Nonetheless, the application of economic and manpower forecasting models has the potential of creating a framework for TVET programming to be designed in such a way as to maximize its contextual effectiveness.

There has been very little diversity in the TVET programmes associated with the Liberian DDRR, with the greatest focus on construction-related industries. This emphasis in construction skills, while well-intentioned, struggled to improve the livelihoods of its participants and often flooded particular labour sectors while others remained under represented. How many plumbers and masons can an economy absorb? This problem is amplified by the fact that the aid system, which is responsible for much of the large-scale post-conflict construction projects, often imports specialized labour, leaving the recently trained workers with even fewer opportunities in an economy plagued by very high rates of unemployment.

The first step in linking training to economic opportunities is a close examination of current and future market opportunities. Linking TVET to planned projects is one way to achieve at least short-term employment for recent trainees, but the long-term success of the economy depends on a skilled labour force that can take advantage of the different sectors within a market economy. As mentioned above, Liberia has a number of attractive resources. It is rich in minerals and timber; there is a large shipping port; the climate is ideal for rubber, coffee, rice and other agricultural products; and the recent advances in information technology open up the potential for new service-oriented markets. Diversifying the implementation of TVET has the potential of producing a much more productive private sector.

In addition to diversifying TVET training, there are a number of support structures that have the potential to promote participant inclusion in the economy. One way to support improved livelihoods is entrepreneurship training and micro-credit schemes. Another avenue that should be explored is partnerships between TVET programmes and the local and international private sector. The potential for client generation, and access to expertise for training purposes, is appealing. On the downside, partnerships are often difficult to establish and businesses may be resistant to investing in a potentially unstable political and economic climate.

Post-conflict scenarios offer both limitations and opportunities in terms of economic growth. The challenges that war-affected populations face should not be under-estimated, but the potential to reshape the social and economic structures are exciting. When properly contextualized, TVET has the potential to aid in this process of post-conflict recovery by building the capacity of the population to improve their livelihoods and take control of their own national development.

References

Ahamad, B.; Scott, K.F.N. 1972. A note on sensitivity in manpower forecasting. *The journal of the Royal Statistical Society*, vol. 135, no. 3, pp. 385–92.

Diebold, F.X. 1998. The past, present and future of macroeconomic forecasting. *The journal of economic perspectives,* vol. 12, no. 2, pp. 175–92.

Ellis, S. 2001. *Mask of anarchy: the destruction of Liberia and the religious dimension of an African civil war.* New York, NY: NYU Press.

Granger, C.W.J. 1996. Can we improve the perceived quality of economic forecasts? *Journal of applied econometrics,* vol. 11, no. 5, pp. 455–73.

Hanke, J.; Weigland, P. 1994. What are business schools doing to educate forecasters? *Journal of economic education,* vol. 26, no. 2, pp. 175–92.

Jain, C.L. 1991. Ivy League business schools far behind the time. *Journal of business forecasting,* vol. 13, no. 4, p. 2.

Kwak, N.K.; Garrett, W.; Barone, S. 1977. A stochastic model of demand forecasting for technical manpower planning. *Management science,* vol. 23, no. 10.

Loomis, D.G.; Cox, J.E. 2000. A course in economic forecasting: rationale and content. *The journal of economic education,* vol. 31, no. 4, pp. 349–57.

Parnes, H.S. 1962. *Forecasting educational needs for economic and social development.* Paris: OECD.

Singer, P.W. 2001. *Children at war.* New York, NY: Pantheon Books.

United Nations Mission in Liberia—UNMIL. 2006a. *Accomplishments and challenges.* <www.unmil.org/documents/insideunmil/presskit0806.pdf>

United Nations Mission in Liberia—UNMIL. 2006b. *Disarmament, demobilization, reintegration and rehabilitation.* <unmil.org/content.asp?ccat=ddrr>

United Nations News Centre. 2005. *Annan calls for urgent aid to Liberia's security agenda; sanctions are not lifted.* <www.un.org/apps/news/story.asp?NewsID=16878&Cr=liberia&Cr1=>

United Nations Office of the Special Advisor on Africa. 2005. *Disarmament, demobilization, reintegration (DDR) and stability in Africa. Conference Report. Freetown, June 21–23, 2005.* <www.un.org/africa/osaa/reports/DDR%20Sierra%20Leone%20March%202006.pdf>

United Nations. Security Council. 2006. *Twelfth Progress Report of the Secretary-General on the United Nations Mission in Liberia.* (Document S/2006/743.) <daccessdds.un.org/doc/UNDOC/GEN/N06/517/11/PDF/N0651711.pdf>

USAID. 2006. *Sub-Saharan Africa: Liberia.* <www.usaid.gov/locations/sub-saharan_africa/countries/liberia>

World Bank. 2006a. *Liberia's President affirms strong partnership with bank, urges women to strive for development.* <web.worldbank.org/WBSITE/EXTERNAL/NEWS/0,,contentMDK:20867632~menuPK:51062077~pagePK:34370~piPK:34424~theSitePK:4607,00.html>

World Bank. 2006b. *Liberia: data and statistics.* <web.worldbank.org/WBSITE/EXTERNAL/COUNTRIES/AFRICAEXT/LIBERIAEXTN/0,,menuPK:356220~pagePK:141132~piPK:141109~theSitePK:356194,00.html>

World Bank. 2006c. *Address to the joint session of the Liberian legislature. Paul Wolfowitz, 21 July 2006.* <web.worldbank.org/WBSITE/EXTERNAL/EXTABOUTUS/ORGANIZATION/EXTOFFICEPRESIDENT/0,,contentMDK:21001978~menuPK:64343258~pagePK:51174171~piPK:64258873~theSitePK:1014541,00.html>

World Bank. 2007. *Liberia at a glance.* <devdata.worldbank.org/AAG/lbr_aag.pdf>

Youdi, R.V.; Hinchliffe, K., eds. 1985. *Forecasting skilled manpower needs: the experience of eleven countries.* Paris: UNESCO-IIEP.

Chapter V.4
Deepening the Divide: The Differential Impact of Protracted Conflict on TVET Versus Academic Education in Palestine

Bilal Barakat

1 Introduction

The effect a conflict has on local TVET need not be the same as its effect on other kinds of education. While this is almost tautological, it is worthwhile examining just how pronounced the difference can be and, by implication, how potentially misleading it would be in conflict and post-conflict settings to generalize from the state of the education sector as a whole to the state of TVET.

In recent years, education generally in and after conflict has been the focus of greater attention than ever before. Given that TVET is often partly incorporated into general education, this means that TVET after conflict is increasingly considered from an educational point-of-view, in addition to the labour-market perspective on economic reconstruction that has dominated in the past. This attention brings with it the promise of best practices and lessons learned for reconstruction in other educational sub-sectors, but TVET's distinct character has important implications.

In some ways, TVET might be expected to be particularly vulnerable to the effects of conflict. It requires more specialized teachers who are difficult to replace if they flee, are killed or injured, or recruited into the armed forces. The classrooms or workshops often involve expensive equipment that is likely to be looted or damaged. In protracted conflicts it might be nearly impossible to obtain and maintain up-to-date equipment in the first place. While there is little hard data on the matter, we might expect a typical TVET student to be more likely to drop-out or participate in hostilities, especially in places where TVET has acquired a reputation for being a second-class option for those who failed for whatever reason to succeed in more academic streams. It also suffers indirect effects. Economic collapse caused by violent or lingering conflict undermines TVET's ostensible rationale, namely the premise that the vocation being trained for will actually offer a livelihood. These notions require careful empirical investigation in a variety of cases in order to yield recommendations for educational reconstruction that are specific to TVET.

The aim of this chapter is to illustrate this differential impact of conflict on TVET compared to general education using the example of Palestine. This is an apt example because the difference between the development under conflict of TVET and other parts of the Palestinian education sector has been particularly pronounced. This example also highlights another important point. Among Palestinians, TVET

R. Maclean, D. Wilson (eds.), *International Handbook of Education for the Changing World of Work*, DOI 10.1007/978-1-4020-5281-1_V.4,
© Springer Science+Business Media B.V. 2009

has been popularly perceived to have a different standing in relation to both national aspirations and personal emancipation than academic education. Under protracted, 'low intensity' conflict, these issues are of great importance. In fact, in such a situation the amplification of this perceived qualitative difference between TVET and academic education can be more critical than the difference in degree in physical vulnerability.

The first section of this chapter provides a brief overview of the interaction of the Israeli-Palestinian conflict with Palestinian education as a whole. Far from merely being 'interrupted' by conflict, throughout the past century Palestinian education has been shaped structurally, ideologically and pedagogically by it.

Against this backdrop, the second section highlights how the conflict's impact on TVET contrasts with its effect on other kinds of education. While higher education, for instance, was boosted by its perceived and actual connection with the nationalist project, even in the absence of clear economic incentives, many forms of TVET have traditionally been neglected and have been particularly vulnerable faced with the effects of economic crises.

The concluding remarks finally depart from the most important observations of the specific case of Palestine to propose questions of more general interest to the problem of TVET in conflict.

2 The Entanglement of Education and Conflict in Palestine

The history of Palestinian education reflects the history of the conflict over Palestine itself (for an overview, see Pappe, 2006; Kimmerling & Migdal, 2003). Before the Oslo Accords in the 1990s, the Palestinians had never controlled their own education system. Within historic Palestine, this control rested first with the Ottomans, then the British and later Israel; Palestinian refugees beyond the borders are subject to the curricula of the respective host countries, even though in their case it is implemented by the United Nations.

Under all these external powers, educational provision was closely linked with the struggle over control of the land. The Ottomans long neglected secondary education and insisted on the unpopular medium of Turkish for instruction (even for the teaching of Arabic!), only to promise reform of both issues during the First World War to shore up Arab support for their failing campaign. During the British Mandate that followed the Ottoman defeat, on the one hand, the increase in schooling helped spread Arab nationalism by bringing young educated men to the countryside as teachers; on the other hand, control over education served the British as both a carrot and a stick to extort local co-operation (Al-Haj, 1995). At the same time, the Arab population keenly felt competition with the education of the Jewish settlers, who were free to link the education of their children with their nationalist ambitions. The Arabs on the other hand felt that their own schools were prevented by the British from playing an equivalent role (Tibawi, 1956; Shepherd, 1999). In popular lore, the Arab defeat in 1948 was attributed in large part to the Zionists' superior education and training (Abu-Lughod, 2000; Graham-Brown, 1984). To what extent the Palestinian refugees' educational achievements in the following decades were spurred on by this conviction and the motivation to overcome this weakness, or were a result of the external circumstances, including a lack of alternative opportunities and favourable access to Arab universities, remains open to debate.

Undisputed, however, is the fact that their educational achievements were remarkable. The United Nations Relief and Works Agency for Palestine Refugees in the Near East (UNRWA) from the start regarded education as a priority and the schools it operated in and near the refugee camps were instrumental in achieving near universal primary enrolment for both genders—at a time when the populations of host and other countries in the region were largely illiterate (Yusuf, 1979). Within a generation, participation in higher education reached levels that were among the highest in developing countries. As a result, educated Palestinians made up large parts of the teaching force and other professional sectors in the Arab Gulf region up until the 1960s (Mazawi, 1994; Badran, 1980). The reputation of Palestinians as the most educated Arabs was cemented; the explanation of their enthusiasm as the natural result of their experience of dispossession and the recognition of education as an asset that could not be taken away became part of Palestinian folklore. Below we will examine to what extent this was true of academic education alone.

While for some the outcome of the 1948 War resulted in improved access to education and labour markets for the highly skilled, after the war of 1967, when Israel gained control over the West Bank and Gaza Strip, the consequences for education were uniformly harmful (Velloso, 2002). For over two decades, school development was neglected despite tremendous population growth. The curriculum was censored. For a long time, the education sector was controlled by military personnel in uniform and teacher appointments were under tight control of the security services and were abused for the recruitment of collaborators.

In East Jerusalem, there was an attempt to incorporate schools into the Israeli 'Arab Education' sector to underline Israeli claims of sovereignty over the city (Masarweh & Salhout, 2002). This attempt failed due to popular non-co-operation; within a short time, most parents had moved their children out of the Israeli-controlled schools and into Islamic charity schools, forcing the Israeli authorities to reverse their policy and reintroduce the censored Jordanian curriculum.

While school development was stifled, the decades following 1967 did see the rise of Palestinian universities. These were barely tolerated by the Israeli military authorities, partly because they had no administrative recourse to prevent their legal establishment as private institutions and partly because it was hoped that the universities would offer young Palestinians an alternative to membership in guerrilla forces or the PLO (Sullivan, 1994). Instead, the universities fermented and became symbols of Palestinian nationalism as the only 'public' institutions not under direct Israeli control (Kimmerling & Migdal, 2003; Sullivan, 1994). As a result, violent and bureaucratic harassment by the authorities increased, culminating in expulsions of students, lecturers and university officials, and complete forced closures for months on end (Baramki, 1987; Assaf, 1997).

These closures reached their peak during the first popular uprising in the Occupied Territories—the Intifada—during the late 1980s and early 1990s (Usher, 1991;

Barber, 1997). Education was effectively taken hostage as a punitive measure by the Israeli military authorities. At times, all educational institutions were closed, ostensibly for security reasons. The security rationale was, however, taken ad absurdum by extending closures to primary schools and kindergartens; even teaching activities in private homes were outlawed under the threat of a prison term. These constraints fermented the creative development of alternative and distance education materials and teaching methods by progressive Palestinian educationalists (Mahshi & Bush, 1989; Fasheh, 1990). Clandestine 'neighbourhood schools' allowed for experimentation with alternative teaching approaches that would have encountered resistance in the formal sector. Later, these experiences were to have an important influence on the development of the first Palestinian school curriculum.

As a result of prolonged closures, the school system was close to collapse when the Palestinian National Authority (PNA) took control of the education sector after the Oslo Accords of 1993 (Assaf, 1997). For several reasons, the education sector continued to be one of the most important arenas for the struggle over political control. Reflecting the combination of an extremely youthful population with high enrolment, a majority of Palestinians in the West Bank and Gaza Strip were directly affected by the education sector as students, teachers and administrators or parents. The fact that universities represented one of the few areas of local independent capacity, they were reluctant to cede this independence to a Palestinian Authority governed principally by returning exiles (Hanafi & Tabar, 2005). And, finally, education was one of the sectors with the greatest international involvement and scrutiny, partly because it was considered 'safe to invest in' and because of the controversy generated by a disinformation campaign accusing Palestinian textbooks of incitement (Brown, 2001, 2002).

Educational attainment remained relatively high and university enrolment continued to reach new records, despite the fact that it offered no substantial economic returns in the depressed economic environment of the Occupied Territories. The lack of employment opportunities also meant women's participation in the labour force remained very low even by regional standards, which might partly explain the exceptional fact that women's education continued to have only a moderate lowering effect on fertility (Goujon, 1997).

Having maintained a leading role in terms of educational attainment in the Arab world throughout decades of conflict and occupation, since the beginning of the second Intifada in 2001, past gains are seriously at risk of being lost. A second generation is growing up with severely disrupted schooling and, when in school, is being taught by teachers who lost years of their own schooling during the first Intifada. Israeli military incursions into Palestinian population centres often result in physical damage to educational infrastructure, as well as the injury or death of students and teachers. Road blocks and other mobility restrictions (including the separation wall) represent a formidable obstacle to attendance (Moughrabi, 2004; Palestinian Authority. MoEHE, 2005; DSP, 2005). Since the international de facto embargo of the Palestinian government elected in early 2006, the situation in the Occupied Palestinian Territories, and Gaza in particular, has suffered further dramatic deterioration, not least long teacher strikes over unpaid salaries. The implications of these developments cannot yet be fully ascertained.

Looking back over the past century, it is clear that the education of Palestinians has not merely been constrained by the unresolved conflict over Palestine, but defined by it. It is equally clear that its future is equally tied up with the fate of a political settlement.

3 'Cinderella' in Times of Conflict

Clearly, Palestinian education as a whole has affected and has been fundamentally affected by the history of the Israeli-Palestinian conflict. However, the impact on different branches of the education system has varied. Simplistically speaking, higher education received a quantitative boost, both in terms of students and in terms of local university development (although quality was naturally negatively affected); primary enrolment leapt ahead of the regional competition, both because of UNRWA's provision to refugees and because of popular demand for education as an asset that could not be appropriated. The effect on TVET development has, however, been unambiguously detrimental.

Already during the British Mandate, TVET for the Arab Palestinians was neglected, a neglect that was interpreted by some as deliberate. The enthusiasm for 'local arts and crafts' on the part of some British officials made them ill-disposed towards the teaching of modern industrial skills (Shepherd, 1999). The provision of specialized agricultural education in the Arab sector was all but non-existent and local initiatives, such as maintaining a school garden, were often the result of individual committed head-teachers. As the conflict with the Zionist project was very much seen as a conflict over land, this neglect was interpreted by the Arab leadership as a deliberate attempt to limit their competitiveness vis-à-vis the technologically advanced Zionist agricultural enterprises.

After the 1948 War, UNRWA did from the start include TVET among the educational services it offered Palestinian refugees (Faherty, 1959), but it was never popular and to this day its TVET offerings remain inadequate in relation to the size and needs of the target population.

In fact, critics in the past accused UNRWA of having biased its educational provision towards helping top achievers gain access to universities (Weighill, 1995). While the number of higher education students among Palestinian refugees was comparatively high, they were still a small minority overall and this 'elitist' approach left the large mass of refugees with an education but limited opportunities.

This outcome is hardly surprising. The refugees' demand for education was driven by the priorities of the bourgeoisie among them, who already had experience in the modern sector and who, keen to stay ahead, devoted 'all their resources to making an economic recovery and to ensuring that their children obtained a university education' (Badran, 1980, p. 52).

Ironically, under the British Mandate, TVET in the form of agricultural education suffered because it was regarded as *more* relevant to effective Arab claims to the land than academic education which was easily 'sanitized' by the mandate authority (Tibawi, 1956). In stark contrast, in the post-1948 period the contribution of education to the nationalist project came to be seen instead in the sum of individual excellence, which was associated strictly with academic attainment. While many Palestinian students did tend to see their pursuit of education as part of the national project, it is debatable whether this was their main motivation. It could be argued that for the nationalists to politically endorse individual higher education as part of the 'liberation through education' slogan was to make a virtue of necessity and to lend patriotic respectability to educational choices motivated rather by individual considerations.

By contrast, TVET was seen neither as a desirable option in terms of personal advancement nor as a valuable contribution to the national project. In fact, it even appeared to some as undermining collective aspirations. In a context where it is not highly regarded, TVET's sole attraction is the prospect of improved employment prospects. In order to achieve these, it must correspond to the de facto economic context. But to adapt to a situation where economic development is deliberately stifled, as has been the case under Israeli occupation (Roy, 1995), can be understood as capitulating before the status quo: 'to restrict the growth of higher education to suit the needs of an exploited and artificially depressed economy would be nothing less than social strangulation. The short-term effects might be defensible (i.e. to discourage emigration), but the long-range impact on society may be disastrous' (Hallaj, 1980, p. 87)

The class-based counter-argument was sure to follow:

> Understandable as such a viewpoint may be, we should not ignore the way it allows a hypothetical *future* disaster to eclipse current actual disaster, such as Israeli exploitation of low-skilled Palestinian workers [. . .] It is through such weighting of priorities that so much Palestinian money has been mobilized for student scholarships, research institutes and universities, and so little for training programs for the poor (Sayigh, 1985, p. 132).

The argument was never settled, and pride in the achievements in higher education continued to dominate the discourse on education and the national project.

The question of to what extent this reflected a cultural bias is a difficult one. By any account, most other Arab countries share entrenched negative social attitudes to blue-collar labour (reflected by low demand for TVET (UIS, 2002)), and this raises the question of whether Palestinian TVET would have stagnated regardless of the conflict. The assumption of an intrinsic negative Arab attitude towards TVET is, however, undermined by the discussion regarding the Palestinian-Arab citizens of Israel. Some have suggested the assumption of low demand for TVET in the Israeli-Arab education sector to be merely a convenient excuse for a lack of Israeli investment, and report a 'positive shift in attitudes towards skilled labour and vocational-technological education' (Mar'i, 1978, p. 165) and that 'Arab parents and pupils alike have a positive attitude regarding vocational-technological education' (Al-Haj, 1995, p. 92).

In assessing this apparent contradiction between 'cultural attitudes' of the same people either side of an armistice line, it is important to take into account the fact that the Palestinian-Arab citizens of Israel have had few alternatives. In the academic stream, the cards have traditionally been and still are heavily stacked against them in terms of funding and appropriate curricula, encouraging extremely high drop-out and failure rates. For those that succeed, there are few employment options (Human Rights Watch, 2001). Likewise, their participation in higher education at Israeli universities remains marginal, even if it is increasing slowly. It should also be taken into account that TVET in Israel includes a number of high-tech branches far removed from the stigma of manual labour, even if in practice—if not in principle—they tend not to be available at Arab TVET institutions.

In any case, because the middle classes were the first to flee, the Palestinian Arabs that stayed behind in 1948 and became Israeli citizens were on average less educated to begin with than the majority of the refugees.

But it is not only the Palestinians' own attitudes towards TVET and blue-collar jobs that enter the picture. The main drive in international support for Palestinian education during the Oslo era came at a time when TVET had recently fallen out of favour with the World Bank and other agencies following its lead. After decades of emphasizing TVET, based on projected manpower requirements for economic de-velopment, studies calling into question fundamental assumptions underlying TVET provision and, more decisively, suggesting it was not cost-effective and offered lower economic returns than an expansion of primary schooling, led to a radical change in lending policy (Middleton, Ziderman & van Adams, 1991). Only recently has this trend been reversed.

Ostensibly, common criticisms of TVET apply even more forcefully in a refugee situation. It has been asserted that training for specific tasks is too specialized, and that general education provides a more flexible preparation for many jobs. Given the uncertainty in refugees' lives, such flexibility is highly desirable. It is also often noted that TVET is more dependent on being regularly updated and made relevant to the shifting economic and technological context. Such updates are expensive in terms of the training of teachers and possibly equipment, making it even more difficult for TVET to remain relevant in the often austere conditions of refugee and conflict-affected education. However, there are also obstacles to the currency of curricula that affect academic subjects more seriously than TVET. Under mili-tary occupation after 1967, censorship of school textbooks meant that even though legally the Jordanian curriculum applied in the West Bank, its changes were not always applied if the new textbooks were banned. This resulted in the teaching and examination of hopelessly outdated material that was known to be false by teachers and students alike (Schiff, 1989). Since TVET curricula are typically considered to be less politically sensitive, this at least is one constraint more likely to affect academic subjects.

In most respects however, it seems TVET remains at least as vulnerable as other branches of education, in particular regarding the effects of physical violence.

During the second Intifada, the education sector had to engage in ingenious planning in order to respond to the challenge of ad-hoc road-blocks and other mo-bility restrictions imposed by the Israeli occupation forces. For example, in order to keep schools running teachers who could not reach their usual place of work were reassigned to a school they could access (World Bank, 2004; Lempinen & Repo, 2002). Again, structural differences between TVET and general education make this kind of attempt to mitigate the effects of conflict more difficult in the case of the former. Not only are there fewer sites that are also further apart, but there are many different providers who cannot easily exchange their staff. Similarly, the clandestine community schools set up during the first Intifada to circumvent school closures are a model that was already problematic with regard to general and academic education, but unfeasible with regard to TVET.

The lack of past opportunity for TVET in the West Bank and Gaza Strip to develop into a viable educational option is reflected in the extremely low enrolment in the vocational secondary stream. The share of secondary students in one of the four vocational streams (industrial, commercial, agricultural, hotel—depending on classification, whether home economics or religious studies are also considered vocational streams) was less than 5% in the 2005/2006 school year overall, and even lower in the Gaza Strip, where there were only a few hundred vocational secondary students among the more than 50,000 secondary students in government schools (Palestinian Authority. MoEHE, 2005). There is also a marked gender differential, with many of the industrial options closed to females. While the overall secondary TVET enrolment represents a considerable increase over previous levels, it falls far short of the target share of 7.5% of all secondary students (Palestinian Authority. MoE, 2000), while the targets for increasing general secondary enrolment have been met even under the most adverse conditions.

As we have seen, the historic development trajectories of TVET and academic education in Palestine have diverged substantially under the political and social pressures of the century-old Palestinian-Israeli conflict. However, it would be a mistake to attribute current gaps between the two purely to this differential. There are certain structural features of TVET provision in the West Bank and Gaza Strip retarding its development; the fact that overcoming them is made no easier by the conflict environment does not mean that they are a result of it.

The problems needing to be overcome are well-known. The Ministry of Education and Higher Education's Human Resource Development strategy for the TVET sector provides a succinct synthesis:

> Lack of participation in community development. Absence of entrepreneurship programs. Lack of business participation in the technical education process. Inadequate vocational guidance and counselling. Absence of information about graduate employability [...] Limited instructional skills & knowledge of trainers. Limited technical skills & knowledge of trainers. Inadequate curricula [...] Lack of public awareness regarding TVET strategy. Inadequate management information system. Unclear vision of TVET development. Limited management skills of TVET staff (Palestinian Authority. MoEHE, n.d.).

Observers of the current state of TVET in the West Bank and Gaza Strip agree that it is heavily fragmented and lacks relevance. In addition to technical and vocational post-secondary formal education at secondary schools and post-secondary community colleges, semi-formal training is available at the Ministry of Labour's and UNRWA training centres. There are also non-formal providers whose exact number is unknown but goes into the hundreds (World Bank, 2006), most offering short courses and lacking economy of scale. Past lack of co-ordination means:

> One can become a carpenter in 9 months, 11 months or 24 months. A person may train for carpentry in vocational secondary schools, or in a training Centre, run by UNRWA, or the Ministry of Labor, or the Ministry of Welfare and Social Affairs, or quite a number of private institutions, and each time using different curricula (Palestinian Authority. MoEHE, 1998).
>
> The relationship between TVET and the labour market has been described as 'almost non-functional'. [Existing TVET is] neither efficient nor relevant to the needs of its target group or the needs of the market [... and] incapable of serving its stated purpose (Abu Nahleh, 1996, p. 144, quoted in Mazawi, 2000, p. 374).
>
> This lack of relevance for employability is invariably confirmed by outside observers. UNRWA likewise admits that because of funding constraints, its TVET centres 'cannot respond to the changing needs of the labour market' (UNRWA, 2005, p. 19).

Unsurprisingly then, demand is very weak. The vocational secondary option is unpopular (see above) and attracts only the academically least able. Reinforcing TVET's stigma, the Ministry of Social Affairs, as yet another provider, offers training specifically for school drop-outs, ex-detainees and other 'social cases' requiring rehabilitation.

Those that do enrol in the vocational secondary stream demonstrate little vocational intent: in a tracer study of industrial school graduates in 2001, nearly half the sample subsequently enrolled in degree and diploma-level higher education courses instead of training-related employment (World Bank, 2006, p. 71).

The popularity of TVET courses varies greatly between different options. In contrast to most courses, nursing stands out as having more applicants than places (World Bank, 2006). Such differences call into question the usefulness of making general statements about the state of TVET as such. The usual caveats apply about overstating the distinction between TVET and academic education. In particular, what is a highly skilled profession in one era might become a low- or medium-qualification skill later, as the relevant technology moves from being high-tech to being routine. Operating computers is a current case in point. What is the appropriate categorization of, for example, tertiary agricultural education leading to a B.Sc. as offered by the College of Agriculture at Hebron University (i.e. the borderline between ISCED 4B versus 5B (UIS, 2002)) depends very much on the question to be answered.

Further calling the distinction into question is the fact that much of what was said about TVET also applies to some extent to science education, with its similar need for equipment and specialized teachers. In fact, the occupation authorities confiscated most chemicals from schools' science laboratories, severely limiting their usefulness (UNESCO, 1991). The detrimental effect of the conflict on Palestinian science education in particular is well known. The disproportion of humanities versus science students carries over from secondary to university level (World Bank, 2006) and this weakness in science and mathematics reinforces the low take-up of TVET at higher levels and constrains the supply of trainers.

This phenomenon is further strengthened by the fact that science education at all levels is more expensive to the student than humanities or social science subjects.

The oversupply of cheap academic alternatives, regardless of their value, reduces the relative attractiveness of TVET, as fees at technical and community colleges are similar to those at traditional universities and actually exceed those at the local Open University (World Bank, 2006). In a vicious circle, the low demand for TVET further drives up unit costs.

It is to their credit that Palestinian educationalists are not content with maintaining the status quo but are trying to advance the development of the education sector, even during times of crisis. These efforts notwithstanding, Palestinian TVET is in a state of arrested development, with reform efforts having been articulated, but stalling in implementation.

Due to the lack of Palestinian statehood, Palestinian participation in some intergovernmental initiatives for co-operation in the field of TVET is difficult. There is no Palestinian presence in the Arab States UNESCO-UNEVOC Network. The question of to what extent Palestinian TVET can, without active participation, benefit from the outcomes of initiatives, such as the 2002 'Regional Expert Meeting on TVET Project Development in the Arab States' (UNESCO-UNEVOC, 2003), remains problematic. This constraint does not however apply to other regional fora, such as the GTZ-facilitated Regional Arab-German Network on TVET (<www.arab-tvet.com>) for the development of shared occupational classification schemes and an Arabic glossary of TVET curricular terms.

Already during the late 1990s, a national TVET development plan and reform scheme was developed (Lempinen & Repo, 2002; World Bank, 2006). It reflected the uncertainty caused be the unresolved conflict in its call for flexibility regarding training for neighbouring labour markets that might or might not be or become accessible to Palestinian labour. Its key themes, however, were: (a) the unification and harmonization of standards and qualifications; (b) the modularization of curricula; (c) responsiveness to demand with a limited role for the ambition to create a small excess supply of skilled labour as a catalyst; and (d) a tighter integration with academic trajectories by providing bridging courses between academic secondary and further education and TVET, between TVET and higher education.

Remarkably, Palestinian educationalists do not lay the blame for the lack of progress in implementing this national TVET strategy directly on the intensification of the conflict. In the 2003/2004 Action Plan (Palestinian Authority. MoEHE, 2003), failure to achieve real change is instead pinned on a lack of management capacity at the systems level, the absence of follow-up, and the neglect of transitional objectives that could serve to connect the ambitious strategic objectives with the levels of funding actually available.

Compared to times past, TVET is enjoying increased attention. The will for reform appears real and co-operation between the concerned ministries has been lauded as exceptional (Lempinen & Repo, 2002). A recent novelty has been public-awareness campaigns, including newspaper supplements, radio and TV advertisements to promote TVET as a valid and rewarding educational choice (the advertisements may be viewed at <www.tvet-pal.org/awareness/awareness.html> [validated 4 August 2008]). To what extent such measures influence public perceptions and behaviour remains, of course, to be seen but, given that students' knowledge about

TVET opportunities used to come mainly from informal sources (Abu Nahleh, 1996, in Mazawi, 2000), represents an important step in the right direction of trying to break TVET's stigma.

4 Concluding Remarks

It is regrettable that TVET is all too often the 'Cinderella' of national systems of education. Even if it is thus neglected in practice, we should not neglect it in our analyses of education sectors in and after conflict. Attention to the specific circumstances of TVET is crucial because, as we have seen, its destiny in and after conflict can diverge significantly from broader trends in the education sector. Reasons for this divergence include both structural effects of the typically greater geographic dispersion of TVET institutions compared to other schools for instance, as well as attitudinal effects. Pre-existing biases are unlikely to be overcome when the stakes are raised in conflict.

In the Palestinian case, the conflict and its political effects provided a boost to primary and higher education enrolment, while constraining their quality. By contrast, the development of TVET was stunted. While a regional comparison suggests that its neglect due to cultural biases would have been likely regardless of the conflict, the fact remains that it neither shared in the mystique of the liberation struggle created around education generally, nor has been able to follow the pace of developments in neighbouring countries where TVET has traditionally been similarly neglected, but is now in the process of being modernized in the face of rising graduate unemployment.

Examining the differences in impact of conflict on TVET and academic education should not obscure but rather sensitize us to the fact that there are large differences *within* either. The interesting question is how these relate and which patterns, if any, are stable across different contexts of conflict. Does prolonged conflict as a rule tend to affect science education more than literacy, and is that one of the factors constraining technology-oriented TVET? To what extent are certain vocations upgraded in status for ideological reasons or because of their practical contribution to the national struggle, say farming or para-medical occupations? And are such attitudes reflected in the enrolment distribution for formal TVET streams?

An interesting question is in what way the relative importance attributed to different forms of education by national movements depends on the existence of a territorial base. A political movement engaged in a violent struggle will endeavour to strengthen its assets that are relevant to the kind of conflict it is fighting. It will be most interested in those kinds of education that contribute to these assets. For a movement with local control, the full range of education and training that contribute to a functioning pseudo-State are desirable and can be actively encouraged. A de-territorialized movement finds itself in a different situation. The need to develop or maintain a national identity through cultural activism and the creation of nationalist literature, the existential need to build political and diplomatic capacity, etc., imply a different set of educational priorities geared more towards the elite end.

Moreover, with less control over the educational trajectories of its client population, it is forced to ideologically accommodate, rationalize or even appropriate the latter's educational choices.

It is important to note that such questions are not merely theoretical. Not only can TVET differ from the academic streams of the education sector in terms of how it is affected by conflict, it also has a specific role to play in reconstruction. General schooling is an important factor in creating confidence in the capacity of emerging authorities to deliver large-scale public services, in keeping children and youth occupied, and in attempting to plant the seeds for long-term societal changes and development. The coverage of TVET is necessarily more limited and does not reach large parts of the population. On the other hand, it offers opportunities for more immediate integration with economic recovery, reconstruction and, most importantly, livelihoods. Improving TVET's contribution to the transition to peace ought to be the raison d'être for our attempts to understand its role in conflict.

References

Abu-Lughod, I. 2000. Palestinian higher education: national identity, liberation and globalization. *Boundary—2*, vol. 27, no. 1, pp. 75–95.

Abu Nahleh, L. 1996. *Gender planning, vocational education, and technical training (VETT) in Palestine*. London: World University Service (UK); Birzeit: Birzeit University, Women's Studies Department.

Al-Haj, M. 1995. *Education, empowerment, and control: the case of the Arabs in Israel*. Albany, NY: State University of New York Press.

Assaf, S. 1997. Educational disruption and recovery in Palestine. *In:* Tawil, S., ed. *Final report and case studies of the Workshop on Educational Destruction and Reconstruction in Disrupted Societies*. Geneva, Switzerland: UNESCO-IBE.

Badran, N.A. 1980. The means of survival: education and the Palestinian community, 1948–1967. *Journal of Palestine studies*, vol. 9, no. 4, pp. 44–74.

Baramki, G. 1987. Building Palestinian universities under occupation. *Journal of Palestine studies*, vol. 17, no. 1, pp. 12–20.

Barber, B.K. 1997. Palestinian children and adolescents during and after the Intifada. *Palestine-Israel journal*, vol. 4, no. 1, pp. 23–33.

Brown, N.J. 2001. *Democracy, history, and the contest over the Palestinian curriculum*. <www.geocities.com/nathanbrown1/>

Brown, N.J. 2002. *The international controversy regarding Palestinian textbooks*. (Lecture delivered at the Georg-Eckert Institute for International Textbook Research.) <www.geocities.com/nathanbrown1/>

Development Studies Programme—DSP. 2005. *Palestine human development report, 2004*. Ramallah: DSP; Birzeit: Birzeit University.

Faherty, R.C. 1959. *In human terms: the 1959 story of the UNRWA-UNESCO Arab refugee schools*. Paris: UNESCO.

Fasheh, M. 1990. Community education: to reclaim and transform what has been made invisible. *Harvard educational review*, vol. 60, no. 1, pp. 19–35.

Goujon, A. 1997. *Population and education prospects in the western Mediterranean region (Jordan, Lebanon, Syria, the West Bank and the Gaza Strip)*. Laxenburg, Austria: IIASA. (Interim Report IR-97-046.)

Graham-Brown, S. 1984. *Education, repression and liberation, Palestinians*. London: World University Service (UK).

Hallaj, M. 1980. The mission of Palestinian higher education. *Journal of Palestine studies*, vol. 9, no. 4, pp. 75–95.

Hanafi, S.; Tabar, L. 2005. *The emergence of a Palestinian globalized elite: donors, international organizations and local NGOs*. Jerusalem: Institute of Jerusalem Studies.

Human Rights Watch—HRW. 2001. *Second class: discrimination against Palestinian Arab children in Israel's schools*. New York, NY: HRW.

Kimmerling, B.; Migdal, J.S. 2003. *The Palestinian people: a history*. Cambridge, MA: Harvard University Press.

Lempinen, J.; Repo, J. 2002. *Palestine (West Bank and Gaza) country report: education and training sector*. Helsinki: Ministry for Foreign Affairs of Finland, Further Education Programme.

Mahshi, K.; Bush, K. 1989. The Palestinian uprising and education for the future. *Harvard educational review*, vol. 59, no. 4, pp. 470–83.

Mar'i, S.K. 1978. *Arab education in Israel*. Syracuse, NY: Syracuse University Press.

Masarweh, I.; Salhout, J. 2002. *The suffering of children under occupation: documentary study*. Jerusalem: Jerusalem Center for Social and Economic Rights.

Mazawi, A.E. 1994. Teachers' role patterns and the mediation of sociopolitical change: the case of the Palestinian school-teacher. *British journal of sociology of education*, vol. 15, no. 4, pp. 497–514.

Mazawi, A.E. 2000. The reconstruction of Palestinian education: between history, policy politics and policy making. *Journal of education policy*, vol. 15, no. 3, pp. 371–75.

Middleton, J.; Ziderman, A.; van Adams, A. 1991. *Vocational and technical education and training*. Washington, DC: World Bank. (A World Bank policy paper.)

Moughrabi, F. 2004. Palestinian universities under siege. *International higher education*, vol. 36, pp. 9–10.

Palestinian Authority. Ministry of Education. 2000. *Five-year education development plan*. Ramallah: Ministry of Education.

Palestinian Authority. Ministry of Education and Higher Education. No date. *Human resource development for technical and vocational education and training (TVET) in Palestine*. Ramallah: Ministry of Education and Higher Education. <www.tvet-pal.org/human/mehe.html>

Palestinian Authority. Ministry of Education and Higher Education. 1998. *Vocational and technical education and training in Palestine: national strategy*. Ramallah: Ministry of Education and Higher Education. <www.tvet-pal.org/about/strategy.html>

Palestinian Authority. Ministry of Education and Higher Education. 2003. *TVET national strategy: proposed implementation plan*. Ramallah: Ministry of Education and Higher Education. <www.tvet-pal.org/about/plan.htm>

Palestinian Authority. Ministry of Education and Higher Education. 2005. *Statistics about general education in Palestine 2005-2006*. Ramallah: Ministry of Education and Higher Education.

Pappe, I. 2006. *A history of modern Palestine: one land, two peoples*, 2nd ed. Cambridge, UK: Cambridge University Press.

Roy, S. 1995. *The Gaza Strip: the political economy of de-development*. Washington, DC: Institute for Palestine Studies.

Sayigh, R. 1985. Palestinian education: escape route or strait-jacket? *Journal of Palestine studies*, vol. 14, no. 3, pp. 127–34.

Schiff, B.N. 1989. Between occupier and occupied: UNRWA in the West Bank and the Gaza Strip. *Journal of Palestine studies*, vol. 18, no. 3, pp. 60–75.

Shepherd, N. 1999. *Ploughing sand: British rule in Palestine*. London: John Murray.

Sullivan, A. 1994. Palestinian universities in the West Bank and Gaza Strip. *Muslim world*, vol. 84, no. 1–2, pp. 168–88.

Tibawi, A.L. 1956. *Arab education in mandatory Palestine: a study of three decades of British administration*. London: Luzac.

UNESCO. 1991. *Palestine: priority projects for educational development. Project report*. Paris: UNESCO.

UNESCO Institute for Statistics. 2002. *Arab States regional report*. Montreal, Canada: UIS.

UNESCO-UNEVOC. 2003. *Regional Expert Meeting on TVET Project Development in the Arab States*. Bonn, Germany: UNESCO-UNEVOC. <www.unevoc.unesco.org/arabstates>

United Nations Relief and Works Agency. 2005. *Medium-Term Plan 2005-2009: a better future for Palestine refugees*. Gaza: UNRWA.

Usher, G. 1991. Children of Palestine. *Race & class*, vol. 32, no. 4, pp. 1–18.

Velloso, A. 2002. Palestinian education: a national curriculum against all odds. *International journal of educational development*, vol. 22, no. 2, pp. 145–54.

Weighill, L. 1995. The future of assistance to Palestinian refugees. *Asian affairs*, vol. 26, no. 3, pp. 259–69.

World Bank. 2004. *Four years: Intifada, closures and Palestinian economic crisis: an assessment*. Washington, DC: World Bank.

World Bank. 2006. *West Bank and Gaza Education Sector Analysis*. Washington, DC: World Bank.

Yusuf, M.D. 1979. The potential impact of Palestinian education on a Palestinian State. *Journal of Palestine studies*, vol. 8, no. 4, pp. 70–93.

Chapter V.5
Co-ordinated Programming for Skills Development and Livelihoods in Post-Conflict Societies: What Promise Does TVET Hold for Southern Sudan?

Zuki Karpinska

> *Inconsistent development over the years [...] means that the new Government of Southern Sudan is confronted by a wide diversity of needs. Nowhere is this more evident than in the education sector, where estimates during the war found that just one child in five attended school and less than 1 per cent of girls completed their primary education (Southern Sudan. MoEST/UNICEF, 2006, p. 2).*

> *Technical education is needed to train Southern Sudanese so the country is rebuilt by its citizens (Southern Sudan. MoEST, 2007b, p. 47).*

1 Introduction

In conflict and post-conflict contexts, international aid agencies often assume responsibility for the delivery of services, such as education. Co-ordination in the field of development and relief aid may be defined as 'the systematic utilization of policy instruments to deliver humanitarian assistance in a cohesive and effective manner' (Minear et al., 1992, p. 3). In other words, both international stakeholders—United Nations agencies, bi- and multi-lateral donors, and international non-governmental organizations (NGOs)—and local stakeholders—government authorities and local NGOs—should strive for cohesion and effectiveness in their approaches to the provision of aid and development programming. However, in their research on United Nations (UN) agency co-ordination in humanitarian response, Reindorp and Wiles (2001) cite from past studies of complex emergencies the following themes that contribute to ineffective interventions: 'turf battles, empire-building, overlapping and conflicting mandates, and ad hoc arrangements' (p. 8). It is this state of affairs that has led Sommers (2004) to ask: 'Why is the act of co-ordinating humanitarian and post-conflict reconstruction activities so difficult?' (p. 17). Sommers goes on, suggesting that:

> In principle, it should be simple and straightforward: the work by different actors in sectors such as education should fit together and complement each other. It does not make sense

R. Maclean, D. Wilson (eds.), *International Handbook of Education for the Changing World of Work*, DOI 10.1007/978-1-4020-5281-1_V.5,
© Springer Science+Business Media B.V. 2009

for them to overlap or leave gaps in service. Working as a team to address the collective needs of people recovering from tragedy and disaster seems the appropriate, logical and humanitarian thing to do (Sommers, 2004, p. 17).

Why, indeed, does co-ordination for cohesive and effective programming seem so elusive?

This chapter examines the difficulties of providing cohesive and effective technical and vocational education and training (TVET) in challenging contexts by looking at government, external agency and NGO co-ordination structures in southern Sudan.[1] TVET in southern Sudan, rather than being 'concerned with the acquisition of knowledge and skills for the world of work' (UNESCO-UNEVOC, n.d.), is currently mainly concerned with the acquisition of skills that could lead to livelihoods—the means of making a living. The term 'world of work' does not currently apply to the context of southern Sudan because too few opportunities for gainful employment exist to make it meaningful; the market for semi-skilled labour of the type that emerges from existing TVET programmes is still too underdeveloped to absorb the few graduates. Thus, for the purposes of this chapter, TVET is defined as any educational opportunity providing training in livelihood skills.[2]

The chapter begins with a brief overview of the Sudanese conflict, as well as the current political and economic context in the region. The subsequent sections offer a description of TVET programmes in southern Sudan to date; an analysis of current steps that the Ministry of Education, Science and Technology (MoEST) is pursuing to better organize these TVET offerings; and a discussion of the mechanisms used to co-ordinate TVET and other programming. The chapter ends with an expression of optimism that these steps will improve co-ordination among TVET-funding donors, TVET-providing agencies and governmental authorities.

2 Overview of the Conflict and Its Aftermath

Sudan is the largest country in Africa and is home to the longest-running conflict on the continent. The north and south of the country have been at war since even before the country gained independence from the British in 1956, due in part to differences in religion, ethnicity and resource availability. After a decade of relative peace between 1972 and 1982, a second civil war broke out in 1983, arguably instigated by the imposition of Shari'a law by the Khartoum-based Government of Sudan (GoS). The Sudan People's Liberation Army (SPLA) and its splinter groups emerged as the main 'rebel' force in opposition to the GoS. The area known as southern Sudan had historically been severely underdeveloped, but—since the fighting took place almost exclusively in the south—what little infrastructure was in place has been completely destroyed. Over the twenty-two years of civil war post-1983, southern Sudan was ravaged in terms of loss of human life, destruction of schools and roads, disruption of agricultural and business activities, as well as massive population displacement. An estimated 2 million people died during the war and approximately 4.5 million Southern Sudanese were displaced.[3]

The Comprehensive Peace Agreement (CPA) (GoS & SPLM/A, 2005) ending the second war was signed on 9 January 2005 by only two of the parties to the conflict: the GoS and the Sudan People's Liberation Movement/Army (SPLM/A). This is significant because most Sudanese, from both the north and the south, did not participate in the peace process. Even other key military groups, such as the South Sudan Defence Force (SSDF) and the National Democratic Alliance (NDA), were not represented during the two-year negotiations led by the Inter-Governmental Authority on Development (IGAD), which enjoyed strong support from the international community, including the so-called 'troika' of the United States, Norway and the United Kingdom (Young, 2005). Under the CPA, southern Sudan—comprising ten of Sudan's southernmost states with two additional states and one area administered jointly with the Khartoum government—became an autonomous region. For all intents and purposes, however, southern Sudan still suffers from insecurity due to continuing occasional skirmishes between the GoS forces and southern armies.

The CPA's power-sharing protocol called for an autonomous Government of Southern Sudan (GoSS) and a Government of National Unity (GoNU), the latter comprising representatives from both the north and the south. The appointed ministers and other executives of the GoSS are almost exclusively former military officials, many of whom lack the administration skills required to lead a civilian nation, resulting in a fledgling government of generally low capacity (International Crisis Group, 2006). Under the CPA, the South will hold a referendum in 2011 to vote on the status of the region, leaving it to the Southern Sudanese to decide whether to continue power-sharing or to secede entirely and establish their own nation-State. According to National Democratic Institute for International Affairs (NDI) focus group data (Cook, 2005) and other sources, the Southern Sudanese will almost certainly vote for the latter option, but the GoS will be reluctant to give up the oil wealth that the south represents. The CPA's wealth-sharing protocol had specified that half of Sudanese oil wealth would be allocated to the south. These funds were to comprise—for now—the sole source of non-donor GoSS revenue, as a tax system is currently unthinkable. As of the time of writing, only a fraction of the *expected* funds have been released by the GoS (Reeves, 2005, *emphasis added*), which—together with the low capacity of the southern government—has delayed full GoSS assumption of responsibility for delivery of services, such as education.

3 The Economic Context and Livelihoods

Muchomba and Sharp (2006) report: 'Livelihoods in southern Sudan are inextricably linked to both a relatively rich and abundant resource base and the terrible consequences of more than two decades of civil conflict' (p. 18). The majority of Southern Sudanese seek livelihoods in animal husbandry, agriculture, fishing on the Nile River and its tributaries, wild food collection and/or trade. Livestock may represent the single greatest material asset of the Southern Sudanese; many of the ethnic groups in southern Sudan are pastoralist, owning vast herds of cattle and goats. The cattle herds, in particular, may sometimes number in the thousands, and are an integral part of both the region's livelihoods and its culture. Both pastoralist and non-pastoralist ethnic groups practice small-scale agriculture, for subsistence and/or as a means of currency. However, crops are affected by the region's periodic droughts (including a recent drought that lasted for three years) and the resultant low yields are often insufficient for even subsistence. Trading and selling of goods from nearby Uganda, Kenya or Ethiopia and even from Khartoum—due in part to improved transportation and demining of key access roads—is increasing rapidly during the time of fragile peace. The rudimentary markets are expanding, with more goods—e.g. plastic sandals, clothing, cigarettes—appearing in an increasing number of locations. The barter system is still widespread, with southern Sudan's three currencies—in addition to those of the neighbouring countries—less commonly used than exchange for cattle, beer or grain (Muchomba & Sharp, 2006).

Very few paid job opportunities exist in southern Sudan, outside of the aid community. NGOs and international organizations employ hundreds of Southern Sudanese as programme managers, project staff, driver/mechanics, security guards, cooks, cleaners, etc. Due to continued inability by the government to pay salaries, teachers are usually unpaid volunteers; a small number of schools receive small incentives for teachers from NGOs like Norwegian Church Aid (NCA), but these are usually in the form of non-cash items, such as soap. Temporary work is sometimes available in select areas for semi-skilled labourers, such as masons or carpenters on construction projects. As a result, many Southern Sudanese are still dependent on humanitarian aid (Marriage, 2006) from organizations such as the World Food Programme.

All of these livelihoods are affected by the reality of the southern Sudanese environment. Lack of roads and periodic flooding mean no access to markets for the vast majority of the population. There are disparities within the region of southern Sudan, however: the southern-most Equatoria states are much less affected by the rains than the rest of the region. The Equatorias have better roads, are closer to the relatively-developed markets of Uganda and Kenya and do not have the swamps of Jonglei or other states. Security is also often an issue that affects access to markets, but in isolated cases rather than as a region-wide phenomenon. Uganda's Lord's Resistance Army (LRA) attacks, for instance, are limited to the southernmost states and can close down markets for weeks. It is important to note that the most significant factor in the economy of southern Sudan is its sheer physical size. The region is massive and distances between points can be unmanageable. Transportation costs are thus staggeringly high, impacting both southern Sudanese livelihoods and international agency programming.

Finally, a significant challenge to the development of livelihoods in post-conflict southern Sudan is lack of education and training. Southern Sudan's 'lost generation' —those denied access to schooling during the war years due to insecurity, displacement and/or lack of resources—comprises the majority of the population. The latest figures show that only one out of every five children attended school during the war, with just 2% finishing the primary school cycle (Southern Sudan. MoEST/UNICEF, 2006). Education and development funding have only been available in the region for the past several years; prior to this, the vast majority of donor funds were solely available for humanitarian relief (Sommers, 2005). Although a few organizations,[4] including UNICEF, offered school 'materials and a little training' prior to 1993, not until then was the need for support for education recognized (Joyner, 1996). And, not until 2000 did long-term development programming in education begin (Sommers, 2005). Any and all educational opportunities in southern Sudan are thus still rare, although the demand for basic education and skills training is high and expected to rise (Southern Sudan. MoEST, 2007a).

4 Definitions of TVET and the New TVET Policy Framework

Until 2007, MoEST offered little guidance for TVET programming. The SPLM Secretariat of Education's *Education policy of the new Sudan and implementation guidelines* (2002), which is still in effect, only notes that vocational training should/will exist in southern Sudan. No further information is provided in the existing education policy as to what TVET will comprise, by whom it will be carried out, or how it will be financed. Only weeks before this writing, however, MoEST published a new policy handbook that includes definitions for TVET and a firm commitment to developing both a TVET policy framework and a system of certification (Southern Sudan. MoEST, 2007a).

MoEST differentiates in the following manner between informal, non-formal, and formal vocational training (Southern Sudan. MoEST, 2007a; 2007b):

1. *Informal vocational education programmes* consist of basic occupational skills training, with a duration of one week to three months. There are no prequalifications to entry and courses are usually taught by 'community members with some years of practical experience in the vocation. The courses do not follow a structured linear progression' (p. 2).
2. *Non-formal vocational education programmes* consist of basic occupational skills training, with a duration of three to six months. There are no prequalifications to entry and courses are usually taught by skilled practitioners.
3. *Formal vocational education programmes* consist of training with 'curricula developed into modules/guides which allow students to build sequentially on their skills', with a duration of nine months to two years. These programmes have 'a written curriculum which contains both theoretical and practical components. The theoretical courses are usually taught by university graduates and practical courses by practitioners with extensive experience' (pp. 2–3).

In practice, however, few *formal* vocational education programmes, such as the ones described above, yet exist. Even the longer training programmes rarely require any secondary education and college-graduate instructors are scarce.

Until 2005,[5] skills training in southern Sudan was only available through NGOs, which—if offered in physical premises—generally only established and operated one centre. This is particularly true of centres operated by Sudanese NGOs. The most common training programming—which would be categorized as informal vocational education by MoEST—involves livelihoods skills training at the community level. Vétérinaires sans frontières-Belgium (VSF), for example, trains pastoralist groups in techniques that improve animal husbandry practices. Other NGOs work with farming communities to increase crop yields. These types of training are shorter, on average, than the non-formal and more formal vocational education described below, with instruction taking place over a period of weeks or several days per month during an entire year, as opposed to training that requires daily attendance for months. Such livelihoods skills-training programmes build on local knowledge or introduce innovation in a skill that is already practised.

Among the NGOs involved in *non-formal* skills training, as described above, Catholic Relief Services (CRS) operated six livelihood skills-training centres,[6] later turned over to the relevant ministries, and currently operates six vocational training centres.[7] Of the approximately two dozen skills training centres that currently exist in southern Sudan, CRS has thus established about half. Due to the high cost of inputs such as electricity—which, since electricity in southern Sudan is produced solely by generators, requires gasoline transported into the region at great cost—these skills-training centres usually focus on skills that do not require heavy investment, such as carpentry or agriculture, rather than computer training or car mechanics. At the moment, in the absence of a southern Sudanese vocational curriculum, NGOs typically establish their own training curriculum at each centre or adapt Kenyan or Ugandan curricula. In 2004, Save the Children Sweden had developed a Sudan-specific curriculum for vocational training in two subjects, with the consent of the then-SPLM Secretariat of Education (currently MoEST). These materials, however, have not been accepted by MoEST as part of the national curriculum for vocational training.

Many of these training centres are nominally managed by boards (boards of governors, management boards, etc.) composed of community-elected representatives. Some NGOs suggest a minimum quota for female representation to dissuade communities from appointing all-male boards, as would otherwise be the case. The boards receive training in educational management and administration in order to build community capacity to make decisions on behalf of the centres, organize assistance in the construction efforts and liaise with the NGOs. However, the boards effectively have little or no power, except over the modest project funding that is channelled to them through the NGOs. The centres managed by boards are frequently expected to assume responsibility for the training when projects end on behalf of the relevant ministry. Since 2006, ministries, such as the Ministry of Agriculture and Forestry, the Ministry of the Environment, Wildlife Conservation and Tourism and the Ministry of Animal Resources and Fisheries, have begun to offer skills training, after having assumed responsibility for several of the training centres formerly operated by NGOs. Due to the difficulties in accessing GoSS resources, as mentioned above, it is unlikely that many of these centres will continue to be operational without additional donor funding in the interim before the flow of GoSS resources becomes more consistent.

Generally, there are no educational requirements for admittance to vocational training programmes, although there are exceptions. Life-skills training is rarely, if ever, incorporated into the curricula, but one-off trainings such as HIV/AIDS awareness may be given to students. Many centres do incorporate business management training or entrepreneurial training into the curriculum, in order to prepare graduates to earn a living from their newly-acquired skills. Apprenticeship programmes are very difficult to establish in southern Sudan because so few people earn a living using a vocational skill. Those who do are located in one of only a handful of 'urban' centres (which are essentially larger villages with some permanent structures). Due to the size of the region, linking graduates with apprenticeships is generally unfeasible.

Assuming that the success of a programme is not measured by completion rates but rather by the number of graduates who use the skills learned in order to earn a living after the programme ends, it would seem that there are not many successful training programmes in southern Sudan. Training programmes that focus on traditional skills—e.g. agriculture or fishing—are more successful than those that focus on trades, such as carpentry or masonry. The truth is that there are few markets large enough in southern Sudan to absorb graduates with skills taught in the more-formal training centres. Logically, a community of 1,000 or even 10,000 people does not need 100 masons. Similarly, a centre that does not have free boarding facilities and daily food rations cannot admit students outside the local community. Available evidence suggests that, with time, the demand for skills will increase, and these training programmes will enjoy more success in terms of the number of graduates who use the skills acquired during trainings in their livelihoods.

A key missing factor in the co-ordination of these TVET offerings in southern Sudan has been the 'utilization of policy instruments' (Minear et al., 1992, p. 3), for the simple reason that none had existed. At the same time as the above-mentioned new policy handbook was published—i.e. only two months prior to this writing—MoEST developed a Draft Background/Policy Technical-Vocational Education Training Policy Framework with the aid of an external consultant. The draft framework provides a situational analysis of planned and existing TVET opportunities in southern Sudan, as well as offering policy briefs on the vision, structure, mandate and resource allocation of current and future TVET programmes. The document also addresses issues of inter-ministerial co-operation, certification and funding challenges. MoEST expects that the framework will 'initiate a policy dialogue between and among education stakeholders at all levels' (Southern Sudan. MoEST, 2007b, p. 1).

Importantly, the draft policy framework proposes definitions of TVET that distinguish between vocational and technical education. According to MoEST, the 'suggested' definition for vocational education comprises 'vocational programs [that] offer individuals, who typically have had little or no access to formal education programs, the opportunity to gain vital skills and be productive members of the community' (Southern Sudan. MoEST, 2007b, p. 46). These are thus the vocational programmes discussed above: training opportunities that do not require prior education. The vision for vocational training in southern Sudan reads: 'to produce a well integrated [*sic*] self-motivated, creative individual equipped with relevant knowledge, skills and attitude through appropriate technology and wise use of available resources while preserving the cultural legacy of the community' (ibid.). The 'suggested' definition for technical education comprises formal training that 'integrates academics with formal skills' (ibid.). These training programmes fall under the MoEST Higher Education Directorate and thus would be akin to polytechnic-level education as practised in more developed countries, i.e. training opportunities that require a secondary-level education. The vision for technical educational is one that is 'both practical and theoretical', with 'a strong academic track to provide a way for individuals with a secondary school degree to progress upward through the formal education ladder' in order to 'train Southern Sudanese so the country is re-built by its citizens' (Southern Sudan. MoEST, 2007b, pp. 46–47). The Draft Background/Policy Technical-Vocational Education Training Policy Framework thus finally clarifies MoEST's understanding of and vision for TVET.

5 Co-ordination Structures for Service Delivery in Southern Sudan

NGOs and international agencies have been responsible for service provision in southern Sudan during the war years and beyond (e.g. drilling wells, operating health clinics). This is not to say that government authorities at all levels have been absent from service delivery planning, but—without financial resources of their own—the southern Sudanese authorities have not provided the services; the aid community has. Even today, however, the vast majority of southern Sudan remains underserved.

The uneven and inadequate (Marriage, 2006) service delivery in southern Sudan is not only due to poor co-ordination. In order to operate in a given location, an organization requires a secure camp to house workers, store supplies and establish communications, which necessitates constructing and maintaining field offices in insecure and/or inaccessible locations at a great expense. Organizations thus have—quite rightly—been accused of 'favouring' particular locations due to the relative ease of travel to and/or relative security of a given site. It is also true that, once a field office is established, NGOs frequently continue to work in that location and do not move to another. Given the considerable transportation costs of operating in southern Sudan, these trends cannot be avoided, though greater co-ordination could help provide a more equitable distribution of resources (e.g. assignment of areas to specific NGOs by the GoSS based on comparative advantage of service delivery). Yet, the less accessible the location, the greater the costs of operation: building one TVET centre in Unity state may cost three times as much as building three in Western Equatoria state. Since the needs in southern Sudan are so great, building the three TVET centres would generally be considered more cost-effective than building the one.

It would be imprudent to write a chapter on co-ordination in southern Sudan without mentioning Operation Lifeline Sudan (OLS), an unprecedented (Lautze et al., 2004) security and information-sharing consortium founded in 1989. Members of OLS were the many (although not all) international agencies and NGOs involved in the humanitarian efforts responding to civilian needs in southern Sudan. OLS co-ordinated with both the GoS and the SPLA/Sudan People's Liberation Movement (SPLM)—the political wing of the SPLA—to gain access to the millions of Southern Sudanese whose livelihoods were in suspension because of the war. While member organizations of the OLS consortium claimed neutrality, it has since been argued that these and other international actors perpetuated the conflict, inadvertently or purposefully supplying the armies with food and non-food rations, along with the targeted civilian beneficiaries (see, for example, Sommers, 2005). The many critics of OLS (e.g. Marriage, 2006) assert that the co-ordination structure failed the Southern Sudanese.

UNICEF, the lead UN agency for OLS, had also been the 'lead agency' for education[8] until its handover to the then-SPLM Secretariat of Education in 2003. Arguably, no overview of the lack of success of co-ordination between international, national and local stakeholders in education could be more persuasive than that of Sommers (2005):

> Among the most staggering failures in the case of education for Southern Sudanese since 1983 has been the widespread and alarming deficiency in the co-ordination of education policies and practices. Across more than two decades of civil war, there has been poor co-ordination of education activities in just about every way imaginable. There has been virtually no co-ordination of education concerns for Southern Sudanese between [...] refugee agencies and those working within southern Sudan, among those working within southern Sudan (for the most part and until recently), [and] within the same agencies working with the same Southern Sudanese population in northern and southern Sudan. [...] On issues as basic as teacher payments and the curriculum, co-ordination has, for nearly all of the past twenty-one years, ranged between flawed and nonexistent (pp. 255–56).

While apt, this assessment reflects a time when far fewer agencies worked in the education sector than exist today; and, the more agencies, the greater is the challenge of co-ordination for cohesive and effective programming. More development programming has become possible since the signing of the CPA and the number of NGOs in the region has multiplied.

In southern Sudan, TVET falls under the purview of MoEST, which for the last few years has also been responsible for the co-ordination of TVET programming. The Education Rehabilitation and Development Forum (ERDF) is the co-ordination meeting for all local and international agencies implementing education, and thus TVET programming in southern Sudan. The ERDF is theoretically a quarterly meeting, but—in the twenty-six months that the author of this chapter worked in southern Sudan—the ERDF has only taken place five times. A joint MoEST-NGO co-ordination body for vocational education was established in 2005. Now called the GoSS-MoEST Vocational-Technical Thematic Group, the co-ordination body meets during the infrequent ERDF meetings. In southern Sudan, currently eleven NGOs, as well as twelve ministries,[9] have reported implementing, or planning to implement, TVET programmes, and more NGOs than this actually operate skills-training programmes. Yet, as mentioned above, every actor involved in TVET appears to be working independently of the others. Importantly, not all of the actors involved in TVET attend ERDF meetings, much less the thematic group meetings. In such a context, TVET programmes differ in terms of duration, content, beneficiary number, quality, certification and approach.

In addition, the ministries of southern Sudan have not co-ordinated well among themselves. Numerous GoSS ministries currently implement vocational programmes, which have not been vetted by MoEST, nor have these programmes 'been integrated into the overarching' education system (Southern Sudan. MoEST, 2007b, p. 54). The ministries also plan to organize additional trainings that are yet to be approved by MoEST, and it is unclear whether there is consensus on the part of the other ministries that their trainings should be subject to MoEST scrutiny. MoEST asserts that it should be responsible for certifying/recognizing vocational curricula of all the ministries, as well as responsible for leading the process of developing a curriculum framework linking all formal and non-formal programmes (Southern Sudan. MoEST, 2007b). A large part of the proposed co-ordination role of MoEST would comprise developing and standardizing a system of certification that is currently lacking in southern Sudan. Presumably, the promise of ensuring recognition for TVET graduates in all sectors could overcome the reluctance, if any, of other ministries to relinquish a degree of control over their training to a parallel ministry.

6 Concluding Remarks

The Draft TVET Policy Framework may well solve the problem of poor co-ordination in TVET among MoEST, other ministries and NGOs. Its very existence has finally provided a structure to a disjointed TVET system. In addition to its clarification of the vision for and understanding of TVET, the document offers a detailed, though somewhat optimistic, account of existing TVET programming in southern Sudan. This stock-taking is an important first step in improving co-ordination among the NGO and ministry service providers. The MoEST Draft TVET Policy Framework, however, makes no mention of whether the stock-taking has been thorough in terms of assessing which of the many interventions described therein are actually operational, much less whether statistics, such as the number of beneficiaries, have been collected. While it is potentially a great opportunity for the southern Sudanese who have not had access to skills training that the number of ministries and NGOs suggested by the document are now involved/plan to be involved with TVET, the author of this chapter remains sceptical that many of these trainings are a matter of fact. Especially at the level of the ministries, the planned trainings may result in programmes that are very limited in terms of numbers of beneficiaries or these trainings may be akin to wish-lists, i.e. training that the ministries would undertake if the technical capacity and funding to implement such projects were available. In order to make these trainings a reality, the most immediate input required will be additional allocated funding for both training and capacity-building by the implementing ministries.

Southern Sudan is certainly not the only region to suffer from co-ordination difficulties (see Reindorp & Wiles, 2001; INEE, 2004; Sommers, 2004), but the lack of a TVET policy or framework surely contributed to the disjointed manner in which TVET has been offered. Yet, it is simplistic to assume that, once the TVET Policy Framework is finalized and disseminated, co-ordination among government ministries and the aid community will suddenly improve. The document will in all likelihood serve as procedural guidelines for the southern Sudanese ministries, leading to cohesion within the GoSS—which is an improvement in and of itself—but may not improve GoSS co-ordination with external agencies.

Smillie & Minear (2003), in a study of donor behaviour in emergency and reconstruction contexts, found that:

> The overall effectiveness of humanitarian assistance is compromised by donor earmarking, by short funding cycles, by unrequited pledges and late funding, by tying contributions to a donor's own nationals, NGOs, and contractors, and by donors' political interests (p. 5).

Sommers (2004) seconds this notion; he posits that, in not co-ordinating among themselves, donors may achieve 'chaotic' and 'contradictory' programming. The personal experience of working in southern Sudan by the author of this chapter, terminating seven months before this writing, is that conflicting donor practices were the factor most responsible for lack of overall co-ordination in TVET programming. She agrees with Sommers (2004) in that donors, more than any other stakeholder, have the greatest power to ensure co-ordination. In the current funding context in southern Sudan, each NGO receives funding from a different source— donors with their own priorities, own reporting requirements, own bureaucratic so-called red-tape and own funding calendars. The 2005 establishment of the South Sudan Multi-Donor Trust Fund (MDTF), a co-operative funding mechanism for reconstruction and development funding administered by the World Bank, was to mitigate these issues, giving more power to the ministries to prioritize their funding needs and choose the implementing agencies for the projects identified to meet those needs. The MDTF was designed to recognize the '*ownership* and leadership' of the GoSS of the reconstruction and development process, 'with full *transparency*', ensuring 'effective *donor co-ordination* within the context of broader aid management structures in order to reduce transaction/duplication costs; provide consistent policy advice; [and] provide common fora for dialogue' (IBRD, 2005, p. 7. *Emphasis in the original*). However, such an arrangement may only work—even in theory—if all donors transmit available resources through the fund; USAID, the single largest bi-lateral donor to education in southern Sudan, does not. Greater co-ordination on the part of donors, among themselves and especially with the GoSS, could lead to interconnected projects aligned with the priorities of the recipient stakeholders, such as those outlined in the Draft TVET Policy Framework.

The importance of the framework cannot be overemphasized. The very definition of co-ordination used in this paper requires actors to systematically utilize policy instruments such as this in a coherent and effective manner (Minear et al., 1992). One of the quotations that opened this chapter comes from the framework itself: 'Technical education is needed to train Southern Sudanese so the country is rebuilt by its citizens' (Southern Sudan. MoEST, 2007b, p. 47). In the framework, MoEST has delineated its vision for southern Sudan, outlined the gaps in TVET offerings and identified the many unmet needs. If donors are willing to fund the interventions necessary and if they and the implementing agencies work together under the aegis of a revitalized ERDF, the co-ordination hitherto lacking in southern Sudan's education sector may transform the course of the reconstruction process. TVET may yet provide southern Sudan with the technical workforce needed to rebuild, and the framework could be the first step in ensuring that TVET programming will educate such a workforce.

Notes

1. For the purposes of this chapter, 'southern', when referring to the area of Sudan, will be written in lowercase, while Southern Sudanese, when referring to the people, will be capitalized. For a full discussion, see Sommers, 2005.
2. As will be discussed later, this definition does not necessarily coincide with the current understanding of TVET of the Government of Southern Sudan's (GoSS) Ministry of Education, Science and Technology (MoEST).
3. These figures are those cited in NSCSE (2004). However, these and other data available for southern Sudan are highly contested and generally considered unreliable.
4. The notable exceptions to 'hit-and-run' educational programming (Sommers, 2005) in the period prior to 2000 have been Christian organizations, such as the Diocese of Torit.
5. The author of this chapter was an educational practitioner in southern Sudan for over two years. Much of the information that follows on TVET and international aid is based on her experience.
6. These centres were financed through the United States Agency for International Development (USAID)-funded South Sudan Agriculture Revitalization Programme (SSARP).
7. These centres were financed through the European Community (EC)-funded Vocational and Adult Literacy Training Project (VOCAL). The author of this chapter helped design the VOCAL Project.
8. While the UN Office for the Co-ordination of Humanitarian Affairs (OCHA) has a presence in southern Sudan, its co-ordination activities are largely limited to the UN agencies in this context and do not extend to co-ordinating sector programmes, such as education or health.
9. These ministries are: Ministry of Agriculture and Forestry; Ministry of Animal Resources and Fisheries; Ministry of Co-operatives and Rural Development; Ministry of Education, Science and Technology; Ministry of Environment, Wildlife Conservation and Tourism; Ministry of Gender, Social Welfare and Religious Affairs; Ministry of Health; Ministry of Industry and Mining; Ministry of Labour, Public Service and Human Resource Development; Ministry of Water Resources and Irrigation; Ministry of Youth, Culture and Sports; and the Southern Sudan Disarmament, Demobilization and Reintegration Commission. The NGOs are: Ananda Marga Universal Relief Team (AMURT); Catholic Relief Services (CRS); Dioceses of Rumbek (DOR); Diar Relief and Development Association (DRDA); Education Base; International Aid Sweden (IAS); Norwegian People Aid (NPA); Norwegian Refugee Council (NRC); Ockenden Plan International; Save the Children Sweden; and Women for Women International (Southern Sudan. MoEST, 2007a).

References

Cook, T.D. 2005. *A foundation for peace: citizen thoughts on the southern Sudan Constitution—findings from focus groups with men and women across southern Sudan.* Washington, DC: National Democratic Institute for International Affairs. <www.access democracy.org/library/1918_su_southernsudan_060905.pdf>

Government of Sudan; Sudan People's Liberation Movement/Army. 2005. *The Comprehensive Peace Agreement between the Government of the Sudan and the Sudan People's Liberation Movement/Sudan People's Liberation Army.* Nairobi: Government of Sudan.

Interagency Network for Education in Emergencies Interagency Network for Education in Emergencies. 2004. *Minimum standards for education in emergencies, chronic crises and early reconstruction.* New York, NY: INEE. <ineeserver.org/page.asp?pid=1240>

International Bank for Reconstruction and Development. 2005. *Memorandum of the President of the International Bank for Reconstruction and Development to the Executive Directors on a proposal for the World Bank to administer two multidonor trust funds for Sudan, 17 March 2005.* <www.unsudanig.org/docs/Sudan_MDTFs.pdf>

International Crisis Group. 2006. *Sudan's Comprehensive Peace Agreement: the long road ahead.* Brussels: Crisis Group. (Crisis Group Africa report, no. 106.) <www.crisisgroup.org/library/documents/africa/horn_of_africa/106_sudan_comprehensive_peace_agreement_long_road_ahead.pdf>

Joyner, A. 1996. Supporting education in emergencies: a case study from southern Sudan. *Development in practice,* vol. 6, no. 1, pp. 70–76. <dx.doi.org/10.1080/0961452961000157614>

Lautze, S. et al. 2004. Assistance, protection, and governance networks in complex emergencies. *The Lancet,* vol. 364, pp. 2134–41.

Marriage, Z. 2006. The comfort of denial: external assistance in southern Sudan. *Development and change,* vol. 37, no. 3, pp. 479–500.

Minear, L. et al. 1992. *United Nations coordination of the international humanitarian response to the Gulf Crisis 1990–1992.* Providence, RI: Brown University, The Thomas A. Watson Jr. Institute for International Studies. (Occasional paper, no. 13.) <hwproject.tufts.edu/publications/abstracts/op13.html>

Muchomba, E.; Sharp, B. 2006. *Southern Sudan livelihoods profiles: a guide for humanitarian and development planning.* Nairobi: Southern Sudan Centre for Census, Statistics and Evaluation (SSCCSE)/Save the Children UK.

New Sudan Centre for Statistics and Evaluation. 2004. *Towards a baseline: best estimates of social indicators for southern Sudan.* Rumbek, Sudan: UNICEF. (NSCSE series paper, no. 1/2004.) <www.reliefweb.int/library/documents/2004/splm-sud-31may.pdf>

Reeves, E. 2005. *The slow collapse of the Comprehensive Peace Agreement for South Sudan.* <www.sudanreeves.org/ Article70.html>

Reindorp, N.; Wiles, P. 2001. *Humanitarian co-ordination: lessons from recent field experience.* London: Overseas Development Institute. (A study commissioned by OCHA.)

Smillie, I.; Minear, L. 2003. *The quality of money: donor behavior in humanitarian financing.* Somerville, MA: Tufts University, Humanitarianism and War Project, Feinstein Famine Center. <hwproject.tufts.edu/new/pdf/donor_behav.pdf>

Sommers, M. 2004. *Co-ordinating education during emergencies and reconstruction: challenges and responsibilities.* Paris: UNESCO-IIEP.

Sommers, M. 2005. *Islands of education: schooling, civil war, and the southern Sudanese (1993–2004).* Paris: UNESCO-IIEP.

Southern Sudan. Ministry of Education, Science and Technology. 2007a. *Ministry of Education, Science and Technology policy handbook (Final draft).* Juba, Sudan: MoEST.

Southern Sudan. Ministry of Education, Science and Technology. 2007b. *Draft background/policy technical-vocational education training policy framework.* Juba, Sudan: MoEST.

Southern Sudan. Ministry of Education, Science and Technology; UNICEF. 2006. *Rapid assessment of learning spaces: Southern Sudan.* Juba, Sudan: MoEST. <www.ungei.org/resources/files/RALS_book_ALL_PAGES.pdf>

Sudan People's Liberation Movement. Secretariat of Education. 2002. *Education policy of the New Sudan and implementation guidelines*. Rumbek, Sudan: SPLM.

UNESCO-UNEVOC. No date. *What is TVET?* Bonn, Germany: UNESCO-UNEVOC.

Young, J. 2005. Sudan: a flawed peace process leading to a flawed peace. *Review of African political economy*, vol. 103, pp. 99–113.

Chapter V.6
Vocational Training in Post-War Sierra Leone and Liberia

Andrew Benson Greene Jr.

1 Introduction

In this ever-changing fast-paced world, technology is becoming more and more important. Each of us will be using some sort of technology everyday of our lives, which means that the field of vocational training has never been as important as it is today.

Current research into how and why we learn as individuals, how groups and organizations learn and the complex ways knowledge is created, shared, communicated and culturally mediated in contemporary society addresses fundamental issues of interest to educators and policy-makers. We need to enhance the breadth and depth of research on education in the context of the new economy. It is vital that we achieve a deeper understanding of new technology as both an opportunity and a challenge for learning and for the delivery of education. Today, more than ever, we expect educational institutions to fulfil major economic and social goals in educating citizens, to respond to the needs of a knowledge-intensive, technology-based labour market, and to prepare individuals for learning and acquiring new skills throughout their lifetimes. We need research to understand how our schools, educators and education systems should respond to these needs, how to assess our existing learning systems and how they might evolve. Let us therefore examine the extent to which vocational training has evolved and its present situation in Sierra Leone.

Sierra Leone suffered nearly ten years of war, which displaced a large proportion of the population and destroyed most of the country's infrastructure. Terrible atrocities were committed against the civilian population by the rebel army. Many children suffered acts of frightening brutality, such as limb amputations. Disabled young people face particular hardships as their chances of employment are severely reduced, particularly those who have had upper limbs amputated. For many, the only option is to beg for food and money.[1]

R. Maclean, D. Wilson (eds.), *International Handbook of Education for the Changing World of Work*, DOI 10.1007/978-1-4020-5281-1_V.6,
© Springer Science+Business Media B.V. 2009

2 Making Amends

The circumstances under which the education system in Sierra Leone has evolved in recent years were the result of skirmishes during a decade-long war. There is now an ever-growing response to skills training in both technology-enhancing learning and non-technological usage through formal and non-formal education. The proliferation of skills and vocational training thriving today are the result of the nationwide realization that, in order for there to be a sustained manpower base, the country must invest in a knowledge-based economy. Partly too, and perhaps the most persistent idea, is the belief that, to make amends for the lost years, the plethora of young people affected by war direly needs these skills. A bold attempt is being made by these young people to catch up with their counterparts in other countries and in the rest of the world, particularly with those skills that will enable them to survive in today's competitive world driven by globalization.

The rebel war in Sierra Leone displaced blacksmiths and farmers resulting in the loss of vital assets, such as their tools. With the signing of the peace accord, these blacksmiths and farmers will return to their homes with no tools to resume their livelihoods. Even though donor assistance is likely to make up for the loss of farm tools, this gesture may not be enough to satisfy all the affected population. Even so, these tools will need frequent repairs. To resettle such a deprived population, blacksmithing skills are going to be essential.

It is estimated that there are 3,000 displaced blacksmiths in the affected areas—the southern and eastern provinces and Tonkolili district in the north. To resettle these blacksmiths, there is a need for basic working tools, such as hammers, locally-made anvils and bellows. It is also proposed to provide them with assistance in setting up their workshops and a seven-day refresher training course.

For more than a decade the Sierra Leone Work Oxen Programme (SLWOP) of the Ministry of Agriculture has been involved in training blacksmiths for the country. The majority of the trainees were sent by the interested organizations, such as development projects and non-governmental organizations (NGOs). The programme has the capacity to train twenty blacksmiths per session, including accommodation and food, at the Rolako Centre (Bombali District, Northern Province). Using local materials and know how, the programme has forged bellows and anvils that are gaining favour among many village blacksmiths.

Blacksmiths will be selected from chiefdoms and trained to become trainers of other blacksmiths in their local area. The trained blacksmiths will be provided with the necessary equipment and assisted to develop tool production centres in the chiefdom. Resource people for this training will be drawn from the private sector, as well as from SLWOP. Training materials, such as tools and steel, will be purchased. The training will involve shaping, tempering techniques, cold and forge work, basic workshop management techniques, introduction to improved tools, group formation, sources of scrap and marketing skills and awareness about emergency repairs for tools. The blacksmiths will be made aware of the rationale and strategy behind setting up chiefdom blacksmith tool-production centres as the centres for training and production of basic tools for the resettling population.

About 400 blacksmiths will be trained and equipped (they, in turn, will be able to train an estimated 2,600 blacksmiths that are required to satisfy the needs of resettlement), 400 tool production and training centres will be established, and four million units of assorted tools adapted to the very specific needs of the farmers in the targeted areas will be produced (each production centre will produce on average 10,000 units per year).[2]

3 The Nehemiah Project

Margaret A. Novicki is the United Nations Information Centre Director for Ghana and Sierra Leone. In an article entitled 'Sierra Leone camps try to rehabilitate child victims and soldiers', she writes:[3]

> Currently the Nehemiah Project accommodates 140 children, but there are thousands of children throughout the country who need rehabilitation. We expect to replicate the Nehemiah Project throughout Sierra Leone, as finance and resources are released and, as the locally recruited staff gain skills and knowledge in this field, that they will train others to staff the additional units.

Novicki describes the circumstances under which amputees live and attempt to acquire skills.

> Maimouna lives with her aunt at the Murraytown Amputee Camp, a squalid shantytown on the outskirts of Freetown, home to over 1,000 amputees, war-wounded and other victims of Sierra Leone's civil war. The camp is managed by Médécins sans Frontiers with the help of Cause Canada and Handicap International. It provides social work services, vocational training, physical therapy, psycho-social counselling and prosthetic aids.
>
> Daniel, aged 15, now lives at St. Michael's Lodge, an interim child-care centre 14 miles from Freetown. A former RUF fighter, he and the other 150 children at St. Michael's are learning vocational skills and receiving psycho-social counselling. Most of the children seem quite small for their ages: years of malnourishment have stunted their growth. When asked what he plans for his future, Daniel says he simply wants to go to school. Even these war-hardened youth are still children at heart. It is estimated that the project for one training session of 20 blacksmiths will cost US$ 3,000, and hopefully, 20 sessions will be organised during the year.

The Nehemiah Project seeks to integrate general education and vocational training within a structure designed to encourage responsible, socially adjusted behaviour, whilst addressing the underlying problems of grief, fear, guilt and depression.

Children impacted by war will be eligible for admission to the vocational training programme in carpentry, tailoring, weaving, soap-making and welding. These children will be referred to CAUSE Canada, a Christian-motivated international relief and development organization, by several agencies including Children Affected by War (CAW), the Sierra Leone Ministry of Health (MOH) and UNICEF. Training will consist of a six-week internship at vocational training facilities in Waterloo, Bo and Makeni.

This project endeavours to promote an atmosphere in Sierra Leone conducive to sustainable peace. Children impacted by war need to receive psycho-social counselling so that they can adapt to peacetime society. Vocational training will help to ensure that they become contributing members of their communities.

Amputees require counselling in order to come to terms peacefully with their disabilities. Occupational therapy will help foster in these victims a new hope for the future. This type of rehabilitation will help them to once again become contributing community members, and this will hopefully lay a foundation helping them to forgive their former adversaries.

4 The Scars of War

Sierra Leone's civil war, and the events following the coup d'état of 25 May 1997, brought unprecedented social and economic disaster to the country. The United Nations Development Programme estimates that 3.2 million people were directly affected by the war and the aftermath of the May coup. UNDP further states that about 700,000 people sought refuge in Guinea and Liberia. An estimated 12,000 people, the majority of them children, lost their lives to this conflict.

UNICEF believes that, as a result of the war, more than 1,000 people had limbs forcibly amputated. About 80% of these have lost either one or both hands. It is also estimated that approximately 2,500 people have endured either severe machete lacerations or permanently debilitating gunshot wounds. Additionally, about 5,000 children between the ages of 7 and 14 years were enlisted into military groups to serve either as combatants, child labourers or sex slaves.

The children impacted by war include those recently orphaned, former child-soldiers, and children who have been either physically or psychologically handicapped by this conflict. This project offers psychological counselling and vocational training for children impacted by war. These children will participate in the manufacturing of appropriate physiotherapy aids and farm tools. They will also take part in activities specifically designed to assist recent amputees.

Handicap International and Médécins Sans Frontiers (MSF) plan to provide prostheses to war amputees. Both of these organizations, as well as government health authorities, have asked CAUSE Canada (CC) to provide occupational therapy and counselling services to complement their work. CC has been asked to provide Canadian occupational therapists and counsellors with expertise in post-traumatic stress disorder. These professionals will be engaged on a short-term basis to upgrade the training of national health practitioners and to assist in the rehabilitation of both war amputees and children affected by war.

Throughout the project, the issue of the repatriation of children impacted by war and the reintegration of amputees will be addressed both in the vocational programmes and in the communities where repatriation will take place. While the acquisition of marketable skills will be the key to the repatriation process for children impacted by war, these students will also be instructed on how to meet and overcome common social obstacles they will face upon their return. Amputees will receive similar instruction appropriate to their unique situation.

Communities will also be prepared to receive these victims of war. Through workshops and other types of consultations held with community leaders in the target regions of Greater Freetown/Waterloo, Bo and Makeni, villagers will be both practically and psychologically prepared to accept amputees and children impacted by war into their ranks.

In order to assist with the reintegration programme, children will be provided with farm tools which can be presented as gifts to the community upon their return. The skills they have developed will assist in the economic recovery of their communities and will help smooth the reintegration process as they become contributing members of their villages. Amputees will benefit from the programme by receiving tools orthopedically designed for their own use as productive members of their community

In Sierra Leone, the United Methodist Church has taken action to improve vocational training for students through Operation Classroom (OC). In the southern head district of Bo in Sierra Leone, the Bo Centenary School has been fortunate in that it is one of the few schools to have remained open and functioning during most of the war. The annual conference and OC have agreed to put together a major vocational training programme at Bo. The school's student enrolment varies from 350 to 450 students in grades 7 to 12.

5 Bridging the Digital Divide

Bridging the digital divide has been a major pre-occupation of the international education and resource network, iEARN Sierra Leone. It aims at promoting e-learning as a first step in speeding up the deployment of a high-quality infrastructure to step up training and overall digital literacy at a reasonable cost. For this purpose, the opening up of a community access centre is planned where young people who have been child-soldiers will be introduced to the necessary technology.

It can be predicted that the youth community access centre will long remain the principle information window to the outside world for war-affected youths and underprivileged children. The participation of more young people in cyberspace and the development of access to the new technologies are desirable, as is access to the Internet, off-line resources, on-line networks and chat capabilities. The acquisition of such skills will be assets in the battle to overcome the digital gap between developed and developing countries—as is the case in Sierra Leone. The transfer of competence from the facilitator to the war-affected youths will allow these children to go on-line with the whole world so as to train them for job prospects in computer-related fields, thereby enhancing sustainable development and social justice for the community and the country.

Friends of Africa are researching a project to set up a special computer-training laboratory for disabled young people. The courses will initially teach the students the basic programmes before moving on to packages for desk-top publishing, computer-aided design, book-keeping and other vocational subjects. The second phase will help these people into jobs using the skills and special equipment available through the centre. The centre itself will also employ several disabled young people on its own income-generating activities. Information technology offers disabled people in Sierra Leone a new opportunity to lead productive and fulfilled lives. Initial basic computer training for fifty students will cost US$8,000 per year.[4]

The expansion of a centre for the youths to obtain access to Internet on a regular basis is a vision that offers the possibility of turning the great challenge of closing the digital gap into reality and permitting every participating youth to be reintegrated not only into a society free from war, but a society full of knowledge. This will be the foundation that leads to the recruitment of additional young people in Sierra Leone to learn the relevant tele-communications and ICTs skills. It will further foster the promotion of peace education amongst secondary and post-secondary schools and inspire the inclusion of peace education in the school curriculum.

This in itself enhances learning and will be a catalyst for social change. Whilst each generation is granted access to the new tools needed for human achievement and progress in their own times, the present young generation is living in the new wave of tele-communication technology that links communities together to make a difference. The child-soldiers, war-affected children and disadvantaged youths/students will also reveal to the world the awful situations they faced as child-soldiers or victims of war to colleagues across the vast cultural divide. In the telling of their stories, their peers will learn what happened to them; the child-soldiers and victims will in turn achieve catharsis through the telling of their stories. It is to be hoped that they will derive positive and encouraging feedback from their colleagues and feel that once again they are not alone. Through multi-media art forms, drawings, paintings, cartoons, creative writing, music and fine arts posted by regular mail or sent through the web as attachments, children will see for themselves the strength of their talents. The projected outcome will be estimated by the extension of the work to be used as a model in four additional countries—Colombia, Palestine, Rwanda and Uganda—having been piloted in a realistic setting. This technology will demonstrate how children of war write for an authentic audience to better communicate with peers about real issues that touched their very lives, families and communities.

To sustain the Internet centre, grants or funds will be utilized to acquire the necessary tools needed for the achievement of the long-range goal of providing the relevant tele-communication kits to equip young people with the necessary skills. The funds will be used to sustain the centre even long after the one-year duration of the implementation time-line has passed.

Finally, even though there are enormous challenges facing young people and all those who access the limited technology available today in Sierra Leone, there are also great hopes embedded in the use of technology in vocational training in the near future for the progress of a country whose economy was destroyed as a result of a decade-long war.

6 Liberia

Furthermore, in the sub-region, the neighbouring country of Liberia has also been confronted by years of violence and war. Here too, vocational skills training has been a major pre-occupation for improving the lives of its inhabitants. The John Tamba Tailoring Shop in Kakata in Margibi County (Liberia) is a cinderblock build-ing just big enough to accommodate six sewing machines and the people who op-erate them. At one of the machines, Musu Yoryor is putting the finishing touches to a pair of drawstring trousers she learned how to make at the Don Bosco Centre for war-affected children. 'I am practising here until I get my own sewing machine,' she said, showing the trousers. 'I feel good about it.'

Yoryor, 19, later completed the vocational training course at Don Bosco and graduated in an official ceremony. She and her 100 classmates are now bud-ding entrepreneurs in the trades of agriculture, masonry, rattan furniture-making, pastry-making and tailoring. Don Bosco is an NGO affiliated with the Catholic Church.

The Kakata centre was established in 1997 as a hostel for boys and girls who were separated from their families during the recent civil war in Liberia. Then, as now, the goal is for these children to be reintegrated into their communities. 'These children carry the stigma of being someone different and we are trying to remove that stigma,' said Alfred Tamba, Don Bosco's project co-ordinator in Kakata.

Liberia's civil conflict (1989–1997) took a particularly brutal toll on children. Thousands were abandoned or otherwise separated from their families. Of the nearly 5,000 documented cases to date, more than 3,000 have yet to be reunited with their families. Many of these children live on their own in the streets, as in Kakata.

Throughout Liberia, UNICEF supports twenty-two centres offering vocational and literacy training and counselling services for war-affected children. Most of the boys participating in the project fought as soldiers in the war and were demobilized with UNICEF assistance. Many of the girls were abducted and raped and are now mothers, some as young as 13 years old. Since 1997, when the project began, about 6,000 children have participated.

The ten-month course at the Kakata centre covers basic vocational skills and small-business management. Another centre in Zwedru (Grand Gedeh County), also operated by Don Bosco, offers courses specifically for teenage mothers, including soap-making, pastry-making and tailoring. It houses a small day-care facility.

Graduates receive tools of the trade—Yoryor will have her sewing machine when funding is secured—and a small cash grant. Under the supervision of a small-business adviser, many of them form miniature co-operatives as a way to minimize start-up costs and maximize capacity.

The business success of these young people hinges on an improvement in eco-nomic conditions, a fact that Alfred Tamba fully acknowledges. Liberia's economy is in a shambles, poverty is pervasive and unemployment is the norm for most adults. Even in the most economically active region of the country, Montserrado County, residents live on less than US$2 per household per day. 'We hope these young people will produce. We hope their products will be purchased,' said Tamba. 'It all depends on the economic purchasing power of the people who live here.'

Another focus of efforts to help war-affected young people in the sub-region gain vocational training skills can be noted in the work of the United Methodist Church in Liberia, The United Methodist Church located in the town of Ganta—GUMS—has an enrolment of over 750 students. The North Carolina conference recently built a new classroom block building for children from kindergarten to grade 9. Ganta has been selected to become one of the Operation Classroom (OC) schools to include a major vocational training programme.

We believe that the best depositories of investment are the young people of our nations. Throughout history and across the world, youthful idealism has reawakened societies and urged them forward to new realizations and new awareness. We believe that these young people are the future leaders of tomorrow and, although they have faced unprecedented violence, skills for vocational training will be a first step towards transforming them into active and responsible citizens. Working with new technologies will enable them to acquire useful skills in critical thinking, cross-cultural awareness and valuable experience. Collaborative educational projects will be favourable for all the youths concerned and will prepare them to face the challenges of globalization.

Notes

1. Sierra Leone News, 2002, vol. 38: <www.sierra-leone.org/slnews.html>
2. Friends of Africa: <www.friendsofafrica.net/main.html>
3. Margaret A. Novicki, Saving a war's traumatized children: Sierra Leone camps try to rehabilitate child victims and soldiers. *Africa recovery*, vol. 14, no. 2, July 2000, p. 10. <www.un.org/ecosocdev/geninfo/afrec/subjindx/142child.htm>
4. <www.childsoldier.net>

Chapter V.7
TVET and Community Re-Integration: Exploring the Connections in Sierra Leone's DDR Process

Julia Paulson

1 Introduction

Disarmament, demobilization and reintegration (DDR) programmes are fast becoming a norm in post-conflict contexts (United Nations, 2000). These programmes are designed to collect weapons from and to demobilize fighting factions and, subsequently, to assist ex-combatants in reintegrating into civilian life. Technical and vocational education and training (TVET) programmes, in the form of skills training and/or apprenticeship schemes, are often included as a central activity in the reintegration phase of DDR in order to equip ex-combatants with skills to help them generate new livelihoods essential for their transition into civilian communities. Humphreys and Weinstein (2005) state that:

> Reintegration packages and training programs enable leaders to deliver concrete benefits to combatants at the conclusion of the fighting, some of which can be designed to address underlying grievances that gave rise to the conflict [...] To the extent that DDR programs reintegrate combatants into non-military life and help them to find gainful employment, we can think of programs as a key element of successful peace-building (p. 6).

This chapter uses the DDR process of Sierra Leone—a nation where grievances about educational exclusion and lack of opportunity have been identified among causes of conflict (see, for instance, Keen, 2005; Richards, 1996)—to explore the reintegration component of DDR, with a particular focus on TVET programmes. It asks if and how TVET programmes contribute to the reintegration of ex-combatants into communities and whether they could be better designed to do so.

2 DDR, Reintegration and TVET

> For individuals who have been armed for a long time, their gun has become a means of livelihood (Pouligny, 2004, p. 4).

Ultimately, the DDR process is expected to be instrumental in transforming conflict livelihoods into post-conflict ones. Through disarmament and demobilization, the process is meant to remove weapons—and war itself—as a means of livelihood

R. Maclean, D. Wilson (eds.), *International Handbook of Education for the Changing World of Work*, DOI 10.1007/978-1-4020-5281-1_V.7,
© Springer Science+Business Media B.V. 2009

and, through the reintegration process, to replace these livelihoods with ones that contribute to stability, peace and growth. It is the reintegration phase of DDR programmes that link them directly to the peace-building process. The extent to which these programmes succeed in integrating combatants into lives (and livelihoods) not embedded in conflict (and in the war economy) is indicative of DDR programmes' success in building peace. Given the scope of this task, it is unsurprising that analysts understand the reintegration phase as 'the toughest part of a DDR effort' (Humphreys & Weinstein, 2005, p. 39) and the 'most challenging component of the DDR program' (Refugees International, 2002).

Given the centrality of recreating livelihoods to the hugely challenging task of reintegration, TVET programming is clearly a very important component of 'doing' this part of DDR. 'The approach,' argue Richards et al. (2003), 'should be to reduce the incentives to selling labour as a fighter by increasing incentives to "legitimate" labour' (p. 6). The facilitation of this move from fighter to civilian is often attempted through the inclusion, in DDR programming, of training courses, apprenticeships and the provision of access to the formal education system. The UN defines the reintegration phase of DDR as:

> the process which allows ex-combatants and their families to adapt, economically and socially to productive civilian life. It generally entails the provision of a package of cash or in-kind compensation, training and job- and income-generating projects (United Nations, 2000).

For Pouligny (2004), reintegration programmes as a part of DDR 'support the immediate and medium-term social and economic inclusion of former combatants into their communities of origin or into new communities' (p. 7).

Since TVET programming—often accompanied by counselling, reinsertion packages (short-term allowances to support ex-combatants) and community activities designed to foster reconciliation—is usually one of the central activities of a DDR process, it is important to ask how successful it has been at contributing to the reintegration of ex-combatants. This question can be broken down further to look at practical as well as theoretical questions surrounding TVET as a part of DDR. Theoretically, it is important to explore how meaningful the connection between learning skills and reintegrating into communities following periods of war really is? Does TVET training contribute to 'social and economic inclusion' of ex-combatants in the communities that they return to? Could it be that skills for employability are one among many barriers to reintegration facing ex-combatants and those affected by war? And could TVET programming designed with a more holistic focus address these further barriers?

Practically, it is important to understand what type of skills training is provided as a part of DDR initiatives and to attempt to evaluate the success of this training in actually generating livelihoods for ex-combatants, particularly given the condition of the economies and labour markets into which ex-combatants are expected to (re)integrate. High unemployment and economic stagnation often characterize the post-conflict environment and certainly do in the case of Sierra Leone. What do 'social and economic' reintegration look like in such circumstances? Richards et al. (2003) found that in Sierra Leone 'disarmament and demobilization have succeeded, but reintegration is far from complete' (p. 4). What was and is the role of TVET in the (incomplete) reintegration process in Sierra Leone?

3 Youth, Education and Conflict in Sierra Leone

For Richards (1996), Sierra Leone's conflict must be understood as a crisis in modernity, central to which were the unfulfilled aspirations of youth. 'In a country built up for two hundred years or more around systems of schooling where Western models have been held out as the ideal,' writes Richards, 'educational issues are one of the key aspects of the present [sic] crisis' (p. 36). In the years prior to Sierra Leone's decade-long conflict, which killed between 50,000 and 75,000 people, displaced nearly half the country and saw the rape and enforced sexual slavery of tens of thousands of women and girls (Dougherty, 2004; Women's Commission for Refugee Women and Children, 2004), the education system in the country suffered serious decline or, in many regions, outright collapse. The 'forgotten aspirants' (Wright, 1997) of this crumbling and exclusionary education system, found—instead of the promises of Western modernity inherent in the education system—a stifling patrimonialism (Richards, 1996) that offered few or no opportunities for Sierra Leonean youth. This sense of disenfranchisement amongst young people has been central to many analyses of the conflict (see, for instance, Keen, 2005; Wright, 1997; Richards, 1996), since joining in the fighting offered youth opportunities where otherwise there were none (for a detailed discussion of education, conflict and youth in Sierra Leone, see Paulson, 2006).

4 The DDR Process in Sierra Leone

Sierra Leone's DDR process, largely considered by the international community to be a successful model that has contributed to Sierra Leone's peace process, has been used to inform similar processes in Liberia, Burundi and Haiti (Humphreys & Weinstein, 2005). The perceived success of Sierra Leone's DDR and its replication as a model of international success offer another reason to explore the process in depth and to question its various dimensions. In addition to using some data from a Government of Sierra Leone sponsored 'Tracer Study' (Stavrou et al., 2003) of 250 ex-combatants, this chapter draws heavily on two studies that have done just this, with a focus on the reintegration phase of the DDR process. One, a largely quantitative study of 1,043 ex-combatants who went through the DDR process and of 200 non-combatants who did not, was undertaken in the summer of 2003 by Humphreys and Weinstein, (2004, 2005). The second, mentioned above, is a qualitative, interview-based investigation that also included those who did and did not participate in the DDR process, conducted by Richards et al. (2003). Both studies were conducted while DDR activities were on-going or shortly after they had been completed, meaning that the longer-term effects of DDR along with longer-term perceptions of reintegration could not be gathered in the studies. This fact is particularly relevant when considering how 'successful' reintegration could be evaluated—a very difficult question, made more difficult when the evaluation is being undertaken in the short term. Sierra Leone's DDR process will be briefly detailed before turning to the findings of these studies—which converge and diverge in interesting ways that are, arguably, informative about their methodological choices.

The DDR process in Sierra Leone, as in many other nations, began and was halted several times by renewed conflict before entering into a period stable enough for co-ordinated demobilization and disarmament to occur. In 1998 the first DDR camp was opened, but the process was suspended with the 1999 attacks on Freetown by the Revolutionary United Front (RUF). DDR camps re-opened following the signing of the Lomé Peace Accord in July 1999, but were again disrupted by fighting in May 2000 and by the national elections of 2002 (Ginifer, 2003; Refugees International, 2002). At its completion in July 2003 (Humphreys & Weinstein, 2004), Sierra Leone's National Committee on Disarmament, Demobilization and Reintegration (NCDDR) had disarmed and registered between 67,260 (Richards et al., 2003) and 76,000 (Humphreys & Weinstein, 2004) ex-combatants (the World Bank (2005) puts the figure at 69,000). The NCDDR established sixteen demobilization centres that covered all of Sierra Leone's twelve districts, and seven interim care centres were also established (World Bank, 2005). The NCDDR was funded primarily through the World Bank's Multi-Donor Trust Fund (Refugees International, 2002) with contributions from the Africa Development Bank, the Islamic Development Bank, the United Nations Development Programme, UNICEF, the World Population Foundation, the United Nations Human Security Fund, the European Development Fund and the United Kingdom's Department for International Development (World Bank, 2005). The United Nations Mission in Sierra Leone (UNAMSIL) was responsible for co-ordinating the demobilization and demilitarization component of the NCDDR, while the reintegration component was contracted out to various international and local NGOs (Refugees International, 2002). Funders of the DDR process in Sierra Leone have been criticized for focusing heavily on the two 'Ds', and leaving a meagre budget for the 'reintegration' phase—a fact that will be crucial in our consideration of the TVET provisions within Sierra Leone's DDR process. Meek and Malan (2004) include, among their recent list of lessons learnt in DDR processes, the need to prioritize and link reintegration more fully to disarmament and demobilization, demonstrating that this has been a problem unique to Sierra Leone.

In order to enter a DDR camp, ex-combatants had either to present a weapon or enter with their commander as a part of a unit to be demobilized. These requirements can exclude many combatants, along with individuals who were involved with the fighting forces in roles other than as weapon-carrying combatants (Humphreys & Weinstein, 2004; Richards et al., 2003; Refugees International, 2002). Child-soldiers, who often did not possess their own weapons, children who worked as cooks and porters, and women who were held as 'bush wives' (women in forced sexual relationships with fighters) were consequently often left out of the DDR process because they could not present a weapon in order to gain access to its programming. Richards et al. (2003) argue that bush wives, whose reintegration following the conflict has been particularly difficult given the stigma attached to their roles in the war and to the children that many had as a result, are the group in the greatest need of reintegration assistance—and are among the groups who have benefited least from the formal DDR.

Another problem associated with the need to turn in a weapon or to demobilize with a commander was the power that this requirement gave to commanders. Richards et al. (2003) heard many reports of commanders and high-powered individuals removing weapons from their rank-and-file fighters and giving them to family members or influential community members close to the commander—thus entitling false ex-combatants to DDR benefits and excluding actual ex-combatants from the process. This problem was not identified in Humphreys and Weinstein's (2004) more quantitative study and as Richards et al. (2003) note, their study cannot quantify the phenomenon. The NCDDR estimates that the number of false ex-combatants registered in the DDR process was low. However, Richards et al. (2003) report that several of their respondents estimated that approximately 50–60% of gun-carrying ex-combatants were excluded from the DDR process in favour of false ex-combatants. 'For every false ex-combatant there must be a real ex-combatant without benefits' (p. 4), a situation that is potentially volatile, especially if numbers of ex-combatants excluded from the NCDDR are as high as Richards' respondents report. The reintegration of this potentially large group of ex-combatants is thus proceeding without the official support and associated training of the DDR process.

Once registered with the NCDDR, ex-combatants received basic necessities and orientation activities, including trauma healing, psycho-social counselling, information and sensitization seminars and short civic education programming (Ginifer, 2003). They were also often involved in destroying their own weapons to add a symbolic dimension to the demobilization. At the end of their time in DDR camps, ex-combatants were transported to the relocation area of their choice, and were highly encouraged to re-settle in their home communities. 'Reinsertion packages' (or allowances) were provided—often with 'significant and unpredictable' delays (Humphreys & Weinstein, 2004)—to support ex-combatants through the first three months in their chosen settlement locations. Humphreys and Weinstein (2004) found that the ex-combatants they surveyed either spent the bulk of their reinsertion packages on living expenses or gave it to family and dependents. Very little of the reinsertion package was kept as savings nor was it seen as a resource for initial livelihood-generating investments.

5 Skills Training and the DDR Process in Sierra Leone

The former Secretary-General, in his 2000 speech on United Nations Peacekeeping and DDR, made the following recommendations for the educational and skills training component of DDR reintegration programmes:

> Provision should be made for education and, as appropriate, for relevant vocational training and opportunities for employment or self-employment, including for children with

disabilities. Traditional apprenticeship models, where the trainee is taken in as part of the master craftsman's family, may prove useful. Upon completion of vocational skills training, trainees should be provided with the relevant tools and, where possible, with start-up loans to promote self-reliance. Reintegration programmes must replace the economic incentives of war for child warriors; at the same time, training or educational programmes should be geared to the existing economy and avoid creating false expectations about the possibilities for economic reinsertion (United Nations, 2000).

Compliance with these—albeit vague—recommendations can be seen within Sierra Leone's DDR process, though provisions for children (and others) with disabilities were minimal (Katie Dimmer, personal communication) and micro-credit loans were not provided following training. According to Humphreys and Weinstein (2004), three-quarters of the ex-combatants who entered the DDR process participated in some form of training programme; however, the World Bank (2005) states that 85% (48,246 ex-combatants) of those registered in the DDR process participated in training. NCDDR's approach to skills training was to target the informal sector through the establishment of apprenticeships, to offer selected in-centre formal skills training courses, and to provide formal educational opportunities, particularly for children (Ginifer, 2003). UNICEF co-ordinated the provision of educational programmes for nearly 7,000 children who had been through the DDR process (Alexander, 2006). Children participated primarily in the Community Education Investment Programme (CEIP), which waived school fees for former child soldiers and provided them with a uniform and school material—notebooks, pencils and paper were also provided to all children at the CEIP schools to minimize the perceived advantage given to former child-soldiers (Alexander, 2006)—or in the Complimentary Rapid Education Primary School (CREPS) programme, which condensed six years of primary schooling into three and was directed towards older children (Alexander, 2006). The support for formal educational opportunities provided through the NCDDR was understood as one of its greatest successes and accomplishments (Ginifer, 2003). However, Humphreys and Weinstein (2004) quote the following excerpt from an interview with a participant in the DDR:

> I'm not happy with DDR because they lied to us. Promised to have us enrolled in schools, I have not seen any such. We need education and jobs. DDR has not registered a good number of us. They promised us educational materials but none have been delivered (p. 33).

In addition to programmes that provided ex-combatants with access into formal education, ex-combatants could access TVET programming, generally lasting for three months to a year and offering courses or apprenticeships in trades such as car repair, carpentry, computers, masonry, bicycle repair, building, plumbing, metalwork, road maintenance, tailoring, agriculture and, primarily for women, soap-making and tie-dying (see Yarrow in this section for a nuanced discussion of TVET programming, gender and the post-conflict context). Whether ex-combatants had a high degree of choice regarding entry into formal education programmes, apprenticeships or skills training is not well documented. However, this appears to be a critical question for ex-combatants' potential reintegration, for their satisfaction with their experience of DDR, and for the livelihoods they may build in the future. Of the 250 ex-combatants surveyed in the tracer study (Stavrou et al., 2003), 76% entered vocational or skills-training courses, 12% undertook apprenticeships, 5% participated in public works schemes, 4% entered formal schooling and 3% engaged in agricultural training.

Those who did enter TVET programmes received training of varying quality, as it was contracted out to local and international NGOs whose capacities, capabilities and commitment varied greatly. Richards et al. (2003) report finding a computer training centre open and receiving NCDDR funding to provide skills training that did not have a single computer. They also report 'common consent' among respondents that skills training was 'too perfunctory and of too low a quality to offer much immediate chance of real employment' (p. 13). The Commissioner of the NCDDR responded to criticism about the TVET component of DDR by positing it as a 'useful first step' (as quoted in Richards et al., 2003) and hoping that ex-combatants would pursue further training. Given the very limited resources of most ex-combatants, one must ask whether further training was among their options upon completing the reintegration phase of the NCDDR.

Those entering apprenticeships and skills training received small stipends to cover their basic living expenses for the duration of their training periods; mentors participating in apprenticeships received tools and other benefits in return for their participation (Refugees International, 2002). The stipend received by trainees is, according to Refugees International (2002), 'one of the very reasons why these programs are essential—they offer a small window that allows former combatants time to be supported while they readjust to civilian life.' Ex-combatants were also to receive, as per the UN's recommendation, a toolkit relevant to their developed skills upon the completion of their training programmes. However, many ex-combatants reported that their toolkits were delivered late or not at all (Humphreys & Weinstein, 2004; Richards et al., 2003). Other ex-combatants sold their toolkits after failing to find employment in their new fields, according to Richards et al. (2003):

> We found some masons, carpenters and tailors reported to be providing a useful service in more remote rural communities where skills shortages are severe. In other cases, however, ex-combatants sold tools packages and moved to the diamond fields, unconvinced they could make a living in their new craft (p. 5).

This situation begs Ginifer's (2003) question of whether the skills included within Sierra Leone's DDR process were in fact appropriate for generating employment, building livelihoods and contributing to reintegration in post-war Sierra Leone. A serious lack of data on the needs of the labour market in Sierra Leone (Ginifer, 2003) is but one challenging feature of what is a very constrained economy, with limited growth and unemployment rates as high as 80% (Refugees International, 2002), dominated largely by patrimonialism and, especially at high levels, corruption (Graybill, 2007). If reintegration is understood, in part, as (re)insertion into the labour market—which it appears to have been within Sierra Leone's DDR process— then one of the largest challenges of reintegration is certainly the very real lack of jobs for ex-combatants, even those trained with what are perceived as marketable skills through TVET programmes.

When Humphreys and Weinstein (2004) surveyed ex-combatants about their reintegration processes, most of their respondents had either just completed their skills training (40%) or were still participating in courses. These respondents, over-all, were satisfied with their training, with 75% reporting that they felt prepared for work; a vast majority felt that the skills with which they had been trained were needed in the regions where they would resettle or had resettled. Some 87% of ex-combatants surveyed felt they were better off socially because of the training that they had received. This is an important finding with regards to our question about the links between TVET training and reintegration as it supports the idea that skills training can have meaningful benefits for ex-combatant's social reintegration. This social aspect of TVET training is reassuring given the dismal prognosis by Refugees International (2002) that only approximately 10% of ex-combatants trained by the NCDDR would find employment upon the completion of their training. It is im-portant to consider the optimism of the ex-combatants surveyed by Humphreys and Weinstein in 2003 about their prospects following skills training in this light, and to take very seriously, as a challenge for reintegration as well as for stability and peace in Sierra Leone, the disillusionment they are likely to now be experiencing.

The NCDDR, rather belatedly, recognized the obstacles to employment for graduates of TVET programmes and 'grappled with alternatives' (Ginifer, 2003) that could provide or build livelihoods for ex-combatants. Thus, it encouraged ex-combatants to form co-operatives or seek avenues for self-employment or in-come generation (Ginifer, 2003). The NCDDR also provided some counselling on job-seeking and accessing employment opportunities, but both Humphreys and Weinstein (2004) and Richards et al. (2003) found that ex-combatants perceived this portion of the programmes to be unsatisfactory and under-prioritized. The most common response (54%) among ex-combatants surveyed by Humphreys and Weinstein (2004), when asked how they would improve the DDR process, was to provide more support for finding jobs once the training periods were completed. The NCDDR did attempt to liaise with UNAMSIL to create 'stop-gap' opportunities for ex-combatants that saw them employed for short-term public work projects, such as road construction (Ginifer, 2003). However, as other contributions to this sec-tion highlight (see, for instance, Kane and Karpinska in this section), tying TVET programming to realistic livelihood and employment opportunities available to par-ticipants upon completion is an essential priority in post-conflict TVET programmes and one that should have been in the forefront of the NCDDR's programme plan-ning, rather than addressed as the ramifications of its neglect became apparent.

The complexities, as well as the need, to tie TVET programmes realistically to market needs and realities are also demonstrated within Sierra Leone's DDR process. Many recognize (Humphreys & Weinstein, 2004; Richards et al., 2003; Ginifer, 2003) that agriculture is the sector in Sierra Leone most likely to be able to reabsorb large numbers of ex-combatants, because: (a) many of them would have left the agricultural sector to join in fighting; (b) agriculture was severely disrupted by conflict; and (c) agriculture was one of the principal livelihood op-tions in Sierra Leone prior to the conflict. However, the agricultural training options provided by the NCDDR were the least attractive to ex-combatants, who mostly preferred options that led to formal education or to computer training, followed by vehicle driving and maintenance, carpentry and tailoring (Richards et al., 2003). Ginifer (2003) explains that 'many ex-combatants had high expectations of acquiring skills and a job, and were disinclined to take up agriculture, the sector most likely to provide opportunities in Sierra Leone.' Such trends point to the continued perceived benefits of formal education—as well as skills training—in Sierra Leone and, unfortunately, to the continuation of these expectations being unfulfilled—a situation that, in the past, has contributed to conflict. In fact, Humphreys and Weinstein (2004) found that those who had more than a primary school education were slightly less likely to find employment than those who had not completed primary schooling, a finding that is indicative of the continued disenfranchisement of youth in Sierra Leone. Educational reconstruction is given considerable priority in post-conflict Sierra Leone. However, policy and programmes initiatives should capture the real disillusionment that has been associated with educational aspirations in Sierra Leone and develop strategies to ensure that education—both academic and TVET —lead to opportunities.

6 Reintegration, Communities and Livelihoods

> The NCDDR is talking about how well it has addressed material need. The ex-combatants are talking about whether or not they have acquired their rights (Richards et al., 2003, p. 9).
>
> The all-encompassing issue of reintegration has much to do with collective self-images and the way local communities are involved in a process of social reconstruction of the memories of violence (Pouligny, 2004, p. 7).
>
> Evidence from Sierra Leone does not support the hypothesis that participation in a DDR program increases the level of reintegration success at the individual level (Humphreys & Weinstein, 2004, p. 39).

The reintegration of ex-combatants following a period of extended conflict is clearly a complicated process. It is also one for which programming is often devised in a rather ad-hoc way, given the urgency of getting DDR processes running quickly so as to consolidate the entry into a 'post-conflict' situation. While the task of those raising questions in retrospect is certainly easier than that of those involved in planning programming in the moment, it is nonetheless important to reflect critically on reintegration processes and to take into account the multitude of issues—several of which are raised in the above quotations—that responsive programming must try to capture. Thus, this section seeks to explore the processes and reported outcomes of reintegration programming in Sierra Leone—with a particular focus on TVET and on the role of building livelihoods for reintegration—while also reflecting on broader social processes—some of which find roots in or around the DDR process—that affect reintegration or its lack thereof.

Some 90% of the respondents to Humphreys and Weinstein's (2004) study reported having experienced no problems in gaining the acceptance of the communities where they re-settled. This is a striking figure, and contrasts sharply to Ginifer's (2003) appraisal of ex-combatants' community reintegration process as 'difficult' and characterized by 'latent hostility to ex-combatants among civilians in Sierra Leone'. Ginifer (2003) reports community members engaging in the reintegration process grudgingly, making comments such as 'we are forgiving them [ex-combatants] because the government says so'. As mentioned above, the benefits provided to ex-combatants by the DDR process could, and did, breed community resentment, as demonstrated by the following comment: 'those who have ruined us are being given the chance to become better persons financially, academically and skills-wise' (as quoted in Ginifer, 2003). It is incredibly difficult to assess the degree of community animosity towards ex-combatants, and it certainly varies across communities and alters depending on the faction and personal role of individual ex-combatants. Both the Humphreys and Weinstein (2004) and the Richards et al. (2003) studies found that ex-Community Defence Force (CDF) fighters had an easier time reintegrating than did members of any other faction. This is probably due to the fact that CDF factions were formed largely by members of the same community united to defend that community against attack and were perceived as heroes in the minds of their communities. Both studies also found that fighters who returned to their home communities reintegrated more successfully than did those who did not return home. This finding must be taken cautiously, as it is likely that those who choose not to return to their home communities were associated with severe violations of human rights that their home communities would be aware of (or have experienced firsthand). Arguably, these combatants were therefore unlikely to return home and may well be among those most likely to experience the greatest challenges in terms of reintegration, regardless of where they settled.

In addition to community animosity, Richards' study points to other, potentially volatile, resentments hindering reintegration. Those ex-combatants excluded from the NCDDR process experience a 'strong sense of disillusionment' (Richards et al., 2003, p. 5) and are subject to the same stigmatization for their role in the conflict as those who did participate in the NCDDR, without the resulting benefits and assistance that comes from participation in DDR. In addition, Richards et al. (2003) argue that 'the reintegration of ex-combatants after the war in Sierra Leone is hindered not so much by negative civilian attitudes, but by a strong sense of grievance among young people who believe that they have not been fairly treated in the DDRP (disarmament, demobilization and reintegration process)' (p. 5). This includes those who were and were not participants in the NCDDR. Richards et al. (2003) highlight the vulnerability of ex-combatants, and especially of those associated with the fighting forces who were not able to access the DDR process (in particular women). They argue that forced rural marriages that virtually indenture women who were associated with fighting factions are common and that those ex-combatants who return to or take up work in the diamond fields often experience very exploitative labour conditions. Interestingly, Humphreys and Weinstein's (2004) study found that non-participants in the DDR process reintegrated as successfully as did participants. This finding must be questioned given the depth of the qualitative evidence to the contrary presented by the study of Richards et al. (2003).

The point that the DDR process itself creates divisions (both between ex-combatants themselves and between ex-combatants and civilians) that hamper the reintegration process (Richards et al., 2003) is an important one. The NCDDR adopted several strategies to address the injustice perceived by community members who watched ex-combatants receive assistance and benefits (Ginifer, 2003) and very few to address the grievances of ex-combatants and those associated with the fighting forces excluded from the NCDDR (Richards et al., 2003). The NCDDR attempted to minimize community animosity by stressing that the skills training and economic reinsertion benefits that ex-combatant received were not meant as compensation for their war activities and by attempting to show that the skills that ex-combatants were gaining would be beneficial for communities as a whole (Ginifer, 2003). Sensitization activities and radio campaigns were carried out to disseminate these messages. The NCDDR also organized some events using traditional reconciliatory practices to encourage the reintegration of ex-combatants and provided ex-combatants with 'pre-discharge counselling' that emphasized reintegration into the community and urged ex-combatants to develop a 'special re-entry plan' (Ginifer, 2003). Ex-combatants were encouraged to participate in tasks that would benefit the communities, such as construction and rehabilitation projects. The NCDDR sought to engage local, community-based social reintegration organizations, providing funding for adult education programmes, civic and peace education and music and sports groups—hoping to rebuild the 'social capital' of ex-combatants (Ginifer, 2003).

The sensitization activities of the NCDDR, along with its community meetings and use of traditional reconciliatory rituals to foster reintegration, overlap in many ways with activities carried out by Sierra Leone's Truth and Reconciliation Commission (TRC), another post-conflict mechanism aimed at contributing in some way to reintegration by creating a forum for acknowledging the human rights abuses that occurred during the conflict and by making recommendations (enabled in the TRC's founding legislation as mandatory) for post-conflict reforms to prevent conflict from reoccurring. Among the TRC's recommendation was a recommendation to implement a package of reparations for victims of human rights violations (Graybill, 2007). Included in these recommendations were educational and skills training programmes, the existence of which—were they to be implemented by the government, that has to date been negligent of its responsibility to take up TRC recommendations (Graybill, 2007)—could address the inequities between survivors and ex-combatants created by the NCDDR process. Closer ties between the NCDDR and other post-conflict mechanisms, such as the TRC, could potentially have led to more holistic programming, capable of addressing the reintegration needs of more diverse communities from a variety of angles.

Fithen and Richards (2005) argue for a more complex understanding of reintegration, pointing out that, in the post-conflict context, reintegrating does not simply mean readapting or 'fitting into' a community as a civilian, but rather being able to participate in reshaping the future and in creating new opportunities—a central task for communities in Sierra Leone given the current economic circumstances. The conflict, they argue, opened spaces for individualism and individual rights (see Archibald & Richards, 2002) in what was a largely patrimonial society. Skills training, along with formal education, could contribute to consolidating this potentially positive impact of Sierra Leone's conflict were they to subsequently open real opportunities for youth. Fithen and Richards (2005) describe a group of ex-combatants who formed a bicycle taxi collective in Boas as an example of ex-combatants reintegrating positively (and profitably) into a community:

> 'reintegration' is not just a matter of 'fitting in' but of spotting and developing new opportunities for self-employment in a changing society. [. . .] Finding such opportunities strengthens social acceptability [. . .] as well as providing livelihood opportunities. Social acceptability, in turn, strengthens chances of winning political battles. [. . .] These ex-combatants are not just 'fitting into' such a society—they are helping to forge it (pp. 134–35).

Seen in this way, TVET programming is an integral part of a reintegration that creates and facilitates new opportunities and livelihoods for ex-combatants and for communities by enabling the possibility of building realities that differ considerably from pre-conflict ones. Seen more narrowly, however, TVET programming as a part of DDR has the real potential to raise expectations, create divisions and—in failing to lead to employment or livelihoods—create potentially dangerous disillusionment among youth. The challenge, therefore, of envisioning and programming for holistic, integrated TVET programming is a central one for DDR processes.

References

Alexander, A. 2006. *Community based reintegration: programme evaluation.* Freetown: UNICEF. [Unpublished evaluation of UNICEF's Community-Based Reintegration (CBR) Programme.]

Archibald, S.; Richards, P. 2002. Converts to human rights? Popular debate about war and justice in rural central Sierra Leone. *Africa,* vol. 72, no. 3, pp. 339–67.

Dougherty, B.K. 2004. Searching for answers: Sierra Leone's Truth and Reconciliation Commission. *African studies quarterly,* vol. 8, no. 1, pp. 39–56.

Fithen, C.; Richards, P. 2005. Making war, crafting peace: militia solidarities and demobilisation in Sierra Leone. *In:* Richards, P., ed. *No war, no peace: an anthropology of contemporary armed conflict.* Oxford, UK: James Currey.

Ginifer, J. 2003. Reintegration of ex-combatants. *In:* Meek, S. et al., eds. *Sierra Leone: building the road to recovery,* pp. 39–52. Pretoria: Institute for Security Studies Africa. (ISS monograph no. 80.)

Graybill, L. 2007. Debt relief: a panacea for Sierra Leone. *In:* Center for Strategic and International Studies, ed. *Africa policy forum.* Washington, DC: CSIS. <forums.csis.org/africa/?p=24>

Humphreys, M.; Weinstein, J.M. 2004. *What the fighters say: a survey of ex-combatants in Sierra Leone. June–August 2003: Interim report: July 2004.* New York, NY: Columbia University. <www.stanford.edu/~jweinst/docs/manuscripts/humphreys_ combatantsurvey.pdf>

Humphreys, M.; Weinstein J.M. 2005. *Disentangling the determinants of successful disarmament, demobilization and reintegration.* [Unpublished manuscript.] <www.stanford.edu/~jweinst/docs/manuscripts/DDR%20IGCC.pdf>

Keen, D. 2005. *Conflict and collusion in Sierra Leone.* Oxford, UK: James Currey.

Meek, S.; Malan, M., eds. 2004. *Identifying lessons from DDR experiences in Africa.* Pretoria: Institute for Security Studies. (ISS monograph, no. 106.)

Paulson, J. 2006. The educational recommendations of Truth and Reconciliation Commissions: potential and practice in Sierra Leone. *Research in comparative and international education,* vol. 1, no. 4, pp. 335–50.

Pouligny, B. 2004. *The politics and anti-politics of contemporary 'Disarmament, Demobilization and Reintegration' Programs.* Paris: Centre d'études et de recherches internationales. <www.ceri-sciencespo.com/cherlist/pouligny/rapportpouligny.pdf>

Refugees International. 2002. *RI Focus: disarmament, demobilization and reintegration in Sierra Leone.* Washington, DC: Refugees International. <www.refugeesinternational.org/content/article/detail/884/?PHPSESSID=5cfliegen3C>

Richards, P. 1996. *Fighting for the rainforest: war, youth and resources in Sierra Leone.* Oxford, UK: James Currey.

Richards, P., et al. 2003. *Where have all the young people gone? Transitioning ex-combatants towards community reconstruction after the war in Sierra Leone.* London: School of Oriental and African Studies. [Consultancy paper, unpublished.]

Stavrou, A. et al. 2003. *Tracer study and follow-up assessment of the reintegration component of Sierra Leone's Disarmament, Demobilization, and Reintegration Program.* Cork, Ireland: University of Ireland, Centre for Sustainable Livelihoods.

United Nations. 2000. *The Role of United Nations Peacekeeping in disarmament, demobilization, and reintegration: report of the Secretary-General.* New York, NY: UN. (Report no. S/2000/101.) <www.smallarmssurvey.org/files/portal/issueareas/measures/Measur_pdf/i_measur_pdf/UN_doc/s_council/S_2000_101.pdf>

Women's Commission for Refugee Women and Children. 2004. *Global survey of education in emergencies.* New York, NY: WCRWC.

World Bank. 2005. Sierra Leone: community reintegration and rehabilitation. *Findings: Africa Region,* May, no. 112. <www.worldbank.org/afr/findings/infobeng/infob112.pdf>

Wright, C. 1997. Reflections on Sierra Leone: a case study. *In:* Tawil, S., ed. *Final report and case studies on educational disruption and reconstruction in disrupted societies.* Geneva, Switzerland: UNESCO-IBE.

Chapter V.8
TVET, Women and Conflict: Palestinians in the Lebanese Civil War

Rachel Yarrow

1 Introduction

That the very different, yet very real, male and female experiences of conflict have frequently been misunderstood is increasingly agreed upon (see UNIFEM, 2004, for example). In particular, attention is being drawn to changes that conflict brings about in women's need to earn a livelihood, changes in the types of livelihood that are acceptable for women, and changes in wider ideas about gender roles and stereotypes (Date-Bah, 2003). This chapter focuses first on the changes that the conflicts in Lebanon of the 1970s and 1980s brought about in ideas about Palestinian women's economic activity; secondly, the effect that conflict had on the provision of technical and vocational education and training (TVET) for Palestinians in Lebanon; and lastly, the extent to which the new TVET provision took account of, and capitalized upon, the changes that had taken place. These changes will be analysed through Buckland's idea of the post-conflict situation as the 'best of times, worst of times', 'both an opportunity and a constraint' (2005, p. 25). In particular, this chapter will focus on case studies of two NGOs that were involved in TVET provision for Palestinian women during the Lebanese Civil War, and the extent to which they effectively capitalized on the 'opportunities' offered by the post-conflict situation.

In reality, the notions of conflict and post-conflict situations are to a large extent co-extensive in the context of Palestinians in Lebanon. At the meta-level, as refugees of a yet-unresolved conflict, their situation is still not truly post-conflict, especially as the threat of impending Lebanese and Palestinian civil war seems very real in the present day. However, armed hostilities are not a daily reality for Palestinian refugees living in Lebanon and, even during the Lebanese Civil War, there were long periods when large numbers of Palestinians were not directly involved in fighting. This chapter focuses primarily on TVET in the period 1976–1988, years which arguably all fall within the boundaries of the Lebanese Civil War and could be regarded as 'conflict' rather than 'post-conflict' times. However, from anecdotal evidence, those who experienced this period at first hand tend not to refer to it as such, but to focus on discrete episodes of conflict which particularly affected them, and which fell several years apart. The periods between these episodes do then become post-conflict. TVET programming that arose as a response to these episodes is, then, interpreted primarily as occurring in a post-conflict situation.

R. Maclean, D. Wilson (eds.), *International Handbook of Education for the Changing World of Work*, DOI 10.1007/978-1-4020-5281-1_V.8,
© Springer Science+Business Media B.V. 2009

TVET is a notoriously difficult concept to define. UNESCO-UNEVOC defines it as being 'concerned with the acquisition of knowledge and skills for the world of work' (UNESCO-UNEVOC, n.d.). TVET definitions usually do not cover such areas as legal, medical or teacher training, however, even though they are concerned with such. For the purposes of this chapter, TVET is defined pragmatically as that which happens in vocational training centres (VTCs), and what is therefore usually recognized as vocational training by most Palestinians. This excludes training for professions, such as law and engineering, but does include many 'semi-professional' courses (such as architectural drawing, computing, or business and office management), as well as the more practical and traditional courses (such as welding, sewing and hairdressing). Teacher training for Palestinians does take place in the VTC run by the United Nations Relief and Works Agency for Palestinian Refugees in the Near East (UNRWA), but will not be included in the considerations of this chapter.

2 A History of Conflict

Following the creation of the State of Israel in 1948, and the ensuing war, around 500,000 to 700,000 Arab Palestinians left their homes in what had become Israel, or Arab Palestinian land seized by Israel (Fisk, 1990, p. 17).[1] Approximately 100,000 of these sought refuge in Lebanon (Ugland, 2003, p. 15). In 1949, UNRWA was established by the United Nations General Assembly in order to provide 'direct relief and works programmes' for the refugees (UNRWA, n.d.). The refugees in Lebanon initially gathered in the South, around the cities of Tyre and Sidon, but were later dispersed to the Beka'a valley and Tripoli, and organized into camps on land leased by UNRWA.

Current estimates of the number of Palestinians in Lebanon range from 200,000 to 600,000 (see Ugland, 2003, p. 18 for a discussion of this). It is probably reasonable to assume that the Palestinians make up slightly under 10% of the population of Lebanon today (see Haddad, 2003, p. 4, for example).

The violence and conflict that has had the most direct effects on the Palestinians still alive in Lebanon today is undoubtedly that which took place during the Lebanese Civil War. After the Cairo Agreement of 1969, the Palestinian Liberation Organization (PLO) was permitted to have a legitimate armed presence in Lebanon and was effectively given autonomy over the Palestinian camps. What resulted is often referred to as the Palestinian 'State within a State', presided over by Chairman Yasser Arafat (Schultz & Hammer, 2003, p. 55), and viewed with much misgiving by the ruling Maronite Christians. The start of the Lebanese Civil War is often cited as the clash between a Palestinian organization and the Phalange, a Maronite militia, in 1975 (ibid.), although the PLO have strenuously denied that they were trying to destabilize the situation. The Palestinian camps had soon become targets, however, and in 1976 the Phalange embarked on a seven-month siege of the camp of Tal al-Zataar, during which 3,000 Palestinians were killed (Schultz & Hammer, 2003, p. 56).

Following the Israeli invasion of Lebanon in 1982, further damage was inflicted on the Palestinian refugees, most notoriously in the massacres in the Beirut camps of Sabra and Shatila, in which up to 2,000 Palestinian men, women and children died at the hands of the Phalange (Fisk, 1990, pp. 359–400).

At this time, too, the PLO was driven out of Lebanon, and the relative autonomy that had been enjoyed by the Palestinians in the camps was over. Moreover, following the expulsion of the PLO, the Shi'ite Amal movement, with Syrian backing, became obsessed with driving out any remaining PLO loyalists suspected of remaining in the camps (Haddad, 2003, p. 34). The resulting 'War of the Camps' consisted of a series of sieges of the Palestinian camps in Beirut and Southern Lebanon, concentrated over the period 1985–87, and resulted in the deaths of many hundreds of Palestinians, the (re-)displacement of thousands more and the near-destruction of many camps.

3 Palestinian Women in the Economic Sphere

Historically, the place of Palestinian women has been regarded as in the home, the ethos of *sitt fil-bait* (the lady in home) (Sayigh, 1993, p. 183). To be a working woman in the 1950s and 1960s was regarded as shameful in the context of Palestinian refugees in Lebanon; in particular, work outside the camp was to be avoided and work *inside* the home much preferred to that outside (Sayigh, 1994, pp. 45–47). A general fearfulness for women's safety and honour when travelling outside the home, and particularly the camp, is still pervasive in Palestinian society, particularly for unmarried girls. Early marriage has traditionally been seen as the primary guarantee of economic security for women, and the expectation of marriage (for men and women) has been near universal (Ugland, 2003, p. 32). Involvement in domestic labour, seasonal agriculture and even factories was not unknown among poor families, though cottage industries centred on the home, such as sewing and embroidery, were more usual and acceptable for women (Peteet, 1991, p. 21, 33).

3.1 The Experience of Conflict: Changing Women's Roles

Changes in the economic and social place of women in Palestinian society were already beginning in the period leading up to the Lebanese Civil War. Of particular importance was the arrival of the PLO in Lebanon, after they were ejected from Jordan in 1970, together with the signing of the Cairo Agreement in 1969. Although Palestinian women in Lebanon never became actively involved as military fighters in the resistance movement, as they had done in Jordan (Sayigh, 1993, p. 177), the institution-building that accompanied the rise of the PLO in Lebanon provided ample opportunities for women to work towards the national struggle, taking up work in, for example, kindergartens, clinics, vocational training centres and sewing workshops (Sayigh, 1993, p. 183). The PLO also brought a heightened sense of the Palestinian cause as a unified struggle, and as the clouds of civil war began to gather in Lebanon, great value was placed on anything that men or women could do to support the national cause. Sayigh reports an interview in which she was told: 'After the battle of Tell al-Zataar [1976], no mother would prevent her daughter from going out. On the contrary, she would tell her to go out and work to help her people' (1993, p. 183).

The PLO left Lebanon in 1983, following the Israeli invasion, and with them a whole range of employment opportunities disappeared, for men and women alike. By this time, however, the civil war had brought about new factors that were changing women's position in the economic and social spheres. The increasing involvement of men in military and conflict-related activities was surely amongst the most significant factors pushing women into work. On the one hand, the number of casualties resulting from active male involvement in battles such as Tell al-Zataar and, later on, in the Camp Wars of 1985–87, led to an increase in female-headed households. Female-headed households in these circumstances are more likely to live in extreme poverty due to the loss of the husband's financial support (Date-Bah, 2003, p. 117). In such circumstances, the social stigma attached to certain types of work for women is likely to have been subjugated to the physical survival needs of the family, particularly important given that remarriage amongst Palestinian women who have been widowed is not common (Sayigh, 1993, p. 189). On the other hand, the absence of male family members, due to, for example, out-migration, death, displacement or imprisonment, particularly of a patriarchal husband or father, may have engendered a lifting of family control over women's activities, including those boundaries that keep women in the home and out of the world of work.

Furthermore, although women were not involved in active military service *en masse*, there are many examples of women undertaking roles in relation to conflict that marked a departure from their normal sphere of activities. Peteet even cites examples of women university students who, although not encouraged by the PLO, underwent military training during the 1981 general mobilization campaign and who fought in Tal al-Zataar as an expression of their commitment to the national cause (1991, p. 149). More common during Tal al-Zataar and the camp wars was involvement in support activities, for example, smuggling ammunition into camps or working as scouts (Sayigh, 1993, p. 189).

However, not all the effects of conflict resulted in women's entry into the world of work. At the political level, the PLO's focus on the 'national struggle' had left little room for arguments about women's issues. Although some 'leftist factions' of the PLO acknowledged 'the woman question', the mainstream Fateh party 'articulated [no] ideology concerning women' (Gluck, 1995, p. 7); the issue was 'left pending' until after national liberation (Sayigh, 1993, p. 177).

On a more practical level, conflict would have also increased the perceived risk to women when travelling outside the home. The displacement caused by the Lebanese Civil War would also have increased the domestic load, which would have impacted much more heavily on women than men, emphasizing their role and work inside the house (Sayigh, 1993, p. 189).

Furthermore, post-crisis societies are often marked by periods of conservatism (see Phillips, 1995, p. 248, for example). Analyses of gender roles after the First and

Second World Wars, for example, point to a re-affirmation of the traditional gender division in employment (Higonnet & Higonnet, 1987). Certainly, while many changes brought about by conflict were encouraging female participation in the workplace, there were strong conservative forces at work.

4 Conflict and TVET Provision

It is difficult to regard TVET as having a purely neutral role with regard to gender, and TVET programmes are accused of perpetuating gender stereotypes in many situations. The World Bank policy paper of 1991 admits that 'broader societal perceptions about the appropriate role of women' often condition the types of training they are offered and notes that, in Israel, of all TVET students, 83% of men train in blue-collar professions, and 89% of women train in white-collar professions (Neuman & Ziderman in World Bank, 1991, p. 64). There is an inherent tension in the dual roles of adapting one's self to what the market needs and wants, and of trying to encourage women and men to take up new types of economic activity, to which the market may well not be receptive.

When it comes to post-conflict situations, this trend is, if anything, exacerbated; Date-Bah argues that many institutions in the post-conflict setting can be seen to 'reintroduce the pre-war gender biased positions' (2003, p. 111) and specifically that: 'experiences show that many [vocational training and skills development programmes] tend to be gender stereotyped focusing on knitting or sewing' (Date-Bah, 2003, p. 142).

However, while many are prepared to criticize the gender divisions that emerge in much TVET programming (both within and without the post-conflict context), nearly all stress TVET's potential for breaking down constrictive gender stereotypes in the sphere of economic activity, particularly for women. The 1991 World Bank policy paper mentions TVET as having an important place amongst a range of strategies designed to help women overcome barriers to entry into the workplace (World Bank, 1991, p. 7). Furthermore, Date-Bah sees in the post-conflict situation a 'window of opportunity' for overcoming 'the gender stereotypes and traditional gender division of labour; if TVET can capitalize on this window of opportunity, then it has the potential to open new doors for women' (Date-Bah, 2003, p. 111).

4.1 TVET for Palestinians Prior to the Civil War

Due to financial constraints, an UNRWA vocational training centre (VTC) was not opened in Lebanon until 1963. The VTC at Siblin constituted virtually the only form of formal TVET provision available for Palestinians in Lebanon for the following two decades. As Graham-Brown pointed out, the numerous private vocational schools around Beirut were all fee-paying, rendering them inaccessible to most Palestinians (1984, p. 120). The alternative to formal vocational education was to undertake apprenticeships, but, according to one interviewee, these were not well-regarded and not undertaken by women. The VTC in Siblin offered mainly two-year courses and was heavily over-subscribed. As a result of this, however, the VTC could afford to be selective about admissions, thus gaining an excellent reputation for the standard and employment prospects of its graduates (UNRWA, 1986, p. 140).

The period of PLO autonomy in Lebanon had several impacts on vocational education, as many political factions opened their own facilities for vocational training. In 1981, Weighill reports that as many as nine political organizations were running workshops in one or more of the camps (1996, p. 30). Anecdotal evidence suggests women were participating in some form of training during this period in fields such as nursing, administration and secretarial work. This period also impacted on the work of the Siblin VTC. It became a 'fertile recruiting ground' for various armed militia, as military training and a year of service in the PLO became required of all students and graduates, although the curriculum remained unchanged (Weighill, 1996, p. 31).

This system of TVET provision could hardly have been designed to be less accessible to women. The Siblin VTC, in common with other UNRWA VTCs in the Middle East, initially oriented its curriculum towards the rapid economic development taking place in the oil-producing countries (UNRWA, 1986, p. 135). This meant that, aside from its teacher-training programmes, the focus was on manual trades such as welding, construction and electricity, which were culturally (if not actually) prohibited for women. Furthermore, as most of the employment opportunities for holders of such qualifications were in the Gulf States, it was even less likely that women would be tempted to undertake such training. The location of the Siblin VTC also lowered female participation in its courses. Whilst it is somewhat centrally located, in the mountains between Beirut and Sidon, travelling times to the centre from camps in the North, the South and the Beka'a valley were up to two hours by bus, which would far exceed what many parents would consider acceptable for their daughters. Dormitory accommodation, available for young men at the centre, was not made available to women—for cultural reasons. This meant that young women had to find lodgings with local families close to the centre. Fears about young women travelling outside the home would surely only have been exacerbated by the deteriorating security situation of the late 1970s and early 1980s.

As a result of this, by 1982–1983, out of the 712 places available at Siblin for non-teacher-training vocational education, just 93 (or 13%) of them were taken up by females (Graham-Brown, 1984, p. 121). Access to TVET for Palestinian women in the pre-civil war period can, therefore, be said to have been limited by geographical location, types of courses offered and the places of employment that such qualifications would lead to.

4.2 The Effect of Conflict on TVET Provision for Women

As will be seen in the following section, the Lebanese Civil War had the effect of both closing down opportunities for vocational training and also, paradoxically, opening up new opportunities, many of which are still in operation over twenty years later. This section will focus on the provision offered by UNRWA, together with two case studies of NGOs that started functioning during this period: the first, an NGO dedicated to the development and empowerment of women, and the second, an NGO dedicated to providing TVET for Palestinians.

UNRWA's VTC at Siblin remained open until the Israeli invasion in 1982, and then struggled to stay open for about another year. Most of its equipment was looted by the Israelis; the buildings were later occupied by a militia group, leading to further damage due to heavy shelling. Graham-Brown reported that, in 1983, staff felt a 'growing sense of isolation from the new industrial and technical developments in Lebanon and elsewhere', particularly as they became unable to offer any sort of on-the-job training (1984, p. 121). The centre ceased to function at this time and remained closed until the end of the 1980s.

Any vocational training offered by political organizations, however haphazard, also disappeared as the PLO was forced out of Lebanon by the Israeli invasion. However, a new breed of overtly non-political, Palestinian-led non-governmental organizations (NGOs) started to emerge at this time, and vocational training was very much of a priority for them.

4.2.1 Case Study A: An NGO Focusing on Women's Empowerment

NGO A was started in 1977 by a group of Lebanese, Palestinian and Italian women, as a direct response to the Tal Al-Zataar massacre. As mainly women and children survived the massacre, and many were left without either husbands or homes, NGO A began with the intention of 'assist[ing] the survivors, socially, psychosocially, and at the economic level'. The women survivors had mostly weak literacy, but were skilled at making traditional Palestinian embroidery. The NGO capitalized on this skill by bringing women together to produce embroidery that could be sold to provide them with immediate income, whilst creating a group dynamic through which they could be provided with psycho-social support. NGO A had a very strong belief that they did not wish to be carrying out 'charity work', but rather sustainable development: 'We should provide tools for them so they can contribute to the development of their society'. In the wake of the massacre, they felt it was important not to make people feel or act like victims.

With this in mind, moving into vocational training provision was the logical next step after facilitating income generation, and they 'decided that some women needed to develop their skills, so they weren't only dependent on the embroidery'. They began offering courses in sewing and typing. Their rationale for offering sewing was that, as women were often not allowed to access work outside the home, sewing would enable women to find a secure income whilst remaining inside the home. The typing course, on the other hand, enabled women to find jobs with the PLO: 'most of the women who graduated from typing already had jobs waiting for them at the PLO offices, all the political and non-political institutions that the PLO opened'. Offering these two courses was a step towards 'empower[ing] women with skills, and tools that are necessary for them to contribute to the well-being and the development of the whole community', and were seen as part of a move from the traditional (embroidery) to the non-traditional (office work).

NGO A has flourished since its establishment and, in 2000, was offering a range of courses from the very traditional (sewing and hairdressing) to the non-traditional, which were increasingly favoured from the early 1990s (office management, accounting, typing, interior decoration, carpentry, electricity and photography).

NGO A has always focused on offering social support along with vocational training. Many trainees are admitted on the basis of their reduced circumstances, and may be assisted with the payment of course fees. Classes on subjects such as human rights, leadership and domestic violence are attached to all the vocational training programmes and form a core part of their vision.

4.2.2 Case Study B: An NGO Dedicated to Providing Vocational Education for Palestinians

NGO B was established by two engineers who were working for UNRWA at the time of the Israeli invasion of Lebanon in 1982, along with staff from UNESCO. They began to realize that TVET provision for Palestinians in the South was inadequate, particularly following the closure of the VTC at Siblin due to damage and looting. Even before the closure, however, the founder of NGO B pointed out that for all the tens of thousands of Palestinians from camps and gatherings in the Tyre area, only about four places would be available in a course such as electricity at Siblin. After the opening of a VTC in the Tyre area, sixteen extra places would be available, thus increasing provision four-fold. The founder felt that it was important for students who wanted to undertake vocational education, and also those who wanted to go to university but did not have the means, to have an opportunity to obtain a good qualification 'based on proper methods, and proper ways, and a good syllabus, and good training', in contrast to the informal and generally poorly respected apprenticeship training of the past.

In 1983, therefore, NGO B opened a VTC in some former PLO offices in al-Bass camp. Of great significance was how, when the Siblin VTC was closed, UNRWA agreed to collaborate with NGO B, providing official certification (which they continue to do to this day), curriculum advice and supervision from their own (temporarily unemployed) staff at Siblin. The first courses offered were architectural drawing, and business and office practice, and in the initial year around twenty-two students graduated from each programme. The courses were chosen both on the basis of what students wanted (particularly business and office practice) and on the basis of market needs and possibilities for employment. Draughtsmen were required in engineering companies in Lebanon and across the Middle East, and business and office practice offered similarly transferable skills. The fact that both of these courses were open (culturally) to men and women increased their attractiveness to the founders of the centre, and they found that male and female enrolments were more or less equal.

Each year, two or three courses were added and new centres were opened in Ein Helweh and Nahr el-Bared camps. Later, courses included tailoring, sewing and design, refrigeration and air conditioning, television and radio maintenance, secretarial and computer studies, and nursing.

From the start, females and males could theoretically be admitted to all courses offered by NGO B. In practice, female enrolment in traditionally male fields (added later) such as industrial electricity, or refrigeration and air conditioning, has been non-existent, although the founder of NGO B remembered that 'about ten years ago, a girl came to the electricity course. She stayed until the middle, and then, I don't know, maybe she got engaged or travelled, but I was very pleased with her, because it was a new step, a new thing happening in the community' (personal communication). The founder of NGO B admitted that he would not actively seek out girls and women to join the more traditionally male courses, but thought he would encourage a girl if she came and enquired about it, and would even provide extra facilities if necessary.

5 'Best of Times, Worst of Times'?

Buckland's phrase (coined in Buckland, 2005, p. 25 and borrowed from Charles Dickens' *A Tale of Two Cities*) touches on the idea that, whilst conflict may have a devastating effect on education, the post-conflict situation may also provide opportunity for change and to capitalize on shifts in previously fixed gender stereotypes affected by the conflict. Certainly, this paradigm can be applied to the situation of vocational training as the Lebanese Civil War unfolded. Although in some ways, vocational training was left in a dire situation by the Israeli invasion, in other ways, the space that opened up presented NGOs with the possibility of experimenting with a different model of TVET provision as the 'inertia and resistance' that usually characterize attempts to reform TVET and remake structural inequalities are overcome (Date-Bah, 2003, p. 212).

Whether the structural inequalities relating to gender really *were* remade in the new system of TVET provision that emerged is, at first glance, somewhat questionable. NGO A, for example, for all its rhetoric of empowerment and development, focused on equipping women with the skills of sewing and typing; certainly, such skills may have led to employment, and typing was not as 'traditional' a form of employment for Palestinian women as embroidery, but women working in these areas could hardly be regarded as breaking gender stereotypes. Similarly, for NGO B, although the courses were theoretically offered to men and women, in reality, in the absence of explicit encouragement and guidance for women thinking about enrolling in traditionally male courses, enrolment patterns remained conventional. While NGO B, therefore, and to a lesser extent NGO A, were offering training that did not reinforce previously held gender stereotypes, neither did they take major steps towards breaking them down. The criticism levelled at training and employment programmes in post-conflict Lebanon seems applicable here: 'the focus of the programme was on meeting immediate/practical needs without consideration of strategic interests or long-term empowerment of women' (Date-Bah, 2003, p. 130).

This seems particularly pertinent in the face of evidence, cited by the World Bank, that women can be encouraged into non-traditional courses even in a country as conservative as Morocco. In 1979, note was taken that, although women were theoretically entitled to enrol in 'industrial training programmes', very few had applied and none had been accepted. Advertisements specifically targeted at women were placed in the media, female instructors were recruited and career counselling services put in place, with the result that enrolment figures rose sharply and have been sustained (World Bank, 1991, p. 218). The cautious approach of the case study NGOs may therefore be thought of as a little disappointing.

However, there are other important ways in which the situation of women's access was very much altered by the newly emerging TVET system. Perhaps most importantly, the NGOs capitalized on the opportunity for change that was presented by the UNRWA Siblin VTC losing its stranglehold on the system. As described above, the Siblin VTC was geographically very difficult to reach; provision in the new, smaller NGOs took place within the camps. As the founder of NGO B explained to me:

> You know our customs here. A lot of families, maybe twenty years ago, don't let their daughters travel away, or take vocational training, or go outside the camps. But inside the camp, it is as though they are still under the supervision of their families (personal communication).

Similarly, in NGO A, the training took place in all-female groups, so there was no risk of exposure to single young men. A particularly important innovation was that of NGO B, when it secured collaboration with and certification of UNRWA on their new courses. This gave their new style of provision a crucial legitimacy which it could carry forward into the post-conflict era, even when Siblin re-opened in 1988.

Another remarkable innovation of both NGOs, particularly NGO B, was the focus on delivering 'modern' courses, rather than 'traditional' courses that brought with them a burden of gender stereotyping. By delivering courses, such as business and office practice and typing, men and women were able to access equal training and employment prospects without struggling against the weight of cultural expectations as they would have in careers such as hairdressing or welding. This was particularly important given the dire economic and employment situation of the time. The barriers to entry for a man or woman with an 'unconventional' qualification would have been even higher than normal, as employers became less inclined to take risks. Looking forward to the 'modern' job market was an inspired way of avoiding the trap of perpetuating and reinforcing gender stereotyping in the workplace. This also had the effect of lessening the notion that vocational training was somehow 'backward' or academically inferior to other forms of study, which increased its attractiveness to parents, sons and daughters alike.

This is not to say, however, that these NGOs have not experimented with breaking down gender stereotypes in TVET, and the comparative flexibility of the new system was another great strength in this respect. With centres in many camps, and with courses lasting less than a year, both NGO A and B have been able to start new programmes for a trial period, in just one camp, before committing to full enrolment. This meant, eventually, that it was possible to experiment with, for example, carpentry courses for women. This course was discontinued, but one can regard the fact that it was at least tried for several years, and that many women passed through it, as something of an achievement in itself. Women are far more likely to enrol in an 'experimental' subject if it is not required that they also travel for several hours every day outside the camp, and commit to a course of two years, as the opportunity costs are lower.

Perhaps most important, however, was that the number of training places rose, and not only in male-dominated areas, meaning that a larger number of women were able to take advantage of training. As a result of training, women are more likely to be able to contribute to household earnings and work outside their immediate home. This may have various empowering effects, such as improved self-confidence, influence in the home, and the possibility of meeting and interacting with a wider range of people, whilst not actively breaking down employment-related gender stereotypes. In this respect, the NGOs were also able to benefit from the increased demand for vocational training in the conflict and post-conflict situations. The founder of NGO B remarked that:

> The Israeli invasion didn't prevent women from leaving their houses and coming to the centre to take vocational training. I think in some points it encouraged them, especially as a lot of men were in prisons. I think families changed their thoughts about continuing teaching their daughters and even they have no problem if they go to work after graduation (personal communication).

Perhaps even more important now is the continuing sense that, in an uncertain world, marriage no longer guarantees long-term economic security for a woman. One young woman explained to me:

> If you have children and your husband dies, you should have a job to work in. Here, you are independent, you must work to earn, the government will not help to support you. You must depend on yourself. Even if you have children, you should work. So I think I should get vocational training, in order that, if anything happens in my life, I have a certain job to work in (personal communication).

6 Conclusions

Buckland's 'best of times, worst of times' analogy works well in this context. The (post-)conflict situation for vocational training was extremely difficult, and there had been many ways in which the situation concerning stereotyped ideas about women in the economic sphere had been worsened by the conflict, as well as some interesting ways in which it had been broken down. Some of the features of the new TVET providers were perhaps disappointingly conservative, and did not do enough to move away from the *status quo ante*. However, to focus on these would be to ignore the ways in which the emerging NGO provision was innovative, both in terms of structure, courses on offer and willingness to take advantage of changes in expectations about women and work brought about by conflict.

There were many real constraints on women which affected their participation in training and in the workforce. Certain conservative ideas about the woman's role in the economic sphere were inscribed rather than loosened by the experience of conflict, which in effect pulled women out of certain types of employment, whilst the economic collapse and resulting lack of employment opportunities for both sexes simultaneously pushed them out of the workforce. Given that the onus on TVET must always be to improve the prospects of earning a livelihood, there are very real arguments in favour of TVET focusing on *any* skills that might provide or increase income, even if they are traditional skills such as sewing or embroidery. After all, it must be recognized that nothing is less empowering for women than extreme poverty.

However, accepting that the post-conflict situation might not be the optimum moment to introduce radical reforms to TVET provision—for example, welding courses for women—does not mean that NGOs and other TVET providers cannot take advantage of the opportunity to innovate and capitalize on societal changes. Some problems with the antecedent TVET provision tackled with particular effect in this context were, as described above, the place and mode of delivery, the reputation of TVET and types of courses offered, all of which had a real and lasting effect on the possibility of Palestinian women to undertake training.

Note

1. This figure is contested; Sayigh, for example, estimates that 590,000 Arab Palestinians were displaced to the West Bank and Jordan, whilst a further 300,000 moved beyond the borders of Palestine altogether (1979, p. 99).

References

Buckland, P. 2005. *Reshaping the future: education and post-conflict reconstruction.* Washington, DC: World Bank.

Date-Bah, E., ed. 2003. *Jobs after war: a critical challenge in the peace and reconstruction puzzle.* Geneva, Switzerland: ILO.

Fisk, R. 1990. *Pity the nation: Lebanon at war.* Oxford, UK: Oxford University Press.

Gluck, S.B. 1995. Palestinian women: gender politics and nationalism. *Journal of Palestine studies,* vol. 24, no. 3.

Graham-Brown, S. 1984. *Education, repression and liberation: Palestinians.* London: World University Service.

Haddad, S. 2003. *The Palestinian impasse in Lebanon: the politics of refugee integration.* Brighton, UK: Sussex Academic Press.

Higonnet, M.R.; Higonnet, P. 1987. The double helix. *In:* Higonnet, M.R. et al., eds. *Behind the lines: gender and the two world wars,* pp. 31–47. New Haven, CT: Yale University Press.

Peteet, J.M. 1991. *Gender in crisis: women and the Palestinian resistance movement.* New York, NY: Columbia University Press.

Phillips, D., ed. 1995. *Education in Germany: tradition and reform in historical context.* London: Routledge.

Sayigh, R. 1979. *Palestinians: from peasants to revolutionaries.* London: Zed Books.

Sayigh, R. 1993. Palestinian women and politics in Lebanon. *In:* Tucker, J., ed. *Arab women: old boundaries, new frontiers*, pp. 175–95. Bloomington, IN: Indiana University Press.

Sayigh, R. 1994. *Too many enemies: the Palestinian experience in Lebanon.* London: Zed Books.

Schultz, H.; Hammer, J. 2003. *The Palestinian diaspora: formation of identities and politics of homeland.* London: Routledge.

Ugland, O.F., ed. 2003. *Difficult past, uncertain future: living conditions among Palestinian refugees in camps and gatherings in Lebanon.* Tøyen, Norway: FAFO.

UNESCO-UNEVOC. No date. *What is TVET?* <www.unesco.unevoc.org>

United Nations Development Fund for Women—UNIFEM. 2004. *Getting it right, doing it right: gender and disarmament, demobilisation, and reintegration.* New York, NY: UNIFEM.

United Nations Relief and Works Agency for Palestinian Refugees in the Near East. 1986. *UN-RWA: a brief history, 1950-1982.* Vienna: UNRWA.

United Nations Relief and Works Agency for Palestinian Refugees in the Near East. No date. *Establishment of UNRWA.* <www.un.org/unrwa/overview/index.html>

Weighill, M.-L. 1996. *Palestinian refugees in Lebanon: the politics of assistance.* (Paper presented at the Palestinians in Lebanon Conference, Queen Elizabeth House, Oxford, United Kingdom, 27–30 September 1996.)

World Bank. 1991. *Vocational education and training: a World Bank policy paper* Washington, DC: World Bank.